Aurora, that is, the day-spring, or dawning of the day in the Orient, or morning-rednesse in the rising of the sun, that is, the root or mother of philosophie, astrologie, & theologie from the true ground, or a description of nature (1656)

John Sparrow

Aurora, that is, the day-spring, or dawning of the day in the Orient, or morning-rednesse in the rising of the sun, that is, the root or mother of philosophie, astrologie, & theologie from the true ground, or a description of nature

Morgenröte im Aufgang.
Böhme, Jakob, 1575-1624.
Sparrow, John, 1615-1665?
Translation by John Sparrow of: Morgenröte im Aufgang.
Errata: p. [27]-[28].
Imperfect: t.p. mutilated.
[28], 939 [i.e. 643] p.
London : Printed by John Streater for Giles Calvert ..., 1656.
Wing / B3397
English
Reproduction of the original in the Henry E. Huntington Library and Art Gallery

Early English Books Online (EEBO) Editions

Imagine holding history in your hands.

Now you can. Digitally preserved and previously accessible only through libraries as Early English Books Online, this rare material is now available in single print editions. Thousands of books written between 1475 and 1700 and ranging from religion to astronomy, medicine to music, can be delivered to your doorstep in individual volumes of high-quality historical reproductions.

We have been compiling these historic treasures for more than 70 years. Long before such a thing as "digital" even existed, ProQuest founder Eugene Power began the noble task of preserving the British Museum's collection on microfilm. He then sought out other rare and endangered titles, providing unparalleled access to these works and collaborating with the world's top academic institutions to make them widely available for the first time. This project furthers that original vision.

These texts have now made the full journey -- from their original printing-press versions available only in rare-book rooms to online library access to new single volumes made possible by the partnership between artifact preservation and modern printing technology. A portion of the proceeds from every book sold supports the libraries and institutions that made this collection possible, and that still work to preserve these invaluable treasures passed down through time.

This is history, traveling through time since the dawn of printing to your own personal library.

Initial Proquest EEBO Print Editions collections include:

Early Literature

This comprehensive collection begins with the famous Elizabethan Era that saw such literary giants as Chaucer, Shakespeare and Marlowe, as well as the introduction of the sonnet. Traveling through Jacobean and Restoration literature, the highlight of this series is the Pollard and Redgrave 1475-1640 selection of the rarest works from the English Renaissance.

Early Documents of World History

This collection combines early English perspectives on world history with documentation of Parliament records, royal decrees and military documents that reveal the delicate balance of Church and State in early English government. For social historians, almanacs and calendars offer insight into daily life of common citizens. This exhaustively complete series presents a thorough picture of history through the English Civil War.

Historical Almanacs

Historically, almanacs served a variety of purposes from the more practical, such as planting and harvesting crops and plotting nautical routes, to predicting the future through the movements of the stars. This collection provides a wide range of consecutive years of "almanacks" and calendars that depict a vast array of everyday life as it was several hundred years ago.

Early History of Astronomy & Space

Humankind has studied the skies for centuries, seeking to find our place in the universe. Some of the most important discoveries in the field of astronomy were made in these texts recorded by ancient stargazers, but almost as impactful were the perspectives of those who considered their discoveries to be heresy. Any independent astronomer will find this an invaluable collection of titles arguing the truth of the cosmic system.

Early History of Industry & Science

Acting as a kind of historical Wall Street, this collection of industry manuals and records explores the thriving industries of construction; textile, especially wool and linen; salt; livestock; and many more.

Early English Wit, Poetry & Satire

The power of literary device was never more in its prime than during this period of history, where a wide array of political and religious satire mocked the status quo and poetry called humankind to transcend the rigors of daily life through love, God or principle. This series comments on historical patterns of the human condition that are still visible today.

Early English Drama & Theatre

This collection needs no introduction, combining the works of some of the greatest canonical writers of all time, including many plays composed for royalty such as Queen Elizabeth I and King Edward VI. In addition, this series includes history and criticism of drama, as well as examinations of technique.

Early History of Travel & Geography

Offering a fascinating view into the perception of the world during the sixteenth and seventeenth centuries, this collection includes accounts of Columbus's discovery of the Americas and encompasses most of the Age of Discovery, during which Europeans and their descendants intensively explored and mapped the world. This series is a wealth of information from some the most groundbreaking explorers.

Early Fables & Fairy Tales

This series includes many translations, some illustrated, of some of the most well-known mythologies of today, including Aesop's Fables and English fairy tales, as well as many Greek, Latin and even Oriental parables and criticism and interpretation on the subject.

Early Documents of Language & Linguistics

The evolution of English and foreign languages is documented in these original texts studying and recording early philology from the study of a variety of languages including Greek, Latin and Chinese, as well as multilingual volumes, to current slang and obscure words. Translations from Latin, Hebrew and Aramaic, grammar treatises and even dictionaries and guides to translation make this collection rich in cultures from around the world.

Early History of the Law

With extensive collections of land tenure and business law "forms" in Great Britain, this is a comprehensive resource for all kinds of early English legal precedents from feudal to constitutional law, Jewish and Jesuit law, laws about public finance to food supply and forestry, and even "immoral conditions." An abundance of law dictionaries, philosophy and history and criticism completes this series.

Early History of Kings, Queens and Royalty

This collection includes debates on the divine right of kings, royal statutes and proclamations, and political ballads and songs as related to a number of English kings and queens, with notable concentrations on foreign rulers King Louis IX and King Louis XIV of France, and King Philip II of Spain. Writings on ancient rulers and royal tradition focus on Scottish and Roman kings, Cleopatra and the Biblical kings Nebuchadnezzar and Solomon.

Early History of Love, Marriage & Sex

Human relationships intrigued and baffled thinkers and writers well before the postmodern age of psychology and self-help. Now readers can access the insights and intricacies of Anglo-Saxon interactions in sex and love, marriage and politics, and the truth that lies somewhere in between action and thought.

Early History of Medicine, Health & Disease

This series includes fascinating studies on the human brain from as early as the 16th century, as well as early studies on the physiological effects of tobacco use. Anatomy texts, medical treatises and wound treatment are also discussed, revealing the exponential development of medical theory and practice over more than two hundred years.

Early History of Logic, Science and Math

The "hard sciences" developed exponentially during the 16th and 17th centuries, both relying upon centuries of tradition and adding to the foundation of modern application, as is evidenced by this extensive collection. This is a rich collection of practical mathematics as applied to business, carpentry and geography as well as explorations of mathematical instruments and arithmetic; logic and logicians such as Aristotle and Socrates; and a number of scientific disciplines from natural history to physics.

Early History of Military, War and Weaponry

Any professional or amateur student of war will thrill at the untold riches in this collection of war theory and practice in the early Western World. The Age of Discovery and Enlightenment was also a time of great political and religious unrest, revealed in accounts of conflicts such as the Wars of the Roses.

Early History of Food

This collection combines the commercial aspects of food handling, preservation and supply to the more specific aspects of canning and preserving, meat carving, brewing beer and even candy-making with fruits and flowers, with a large resource of cookery and recipe books. Not to be forgotten is a "the great eater of Kent," a study in food habits.

Early History of Religion

From the beginning of recorded history we have looked to the heavens for inspiration and guidance. In these early religious documents, sermons, and pamphlets, we see the spiritual impact on the lives of both royalty and the commoner. We also get insights into a clergy that was growing ever more powerful as a political force. This is one of the world's largest collections of religious works of this type, revealing much about our interpretation of the modern church and spirituality.

Early Social Customs

Social customs, human interaction and leisure are the driving force of any culture. These unique and quirky works give us a glimpse of interesting aspects of day-to-day life as it existed in an earlier time. With books on games, sports, traditions, festivals, and hobbies it is one of the most fascinating collections in the series.

The BiblioLife Network

This project was made possible in part by the BiblioLife Network (BLN), a project aimed at addressing some of the huge challenges facing book preservationists around the world. The BLN includes libraries, library networks, archives, subject matter experts, online communities and library service providers. We believe every book ever published should be available as a high-quality print reproduction; printed on-demand anywhere in the world. This insures the ongoing accessibility of the content and helps generate sustainable revenue for the libraries and organizations that work to preserve these important materials.

The following book is in the "public domain" and represents an authentic reproduction of the text as printed by the original publisher. While we have attempted to accurately maintain the integrity of the original work, there are sometimes problems with the original work or the micro-film from which the books were digitized. This can result in minor errors in reproduction. Possible imperfections include missing and blurred pages, poor pictures, markings and other reproduction issues beyond our control. Because this work is culturally important, we have made it available as part of our commitment to protecting, preserving, and promoting the world's literature.

GUIDE TO FOLD-OUTS MAPS and OVERSIZED IMAGES

The book you are reading was digitized from microfilm captured over the past thirty to forty years. Years after the creation of the original microfilm, the book was converted to digital files and made available in an online database.

In an online database, page images do not need to conform to the size restrictions found in a printed book. When converting these images back into a printed bound book, the page sizes are standardized in ways that maintain the detail of the original. For large images, such as fold-out maps, the original page image is split into two or more pages

Guidelines used to determine how to split the page image follows:

• Some images are split vertically; large images require vertical and horizontal splits.
• For horizontal splits, the content is split left to right.
• For vertical splits, the content is split from top to bottom.
• For both vertical and horizontal splits, the image is processed from top left to bottom right.

John Sullivan
&c

to

Owen Crane
&c

Rev. 1. 4.

4. John to the Seven Churches in Asia, Grace be unto you, and Peace from him which is, and which was, and which is to come, and from the seven Spirits which are before his Throne.

Rev. 4. part of the 3. vers. & 5, to the 11.

3. —— And there was a Rainbow round about the Throne, in sight like unto an Emerald.

5. And out of the Throne proceeded Lightenings and Thundrings, and Voyces: and there were seven Lamps of Fire Burning before the Throne, which are the Seven Spirits of God.

6. And before the Throne there was a Sea of Glasse like unto Crystal: and in the midst of the Throne and round about the Throne, were four Beasts full of Eyes before and behind.

7. And the First Beast was like a Lyon, and the Second Beast like a Calf, and the Third Beast had a Face as a Man, and the Fourth Beast was like a flying Eagle.

8. And the Four Beasts had each of them fix wings about him, and they were full of Eyes within, and they rest not Day and Night, saying, Holy, Holy, Holy, Lord God Almighty, which was, and is, and is to come.

9. And when those Beasts give glory and honour and thanks to him that sate on the Throne, who liveth for Ever and Ever,

10. The Four and twenty Elders fall down before him that sate on the Throne, and worship him that liveth for Ever and Ever, and cast their Crowns before the Throne, saying,

11. Thou art worthy, O Lord, to receive Glory and Honour and Power; for thou hast Created all things, and for thy Pleasure they are and were Created.

Rev. 5. 6, 8, to the 10.

6. And I beheld, and Lo, in the Midst of the Throne and of the Four Beasts, and in the midst of the Elders stood a Lamb as it had been slain, having seven Horns, and seven Eyes, which are the seven Spirits of God sent forth into all the Earth.

8. And when he had taken the Book, the four Beasts and four and twenty Elders fell down before the Lamb, having Every one of them Harps and Golden Vialls full of Odours, which are the Prayers of Saints.

9. And they sung a New Song, saying, Thou art worthy to take the Book, and to Open the Seals thereof: for thou wast slain, and hast redeemed us to God by thy Bloud, out of Every Kindred, and Tongue, and People, and Nation.

10. And hast made us unto our God Kings and Priests, and we shall reign on the Earth.

Isaiah 9. 2.

2. The People that walked in Darknesse, have seen a great Light: they that dwell in the Land of the shadow of Death, upon them hath the Light shined.

Matth. 4. 16.

16. The People which sate in Darknesse saw great Light: and to them which sate in the Region and shadow of Death, Light is sprung up.

Ἀποκάλυψις πασῶν Ἀποκαλύψεων.

חזון הבל חזיונות

Revelatio Omnium Revelationum.

This A V R O R A, or
Rednesse of the Morning
Is the WONDER of the World.

Rev. 1. 4.

Rev. 3. 10.

W. Hollar fecit.

Note.

It is *necessary* for the Reader, to *peruse* the Book of the three Principles, and the Book of the threefold Life of Man, also with *this*; and then he will be able to conceive aright of the Ground in *this Booke* Aurora.

For *since* the time of the writing of *this* Booke Aurora, Day-spring or Morning Rednesse; the lovely *Bright Day* hath appeared unto the Author. And *all* that which is too obscure here, is held forth *most cleerly* in them; which is truly a great WONDER, as the Reader who loveth God, will find.

Although the Authour indeed had written this Book only *for himselfe*, according to the gift of Gods Spirit, but knew not *then* the Counsel or will of God concerning it.

Begun the 27 of *January*, in the yeare 1612. on the *Friday after* the Conversion of *Paul*.

A   The

The Preface to the Reader.

Reader,

THe Books of this Author, that are already published, declare sufficiently the high worth of his deepe writings: But of all the benefits that doe accrue thereby, it is one inestimable Excellencie of them, that they helpe the Mindes of all sorts of people, that will take paines to reade and to consider them; in the understanding of the Holy Scriptures: and that satisfactorily and convincingly, without neede of having any reference to the vast Commentaries of Authours, either in the Learned or Moderne Tongues; and they will help Men to be able to discerne the truth in the various Expositions and Opinions of all Parties, also to still the differences debates controversies disputes and contests; that all may be satisfied in a Loving friendly way, and so agree in one and the same Truth together.

And among many differences in Opinion that Spring up, there is one weighty and remarkable, arisen, since the Light within, and Christ within, hath been pressed more then Ordinary; one sort being judged to deny, a Christ without, and the other, a Christ within; whereas it might be considered, that * Christ is not divided, though he be every where in all places, and in all things, and yet but once manifested in ‡ the likenesse of sinfull Flesh: Suffering, Dying, Rising from the dead, Ascending into Glory; yet he that is not partaker of the same Christ within, or is not made conformable in his soul and spirit to him in his suffering Death and Resurrection, in this Life, in some measure, shall never be partaker with him in his glory in the Life to come; But if wee † Suffer with him, we shall also be glorifyed with him, at his appearing: Pauls desire to

*1 Cor.i.13.

‡ Rom.8.3.

† Rom.8.17.

know

know nothing but * Christ and him crucified *among the* * 1 Cor. 2. 2.
Corinthians ; was not to know them to crucifie Christ, but
the vertue and Power of Christ crucified in them : and if the
same Christ that suffered at Jerusalem were not in every
one, the wickedest Man in the world could not † crucifie † Heb. 6. 6.
to himselfe the Lord of glory: *And what Christ did*
in the Flesh once, alwaies had and hath its powerfull effect
in the Spirit of every Soul that is united to him within it
selfe, and not otherwise: Therefore we should learne to
understand, how, it is Christ, that was * the Lamb slain * Rev. 13. 8.
from the beginning of the World, *and then also in*
Abel *when he was slain by* Cain : *also in his own Body*
when Jesus *himselfe was nailed on the Crosse and gave up*
the Ghost : and still suffers and is slain ‡ *in his Members*; ‡ Eph. 5. 30.
and as he will say at the Judgment, when all shall appeare,
from Adam *to the last Man that is borne of a Woman*,
* whatsoever is done to the Least of those that be- * Math. 25.
lieve in him, *it is done to Christ himselfe, in them ; and* 40. 45:
not that he will, only, take it as done to him, as his words
are commonly expounded ; but it is really done to him:
† His Flesh is meat indeed, *&* his Blood is drink in- † Joh. 6. 55.
deed, *and they that did not eate and drink it, though it*
were within them (*otherwise they could not doe so*) had
no part in him : *and this he said when himselfe was con-*
versant with his Disciples before his Suffering and Death;
Therfore there cannot be a Christ within, a Christ without,
but one and the same Christ within and without, now and
then, and alwaies, from Eternity to Eternity.

There is another great difference, concerning Perfection
and the attaining to it in this Life : one sort condemning
the otherf, or speaking that which they understand to be spo-
ken in the Scripture ; but they doe not endeavour to recon- * Math. 5.
cile the meaning of those Texts, which seeme so extreamely 48.
to differ. For perfection; * Be ye perfect *as your* Luk. 6. 32.
heavenly Father is perfect, † Job *was a perfect and* † Job. 1. 1.
&. 2. 3.

A 2 up-

*James.3.2. upright Man. *If any Man sin not in word he is a per-
†James1.25 fect *Man. And there is mention made of the* †perfect Law
* 1 Joh. 3.9. of Liberty: also, *he that is borne of God sinneth not,
ne ither can he, because the seed of God remaineth in
‡ Phil.3.15. him. ‡ As many as be perfect, let them be thus
* Phil. 3.14. minded, viz: *to presse for the Prize of the high call-
† Rom.3.10. ing of God in Christ Jesus. On the other side: †There
* 1 Kings 8. is none righteous, no not one, *there is not a Man
46. that sinneth not, ‡ in many things WEE sin all. And
2 Chron.6. the Apostle John, who no doubt was then borne of God,
36. saith: *If WEE say we have no sinne we deceive
Prov. 20.9. our selves, and there is no truth in us; if [wee] say, not
Eccles.7.22. if he or they say, or whosoever saith: And while he was in
‡ James 3.2. the instant of high Revelations, †he fell down before the
* 1 Joh.1.8. Angel to worship him, thinking it had been God, but
† Rev.19.10. the Angel said to him, See thou doe it not, for I am thy
fellow servant.

   And these great differences cannot be reconciled by the
distinction of a time or condition of Men unconverted, before they have attained Perfection, before they are righteous
or before they are sanctified: but they may be decided by the
understanding, what it is that sinneth in Man; and
what it is in Man that is perfect and cannot sinne: For
as the Soul in this Life entereth into the one or the other
through obedience to it; that Soul is either righteous and
perfect, or wicked and imperfect, as the Scriptures testifie:
* Col.1.28. And *every one that shall be presented perfect, is to
be presented perfect in Christ Jesus, so that our perfection
consisteth in him not in Selfe: and so the Gifts of God are
‡ Eph. 2.8. perfect, or else we could not be ‡ saved by Faith, for that
is not of our selves, but is the gift of God: and therefore it may well be said by the Apostle Paul, after his high
* Rom.7.18. Revelation: *I know that in me, that is in my Flesh
dwelleth no good thing; dwelleth, not did or hath
dwelt,

dwelt, *before his conversion or at the beginning of the writing that Epistle:* but *at that instant dwelleth in him no good thing in his Flesh:* also, *saies he,* † I doe find a Law in my Members rebelling againſt the Law of my mind, and leading me into captivity to the Law of ſinne : *So that* * the good which he would doe, that he did not, but the evil which he would not doe, that he did. ‡ To will was preſent with him, but how to performe it, that he did not know: *and then ſaies,* So in my mind I ſerve the Law of God, *which is perfect,* but in my Fleſh I ſerve the Law of ſin, *Alſo the Apoſtle John ſaith,* * Let no man deceive you, he that doth righteouſneſſe, is righteous : and the Apoſtle *Paul* again ſaith,† as many as are led by the ſpirit of God they are the Sons of God : *and* * his ſervants ye are to whom ye obey ; whether of obedience unto righteouſneſſe or of ſin unto Death. *Alſo it is ſaid,* † The Soul that ſinneth it ſhall die. * If a righteous Man (*which is indeed a perfect Man ſo long as he is a ſervant to righteouſneſſe*) departeth from his righteouſneſſe, and doth that which is wicked ; in the wickedneſſe which he doth he ſhall die : *and yet that which is perfect cannot die. And on the other ſide ;* ‡ If a wicked Man turne from his wickedneſſe and doth the thing which is good and righteous, in the righteouſneſſe which he doth, he ſhall live, ſaith the Lord : *Thus, a righteous Man can ſin, and a wicked Man can doe that which is righteous : yet it is the Soul in the wicked Man that turneth and doth righteouſneſſe in the minde, and the will, and the Spirit, and the heart, and the Life, through Chriſt in the Soul: And it is the Soul in the Righteous Man that doth that which is wicked, in the minde and will, and ſpirit and heart and life, through the Power of Sin, corruption, and imperfection, alſo of the Fleſh*

† Rom. 7.23.

* Rom. 7.19.

‡ Rom. 7.18

* 1 Joh. 3. 7.

† Rom. 8.14

* Rom. 6.16.

† *Ezek.* 18. 20.

* Ezek. 18. 24. 26.

‡ Ezek: 18. 21 22. 27. 28.

on

* Rom.7.24.	or the * body of Death, which is this mortal flesh and bloud:
† Rom.6.12.	therefore we should † not let sinne Reigne in our Mor-
	tal Bodies, that we should obey it in the Lusts there-
* Col.1.29.	of. But we should * strive after perfection ; that
† Gal.4.19.	† Christ may be formed in us: we should * give God our
* Prov.23.	Hearts, and he will clense them for us, & make us † after his
26.	own heart, and will make our Hearts desires and minds
† 1 Sam.13.	pure, and then they are * perfect ; for nothing that is
14.	† Impure, and so, imperfect, can enter into the King-
* 1 Cron.28.	dom of God. Thus, in our Minds, † if we do the will
9.	of our Father which is in Heaven, we shall know of
† Rev.21.27	the words of Christ, whether they be of God or no :
† Joh.7.17.	which they that heard them from his owne mouth and did
	not so, could not know. But we are not to condemne those
	that have not attained to our mesure of Light, Grace, Know-
* Math.5.16	ledge, or Perfection : but to let our * Light so shine be-
	fore Men, that they may see our good works, and glo-
	rify our Father which is in Heaven : and then they
† 1 Cor.14.25	will say, † God is in us of a Truth : they will be able to
	understand it. If we be * strong, we should help those that
* Rom.15.1,	are weak in Light or understanding, and should declare
† Luk.1.79.	the † Gospel to those that sit most in Darknesse and in
	the shadow of Death, and guide one anothers feete
	into the way of Peace, and then we shall be like him who
* Math.11.	is in our hearts, * meeke and lowly, and so wee shall
29.	find rest unto our Sou's ; and then, when He who is
† Col.3.4,	now our † Life, shall appeare, we shall also ap-
	peare with him in Glory. And when we have re-
* 1 Joh.2.	ceived * the unction of the Holy one, in our Souls, we
27.	are then † come to the spirits of Just men made per-
† Heb.12.23	fect, and to the Church of the first-Borne which are
	written in Heaven : and yet some that were so, did not
	know by what Death they should glorifie God : and
* 1 Cor.15.	in Death the Body is * sown in Corruption, it is rais-
42.43.	ed in Incorruption, sown in Dishonour, raised in Glo-
	ry

ry, sown in weaknesse, raised in power: *sown in imperfection raised in perfection;* for ǂ this Mortall ǂ 1 *Cor.* 5. must put on immortality. *Thus though we are risen* 53, 54. *with Christ in our Souls, Spirits, and Minds, serving the Law of God in this Life with a perfect Hear , say though sinne dwell in our flesh, yet if we let it* not r.igne *in our Mortall or imperfect Bodies, so that we* obey it not *in the Lusts thereof; then the Holy Spirit dwelleth in our minds, and in our bodies, which are the Temples of the Holy Ghost: but if we let sin raigne, then our Souls and Bodies are Denns of Theeves and Murtherers, and the habitations of all Devills.*

This for the present is my *understanding, which I pray may be enlightened and helped by the Father of Lights, from whom is every perfect Gift to my selfe and all mankinde my brethren: who have severall measures of the same Light, and divers Gifts by the same Spirit: of which I desire to be made partaker from themselves, and shall highly rejoyce my selfe therein, with them.*

But the Ground *to the understanding the things here mentioned, and of all things contained in the Scriptures, is exactly described in this Authors writings.*

For, they *discover both where the* Things *themselves are to be found, in which are hidden all Divine and Naturall Mysteries, and likewise shew, as with the finger, how those secret things have proceeded to their Being and manifestation, from the infinite* Incomprehensibility, *wherin* Nothing *can be perceived, and yet* All things *have proceeded from thence; and how they have come to be as they Are; to the discerning what the Essatle Manifested Revealed* God *is, and all* Creatures *whatsoever: and amongst the rest, what we* our selves *are, and how we may attain the true only and eternal happinesse and blessednesse of Life everlasting, with and in God.*

                                                            And

And can there be any thing more usefull beneficiall necessary and worthy then this?

Also further by his writings we may come to understand, how *Christ is the Saviour of* All *Men: and yet all* will *not attaine salvation. Though it be confessed. and must be granted, that Eternal Salvation is attained by some* Infants, *also by some innocent ignorant* Persons *of yeares, that have been torn of Hethenish, Jewish, and Christian Parents; being such as have served God according to the Law of their fore-fathers with an upright Conscience: as* Paul *who was a Jew: and so the* Eunuch, Servant *to* Candace Queen *of Æthiopia, a stranger; and* Cornelius the Centurion, *and all others fearing God, and working Righteousnesse, in every Nation, are accepted of him, though they know nothing of the Great, and Common Salvation that hath appeared to all Men; as the Apostles knew it.*

For, if any be cleansed from his Sinnes, it is done by the blood of JESUS CHRIST *which clenseth us from all Sinne, and this is effected in us and for us, when we knew not, and though we know not of it, nor* how *it is done, in the least, to satisfie a Soul that it may undoubtedly be convinced thereof.*

And indeed, had not the Holy Scripture *mentioned this thing concerning the* Blood of Christ; *it had not been possible for any Man but such as the Prophets and Apostles were, to have procured any that are* now called Christians *to Believe and Confesse it.*

Neither can any understand this though he reade of it in the Scriptures; but by the Holy Spirit *within himselfe, which proceedeth from the Father and the Sonne in the Soul of every one, and by the word in the Heart, the word*

of

of Faith, which is God and Christ, even that true [Divine] Light which lighteth every one that cometh into the world.

The same also may be said concerning all those that have been, are, or shall be saved, though they attain not the understanding of the mysteryes of Salvation, in this Life, as those did who wrote the Holy Scriptures, neither can any understand them as they did, but by the same Gifts of the Holy Spirit in the Soul.

Therefore let none boast that he is not born among those, that are called Heathens, but among those, that were outwardly called Jewes of old, or Christians now, or of the Church of Rome, or Protestants or of the Reformed Religion or Presbyterians Independents Separatists Seekers or Perfectists: though every one of these have outwardly a high Prerogative and Excellency above the Heathen, yet the lives and fruits of these not exceeding their's, they will rise up in Judgment against these: but let every Soule, in Love, rejoyce, with all other Soules, in this, that God is our Father, in whom wee live and move and have our Beings, ruling in our Soules' and manifesting his infinite Grace and Mercy, and bringing all things to passe, according to his unconceivable Wisdome and Goodnesse, and according to the purpose of his good will towards Men, which is his Eternall Gospell: To those that hearken and yeeld, to his will and word of Life, alwaies calling, in the Soul of every one, or else none could be condemned for neglecting and contemning it, as they shall be: also provoking the Soul to forsake that which it perceiveth to be evill, and embrace and Co-work with that which it perceiveth, to be good Holy and divine within it selfe: therefore also let every Soul, †groape after God in its Heart, that it may feele and know him whom to know is Life Eternall, and feele the Hope of enjoying the inestimable good things that are laid up for them that

Love

Love God, though few here know any thing thereof: and yet he will certainly give them unto us at that *Day*, which himselfe hath appointed, which will also assuredly come, though no man knoweth when nor what that day will be or bring forth, but he to whom God doth reveale it.

And indeed such Person's writings, whose understandings have been filled with Spirituall *Divine* wisdome, are to be prized above all others.

And though it be an exceeding happinesse and joy to us that God hath bestowed so large understanding to those that have written the Scriptures, and therefore we ought diligently and frequently to read and deeply consider them, yet in most of the Mysteries thereof it remaineth very dark to us, we having so little knowledge of the things it speaketh of: therefore how highly, in exceeding *Love* to the * Scriptures, should we value and esteeme the writings of this *Author Jacob Behme*, which disclose the very things which are but briefly hinted therein, and so fundamentally as to satisfie all the objections, of *Reason* that can be made, and which do also direct us plainly in the way to find the infallible *Conductor the Holy Spirit*, which will open our understandings, to discerne those hidden *Mysteries* mentioned in the Scriptures so long agoe; that † we through patience and ‡ **comfort of them** might have Hope; And yet but darkly, of purpose that some things should be kept secret from the beginning of the world, and not revealed till the due time and season in every Age, and some not till this last age which is appointed for the manifesting of all mysteries.

And because this *Author* could not so deeply and fundamentally disclose these mysteries, but in such significant though hard *Termes* of expression as he * useth; he wrote therefore for the satisfaction of his loving friends, some explanator

that the Deepe and Glorious misteries therein couched may themore cleerely be understood by us. See his Aurora. Chap.9 v. 14.

† Rom. 15.4.
‡ This true comfort of the Scriptures in the Soul, comes by understanding the spirituall sence of the Mysteries of the Scripture, not the bare litterall sence or History.

* See the preface to Jacob Behmes clavis, verf. 10. 11,

planatory Tables, and a Clavis; which are already printed in English: yet still for all that, they are accompted very difficult to be understood.

And I also, who have much and studiously traced his writings over, have found them difficult, but far exceeding in recompence, the utmost paines that I could possibly bestow upon them; I find also that the understanding of them cometh by Degrees, and frequent Loving conversation in all the parts and pieces he hath written; and yet also I must say that this book *Aurora* hath conduced more to open my mind to the understanding of all his writings, and of all Mysteries, both Naturall and Divine, and so consequently of the Holy Scriptures, then any other helps and books which I could ever meete withall besides.

which the Reader will also perceive, by the diligent perusall of this book, in a continued order, from the Beginning and so on: & find* **whatsoever his heart desireth or ever longed for**, and that *See this Aurora, Ch. 3. verf. 96.* it is, as this Author says neere the end of the Preface to this Book,

The Wonder of the World.

And though it was not quite finished at the time when he wrote it, nor ever after, being it was taken away and kept from him till he had written severall compleate Treatises, and so in them that defect of the Aurora was supply'd in abundant measure: for, instead of 30. Sheets which that book wanted to the end; there are written of the same Mysteries, when he had more full knowledge, and leave to declare it and set it down in writing, more then 300. Sheetes of Paper, which containe all Mysteries in

succinct

succinct Termes very deeply _expressed : but in this, the_ Ground _of those Termes are largely and plainly described after the manner of the_ Infancy _of his high_ Manifestation _in a_ Childish _way, so that it is a large and most cleere_ A B C, _being the fitter and plainer for Beginners, with which his other books may the easier be understood, and is a summary contents of all his_ Mysteries, _and may serve instead of a_ Manuduction, _introduction, and key to unlock all the difficult expressions, in his other Books._

And that because it explaines the first Ground concerning the Seaven Properties _of the_ Eternall Nature, _which here he calleth the_ Seaven Qualifying, _or fountaine Spirits or Qualities, which are the_ Seaven Spirits _of God, in and from and to All Eternity, with Notes of_ Reference _to the Book of the three_ Principles, _and threefold Life of Man; which are the supply to the want of finishing this Book, and which he wrote down with his own hand, in their severall proper places by way of exposition in a manuscript of_ Michael von Enderns, _his own written Copy being kept from him, by_ Gregory Rickter _the superintendent at_ Gerlitz, _and published in Print with many whole verses Lines and words left out, printed in high Dutch, 1634. But these Notes were added by the Author, in the yeare 1620. and are here inserted, with Alphabetical marks, in this translation into_ English, _which is made from a Copy taken from that of his own hand writing, which was kept laid up for 27 yeares together, till the 26 of_ November, _in the yeare 1641, when it was brought to Light by_ D. P. S. A _Burgomaster, at_ Gerlitz: _and presented, to the Prince Elector of Saxonies_ Marshall of his House, _George_ Pflugen, _in Dresden : But is now in the Hands of a worthy Person in Holland, and lately printed in High Dutch : and so the rest of this Authors Manuscrips in his Hands, will be printed_

b.

by degrees in Nine parts, *in the same Order the Author hath written them in* : This Aurora *being the* first.

But the Author was *resolved to leave it unfinished to remaine as an* Eternall remembrance *of the endeavour to* suppresse *and* quash this Revelation *in its* first dawning : *which will also be* manifested *at the* Last Day *, when all things shall appeare, to be judged whether they be* Good or Evill ; *and every thing receive its just recompence of reward.*

Therefore,

Deare Reader,

In true sincere Love *to thee as to my* self *I commend this Book the* Aurora *to thy* reading *whosoever thou* art ; *desiring thy* Prayers *, that is , thy* good desires *, that I with thee may be received into the* Grace *and* Mercy *of the* All-mighty Omni-present God *, whose whole* fullnesse *is all-*waies with and in himself *every where , and so be* pro-tected *through this* miserable Pilgrimage *, under* corrup-tion *, in the vale of* sinfull Flesh *, and that* most hurting us *, in the* greatest Pleasure *,* Honour *,* Pomp *,* Riches *and* fullnesse *of* Worldly content *, in this transitory Life , till we awak and meete together , in the everlasting joy of our* ever blessed God *, who* filleth us *throughout and all things else with* himselfe *, within and without , which we* should perceive *, if we would learne to* distinguish *,* Him *from the* Creature *in every thing.*

I willingly yeeld *my* self *to be thine , though with the acknowledgment that I am* one of the unworthiest *of the* Children of Men,

John Sparrow.

The Brief Contents of the 26. Chapters of the First Book of the Author, called, the

Aurora.

The Contents.

The Contents.

[b]   Chapter

The Contents.

Chapter

The Contents.

The Contents.

The Contents

Chapter

The Contents.

These

These Errours are so many, because, after the Book was Printed in English, there came over from beyond Sea a New Copie of the *Aurora* in High-Dutch, printed, and compared with that of the Authors own hand-writing: And so also it was compared here with this printed Copie in English, wherein most of these differences were found.

And therefore the Reader is desired to mend his Book before he reads it, for it will render many of the Obscure places cleer to be understood.

J. B. Preface, Page 4. line 6. for *to*, read in, p. 5 l. 28 r. Gen. 25. 23. p. 6. l. 14 l. 19 l. 33 f. *Nature*. r. kind. l. 24 r. *Mahalaleel*. p. 16 l. 9 s. *Evil Quality*. p. 18 l. 14 r. *Tree*, and spoyled many Twegges in the Holy Tree. p. 20 l. 12 f. *dwell*. r. flow. p. 26 l. 31 f. *yet beheld*. r. behold. p. 28 l. 5 f. *fist*. r. for. p. 30. l. 10 r. *see* 10, the p. 36 l. 28 r. *eth* in winter. p. 47 l. 3 r. *as if God were*. p. 57 l. 13 f. *the very*. r. every. p. 62 l. 2 r. *World*, and is the King and the Heart of all things of this world: and. p. 63 l. 5 put out, *is*. l. 6 r *but is*. l. 19 f. *onne*. r. *Sonne*. p. 64 l. 13 f. *out of*, r. And is. p. 64 l. 31 r. *other*, and is the Spirit and Life of all powers of the whole Father. p. 68 l. 17 f. must. r. will. p. 82 l. 50 f. *to*. r. into. p. 85 l. 23 r. *out of the Seed of the Mother*. p. 97 l. 24 f. *Eternity to Eternity*. p. 98 l. 18 r. *As by*. l. 28 f. *br*. r. by. p. 100 l. 6 f. *Radox*. r. *Rednes*. p. 100 l. 10 f. *Liberty*. r. *Ternary*. p. 111 l. 30 r. *that in the divine power they should*. p. 114 margin. f. *Part*. r. *Port*. p. 115 l. 13 r. *up, in the moving of the Holy*. p. 117 l. 20 r. *Nativities or Genitures of the*. l. 30 r. *Head and General or Leader*, the beautifullest and most powerful *Cherubin*. or, p. 119 f. bad. r. had. p. 141 l. 13 f. *cannot*. r. come to. p. 156 l. 24 f. *valley*. O *Potency & Dominion*, thou art a Raging and tearing of the Hellish fire. p. 159 l. 6 r. *Pitty*. r. complain on. p. 161 l. 20 r. *delightfull* habitation. l. 25 f. *creatures* in this world. p. 166 l. 23 f. *Life*. r. *Light*. p. 174 l. 6 r. thick and stinking; and. l. 16 f. *brittle*. r. spoyled or corrupt. p. 176 l. 22 r. *as well the fist as the*. p. 177 l. 1 r. the *Second, third, fourth*. p. 180 l. 30 f. *Light*. r. *Sight*. p. 188 l. 12 f. *world*. r. wood. p. 191 l. 2 f. *thou lovest*, r. pleaseth thee. p. 197 l. 8 r. *Smelling, All-Tasting, All-* p. 200 l. 17 r *and all*. f *Deity*. r. God. p. 203 l. 27 f. *a*. r. one. p. 205 l. 13 r. *Center*, as a Heart. p. 208 l. 4 f. *half*, r. cleer. p. 216 l. 10 f. *the six*. r. the Seven. p. 231 l. 16 r. one for *from*. p. 245 l. 12 r. and Habitation of all. p. 253 l. 1 r. *God*, hath; for, the Ternary of God riseth up in the Seven Spirits of God; and is. l. 16 r. the One Body. l. 30 f. Spirit. r God. p. 272 l. 16 f. *Warres*, r. *Wares*. l. 26 for, a dull Humour, r. drunkennesse or fulnesse. p. 282 l. 4 f. fiery, r. fierce. p. 288 l. 15 r. *Spirits* one in another, where alwaies one generateth the other. p. 289 l. 23 r. the *other*, and in the sound one heareth the other. p. 292 l. 19. r. *as the* whole Deity. l. 24 f. *Deity*, r. God. p. 317 l. 25 *Mark*: to which it is the whole desire, longing and delight of my heart, to reach fully. p. 321 l. 23 f. er. r. and.

p. 322.

J. B. Preface for the *Aurora*.

To the Courteous Reader.

1.

Courteous *Reader*, I compare the whole *Philoso-phie Astrologie* and *Theologie*, together with their Mother; to a goodly Tree, which grow-eth in a fair Garden of pleasure.

2. Now the Earth, in which the Tree standeth af-fords sap continually to the tree, whereby the tree hath its living *Quality*: but the tree in it self groweth from the *Sap* of the earth, becomes Large, and spreadeth it self abroad with its branches: And then as the Earth worketh with its power upon the tree, to make it grow and encrease; so the Tree also worketh continually with its *branches* with all its strength, that it might still bear good fruit abundantly.

3. But when the Tree beareth few fruit, and those but small ones neither, shrivelled *rotten* and worm-eaten, the fault doth not lye in the will of the tree, as if it desired *purposely* to bear evill fruit, because it is a goodly Tree of good *Quality*; but here lyeth the fault, because there is often great cold, great heat, mildew, caterpillars and other worms happen to it: for the *Quality* in the Deep, from the influence of the Stars, spoileth it, and that maketh it bear but few good fruit.

4. Now the Tree is of this condition, that the bigger and older it is, the sweeter fruit it beareth: in its youn-ger years it beareth few fruit, which the crude and

wild

wild nature of the ground or earth caufeth, and the *fu-perfluous* moifture in the tree : and though it beareth many and fair bloffoms, yet the moft of its Apples fall off whileft they are growing, which is not fo, when it ftandeth in a very good foyl or mould. Now this tree alfo hath a good fweet quality, but there are *three* other which are contrary unto it, namely, the bitter, fowre, and aftringent.

5. And as the Tree is, fo will its fruit be, till the Sun worketh on them and maketh them fweet, fo that they become of a fweet tafte, and its fruit muft alfo *hold out* in rain, wind and tempeft.

6. But when the tree groweth old, that its branches wither, and the fapp afcendeth *no more*, then below the ftemm or ftock there grow many fuckers, at laft from the root alfo twiggs grow, and make the old tree flou-rifh, fhewing that *it* alfo was once a green twigg and young tree, and is now become old. For Nature, or the fapp, ftruggleth fo long till the Stock groweth quite dry, and then is to be cut down and burnt in the fire.

7. Now obferve, what I have fignified by this *fimilitude* : the Garden of this tree fignifieth the *World*; the foyl or mould fignifieth *Nature*, the Stock of the tree figuifies the *Starres*, by the *Branches* are meant the *Elements*, the fruit which grow on this tree fignifie *Men*, the fapp in the tree refembles the pure *Deitie*. Now Men were made out of Nature the *Starrs* and *Elements*, but God the Creator raigneth in all : even as the *fapp* doth in the whole tree.

8. But there are *two Qualities in Nature*, even untill the *Judgment* of God : the One is pleafant, heavenly and holy, the other is fierce, wrathfull, hellifh and thirfty.

9. Now

9. Now the good one qualifieth and worketh continually with all industry, to bring forth *good* fruit, and the *Holy Ghost* raigneth therein, and affords thereunto sapp and life: the bad one Springeth and driveth with all its endeavour to bring forth *bad* fruit continually, to which the devil affordeth sap and *hellish* flame. Now both are in the tree of Nature, and *Men* are made out of *that* tree, and live in this world, in this garden, *betwixt* both, in great danger; suddenly the Sun shineth on them; by and by, winds, rain and snow, fall on them

10. That is, if man elevateth his Spirit into the *Deity*, then the Holy Ghost moveth springeth and qualifieth in him: but if he permit his spirit to sink into the world, in lust towards *evil*, then the Devil and hellish sapp stirreth and raigneth in him.

11. Even as the Apple on the tree becometh corrupt rotten and worm-eaten, when frost, heat, and mill-dew fall on it, and easily falls off and perisheth: so doth Man also when he suffers the Devill to rule in him with his *poysson*.

12. Now as in Nature there is, springeth, and raigneth, good and bad; even so in Man: but Man, is the *Child of God*, whom he hath made out of the best Kernel of Nature, to raign in the good, and to overcome the bad; though evill sticketh unto him, even as in *Nature* the evill hangeth on the good, yet he can overcome the evil, if he elevateth his spirit in God; for then the *Holy Ghost* stirs and moveth in him, and helps him to overcome.

13. As the good quality in Nature is potent, to overcome the evill, for it is and cometh from God, and the Holy Ghost is the *Ruler* therein: even so is the fierce wrathful Quality, powerful to overcome in a *malicious*

wicked

wicked foul: for the Devil is a potent *Ruler* in the wrath or fierceneſs, and is an eternal Prince of the ſame.

14. But Man hath caſt himſelf into fierce wrathfulneſſe through the *fall* of *Adam* and *Eve*, ſo that the evill hangeth on him; otherwiſe, his moving and driving would be *only* to the good. But now it is in *both*, and it is as St. *Paul* ſaith, *Know ye not, that to whom you yield your ſelves ſervants in obedience, his ſervants ye are, to whom ye obey, either to ſinne unto death, or to the obedience of God unto righteouſneſs,* Rom. 6. 16.

15. But becauſe man hath an *impulſe* or inclination to both, he may lay hold on which he pleaſeth; for he liveth in this World betwixt *both*, and both *Qualities*, the good and the bad are in him, in which ſoever man moveth, with that he is indued, either with a Holy or a Helliſh Power. For Chriſt ſaith, *My Father will give the Holy Ghoſt to thoſe that ask him,* Luk. 11. 13.

16. Beſides, God commanded man to do good, and did forbid him to do evill; and now doth daily call and preach, and exhort man unto good; Whereby we ſee, well enough, that God *willeth not evil*, but his Will is, That *His Kingdom* ſhould *come*, and *his will be done, on earth as it is in heaven.* Now ſince man is poiſoned through ſinne, that the fierce wrathful quality, as well as the good, reigneth in him, and is now *half* dead, and in his groſſe ignorance can no more know God his Creator, nor Nature and its operation; yet hath Nature done its *beſt* endeavour from the beginning till now, to which God hath given his Holy Ghoſt, ſo that it hath at all times generated wiſe, holy and *underſtanding* men, which did learn to know Nature and their Creator, who alwayes in their Writings and Teachings have been *a Light* to the World, whereby
God

God hath raised his Church on Earth, to his eternal praise. Againſt which the Devil hath *raged*, and ſpoiled many a noble Twigg, through the wrathfull fierceneſs in Nature, whoſe *Prince* and God he is.

17. For Nature hath many times prepared and fitted a learned judicious man with good gifts, and then the Devil hath done his utmoſt to ſeduce that man, and bring him into *carnal pleaſures*, to pride, to a deſire to be rich, and to be in authority and power. Thereby the Devil hath ruled in him, and the fierce wrathfull *Quality* hath overcome the good; his Underſtanding, his Knowledge and Wiſdome hath been turn'd into *Hereſie* and Errour, who hath made a mock of the Truth, and been the Author of great Errours on earth, and a good Leader of the Devils Hoſt.

18. For the bad quality in Nature hath wreſtled, and doth ſtill wreſtle with the good, ever ſince the beginning, and hath elevated it ſelf, and ſpoiled many a noble fruit even in the mothers *womb*, as it plainly appeareth, firſt by *Cain* and *Abel*, which came from one womb. *Cain* was from his mothers womb a deſpiſer of God, and proud; but *Abel*, on the contrary, was an humble man, and one that feared God.

19. The ſame is ſeen alſo in the *three* ſons of *Noah*; as alſo by *Abraham*'s ſons *Iſaac* and *Iſmael*, eſpecially by *Iſaac*'s in *Eſau* and *Jacob*, which ſtruggled and wreſtled even in the mothers womb: therefore ſaid God, *Jacob have I loved, and Eſau have I hated*, Gen. 25. which is nothing elſe, but that both qualities in Nature have vehemently wreſtled one with another.

20. For when God at that time moved in Nature, and would *reveal* himſelf unto the world through righteous *Abraham Iſaac* and *Jacob*, and would raiſe a Church to himſelf on earth for his glory, then in Nature

ture Malice alfo moved, and its Prince *Lucifer*. See-
i g there was good and bad in man , therefore both
Qualities could raign in him , and therefore there was
born at *once* in one womb an evill and a good Man.

21. Alfo it is cleerly feen by the *firft* world, as alfo
by the *fecond*, even unto the end of our time, how the
Heavenly and Hellifh Kingdom in Nature hath alwayes wreftled one with another, and ftood in great
travel, even as a woman in the birth.   This doth moft
cleerly appear by *Adam* and *Eve*.   For there grew up
a tree in Paradife of both *Qualities* of good and bad,
wherewith *Adam* and *Eve* were to be tempted, to try
whether they would hold out in the *good Quality* in
the Angelicall nature and form.   For the *Creator did
forbid* Adam *and* Eve *to eat of the fruit* : but the evill
quality in Nature did wreftle with the good, and
brought *Adam* and *Eve* into a luft and longing to eat
of both.   Thereupon they prefently became of a beaftial form and nature, and did eat of good and bad, and
muft increafe and live in a *beaftial* manner, and fo many
a noble twigg begotten or born of them perifhed.

22. Afterward it is feen, how God did work in Na-
ture, when the Holy Fathers in the firft world were
born :   as *Abel, Seth, Enos, Kenan, Mahaleel, Jared, Henoch,
Methufalah, Lamech,* and Holy *Noah*.   Thefe made the
Name of the Lord known to the world, and preached
Repentance : for the Holy Ghoft wrought *in* them.

23. On the contrary, the Hellifh God alfo wrought
againft it, *in* Nature, and begot Mockers and Defpifers,
firft *Cain* and his Pofterity :   and it was with the firft
world as with a young tree, which groweth, is green,
bloffometh fairly, but bringeth little good fruit, by
reafon of its *wild* Nature.   So Nature in the firft world
brought forth but little good fruit, though it bloffomed
                                                     fair

fair in *worldly* knowledge and luxury or wantonesse, *which* could not apprehend the Holy Spirit, who wrought in Nature then, as well as now.

24. Therefore said God, *It repents me, that I have made man,* Gen. 6. 6. and he stirred up Nature so, that all flesh dyed, which lived on dry Land, excepting the root and stock, that remained in vertue : and so he hath hereby *Dung'd* the wild Tree, and manured it, that it should bear *better* fruit. But when the same sprung up again, it brought forth also good and bad fruit again ; Among the sons of *Noah,* there were found again Mockers and Despisers of God, and there *hardly* grew any good branch on the tree, which brought forth any *holy* and good fruit : the other branches were bearing also, and brought forth wild Heathens.

25. But when God saw, that man was thus dead in his Knowledge, He moved Nature again, and *shewed* unto *man,* how there was *good and bad* therein, that they should *avoid evill,* and *live unto the good* ; and he caused fire to fall down out of Nature, and fired *Sodom* and *Gomorah,* for a terrible example to the world. But when the blindnesse of men grew predominant, and refused to be taught by the Spirit of God, he gave *Laws* and *Precepts* unto them, shewing how they should behave themselves, and confirmed them with *wonders* and Signs, lest the knowledge of the true God should be quite extinct. But for all this, the light did *not* manifest it self, for the darknefs and wrathful fiercenefs in Nature struggled against it, and the Prince thereof ruled powerfully.

26. But when the Tree of Nature came to its middle age, then it began to bear some *mild* and sweet fruit, to shew , that it would henceforth bear pleasant fruit. Then were born, the *Holy Prophets,* out of the sweet branch of the tree, which taught and preached

of

of the *light*, which hereafter fhould overcome the wrathful fierceneſs in Nature. And then there aroſe a light in Nature among the Heathens, ſo that they knew Nature, & her operation, although this was *only a* light in the *wild* Nature, and was not yet the *holy* light.

27. For the wild Nature was not yet overcome, and light and darkneſſe wreſtled ſo long one with another, till the *Sun* aroſe, & forced this tree with its heat, ſo that it did bear pleaſant ſweet fruit : that is, till there came the Prince of Light out of the heart of God, and *became Man* in Nature, and wreſtled in his humane body in the power of the Divine light in the wild Nature. That ſame Prince and *Royal* twigg grew up in Nature, and became a tree in Nature, and ſpread its branches abroad from the Eaſt to the Weſt, and encompaſſed the whole Nature, and wreſtled and fought with the fierce wrath which was in Nature, and with the Prince thereof, till he overcame and triumphed as a King in Nature, and took the *Prince of wrath* or fierceneſſe, *Captive* in his own houſe, *Pſal.* 68.

28. This being done, there grew out of the Royal Tree, which was grown in Nature many thouſand *Legions* of precious ſweet twigs, all which had the ſcent and taſte of that precious Tree. Though there fell upon them, rain, ſnow, hayl and tempeſtuous ſtorms, ſo that many a twigg was *torn* and beaten off from the tree, yet ſtill others grew in their places. For the Wrath or fierceneſſe in Nature, and the Prince thereof, raiſed great *tempeſts*, with hayl, thundring, lightning and rain, ſo that many glorious twiggs were torn from the ſweet and good Tree.

29. But theſe twiggs were of ſuch a pleaſant ſweet and curious taſte, that no humane nor Angelical tongue is able to expreſſe it : for there was great *power* and vertue

vertue in them, they were good to *heal* the wild Heathens. Whatever Heathen did eat of the twigg of this tree, he was *delivered* from his wild nature, in which he was born, and became a sweet tree in this pretious Tree, and sprung up in that tree, and did bear pretious fruit, like the Royal tree. Therefore many Heathens *resorted* to the pretious tree, where the pretious twiggs lay, which the Prince of darknesse by his storms and tempestuous winds had torn off; and whatever Heathen did smell to the twigg so torn off, he was healed of his wild wrath or fiercenesse, which he had brought from his Mother into the world.

30. But when the Prince of darknesse did see, that the Heathens *strove* and contended about these *twiggs*, and not about the *Tree*, therein he found great losse and dammage, and then he ceased with his storms toward the East and South, and placed a Merchant under the tree, who gathered up the twiggs, which were fallen from the pretious tree : and then when the Heathens came, and enquired after the good and vertuous twigs, then the Merchant presented and offered them, for money, to make gain of the pretious *Tree*. For, this, the Prince of wrath or fiercenes required at the hands of his Merchant, because the tree was grown upon his ground and land, and spoyled his soyl.

31. And so when the *Heathens* did see, that the fruit of the pretious tree was put to *sale*, they flock'd to the Merchant, and bought of the *fruit* of the tree, and they came also from forraign Islands to buy, even from the Ends of the world. Now when the Merchant saw, that his Wares were in request and esteem, he plotted, how he might gather a great treasure to his *Master*, and so sent *Factors* abroad, every where, to offer his Wares to sell, praising them highly : but he *sophisticated* the
C   wares,

wares, and sold other fruit instead of the good, which were not grown on the good Tree; this he did to encrease his Masters treasure.

32. But the Heathens and all the Islands and Nations, which dwelt on the earth, were all grown on the *wild* tree, which was good and bad: and therefore were half blind, and did not discern the good tree, (which however did spread its branches from the East to the West,) else they would *not* have bought of the *false* wares.

33. But because they knew not the pretious Tree, which spread its branches over them all; *all of them ran after, and to, the Factors,* and bought of them *mix'd* false wares instead of good; and supposed they served for health: but because *all* of them did *long* after the good tree, which however moved over them all, many of them were healed, because of their great desire they had to the Tree. For the fragrancy of the tree, which moved over them, healed them of their wrath or fiercenesse and *wild* nature, and not, the false wares, of the Factors: this continued a long time.

34. Now when the Prince in the darknesse, who is the Source of wrath or fiercenefs, malice and perdition, *perceived,* that men were healed of their poison and wild nature by the fragrancy of the pretious Tree, he was enraged, and planted a wild tree toward the North, which sprung up and grew in the fiercenesse or wrath of Nature, and made proclamation, saying: *This is the Tree of Life, he that eateth of it, shall be healed and live eternally.*

35. For in that place, where the wild tree grew, was a wild place, and the people there had the true light of God from the beginning even unto that time, and to this day, though unknown: and the tree grew

on

on the Mount *Hagar* in the house of *Ifmael* the mocker.
But when Proclamation was made of the tree, *Behold
this is the tree of life*! then the wild people *flocked* unto the tree, which were *not* born of God, but of the
wild Nature, and *loved* the wild tree, and did eat of
its fruit.

36. And the tree grew to a mighty bigneſſe, by the
ſap of *wrath* or fierceneſſe in Nature, and ſpread abroad
its branches, from the North to the Eaſt and Weſt:
but the tree had its ſource and Root from the wild
Nature, which was good and bad, and as the tree was,
ſo were its fruits. But though the men of this place
were grown out of the wild Nature, yet the tree grew
over them all, and grew ſo huge, that it reach't with
its branches even unto the Eſteemed *pretious Land* or
Country under the Holy Tree.

37. But the cauſe, that the wild tree grew to ſuch a
huge bigneſſe, was, becauſe the Nations under the
good Tree ran all after the *Factors*, which ſold the
falſe Wares, and did eat of the falſe fruits, which
were good and bad, and ſuppoſed they were healed
thereby, and medled *not* with the holy good effectuall
Tree.

38. In the mean while they grew more blind, weak
and faint, and were *diſabled* to ſuppreſſe the growing
of the wild tree toward the North: for they were too
weak and faint, and they ſaw well enough, that the
tree was wild and naught, but they wanted ſtrength,
and could not ſuppreſſe the growing of the tree.

39. Yet if they had not run after the falſe Wares
thoſe Factors *ſold*, and had not eaten of the *falſe* fruits,
but rather eaten of the pretious tree, then they might
have gotten ſtrength to oppoſe the wild tree. But becauſe they ran a whoring after the wild Nature in

Humane

Humane *conceits* and opinions, in the lusts of their hearts, in a hypocritical way, therefore the wild Nature did predominate over them, and the wild tree grew high and large over them, and spoiled them with its wild *rankneſſe*.

40. For, the Prince of Wrath or fierceneſs, in Nature, gave his power to the tree, to ſpoil men, which did eat of the wild fruits of the Factors: Becauſe they forſook the Tree of life, and ſought after their own fancie, as Mother *Eve* did in Paradiſe, therefore their own *innate quality* predominated in them, *and brought them into ſtrong deluſions,* as St. *Paul* ſaith, 2. *Theſ.* 2. 11. And the Prince of Wrath or fierceneſſe, did raiſe *warrs* and tempeſts from the wild tree toward the North againſt the people and Nations, which were *not* born of the wild tree, and the tempeſt which came from the wild tree overthrew them in their weakneſſe and faintneſſe.

41. And the *Merchant* under the good Tree diſſembled with the Nations of the South and Weſt, and toward the North, and commended his Wares hugely, and deceived cunningly the ſimple ones; and thoſe that were witty, he made them his Factors, that they alſo might have their *livelihood* or livings out of it, and he brought it ſo far, that no body did ſee or know the holy tree any more, and ſo he got all the Land to himſelf, and then made Proclamation, 2 *Theſſ.* 2. *I am the ſtock of the good tree, and ſtand on the root of the good tree, and am ingrafted into the Tree of Life, buy my Wares which I ſell* : and then you ſhall be *healed* of your wild birth, and live for ever.

42. I am grown out of the root of the good Tree, and the fruit of the holy tree is in my power, and I ſit on the *Throne* of the divine power, I have power in heaven

ven and on earth, *Come unto me,* and buy for money, the fruit of life.

43. Whereupon all Nations flocked unto him, and did buy and eat, even till they fainted: all the Kings of the South, Weſt, and toward the North did eat the fruits of the *Factor,* and lived under a great faintneſſe; for the wild tree of the North grew more and more over them, and made *waſte* of them a long time. And there was a miſerable time upon earth, ſuch as never was, ſince the world ſtood, but men thought that time to be *good;* ſo terribly the Merchant under the good tree, had *blinded* them.

44. But in the *Evening* God in his mercy took *pity* on mans miſery and blindneſſe, and ſtirr'd up the good tree again, even that glorious *Divine* Tree, which did bear the fruit of life; then there grew a twigg *nigh* unto the root, out of that pretious tree, and was green, and to it was given the *ſap* and ſpirit of the tree, and it ſpoke with the tongue of Man, and *ſhewed* to every one the pretious tree, and its voice was heard in many Countreys.

45. And then men reſorted thither to ſee and to hear what the matter was, and there was ſhewed unto them the pretious and vigorous Tree of Life, of which men had eaten at the beginning, and were *delivered* of their wild nature, and they were mightily rejoyced, and did eat of the Tree of life with great joy, and refreſhing, and ſo got new ſtrength from the Tree of life, and ſung a new ſong concerning the *true real Tree of Life,* and ſo were delivered from their wild birth, and then hated the Merchant and his Factors, as alſo their falſe Wares.

46. But all thoſe came, which did hunger and thirſt after the Tree of life, and thoſe that ſate in the *Duſt,* and they did eat of the holy Tree, and were healed of their

impure

impure birth and wrath or fierceneſs of Nature, in which they lived, and ſo were *ingrafted* into the Tree of life. But onely the Factors of the Merchant, and his and their Diſſemblers, and thoſe that made their gains with falſe wares, and had gathered Treaſure together, *came not*, for they were drown'd and quite dead in the gain of the Merchants whoredom, and lived in the wild nature, and ſo their anguiſh and ſhame, which was diſcovered, *kept* them back, becauſe they went a whoring ſo long with the Merchant, and ſeduced the ſoules of men, notwithſtanding they gloried, that they were ingrafted into the tree of life, and lived in ſanctity by a divine power, and ſet to ſale the fruit of life.

47. Now becauſe their ſhame, deceit, covetouſneſs, knavery and wickedneſſe was diſcovered, they waxed dumb, and ſtayed behind, they were aſhamed, and repented of their abominations and *Idolatry*, and ſo went with the hungry and thirſty to the Fountain of Eternal life ; and therefore they grew faint alſo in their thirſt, and their plague riſeth up from eternity to eternity, and they are gnawed in their conſcience.

48. Now the Merchant ſeeing that the deceit of his falſe Wares was *diſcovered*, he grew very wroth, and deſpaired; and bent his Bow againſt the holy people, which would buy no more of his Wares, and ſo deſtroyed many of the *holy* people, and blaſphemed the *Green-twigg, which was grown up out of the Tree of life.* But the *Great Prince* MICHAEL which *ſtandeth before God*, came and fought for the Holy people, and overcame.

49. But the prince of darkneſſe perceiving, that his Merchant had a Fall, and that his deceit was diſcovered, he raiſed a *tempeſt* from the North out of the wild Tree againſt the holy people, and the Merchant of the

South

South made an affault upon *them* : then the Holy people grew hugely in their Bloſſom, even as it was in the
beginning, when the holy and pretious tree grew, and
that overcame the wrath or fierceneſſe in Nature and
its Prince ; thus it was at that time.

50. Now, when the noble and holy Tree was revealed
to *all* Nations, ſo that they ſaw how it moved over them,
and ſpread its fragrancy over all people, and that any
one that pleaſed, might eat of it ; then the people grew
weary of eating its *fruit*, which grew on the tree, and
long'd to eat of the *Root* of the Tree; and the cunning
and wiſe people ſought after the *Root*, and contended
about the ſame : ſo the ſtrife was great about the root
of the tree, inſomuch, that they *forgot* to eat of the
fruit of the ſweet tree, by reaſon of the *controverſie* about
the root of the tree.

51. And now they minded *neither* the Root nor the
Tree, but the prince of darkneſſe had another deſign,
intending ſomething elſe : when he ſaw, that they
would eat no more of the good Tree, but contended
about the Root, he perceived, that they were grown
very weak and faint, and that the wild Nature predominated in them again;

52. And therefore he ſtirred them up to pride, ſo that
every one ſuppoſed, he had the Root at hand, every one
muſt look after and hear him, and reverence him :
Whereby they built their Palaces and great Houſes,
and ſerved in ſecrecie their Idol *Mammon*, whereby
the Lay people were troubled and cauſed to offend, and
ſo lived in carnal pleaſures, in the deſire of the *wild* Nature, and ſerved their belly in wantonneſſe, confiding
in the fruit of the tree, which moved over them all,
though they fell into miſery, that *thereby* they might be
healed.

53. And

53. And in the mean while they ferved the prince of darkneſſe according to the impulſe of the wild nature, and the pretious tree ſtood there onely for a Maygame or mocking ſtock, and many lived like *wild beaſts*, and did lead a wicked life, in Pride, Pomp, Statelineſſe and Laſcivioufneſſe, the rich confuming the labour and ſweat of the poor, forcing them thereunto.

54. All evill actions were approved of for Bribery: the *Lawes* iſſued forth out of the *evill* in Nature, and every one ſtrove after *riches* and goods, after pride, pomp and ſtatelineſſe, there was *no* deliverer for the poor; ſcolding, railing, curſing, and ſwearing were *not* diſapproved nor held vitious, and ſo they defiled themſelves in the wrathful or fierce *Quality*, even as a ſwine tumbleth in the dirt and Mire.

55. This did the Shepherds with the ſheep, they retained no more but the bare *name* of the noble tree, its fruit, vertue and life was only a cover to their *Sins*. Thus the world lived at that time, ſaving a ſmall remnant or number, which were generated in the midſt among the Thorns in great *tribulation* and contempt, out of all Nations upon the Earth, from the Eaſt to the Weſt.

56. There was no difference, they all lived upon the impulſe of the wild nature in *faintneſſe*, even unto a little number, which were delivered out of all Nations, as it was before the *Deluge*, and before the growing of the noble tree in Nature; and thus it was alſo at that time.

57. But why men in the end, did long ſo eagerly after the *Root* of the tree, is a *Myſtery*, and hitherto it was concealed from the wiſe and prudent; neither will it riſe up to the height, but in the Deep, in great ſimplicity.

58. As

58. As indeed the noble tree with its kernel and heart, hath *alwayes* been concealed from the worldly wise: though they suppofed they ftood fome at the root, and fome at the very Top of the tree, yet this was no more then a fhining Mift before their eyes.

59. But the noble tree from the beginning till now ftrove in Nature to its utmoft, that it might be revealed to *all people* Tongues and Languages, againft which the Devil in the wild nature raged, and fought like a fierce Lyon.

60. But the noble tree bore the more and the fweeter fruit, and revealed it felf more and more againft all the fury and madneffe of the Devill, even unto the end; and *then it was light.* *For there grew a green twigg at the Root of the nobleTree,* which gat the fap and life of the root, to which was given the *Spirit* of the Tree; fo it encreafed and multiplyed the noble tree in its glorious vertue and power, and nature alfo, in which it grew.

61. Now when this was done, then *both the Gates* of Nature were opened, the knowledge of the *two Qualities* of good and bad, and fo the *Heavenly Jerufalem* was manifefted, and the *Kingdom of Hell* alfo, to all men upon Earth. And the Light and voice was heard in the *four winds,* and the falfe Merchant in the South was quite revealed, and his *own* hated him, and rooted him out from the whole earth.

62. This being done, the wild tree toward the North *withered,* and all people beheld the holy tree, even in *forraign* Iflands, with admiration. And the Prince in the darkneffe was revealed, and his Myfteries were difcovered, and his fhame, ignominy and perdition, the men upon earth did *fee* and *know,* for it was *Light.*

D

63. And

63. And this lasted but a little time, for men forsook that light, and lived in carnal pleasures to their own perdition: for as the gate of light had opened it self, so did also the gate of darknesse, and from them both went forth all manner of powers and Arts, that were therein.

64. For as men had lived from the beginning in the growth of the wild nature, and hunted only after earthly things; so in the end, things were not mended but rather worse.

65. In the middle of this time were raised many great stormy winds from the West toward the East and North: but from the North there went forth a great *stream of water* toward the holy tree, and in the *midst* of the stream it was light, and so the wild tree toward the North withered.

66. And then the Prince in the darknesse was enraged in the great motion of Nature. For the *Holy Tree* moved in Nature, as one that would by and by be elevated, and kindled, in the *glorification* of the holy Divine *Majestie,* and cast the wrath or fiercenesse from it, which had so long stood against it, and had wrestled with it.

67. In like manner, the tree of darknesse wrath fiercenesse and perdition, moved furiously, as one that would be kindled by and by, and therein the Prince with his *Legions* went forth to spoyl the noble fruit of the good tree.

68. And it stood horribly in Nature in the fierce quality, in that quality, wherein the prince of darknesse dwelt, to speak after the manner of men; even as when men see terrible weather coming on, which maketh a horrible appearance with lightening and tempestuous winds, at which men stand amazed.

69. On

69. On the other side in the good quality, in which the *holy tree of life* stood, all was pleasant sweet and delightful; like an heavenly joyfulness. These two moved furiously one against another, till the whole nature was kindled of both qualities in one moment.

70. And the tree of life was kindled in its own quality, by the fire of the *Holy* Ghost, and its quality burnt in the fire of heavenly joyfulness, in an unsearchable light and glory.

71. All *voyces,* of the heavenly joyfulnesse qualified mixed or harmonized in this fire, which have been from eternitie in the good qualitie; and the Light of the holy Trinity *shined* into the tree of life, and replenished or filled the whole quality, in which it stood.

72. And the tree of the fierce quality which is the other part in Nature, was kindled also and burnt in the fire of *Gods wrath* in a hellish flame, and the fierce source rose up into eternity, and the Prince of darknesse with his Legions did abide in the fierce wrathfull quality, as in his own Kingdom.

73. In this fire were consumed, the *Earth, Starres* and *Elements,* for all were on fire at once, each in the fire of its own quality, and all was separable. For the Ancient of Dayes moved himself in it, wherein every power and all the Creatures, and whatsoever can be *named,* even the powers of Heaven, of the Stars and of the Elements, became thin again, and fashioned according to that form, which they were in from the beginning of the Creation.

74. Only the *two qualities,* good and bad, which have been in Nature one in another, were separated, and the bad one, was given to the prince of malice and wrath or fiercenesse for an eternal habitation; and that

is called *Hell*, or a *Rejection*, which in eternity, no more apprehends or toucheth the good quality ; but is an oblivion of all good, and that unto its eternity.

75. In the other quality ftood the Tree of eternal Life, and its fource and off-fpring defcended from the holy *Trinity*, and the Holy Ghoft did fhine into the fame. And all men came forth which defcended from the loynes of *Adam*, who was the firft man, Each in its vertue, and in that quality, in which each did grow on earth.

76. Thofe that on earth had eaten of the good Tree, which is called *JESUS CHRIST*, *in them* did dwell the *Mercy* of God unto eternal joy ; they had in them the power of the good quality, they were received into the good and holy quality, and they fung the Song of their *Bridegroom*, each in his voyce according to his own Holineffe.

77. But thofe that were born in the *Light of Nature*, and of the Holy Ghoft, and on earth never *fully* knew the Tree of Life, but were grown in its power, which overfhadowed all men upon earth, as very many Nations, Heathens and Babes, which were alfo received into the fame power wherein they were grown, and wherewith their fpirit was cloathed, and they fung the fong according to their power and meafure in the noble tree of eternal life, for every one was glorified according to his power vertue meafure and proportion.

78. And the Holy Nature Generated joyfull heavenly fruit, even as on earth it had generated fruit in both the Qualities, which were both good and bad, fo now it did generate heavenly fulneffe of Joy.

79. And thofe men, that were now like Angels did each eat the fruit of his *Quality*, and they fung the fong

of

of God, and the fong of *the Tree* of eternal *life.*

80. And that was in the Father as a holy Sceane, a triumphing joy ; for to that end all things at the beginning were made out of the Father, and now they abide fo to all eternity.

81. But thofe that were grown on earth in the power of *the tree of wrath,* that is, which the fierce quality had overcome, and were withered in the wickednelle of their fpirit, in their *Sins,* all thofe came forth alfo each in his power or faculty, and were received into *the Kingdom of Darknelle,* and each was indued in that power, in which he was grown up, and their King is call'd *Lucifer,* viz. one expell'd or driven forth from the Light.

82. And the hellifh quality brought forth fruit alfo, as it had done upon earth, onely the good was fevered or parted from it, and therefore it brought forth fruit now in its *own* quality. And thefe Men alfo, which were now like the fpirits, did each eat the fruit of his quality, and fo did the Devils alfo.

83. For as there is a difference in men upon earth in their qualities, and all are not of one Quality Condition or Difpofition, even fo among the rejected reprobate fpirits, and fo in the heavenly pomp in Angels and Men, and that lafteth unto its eternity. *AMEN.*

84.

Courteous Reader, This is a fhort information concerning the *two* Qualities in Nature from the beginning to the end, how there arofe from thence *two Kingdoms,* a heavenly and a hellifh, and how they ftirre in this time and ftrive one againft another, and what the iffue of it will be in the time to come.

The Contents of this Book, by way of Introduction.

To this Book I have given this Name, viz.

The Root or Mother of

Philosophie, Astrologie, and Theologie.

And that you may know what this Book doth treat of,

Observe,

I.

1. In the *Philosophie,* is treated concerning the Divine power,

I. *What God is ;*
II. *How in the Being of God, is created, Nature the Stars and the Elements.*
III. *From whence every thing hath its Original.*
IIII. *How Heaven and Earth were created.*
V. *How Angels, Men, and Devils, were created.*
VI. *How Heaven and Hell, and whatever is creaturely, were created, and what the Two Qualities are in Nature.*

All out of a true ground in the knowledge of the Spirit, by the impulse and motion of God.

2. In

II.

2. In the *Astrologie*, is treated,

   I. *Of the powers of Nature, of the Stars, and of the Elements.*

   II. *How all Creatures proceeded from thence.*

   III. *How the same do impell and rule all.*

   IIII. *And work in all, and how good and bad is wrought by them in Men and Beasts.*

   V. *whence it cometh, that Good and Bad is, and raigneth in this world.*

   VI. *Also how the Kingdom of Heaven and of Hell consisteth therein.*

3. My purpose is not to describe the course, place and Name of all Stars, and what their Annual Conjunction, Opposition, Quadrat, is, or the like; what they yearly and hourly operate, which by a long processe of time hath been observed, by the wise, skilful and Expert Men, who were rich and large in spirit, by their diligent contemplation, observation, deep sense, Calculation and Computation.

4. Neither have I studied or learned the same, and I leave that to the Learned to discourse of: but my intention is to write according to the Spirit and sense; and not according to Speculation.

III.

5. In the *Theologie* is handled.

   I. *Of the Kingdom of Christ, of what condition the same is.*

   II. *How it is set in opposition to the Kingdom of Hell.*

                     III. *How*

III. *How in Nature it fighteth and striveth against the Kingdom of Hell.*

IIII. *How men through Faith and Spirit are able to overcome the Kingdom of Hell, and triumph in Divine power , and obtain eternal salvation, and all this as a victory in the Battel.*

V. *Also how Man through the operation or working in the hellish quality , casts himself into perdition.*

VI. *And what the issue of both will be at last.*

6.

The Supream Title is,

AVRORA.

That is,

The Dawning of the Day in the East:

or

Morning-Redneſſe in the Riſing

of the

SVN.

And is a ſecret Myſtery concealed from the wiſe and prudent of this world, which themſelves ſhall ſhortly be ſenſible of : but to thoſe, which read this book in *ſingleneſſe* of heart, with a deſire after the holy Spirit, who

E

place

place their hope *onely* in God, it will *not* be a hidden fe-cret, but a manifeſt knowledge.

7. I will not explain this Title, but commit it to the judgment of the *impartial* Reader, who wreſtleth in the good quality of this world.

8. Now if Mr. Critick, which qualifieth or work-eth with his wit in the fierce quality, gets *this book* into his hand, he will oppoſe it, as there is alwayes ſtir-ring and Oppoſition between the Kingdom of Heaven and the Kingdom of Hell.

I. Firſt he will ſay, that I aſcend *too high* into the Deity, which is not a meet thing for me to do.

II. Then Secondly, he will ſay, that I boaſt of the Holy Spirit: I had more need to live ac-cordingly, and make demonſtration of it by wondrous Works or Miracles.

III. Thirdly he will ſay; that I am not learned *enough.*

IIII. Fourthly he will ſay; that I do it in a vain-glorious way.

V. Fifthly he will be much offended at the *ſim-plicity* of the Author: as it is uſual in the world, to gaze onely upon *high* things, and ſimpleneſſe is a ſcandal and offence unto it.

9.

To theſe partial worldly Criticks, I ſet in oppoſition the *Patriarchs* of the firſt world, which were mean de-ſpiſed Men, againſt whom the world and the Devil ra-ged as in the time of *Henoch,* when the holy Fathers preached powerfully of the name of the Lord, they did not aſcend with their Bodies into Heaven, and yet be-held all with their *Eyes,* Only the Holy Ghoſt revealed himſelf in *their Spirits.*   10. After-

10. Afterward it is seen in the next world among the holy Patriarchs and *Prophets,* all which were mean simple Men, and some of them were *Herds-men.*

11. Also when the *MESSIAS CHRIST* the Champion in the Battle in Nature, assumed the humanity, though hee was the King and Prince of Men, yet he kept himselfe in this world in a low estate and condition : and was a *Stranger* to the world. And all his *Apostles* were poor despised Fisher-men.

12. Nay Christ himselfe returneth *thanks to his heavenly Father, that he hath concealed it from the worldly wise men, and revealed the same to Babes.* Math. 11.

13. Besides it is seen, how they also were *poor Sinners,* having both the impulses of good and of bad, in Nature. And yet they reproved and preached against the Sinnes of the world, yea against their own Sins, which they did by the impulse of the holy Spirit, and not in vain glory.

14. Neither had they any Ability from their own strength and power, to teach of Gods Mysteries in that kind, but all was by the impulse of God.

15. So I can say nothing of my self neither, nor boast or write of any thing, save this, that I am a *simple* man, and besides a *poore sinner,* and have need to pray daily ; *Lord, forgive us our sins,* and say with the Apostle : *O Lord, thou hast redeemed us with thy Blood.*

16. Neither did I ascend into heaven, and behold all the works and creatures of God ; but the same heaven is *revealed* in my spirit, so that I know in the spirit the works and creatures of God.

17. And besides, the will to that, is not my naturai will, but it is the *impulse* of the Spirit: and I have endured many an assault of the Devil for it.

18. But the spirit of man is descended not only

E 2

from

from the Starrs and Elements, but there is hid therein, a spark of the light and power of God.

19. It is *not* an empty Word, which is set down in *Genesis*, the 1. ch. *v.* 27. *God created man in his own Image, in the Image of God created hee him.* Firſt it hath this ſence and meaning *viz.* that he is created out of the *whole Being* of the Deitie.

20. The *Body* is from the Elements, therefore it muſt have Elemental food.

21. The *Soule* hath its Original, not only from the Body, though it be in the Body, and hath irs firſt beginning in the Body ; yet it hath its ſource alſo from without in it, by and from the Ayr, and ſo the Holy Ghoſt ruleth in it, in that maner, as he repleniſheth and filleth all things, and as all things are in God, and ſo God himſelf is all.

22. Seeing then the Holy Spirit in the Soule is creaturely, *viz.* the proprietie or Portion of the Soul; therefore it ſearcheth even into the *Deitie*, and alſo into *Nature*, for it hath its Source and deſcent from the *Being* of the whole Deitie.

23. When it is kindled or enlightened by the Holy Ghoſt : then it beholdeth what God its Father doth, as a ſon beholdeth what his Father doth at home in his houſe.

24. It is a *Member* or child in the houſe of the heavenly Father.

25. And as the Eye of man ſeeth even unto the Stars, from whence it hath a *finite* original and begining : So the ſoul alſo ſeeth even *into* the Divine Being, wherein it liveth.

26. But the Soul having its ſource alſo out of Nature, and that in Nature there is good and bad; alſo, in that man hath caſt himſelf, through Sin, into the fierceneſſe or wrath of Nature, ſo that the ſoul is daily and
hourly

hourly defiled with *Sins*, therefore it knoweth but in part.

27. For the wrath or fiercenesse in Nature *raigneth* now also in the soul. But the Holy Ghost doth not go into the wrath or fiercenesse, but raigneth in the *source* of the soul which *is* in the light of God, and fighteth against the wrath or fiercenesse in the Soul.

28. And therefore the soul *cannot* attain unto any *perfect* knowledge in this life, till at the end, when light and darknesse are separated, and wrath or fiercenesse, is, with the Body, consumed in the Earth, and then the soul seeth clearly and perfectly in God its Father.

29. But when the soul is kindled or enlightened by the Holy Ghost, then it *triumpheth* in the Body, like a huge fire, which maketh the heart and reins tremble for Joy.

30. But there is not presently a great and deep knowledge in God its Father, but its love towards God its Father, triumpheth thus in the fire of the Holy Spirit.

31. But the knowledge of God is sowen in the fire of the Holy Ghost, and at first is as small *as a Grain of Mustard seed*, as Christ makes the comparison, *Matth.* 13. *afterward it groweth large, like a tree, and spreadeth it self abroad* in God its Creator.

32. Just as a Drop of water in the Ocean cannot avail much; but if a great River runneth into it, that maketh a greater commotion.

33. But the time past, present, and to come, as also depth and heighth, near and afar off, is all *one* in God, one comprehensibility.

34. And the holy Soul of man seeth the same also; But in this world in part only: it happeneth *some times,* that it seeth nothing at all : for the Devil doth assault it
furiously

furiously in the fierce wrathful source which is in the soul, and oftentimes covereth the noble Mustard seed, and therefore Man must alwayes be in fight and war.

35. In this manner, and in this knowledge of the Spirit, I will write in this book, concerning God our Father, in whom are all things, and who himself is all: And will handle, how all is become *distinct* and creaturely, and how all driveth and moveth in the *whole* tree of life.

36. Here you shall see the 1° true ground of the Deity ; 2° how all was *One* Being before the Time of the world ; 3° how the *holy Angels* were created also ; and out of what : 4° Also how the terrible Fall of *Lucifer* together with his *Legions* hapned : 5° How Heaven, Earth, Stars, and the Elements, were made: 6° how metals, stones and other creatures in the earth are generated; 7° How the birth of life is, and the corporeity of all things ; 8° Also what the true *heaven* is, in which God and his Saints do dwell: 9° And what the *wrath* of God is, and the *Hellish* fire.   10°   And how all is become kindled and enflamed.

In brief,

How, and what, the Being of all Beings is.

37.

The *First Seven* Chapters treat very plainly and comprehensibly of the Being of God and of Angels,

Angels, by *similitudes*, that the Reader may from one step to the other at last come to the *deep sense* and true ground.

38. In the *Eighth* Chapter, beginneth the depth in the Divine Being, and so on, the further, the deeper.

39. One thing is often repeated, and still more deeply described, for the Readers sake, and by reason of my slow and dull apprehension.

40. That which you do not find sufficiently explained in *this* book, you will find more clearly in the *second* and † *third*.

41. For, corruption is the cause, why we know but in part, and have not perfect knowledge at once.

* Of the Three Principles
† Of the Threefold Life of Man.

42 Yet

42. Yet this Book is *the WON-DER of the World*, which the holy Soul will underſtand well enough. Thus I commit the Reader into the meek and *holy Love* of God.

The

The First Chapter.

Of Searching out the Divine Being in Nature, of both the Qualities; the Good *and the* Evil.

1.

THough Flesh and Blood cannot conceive or apprehend the Being of God, but the Spirit only when enlightned and kindled from God:

2. Yet if a man will speak of God, and say : What GOD is, Then,

    I. A man must diligently consider the *Powers* in Nature.

    II. Also the whole Creation, Heaven and Earth.

          F   III. The

III. The Stars, the Elements, and the Creatures, which are proceeded from them. As also the holy Angels, Devils, and Men ; moreover, Heaven and Hell.

Of the Two Qualities in One.

3.

In this Confideration are found, *Two Qualities*, a *Good* one and an *Evil* one, which are in one another as One thing, in this world, in all Powers, in the Stars and the Elements, as alfo in all the Creatures : and no Creature in the Flefh, in the Natural Life, can fubfift, unleffe it hath the Two Qualities.

*What a * QVALITY is.*

* The *understanding* of the Thing here called QVALITY, is the foundation of that whole Revelation of *Jacob Behme's* : and of all *Myfteries* ; of which his Writings are only a defcription. For all along, the feven Qualities are called fometime Seven Sources, Seven Species, Kinds, Manners, Circumftances, Conditions, Powers, Operations, or Faculties, of a Thing : Alfo, the Qualifying or Fountain Spirits, which give, model, Image, or frame, the Power, Vertue, Colour, Tafte, figure, fhape, Conftitution, Subftance, Effence, & diftinct Beeing, of All Things ; which ever were, are, fhall be, or can be ; in, from, and to, ALL Eternity ; in God, and all Creatures ; in Heaven, in Hell, or in this World : Alfo, the Forms or Properties, of Nature which is the *Salitter* or Power, of God ; And fo, they are, the feven Spirits of God : as in the Revelations of *John*, Chap. 1. 4. Ch. 3. 1. Ch. 4. 5. Ch. 5. 6.

° Sound, Smell,

4.

Now here a man muft confider, What the word QVALITY meaneth, or is.

A Quality is the Mobility boyling fpringing and driving of a thing.

Of

Of Heat.

5. As, for Example, *Heat,* which burneth, *confumeth* and driveth forth all, whatfoever cometh into it which is not of the fame property: and again it *enlightneth* and warmeth all cold, wet, and dark things, it compacteth and hardneth foft things.

Of Light and Fierceneſſe.

6.

It containeth likewife two other kinds in it, namely, 1° Light, and 2° Fierceneffe: of which take notice in this manner. The light or the heart of the heat is in it felf a pleafant joyfull Glance or Luftre, a power of *life,* an inlightening and glance of a thing which is afar off, and is a piece or fource of the heavenly Kingdom of Joy.

7. For it maketh all things in this world *living* and moving; all fleth, trees, leaves, and graffe, grow in this world in the power of the light and have their life therein, *viz.* in the Good.

8. Again it containeth, alfo a fierceneffe or *wrath* which burneth, confumeth, and fpoileth: this wrath or fierceneffe fpringeth, driveth, and elevateth it felf in the Light, and maketh the light moveable.

9. It wreftleth and fighteth together in its two-fold fource, as one thing; It is alfo one thing, but it hath a double fource: The *light* fubfifteth in God without heat, but it doth not fubfift fo in Nature.

10. For all Qualities in nature are one in another as one *Qualitie,* in that maner, as God is all: and

as all things descend and come forth from him : For God is the *Heart* or fountain of Nature, from him cometh all.

11. Now the *Heat* reigneth and predominateth in all powers in Nature, and warmeth all, and is *one* source or spring in *all* ; for if it were not so, the water would be too cold : and the Earth would be congealed, and there would be no Ayr.

12. The Heat is *predominant* in all, in trees, herbs and graffe, and maketh the water moveable, so that, through the waters Springing out of the earth, there groweth herbs and graffe, and it is therefore called a Quality, because it operateth moveth and boyleth in all, and elevateth all.

13. But the *Light* in the Heat giveth power to all qualities, so that all groweth *pleafant* and joyful. Heat without Light availeth not the other qualities, but is a *perdition* to the Good, an evil source or Spring : for all is spoiled in the fierceneffe or wrath of the Heat. Thus the light in the heat is a quick Spring or living fountain ; into which the Holy Ghoft entreth, but not into the fierceneffe or wrath.

14. Yet the heat maketh the light moveable, so that it springeth and driveth forth, as is seen in winter ; when the Light of the Sun is *likewife* upon the earth, but the *hot* Rayes of the Sun cannot reach into the earth, and that is the reason why no fruit groweth.

Of

Of the qualification of the Cold Quality.

15.

Cold is a Quality also, as well as *Heat*, it qualifieth or operateth in all creatures, whatsoever come forth, in *Nature*, and in all whatsoever doth move therein, in Men, Beasts, Fowles, Fishes, Worms, Leaves, and Grasse.

16. And Heat is set in *opposition* unto it, and qualifieth therein as if it were one and the same thing, but it opposeth the fiercenesse or rage of the Heat, and *allayeth* the Heat.

17. It containeth also two sorts or Species in it, which is to be Observed, *viz.* It *mitigateth* the heat, and maketh all things pleasant, and is in all creatures, a quality of life ; for no creature can subsist without *cold*, for it is a springing driving Mobility in every thing.

18. The other kind or Species is *Fiercenesse* : for where it getteth power, it suppresseth all, and spoileth all, even as the Heat doth; no life can subsist in it, if the Heat did not hinder that. The fiercenesse of Cold is a destruction to every life, and the house of Death, even as the Hot fiercenesse also is.

Of the qualification of the Ayr and the Water.

19.

Ayr hath its original from Heat and Cold ; for

Heat.

Heat and Cold work powerfully, and replenish all, whereby is caused a lively and *stirring* motion ; but when cold allayeth or *mitigateth* the Heat, then both their qualities are rarified and made thin ; and the *Bitter* quality drawes them together, so that they become Dewey.

20. But the Ayr hath its original and greatest motion from *Heat*, and the water hath it from *cold*.

21. Now these Two Qualities wrestle continually one with another, the Heat *consumeth* the water, and the Cold condenseth or crowdeth the Ayr. Now ayr is a cause and the spirit of every *life* and motion in the world, be it in flesh, or in any of the vegetables ; all whatever is, hath its *life* from the Ayr, and nothing can subsist without ayr, whatsoever moveth and is in this world.

22. *Water* also Springeth in every living and moving creature in this World ; in the water consisteth the Body of every thing, as the Spirit consisteth in the

or in Flesh;   Ayr : be it * in animals, or vegetables.

23. And these two are caused by heat and cold, and qualify or mix and operate together as one thing.

24. Now in these two qualitis two other Species or kinds are to be observ'd, *viz.* a *living* and a *dead* operation. The Ayr is a living quality, if it be temperate or moderate in a thing, and the Holy Ghost reigneth in the Calmnesse or *Meeknesse* of the Ayr, and all the creatures rejoyce therein.

25. But there is a *fiercenesse* or wrath also in it, so that it killeth & destroyeth by its terrible disturbance. But the qualification taketh its original from the fierce disturbance or elevation, so that it moveth and driveth in every creature, from whence *life* hath its originals

and

and doth exist: and therefore both of them must be in this life.

26. The Water also hath a fierce *deadly* Spring, for it killeth & consumeth: and so, all things that have a life and Being, must *Rot* and perish in the water.

27. Thus is the Heat and the Cold a cause and original of the Water and of the Ayr, in which every thing *acteth* and *standeth*, every life and mobility standeth therein. Of which I shall write plainly, Concerning the Creation of the Stars.

Of the Influences of the other Qualities in the Three Elements, Fire, Ayr, and Water.

Of the Bitter Quality.

28.

The *Bitter* quality is the heart in every life : for, as it draweth together the Water in the Ayr, and also dissipateth the same, so that it becometh *separable*; so also in other Creatures, as in vegetables of the Earth. For Leaves and Grasse have their *green colour* from the Bitter quality.

29. Now if the Bitter quality dwelleth meek *l*y and Gently in any Creature, then it is the *Heart* or joy therein : for it dissipateth all other Evil Influences, and is the beginning or cause of joy or of *Laughing*.

30. For, being moved, it causeth the Creature to tremble and be joyful, and raiseth it up in its whole Body : for it is as it were a glimpse or Ray of the *heavenly* joyfulnesse, an elevation of the spirit, a spirit and power or vertue in all vegetables of the Earth, and a mother of the life.

31. The Holy Ghost springeth moveth and driveth
vehemently

vehemently in this quality, for it is a part of the heavenly *joyfulnesse*, as I shall demonstrate afterward.

32. But it hath also in it another Species or kind, namely, the fiercenesse or wrath, which is the very House of Death, a *Corruption* of all Good, a perdition and destruction of the Life in the Flesh.

33. For if it be elevated too much in any creature and be inflamed in the Heat, then Flesh and Spirit separateth, and the Creature loseth its Life and must Die: for it moveth and kindleth the Element of *Fire*, for in the great Heat and Bitternesse no Flesh can subsist.

Of the Sweet Quality.

34.

The *Sweet* Quality is set opposite to the *Bitter*, and is a *gracious* amiable blessed and pleasant quality, a refreshing of the Life, an allaying of the Fiercenesse, it maketh all pleasant and *friendly* in every Creature, it maketh the Vegetables of the Earth fragrant and of good taste, affording fair, yellow, white and ruddy *Colours*.

35. It is a glimpse and source of meeknesse, a pleasant Habitation of heavenly joyfulnesse, a House or Mansion of the Holy Ghost, a qualification of Love and *Mercy*, a joy of the Life.

36. But on the other side, it hath also a fierce or wrathful source, a source of Death & Corruption: For if it be *kindled* in the Bitter Quality in the Element of Water, then it breedeth diseases, and the botchey Plague or Pestilence, and corruption of the Flesh.

37. But if it be kindled in the Heat and Bitternes, then it infecteth the Element of Ayr, whereby is ingendred a suddain spreading Plague, and suddain Death.

Of

Of the Soure Quality.

38.

The *Soure* Quality is set opposite to the Bitter and Sweet, and is a good temper to all , a *refreshing* and cooling when the bitter and sweet qualities are elevated too much; it is a longing delight in the Taste, a pleasure of life, a stirring Boyling flowing joy in every thing ; a desire longing and lust of joyfulness, a still Joy or habitation of the *Spirit* : thus it is a temperature to all living and moving creatures.

39. It containeth also a source of evil and corruption : For if it be too much elevated , or stirreth too much *in any thing*, so that it be *inflamed*, then it engendreth *sadnesse*, and Melancholy.

40. In the water it causeth a stinck , putridnesse, and ranknesse, a forgetfulnesse of all good things, a melancholy or sadnesse of life, a House of Death, a *Beginning* of Sorrow; and an *End* of joy.

Of the Astringent or Saltish Quality.

41.

The *Saltish* quality is a good * Temperature in the bitter, sweet, and soure , making every thing pleasant ; it opposeth the *rising* of the bitter Quality, as also of the sweet, and soure; *left* they should be inflamed : it is a sharp quality, a delight in the taste , a source of life and joy.   * or Temper.

42. It containeth also fiercenesse and corruption : Being inflamed in the *fire*, it engendreth a hard, tearing and stony nature , a fierce wrathful
G   source,

source, a *destruction* of life, whereby the Stone or Gravel is engendred in the Reins, causing great pain and torment to the flesh.

43. But if it be inflamed in the *water*, then it engendreth in the flesh, scabs, sores, pox, leprosie, and is a *mourning* house of Death, a misery, and forgetting of all good things.

The Second Chapter.

An Introduction, shewing how men may come to apprehend The Divine, and Naturall, Beeing. And further of the two Qualities.

1.

ALl whatsoever hath been above mentioned is *therefore* called *Quality*, because it qualifieth operateth or frameth all in the Deepe above the earth, also upon the earth, and in the earth, in one another, as *ONE* thing; and yet hath severall distinct vertues and operations, and but one mother, from whence descend and Spring all things.

2. And all the creatures are made and descended from *these qualities*, and live therein as in their mother : and the earth and Stones descend or proceed from thence also ; and all that groweth out of the earth, liveth and Springeth forth out of the vertue of these qualities; no *rational man* can deny it.

3. Now This two-fold Source, Good and Evil in every thing, is caused by the Stars : for as the Creatures in the Earth are in their Qualities, so also are the Stars.

4. For from the two-fold Source, every thing hath its great Mobility, running, Springing, driving and growing. For meeknesse in nature is a Still *Rest*, but the fiercenesse in every power, maketh all

things

things moveable, running, and Generative.

5. For the driving qualities cause a lust in all creatures unto evil and good, so that every thing is *desirous* one of the other, to copulate and encrease, decrease, grow fair, perish, love, and hate.

6. In every Creature in this World is a *Good* and *Evil* will and source; in Men, Beasts, Fowles, Fishes, Wormes, and in all that which is upon the earth; in Gold, Silver, Copper, Tinn, Iron, Steel, Wood, Herbs, Leaves, and Grasse; As also in the earth, in stones, in the water, and all whatsoever can be thought upon.

7. There is nothing in Nature, wherein there is not Good and Evil: every thing moveth and liveth in this double impulse working or operation; be it what it will.

8. But the holy Angels and the fierce Wrathful Devils are here to be excepted, for these are severed apart: Each of these liveth, qualifieth and ruleth in his own peculiar quality.

9. The holy Angels live and qualifie in the *light* in the *good* quality wherein the Holy Ghost raigneth. But the Devils live and raign in the *fierce* wrathful quality, in the Quality of fiercenesse and wrath, destruction or perdition.

10. Yet both of these the good and the evil Angels were made out of the qualities of Nature, from whence all things existed, only they differ in their qualifying or Condition.

11. The Holy *Angels* live in the power of meeknesse, of the Light and joyfulnesse, and the *Devils* live in the power of the rising or elevating quality of fiercenesse, terrour and Darknesse, and cannot comprehend the light, into which condition they precipitated

pitated and caft themfelves through their pride and elevating of themfelves, as I fhall fhew afterward, when I fhall write of the Creation.

12. But if thou wilt not believe, that in this world all defcendeth or cometh from the Stars, I will demonftrate it to thee : if thou art not a Sot or Stock, but haft fome little Reafon and underftanding left, therefore take notice of that which followeth.

13. Firft behold the *Sun*; It is the Heart or *King* of all Stars, and giveth *light* to all ftars from the Eaft to the Weft, it enlightneth and warmeth all, all liveth and groweth by its power ; befides, the joy of all creatures ftandeth in its power.

14. If that fhould be taken away or Extinct, then all would be dark and cold, neither would there grow any fruit, and neither man nor beaft could *propagate* and increafe, becaufe their heat would be extinguifht, and their *Seed* would be cold and chilled.

Of the Quality of the Sun.

15.

If thou wilt be a Philofopher, and *Naturalift,* and fearch into *Gods Being in Nature,* and difcern how all is come to paffe, then pray to God for the holy Spirit, to enlighten thee with the fame.

16. For in thy Flefh and Blood thou art not able to apprehend it, and though thou doft read it, yet it is but as a Fume or Mift before thine Eyes.

17. In the Holy Ghoft alone, who is in God and alfo in the whole Nature out of which all things were made ; in him alone thou canft fearch into the whole Body or Corporeity of God, which is *Nature,* as alfo into the holy Trinity it felf. 18. For

18. For the Holy Ghoſt goeth forth from the holy Trinity, and reigneth and ruleth in the *whole Body* or *Corpus* of God; that is, in the whole Nature.

19. Even as the ſpirit of Man ruleth and reigneth in the whole body in all the Veins, and repleniſheth the *whole Man*: even ſo the Holy Ghoſt repleniſheth the whole Nature, and is the *Heart* of Nature, and raigneth in the good Qualities of every thing.

20. Now if thou haſt that ſpirit in thee, ſo that it enlightneth, *filleth* and repleniſheth thy ſpirit, then thou wilt underſtand what followeth in this writing.

21. But if not, then it will be with thee, as it was with the *wiſe* Heathens, who gazed and ſtared on the Creation, and would ſearch and ſift it out by their *own Reaſon*, and though with their fictions and conceits they came before Gods countenance or Face yet they were not able to ſee it; but were ſtark *blind* in the knowledge of God.

22. And as the children of *Iſrael* in the Deſart could not behold *Moſes* his countenance, and therefore he muſt put a Vail before his face, when he drew near to the people.

23. The cauſe of it was, they neither underſtood nor knew the true God and his Will, who *notwithſtanding* walked among them, and therefore that Vail was a ſign and type of their blindneſſe and miſ-underſtanding.

24. As little as a peece of work can apprehend him that made it, ſo little alſo can *Man* apprehend and know God his creator, unleſſe the Holy Ghoſt *enlighten* him; which hapneth only to thoſe, that rely not upon themſelves, but ſet their *hope* will and
desires,

desires, only upon God, and move in the Holy Ghost, and these are *one Spirit* with God.

25. Now if we consider rightly of the Sun and Starrs, with their *Corpus* or Body, operations and Qualities, then the very divine Being may be found therein, and that the vertues of the stars are Nature it self.

26. If the whole Wheel *Circumference* or Sphear of the stars be well considered, then it is soon found, that the same is the mother of all things: or the Nature out of which all things are come, and wherein all things stand and live, and whereby every thing moveth, all things are made of these powers, and therein they abide *eternally*.

27. And though, indeed *they shall be changed* at the end of this Time, when good and evil shall be separated; And so in like manner Angels and men, *in the power of Nature* out of which they had gotten their first beginning, shall subsist in God, eternally.

28. But here thou must elevate thy minde in the *Spirit*, and consider, how the *whole Nature* with all the powers, which are in Nature, also the widenesse, depth and height, also heaven, and earth, and all whatsoever is therein, and all that is above the heavens, is together, the *Body* or Corporeity of God; and the powers of the Starres are the fountain Veins, in the naturall body of God, *in this world*.

29. Thou must not conceive, that in the Body of the Stars, is the *tryumphing* Holy Trinity, God the Father Sonne and Holy Ghost, in which there is no evil, but is the Light-holy eternal fountain of joy, which is undividable, and unchangeable, which no creature can sufficiently apprehend or expresse: which dwelleth

ethand is above the Body of the Stars in it self, whose depth no creature is able to measure or fathom.

30. But we must not so conceive, as if God were not at all in the *Corpus* or Body of the Stars, and in this world: for when we say, **ALL, or from Eternity to Eternity, or All in All** then we understand, the Entire GOD.

31.

Take *Man* for a Similitude or Example, *who is made after the Image or Similitude of God*, as it is written in *Moses*, *Gen.* 1. 27.

32. *The Inward or hollownesse in the Body of Man*, is and signifieth the Deep betwixt the Stars and the Earth.

33. *The whole Body with all its parts*, signifieth Heaven and Earth.

34. *The Flesh* signifieth the Earth, and is also from Earth.

35. *The Blood* signifieth the Water, and is from the Water.

36. *The Breath* signifieth the Ayr, and is also Ayr.

37. The *Wind-Pipe and Arteries*, wherein the Ayr qualifieth or operateth, signifieth the Deep betwixt the Stars and the Earth, wherein fire, ayr and water qualifie in an elementary manner, and so the warmth, the Ayr, and water, qualifie also in the *Wind-Pipe and Arteries*, as they do in the Deep above the Earth.

38. The *Veins* signifie the powerfull flowings out from the Stars: and are also the powerful outgoings of the Stars: for the Stars with their powers raign in the Veins, and drive forth the Forme, shape and condition in Men.

39. The *Entrails* or *Guts* signifie the operation of
the

the *Stars*, or their confuming of all that which is proceeded from their power, for whatfoever *themfelue* have made, that they confume again, and remain ftill in their vertue and power, and fo the Gutts alfo are the confuming of all that, which man Thrufteth and ftuffeth into his *Gutts*, even all whatfoever groweth from the power of the *Stars*.

40. *The Heart* in man Signifieth the Heat, or the Element of Fire, and it is alfo the Heat : for the Heat in the whole Body, hath its Original in the *Heart*.

41. *The Wind-Pipe* and *Arteries*, fignifie the Element of Aire, and the Aire ruleth alfo therein.

42. *The Liver* fignifieth the Element of water, and it is alfo the water : for from the Liver cometh the Blood in the whole Body into all the Members. The Liver is the Mother of the Blood.

43. *The Lungs* Signify the Earth, and are alfo of the fame Quality.

44. *The Feet* Signify near and afar off, for near and afar off, are all one in God : and fo man by means of his Feet can come and go *near* and *far off* : let him be where he will, he is in Nature, neither near, nor *afar off* ; for in God thefe are *one* thing.

45. *The Hands* fignifie Gods Omnipotence : for as God in Nature can *change* all things, and make of them what he pleafeth : fo man alfo can with his Hands *change* all that which is grown in Nature, and can make with his Hands out of them what he pleafeth : he ruleth with his Hands the *work* and Being of the whole Nature, and fo they very well fignifie the Omnipotence of God.

How

Now observe here further;

46.

The *whole Body, to the Neck*; signifieth, and is, the round circle or Sphear of the Starres, as also the Deep within or between the Stars, wherein the *Planets* and *Elements* reign.

47. *The Flesh* signifyeth the Earth, which is congealed, and hath no motion: and so the flesh in it self hath no Reason, Comprehensibility, or Mobility, but is moved only by the power of the *Stars*, which raign in the flesh and veins.

48. No more could the earth bring forth any fruit, neither could there grow any Metals, as Gold, Silver,, Copper, Iron, or stones, if the *Starrs* did not work in them; neither could there grow any Grasse, without the operation of the Starrs.

49. The *Head* signifieth Heaven; the same is grown on the Body, by the veins, passages and going forth of powers; and so all the powers come again from the Head and *Brain* into the Body, into the fountain-veins or Arteries of the flesh.

50. Now Heaven is a pleasant Pallace of joy, wherein all the powers are, as in the whole nature in the Starrs and Elements, but not *so hard* working and Springing. For every *power* of *Heaven*, hath but one Species kind or form of power, Springing very *bright* and *meek*, not promiscuously Evil and Good one in another, as in the Starrs and Elements, but very *pure*.

51. It is made out of the Midst of the *waters*, but not qualifying in such a manner, as the *water* in the *elements*, for fiercenesse or wrath is not therein. However. Heaven belongeth to Nature, because the Stars and Elements have their original and power from the *Heaven*.

H

52. For Heaven is the *Heart* of the water, as in all creatures, and in all that, which is in this world, the water is the *Heart* thereof and nothing can Subfist without water, be it in the flesh or out of the flesh, in the Vegetables of the earth, or in Metals and Stones, in every thing the water is the kernel or the Heart of it.

53. And so Heaven is the Heart in Nature, wherein all the powers are, as in the Stars and Elements, and it is a soft supple and meek matter of all powers, as the Brain, in mans Head, is.

54. Now Heaven kindleth with its power, the Stars and Elements, so that they move and work : And so the *Head* of man is also like Heaven.

55. For as in Heaven all powers are meek and full of joy; And as Heaven hath a *Closure* or *Firmament* above the Starrs; and yet all powers go forth from Heaven into the Stars : so the Brain also hath a Closure or Firmament between it and the body, and yet all the powers go forth from the Brain into the Body, and into the whole man.

56. *The Head Containeth the five Senses,* viz. Seeing, Hearing, Smelling, Tasting, and Feeling, wherein the Stars and Elements qualify, and therein exifteth the Sydereal or Heavenly Starry or Astral and Natural spirit in Men and Beasts, in this floweth forth Good and Evil, for it is the *House* of the Stars.

57. Such power the Stars borrow from Heaven, that they can make in the flesh a Living and moving *Spirit* in Man and Beast. The moving of the Heaven maketh the Stars moveable, and so the Head also maketh the Body moveable.

58.

Now open here the eyes of thy Spirit, and behold God thy Creator. Question.

Question.

Here Now the Question is, From whence hath Heaven, or whence Borroweth it this power, that it causeth such *Mobility* in Nature?

Answer.

59. Here you must Lift up your Eyes Beyond Nature, into the Light-holy Tryumphing divine power, into the unchangeable holy Trinity, which is a triumphing Springing moveable Being, and all powers are therein, as in Nature.

60. For this is *the Eternal Mother of Nature,* of which Heaven, Earth, Stars, Elements, Angels, Devils, Men, Beasts, and all have their being, and therein *ALL* standeth.

61. When we nominate Heaven and Earth, Stars and Elements, and all that is therein, and all whatsoever is above the Heaven, then thereby is nominated the *Totall God,* which hath made himself *Creaturely,* in these above mentioned Beings, in his power which goeth forth from him.

62. But *GOD* in his *TRINITY* is unchangeable, and whatever there is in Heaven and upon Earth, and above the Earth, hath its Spring Source and Original, from the *Power* which proceedeth from God.

63. Yet you must *not* therefore conceive, that in God, there is Good and Evil, for God Himself is the *Good,* and hath the *Name* from good, which is the triumphing Eternal Joy: only *all* the *powers* proceed from him, which you can search out in Nature, and which are in *all* things.

Question.

64. Now perhaps you may say: *Is there not good*

and

and *Evil in Nature* : and so *seeing every thing cometh from God, needs must then the Evil also come from God* ?

Answer.

65. Behold there is a *Gall* in mans Body, which is *Poison,* and he cannot live without this Gall ; for the Gall maketh the *Astral spirits* moveable, joyous, triumphing or laughing : for it is the source of joy.

66. But if it be inflamed or kindled in one of the Elements, then it *spoileth* the whole Man, for the wrath in the Astral spirits cometh from the Gall.

67. That is, when the Gall overfloweth, and runneth to the Heart, then it kindleth the Element of *fire,* and the fire kindleth the Astral *spirits,* which *raign* in the *Blood* in the veins and in the Element of *Water;* and then the whole Body trembleth by reason of the wrath and the poyson of the Gall.

68. And such a source hath *Joy,* and from the same substance as also the *wrath.* That is, when the Gall in the *Loving* or Sweet quality is inflamed, in that, which man is in love withall, then the whole body trembleth for joy, in which many times the *Astrall* spirits are affected also, when the Gall is overflown, and is kindled in the *Sweet* quality.

69. *But it hath no such Substance in God, for he hath not flesh and blood, but he is a Spirit, in whom all powers are* ; as we pray in the Lords Prayer, *Thine is the power.* (John 4.24. Matth.6.)

70. And as it is written of him in *Isaiah 9. He is Wonderful, Counsel, Power, Champion, Eternal Father, Prince of Peace.*

71. The *Bitter* quality is in God also, but not in that manner as the Gall is in Man, but it is an *everlasting*

lasting power, in an elevating triumphing spring or source of Joy.

72. And though it be written in *Moses, I am an angry zealous God,* Exod.20. *Deut.*4.24. yet the meaning of it is *not,* that God is angry *in himself,* and that there ariseth a fire of anger in the *Holy Trinity.*

73. No; that cannot be, for it is written, *against those that hate me,* in that same Creature, *the fire of anger riseth up.*

74. But if God should be angry in Himself, then the *whole Nature* would be on fire, which will come once to passe *On the Last Day* in *Nature,* and *Not* in *God,* but *in God, the triumphing Joy will burn;* it was never otherwise from eternity, nor will it Ever be otherwise.

75. But now the elevating springing triumphing joy in God maketh Heaven triumphing and *moveable,* and *Heaven* maketh the *Stars* and *Elements* moveable, and the Stars and the Elements make the *Creatures* moveable,

76. Out of the *Powers* of God, are the Heavens proceeded : out of the *Heaven* are the Stars; out of the *Stars* are the Elements ; out of the *Elements* are the *Earth* and the *Creatures* come to be.

77. Thus all had its beginning even to the Angels and Devils ; *which,* before the Creation of Heaven, Stars, and the Earth, were proceeded out of the same power out of which the Heaven, the Stars, and the Earth were proceeded.

78. This is a short Entrance or Introduction, shewing how the Divine and Natural Being is to be considered. Henceforth I will describe the true Ground
and

and Depth concerning What God is, and how all things are framed in Gods Being.

79. Which indeed hath been partly concealed from the beginning of the World to this time, and Man with his *Reason* could not comprehend it.

80. But seeing God is pleased to reveal Himself in Simplicity in this last Time; I shall give way to his Impulse and Will; I am but a very little Spark of Light. *AMEN.*

The Third Chapter.

Of the most blessed Triumphing, Holy Holy Holy Trinity, GOD the Father, Sonne, and Holy Ghost, ONE onely God.

1.

COurteous Reader, here I would have you faithfully *admonished*, to let go your Opinion and Conceit, and not to Gaze after the *Heathenish* wisdome, nor be offended at the simplicity of the Authour: for this work comes not from *his Reason*, but from the impulse of the Spirit.

2. Onely be thou careful to get into thy spirit the Holy *Ghost*, which issueth forth from God, and He will lead thee into all truth, and reveal *Himself* unto thee.   3. And

3. And then thou wilt fee well enough in his Light and Power; even into the holy *Trinity*, and underftand thofe things which are written hereafter following.

Of GOD *the* FATHER.

4.

When Our Saviour JESUS CHRIST taught his Difciples to pray, he faid; *when ye pray, fay thus: Our Father, which art in Heaven*, Matth. 6.

5. The meaning is not, as if Heaven could comprehend encompaffe or contain God the *Father*: for *it felf* is made by the Divine power: for *Chrift* faith, *My Father is greater then all*, Joh. 10.29.

6. And God faith in the Prophet, *Heaven is my Throne, and the Earth is * my footftool*, Efa. 66. *What houfe would you build for me? I compaffe the Heaven with a Span, and the Earth with three Fingers*, Efa. 40. 12. Alfo, *I will dwell in Jacob, and Ifrael fhall be my Tabernacle*, Pfal. 135.4. Syrac. 25.13. * The Durt under my Feet,

7. But in that Chrift calls his Father a *Heavenly* Father, his meaning is, that his Fathers *luftre* and power appeareth and fhineth very *bright* and pure in Heaven; and that, *above* the circle or inclofure, which we behold with our Eyes, and which we call *Heaven*, doth appear the totally *Triumphing* Holy Trinity, The *Father Sonne* and *Holy Ghoft*.

8. Chrift alfo thereby diftinguifheth his *Heavenly* Father from the Father of *Nature*, which is indeed the Stars and the Elements, thefe are our Natural Father, out of which we are made, and by whofe impulfe

impulfe we live here in this world, and from whence we have our food and nourifhment.

9. But God is *therefore* Our Heavenly Father, in that our *Soul* continually longeth after him, and is defirous of him, yea it thirfteth and hungreth continually after him.

10. The *Body* hungreth and thirfteth after the Father of Nature, which is *viz.* the Stars and the Elements, and *that Father* alfo feedeth and nourifheth the Body.

11. But the Soul thirfteth after the heavenly Holy Father, and he alfo giveth meat and drink to it, feeding it with his holy Spirit, and the fpring fource or fountain of joy.

12. Yet we have *not two* Fathers, but only *One*: for Heaven is made by his Power, and the Stars out of his Wifdome, which is *in him*, and proceedeth forth *from him.*

Of the Subftance and Property of the Father.

13.

When we confider the whole Nature and its property, then we fee the Father.

14. When we behold Heaven and the Stars, then we behold his eternal *Power* and Wifdom: fo many Stars as ftand in the whole Heaven, which are innumerable and incomprehenfible to *Reafon*, and fome of them are not vifible; fo manifold and *various* is the Power and Wifdome of God the Father.

15. But Every Star in Heaven Differeth in its power and

and *Quality*, which also maketh so many Distinctions in and among the Creatures upon the Earth, and in the whole Creation.

16. But all the *Powers*, which are in *Nature*, proceed from God the Father; All Light, Heat Cold, Ayr, Water, and all the powers of the Earth; Bitter, Sowre, Sweet, Astringent, Hard, and Soft, and more then can be Reckoned; all have their *beginning* from the Father.

17. Therefore if a Man would liken the Father to any thing, he should liken him to the Round Globe of Heaven.

18. Thou must not conceive here, that the very power, which is in the Father, standeth in a Peculiar severed or divided part and *place* in the Father, as the Stars do, in Heaven.

19. No! but the Spirit sheweth that *all* the powers in the Father are one in another, as one power.

20. A Resemblance Image or Figure whereof, we have in the Prophet *Ezekiel the 1.Chap.* Who seeth the Lord in the Spirit and resemblance, like a wheele, having *Four other wheels* one in another, the Four being like one another, and when they moved, they went Strait forward, which way soever the Wind did sit, or Blow, and that way they went all forward, having no cause of returning.

21. And thus it is with God the Father; for all the powers are in the Father, one in another, *as one power*; and all powers Consist in the Father, in an unsearcheable Light and Clarity, or Brightnes and Glory.

22. Yet thou must not think, that God who is in Heaven and above the Heaven, doth there stand and

I   hover,

hover, like a power and quality which hath in it *neither* Reafon, nor knowledge in it.

23. As the Sun which turneth round in its circle, and fhooteth forth from it felf Heat and *Light*, whether it be for benefit or hurt to the Earth and Creatures, which indeed would be for hurt, if the other Planets and Stars did not hinder.

24. No! the Father is *not fo*, but he is an All-mighty, All-wife, All-knowing, All-feeing, All-hearing, All-fmelling, All-feeling, All-tafting God, who in himfelf is meek, friendly, gracious, merciful, and full of Joy, yea Joy it felf.

25. And he is thus from Eternity to eternity unchangeably : He never changed himfelf in his *Being*, neither will he change himfelf in all *Eternity*.

26. He is proceeded or born of nothing, but *Himfelf* is all in Eternity ; and all whatfoever is, is come from his power, which from Eternity goeth forth from *him*.

27. His Immenfeneffe Heighth and Depth, *no Creature*, no not any Angel in Heaven, can fearch into it, but the Angels live in the *power* of the Father very meekly, and full of Joy, and they alwaies *Sing* in the power of the Father.

Of GOD *the* SONNE.

28.

If a Man will fee *God* the *Sonne*, he muft once more look upon natural things, otherwife I *cannot* write of him : the Spirit indeed beholdeth him, but that can neither be fpoken nor *written* ; for the Di-

vine

vine Being confifteth in power, which can neither be written nor fpoken.

29. Therefore we muft ufe *Similitudes,* if we intend to fpeak of God : for we live in this world, as men who know *but in part,* and are made of that which is but in part. Therefore I cite the Reader into *the life to come,* where and when I fhall fpeak more properly and more clearly of this high Article.

30. In the mean while, the loving Reader is to attend to the fenfe and *meaning of the Spirit,* and then he will not fail to get a little refrefhing, if he hath but any *hunger* in him.

Now Obferve.

31.

The Turks and Heathens fay, *God hath no Sonne* : Set Open your Eyes wide, here ; and do not make your felves *ftark* blind, and you will fee the Sonne.

32. The Father is all, and all power Subfifteth in the Father : He is the Beginning and the End of all things ; and befides and beyond him is nothing ; and whatever is, is from the Father.

33. For *before* the beginning of the Creation of the Creatures, there was nothing but only GOD ; and where there is nothing, out of that nothing will be. All things muft have a Caufe or Root, or elfe Nothing will be.

34. Yet you are not to think that the Sonne is *another* God, then the Father. Neither fhould you think, that the Sonne is without or *befides* the Father, and that he is a fevered part or divided piece; as when

two men stand one by another, where one comprehendeth not the other.

35. No! the Father and the Sonne is not of *such* a substance, or such a kind of thing : for the Father is not an *Image*, to be likened to any thing; but the Father is the *fountain* of all powers, and all the powers are one in another as one power, and therefore he is said to be ONE onely GOD.

36. Otherwise if his powers were *divided*, then he were not Al-mighty, but now he is the Self-subsisting, All-mighty, and All-powerful God.

37. And the *Sonne* is the *Heart* in the Father, all the powers, which are in the Father, are the *propriety* of the Father; and the Sonne is the *Heart* or the Kernel or Pith, in all the powers, in the whole Father, and he is the *cause* of the springing Joy in all powers in the whole Father.

38. From the Sonne, who is the Fathers Heart in all his powers, the Eternal Joy ariseth and springeth in all the powers of the Father, such a joy, *as no eye hath seen, nor ear heard, neither hath ever entred into the Heart of any Man,* as St. *Paul* saith, 1 *Cor.* 2. 9.

39. But if a man here on Earth be enlightned with the Holy Ghost from the fountain of JESUS CHRIST, so that the spirits of Nature, which signifie the Father, be kindled in him, then there ariseth such a Joy in his *Heart,* and it goeth forth into all his *veins,* so that the whole body trembleth, and the Soulish animal spirit triumpheth, as if it were siting in the holy Trinity, which is understood onely by those, that have been Guests in that place.

40. And this is but a Type or Glimpse of *the Sonne*

of God in Man, whereby *Faith* is ſtrengthened and preſerved : for the joy cannot be ſo great in an earthen *veſſel*, as in a heavenly, wherein the perfect power of God is fully.

Now here I muſt write a Similitude.

41.

I will ſhew thee a Similitude in Nature, ſignifying how the holy Being in the holy Trinity, is.

42. Conſider Heaven, which is a round *Globe*, having neither beginning nor end, but its beginning and end is every where, which way ſoever you look upon it : and ſo is *God*, who is in and above the Heaven, he hath neither beginning nor end.

43. Now conſider further ; the Circle or Sphear of the Stars, they denote the *various* Powers and Wiſdome of the Father, and they are made alſo by the Power and Wiſdom of the Father.

44. Now the Heaven, the *Stars*, and the whole *Deep* between the Stars, together with the *Earth* ; ſignifie, the Father.

45. And the *Seven Planets*, ſignifie, the ſeven Spirits of God, or the Princes of the Angels, among which alſo Lord LUCIFER was one, before his Fall ; which all were made out of the Father in the beginning of the creation of Angels, before the Time of this World.

46. *Now Obſerve* : The Sun ſtirreth in the midſt in the Deep between the Stars in a round circle, and is the heart of the Stars, and giveth Light and power to all the ſtars, ſo *tempering* the power of the ſtarres, that all becometh pleaſant and joyfull.

47. It *enlighteneth* alſo the Heaven, the Stars, and the

the Deep above the Earth, working in all things that are in this world, and so rightly signifieth, the *Sonne* of God.

48. For, as the *Sun* standeth in the midst betwixt the Stars and the Earth, enlightening all powers, and is the Light and *Heart* of all the powers, and is all the Joy in this world ; besides, all beauty and pleasantnesse standeth in the light and power of the Sun. ---

49. Even so, the Sonne of God *in* the Father, is the Heart in the Father, and shineth in all the powers of the Father ; his power is the moving *springing joy* in all the powers of the Father, and shineth in the whole Father, as the Sun doth in the whole world.

50. If the Earth should be taken away, which signifieth, the *House* of Misery Trouble or of Hell ; then the whole Deep would be Light in one place, as well as in another : as indeed the whole Deep in the Father is as light in one place as in another, from the *Lustre* of the Sonne of God.

51. And as the Sun is a Self-subsisting creature, power, and Light; which shineth not *forth from* or out of all creatures, but *in* and into all creatures, and all creatures rejoyce in its power :

52. So the Sonne in the Father, is a self-subsisting person, and enligheneth all the powers in the Father, and is the Fathers joy *or Heart* in his Centre, or the Midst of him.

Observe here the Great Mystery of God.

53.

The Sun is made or Generated from all the Stars, and is a Light, taken from the whole Nature, and shineth

ted

again, into the whole Nature of this World, it is *united* with the other Stars, as if it self together with all the stars, were but *one* starr.

54. And so the Sonne of God is Continually Generated from all the powers of his Father, from Eternity, is not made, but the Heart and *Luſtre* ſhining forth from the powers of his Heavenly Father; a ſelf-ſubſiſting Perſon, the Center, or Body of the Luſtre in the deep.

55. For the Fathers power Generateth the Sonne continually from Eternity, to Eternity: but if the Father ſhould *ceaſe* to *Generate*, then the Sonne would be no more: alſo if the *Sonne* ſhould ſhine no more in the Father, then the Father would be a dark valley: alſo then the Fathers power would not riſe from Eternity, to Eternity, and ſo the Divine Being would not *Subſiſt*.

56. Thus the Father is the *ſelfe-ſubſiſting* Being of all powers, and the ſonne is the heart in the Father, which is Generated continually out of all the powers of the Father, and who again *enlightneth* the powers of the Father.

57. Do not conceive, that the *Sonne* in the Father is ſo mix'd, that his *Perſon* can neither be ſeen nor known: No; for if it were ſo, then it were but one Perſon.

58. For as the *Sun* ſhineth not from or out of the *other* ſtars, though it had its original from the *other* ſtars; ſo alſo the Sonne ſhineth not from or out of the powers of the Father, as to his Body or *Corporeity*.

59. And though he be generated continually out of the powers of the Father; And yet he ſhineth back again into the powers of the Fahter, for he is *another* Perſon' than the Father, but *not* another God.
                                                                60. He

60. He is eternally *in* the Father, and the Father genereateth him continually from eternity to eternity, and the Father and the Sonne is ONE *God,* of an Equall Being in Power and Omnipotence.

61. The Sonne feeth, tafteth, heareth, feeleth, fmelleth and comprehendeth *All*, as the Father doth; in *His* power, all liveth and is, whatfoever is Good, as in the Father; But that which is Bad or Evill is *not* in *Him*.

Of GOD *the Holy* GHOST.

62.

God the Holy Ghoft, is the Third Perfon in the triumphing holy Deity, and proceedeth from the Father and the Sonne, ~~and is~~ the holy moving fpring or *fountain* of Joy in the whole Father.

63. He is a pleafant, meek quiet Wind or whifpering Breath or *Still voyce*, out of all the powers of the Father and of the Sonne; as, *on Mount Horeb* with the Prophet *Eliah*, 1 Kings 19.12. And on *Whitfunday* or the Day of Pentecoft, with the Apoftles, *Act.* 2. may be perceived.

64. Therefore if we will defcribe his Perfon, fubftance and property from the true Ground; it muft be reprefented in a *Similitude*. For the Spirit cannot be written down, being no Creature, but the moving flowing boyling power of God.

65. Confider, the Sun and Stars again; the *Stars* being many and feveral, inexpreffible and innumerable, they fignifie the Father: out of the ftars the *Sun* is come to be; for God hath made it out of *them*, and it fignifieth the Sonne of God.

66. And from the Sun and ftars proceed the *four*

Elements,

Elements, Fire, Ayr, Water, and Earth : as hereafter I shall demonstrate plainly, when I shall write of the *Creation.*

Now Observe:

67.

The three Elements, Fire, Ayr and Water; have a *threefold* moving or qualification, but proceed from one Body : and consider, the fire or heat swells and flies aloft from the Sun and stars; and from the Heat the Ayr * swells and flies aloft ; and from the Ayr comes the Water.

> * or Expandeth it self.

68. And in *this* motion or qualification consisteth the life and spirit of all creatures, and whatever can be named in this world ; and *that* signifieth the Holy Ghost.

69. And as the three Elements, fire ayr and water, proceed from the Sun and stars, and are *one Body* in one another, and cause the *living motion*, and the spirit of all the Creatures of this world :

70. So the Holy Ghost proceedeth from the Father and the Sonne, and causeth the *living motion* in all the powers of the Father.

71. And as the three Elements move in the Deep, as a *self-subsisting* spirit, and cause heat, cold, and clouds, and do flow forth from the power of all the stars; and as all the powers of the Sun and stars are in the three Elements, as if they *themselves were* the Sun and stars, from whence is the life and spirit of all Creatures, and doth consist therein.

72. Just so the Holy Ghost proceedeth from the Father and the Sonne, and moveth in the whole Father.

and is the Spirit & life of all pooor of that wholl fath Observe

Obſerve here, the deep Myſtery.

72.

All the *Stars* which men ſee, and thoſe which they do not ſee, they all ſignifie the *Power* of God the Father: and out of theſe ſtars is Generated the *Sun,* which is the *Heart* of all the ſtars.

73. Alſo there goeth forth from all the ſtars, the *Power* which is in every ſtar, into the Deep: And the Power, Heat and ſhining of the Sun goeth like-wiſe into the Deep.

74. And in the Deep, the power of all Stars, to-gether with the Heat and luſtre of the Sun, are all but *one thing* : a moving boyling *hovering,* like a Spi-rit or Matter. Onely it hath not Reaſon, for it is not the Holy Spirit ; and thus alſo the fourth Element muſt adhere or belong to a natural ſpirit ; or it is not capable of Reaſon.

" [75. *And thus God the* Father *goeth forth in his*
" *Deep out of all his powers, and Generateth the*
" *Splendor the Heart or the Sonne of God in*
" *his Center.*]

76. Which may be likened to the round *Globe* of the *Sun,* which ſhineth upwards, downwards, and on every ſide ; And ſo the ſplendor together with all the powers, goeth forth from the Sonne of God in the whole Father.

77. Now, in the whole Deep of the Father, Ex-ternally without the Sonne, there is nothing but the manifold and unmeaſurable, or unſearchable *Power* of the Father.

78. And the unſearchable Power and *Light* of the Sonne, is in the Deep of the Father, a living, all-pow-erful,

erful, all-knowing, all-hearing, all-seeing, all-smelling, all-tasting, all-feeling *Spirit*, wherein is all power splendor and wisdom, as in the Father and the Sonne.

79. And as in the four Elements, there is the power and splendor of the Sun and *all* the stars: so it is in the whole *Deep* of the Father: and that is, and is rightly called, *the Holy Ghost*, which is the third self-subsisting *Person* in the Deity.

Of the Holy TRINITY.

80.

Now when we speak or write of the *Three Persons* in the Deity, you must *not conceive* that therefore there are three Gods, each Raigning and Ruling by himself, like temporal Kings on the Earth.

81. No. * Such a Substance and Being, is not in God: for the Divine *Being* consisteth in power and not in Body or flesh.

82. The Father is the whole Divine power, whence *all creatures* have proceeded; and hath been alwayes from Eternity: He hath neither beginning nor end.

* or the Trinity hath no such substance and Being in God.

83. The Sonne is in the Father, being the Fathers Heart or Light, and the Father generateth the Sonne continually from Eternity, to Eternity; and the Sonnes *Power* and Splendor shineth back again in the whole Father, as the Sun doth in the *whole* World.

84. Also the Sonne is *another* person then the Father, but not Externally without or severed from the Father, *nor* is he any other God then the Father is;

K 2   his

his power, Splendor, and Omnipotence *is no leſſe* then the whole Father.

85. The Holy Ghoſt *proceedeth* from the Father and the Sonne, and is the *Third* ſelf-ſubſiſting perſon in the Deity: As, the *Elements* in this World go forth from the Sun and the Stars, and are the moving Spirit, which is in every thing in this world.

86. So the Holy Ghoſt is the moving Spirit in the whole Father, and proceedeth or goeth forth from Eternity to Eternity *continually* from the Father and Sonne, and repleniſheth the whole Father; he is nothing Leſſe, or Greater then the Father and Sonne; His *moving power* is in the whole Father.

87. *All things* in this World are according to the ſimilitude of this *Ternary.* Ye blind Jewes, Turks, and Heathens, open wide the Eyes of your Mind: I muſt ſhew you, in your Body, and in every Natural thing, in Men, Beaſts, Fowles, and worms; alſo in wood, ſtone, leaves and graſſe, the Likeneſs of the Holy Ternary in God.

Objection.

88. Ye ſay, there is but *One* Being in God, and that, God hath no Sonne.

Anſwer.

89. Open your Eyes, and conſider your Selves: Man is made according to the ſimilitude, and out of the power of God in his Ternary. Behold thy inward man, and then thou wilt ſee it moſt plainly, and clearly, if thou art *not* a fool, and an irrational Beaſt; therefore obſerve.

60. In thy Heart, in thy Veins, and in thy Brain, thou haſt thy ſpirit; and all the powers which move

in

in thy heart, in thy Veins, and in thy Brain, wherein thy Life confisteth, fignifieth God the Father.

91. From that power fpringeth up thy *Light*, fo that thou feeft, underftandeft and knoweft in the fame power, what thou art to do; for that Light glimmereth in thy whole Body: and the whole Body moveth in the power and knowledge of the *Light*, for the Body helpeth all the Members in the knowledge of the Light: which fignifieth, God the *Sonne*.

92. For as the *Father* generateth the *Sonne* out of his power, and as the Sonne fhineth back in the whole Father: fo in like manner the *Power* of thy Heart, of thy Veins, and of thy Brain, generateth a *Light* which fhineth in all thy powers in thy whole Body: Open the Eyes of thy Mind, confider it, and you fhall find it fo.

93. *And Obferve :* As from the Father and the Sonne there *goeth forth* the Holy Ghoft, and is a felf-fubfifting Perfon in the Deity, and moveth in the whole Father ; fo alfo out of the powers of thy heart, veins and thy brain, goeth forth the *Power* which moveth in thy *whole* Body; and out of thy *light* goeth forth in the fame Power, Reafon, Underftanding, skill, and Wifdom, to govern the whole body, and to diftinguifh all whatfoever is Externally with- *Extra Corpus* out the Body.

94. And both thefe are but one in the government of thy Mind, *viz.* thy *fpirit*, which fignifieth God the Holy Ghoft : alfo the Holy Ghoft from God *ruleth in* this fpirit in thee ; if thou art a child of *Light* and not of *darkneffe.*

95. For in refpect of *this* light underftanding and government, is man *diftinguifhed* from Beafts, and is an Angel of God, as I fhall clearly fhew, when I fhall write of the Creation of Man.   96. There-

96. Therefore obferve exactly, and take notice of the order of this Book, and thou wilt find,

Whatfoeve thy Heart defireth, or ever longed for.

97. Thus you find in Man *three* fountains. Firft the *Power* in thy whole Mind, which fignifieth, God the Father; Then fecondly, the *Light* in thy whole mind, enlightening the whole Mind, which fignifieth, God the Sonne : Then thirdly, there goeth forth out of all thy powers, and out of thy light alfo, a *fpirit*, which hath underftanding.

98. For, all the Veius together with the Light in thee, as alfo thy Heart and thy Brain, and all whatfoever is in thee, make or Conftitute *that* fpirit, and that is thy *Soul*; and it well fignifieth, the Holy Ghoft, which goeth forth from the Father and the Sonne, and raigneth in the whole Father : for the *Soul* of Man raigneth in the *whole* Body.

99. But the Body or the beaftial flefh in man, fignifieth, the *dead* corrupted Earth, which Man through his *Fall* hath fo framed it to himfelf, as more fhall be fpoken of in its due place.

100. The *Soul* containeth the firft Principle, and the *Soul's fpirit* the fecond principle, *in Ternario fancto*, in the Holy Ternary; and the *outward fpirit*, viz. the Aftral, containeth the third principle of this world.

101. Thus you find alfo the Ternarie of the Deity, in Beafts : for as the Spirit of a man, is, and Exifteth, fo it is alfo in a Beaft, and therein is no difference.

102. But the difference, lyeth in *this*, that Man is made by God himfelfe out of the beft Kernel or

Pith

pith of Nature, to be his Angel and Similitude, and *God Ruleth* in man with his holy Spirit; so that Man can Speak discourse distinguish and understand all things.

103. But a Beast is made of the *wild* Nature of this World; the *Stars* and *Elements* have generated Beasts through their motion, according to the will of God.

104. And so the spirit in Birds, Fowles and Wormes, Existeth also : and *all* hath its three-fold source in *similitude* to the Ternary in the Deity.

105. And you see also the Ternarie of the Deity in Wood and Stones, as also Herbs, Leaves, and in Grasse : only *these* are *all* Earthly.

106. However Nature Generateth nothing, be it what it will in this World, and though perhaps it should stand or continue, but scarce a Minute, yet it is all generated in the Ternarie, or according to the similitude of God.

107. *Now Observe* : In either wood, stone or herbs, there are three things contained, neither can any thing be generated or grow, if but one of the three should be left out.

108. I. First there is the *Power*, from which *a Body* comes to be, whether wood, stone, or herbs.

II. After that in the same, there is a *Sap* in that thing, which is the *Heart* of the thing :

III. And thirdly, there is in it a *springing* flowing Power, Smell or Taste, which is the *spirit* of the thing, whereby it groweth and encreaseth. Now if any of these three fail, the thing cannot subsist.

109. Thus

109. *Thus* you find in Every thing a Similitude of the *Ternarie* in the Divine Being; look upon what you will; let no man make himself so stark blind, as to think *otherwise*, or to think that God hath no Sonne and Holy Ghost.

110. I shall make this *more* plain and clear, when I come to write of the *Creation*: for I do *not borrow* of other men in my Writings: And though indeed I quote many Examples and Testimonies of Gods Saints; Yet all is written by God in my Mind, so that I *absolutely* and infallibly believe, know, and see it, yet not in the flesh, but in the spirit, in the *impulse* and motion of God.

111. It is not so to be under-stood,

stood, that my Reason is greater or higher than all other mens living, but I am the Lords *Twigg* or Branch, and am a very mean and little Spark of his; he may set me where he pleaseth, I cannot *hinder* him in that.

112. Neither is this my *Natural will*, that I can do it by my own small ability, for if the Spirit were withdrawn from me, then I could neither know nor understand *my own Writings*, and I must on every side fight and struggle with the Devill, and lye open to temptation and affliction as well as other men.

113. But in the following Chapters you will *soon see* the Devil and his Kingdom *laid naked,*

L

ked, his **Pride** and **Reproach**
shall suddenly *be discovered.*

The Fourth Chapter.

*Of the Creation of the Holy
Angels.*

An Instruction, or open Gate of Heaven.

1.

THe Learned, and almost all Writers, have
very much *Cumbred*, and troubled their
Heads mightily, to *search contrive* and conceive in Nature, (and have brought forth
many and sundry *Opinions*) concerning How, and Of
what, the Holy Angels were framed : And on the
other side, what that horrible *Fall* of the Great Prince
Lucifer was: or, How he became so *base* a wicked and
fierce wrathful Devil ; From whence that *Evil Quality* should Spring, or, What drove him to it ?

2. And although this ground and great Mystery
hath remained hidden from the beginning of the
world, and that humane flesh and blood is *not able*
to conceive or apprehend it :

3. Yet God, who created the world, will reveal
himself, *now* at the End, and all great Mysteries will
be manifested or revealed : to intimate, that the
great Day of Revelation and the Final Judgment, is
near, and *daily* to be expected.

4. On which, will be restored again all that which hath been lost through *Adam*, and in which the Kingdome of Heaven, and the Kingdom of the Devill shall be *severed asunder*, in this world.

5. But *How* all this will be done, God will reveal, in the highest plainesse, and simplicity, so that no man will be able to Oppose Him.

6. Therefore every one should lift up his Eyes, for his Redemption draweth near; And not *seek after* base covetousnesse, pride and wanton luxurious statelinesse, supposing it the best life to be Here; whereas in their luxury, they *sit* in the midst of Hell, to wait upon *Lucifer* as *his Guard*.

7. Which themselves shall suddenly be *sure to see* with great terrour, anguish and eternal despair, as also to their shame and scorn: whereof the Devils are *a terrible* Example, who were once the fairest and *brightest* Angels in Heaven, as I shall reveal write and *manifest* here following; I will suffer Gods impulse, I am not able to withstand it.

Of the Divine Quality.

8.

Since thou hast perceived, in the *Third* Chapter, the Ground of the Ternarie in the Divine Being, I shall here shew plainly, the *power* and operation, as also the Qualities or qualification in the Divine Being; or, *from what* the Angels were properly and peculiarly created, or what their *Body* and Power is.

9. And as I said before: All the powers or vertues are in God the Father, and no man with his sense and thoughts can *reach* to apprehend

hend it. But in the *Stars* and the Elements, as also by all the creatures in the whole creation of this World, a Man may *clearly know* it.

10. All power and vertue is in God the Father, and proceedeth also forth from him, as Light, Heat, Cold, Soft, Gentle, Sweet, Bitter, Sowre, astringent or harsh, sound or noise, and much more that is not possible to be spoken or apprehended. *All these* are in God the Father, one in another as one power, and yet all these powers move in his *Exit*, or going forth.

11. But the powers in God do not operate or qualify in that *maner*, as in Nature, in the stars, and Elements, or in the creatures.

12. No; you must *not* conceive it so: For Lord *Lucifer* in his Elevation made the powers of impure Nature *thus* burning, bitter, cold, astringent, soure, dark and unclean.

13. But in the Father, all powers are mild, soft, like Heaven, very full of joy, for all the powers tryumph in one another, and their voice or sound riseth up from Eternity, to Eternity.

14. There is nothing in them but Love, meeknesse, mercy, friendlinesse, or courtesie; even such a tryumphing, rising source or fountain of joy wherein all the voices of Heavenly joyfulnesse *found* forth, so as no man is able to expresse it, nor can it be likened to any thing.

15. But if a man *will* Liken it to any thing, it may *nearest* be Likened to the Soul of Man, when *kindled* or enlightened by the Holy Ghost.

16. For *then* it is thus joyful and tryumphing, and all powers rise up in it, and tryumph, and so raise the Bestial Body, that it trembleth: this is a true

glimpse

glimpse of the *divine* Quality, as the quality is in God ; But in God all is Spirit.

17. The quality of water, is not of *such* a running and Qualifying condition or maner in God, as it is in *this* World ; but is a Spirit, very bright cleare and thinne, wherein the Holy Ghost riseth up ; a *meer power.*

18. The bitter Quality Qualifieth in the sweet, astringent or harsh and sowre Quality, and the *Love* riseth up therein from Eternity, to Eternity.

19. For the Love in the Light and clarity or Glorious Brightnes goeth forth from the *Heart* or Sonne of God, in all the powers of the Father, and the Holy Ghost moveth in them all.

20. And this, in the Deep of the Father, is Like a Divine * SALITTER, which I must needs liken to the *Earth,* which before its corruption was even such a *Salitter.*   ** or SALNI-TRIUM.*

21. But not so Hard, Cold, Bitter, Sowre, and Dark, but like the Deep or like Heaven, very clear and pure, wherein all powers were *Good* fair and Heavenly : But that Prince Lucifer thus *Spoiled* them ; as you shall perceive here following.

22. This Heavenly Salitter, or powers one in another, generate Heavenly joyful fruits and colours ; all manner of Trees and Plants, on which do *grow* the fair pleasant and lovely fruits of *life.*

23. There Spring up also in these powers and vertues, all manner of Blossoms and *Flowers,* with fair Heavenly colours and smells.

24. They are of *Several* Tastes, each according to its Quality and kind, very *Holy, Divine,* and full of joy.

25. For every Quality beareth its own fruit, *as it is*

is in the corrupted murtherous Den or dark Valley and Dungeon of the Earth; there spring up all manner of Earthly Trees, Plants, Flowers, and Fruits.

26. Also *within the Earth, Grow* curious pretious Stones, Silver, and Gold, and these are a *Type* of the Heavenly Generating or Production.

27. Nature *Laboureth* to its utmost diligence upon this corrupted Dead Earth, that it might generate Heavenly forms and Species or Kinds; but it generateth *only* Dead, Dark, and Hard fruit, which are no more then a meer shadow or Type of the Heavenly.

28. Moreover its fruit is *altogether* fierce, or biting, Bitter, Sowre, astringent or harsh and Hot, also Cold, hard and naught; they have *Scarce* any spark or spice of Goodnesse in them.

29. Their Sap and spirit is *mix'd* with hellish quality, their scent or smell is a very *stink*; thus hath Lord *Lucifer* caused them to be, as I shall clearly shew hereafter.

30. Now when I write of Trees, Plants and Fruits, you must *not* understand them to be *Earthly*, like those that are in this world: for it is *not* my meaning, that there should grow in heaven, such Dead hard Trees of wood; or *such* stones, as consist of an earthly Quality.

31. No; but my meaning is heavenly and spiritual, yet *truly* and *properly such*: I mean no other thing, Then what I set down in the Letter.

32. In the Divine Pomp and State are especially *two* things to be considered: *first* the *Salitter* or the Divine powers, which are moving springing powers.

33. In *that* same power groweth up and is generated

ted fruit according to every quality and species or kind, *viz. heavenly* Trees and Plants, which without ceasing bear fruit, fairly bloffom, and grow in divine power; fo Joyfully, that I can neither fpeak nor write it down:

34. But ftammer it like a *child*, that is learning to fpeak, and can by *no means* rightly call it, as the Spirit giveth it forth, to be known.

35. The *second* form or property of Heaven in the divine pompe or ftate is *Mercurius*, or the Sound, as, in the *Salitter* of the Earth, there is the Sound, whence there groweth Gold, Silver, Copper, Iron, and the like; of which men make all manner of *Mufical Inftruments* for founding; or for mirth, as Bells, Organ-Pipes, and other *things* that make a found: Alfo there is likewife a Sound in all the creatures upon earth, elfe all would be in ftillnefle and *filence*.

36. By that found in *Heaven* all powers are moved, fo that all things grow Joyfully, and generate very beautifully: And as the Divine power is manifold and various, fo alfo the found or *Mercurius* is alfo manifold and various.

37. For, when the powers fpring up in God, they *touch* and ftirre one another and move one in another, and fo there is a conftant harmony, *mixing* or Confort, from whence go forth all manner of colours.

38. And in thofe Colours grow all manner of *Fruits*; which rife or fpring up in the *Salitter*, and the *Mercurius* or found mingleth it felf therewith, and rifeth up in all the powers of the Father, and then founding, and *Tunes*, rife up in the heavenly joyfulnefle.

39. If you fhould in this world bring many thoufand kinds of mufical Inftruments together, and all

should be tuned in the best manner most artificially, and the most skilful Masters of Musick should play on them in consort together, all would be no more then the *Howlings* and barkings of Dogs in *comparison* of the *Divine Musick*, which riseth up through the Divine Sound and Tunes from Eternity to Eternity.

40. Further, if thou wilt consider the heavenly Divine Pomp State and *Glory*, and conceive how it is, and what manner of Sprouting Branching delight and joy there is in it ;

41. View this world diligently, and *consider* what manner of fruit sprouts branches and encreases, groweth out of the *Salitter* of the Earth, from Trees, Plants, Herbs, Roots, Flowers, Oyles, Wine, Corn and whatever else there is that thy *heart* can find out : *all* is a *Type* of the heavenly Pomp.

42. *For,* the *earthly* and corrupt nature hath continually laboured from the beginning of its Creation to this day to bring forth *heavenly* forms or shapes in the Earth, as also in Man and Beasts : as men very well see that every year *New Arts* are invented and brought to Light, which hath been constantly so from the beginning to this time.

43. But yet Nature hath *not* been *able* to bring forth heavenly power vertue and qualities, therefore its fruit is half dead, corrupt, and impure.

44. You must *not think,* that in the divine pomp, there cometh forth, Beasts, Worms and other creatures in flesh, as in this World they do : No; but I mean only the *wonderful* proportion, power, vertue, and comelinesse of feature in them.

45. And Nature laboureth with highest diligence, to produce in its Power *heavenly* figures shapes or

forms,

forms, as we fee in Men, Beafts, Fowles and Worms, as alfo in the encreafe or growth of the Earth, that all things are done, fhew, and appear moft curioufly, Artificially, and delicately.

46. For *Nature would fain be delivered from this Vanity, that it might procreate heavenly forms in the holy Power.*

47. For, in the Divine Pomp likewife go forth *all manner* of Sprouting and Vegetation of Trees, Plants, and all manner of fruit, and every one beareth *its own* fruit, yet not in an earthly quality and kind, but in a *Divine* quality form and kind.

48. Thofe fruits are not of fo dead, hard, bitter, foure and aftringent a relifh for *food*; nor do they *rot* and grow ftinking, as thofe in this world do; but all confift in holy Divine power.

49. Their Conftitution or *compofition* is from Divine power, from the *Salitter* and *Mercurius* of the divine pomp, and are the food of the holy Angels.

50. If mans *abominable* Fall had not fpoiled it, he would have been feafted, in *fuch* a manner, in this world, and have eaten fuch fruit as indeed they were prefented to him in Paradife, in a *twofold* manner.

51. But the infectious *Luft*, longing and Malady of the Devil, who had infected and fpoiled the *Salitter*, of which *Adam* was made, that brought Man into an *Evil Longing* or Luft *to eat* of both the Qualities the *Evil* and the *Good*, whereof I fhall write clearly here following, and demonftrate it.

Of the Creation of Angels.

52.

The Spirit sheweth plainly and clearly, that *before* the Creation of the *Angels*, the Divine Being with its rising and qualifying was from eternity, and remained so *in* the Creation of Angels, as it is also at *this day*, and will so continue in and *to* Eternity.

53. And the Space Room or *place* of this *world*, together with the creaturely heaven, which we behold with our eyes, as also the Space or Place of the *Earth* and Stars together with the Deep, *was* in such a form as now at *this day* it *is* in, aloft, above the Heavens, in the Divine Pomp.

54. But *was* the Kingdom of the Great Prince Lucifer, in the Creation of the Angels: [" *Understand* " *according to the* second Principle, *out of which he was* " *thrust forth into the outermost, which also is the very in-* " *nermost of all.*

55. Who by his proud elevation in his Kingdom, *kindled* the qualities, or the divine *Saliter*, out of which he was made; [" *Understand the* Center *of* " his Nature, *or the* first Principle:] *and set it on fire.*

56. Supposing thereby he should grow hugely and highly *light* and qualifying, *above* the Sonne of God: but he became a Fool, therefore *this place* or space in its burning quality could *not* subsist in God, whereupon the Creation of this world ensued.

57. But this world at the End, in *God's* appointed Time, will be *set* again to its first place, as it was be-

fore the Creation of Angels, and Lord Lucifer will have a *hole* or dungeon for his eternal habitation therein, and he will *remain* eternally in his kindled quality, which will be an eternal base filthy reproachful Habitation, an empty void dark valley or dungeon, a hole of fiercenesse or *wrath*.

Now Observe;

58. God in his moving, created the holy Angels at once, not out of a strange *matter*, but out of himself, out of his *own* power, and eternal wisdom.

59. But the Philosophers had *this opinion, as if* God had made the Angels only out of the light: but they *erred therein*, for they were made not only out of the light, but out of *all* the Powers of God.

60. And as I have shewed *before*, there are *two* things especially to be observed in the Deep of God the Father : first the power, or all Powers of God the Father, of the Son and of the Holy Ghost, are very lovely, pleasant and various, and yet are all *One in another* as one power.

61. And as the powers of all the stars *rule* in the Ayre, so also in God : but every power in God *sheweth* it self with its operation, feverally and diſtinctly.

62. Then afterward the Sound is in every power, and the Tone or tune of the Sound is according to the quality of every power ; and therein conſiſteth the total Heavenly Kingdom of Joy, and ſo from this divine *Saliter* and *Mercurius* all Angels are made, viz. out of the Body of Nature.

Queſtion.

Question.

63. But thou mayeſt here ask: *How* are they made or generated ; or in what way and manner ?

Anſwer.

64. If I had the *tongue* of an Angel, and thou hadſt an Angelical *underſtanding,* we might very finely diſcourſe of it. But the Spirit only doth ſee it, and the tongue cannot advance towards it. For I can uſe *no other* words, then the words of this world: but now the Holy Ghoſt being in thee, thy *Soul* will well apprehend it.

65. For behold the totall holy Trinity hath with its moving Compoſed *compaƈted* or figured a Body, or Image out of it ſelf, like a *little* God, but not ſo fully or *ſtrongly* going forth, as the whole Trinity, yet in ſome meaſure according to the *extent* and Capacity of the Creatures.

66. For in God there is *neither* beginning nor end, but the Angels *have* a beginning and end, but not circumſcriptive apprehenſive palpable or *concluſive*: for an Angel can ſometime be great, and ſuddenly little again, their alteration is as ſwift as mans thoughts are. All *qualities* and powers are in an Angel, *as* they are in the whole Deity.

67. But thou muſt rightly underſtand this. They are made and compaƈted together, or figured out of the *Salitter* and *Mercurius*, that is, out of the *exit* or excreſcence,

68. Conſider this *Similitude*: Out of the Sun and Stars, go forth the Elements, and they make in the *Salitter* of the Earth a *living* ſpirit, and the ſtars remain in their Circle or *S*phear, and *that* Spirit likewiſe

wise getteth the quality of the starres.

69. But now the Spirit after its compaction, is a severed *distinct* thing, and hath a substance of its own as all the Stars have, and the stars also are and remain *severed* and distinct things, each of them is free to it self.

70. Neverthelesse the quality of the Stars *reigneth* in the Spirit; yet the Spirit can and may raise or demerse it self in its own qualities, or may live in the *influences* of the stars, as it pleaseth: for it is free, for it hath gotten the qualities which it hath in it self, for its *own*.

71. And though it *had them* at the beginning from the stars, yet they are now its proper *own*: Just as a mother when she hath the seed in her self, as long as she hath it in her, and that it is *a seed*, it is hers: but when the seed is become a *child*, then it is no more the mothers, but is the childs proper own.

72. And though the child be in the mothers *house*, and the mother *nourisheth* the child with her food, and that the child could *not* live without the mother, yet both the Body and the Spirit, which are generated out of the mother, are the *Childs* proper own, and it retaineth its corporeal right to it self.

73. And in this *manner* it is with the Angels, they are also all composed framed or figured out of the *Divine Seed*, but every one hath his own *Body* to it self, though they are in Gods house, and feed on the *fruit* of their mother, out of which they were made, yet their Bodies are their *proper* own.

74. But the quality *Externally* without them, or externally without their Bodies, *viz.* their mother; is *not* their propriety, as also their mother is not the childs propriety; also the *mothers* food is not the
childs

and then we shall get the Angelical Clarity or Glory and Purity again.

Question.

11. *Now thou wilt ask ; How are the Angels then Created according to the Image of God ?*

Answer.

12. First, the compacted figured Body is indivisible and incorruptible, and not to be *felt* by Mans Hands ; for it is constituted or composed out of the *Divine* power, and that power is so knit and *bound* together, that it can never be destroyed again.

13. For as *none*, no *not* any thing, can destroy the whole Deity, so also there is *not* any thing can destroy an Angel ; for every Angel is formed figured set together or composed out of *all* the powers of God, not with flesh and blood, but out of the *Divine* power.

14. And first the Body is out of all the *powers* of the Father, and in those powers is the *light* of God the Sonne ; and now the powers of the Father and of the Sonne, which are in an Angel creaturely, generate an understanding *spirit*, which riseth up in that Angel.

15. First of all the powers of the Father, generate a light, whereby an Angel seeth into the *whole* Father, whereby he can see the *outward* power and operation of God, which is Externally without its own Body, and thereby can *see* its fellow-brethren, and can see and *enjoy* the glorious fruit of God, and therein consisteth its Joy.

16. And that light at *first* came out of the Sonne
of

of God in the powers of the Father, into the Angelical Body creaturely, and is the *Bodies* proper own, which cannot be withdrawn from it by any thing, *unlesse* it self extinguisheth it, as *Lucifer* did.

17. Now all the powers, which are in the whole Angel, generateth that light ; and as God the Father generateth his Sonne to be his *Heart*, so the power of the Angel generateth also *its* Sonne and Heart in it self, and that *again* enlightneth all powers, in the whole Angel.

18. After that there goeth forth out of all the powers of the Angel, and also out of the Light of the Angel ; a *fountain*, which springeth or boyleth in the whole Angel : and that is its *spirit*, which riseth up into all eternity : for in that spirit is all knowledge and *skill* of all the powers, which are in the total God.

19. For, that spirit springeth up out of all the powers of the Angel, and goeth up into the *Mind*, where it hath *five* open Doors, there it can look round about and *see* whatsoever is in God, and also whatsoever is in it self.

20. And so goeth forth from all the powers, of the Angel, as also from the light of the Angel : *as the* Holy Ghost *goeth forth from the Father and the* Sonne, *and* filleth *the whole* Corpus *or Body.*

Now Observe the Great Mystery.

21. As there are *Two* things to be observed in God: the *first* is the *Salitter*, or the Divine powers, out of which the Body or Corporeity, is : and the *second* is the *Mercurius*, Tone, Tune or Sound. Thus also it is in *like manner* and form, in an Angel.

N   22. First

22. Firſt there is the *power*, and in the power is the Tone or *Tune*, which riſeth up in the ſpirit, into the Head, into the *Mind*, as in man in the Brain, and in the Mind it *hath its open Doors or Gates*; but in the *Heart* it hath its *Seat* Reſidence and Original, where it exiſteth out of all powers.

23. For the fountain of all powers floweth * in the Heart, as it doth alſo in man, and in the Head it hath its *Princely* ſeat, where it ſeeth all, ſmelleth all, and feeleth all.

24. And now when it ſeeth and heareth the *divine* Tone Tune and Sound riſe up, which is externally without it, then is its ſpirit *affeſted*, and kindled with joy, and elevateth it ſelf in its Princely ſeat, and *Singeth* and ringeth forth very joyful words concerning Gods Holineſſe, and concerning the fruit and vegetation of the *Eternal Life*.

25. Alſo concerning the ornament colours and Beauty of the eternal *Joy*, and concerning the amiable bleſſed glance or gracious *aſpeſt* and Countenance of God the Father, Sonne, and Holy Ghoſt; alſo concerning the excellent fraternity fellowſhip and *communion* of Angels, concerning the continual everlaſting joyfulneſſe, concerning the holineſs of God, and concerning the *Angels own* Princely Government.

26. In brief, concerning *all powers*, and that which proceedeth *from* all Gods powers, which in regard of the untowardneſſe of my corruption in the fleſh I *cannot* write; I would much rather be there preſent my ſelf.

27. But what I cannot write here, I will commit to *thy Soul* to conſider further of it: and at the day of the *Reſurreſtion* you ſhall ſee it moſt plainly and clearly.

28. You

28. You fhould not here fcorn my fpirit, for it is *not* fprung forth from the wild Beaft, but is generated from my power and vertue, and *enlightened* by the Holy Ghoft.

29. I write not here without knowledge; but if thou, like an *Epicure* and Fatted Swine of the Devill, from the Devils inftigation fhouldft *mock* at thefe things, and fay :

30. The Fool furely hath *not* gone up to heaven, and feen or heard them : *thefe* are meer *Fables:* therefore in the power of my knowledge, I would have you warned and *Cited* before the fevere Judgment of God.

31. And though in my body I am *too weak,* to bring thee thither; yet *That* from which I have my knowledge, is mighty and potent enough to caft thee even into the Abyffe of Hell.

32. *Therefore* take warning, and confider, that thou alfo belongeft to the Angelical *Quire,* and read the following *Hymne* with longing delight, and then the Holy Ghoft will be awakened and ftirr'd up in thee, and thou alfo wilt get a defire and Longing after the heavenly *Chorus* and Quire of Dancing. *Amen.*

33.

The Mufician hath wound up his Pegs and tuned his Strings; the Bridegroom cometh, take *heed* thou doft not get the *hellifh* * *Gout* in thy feet, when the * *podagra.* Round beginneth, left thou be found uncapable or *unfit* for the Angelical Dance, and fo be thruft out from the *wedding,* feeing thou haft no *Angelical Garment* on.

34. Surely the Gate will be lock'd upon thee, and fo thou wilt not enter in any more, but wilt *Dance*

with

with the He*lliſh wolves* in the helliſh fire : truly thou wilt forget then to mock, and ſorrow will *gnaw* thee.

Of the *Qualification* of an *Angel.*

Queſtion.

35. The Queſtion now is , What manner of *qualification* hath an Angel ?

Anſwer.

36. The *Holy Soul* of a man, and the ſpirit of an Angel, is and hath one and the ſame Subſtance and Being, and there is no difference therein, but onely in the *quality* it ſelf, or their corporeal government, that which qualifieth *outwardly* or from without in man, by the Ayr, hath a *corrupt earthly* quality ; yet on the other ſide it hath alſo a *Divine* and *heavenly* quality hidden from the Creatures.

37. But the *holy* Soul underſtandeth it well, as the Kingly Prophet *David* ſaith, *The Lord rideth on the wings of the wind,* Pſal. 104.3.

Queſtion.

38. But a ſimple man may ask : What do you mean by the word *qualifying,* or, what is that ?

Anſwer.

39. I mean thereby the power, which in the Body of the Angel *entereth in* from without, and commeth forth again : As in a Similitude ; When a a man fetcheth breath and breatheth it forth again : for *therein* ſtandeth the life both of the Body and of the Spirit.

40. The

40. The quality from without, *kindleth* the spirit in the heart, in the first fountain; whereby all the powers in the whole Body become stirring, and then that quality in the corporeal spirit, which is the *natural Spirit* of an Angel or Man, riseth up into the Head where it hath its Princely Seat or *Throne* and Government, and there it hath its *Counsellours*, whose advice it taketh.

41. The *first* Counsellour is the *Eyes*, they are affected with every thing they look upon, for they are the *Light*.

42. For, as the Light goeth forth from the Sonne of God in the whole Father into all the powers, and *affecteth* all the powers of the Father, and on the other side all the powers of the Father affect the *Light* of the Sonne of God:

43. So do the Eyes work in the thing they look upon, and the *thing* worketh again in the Eyes, and the Counsellor, the Eyes bringeth it into the *Head* before the Princely Seat or Throne; and there it is to be approved of.

44. Now if the spirit is *pleased* therewith, then it bringeth the same to the heart, and the heart giveth it to the passages or *Issuings* forth of the powers or fountain-veins in the whole Body; and then the Mouth, and Hands, and Feet, fall to work.

45. The *second* Counsellour is the *Ears*, which have their rise also from all the powers in the whole body through the spirit, their fountain is *Mercurius* or the *Sound*, which ariseth from all the powers.

46. And as in all the powers of God the *Mercurius* riseth and soundeth, wherein the heavenly Tone Tune or Joy consisteth, and the Tone or Tune goeth forth out of all the powers, and so in the *attraction* of
the

the Spirit in God, is *elevated* or raised up :

47. And when one power toucheth or stirreth the other, and tuneth or soundeth ; Then the Tune or Sound *goeth forth*, and riseth up *again* in all the powers of the Father ; and so all the powers of the Father are *again* affected therewith, whereby they are always impregnated with the Tune, and *continually* generate it again in every power.

48. Thus also the second Counsellour in the Head, is the *Eares*, they stand open, and the *sound* goeth forth through them, in all that soundeth.

49. Now where the *Mercurius* soundeth, and is elevated, there the *Mercurius* of the spirit goeth also in, and is thereby affected, and *bringeth it* before the Princely Throne in the Head, where it is to be approved by the *other* Four Counsellours.

50. And if the Spirit is pleased therewith, then it bringeth the same before its Mother into the Heart, and the Heart or the fountain of the heart *giveth it* to all the powers in the whole Body ; and then the Mouth and Hands lay hold on it.

51. But if the *whole* Princely Counsel in the head Be *not* pleased, so that it is approved, then it lets that go again, and bringeth it not to the Mother the Heart.

52. The *third* Princely Counsellour is the *Nose*, there the fountain riseth up from the Body in the Spirit into the Nose, and there it hath two open Doores or Gates.

53. And as the Excellent pretious and amiable *blessed* savour or smell goeth forth from all the powers of theFather and of the Sonne, and *tempereth* it self with all the powers of the Holy Ghost, whence the *Holy Spirit* and most pretious Savour riseth up from the

fountain

fountain of the Holy Ghoſt: And floweth or boyleth in all the powers of the Father, and *kindleth* all the powers of the Father, whereby they are impregnated *again* with the amiable bleſſed ſavour or *Saving Smell*, and ſo generate it in the Sonne and Holy Ghoſt:

54. *So alſo* in Angels and Men, the power of the ſmell riſeth up out of all the powers of the *Body* by and through the *Spirit*, and cometh forth at the *Noſtrils* of the Noſe, and is affected with all Smells or ſavours, and bringeth them through the Noſtrils of the Noſe, which is the third counſellour, into the Head; before the Princely Seat, or Throne.

55. And there it is to be proved, *whether* it be a good ſmell or ſavour pleaſing to its Conſtitution and Complexion, or no: if it be *good*, then it bringeth the ſame to its mother, that it may be brought to effect; if not, then is it expelled and thruſt away.

56. And *this* Counſellor of the Smell, which is generated out of the *Salitter*, is alſo mix'd with *Mercurius*, and ſo belongeth to the heavenly joyfulneſſe, and is a glorious, *Excellent* and fair fountain in God.

57. The *fourth* Princely Counſellour is the *Taſte*, on the *Tongue*, which alſo ariſeth from all the powers of the Body through the ſpirit into the Tongue: for all *fountain-veins* of the whole Body go into the Tongue, and the tongue is the ſharpneſſe or *Taſte* of all the powers.

58. As the Holy Ghoſt goeth forth from the Father and the Sonne, and is the ſharpneſſe or *proof* of all powers, and in his moving or riſing up; bringeth all that which is good, *again* into all the powers of the Father, whereby the powers of the Father are *impregnated* again, and ſo continually generate the Taſte.

59. But

59. But that which is *not good*, the Holy Ghost *speweth that out*, as a loathsome *abomination*, as it is written in the *Apocalypse the 3. Chap. v. 16.* and as he spewed out the Great Prince *Lucifer* in his pride, and perdition. For he could no more endure to Taste the fiery proud *stinking* quality : and thus it is also as to all Proud stinking Men.

60. O Man let this be told thee, for the Spirit is earnestly *Jealous* in this thing especially : *desist* from Pride, or else it will be with you, as it befell the De-vils : there is no jesting or *trifling* herein; the Time is very short, thou wilt suddenly Taste it, I mean the hellish fire.

61. Now as the Holy Ghost proveth all ; so the *Tongue* also proveth all Tastes : and if the same plea-seth the Spirit, then it bringeth the same into the head ; to the *other four* Counsellours before the Princely Seat, and there it is proved, whether it be profitable or wholsome for the qualities of the Body.

62. If so, then is it brought to the Mother, the *Heart*, which giveth it to all the *veins* or powers of the Body, and then the Mouth and Hands lay hold on it.

63. But if it be *not* good, then the tongue *spits* or speweth it out, before it comes to the Princely Coun-sel.

64. But *though* it be pleasant to the Tongue, and is of a good Taste, and yet is not *serviceable* and use-ful for the whole Body, then it is *rejected* neverthe-lesse, when it comes before the Councell, and the Tongue must spit or *spew* it out , and touch it no more.

65. The *fifth* Princely Counsellour is the *Feeling*;
which

which fifth Counsellour ariseth also from all the powers of the Body in the spirit, into the Head.

66. For as *all powers* go forth from God the Father and Sonne, in the Holy Ghost, and so one toucheth the other, from whence existeth the *Tune* or *Mercurius*, so that all the powers do sound and move themselves.

67. Else if one did not touch the other, nothing would stir *at all*, and so this touching maketh the Holy Ghost *stir*, so that he riseth up in all the powers, and toucheth all the powers of the Father, wherein then existeth the heavenly joyfulnesse or *triumphing* ; as also tuning, sounding, generating, blossoming, and vegetation or Springing, *all* which, hath its rising from this, that one power *toucheth* the other.

68. For Christ saith in the Gospel, *John* 5. *v.* 17. *I work, and my Father worketh also.* And he meaneth this very touching and working, in that every power goeth forth from him, and generateth the Holy Ghost, and in the Holy Ghost all the powers are *already* clearly *stirr'd*, by the going forth of the Father.

69. And therefore the Holy Ghost floweth *boyleth* and riseth up from eternity, and kindleth again, all the powers of the Father, and maketh them Stirring, so that they are alwayes impregnated.

70. In such a manner it is *also* in Angels and Men: for all powers in the Body arise, and *touch* one another, or else Angels and Men could Feel nothing.

71. But if one member be too much *stirr'd*, it cryeth to the whole Body for Help, and the whole Body stirs, as if it were in a great commotion or *Uproar*, as if the *Enemy* were at hand, and cometh to help that

O   Member,

Member, and to deliver and releaſe it from the Pain.

72. This you may ſee if a *Finger* be but hurt, cruſh'd or wounded, or any other member of the Body, be it which it will; preſently the Spirit in that place *runneth* ſuddenly to the mother the Heart, and complaineth to the Mother; and if the pain do but a little *exceed*, then the mother rouzeth up and awakeneth all the members of the Body, and *all* muſt come to help *that* Member.

Now Obſerve :

73. Thus *one* power continually toucheth and ſtirreth the *other* in the whole Body, and all the powers riſe up into the head before the Princely Councell, which proveth the ſtirring of all the powers.

74. Now if one member ſtirreth *too much*, and at any time *hurteth* a princely Counſellour; *viz.* by *Seeing*, it would be in Love with that which it *ought not* be in love withall.

75. As Lord Lucifer did, who ſaw the Sonne of God, and fell in love with that *high light*, and moved and ſtirred himſelf ſo very much, intending to be *equal* with him, or indeed to be *higher* and brighter then He; ſuch ſtirring or medling, the Counſellours reject.

76. Or if it would ſtir and move too vehemently, br *Hearing*, and would fain hear falſe and wicked Tongues in talking Lies and Fictions, and bring that to the *heart*, this alſo is rejected by the Counſellours.

77. Or

77. Or if it would by the *Smelling* get a Longing or Lusting after that which is none of its own, as Lord *Lucifer* did also, who longed after the *holy* Savour or *Sweet Smell* of the Sonne of God, and intended in his elevation and kindling to smell and savour yet *more pleasantly.*

78. In that manner as he deceived our Mother *Eve* also, saying ; *If she did but eat of the forbidden Tree,* then *she should be wise* or witty, *and be like God,* Gen. 3. 5. But this smelling or *stirring,* the Councell rejected also.

79. Or if by *Tasting* it should fall into a desire and longing, to *eat* that which is *not* of the quality of the Body, or is none of its own ; as Mother *Eve* in Paradise, fell a longing to eat of the Devils Swine-Apples, and *did* eat thereof ; such stirring in lust the Councel also rejecteth.

80. In brief: There are therefore *Five* in the princely Councell, that one should *advise* the other ; and every one is of a peculiar *sundry* Quality, and that compacted or concreted spirit which is *generated* out of all the powers, He is their King or Prince, and he sitteth in the *Head* in the Brain of a Man, and in an Angel in that Power which is instead of the Brain of a Man, and in the Head also upon his Princely Throne, and executeth every thing, which was concluded and decreed by the whole Princely Councell.

The

The Sixth Chapter.

How an Angel, and a Man, is the Similitude and Image of God.

1.

BEhold ! as the *Being* in God, is, so is the Being also in *Man* and *Angels* ; and as the Divine Body is, so is also the Angelicall and humane Body or Corporeity.

2. But with this difference only, that an Angel and a Man is a *Creature*, and *not* the *whole* Being, but a Sonne of the whole Being, whom the whole being hath generated : and therefore it is fit that it should be in *subjection* to the whole Being, seeing it is the *Sonne* of its Body.

3. Now if the Sonne resist and *oppose* the Father, it is but right, that the Father should cast him away out of the House : seeing the *Sonne* sets himself against him that hath generated him, and from whose power he is *become* a Creature.

4. For if any make somewhat out of that, which is his own, he may, if it doth *not* prove according to his will, do with it what he pleaseth, *and make it either a vessel of honour or dishonour* ; which was done even so to *Lucifer*.

Now Observe :

5. The *whole* Divine power of the Father speaketh forth from all Qualities, the WORD ; that is, the Sonne of God. 6. Now

6. Now that Voice or *that* WORD, which the Father speaketh, goeth forth from the Fathers *Salitter* or powers, and from the Fathers *Mercurius* Sound or Tune: And the Father speaketh this forth in himself, and *that* WORD is the very splendor or Glance proceeding from all his powers.

7. But when it is spoken forth, it stayeth or sticketh *no more* in the powers of the Father, but soundeth or tuneth back again in the whole Father in *all* powers.

8. Now that WORD, which the Father *pronounceth* or speaketh forth, hath such a *sharpnesse*, that the Tone of the WORD goeth swiftly in a moment, through the whole *Deep* of the Father, and that sharpnesse is *the Holy Ghost.*

9. For the WORD, which is spoken forth, or outspoken, abideth as a splendor or glorious * *Edict*, before the King;

* or *Proclamation.*

10. But the Tone or Sound, which goeth forth through the *Word*, *executeth* the Edict of the Father, which he had outspoken through the Word, and that is the *Birth* or Geniture of *the holy Trinity.*

11. Now behold! An Angel and a Man is thus also: the power in the whole Body hath all the *Qualities*, as it is in God the Father.

12. And as all the powers in God the Father, rise up from eternity to eternity: so all the powers rise up also in an Angel and in a Man, into the *Head*, for higher they cannot rise: for they are but Creatures, which have a Beginning and End.

13. And in the Head is the *divine* Councel-Seat or Throne, and it signifieth God the Father, and the *Five Senses* or qualities are the Counsellours, which have

have their influences out of the *whole* Body out of all the powers.

14. Now the *Five Senses* alwayes sit in Councel in the Power of the whole Body, and when the Councels *Decree* is concluded, then the compacted or concreted *Judge* speaketh it out into its Center or midst of the Body; as a *WORD*, into the Heart; for that is the fountain of all powers, from which also it taketh its rise.

15. Now it standeth there in the Heart, as a *self-subsisting Person*, composed out of all powers, and is a Word; and signifieth God the Sonne; and now it goeth out from the *Heart* into the *Mouth* on to the *Tongue*, which is the sharpnesse, and that so sharpeneth it, that it soundeth forth and is distinguished according to the *Five Senses.*

16. From what Quality soever the word taketh its original, in that quality it is thrust forth upon the Tongue, and the power of the *distinction* or difference goeth forth from the *Tongue*; and that signifieth the Holy Ghost.

17. For as the Holy Ghost goeth forth from the Father and the Sonne, and *distinguisheth* and sharpneth all, and effecteth or produceth that, which the Father speaketh through the Word.

18. So also the Tongue sharpneth *articulateth* and distinguisheth all that, which the *Five Senses* in the head bring through the heart on to the Tongue, and the Spirit goeth forth from the Tongue through the *Mercurius* or Tone in *that* place, as it was decreed or concluded by the Councel of the *five Senses*, and executeth it all.

Of the Mouth.

19.

The *Mouth* fignifieth, that thou art an un-allmighty Sonne of thy Father, whether thou art an Angel or a Man. For through the Mouth thou *muſt* draw into thee the power of thy Father, if thou wilt *live*.

20. An Angel muſt do fo, *as well* as a man, though indeed he needs not to uſe the Element of *Aire*, in that manner *as* a man doth ; yet he muſt attract into himfelf, through the Mouth, *the Spirit*, from which, the *Ayr* in this world exiſteth.

21. For in Heaven there is *no* fuch Ayr, but the qualities are very meek and joyful, like a pleaſant cheering *Breath* of wind, and the Holy Ghoſt is among all the qualities in the *Salitter* 2nd *Mercurius.*

22. And this the Angel *alſo* muſt make uſe of, or elfe he cannot be a *moveable* creature, for he muſt alſo eat of the heavenly fruit, through the Mouth.

23. Thou muſt *not* underſtand this in an *earthly* manner, for an Angel hath no Guts, neither Flefh nor Bones, but is conſtituted or compoſed by the Divine power, in the fhape *form* and manner of a man, and hath all members, like Man, *except* the Members of Generation and the Fundament or *going out of the Draſſe*, neither hath an Angel need of them.

24. For Man gat his members of Generation and Fundament firſt in his dolefull and *lamentable* fall. An Angel ſendeth forth nothing, but the *Divine* power;

er, which he taketh in at his Mouth, wherewith he kindleth his heart, and the heart kindleth all the *members*, and *that* he sendeth forth from himself again at the Mouth, when he speaketh and praiseth God.

25. But the heavenly fruits which he eateth, are *not* earthly ; and though they are in such a *form* and shape as the earthly are, yet they are meer *Divine* power, and have such a pleasant Lovely Taste and Smell, that I cannot liken it to any thing in this world : for they *Taste* and *Smell* of the *Holy Tri-nity.*

26. Thou must not think, that they are there only as it were a Type or *shadow* of things ; *no* : for the Spirit sheweth plainly, that in the heavenly pomp in the heavenly *Salitter* and *Mercurius*, do grow *Divine* Trees, Plants, *Flowers*, and all *sorts*, of whatsoever is in this world but as a type and resemblance: And as the Angels are, so are the vegetation and fruits, all *from* the Divine power.

27. These heavenly Sprouts and Springings thou must *not wholly* liken to this world : *For* there are two Qualities *in this world*, a *Good* and an *Evil* : and many things grow through the power of the Evill quality, which doth *not* so in Heaven.

28. *For* Heaven hath but *one* form or manner, nothing groweth there, which is *not good* : Only Lord Lucifer hath deform'd and dress'd this world in that manner : And therefore was Mother *Eve ashamed,* *when she had eaten* of that which was dress'd by the *Evil* quality, in like manner also she was ashamed of her members of Generation, which she had caused by biting of *this Apple.*

29. The Angelical and Heavenly fruit hath *not*
such

such a substance : indeed it is most certain and true, that *there are* all manner of fruits in *heaven*, and *not* meerly Types and Shadowes : also the Angels *pluck* them with their Hands, and eat them, as we do that are Men, but they need *not* any Teeth to do it withall, *neither* have they any, for the fruit is of a divine power.

30. Now all this, whatsoever an Angel maketh use of, which is Externally *without* him, for the supporting of his life, is *not* his corporeal propriety, as if he had it by a Natural right, but the *Heavenly* Father giveth it them in love.

31. True it is, their Body is their own propriety, for God hath given it to them for a propriety: Now whatsoever is given to any for his *own* or for propriety, that is his by *right* of *Nature*, and he doth not deal righteously which taketh it from him again, unlesse upon condition and agreement : And thus God doth *not neither*, and therefore an Angel is an eternal incorruptible Creature which standeth or subsisteth in all Eternity.

32. But what would the Body *profit* him, if God did *not feed* it, for then it would have no mobility, and would lye still like a dead Block. Now *therefore*, the Angels are obedient to God, and humble themselves before the *powerful* God, they honour laud and praise him in his Great Deeds and Works of *wonder*, and sing continually of Gods *Holinesse*, *Because* He feedeth them.

Of the Gracious Blessed and Joyfull Love, of the
Angels, toward God, from a true
Ground.

33.

The right *Love* in the *divine* Nature cometh from the *fountain* of the Sonne of God. Behold thou child of man, let this be told thee; the Angels know *already* what the right Love toward God is, but thou needest it in thy *cold Heart.*

34. Observe: when the gracious *amiable* blessed Joyful Glance and Light, together with the *sweet* power out of the Sonne of God, shineth into all powers in the whole Father: then *all* the powers are kindled by the Gracious amiable blessed lovely *Light* and sweet power, in a triumphing and joyful manner.

35. So also, when the Gracious amiable Blessed and joyful Light of the Sonne of God *shineth* on the loving Angels, and casteth its Beams into their Heart, then all the powers in *their* Body are kindled; and there riseth up such a *Joyful* Love-fire, that for great joy they sing and ring forth Praises, and that which neither I nor *any* other Creature is able to express.

36. With this *Song* I would have the Reader *cited* into the other life, where he will have *experience* thereof: I am not able to set it down in Writing.

37. But if thou wilt have experience of it in *this* world, *give over* thy Hypocrisie, Bribery and Deceit and thy Scorning: and turn thy heart in all seriousnesse

neſſe to God: *Repent* thee of thy Sins, with a true intention and reſolution to live Holily, and pray to God for his holy Spirit.

38. *Wreſtle* with him, as the Holy Patriarch *Jacob* did, *who wreſtled with him all night, till the dawning of the Day,* or Morning *Radius* brake forth, *and would not give over till God had bleſſed him* (Gen. 32.) Do thou ſo like wiſe with him, and the Holy Ghoſt will get a form in thee.

39. If thou holdeſt on in thy earneſtneſſe, and wiltnot give over, then will *this* fire come ſuddainly upon thee, like lightning and ſhine into thee, and then thou wilt well *experiment* that, which I have here written, and wilt *eaſily* beleeve that which is in my Book.

40. Thou wilt alſo become quite *another* man, and wilt think thereon all the dayes of thy life; thy delight will be *more* in Heaven, then on Earth.

41. For the *converſation* of the Holy Soul *is in Heaven,* and though indeed it converſeth in the body on earth, yet it is alwayes *continually* with its Redeemer JESUS CHRIST, and eateth as a gueſt with him. Note this !

The

The Seventh Chapter.

Of the Court Place and Dwelling, also of the Govern-
ment of Angels, how it stood at the beginning,
after the Creation, and how it is become
as it is.

1.

HEre the Devil will *oppose* like a Snarling Dogg, for his shame will be discovered: and he will give the Reader many a sore stroake, and always put him in *doubt* that these things are not so.

2. For nothing doth torment him more, then when his Glory is *upbraided* to him, by signifying what a Glorious King and Prince he hath been: when this is objected to him, then he is in a *rage*, and madnesse, as if he would storm and overthrow all the world.

3. If this Chapter, should be lighted upon by a Reader in whom the fire of the Holy Spirit should be somewhat *weak*, I fear the Devil would be very busie to set upon him, tempting him to *doubting* whether the things, set down here, be so or no, that his kingdome might not stand so very naked, nor his shame be so *quite* discovered.

4. Now if he can but suppose he shall bring it to pass to be doubted of in any heart, he will not *fail* to use his *utmost* skill pains and labour therein. I see very well *already*, that he hath it in his purpose.

5. Therefore I would have the Reader warned, that he be *diligent* in the reading here of, and patient,

so

fo long, till he cometh to the reading of the *Creation* and of the *Government* of this world, and then he will find it plainly and clearly demonftrated from *Nature.*

Now Obferve :

6. When God Almighty had *Decreed* in his Counfel, that he would make Angels or Creatures out of himfelf, then he made them out of his eternal power and *wifdom,* according to the form and manner of the Liberty in his Deity, and according to the *Qualities* in his Divine Being.

7. At firft he made three Kingly Governments or Dominions, anfwerable to the *number* of the Holy Trinity, and each Kingdom had the Order or Ordnance, power and *quality* of the divine Being.

8. Now elevate thy Senfe Thoughts and Spirit into the Deep of the Deity, for here a Gate is *opened.* The Place or Space of this world the Deep of the Earth, and above the Earth even to Heaven, as alfo the created *Heaven,* which was made *out of the* * *midft of the waters,* which moveth above the Stars, *or Centre.* and which we behold with our Eyes, whofe depth we cannot found or reach with our fenfe : *all* this place or room together was one Kingdom, and *Lucifer* was King therein *before* his being thruft out.

9. The other two Kingdoms, that of *Michael* and that of *Uriel,* thofe are *above* the created Heaven, and are like that other Kingdom.

10. Thefe three Kingdoms together contain fuch a Deep, as is not of any *humane* Number, nor can be meafured by any thing.

11. Yet you muft know, that thefe *three* Kingdoms
have

have a Beginning and End: But that God, who hath made these three Kingdoms out of himself, is infinite, and hath no End.

12. Yet, without and beyond and besides these three Kingdoms there is likewise the *power* of the Holy Trinity, for God the Father hath *no End*.

13. But thou art to know this Mystery, that in the Center or *Midst* of these three Kingdoms is generated the splendor or Sonne of God.

[*14. This needs explanation : Read the * Second and*
" † *Third part of these writings, where it is described*
" *more fundamentally: for nothing that is divisible mea-*
" *surable or circumscriptive, is here meant or understood,*
" *only it was in simplicity and plainnesse set down so at*
" *the first, because of the slow and dull apprehen-*
" *sion.*]

15. And the three Kingdoms are *circular* round about the Sonne of God, *neither* of them is further or nearer to the Sonne of God, for the one is equally as near about the Sonne of God as the other.

16. From *this* * fountain and from all the powers of the Fether goeth forth the Holy Ghost, together with the Light and power of the Sonne of God in and through all *Angelical* Kingdomes or Dominions : and without *beyond* and besides all the Angelical Kingdoms, which no Angel or man is able to dive or search into.

17. Neither have I any purpose to consider of it *further*, much lesse to write, but *my Revelation* reacheth even into the three Kingdoms, like an Angelical Knowledge.

18. But *not* in my Reason or apprehension or in *perfection* like an Angel, but *in part*, and so-long only, as the Spirit tarrieth in me, further I know it not.

19. When

19. When he parteth from me, I know nothing, but the Elementary and earthly things of this world: but the Spirit seeth even into the *depth* of Deity.

Question.

20. Now one may ask, what manner of Substance or thing it is ? that the Sonne of God is Generated in the Center or *midst* of these Three Kingdoms ? *Surely* one Angelical Hoast must needs be nearer unto him then the other, seeing their Kingdom hath so great a Deep ?

21. Also then the Glory Clarity or *brightnesse* and power of the Sonne of God would not be so great without *beyond* or besides those Kingdoms, as in with and *among* those that are near him, and as in the Angelical Circuit or Court ?

Answer.

22. *Answ.* The holy Angels were made to be creatures from God: that they should *praise sing* ring forth and Jnbilate before the Heart of God, which is the Sonne of God, and *increase* the heavenly joy.

23. *where* then should the Father else place them, but before the Gate of his Heart ? Doth not all joy of Man, which is in the *whole* man, arise from the fountain of the Heart : so in God also then there ariseth the gyeat joy out of the fountain of his Heart.

24. And *therefore* hath he created the Holy Angels out of himself, which are as it were *little* Gods, answerable to the Being and qualities of the whole God; that in the power should Act *forth* the praise, and sing and ring forth in the power, and *increase* the arising joy from the heart of God.

25. But

25. But the Splendor and the power of the Sonne of God, or heart of God, which is the *Light*, or source and fountain of joy, taketh up his *fairest* and most joyfull original; in the center or *midst* of these kingdoms, and shineth into, and *through* all the Angelical Gates.

26. Thou must understand this *properly*, what the meaning of it is: for when I speak by way of similitude, and *liken* the Sonne of God to the Sun or to a round Globe; it hath not that meaning as if he were a circumscriptive fountain, which can be *measured*, or whose depth, beginning, or end, could be fathomed. I write so only by way of similitude, till the *Reader* may come to the true understanding.

27. For the meaning is not here, that the Sonne of God should be generated *only* in the Center or midst of these Angelical Gates, and no where else without beyond or *besides* these Angelical Gates.

28. For the powers of the Father are *every where*, from and out of which the Sonne is generated and from which the Holy Ghost goeth forth; *how* should he then be generated only in the Center of these Angelical Gates?

29. This therfore is the only ground and *meaning*, that the Holy Father, who is ALL would *have* in these Angelical * Gates, his most joyful and most richly loving Qualities, out of which the most joyful and most *richly loving* Light, Word, heart, or fountain of powers; is Generated: and therefore hath created his Holy Angels in *this* place for his joy honour and Glory.

[30. *In the Abyssal or bottomlesse Eternity indeed, it is in one place as well as in another: but where there are no Creatures, it cannot be known but by the Spirit in its wonders.*]

31. And

31. And this is the *Select* place of the glory of God, which God the Father, in himself, hath made choise of, *wherein* his Holy WORD, or heart is generated in *highest* glory Clarity or brightnes, power and tryumphing joy.

32. For, Observe this Mystery; The Light, which is generated out of the powers of the Father, which is the true fountain of the Sonne of God, is generated *also* in an Angel, and a Holy Man, so that in the same light and knowledge he tryumpheth in *great* joy;

33. How then is it that he should *not* be generated every where, in the *whole* Father? For his power is ALL, and every where, even there, where our heart and sences or Thoughts cannot reach.

34. And so Now, *where* the Father is, *there* is also the Sonne and the Holy Ghost: for the Father every where *generateth* the Sonne, his holy WORD, power light, and sound, and the Holy Ghost, goeth every where forth, from the Father and the Sonne, even *within* all the Angelical gates, and *without* besides or beyond the angelical gates also.

35. Now if a Man likeneth the Sonne of God to the *Globe* of the Sun, as I have often done in the foregoing Chapters; that is spoken in the way and manner of Natural similitudes, and I was *constrained* to write so, because of the mis-understanding of the Reader, that so he might raise his Sense or Thoughts in these natural things, and climbe from step to step, from one *degree* to another, till he might come into the high mysteries.

36. But it hath not this meaning, that the Sonne of God is a circumscribed compacted figured Image, like the Sun.

Q   37. For

37. For if it were so, then *must* the Sonne of God have a beginning, and the Father must have generated him at *once*, and then he could *not* be the Eternal Almighty Sonne of the Father, but were like a King, who had yet a *greater* King *above* him, who had generated him in Time, and in whose power it were to alter and to *change him*.

38. This were such a Sonne, as had a beginning, and his power and splendor were *like* the power of the Sun which goeth forth from the Sun ; the Body or Globe of the Sun standing still in its place : And if this were so, then indeed one Angelical * Gate would be *nearer* to the Sonne of God, then another.

39. But here I will shew to thee the highest Gate of the divine Mystery, and thou needst seek no higher, for there is no higher.

Obſerve:

40. The Fathers power is all, in and above all Heavens, and the same power every where generateth the Light. Now this ALL-POWER, is, and is called, the *all-power* of the Father ; and the Light which is generated out of that all-power, is, and is called the Sonne.

41. But it is therefore called the Sonne, in that it is generated out of the Father, so that it is the *Heart* of the Father in his powers.

42. And being *generated*, so it is another Person, then the Father is : for, the Father is the *power* and *Kingdom*, and the Sonne is the *Light* and Splendor in the Father, and the Holy Ghost is the *moving* or *exit* out of the powers of the Father, and of the Sonne,

Sonne, and formeth figureth *frameth* and Imageth all.

43. As the *Ayr* goeth forth from the power of the Sun and Stars, and moveth in this world, and causeth that all creatures are generated, and that the Grasse Herbs and Trees spring and grow; and causeth *all* whatsoever is in this world to be:

44. So the Holy Ghost goeth forth from the Father and the Sonne, and moveth or acteth, formeth or frameth and Imageth all that is in the *whole God*.

45. All growing or vegetation and forms in the Father arise and spring up moving in the Holy Ghost; therefore there is but ONE only GOD, and *three* distinct *Persons* in one divine Being, Essence or substance.

46. Now if a Man should say, the Sonne of God were an Image, circumscriptive or measureable like the sun, then the Three Persons would onely be in that place where the Sonne is, and his splendor or *shining* would be without or beyond him, and as gone forth from the Sonne, and the Father would be One, onely Externally without or besides the Sonne, and then the power of the Father, which would be afar off, and wide distant from the Sonne, *would not* generate the Sonne and Holy Ghost, externally without and beyond the Angelical Gates; and so there would be an *un-almighty* Being, Externally without or besides this place of the Sonne; and moreover the Father would be a Circumscribed or measurable Being.

47. Which is *not* so: but the Father every where generateth the Sonne out of all his powers, and the Holy Ghost goeth every where forth from the Fa-

*ther

ther and the Sonne, and so *there is* but ONE onely God in one Being with three distinct Persons.

48. Of which you have a similitude in the precious Gold-Oar or a Gold-Stone, unseparated. First there is the matter, that is, the *Salitter* and *Mercurius,* which is the *Mother* or the whole stone, which generateth the Gold every where in the whole *Stone,* and in the Gold is the glorious power or vertue of the Stone.

49. Now the *Salitter* and *Mercurius* signifie the Father, the Gold signifieth the Sonne, and the power or vertue signifies the Holy Ghost : in such a manner also is the *Ternarie* in the holy Trinity onely, that all moveth and goeth forth therein universally.

50. Men find also in a Gold stone a little bit of it in some place wherein there is more and *purer* Gold, then in another not discerned, though there is Gold in the *whole* stone or Oare.

51. Thus also is the Place or Space in the *Center* or midst of the Angelical Gates a more pleasant, more gracious amiable and blessed Place, to the Father, wherein his Sonne and Heart is generated in the most richly and fully loving manner, and wherein the Holy Ghost goeth forth from the Father and the Sonne, in the most richly and fully loving manner.

52. Thus you have the right ground of this mystery, and you *ought not* to think, that the Sonne of God was generated of the Father, at *once* at a *certain time,* as one that hath a beginning, and that he standeth now as a *King,* and will be worshipped.

53. No; this were *not* an Eternal Sonne, but one that had a beginning, and were under beneath or *inferiour* to the Father, that had generated him.

54. *Neither*

54. *Neither* would he be all-knowing, for he could not know how it was before his Father had generated him.

55. But the Sonne is allwayes generated *continually* from eternity unto eternity, and reshineth alwayes continually from eternity, into the powers of the Father again, whereby the powers of the Father are alwayes from Eternity to Eternity *continually* impregnated with the Sonne, and generateth him continually.

56. Out of which, the Holy Ghost *continually* Existeth from eternity to eternity, and so continually from eternity to eternity goeth forth from the Father and the Sonne, and hath neither Beginning nor End.

57. And *this* Being, is not onely so, in *one* place of the Father, but *every where*, in the whole Father, who hath neither beginning nor end; into which, no creature can reach with its *Senses* or thoughts.

Of the Nativity or Geniture *of an Angelical Kings, and how they came to be.*

58.

[" *This also is more fundamentally described in the* " * *Second and* † *Third Book.*]

59. The Person or *Body* of a King of Angels is generated out of all the qualities and out of all the powers of his *whole* Kingdom, through the moving boyling spirit of God, and therefore such a one is their King, in that his power reacheth into all the Angels of his whole Kingdom, and he is the Head or *Throne-Angel.* And such a one was Lord Lucifer also, before his fall.

E.
* Three Principles.
† Threefold Life.

[" 60. *And*

[" 60. *And this also is more fundamentally described*
" *in our* second *and* third *book ;* viz. *in*
" *The three Principles of the Divine Being ;*
" *And in the Threefold Life of Man.*

Of the Ground or Foundation and Mystery.

61.

If a man will find out the mystery, and deepest Ground; he must diligently and *exactly* view and consider the Creation of this world, the Government or Dominion and order or *Ordinance,* as also the Qualities, of the stars, and the elements.

62. And although these are of a *corrupted* and twofold Being, which is not living nor hath understanding : for it is but the corrupt *Salitter* and *Mercurius,* in which King Lucifer kept House, wherein is both Evil and Good, though it be indeed the *reall* power of God, which before its corruption was bright and pure, as now it is, in *Heaven.*

63. This power of the Stars and Elements, did the Creator, after the horrible fall of Lucifers Kingdome, *frame* and put into such order again, as the Kingdome of the Angels *stood in,* in the Divine pomp, before his fall.

64. Only thou must *not think,* that the Angelical Kingdom with its creatures, were so rolled wheeled and turn'd round about, as now the Stars are, which are only powers, and *in regard* of the birth or geniture of this world are thus wheeled or turn'd about, whose birth or geniture standeth in the moving *boyling*

ing

ing anguish in Evil and Good, in Corruption and Redemption, till the End of this enumeration, or the Last Day.

Now Observe:

65. The Sun *standeth* in the Center or *Midst* of the Deep, and is the light or heart which proceeded out of all stars: For when the *Salitter* and *Mercurius*, before the Creation of the world, in the Kingdome of Lucifer became thin or dim and bad qualified one with the other: *then* God extracted the Heart out of all the powers, and made the Sun thereof.

66. And *therefore* the Sun is the most shining and brightest of all, and re-enlighteneth all the starres again, all the stars *work* in its Power, and it self hath the power of all the stars, it *kindleth* all the powers of the stars with its splendour and heat, and so every Star receiveth from the Sun, according to its power and condition, or *Kind*.

67. *Thus* also is the Frame and Constitution of the Angelical Kingdom: The Sun signifieth the Supreamest Throne-Angel, the *Cherubin* or King, in an Angelical Kingdom: such a one as Lord Lucifer also was, before his fall: He had his *seat* in the Center or Midst of his Kingdom, and raigned by his power *in* all his Angels.

68. As the Sun ruleth in all the powers of this world in the *Salitter* and *Mercurius*, that is in softnesse and hardnesse, in sweetnesse and sowrnesse, in bitternesse and astringency, in heat and cold, in Ayr and Water.

69. As is *apparent* in Winter, when there is so hard Cold or Frost, that the water becometh Ice; though the Sun shineth somewhat warm through all

the

the cold froſt, yet for all its beams by which it ſhineth on them, it *freezeth* into Snow and Ice.

70. But *here* I will ſhew thee the right Myſtery. Behold; the Sun is the Heart of all powers in this world, and is compacted framed or compoſed out of all the powers of the ſtars, it *re-enlightneth* all the ſtars, and all the powers in this world again, and all powers grow *active* operative or qualifying in its Power.

71. [" *Underſtand it* Magically : *for it is a Mirrour* " *Looking-Glaſſe or Similitude of the Eternall* " *world:*]

72. As the Father generateth his Sonne, *that is*, his Heart or light, out of all his powers, and that *light* which is the Sonne, generateth the *life* in all the powers of the Father, ſo that in the ſame light, in the Fathers powers goeth forth all *manner* of growing vegetation ſpringing, Ornaments and Joy : of ſuch a condition is the Kingdom of Angels, all, according to the *Similitude* and Being of God,

73. A Cherubim or *Leader* of a Kingdom of Angels, is the *Fountain* or Heart of his whole Kingdom, and is made out of all the powers, out of which his Angels are made, and is the moſt powerfull and brighteſt of them *all*.

74. [" *The Angelical King is the Center or fountain:* " *as* Adams *Soul is the Beginning and Center of all ſoules,* " *and, As ; from the Place of the Sun was created and* " *generated the Planetick wheel or Sphear, wherein each* " *Star is deſirous of the Splendor and Power of the Sun ; ſo* " *the Angels are deſirous of their Cherubim or Prince :* " *all according to God and to his Similitude.*

75. For the Creatour hath extracted the heart out of the *Salitter* and *Mercurius* of the Divine powers.

[" *Under-*

" *Understand he hath composed it by the* Fiat, viz. *the Center of Nature.*]

76. And hath formed out of that the Cherubim, or *King*, that he might preffe or penetrate again with his power into all the Angels, and *affect* them all, with his power.

77. As the Sun with its power preffeth into all the *Stars*, and affecteth them all ; or as the power of God the Son, preffeth into all the powers of God the Father, whereby they are *all* affected, wherein the Birth or Geniture of the heavenly Joyfulneffe fpringeth up.

78. In this form condition and *manner* it is alfo with the Augels. All the Angels of one Kingdome, fignifie, the many and *various powers* of God the Father ; the Angelical King, fignifieth, the Sonne of the Father, or the *Heart* out of the powers of the Father ; out of which the Angels are made ; The *Exit* out of the King of Angels, or his going forth into his Angels, or his *affecting* of his Angels, fignifieth God the Holy Ghoft.

79. And as the Holy Ghoft goeth forth from the Father and the Sonne, and affecteth all the powers of the Father, as alfo all heavenly *fruits* and *forms*, from whence all hath its rifing, and wherein the heavenly joyfulneffe doth confift :

80. Juft in fuch a manner is the *operation* or power of a Cherubim or Throne-Angel, which worketh or operateth in all his Angels, as the Sonne and Holy Ghoft *operateth* in all the powers of the *Father* ; or as the Sun operateth in all the powers of the Stars.

R   81. Where-

81. Whereby all Angels *obtain* the will of the Throne-Angel, and are all *obedient* to him; for they all work in his power which is *in them* all.

82. For they are the *Members* of his body: as all the powers of the Father, are *Members* of the Sonne, and he is their Heart: and as all heavenly forms and fruits are Members of the Holy Ghoſt, and he *their* heart, in whom they riſe up.

83. Or as the Sun is the heart of all the ſtars, and all ſtars are Members of the Sun, and work one *among* another as one Star, and yet the Sun is the Heart *therein*, though indeed there are many and various powers yet *all* worketh in the power of the Sun; and all hath its *Life* from the Power of the Sun. Look on what you pleaſe; be it in * Animals, Metals, or † Vegetables, of the *Earth*.

The

The Eighth Chapter.

Of the whole Corpus *or Body of an* Angelical
Kingdome.

The Great Mysterie.

1.

THe Angelical Kingdoms are *throughout* formed according to the Divine Being, and
they have no other form or Condition, then
the *Divine* Being hath in its Trinitie.

2. Onely this is the difference; that their Bodies
are *creatures*, which have a Beginning and End, and
that the Kingdom, where their Locality *habitation* or
Court is, is not their corporeal propriety or proper
own, having it for their Natural right, as they have
their bodies for a *Natural right*.

3. But the Kingdom belongs to God the Father,
who hath made it out of his powers, and he may set
it and *dispose* it which way he pleaseth; otherwise
their Body is made according to all, and out of all,
the *powers* of the Father.

4. And their power generateth the light and
knowledge *in them* : and as God generateth his
Sonne out of *all* his powers; also as the Holy Ghost
goeth forth out of *all* the powers of the Father and
the Sonne : so also in an Angel the Spirit goeth forth
from their Heart, from their light, and from *all*
their powers.

Now

Now Observe :

5. As the condition and *constitution* of an Angel is in his *Corporeal* Body, with all the Members thereof; such is the condition of a whole Kingdom, which together is as it were one Angel.

6. If a man rightly considereth all circumstances, he will find, that the whole government in its locality circumference or *Region* in a Kingdom, is of the same Condition or Constitution as the body of an Angel is, or as the *Holy Trinity*.

Observe here the Depth.

7. *All power* is in God the Father, and he is the *fountain* of all powers in his Deep ; in *Him* is Light and Darknesse, Ayr and Water, Heat and Cold, Hard and Soft, Thick and Thin, Sound and Tone, Sweet and Soure, Bitter and Aftringent, and that, which I *cannot* number or rehearse.

8. Onely I *conceive* of it in my Body, for That is originally from *Adam* to this time made out of *all powers*, and *according to the Image of God.*

9. But here thou muft *not* think, that the powers in God the Father are in such wife, or qualifie in such a *corrupt* manner and kind, as in man, which Lord Lucifer hath so brought to paffe ; but it is all very lovely pleafant *delicious* and joyfull, very Gentle and Meek or Mild.

10. Firft there is the Light : (as I may *naturally* compare or refemble it) like the light of the Sun, but not fo *intolerable* ; as the light of the Sun is intolerable to our corrupted perifhed Eyes, but very

lovely

lovely pleaſant and delightful an *Aſpect* or Glance of Love.

11. But the darkneſſe is *hidden* in the Center of the light, that is, when a creature is made out of the power of the light, and would move and boyl *higher* and faſter in that light then God Himſelf doth ; then that light would go out and be *extinguiſhed* in that Creature.

12. [" *Undeſtand,* the *Creature kindleth the fire, if*
    " *its ſpirit elevateth it ſelf beyond the* Hu-
    " mility that is *from Love : Read the Se-*
    " cond *and* Third Book, *viz. the Three*
    " *Principles, and the Three-fold Life of*
    " *Man.*]

I.

13. And inſtead of Light it hath *darkneſſe,* and therein the Creature is *ſenſible* by experience, that there is a darkneſſe, hidden in the Center.

14. As when a man kindleth a Wax *Candle,* it giveth Light, but when it is put out, then is the Snuffe or Candle, darkneſſe : *Thus* alſo the light ſhineth from all the powers of the Father : but when the powers are periſhed or *corrupted,* then the light is extinguiſhed, and the powers would remain in darkneſſe, as is apparant by *Lucifer.*

15. The Ayr alſo is not of ſuch a kind *in God,* but is a lovely pleaſant ſtill breath or voyce blowing or moving ; that is ; The *exit* going forth, or moving, of the powers, is the *original* of the Ayr, in which the Holy Ghoſt riſeth up.

16. Neither is the water of ſuch a kind in God, but it is the *ſource* or fountain in the powers, *not* of an elementary kind, as in this world ; if I ſhould liken it to any thing, I muſt liken it to the Sap or *Juyce*

in

in an Apple, but very bright and *lightfome* like Heaven, which is the Spirit of all powers.

17. It is Lord Lucifer which hath thus *fpoiled* it, that it rageth and raveth fo in this world, which fo runneth and floweth and is fo thick and dark, and moreover *if it runneth not* it becometh ftinking ; of which I fhall treat more largely, when I fhall write of *the Creation.*

18. The Heat is in God a moft lovely pleafant foft gentle mild meek warmth, an *exit* or going forth of light, which expandeth it felf rifing up *from* the light, wherein the fource or fountain of Love Springeth up.

19. The Cold alfo in God is not of fuch a kind, but is a cooling or refrefhing of the Heat, a mollifying or allaying of the Spirit, a rifing up boyling or moving of the Spirit.

Note here the Depth.

20. God faith in *Mofes,* when he gave the *Law* to the children of *Ifrael* ; *I am an angry jealous God to thofe, that hate me :* afterward he calls himfelf alfo, *a merciful God to them that fear him,* Exod. 20. 5, 6. Deut. 5.9, 10.

Queftion.

21. Now the Queftion is : What is the wrath of God, in Heaven ? And whether God be angry in himfelf ? or how is God moved to Anger ?

Anfwer.

Answer.

Here there are chiefly *Seven* sorts of Qualities or Circumstances to be observed.

I.

Of the First Species or Circumstance.

22.

First there is in the Divine power hidden in Secret, the astringent Quality, which is a Quality of the *Kernel* Pith or hidden Being, a sharp compaction or penetration in the *Salitter* very sharp and harsh or astringent, which *generates* hardnesse and also coldnesse; and when that heat is *kindled*, it genereateth a sharpnesse like to *Salt*.

23. This is one *Species* or source of wrath in the Divine *Salitter*, and when this source is kindled, which may be done by *great motion* or elevation, touching or stirring, then the astringent causeth, or qualifieth in, great *coldnesse*, which is very sharp, like to *Salt*, very hard binding knitting and *attracting* together like a Stone.

24. But in the heavenly Pomp or State it is not so elevating; for it doth *not elevate* it self, neither doth it kindle it self; Onely, King *Lucifer* hath kindled this quality in his Kingdom, through his Elevation and *Pride*, whence this quality is *burning* even till the Last Day.

25. And by this now, in the Creation of this world,

world, the Stars and the Elements, as also the Creatures *tremble* and burn, out of which existeth also the House of Death and of Hell, also an Eternal Base loathsome Habitation for the Kingdom of *Lucifer* and for all *wicked* Men.

26. This Quality generateth in the heavenly Pomp, the *sharpnesse* of the spirit, out of which, and whereby, the creaturely Being is so formed or constituted, that a heavenly *Body* may be framed, as also all manner of colours, forms and sprouts or vegetation.

27. For it is the contraction *compacting* or Imaging of a thing, and therefore it is the first Quality, and a *beginning* of the Angelical Creatures, and of all Images or figurations which are in Heaven, and which are in this world, and all *whatsoever* can be named or expressed.

28. But if it be kindled through elevation, which those creatures *onely* can do in their own Kingdome, which are created out of the *Divine Salitter*, then it is a burning source-vein of the wrath of God.

29. For it is one of the *seven Spirits of God*, in whose power standeth the Divine Being in the whole or *total* Divine Power and heavenly Pomp.

30. And so if it be kindled, then it is a *fierce* source of wrath, and a beginning of hell, and a torment and woe of the hellish fire, also a quality of *darknesse*; for the Divine Love, and also the Divine Light are extinguished *therein*.

31. [" *It is a Key, which locketh in to the Chamber of* " Death, *and generateth Death, from* " *whence proceedeth Earth, stones, and all* " *hard things.*]

I I.
Of the Second Species or Circumstance.

32.

The *Second* Quality or Second Spirit of God in the Divine *Salitter*, or in the Divine power, is the *sweet* quality, which worketh in the astringent, and mitigateth the astringent, so that it is altogether lovely pleasant and mild or meek.

33. For it is the *overcoming* of the astringent quality, and is the very source or *fountain* of the Mercy of God, which overcometh the wrath, whereby the astringent harsh source is *mollified*, and Gods Mercy riseth up.

34. Of this you have a *Similitude* in an Apple, which at first is astringent *harsh* or choaky, but when the sweet quality forceth and overcometh it, then it is very soft lovely and pleasant to *eat* : and thus it is also in the Divine power.

35. For when Men speak of the mercy of God the Father, they speak of his *power*, of his *fountain* spirits of the qualities, which are in the *Salitter* out of which his most richly loving *Heart* or Sonne is generated.

Observe here.

36. The astringent or harsh Quality is the Heart Pith or *Kernel* in the Divine power, the contraction compaction or imaging forming or impression; for it is the sharpnesse and *cold*, as is seen, that the harsh

S   astringent aftringent cold *dryeth* the water, and maketh it sharp Ice.

37. And the sweet Quality is the *allaying* or warming, whereby the harsh or aftringent and cold quality becometh thin and *soft*, whence the water taketh its original.

38. Thus the aftringent quality *is*, and *is called* the Heart; and the sweet, is called *Barm*, or *Warm*, or softening or *mitigating* : and they are the two Qualities, out of which the Heart or the Sonne of God is generated.

Germanicè Barm-Hertz-igkeit, Warm-Heart-ednesse. Mercy.

39. For the aftringent or *harsh* quality, in its stock or kernel when it qualifieth or operateth in its own Power, is a Darknesse : And the sweet Quality, in its own power is a moving boyling warming and rising Light, a source or *fountain* of meeknesse and well-doing.

40. But while both of them qualifie or operate one in another, in the Divine power ; as if they were but *one* power, they are a meek mild lovely pleasant *merciful* qualifying.

41. And these two Qualities are *two* of the spirits of God among the *Seven* qualifying or fountain-Spirits in the Divine power.

42. Whereof you have an Image in the Revelation of *John* : Apocalypse, Chap. 1. where he seeth *seven Golden Candlesticks* or Lights *before the Sonne of God*, which signifie *the seven spirits of God*, which shine in great clarity brightnesse or lustre before the Sonne of God, out of which the Sonne of God is continually generated from eternity to eternity, and is the Heart of the seven Spirits of God, which I will here describe in *order* one after another.

43. You must here elevate your sense or mind : in the

the *Spirit*, if you intend to underſtand and *apprehend* it: Or elſe in your own ſenſe or mind you will be an aſtringent hard blind Stock.

III.

Of the Third Circumſtance or Species.

44.

The Third Quality or the Third Spirit of God, in the Fathers power, is the bitter quality; which is a penetrating or *forcing* of the ſweet and aſtringent or harſh Quality, which is *trembling*, penetrating, and riſing up.

Obſerve here:

45. The aſtringent or harſh quality is the kernel or ſtock, or ſoure or *attractive*, and the ſweet is the light *mollifying* and ſoftning, and the bitter is *penetrating* or triumphing; which riſeth up and triumpheth in the aſtringent or harſh and ſweet quality.

46. This is the ſource of joy, or the cauſe of the *laughing* elevating Joy, whereby a thing trembleth and Jubilateth for Joy; whence the heavenly joy exiſteth.

47. Moreover, it is the Imaging or forming of all ſorts of *Red* colours in its own quality: in the ſweet it Imageth or formeth all ſorts of *white* and *Blew*: in the aſtringent or harſh and ſoure, it formeth all ſorts

of *Green Dusky* and mix'd colours, with all manner of forms or *Figures* and *Smells*.

48. The bitter quality is the first spirit, whence the *life* becometh stirring, from whence mobility taketh its original, and is well called *Cor* or the Heart, for it is the trembling shivering elevating penetrating spirit, a triumphing, or Joy, an elevating source of *laughing*, in the sweet quality the bitter is mollified, so that it becometh very richly loving and Joyfull.

49. But if it be moved, elevated and kindled too much, then it kindleth the sweet and astringent or harsh quality, and is like a tearing, stinging and *Burning* Poyson, as when a man is tormented with a raging plague-sore, which maketh him *cry out* for woe and misery.

50. This quality in the Divine power, when it is kindled, is the spirit of the Zealous or Jealous and bitter *wrath* of God, which is unquenchable, as may be seen by the Legions of *Lucifer*.

51. Yet further, this quality, when it is kindled, is the bitter *hellish* fire, which putteth out the Light, turning the sweet quality into a *Stinck*, causing a sharpnesse and tearing, a hardnesse and coldnesse, in the astringent or harsh quality.

52. In the sowre quality it causeth a *ranknesse* and brittlenesse, a stinck, misery, a house of mourning, a house of darknesse, of Death and of Hell, an End of Joy, which therein can no more be thought upon : for it cannot be quieted, or *stilled* by any thing, nor can be enlightned again by any thing, but the dark, astringent or harsh, stinking, sowre, torn, bitter *fierce* quality riseth up to all Eternity.

Now Obſerve:

53. In theſe three Species or Qualities ſtandeth the Corporeal Being, or the *Creatural* Being of all Creatures in heaven and in this world, whether it be Angel, or Man, Beaſt, or Fowl, or Vegetable, of a heavenly or earthly form, quality, and kind, as alſo *all* colours and forms.

54. Briefly, whatſoever Imageth it ſelf, ſtandeth in the power and authority of theſe three *head Qualities,* and is formed by them, and alſo is formed out of its own power.

55. Firſt the aſtringent and ſowr quality is a *Body* or ſource, which attracteth the ſweet power, and the cold in the aſtringent or harſh quality maketh it *Dry.*

56. For the ſweet quality is the heart of the water, for it is thin and light or bright, and is like Heaven : and the bitter quality maketh it ſeparable or *diſtinct,* ſo that the powers form themſelves into *Members,* and cauſeth mobility in the Body.

57. And when the ſweet quality is dryed, then it is a *Corpus* or Body, which is perfect, but wanting Reaſon.

58. And the Bitter quality penetrateth into the *Body,* into the aſtringent ſowre and ſweet quality, and frameth all ſorts of Colours according to that quality which the Body is *moſt eagerly* inclined to, or to that quality which is ſtrongeſt in the Body: according to that the bitter quality frameth the Body with its *colours,* and according to that quality the creature hath her greateſt impulſe and inclination, motion, boyling and will.

IIII, *of*

IIII.

Of the Fourth Circumstance or Species.

59.

The fourth Quality, or the fourth fountain-Spirit in the Divine power of God the Father is the Heat, which is the true *Beginning* of life, and also the true *Spirit* of Life.

60. The aftringent or harfh, fowre, and fweet, quality is the *Salitter*, which belongeth to the *Body*, out of which the Body is framed.

61. For coldneffe and hardneffe ftandeth in the aftringent quality, and is a *contraction* and Drying; and in the *fweet* quality ftandeth the water, and the light or fhiningneffe, and the whole matter of the Body.

62. And the bitter quality is the *feparation* and forming, and the Heat is the Spirit or the kindling of the life, whereby the Spirit exifteth in the Body, which fpringeth or moveth in the whole Body, and fhineth out from the Body; alfo maketh the *living motion* in all the qualities of the Body.

63. Two things are chiefly to be eyed in *all the qualities* : if you look upon a Body, you fee firft the Stock Pith or the Kernel of all the qualities, which is framed or *Compofed* out of all the qualities : for to the Body belong the aftringent or harfh, foure, fweet, bitter and hot qualities ; Thefe qualities being *dryed together*, make the Body or Stock.

The

The Great Mysterie of the Spirit.

64.

Now these Qualities are *mix'd* in the Body, as if they were all but *one* quality ; and yet each quality moveth or boyleth in its own power, and so goeth forth.

65. *Each* quality goeth forth from it self into the other, and *toucheth* or stirreth the other, that is, it *affecteth* the other, whereby the other qualities get the will of this ; that is, they prove the sharpnesse and spirit of this quality, as to what *is in it*, and alwaies mix with it continually.

66. Now the astringent or harsh quality together with the sowre, alwaies *contract* or attract the other qualities together, and so apprehend and retain the Body, and Dry it.

67. For it dryeth all the other powers, and *retaineth* them all through its infection or *influence,* and the sweet softneth and moistneth all the other, and so blendeth and tempereth it self with all the other, whereby they become daintily pleasant and mild or soft.

68. And the bitter maketh all the other *stirring* and moveable, and parteth or distinguisheth them into members; so that every member in this tempering obtaineth the *fountain* of all the powers, whence mobility existeth.

69. And the Heat kindleth all the qualities, out of which the light riseth up and expandeth it self
aloft

aloft in *all* the qualities, fo that the one feeth the other : for when the *Heat* worketh in the fweet Moifture, then it generateth the Light in all the Qualities, fo that the one feeth the other.

70. From whence the Senfes and Thoughts exift, fo that the one quality feeth the other, which is alfo in it and *tempered* with it felf, and *proveth* it with its fharpneffe, fo that it becometh to be a will, which in the Body rifeth up in the firft fountain fource or well-fpring in the *aftringent* or harfh quality.

71. And there the bitter quality penetrateth in the heat through the aftringent, and the fweet in the water letteth it *eafily* or Gently through; and there the bitter in the heat goeth *through* the fweet water forth from the Body, and maketh *two* open *Gates*, which are the Eyes, the firft Senfe, or Senfibility.

72. You have an example and type or *refemblance* of this; If *you* behold and confider this world, efpecially theEarth, which is of the *kind and Condition* of all qualities, and all *manner* of figures or fhapes are formed and Imaged therein.

73. Firft the aftringent quality is therein, which attracteth the *Salitter* together, and *fixeth* or maketh the Earth firm and compact, fo that it cometh to be a folid *Body*, which holds together and doth not break afunder, and Imageth or frameth or formeth therein *all manner* of Bodies, according to the kind of each quality, *viz.* all manner of Stones and Oares of Minerals, and all manner of Roots, according to the *condition* or kind of each quality.

74. Now when that is Imaged or formed, there it lyeth as a *corporeal* fpringing boyling mobility, for it moveth or boyleth *thorough*, and *in* the bitter quality,

lity, in it self, as in its own Imaged formed or framed Body : But hath *as yet* no life to growing vegeration springing or spreading abroad *without* the Heat, which is the * *Spirit* of Nature.

* or Nature-Spirit.

75. But when the heat of the Sun *shineth* upon the Earth, then there spring and grow in the Earth all manner of Images or Figures of Oares or Minerals, Herbs, Roots and Worms, and *all whatsoever is* therein.

Understand this aright :

76. The heat of the Sun kindleth, in the earth, the sweet quality of water, in all Imaged or framed *figures* : and then through the heat the light cometh to be in the sweet water, and that *enlightneth* the astringent, sowre, and bitter, qualities, so that they see *in* or *by* the light : and in that seeing the one riseth up into the other, and *proveth* the other ; that is, in that seeing, the one tasteth of the others sharpnesse, from whence cometh the Taste.

77. And when the sweet quality tasteth the *Taste* of the bitter quality, it * caggs at it, and giveth back even as a man when he tasteth astringent harsh or bitter *Gall*, he openeth both the † Gummes of his *Pallate* in his Mouth in his * Cagging, and wideneth his Pallate *more* then it is of it self ; and just so doth the sweet Quality against the Bitter.

* Checks or stops it. Flend flemmet undweich.
† Throat or Jawes.
* or checking.

78. And when the sweet quality thus stretcheth or *wideneth* it self, and retireth from the bitter, then the astringent alwayes presseth after it, and *would* also fain taste of the sweet ; and alwaies maketh the Body that is behind it, and *in* it, to be Dry : for the sweet quality is the Mother of the water, and is very meek mild soft and Gentle.

T　　　　　　　79. Now

79. Now when the aftringent or harfh and bitter quality get *their* light from the Heat, then they *fee* the fweet quality, and tafte of its fweet water, and then they continually make *hafte after* the fweet water, and drink it up, for they are very Hard, rough, and thirfty, and the Heat dryeth them *quite up*.

80. And the fweet quality alwaies flyeth from the Bitter and Aftringent, and ftretcheth its *Pallate alwayes *wider*, and the Bitter and aftringent continually haften after the fweet, and *refrefh* themfelves from the fweet, and dry up the Body.

* Throat or Jawes.

81. Thus is the true Springing or *vegetation* in Nature, be it in Man, Beafts, Wood, Herbs, or Stones.

Now obferve the End of Nature in this World.

82.

When the fweet quality thus flyeth from the bitter, fowre and aftringent, then the aftringent and bitter make *all the hafte they can* after it, as their beft treafure; and the fweet preffeth vehemently from them, and ftriveth fo much, that it *driveth* and Penetrateth through the aftringent or harfh quality, and *rends* the Body, and goeth forth from the Body, out above the earth, and hafteneth fo faft, till a long *ftalk* groweth up.

83. And then the heat above the earth preffeth upon the ftalk, and fo the bitter quality is then kindled by the Heat, and * it receiveth a *repulfe*

* the Stalk.

from

from the Heat, so that it is terrified, and the astringent quality dryeth it.

84. And therein the astringent, the sweet, the bitter, and the Heat, *struggle* together, and the astringent quality in its coldnesse continually maketh its drinesse, and so the sweet withdraweth on the *sides*, and the other hasten after it.

85. But when it seeth that it is *like* to be taken or captivated, the bitter quality from *within* pressing so hard upon it, and the heat from *without* pressing upon it also, it maketh the bitter, fervent, or burning, and inflameth it, and there it *leapeth*, springing up through the astringent quality, and riseth up again aloft, so there cometh to be a hard *knot* behind it in that place, where the struggling was, and the knot gets a Hole or *Orifice*.

86. But when the sweet quality leapeth or springeth up through the knot, then the bitter quality had so much *affected* or wrought upon it, that it was all in a trembling; and as soon as it cometh *above* the knot, it suddenly stretcheth it self forth on *all* sides, striving to flie from the bitter quality: and in that stretching forth, its Body keepeth *hollow* in the middle, and in the trembling leaping or *springing up* through the knot, it still gets more Stalk or leaves, and now is frolick or cheerly that it hath escaped the *Battle*.

87. And so when the heat from without, thus presseth upon the stalk, then the qualities become *kindled* in the stalk, and presse through the stalk, and so become affected or wrought upon in the external light of the Sun, and generate *colours* in the stalk, according to the kind of its quality.

88. But so long as the Sweet water is in the stalk,

the ftalk *retaineth* its greenifh colour according to the kind of the fweet quality.

89. And fuch matters the qualities alwaies bring to paffe with the heat in the ftalk, and the ftalk alwayes groweth *further*, and always one *Storm* or affault is held after another, whereby the ftalk alwayes getteth *more* knots, and ftill fpreadeth forth its branches further and further.

90. In the mean while, the heat from without alwayes dryeth the fweet water in the ftalk, and the ftalk alwaies is *fmaller* at the Top; the higher it groweth, the fmaller it is, *growing on* fo long, till it can efcape or run *no* further.

91. And then the fweet quality yieldeth to be taken *captive*, and fo the bitter, fowre, fweet, and aftringent, do raign joyntly together, and the fweet ftretcheth it felf a little forth, but it can *efcape* no more, for it is captivated or caught.

92. And then from all the qualities, which are in the Body, there groweth a *Bud* or Head, and there is a new Body in the Bud or head, and is formed or figured *anfwerable* or like to the firft Root in the Earth, onely now it gets another more fubtile form.

93. And then the fweet quality extends it felf Gently or mildly, and there grow little *fubtile* leaves in the Head which are of the kind of all the qualities, and then the fweet water is as it were a pregnant woman new with child, having *conceived* the Seed, and it alwaies preffeth onward, till it openeth the Head.

94. And then alfo it preffeth forth in *little* leaves, like a woman which is in travel and bringing forth, out the little Leaves or *Bloffoms* have no more its colour

lour and form, but the form of all the Qualities: for now the sweet quality must bring forth the *children* of the other Qualities.

95. And when this *sweet Mother* hath brought forth the Fair, Green, Blew, White, Red, and Yellow, Flowers Blossoms or Children, then she groweth *quite* weary, and cannot long nourish or Nurse these children, neither can she have them long, seeing they are but her *step-children,* which are very tender.

96. And so when the *outward* heat presseth upon these tender children, all the qualities in the children cannot be kindled, for the Spirit of Life qualifieth or floweth in them.

97. And seeing they are *too weak* for this strong Spirit, and cannot elevate themselves, they yeeld or surrender their Noble power, and that smells so *lovely* and with so pleasant a savour, that it rejoyceth the very Heart, and maketh it Laugh: but they *must wither* and fall off, because they are too tender for this Spirit.

98. For the Spirit draweth from the *Head* or *Bud* into the Blossoms, and the Head or Bud is formed according to the *kind* of all the Qualities; the astringent quality attracteth or collecteth the Body of the Bud or Head, and the sweet quality softneth it and spreadeth it abroad, and the Bitter quality parteth or *distinguisheth* the matter into Members, and the Heat is the *living* spirit therein.

99. Now all the qualities labour or work therein, and bring forth their fruit or children, and *every* child is qualified or conditioned according to the kind and property of *all* the Qualities.

100. This they drive and act so long till all the
matter

matter be quite dryed, till the sweet quality or sweet water be dryed up, and then the *fruit falls off*, and the *stalk* dryeth also and falleth down.

And this is the end of Nature in this World.

101.

Concerning this, much higher things are to be written, which you will find concerning the Creation of this world : this is *only* brought in for a *Similitude*, and described in the briefest manner.

102.

Now the *other* form or kind of Qualities or of the Divine Powers, or of the Seven Spirits of God, are especially to be observed or known by the *Instance* or Example of Heat.

103. First there is the ground, or the corporeall Being, although in the Deity or in the Creatures either, it hath no peculiar or *several* Body, but all the Qualities are in one another as *One*, however the operation of every quality is perceived in particular and *severally*.

104. Now in the Body or fountain is the Heat, which *generateth* the *fire*, which is a form or kind of thing which a man *can* search into, and out of the heat goeth the light *through* all the Spirits and Qualities ; and the light is the *living* Spirit, which a man *cannot* search into.

105. Bnt a man *can* search into its *will*, and know what it willeth, or *how* it is : for it proceedeth in

the

the sweet quality, and the Light riseth up in the *sweet* Quality in the sweet water, and *not* in the other qualities.

106. For Example; thou *canst* kindle *all things* in this world, and so make them give light and burn, if the *sweet* Quality have the predominancy in it; and where the other qualities are predominant in it, thou *canst not* kindle *that*: And though thou *mayest* bring Heat into it, yet thou canst *not* bring the Spirit into it, to make it give *light*: therefore all qualities, are the children of the sweet quality, or of the sweet water, because the spirit riseth up onely in the *water*.

108. Art thou a rational Man, in whom is the Spirit and *understanding*, then look all about in the world, for there thou wilt find it *thus*.

109. Thou *canst* kindle wood, that it give *light*, for the water is chief upper Regent or predominant therein; so likewise in *all* sorts of Herbs on Earth, wherein the *sweet* water is predominant.

110. Thou canst *not* kindle light in a *stone*, because the astringent or *harsh* Quality is chief or predominant therein: neither canst thou kindle light in *Earth*, unlesse the other qualities be first vanquished and boyled out of it, which is seen in the *Gun-powder*, which yet is but a flash or a spirit of *terrour*, wherein the Devil in the Anger of God representeth himself, which I will describe and *demonstrate*, more largely in another place.

Objection.

111. But thou wilt say; That a man *cannot* kindle the *water* to make it give *light*.

Answ.

Answer.

Yes, Dear Man. Here lyeth or ſticketh the myſtery. The wood which thou kindleſt, is not very *Fire*, but a Dark or Opake *ſtock*, onely the fire and light taketh their original from thence.

112. But thou muſt underſtand this, concerning the *ſweet* quality of the *water*, and not concerning the ſtick or block ; but it is to be underſtood concern-

* or Oyli-neſſe.

ing the * *Unctuoſitie* or fatneſſe which is the ſpirit therein.

113. Now, in the Elementary water on earth, the ſweetneſſe is *not* the Chief, or Upper Regent, but the aſtringent, bitter, and ſowre quality ; elſe the water were not *mortale*, but were as *that* water is, out of which Heaven is created.

114. And that I will demonſtrate to thee *thus*, viz. that the aſtringent, ſowre and bitter Quality is predominant in the *Elementary* water on Earth.

115. Take Rie, Wheat, Barley, Oates, or what you will, wherein the ſweet quality is *predominant*, ſoak or ſteep it in the Elementary water, afterward *Diſtill* it, then the ſweet quality will *take away* the predominancy from the other, and afterward kindle that water, and then you will *ſee* the ſpirit, which

† or Oyli-neſſe.

is remaining in the water of the † unctuouſneſſe or fatneſſe of the Corn, which did overcome the water.

116. This thou *ſeeſt* alſo in Fleſh : the fleſh neither burneth nor ſhineth, or giveth Light, but its

* or Oyl, or Tallow.

* *Fat* burneth and ſhineth or giveth Light.

Queſtion.

Question.

117. Thou mayst perhaps ask : How comes that to passe ; or, In what manner is it so ?

Answer.

118. Behold ; in Flesh, the *astringent*, sowre and bitter quality is predominant ; and in the fat, the *sweetnesse* is chief and predominant ; Therefore fat creatures are alwaies Merrier and frolicker then the lean, because the *sweet Spirit* floweth more abundantly in them then in the Lean.

119. For the light of Nature, which is the Spirit of life, shineth more in them, then in the lean : For in that Light in the sweet quality, standeth the *tryumphing* or the Joy, for the astringent or harsh and bitter quality triumph therein, for they rejoyce that they are refresh'd, fed, given to drink, and enlightned from the *sweet* and *light* quality.

120. For in the astringent or harsh quality there is *no* life, but an astringent cold hard Death ; and in the bitter quality there is no Light, but a *dark*, bitter, and raging Pain, a house of Trembling Horrour and fierce wrathful fearful *Misery*.

121. Therefore when they are Guests *feasting* at the sweet and Light quality, then are they affected, and pleasant, very joyful and triumphing *in* the Creature.

122. And therefore *no* Lean creature is merry, unlesse it be so that *Heat* be predominant therein : that is, though it be Lean, and hath *little* of the fat, or oyl in it ; yet perhaps *sweetnesse* is very abundant there.

123. On the other side, many Creatures have

V

much

much fatneſſe and yet are very Melancholy or ſad ; which is, becauſe their fatneſſe is *inclined* to the condition of the Elementary water, wherein the aſtringent or harſh and bitter quality is ſomewhat *ſtrong.*

Of the Language of Nature.

124.

Art thou a rational man, then Obſerve this ; the Spirit, which moveth on high aloft, from the heat, taketh its *Exit*, riſing, and ſhining, in the ſweet quality ; therefore the *ſweet* qualities, is its friendly or kind *will* , and raigneth in meekneſſe ; and meekneſſe and humility are its proper Houſe or *Habitation.*

125. And this is the Pith or *Kernel* of the Deity, and therefore IT is called GOTT, God, becauſe it is ſweet, meek, friendly and Bounteous or Good, GUTIG ; and therefore is IT called $\left\{\begin{array}{l} \textit{Barm-hertz-ig} \\ \text{Warm-Heart-ed} \end{array}\right\}$ or Merciful, becauſe its ſweet quality *riſeth up* in the aſtringent, ſowre, and bitter qualities, and refreſheth moiſtneth and *enlightneth* them, that they might *not* remain a dark valley.

126. For underſtand but thy † *Mother Tongue* aright ; thou haſt as deep a Ground *therein*, as there is, in the *Hebrew*, or *Latine* : Though the Learned elevate themſelves therein, like a proud arrogant * Bride ; it is no great matter, *their* Art is now on the Lees, or bowed down to the Duſt.

The Mother Tongue expounded according to the Language of Nature.
* *Braut.*
Turba.

127. *The Spirit sheweth and declareth, that yet before the End, many a Layman, will know and understand more, then now the Wittiest or Cunningest Doctors know: for the Gates of Heaven set open themselves, those that do not blind themselves, shall and will see it very well, the Bridegroom Crowneth his Bride.*

AMEN.

BARM-HERTZ-IG.

128. Observe! the word BARM- is chiefly formed upon thy *Lips*, and when thou pronouncest BARM- then thou shuttest thy Mouth, and snarlest in the hinder part of the Mouth: and this is the Astringent quality, which environeth or *incloseth* the word; that is, it figureth *compacteth* or contracteth the word together, that it becometh hard, or soundeth, and the Bitter quality separateth or cutteth or *distinguisheth* it.

129. That is, when thou pronouncest BAR, the last letter R snarleth, and murmureth like a *trembling*

Barm--Hertz--zig. Warm-hearted, or Mer-ci-full.

V 2   *bling*

bling Breath, and thus doth the bitter quality which is a trembling.

130. Now the word BARM- is a dead word, void of understanding, so that no man understands what it meaneth: which signifieth, that the *Two* Qualities, Astringent, and Bitter, are a hard dark cold and Bitter Being, which have *no* Light in them: And therefore a man cannot understand their power *without* the Light.

131. But when a man saith BARM- HERTZ-, he fetcheth or presseth the second syllable out from the *Deep* of the Body, out from the Heart, for the *right* Spirit speaketh forth the word HEARTZ , which riseth up aloft from the *heat* of the Heart, in which the Light goeth forth and floweth.

132. Now Observe , when thou pronouncest BARM, then the two qualities, the astringent, and bitter , form frame or *compact* together the word BARM, very leisurely or slowly : for it is a long *impotent* feeble syllable, because of the weaknesse of the qualities.

133. But when thou pronouncest -HERTZ- then the spirit in the word -HERTZ- (Heart) goeth forth *suddenly* , like a flash of lightning, and giveth the † distinction and understanding of the word.

† *or the distinct sense or meaning of the word.*

134. But when thou pronouncest -IG, then thou *catchest* or captivatest the spirit in the midst of the other two qualities, so that it *must stay* there and form the word.

135. And thus is the Divine power also ; the Astringent and Bitter quality, are the *Salitter* of the Divine Omnipotence, the sweet quality is the Pith or Kernel of the *Barm-hertz-ig-keit,* Warm-heart-ed-nesse

neſſe or Merci-ful-neſſe, according to which the whole Being with *all* the Powers, is called

{ GOTT. }
{ GOD. }

136. The *heat* is the Kernel of the Spirit, out of which the *light* goeth, and kindleth it ſelf in the *midſt* or Center of the ſweet quality, and becometh captivated by the aſtringent and bitter quality, as in the midſt or center *wherein* the Sonne of God is generated, and that is the very { *Hertz*, } { Heart, } of God.

137. And the Lights Flame or Flaſh; which in the twinkling of an Eye or Moment, ſhineth into all the powers, even as the Sun doth in the whole world; is the *Holy Ghoſt*, which goeth forth from the clarity or brightneſſe of the Sonne of God, and is the flaſh of Lightning and ſharpneſſe: for the *Sonne* is generated in the midſt or Center of the other qualities, and is catched by the other qualities.

Underſtand this high thing, rightly.

138. When the Father ſpeaketh or pronounceth the WORD, that is, generateth his *Sonne*, which is alwaies done for ever and Eternally: then that *word firſt* taketh its Original in the aſtringent quality, therein it fixeth conceiveth or *compacteth* it ſelf, and in the ſweet quality, it taketh its fountain ſpring or ſource, and in the bitter quality it *ſharpeneth*, and moveth it ſelf, and in the heat it riſeth up, and *Kindleth* the middle ſweet fountain or ſource.

139. And now it burneth *joyntly* or equally alike in all the qualities of the kindled fire, and the fire
burneth

burneth forth from the qualities : for *all* qualities burn, and that fire is one fire and not many several Fires.

149. And that fire is the very *Sonne of God,* which is thus generated alwaies from eternity to eternity : this I can *demonstrate* by the Heaven and the Earth, the Stars and the Elements, and by all the Creatures, Stones, Leaves and Graffe, yea in the Devill himself; and that not with Dead flight unsignificant Arguments *void of understanding,* but with cleer quick *living* and invincible firm Arguments, even *above,* beyond, and to the Refutation of, all mens Reason convincingly and undeniably, and lafty in opposition againft all the devills and the Gates of Hell ; and would do it here, if it would not take up *too* much room.

141. Yet it fhall be *treated of* all along in *this* whole book in all the Articles and *parts* thereof; but you fhall find it more particularly in that part concerning the Creation of the *Creatures,* as alfo, conconcerning the Creation of *Heaven* and *Earth* and of all things, which will be fitter to be done *then,* and *eafier* apprehended by the Reader.

Now Obferve :

142, Out of that fire goeth the *flafh* or the light, forth, and moveth or boyleth in all the powers, and hath or *containeth* the fountain and fharpneffe of all the powers in it felf : becaufe it is generated, through the *Sonne,* out of all the powers of the *Father,* and fo then it reciprocally maketh all the powers in the Father *living* and moving, and through that *Spirit* are all the *Angels* formed and Imaged out of the Fathers *Powers.* 134. And

143. And that Spirit preserveth and *supporteth all,* formeth all, all vegetation, colours and Creatures both in heaven and in this world, and *above* all the Heaven of Heavens. For the Birth or *Geniture* of the Holy *Trinity* above all is thus, and no otherwise, neither will it be otherwise in all Eternity.

144. But when the fire isKindled in a Creature; that is, when a Creature elevateth it self *too high* or too much, as Lucifer and his Legions did, then the light extinguisheth or goeth out, and the *fierce* wrathfull and hot source, the source of the hellish fire riseth up, that is, the Spirit of the fire riseth up in the fierce Quality.

145. Observe here the *Circumstances,* how this is done, or how it can come to be done. Therefore consider an Angel, is formed figured composed or compacted together out of *all* powers, as I have described it at large.

146. Now when he elevateth himself, he elevateth himself *first* in the astringent quality, which he gripeth close together, as a woman, which is in travel; and *presseth* himself, whereby the hard quality becometh so hard and *sharp,* that the sweet water can force or prevail with it *no more,* and so can rise up no more meekly or mildly in the Creature; but is captivated and *dried up* by the astringent quality, and changed into a hard, sharp fierce Coldnesse.

147. For it becometh too **empty* and dry by the astringent *contraction,* and loseth its bright lustre, and its unctuosity, fatnesse or Oylinesse (wherein the *light Spirit* riseth up, which is the Spirit of the Holy *angelical* and *divine* life) becometh so hard compacted

* *Derb.*

pacted

pacted and preſſed together by the aſtringent qualitie, whereby it is dried up like ſweet dry
wood.

148. And ſo when the bitter quality riſeth up in
the exſiccated or dryed ſweet quality, then *cannot* the
ſweetneſſe mollifie it, and imbibe it with its ſweet
light-water, becauſe it is dried up.

149. And there the bitter quality raveth and *rageth*, and ſeeketh for reſt and food, and finds it not,
and moveth or boyleth in the Body as a faint Poy-
ſon.

150. And now, when the heat *kindleth* the ſweet
quality, and would mitigate its heat in the ſweet
water, whence it riſeth up, and *ſhineth* in the whole
Body, there it finds nothing but a hard dry ſweet
ſource or quality, there is no ſap, or *moiſture*, it being
quite exſiccated or dryed up, by the aſtringen-
cie.

151. Then it kindleth the ſweet ſource or quality
with an intent to be *refreſhed*, but there is no ſapp
left, only the ſweet ſource or quality is now burning and *glowing*, even as a *hard* dryed or burnt ſtone,
and can *no more* kindle its light, and ſo the whole Body remaineth now a Dark valley, in which there is
nothing, but a fierce hard coldneſſe in the aſtringent quality, and in the ſweet, a hard glowing fire
only, wherin the fierce *wrathful* heat riſeth up in all
Eternity, and in the bitter quality there is a raving
raging, ſtinging and *burning*.

152. And thus you have here the true deſcription of an *Expulſed* Angel or Devill, as alſo the Cauſe
thereof, and that not written in a ſimilitude *only*, but
in the Spirit, through *that power*, out of which all
things are come to be.

153. O man! behold thy self herein, look before thee, and behind thee, it is not in vain.

154. This great History or *Action,* how it came to passe, and how it went, you will find it at large, concerning the Fall of the Devill.

V.

Of the Fifth Circumstance or Species.

155.

The Fifth Quality, or the fifth Spirit of God among the the Seven Spirits of God, in the Divine power of the Father ; is, the *gracious amiable* blessed friendly and joyful *Love.*

156. Now observe ; what the fountain of the *gracious amiable* blessed and friendly love of God is : Observe it exactly, for it is the very Pith Marrow or *Kernel.*

157. When the heat in the *sweet* quality riseth up, and kindleth the sweet source fountain or spring, then that fire burneth in the sweet quality : now seeing the sweet quality is a thin or transparent lovely *pleasant* sweet fountain or spring-water, it allayeth the heat, and *quencheth* the fire, and so there remaineth in the sweet fountain spring of the sweet water, only the *joyful* light.

158. And the heat is only a gentle soft *warming,* even as it is in a man, which is of a *Sanguine* Complexion, wherein also the heat is only a friendly

X

cheerly

cheerly warming, if the party liveth temperately, and keepeth a *due Measure*.

159. That friendly *Courteous* Love-Light-fire, goeth along in the sweet quality, and riseth up into the bitter and astringent quality, and so *kindleth* the bitter and astringent quality, *feeding* them with its sweet *Love-sap*, refreshing quickning and enlightning them, and making them *living* or lively, cheerfull and friendly.

160. And when the Light-love-power cometh at them, so that they *taste thereof*, and get its life; O there is a friendly Meeting *Saluting* and Triumphing, a friendly wellcoming and great love, a most friendly and *gracious* amiable and blessed kissing and well relishing taste.

161. There the Bridegroom kisseth his Bride: O gracious amiable *Blessednesse* and great love! how sweet art thou? how friendly and Courteous art thou? how pleasant and *lovely* is thy rellish and taste? how ravishing sweetly dost thou smell? O noble light, and *bright* glory, who can apprehend thy *exceeding* Beauty! how comely *adorned* is thy love? how *curious* and dainty are thy colours? and All this *Eternally*! who can expresse it?

162. Or why, and what do I write? whose Tongue doth but *stammer* like a child, which is learning to speak! with *what* shall I compare it? or to what shall I liken it? Shall I compare it with the love of this world: *No*, that is but a meer dark valley to it.

163. O Immense greatnesse! I *cannot* compare thee with any thing, but *only* with the Resurrection from the Dead, there will the love-fire rise up *again*
in

in US, and embrace Man courteously and friendly, and re-kindle again, our astringent bitter and cold dark and *dead* Quality, and embrace us most friendly.

164. O noble Guest! O, *why* didst thou depart from us! O fiercenesse wrath and astringency or severity, *thou* art the cause of it! O fierce wrathfull Devil! O, what hast *thou* done, who hast *sunk down* thy self and beautiful bright Angels, into darknesse? woe, woe for Ever!

165. O, was not the gracious amiable blessed and fair Love in *thee*, also? O thou High and Lofty minded Devil! *why* wouldst thou not be contented! wert thou not a Cherubin? and was there any thing *so* beautiful and bright in heaven as *thou*? what didst thou seek for? wouldst thou be the whole or *Total* God? didst thou not know, that thou wert a *Creature*, and hadst *not* the Fan and Casting shovel in thy own hand, or Power?

166. O, *why* do I pity thee, thou stinking Goat? O, thou cursed stinking Devil! how hast *thou* spoiled us? how wilt thou excuse thy self! What wilt thou *Object* to me?

Objection.

167. Thou Sayst, If thy Fall had not been; Man would never have been thought of.

Answer.

O, thou Lying Devil! Though that should be true, yet the *Salitter*, out of which Man is made, which is also from eternity, as well as *that*, out of which thou art made, had stood in *eternal Joy* and Bright Glory, and had likewise risen up in God, and had tasted of

the

the *gracious* amiable blessed love *in* the seven Spirits of God, and enjoyed the heavenly Joy!

168. O thou lying Devil, stay but a *little*, the spirit will discover thy shame to thee, tarry but a little while *longer*, and thy pomp pride and Pageantry will be at an *End*. Stay, the Bow is bent, the Arrow will *hit* thee, and then *whither* wilt thou fall? the place is ready provided and prepared, it wanteth only to be kindled, wilt thou bring fewel lustily to it, that thou be not frozen with cold? thou wilt *sweat* very hard: dost thou suppose thou shalt *obtain* the light again? *No*, but Hell fire. Smell to thy sweet Love, *Guesse* at it, what is *that* called? *Gehenna*; yes, *that* will be in love with thee, Eternally.

169. Woe, woe, poor miserable *blinded* Man, why suffereft thou the Devil to make thy Body and Soul *so* dark and blind! O temporal Good, and the pleasure and voluptuousnesse of *this life*, thou Blind *whore*, why doest thou go a wooing and *whoring* to the Devil.

170. O, *Security*! the Devil watcheth for thee! O, *High-mindednesse*, thou art a hellish Fire. O, Beauty Pomp or *Bravery*! thou art a dark valley. O self-vindication or *Vengeance*! thou art the fierce wrath of God!

171. O *Man*, why will the world be too narrow, for thee! thou wilt needs have it *all* for thy *self*; and if thou hadft it, thou wouldft not have *Room* enough! O this is the Devils high-mindednesse, who *fell* out of Heaven into Hell.

172. O, Man! Alas, O man! why dost thou *Dance* with the Devil, who is thine enemy? Art thou not afraid, that he will *thrust* thee into Hell? why dost

thou

thou go on fo fecurely! Is it not a very narrow *ftick*, on which thou Danceft, under that fmall narrow Bridge is *Hell!* doft thou not fee how high thou art, and how dangeroufly and defperately thou goeft ? thou Danceft *betwixt* Heaven and Hell.

173. O thou blind Man ! how doth the Devil *Mock* at thee ! O, wherefore doft thou trouble heaven ! doft thou think thou fhalt *not* have enough, in *this* world ? O, blind man ! is not Heaven and Earth thine ? nay *God* himfelf too ! What doft thou bring into this world , or what doft thou take along with thee at thy going out of it ? thou bringeft an *Angelical* Garment into this world, and with thy wicked life thou turneft it into a Devils Mask or *vizard.*

174. O thou miferable Man ! Turn Convert, the heavenly Father hath ftretched forth both his Arms, and calleth thee, do but *Come*, he will take thee *into* his Love : art thou not his child ? He *doth* Love thee : if he did hate thee, he muft be at *odds* with himfelf : O no, it is not fo : there is nothing in God, but a *mercifull* amiable love and Bright glory !

175. O ye *watchmen* of Ifrael ! why do ye *fleep* ? Awake from the fleep of whoredom, and dreffe or trim your *Lamps* : the Bridegroom cometh, *Sound* your Trumpets.

176. O ye covetous ftiffnecked and drunken *Royfters* ! how do you wooe and go a whoring after the covetous Devil ! Thus faith the LORD : Will ye *not* feed my people, which I have committed to your charge ?

177. Behold I have fet you upon *Mofes* his chair, and

and entrusted you with my flock; but you mind nothing but the wooll, and mind *not* my sheep, and therewith, you build your great Palaces. But I will set you on *the Stool of Pestilence*, and *my* own Shepherd, shall feed my sheep, *Eternally*.

178. O thou fair world, how doth Heaven *pity* thee? How dost thou trouble the Elements! O, wickednesse and malice! *when* wilt thou leave, and give over? Awaken! awaken! and, bring forth, thou sorrowfull *woman*, behold thy *Bridegroom* cometh, and requireth *fruit* at thy Hands: Why dost thou sleep? *behold he knocketh!*

179. O gracious amiable blessed Love and clear bright Light, *tarry* with us I pray thee, for the evening *is* at hand! O, Truth! O, Justice, and *righteous* Judgment! what is become of thee? doth not the Spirit *wonder*, as if he had never seen the world before now! O, *why* do I write of the wickednesse of this world? I *must* do it, and the world † curseth me for it. *Amen.*

† or giveth me the Devils thanks for it.

The

The Ninth Chapter.

Of the Gracious amiable blessed friendly and Merciful Love of God.

The Great *Heavenly and Divine* Mystery.

I.

Because I write here of heavenly and Divine things, which are *altogether strange* to the *corrupted* perished Nature of Man; the Reader doubtlesse will wonder at the *simplicity* of the Authour, and be offended at it.

2. Because the condition and inclination of the corrupted Nature is, to gaze *onely* on *high* things, like a proud, wild, wanton and *whorish* woman, which alwayes gazeth in her heat or burning Lust after *Handsome* men, to act wantonnesse with them.

3. Thus also is the Proud corrupted perished Nature of Man, it stareth only upon *that*, which is glittering and in *Fashion* in this world, and supposeth, that God hath forgotten the afflicted, and therefore plagueth them so, because he mindeth them not.

4. Corrupt Nature imagineth, that the Holy Ghost regardeth onely *high* things, the high Arts and Sciences of *this world*, the profound studies and Great Learning.

5. But

5. But whether it be fo, or no; look but back and then you will find the true *Ground* : *what was* Abel ? A fhepherd. *what was* Enoch *and* Noah ? plain fimple men. *what were* Abraham, Ifaac, *and* Jacob ? Herdfmen.

6. *What was* Mofes, that dear man of God ? A Herdfman. *what was* David, when the Mouth of the Lord call'd him ? A fhepherd.

7. *What were* the Great, and Small Prophets ? Vulgar plain and mean People : *fome of them* but Countrey people, and Herdfmen, *counted the under-lings or footftooles of the world*: men counted them but meer fooles.

8. And though they did Miracles Wonders and fhewed great figns, yet *the world* gazed only on high things, and the Holy Ghoft muft be as the Duft under their feet : for the proud Devil *almaies endea-voured* to be King in this world.

9. *And how came* Our King JESUS CHRIST into this world ? Poor and in great trouble and mi-fery, and *had not whereon to lay his head,* Matth. 8. 20.

10. *What were* his Apoftles ? Poor, defpifed, illi-terate Fifhermen, *and what were* they that believed their preaching ? The poorer and meaner fort of the people. The High Priefts and Scribes *were the* Exe-cutioners of Chrift, who *cryed out, Crucifie him, cruci-fie him,* Luk. 23. 21.

11. *What were they* that in all Ages in the Church of Chrift ftood to it moft ftoutly and conftantly ? The poor contemptible defpifed people, who fhed their Bloud for the fake of Chrift.

12. *But who were they* that falfified and adulterated the right pure Chriftian Doctrine, *and alwayes fought*
against

against and opposed it ? *Even* the Learned Doctors
and Scribes, Popes, Cardinals, Bishops and great
Dons, or Masters and Teachers ; *And why did the
world* follow after them, and depend on them ? But
becauſe they had great reſpect, were in great *authority,* and *power*; lived ſtately and carried a Port in the
world ; Even ſuch a *Proud Whore*, is the corrupt periſhed humane nature !

13. *Who was it* that purged the Popes Greedineſſe
of Money, his Idolatry, Bribery, deceit and Cheating; *out of* the Churches in *Germany* ? A poor de-
ſpiſed * Monk or Fryer. *By what* power and might ? * Luther.
by the power of God the Father, and by the power
and Might of God the Holy Ghoſt.

Queſtion.
14. *Then what is* yet concealed or remains hidden?
The true doctrine of Chriſt ?

Anſwer.
No ; but the (°) Philoſophie ; and the *deep
Ground* of God ; the heavenly Delight and Pleaſure;
the revelation of the Creation of *Angels* ; the revelation of the horrible *Fall* of the Devil; From whence
Evil proceedeth : The Creation of this world ; The
deep ground and myſtery of Man and of all Creatures; The Laſt Judgment, And Change of this
world; The Myſtery of the Reſurrection of the
Dead ; And of Eternal Life.

15. *This* ſhall ariſe in the Depth, in great plainneſſe and *ſimplicity*: *But why not* in the heighth in
Art ? That no man ſhould dare to boaſt, that he
himſelf hath done it, and that *hereby* the Devils
pride ſhould be diſcovered and brought to Nothing.

Y   16. But

(o) That is the real knowledge, of the manner how the Myſteries, ſpoken of in the Doctrine of Chriſt, as they are in Nature, Phyſically or Metaphyſically in Supernatural things, are to be underſtood convincingly according to its true Ground ; and the Capacity of the Humane Mind.

116. But why doth God so? *Of his great love* and † Mercy towards all People and Nations, and to shew hereby, that now, is *near at hand,* The Time of the Restitution of all *whatsoever* is lost, wherein men shall behold and enjoy the *perfection,* and move in the *pure* Light and Deep Knowledge of God.

17. Therefore *before hand will arise* the Dawning of the Day, or Morning Rednesse, whereby the *Day may be known or taken notice of.*

18. *He that will now sleep, let him sleep still; and he that will awake and trim his Lamp, let him awake still: Behold the Bridegroom cometh, and he that is awake and is ready, accompanieth into the* eternal heavenly *wedding: But he that sleepeth at his coming, he sleepeth for ever* Eternally in the dark prison of fiercenesse or wrath.

19. Therefore I would have the Reader warned, that he read *this Book* with diligence, and not be *offended* at the meannesse or simplicity of the Author, for God looketh *not* at high things, for He *alone* is High: but *he careth for the Lowly,* how to help them.

20. If you come *so far,* as to apprehend the spirit and sense of the Authour, then you will need no *admonition,* but will rejoyce and be Glad in this light, and thy Soul will Laugh and *Triumph* therein.

21. *Now Observe:* the Gracious amiable blessed Love, which is the *fifth* fountain-spirit, in the divine power, is the *hidden* source fountain or Quality, which, the corporeal being *cannot* comprehend or apprehend, *but* onely, when it riseth up in the body, and *then* the Body triumpheth therein, and behaveth it self friendly lovely and *Courteously,* for that Quality

or

or spirit belongeth *not* to the Imaging or *framing* of a Body, but riseth up in the Body, as a *flower* springeth up out of the Earth.

22. Now this fountain-spirit taketh its original at *first* out of the *sweet* Quality of the water.

Understand this, how it is, and observe it exactly.

23.

First, there is the astringent quality, *then* the sweet, *next,* the bitter : the Sweet is in the *midst* between the Astringent and Bitter. Now the Astringent causeth things to be hard, cold, and dark, and the bitter *teareth,* driveth, rageth, and divideth or *distinguisheth.* These two Qualities *rub* and drive one another so hard, and move so eagerly, *that* they generate the Heat, which now in these two Qualities is *dark,* even as Heat in a *Stone* is.

24. As when a man taketh a stone, or any hard thing, and *rubbeth* it against wood, these *two* things are heated : now this heat is but a darknesse, having *no* light therein : and so it is also, in the Divine power.

25. Now the astringent and bitter quality *without* the sweet water, rub and drive themselves *so hard* one against another, that they generate the dark heat, and so are *kindled* in themselves.

Y 2   26. And

26. *And this Together is the Wrath or Anger of God, the source and originall of the hellish Fire.*

As we see by *Lucifer*, who *elevated* and compressed himself so hard together, with his *Legions*, that the sweet fountain-water in him was *dryed up*, wherein the light kindleth, and wherein the Love riseth up.

27. *Therefore* now he is *Eternally*, an Astringent, Hard, Cold, Bitter, Hot and Sowre stinking fountain-*source*: For when the sweet quality in him, was dryed up, it *became* a sowr stinck, a valley of misery, and a House of perdition and woe.

Now further into the Depth.

28. When the astringent and bitter quality *rub* themselves so hard one upon another, that they generate Heat, and so now the sweet quality, the sweet fountain-water, is therein in the midst or center *between* the astringent and bitter quality, and the *heat* becometh generated between the astringent and bitter quality, in the sweet fountain-water, *through* the astringent and bitter Quality.

29. And there the Light kindleth in the heat in the sweet fountain-water, and *this is the beginning of Life*: for the astringent and bitter Qualities, are the beginning and cause of the heat and of the Light, and *thus* the sweet fountain water becometh a *shining light,*

light, like the Blew or *Azure* Light of heaven.

30. And that bright-Light fountain-water *kindleth* the aftringent and bitter quality, and the heat, which is generated by the aftringent and bitter quality in the fweet water, *rifeth up* out of the fweet fountain-water through the aftringent and bitter quality, and in the aftringent and bitter quality the light *firft then* becometh dry and fhining, as alfo moveable and triumphing.

31. And when the light rifeth up out of the fweet fountain water *in the heat* in the aftringent and bitter quality, then the bitter and aftringent quality *tafteth* the light and fweet water, and the bitter quality *catcheth* the tafte of the fweet water, and in the fweet water is the *light,* but only of a skie-colour or *Azure* which is Blew.

32. And then the bitter quality trembleth, and *diffolveth* the hardneffe in the aftringent Quality, the Light becometh dry in the Aftringent, and fhineth clear, *much brighter* then the Light of the Sun.

33. In this rifing up, the aftringent quality becometh meek, light, thin or *tranfparent,* and pleafant or lovely, and obtaineth its life, whofe *original* rifeth up out of the heat in the fweet water, and this now is *the true fountain or well-fpring of Love.*

Obferve this, in the deep Senfe.

34. How fhould Love and Joy *not* be there? where life is generated in the very Center or midft of Death, and Light, in the midft of darkneffe?

Queftion.
Thou askeft, *How* comes *that* to paffe?

Anfw.

Answer.

35. Indeed, if *my* spirit did sit in *thy* heart, and spring up in thy heart, then *thy* Body would find, feel, and apprehend it.

36. But *otherwise* I cannot bring it into thy sense, neither canst thou apprehend or understand it, *unlesse* the Holy Ghost kindle thy soul, so that *this* light it self shine in *thy* Heart.

37. And then will this light it self be generated *in thee*, as in God; and rise up in *thy* astringent and bitter quality, in *thy* sweet water; and triumph, as in God: Now when *this* is done: then you will *first understand my Book*, and not before.

Observe:

38. When the light is generated in the Bitter quality, that is, when the bitter and dry fountain-sources *catch* the sweet fountain water of Life, and *drink* it, then the bitter spirit becometh Living, in the astringent spirit, and the astringent spirit which is as a spirit impregnated with child, is impregnated with life, and must continually generate the Life.

39. For, the sweet water, and the life in the sweet water rise up *continually* in the astringent quality, and the bitter quality triumpheth continually *therein*, and so there is nothing else but meer laughing, and Joy, a meer being in Love.

40. For the astringent quality *loveth* the sweet water.

41. And First, because, in the sweet water, the Spirit of Light is generated, and *imbibeth* or giveth

Drink

Drink to the astringent hard and cold Qualities; also it enlightneth them, and warmeth them: for in Water, Light, and Heat, The *Life consisteth.*

42. And secondly, the astringent Quality loveth the bitter; because, the bitter Quality in the sweet water, that is, in water heat and light, *triumpheth* in the astringent Quality, and maketh the astringent, moveable or stirring, *wherein* the astringent also can triumph.

43. And thirdly, the astringent quality loveth the Heat, because in the heat the light is Generated, *whereby* the astringent quality is enlightned and warmed.

44. And the sweet quality also loveth the astringent.

45. And first, because it drieth up the astringent *that* it become *not* thinne or dimme *like* the elementary water, and that its quality consisteth in Power, and *because,* that in the Astringent Quality the *light,* which is generated therein, becometh *shining* and *dry.*

46. Besides, the astringent quality is a cause of the heat, which is generated in the sweet water, wherein the light riseth up, and wherein the sweet water standeth in great *clarity brightnesse or* glory.

47. And secondly, the sweet quality also loveth the bitter, because it is a cause of the *heat,* and also therefore, because the bitter spirit triumpheth and *trembleth* in the sweet water, heat, and light, and so maketh the sweet water moveable or stirring, and *living.*

48. And thirdly, the sweet quality loveth heat *exceedingly,* and so very much, that I cannot compare

it

it with any thing : but you may take this for a *Simi-litude*, though it comes very short thereof : Suppose *two* young People of a noble *Complexion*, these being kindled in the Heat and fervour of burning Love one to another, there is such a fire as this ; so that if they could creep into the Bodies and *Hearts* one of another, or transmute themselves into *one* Body, they would do it.

49. But this *Earthly* love is only cold Water, and is not true Fire : A man cannot find any *full* similitude of it in this *half-dead* world ; Onely the Resurrection of the Dead at the Last Day, is a *perfect* Similitude in all *divine* things, which receive the *true Love-fire*.

50. But the sweet quality doth thus love the Heat *because* it generateth therein the light-spirit, which is the Spirit of Life. For *life* existeth in the heat ; for if the Heat were not, all would be a dark valley : Now *so dear* as the Life is, so dear is also the Heat, to the sweet spirit, and the light, in the Heat.

51. And the bitter quality also loveth *all* the other fountain-spirits. And first the sweet. For in the sweet water, the bitter spirit is *refreshed*, and therein it *quencheth* its great thirst ; and its bitterness is therein mitigated, also it obtaineth its light-Life *therein :* in the astringent it hath its Body, wherein it triumpheth cooleth and mitigateth it self ; and in the Heat it *hath* its power and strength, wherein its Joy standeth.

52. And the hot quality also loveth *all* the other qualities, and the love is so *great* therein toward, and in the other, that it cannot be likened to any thing, for it is generated from and out of the other.

53. The astringent and bitter qualities are the
Father

Father of the heat, and the sweet fountain water, is
its *Mother*, which conceiveth, retaineth, and generateth it : for the heat existeth through the astringent and bitter hard driving, which riseth up in the
sweet quality, as in wood, or fewel.

54. Wilt thou *not believe* this ? then open thy
Eyes, and go to a *Tree*, look upon it, and bethink
thy self; there you see first the *whole* Tree, take a
knife and cut a *Gash* in it, and taste how it is ; then
you *first* taste the astringent harsh *choaky* quality,
which draweth thy Tongue together, and that also
draweth and holdeth together all the powers of the
Tree.

55. Then you taste the bitter quality, which maketh the Tree moveable or stirring, so that it *springeth* and groweth green and flourisheth, and so getteth
its Branches Leaves and Fruit.

56. *After that* you taste the sweet, which is very
Gentle and sharp : for it getteth the *sharpnesse* from
the astringent and bitter Quality.

57. Now these *three* Qualities would be Dark
and Dead, if the *Heat* were not therein : but as soon
as the *Spring* time cometh, that the Sun with its
Beams suppleth and warmeth the Earth, the spirit
becometh living by the Heat in the Tree, and the
spirits of the Tree begin to grow green, *flourish* and
Blossom.

58. For the spirit riseth up in the heat, and *all*
the spirits rejoyce therein, and so there is a hearty
love between them.

59. But the heat is generated through the power
and *Impulse* of the astringent and bitter qualities in
the sweet water.

60. But they must use the Heat of the Sun to
their

their kindling, becaufe the qualities *in this world* are half dead, and are too weak, of which King Luci-fer was the caufe, which you will find, here follow-ing, concerning *his Fall*, and concerning the Crea-tion of this world.

Of the friendly Love, gracious amiable bleffed-neffe, and Unity, of the Five qualifying or fountain-fpirits of God.

61.

Though it be impoffible for the hands of men to defcribe this fufficiently, yet the *enlightned* fpirit of *Man* feeth it : for it rifeth up juft in fuch a form and Birth, as the light in the Divine power, and al-fo in the qualities, which are *in God*.

62. Onely this is to be Lamented concerning Man, that his qualities are corrupted, perifhed and *half* Dead, and therefore it is that mans fpirit or his qualities, rifing, or kindling in this world, can come or attain to *no perfection*.

63. On the Other fide, again it is highly to be rejoyced at, that Mans fpirit, in his neceffity becom-meth *enlightned* and kindled by the Holy Ghoft : As the Sun kindleth the cold heat, in a Tree or Herb, whereby the cold *chilled* Heat becometh living.

Now Obferve :

64. As the members of Mans Body love one an-other, fo do the fpirits alfo in the *Divine* power; there is nothing elfe but a meer longing defiring and well liking acceptation, as alfo a *triumphing* and rejoy-cing the one in the other : for through thefe fpirits

cometh

cometh the *understanding* and diftinction in God, in Angels, Men, Beafts, and Fowles, and in *every thing* that liveth.

65. For in *thefe Five* Qualities rifeth up the feeing, fmelling, tafting and feeling, and fo a *Rational* fpirit cometh to be.

66. As when the light rifeth up, then one fpirit feeth the other.

67. And when the fweet fpring or fountain water rifeth up *in the light*, through all the fpirits, then the one tafteth the other, and then the fpirits become *living*, and the power of life penetrateth through all.

68. And in *that* power the one fmelleth the other; And through this qualifying *influence* and penetrating, the one feeleth the other.

69. And fo there is nothing elfe, but a *Hearty* loving, and friendly afpect or feeing, curious fmelling, a good relifhing or tafting and lovely feeling, a gracious amiable *bleffed* kiffing, a feeding upon and drinking of one another, and lovely walking and *converfing* together.

70. This is the gracious amiable bleffed BRIDE, which *rejoyceth in her* BRIDEGROOM, herein is love, joy and delight, here is light and brightneffe or clarity, here is a pleafant and lovely fmell, here is a friendly and fweet tafte.

71. And this for ever *without End*! How can a Creature fufficiently rejoyce therein? O Dear love and gracious amiable bleffedneffe! Surely thou haft no End, No man can fee any End *in thee*, thy profound Deep is unfearchable, thou art *every where* all over thus, onely in the fierce Devil thou art *not*

Z 2   thus,

thus, they have spoiled, and perished, thee in *them-selves.*

Question.

72. Now thou wilt say ; *where* then are these gracious amiable and blessed spirits to be met with? Do they dwell onely in themselves in *Heaven* ?

Answer.

73. This is the other open Gate of the Deity, here thou must set thy eyes *wide* open, and rouze up or awaken the spirit in thy *half* dead heart : for this is not an Obscure Fiction Contrivance or *Phantasie.*

Observe :

74. The Seven Spirits of God contain or comprehend in their circumference, and *space,* Heaven and this world, also the *wide breadth and depth* without and beyond the heavens, even above and beneath the world, and in the world, yea *the whole Father,* which hath neither Beginning nor End.

75. They contain also *all* the *Creatures* both in heaven and in this world, and all the Creatures in heaven and in this world are imaged fashioned or framed out of these spirits, and live in them as in their own *propriety.*

76. And their Life and *Reason* is generated in them, in such a manner, as the Divine being is generated, and also in the *same* power.

77. And out of and from the same *Body* of the seven Spirits of God, are *all things* made and produced, all Angels, all Devils, the Heaven, the Earth, the Stars, the Elements, Men, Beasts, Fowles, Fishes all;

all Worms, Wood, Trees, alſo Stones, Herbs and Graſſe, and *all* whatſoever is.

Now thou wilt ask.

Queſtion.

78. Seeing God is *every where,* and is himſelf *All,* How cometh it then that there is in this world, ſuch Cold and Heat, ſuch biting and ſtriking among all Creatures, and that there is nothing elſe almoſt but meer *fierceneſſe* or wrath in this world ?

Anſwer.

79. [" *The cauſe is, that the firſt four Forms of Na-* " *ture, are one at Enmity againſt the other* " *without the light; and yet they are the* " *cauſes of Life.*]

80. Behold, here the wickedneſſe and malice which is the Cauſe; *viz.* when King *Lucifer* did ſit in his Kingdom, like a *high-minded* proud Bride, then his Circuit Circle or Orbe, contained or comprehended the place or *ſpace,* where *now* the Created Heaven is, which is made out of the water;

81. And the *place alſo* of the created world, even unto heaven, as alſo the *Deep* where now the Earth is, that was *all* a pure and holy *Salitter,* wherein the Seven Spirits of God were *Compleat* and Pleaſant, as now in Heaven, although they are *ſtill* compleat and *full,* in this world.   But obſerve the Circumſtances rightly.

82. When *King Lucifer* elevated himſelf, then he elevated himſelf in the ſeven qualifying fountain-ſpirits, and *kindled them* with his elevation, ſo that
all

all was wholly *burning*, and the aftringent quality was fo *hard* and Compact, that it generated ftones; and was fo *cold*, that it made the fweet fpring or fountain-water turn *to Ice*.

83. And the fweet fpring water became very thick *brittle*, and as * in many pieces; and the bitter quality became very *raging*, tearing and raving, whence *Poyfon* arofe aloft, and the fire or heat was violently and zealoufly or fervently *burning* and *confuming*, and fo there was a very great diftemper and confufed *Mixture*.

84. *Upon this*, King Lucifer was thruft out of his Royal Place or Kingly *Throne* which he had in *that place*, where now the created Heaven is, and thereupon *inftantly enfued* the Creation of this world ;

85. And the hard Brittle matter, which had *wrought forth it felf* in the kindled feven qualifying or fountain-fpirits, was *driven* together, from whence the Earth and Stones came to be, and after that, all the Creatures were created out of the *kindled Salitter* of the feven Spirits of God.

86. Now the qualifying or fountain Spirits became *fo fierce* and wrathfull in their kindling, that the one continually fpoileth the other with its evill naughty quality or fource, and fo alfo now do the creatures, which *were made out of* the qualifying or fountain fpirits, and *live* in the fame impulfe, the one biting beating worrying and annoying the other, all according to the kind or *difpofition* of the Qualities.

87. Upon this now the *Totall* or Univerfall God hath Decreed *the Laft Judgment*, wherein he will feparate the Evil from the Good, and fet the good
again

again in the meek mild and Pleasant delight, as it *was before* the horrible kindling of the Devill, and will give that which is fierce or *wrathfull* to King *Lucifer* for an *Everlasting* Habitation.

88. And then there will be *two Parts* or divisions of this Kingdom, the one, *Men* will get, with their King J E S U S   C H R I S T; the other, the *Devills* shall have with all ungodly Men and wickednesse.

89. This is a *short* Introduction, that the Reader might the better understand the Divine Mystery: concerning *the Fall of the Devil,* and concerning the *Creation* of *this* world, you will find all more at large particularly described. Therefore I would have the Reader admonished, that he read *all in order,* and so he will come to the true ground.

90. It is true, that from the beginning of the world it was *not so fully* revealed to any Man; but seeing God will have it so, I submit to his Will, and will see, what *God* will do with it.

91. For his way which is *before* him is for the *most part* hidden to me: but *after* him the Spirit seeth, even into the highest and profoundest Depth.

The

The Tenth Chapter.

Of the Sixth qualifying or fountain Spirit in the Divine Power.

1.

THe *Sixth* qualifying or fountain Spirit in the Divine Power, is the Sound Tone Tune or Noise, wherein all foundeth and Tuneth, whence enfued *Speech*, Language, and the *diftinction* of Every thing, as alfo the ringing melody and *Singing* of the holy Angels, and therein confifteth the forming or framing of all *Colours*, Beautie, and Ornament, as alfo the heavenly *Joyfulneffe*.

Queftion.

2. But thou wilt ask : What is the Tone or Sound? or how taketh this fpirit its fource and Original ?

Anfwer.

Obferve.

3. *All* the *Seven* Spirits are generated in one another, the one continually generateth the other, *neither* of them is the firft, neither is any of them the laft ; for the laft generateth as well as the firft *viz.*

the

the firſt, ſecond, third and fourth, and ſo to the laſt.

4. But why one is called the *firſt*, another the *ſecond*, and ſo *on*, that is in reſpect to that which is the firſt in order to the imaging framing and *forming* of a Creature.

5. For all the ſeven are *Equally* Eternal, and none of them hath either Beginning or End; and therefore, in that the ſeven Qualities are continually *generating* one another, and that none is without the other; it followeth, that there is ONE *Only Eternal Almighty* GOD.

6. For, if any thing be generated out of or in the Divine Being, that thing is not formed or framed by or through *one* ſpirit alone, but by *all* the ſeven.

7. And if a Creature, which is like or as the whole Being of God, ſpoileth, elevateth and *kindleth* it ſelf in a Qualifying or fountain-ſpirit, yet it kindleth not one ſpirit alone, but *all the ſeven* ſpirits.

8. And therefore that Creature is a loathſome abomination before the *Total* God, and all his creatures, and muſt ſtand in eternal Emnity and ignominy or ſhame, *before* God, and all the Creatures.

9. The Tone or *Mercurius*, taketh its originall in the *firſt*, that is, in the Aſtringent and Hard Quality.

Obſerve in the Depth.

10. Hardneſſe is the Fountain or Well-ſpring of the Tone; but it cannot generate the ſame *alone*, yet it is the Father thereof, and the whole *Salitter* is the Mother; otherwiſe if the hardneſſe were both Father and Mother of the Tone, then a hard Stone alſo muſt

A a   have

have a Ringing found. But it doth only make a Noife, like knocking, as a feed or *beginning* of a Tone, and that, it is, certainly.

11. But the Tone or voice rifeth up in the middle center in the flafh or *Lightening,* where the Light is generated out of the *Heat,* where the flafh or Lightening of life rifeth up.

Obferve, how this is done :

12. When the aftringent quality *rubbeth* it felf with the bitter, fo that the Heat rifeth up in the fweet fpring or fountain-water, then the heat kindleth the *fweet* fpring or fountain water, like a flafh of Lightning, and that flafh is the *light* ; which in the Heat goeth into the bitter quality, and there the Flafh is *diftinguifhed* according to all the Powers.

13. For all powers are difcerned or diftinguifhed in the bitter, and the bitter receiveth the flafh of the light, as if it were *horribly* terrified ; and goeth with its trembling and terrour, into the aftringent and hard quality, and there it is *bodily* captivated.

14. And the bitter quality is now *impregnated* with the light, and fo trembleth in the Aftringent and Bitter quality, and ftirreth therein, and is *captivated* in the aftringent quality, as in a Body.

15. And now when the fpirits do move, and would *fpeak,* the hard quality muft open it felf ; for the bitter fpirit with its flafh breaketh it open, and then *there* the Tone goeth forth, and is impregnated *with* all the feven Spirits, which diftinguifh the Word, as it was *decreed* in the Center, that is, in the middle of the Circle ; whileft it was yet in the *Councel* of the feven Spirits. 16. And

16. And therefore the seven Spirits of God have created a *Mouth* for the Creatures, that when they would utter their voyce which is their speaking, or make a noise, they need not first tear open themselves; and therefore it is that all the veins and powers or * qualifying or fountain spirits *go* into the Tongue, that the Tone or noise may come forth *gently*.

* *conditionating.*

Here Observe exactly, the † *Sense*, and Mysterie.

† *Mind or meaning.*

17. When the flash riseth up in the heat, then first the sweet water *catcheth* or captivateth it, for therein it becometh shining. Now when the water catcheth the flash, that is, the *birth* of the light, then it is terrified, and being so thin and pliant or feeble, it giveth *back* very much trembling : for the heat riseth up in the light.

18. And now when the astringent quality, which is very cold, catcheth the heat and flash, then it is *terrified*, as in a Tempest of lightning ; for when the heat cometh with the Light into the hard cold, then it maketh a *fierce* flash, of a very fiery and light colour.

19. And then that flash *retireth* back, and the sweet water catcheth it, and riseth up in that *fiercenesse*; and in that rising and terrifying, changeth it self into a Green or Azure, or Blew Colour, and trembleth, because of the fierce flash.

20. And the flash in it self *keepeth* its fiercenesse, from whence existeth the Bitter Quality, or the Bitter Spirit, which *now* riseth up in the astringent quality, and inflameth or *kindleth* the hardnesse with its fierce quality, and the light or flash *dryeth* it self in

the

the hardneſſe and ſhineth clear and bright, *far brighter* then the Light of the Sun.

21. But it is caught in the hard quality, ſo that it ſubſiſts in a Bodily manner, and *muſt* ſhine *ſo* Eternally, and the flaſh trembleth in the Body, like a fierce riſing up, whereby all the qualities are ſtirred alwaies and Eternally.

22. And the flaſh of fire in the light trembleth and *triumpheth* thus continually, and the hardneſſe is alwayes the *Body*, which retaineth preſerveth and dryeth it.

23. And this ſtirring in the hardneſſe, is the Tone, ſo that it ſoundeth, and the light or flaſh maketh the ringing, and the ſweet water mitigateth the ringing: ſo that a man can uſe it to the Diſtinction of Speech, or *Articulation of Syllables.*

Here Obſerve *the Nativity* or Birth *of the Bitter* quality, *yet more plainly.*

24. The *original* of the bitter quality, is, when the flaſh of life in the heat riſeth up in the aſtringent quality, and now when the flaſh of fire in the mixture of the water cometh *into* the aſtringent quality, then the ſpirit of the fiery flaſh *catcheth* the aſtringent and hard ſpirit, and both theſe together are an earneſt *ſevere* fierce quality, which rageth and teareth vehemently like a fiery violent fierceneſſe.

25. I can liken it to nothing elſe, but to a *Thunder-Clap*, when the fierce fire firſt falls down, ſo that it *dazzleth* the light; that fierce fire is like the manner of the conjunction of theſe two.

Now Observe :

26. Now when the fire-spirit and the aftringent spirit *ftruggle* and wreftle thus together, then the aftringent maketh a vehement hard *Cold* aftriction, and the fiery maketh a terrible fierce *Heat.*

27. And now the rifing up of the heat and of the aftriction maketh a trembling fierce *terrible* spirit, which raveth and rageth, *as if* it would tear the Deity afunder.

But thou muft underftand this, exactly,
and properly.

28. This is *thus,* in the Original of the Quality in it felf, but in the *midft* in the rifing up of this *fierce* spirit, this spirit is *caught* and mitigated in the fweet water, where its fierce fource or fountain is *changed* into a trembling, bitter, and greenifh Colour like a greenifh duskineffe, and retaineth in it felf the *condition* and property of all *three* Qualities, *viz.* of the fiery, aftringent, and fweet, and fo from thefe three exifteth the *fourth* Quality, *viz.* the Bitter.

29. For from the fiery quality the spirit becommeth *trembling* and *Hot,* and from the aftringent it becometh *fevere* aftringent, hard and *corporeal,* fo that it is a spirit ; which alwayes fubfifteth, and from the fweet it becometh meek or *mild,* and the fierceneffe changeth it into a gentle bitterneffe : which ftandeth now in the Fountain or *well-fpring* of the feven Spirits of God, and helpeth continually to generate the other fix spirits.

Under-

Underſtand this rightly.

30. It doth *as well* generate its Father and Mother, *as* its Father and Mother doth generate it, for after that it is *corporeally* generated, it then, with the aſtringent Quality *alwayes* generateth the fire *again*, and the fire generateth Light, and the light *is* the *Flaſh*, which alwaies generateth the *Life* again in all the qualifying, or fountain ſpirits ; whence the ſpirits have *life*, and alwaies generate one another *again*.

31. But here thou muſt know, that *one* ſpirit *alone* cannot generate another, neither can *two* of them do it, but the birth of a ſpirit ſtandeth in the operation of *all* the *ſeven* ſpirits, *ſix* of them alwayes generate the *ſeventh*, and ſo if *one* of them were not, then the *other* would not be, neither.

32. But that I ſometimes take onely two or three to the Nativity or birth of a ſpirit, I do that, becauſe of my *own weakneſſe*, for I cannot bear them all ſeven at *once* in their perfection, in my † corrupted Brain.

† the Humane Nature being corrupted and periſhed in the Fall of *Adam*.

33. I ſee them *all ſeven*, very well, but when I ſpeculate into them, then the ſpirit riſeth up in the *middlemoſt* fountain or well-ſpring, where the Spirit of life generateth it ſelf, which goeth now *upwards*, now *downwards*, it cannot apprehend all the ſeven ſpirits in *one* thought or at once, but only in *Part*.

34. Every Spirit hath its *own* quality or ſource, though indeed it is generated of the other ; and ſo it is with the *apprehenſion* of Man, he hath indeed the fountain of all ſeven ſpirits *in* him, but in what quality or fountain ſoever the ſpirit riſeth up, the qualifying

lifying or fountain spirit *thereof*, wherein that same spirit is most *strongly* Imaged, that is it which he comprehendeth most sharply in *that* rising up.

35. For even in the Divine power one spirit doth *not go* through all the spirits equally *at once* in its† rising up: for when it riseth up, then indeed it toucheth or *stirreth* them all at once, but it is caught in its rising up, so that it must lay down its statelinesse and Pomp, and not *triumph over all the seven.*

† or *Ascention.*

36. [" *It is the Being or Substance of the Senses and* " *Thoughts, otherwise, if a Thought through* " *the Center of Nature could penetrate all* " *the forms, then it were* Free *from the* " *Band of Nature:*]

M.

37. Thus it is also in Man, when *one* qualifying or fountain spirit riseth up, then it toucheth *all* the other, and seeth all the other, for it riseth up in the middle or central Fountain or Well-spring of the Heart, where, in the *Heat,* the flash of Light kindleth it self, wherein the spirit in its rising up, in the same flash, seeth through *all* the spirits.

38. But, in our corrupted flesh, it is only like a Tempest of *lightning*: for if I *could*, in my *flesh*, comprehend the flash, which I very well see and know *how it is*, I could clarifie or transfigure my Body therewith, so that it would shine with a *Bright* Light and Glory.

[" *For from the Flash cometh the* Light *of the Ma-* *jestie:*]

N.

And then it would no more resemble and be conform to the Bestial Body, but to the Angels of God.

39. But hearken friend, tarry yet a *little* while, and then give the bestial Body, for food, to the Worms:

Worms: but when the Total God shall *kindle* the Seven Spirits of God in the *corrupted* Earth, then if that same *Salitter*, which thou sowest in the earth, will not be capable of the fire, then thy qualifying or fountain-spirits, which thou didst sowe in thy life-time, and is sowen in thy *departure* from hence, will *rise* again in the same *Salitter* which thou hast sown, and will triumph therein, and become *a Body* again.

† or whose Sa-
litter. See
Ch.10: verse
110. the Sa-
litter which
they have
Corrupted.
and Ch. 11.
vers.115. the
Corrupted
Salitter.

40. But he † that will be *capable* of the kindled fire of the seven Spirits of God, he shall *abide* therein, and his qualifying or fountain spirits shall rise in *hellish* pain, which I shall demonstrate clearly in its due place.

41. I cannot describe unto thee the whole Deity by the Circumference or extent of a Circle, for it is unmeasurable; but to *that Spirit* which is in Gods Love it is *not* incomprehensible: it comprehends it well, yet but in Part; therefore take one part after another, and then you will see the *whole*.

42. In this corruption we cannot get higher, then with such a Revelation, neither doth this world inclose it self any higher, both as to the Beginning and the End.

43. I would very fain see *somewhat higher* in this my anxious generating or Birth, whereby my sick Adam might be refreshed.

44. But I look round about me in all the world, and can find out *nothing*; all is sick, lame and wounded; moreover Blind, Deaf, and Dumb.

45. I *have read* the Writings of very high Masters, hoping to find therein the ground and true depth: but I have found nothing, but a *half dead* Spirit, which in anxiety travelleth and laboureth for

health,

health, and yet becaufe of its great weakneffe *cannot* attain perfect power.

46. Thus I ftand yet as an anxious woman in travell, and feek *perfect* refrefhing, but find onely the fcent or fmell or favour in its rifing up, wherein, the Spirit examineth, what power *ficketh* in the true cordial ; and in the mean while refrefheth it felf in its ficknefle with that *perfect fmell* or favour, till the true *Samaritan* doth come, who will dreffe and bind up its wounds and heal it, and bring it to the eternal *Inne* or Lodging, then it fhall enjoy the *perfect Tafte.*

47. This *Herb,* which I mean here, from whofe Fragancy my fpirit taketh its refrefhing, Every Countrey Plowman doth *not* know it, *nor* Every Doctor; the one is as Ignorant of it, as the other; it groweth indeed in *every* Garden, but in many it is quite fpoyled and naught : for the quality of the Soyl or Ground is in *fault.* And therefore men do not know it, nay the *Children of this Myftery* do hardly know it : for, this knowledge hath been very rare dear and pretious, from the beginning of the world to this *Time.*

48. Though in Many, a fource or fountain and quality hath rifen up, but then fuddenly Pride preffed after it, and *fpoyled* all ; whereupon it was *loath* to write it down in its mother-Tongue ; it fuppofed, that was *too* childifh a thing , it muft fhew it in a *deeper* Language, that the world fhould fee, that it is Manly ; and for its *advantage* it kept it in fecret, and *dawbed* it with deep ftrange names, that men might not know it : fuch a *Beaft* is the Devil's Proud difeafe.

49. But hear, thou fimple Mother, which bringeft
all

all the children into this world, which afterward in their rising up are *afhamed* of thee, and despise thee, and yet are *thy* children, which thou haft brought forth.

50. *Thus faith the Spirit, which rifeth up in the feven fpirits of God, which is thy Father, Defpair not, behold I am thy ftrength, and thy power, I will fill to thee a mild draught in thy Age.*

51. Seeing all thy children defpife thee; whom thou didft bear, and haft given them fuck in their Childhood, and will not give thee any attendance, or minifter to thee in thy high or old Age.

52. Therefore I will comfort thee, and will give unto thee a Young SONNE in thy high or old Age; he fhall abide in thy Houfe, as long as thou liveft, and attend thee or minifter to thee, and

and comfort thee, against all the raving and raging of thy proud Children.

Now here Observe further, concerning the Mercurius Tone or Sound.

53. All Qualities take their † beginning-original in their *middle* or center : Therefore Observe, *where* the Fire is generated; for, *there* riseth up the flash of the life of all the qualities, and is *caught* in the water, so that it remaineth *shining,* and is dryed in the astringency, so that it remaineth *corporeal,* and becomes shining Bright and Clear.

† finite or transitory original.

Observe here :

54. For Instance : kindle some wood, and *then* you will see the mysterie ; the Fire kindleth it self in the *hardnesse* of the wood : and this is now the astringent hard quality, The quality or source *Saturnus,* which *maketh* the wood hard and dry.

55. But now, the *light,* that is, the flash, doth not consist in the hardnesse; otherwise a stone also would burn and give Light, but the light subsisteth onely in the *Sap* of the wood, that is, in the * water.

* or Oylinesse.

56. Whilest there is Sap in the wood, the fire shineth, as a shining Light : but when the sap is consumed in the wood, the shining Light *goeth out,* and the wood becometh a glowing Coal.

57. Now behold, the fiercenesse, which riseth up in the light ; consists *not* in the water of the wood,

but

but when the heat riseth up in the hardnesse, then is the flash *generated*, which the sap in the wood first catcheth, whereby the *water* becomes shining.

58. The Fiercenesse or Bitternesse is generated in the midst or center of the hardnesse, and the *heat* is generated in the flash, and therein also it subsisteth: and so far as the flash, that is, the *flame* of the fire, reacheth, so far also reacheth the *fiercenesse* of the bitternesse, which is the sonne of the hardnesse and heat.

59. But thou must know this mystery, that the bitternesse is *already* in the world, Else the fierce bitternesse would not so suddenly generate it self like *lightning* in the natural fire.

60. For, as the Body of the fire generateth it self, when wood is kindled, in such a manner likewise is the *wood* generated in and above the earth.

61. But if the fiercenesse should be generated in the shining light, then surely it would reach *as far* also, as the splendour or shining of the Light, but it doth not so.

62. But thus it is; the flash is the *mother* of the light: for the flash generateth the light, and is the *Father* of the fiercenesse, for the fiercenesse abideth in the flash as a *feed* in the Father, and that flash generateth also the Tone or Sound.

63. When it goeth from the hardnesse and heat, then the hardnesse maketh a thumping *knocking* found in the flash, and the heat ringeth forth, and the light in the flash maketh the ringing *shrill,* and the water mitigateth it, and then in the astringency and hardnesse it is caught and dryed up, so that it is a *corporeal* spirit in all the qualities.

64. For

64. For, *every* Spirit in the seven Spirits of God is impregnated with *all* the seven spirits, and they all are one in another as *one* spirit, neither of them is without the other.

65. Only the Birth therein is *thus*, and so the one generateth the other, in and through it self, and the Birth *lasteth* or continueth thus from Eternity to Eternity.

66. Here I will have the Reader warned, that he rightly *confider* the Divine Birth. Thou must *not* think, that one spirit standeth *by* another, as you see the Stars of Heaven stand one by another.

67. But all the seven are *one in another* as one spirit: as this may be conceived in Man, who hath *several* Thoughts because of the operation of the seven Spirits of God, which keep and reside in, the *humane Body*.

68. But you may say to me, Thou art foolish in this, for *Any Member* of the whole body hath the *power* of the Other.

69. Yet in what quality foever thou excitest or *awakenest* the spirit, and makest it operative or qualifying, according to that same quality, the Thoughts rise up, and *govern* the Mind.

70. If thou stirrest or awakest the spirit in the fire, then there riseth up in thee the bitter and harsh *Anger*; for as soon as the fire is kindled, which is done in the hardneffe and fierceneffe, *then* springeth up the bitter fierceneffe or wrath in the flash.

71. For when thou elevatest thy felf in thy Body towards or *against* any thing, be it in Love or in Anger, now *that* which thou liftest up thy felf towards or against, thou Kindlest the *Quality* of that, and that it is, which *burneth* in thy compacted incorporated

rated Spirit, but that qualifying or conditionating spirit is *excited* in the Flash.

72. For when thou lookest upon any thing, which doth *not please* thee, but is *against* or contrary to thee, then thou *raisest up* the fountain of thy heart; as when thou takest a stone, and therewith strikest fire on a Steel, and so when the *spark* catcheth fire in the heart, *then* the fire kindleth.

73. At first it *gloweth,* but when thou stirrest the source or fountain of the heart more violently, then it is as when thou *blowest* the fire, so that the *flame* is kindled; and then it is high time to quench it, else the fire will be too great, and then *burneth* and consumeth, and doth hurt to *its Neighbour.*

Question.

74. Thou askest : *How* can a man quench this kindled fire ?

Answer.

75. Hearken, Thou hast the *sweet* water in thee, pour that into the fire, and then it goeth out ; if thou *letst* it burn, then it consumeth in thee the Sap that is in all the seven qualifying or fountain Spirits, so that thou wilt become dry.

76. *When that is done, then thou art a hellish fire-Brand, and a Billet or Faggot to lay upon the hellish fire, and then there is no remedy for thee Eternally.*

77. But

77. But when thou lookeſt upon a thing which thou *loveſt* and awakneſt the ſpirit in thine heart, then thou *kindleſt* the fire in thine heart, which burneth firſt in the ſweet water, like a *Glowing* coal.

78. And whilſt it is but *glimmering,* it is only a gentle ſoft longing delight or pleaſing Luſt in thee, and doth *not* conſume thee; but if thy heart be in a greater commotion, and thou kindleſt the ſweet quality or fountain, ſo that it becomes a *burning flame,* then thou kindleſt all the qualifying or fountain ſpirits, and then the whole body burneth, and ſo Mouth and Hands fall on to work.

79. *This fire* is the moſt dangerous and hurtful, and hath ſpoiled Moſt, ſince the world began, and it is a *very hard* matter to quench it : for when it is kindled, it burneth in the *ſweet* water in the flaſh of Life, and muſt be quenched through *Bitterneſſe,* which is ſcarce a water, but much *rather* is a fire.

80. *Therefore* alſo there followeth a heavy ſad ſorrowful Mind, when one is to forſake that, which burneth in his Love-fire in the ſweet fountain water.

81. But thou muſt know, that thou, in the Government of thy Mind, art *thine own* Lord and Maſter, there will riſe up *no* fire to thee in the circle or whole circumference of thy Body and Spirit, *unleſs* thou awakneſt it *thy ſelf.*

82. It is true, all thy ſpirits ſpring and move in thee, and riſe up in thee, and indeed *alwaies* One ſpirit hath *more* power in thee then another.

83. For if the Government of the ſpirits were in one man as in another, then we ſhould *all* have one
will

will and form : but they are all seven in *the power* of thy compacted incorporated spirit, which spirit is the *S O U L.*

84. [" *It hath in it the* first principle ; *the spirit of*
" *the soul hath the* second; *and the Astral or*
" *starry spirit in the Elements, hath the*
" *Third, viz. this VVorld*:]

85. Now if a fire riseth up in one qualifying or fountain spirit, then that is *not concealed* or hidden from the soul, It may instantly awaken the other qualifying or fountain spirits, which are *contrary* to the kindled fire, and *may* quench it.

86. But if the fire will be, or become, *too big*, then hath the soul *a Prison*, wherein it may shut up the kindled spirit, *viz.* in the hard astringent quality, and the *other* spirits must be the Gaylors, till their wrath be allayed, and the fire be *extinguish'd.*

Observe, what that is.

8. When *One* qualifying or fountain spirit driveth thee too strongly, or presseth thee *too hard* to a thing, which is against *the Law of Nature*, then thou must turn thine *Eyes* away from it : if that will not help, then take *that spirit*, and cast it into prison :

88. That is, Turn thy heart *away* from temporall Pleasure and voluptuousnesse, from fulnesse of eating and drinking, from the *Riches* of this world ; and think : that, To day is the *last* Day of the *End* of thy *Body*: turn away from the *wantonnesse* of the world, and call *earnestly* to God, and yield or submit thy self to Him.

89. When

89. When thou doſt ſo, then the world mocketh thee, and thou art a *fool* to them. But bear *this* croſſe patiently, and let not the impriſoned ſpirit get out of Priſon again, but truſt in God, and *he will ſet upon thee, the Crown of the divine Joy.*

90. But if the ſpirit *breaketh out* of Priſon, then put it in again, *make good* thy Part againſt it as long as thou liveſt, and if thou getteſt ſo much advantage, that it do not *wholly* kindle the ſource or fountain of thy heart, whereby thy ſoul *would* become a dry firebrand of wood, each fountain or ſource having *yet* its Sap, *when* thou departeſt from hence:

91. Then will not that kindled fire at the Laſt Judgment Day, hurt thee ; nor will it cleave or *ſtick* in thy Sappy-ſpirits, but after this anxious affliction, and trouble, thou wilt be in the Reſurrection, *A triumphing Angel of God.*

Queſtion.

92. But now, thou maiſt ſay ; Is there in God alſo a *contrary* Will or Oppoſition, amongſt or between the ſpirits of God ?

Anſwer.

93. No : though I ſhew here their *earneſt* Birth, how earneſtly and ſeverely the ſpirits of God are generated, whereby every one may very well underſtand the great earneſt *ſeverity* of God:

94. Yet it doth *not therefore follow,* that there is a diſunion or *diſcord* amongſt them : For the very innermoſt

C c

nermoſt *deepeſt* Birth or Geniture in the heart or kernell, is onely and altogether *ſo,* which no creature
can apprehend in the Body, but in the *flaſh,* where
the hidden ſpirit is generated, there it will be apprehended : for that is alſo generated in *ſuch* a manner
and in ſuch a power, as is here mentioned.

95. But unto me is opened the Gate of my *Mind,*
ſo that I *can* ſee and diſcern it, elſe it would indeed
remain concealed with and hidden to me, *till* the *day*
of the reſurrection from the dead ; yea it hath been
concealed from *all men,* ſince the beginning of the
world : but I ſubmit my will to Gods Will, let him
do what he pleaſeth.

96. In God *all* the ſpirits do triumph, as *one* ſpirit,
and one ſpirit alwaies mitigateth and loveth the
other, and ſo there is nothing but meer Joy and Delight : but their *ſevere* Birth or Geniture which is
effected or done in *ſecret,* muſt be ſo : for life, underſtanding, and † Omniſcience is *thus* generated :

† or *All-
knowing-
neſſe.*

*and this is an eternall Birth or
Geniture, which is never otherwiſe.*

97. Thou muſt not think, that perhaps in Hea-
ven there is *ſome* manner of Body which *onely* is thus
Generated, *which* above all other things, is called
God.

98. No; but the whole Divine Power, which it
ſelf is heaven, and the Heaven of *all* Heavens, is *ſo*
generated, and that is called GOD *the Father*; of
whom all holy Angels are generated, and live alſo
in the ſame power, alſo the ſpirit of all Angels in
their Body is alwayes continually and eternally *thus*
genera-

generated, in like manner also is the *Spirit* of all Men.

99. For this world belongeth as well to the Body or * *Corpus* of God the Father, as the Heaven doth; but the *spirits* which are in the locality or space of this world, were kindled through King *Lucifer*, in his elevation, so that all things in this world are as it were *half* Faint and Dead: And *therefore* it is, that we poor men are so very much blinded, and live in so great and *desperate* Danger.

* *Substantiality* or *Corporeity*.

100. Yet thou must *not* therefore think, that the heavenly light in this world, in the qualifying or fountain spirits of God is *quite* extinct: no; there is onely a duskishnesse or dimme *Obscurity* upon it, so that we cannot apprehend it with our *corrupted* Eyes;

101. But if God did *once* put away that duskishnesse, which moveth about the light, and that thy eyes were opened, then, in *that* very place, where thou standest, sittest, or lyest: thou shouldest see;

the glorious Countenance or Face of God and the whole heavenly Gate.

102. Thou needest not first to cast thine eyes up into Heaven, for it is written: *The word is near thee, viz: on thy Lips, and in thy Heart,* Deut. 30. 14. Rom. 10. 8.

103. *Yea God is so near thee, that the Birth or Geniture of the Holy Trinity is done or wrought,*

Cc 2 *even*

even in thy heart , yea all the Three Persons are Generated in thy heart, even God the Father, Sonne, and Holy Ghost.

104. Now, when I write here, concerning the midst or *Center*, that the fountain of the Divine Birth or Geniture is in the midst or Center ; the meaning is *not*, that in Heaven there is a peculiar or *severall* place, or a peculiar *several* Body, wherein the fire of the divine life riseth up; out of which the seven spirits of God go forth into the whole *Deep* of the Father.

105. No ; but I speak in a corporeal, or Angelical or Humane way, that the *Reader* may the better understand it ; in such a manner, as the Angelical Creatures were Imaged or framed, and as it is in God every where, *universally*.

106. For thou canst not nominate any place either in heaven or in this world, wherein the divine Birth or Geniture is *not thus,* be it in an Angel, or Holy man, or any where else.

107. Wheresoever one qualifying or fountain-spirit in the divine power is *touched* or stirred, let the place be where, or thing what, it will, *except* in the Devils and all wicked damned Men ; there is the fountain of the divine Birth or Geniture, clearly at hand, and there *already* are all the seven qualifying or fountain-Spirits of God.

108. As when thou wouldst make a spacious *creaturely* circumscribed circle , and hadst the whole Deity peculiarly *apart* therein, Then Just so as it is

generated

generated in a Creature, so it is also in the whole Deep of the Father in all places and parts thereof, and in all *things*.

Note.

109. And in such a manner, is God, an All-mighty, all-knowing, all-seeing, all-hearing, all-smelling, all-feeling God, who is every where, and proveth the Hearts and Reines of the Creatures.

110. And in such a manner, Heaven and Earth is *His*; Also in such a manner all the Devils, together with all wicked Men; must be *his* Eternal *Prisoners*; and in the *Salitter*, which they have corrupted and kindled in their Place or Space; must endure eternal Pain and Torment, and moreover Eternal shame and Reproach.

111. For the Total *glorious* face of God, together with all the holy Angels, will shine bright and gloriously, above them and under them, and round about *them* on Every side.

112. And all holy Angels together with all holy Men, will eternally triumph above them, below them, and round about *them*, and for great Joy, delight, and Pleasantnesse; sing of Gods *Holinesse*, of their Royall Kingly Government or Regiment, and of the gracious amiable blessed fruit of the heaven-

ly

ly Spring or *Vegetation* ; and that wil go forth according to the qualities of the seven Spirits of God, in many various *Voices*.

113. On the contrary, the Devils with all wicked Men will be *forced* into a Hole, where a hellish stinck will burn boyl and rise up, and the hellish fire, and hellish coldnesse, and bitternesse, will *burn* after the manner of the kindled spirits of God, eternally, in their Body, as also in their *Courts* Dominions Regions Space or Circumference.

114. Nay, if they could be lock'd in or barred up into a *Hole*, that the angry face of God might *not* touch them, then they might be Quiet and contented ; and would not be necessitated to endure eternal Ignominie, shame, and reproach.

115. But here is no help, their *Torment* encreaseth and becometh but the greater ; the more they bewail it, the *more* doth the hellish fiercenesse or wrath kindle it self, they must lye in Hell, as dead Bones, like sindged scorched Sheep in the fire, their *stink* and abomination *gnaweth* them.

116. They dare not lift up their Eyes for shame, for they see in their Circumference Courts or *Regions* nothing else, but onely a severe Judge, and above them and on all sides of them they *see* the Eternal Joy.

117. " [*Not that they apprehend and behold it,* but
    " *they have a kind of knowledge thereof*
    " *in the* Center.]

118. Here is Lamentation and Woe, *yelling* and crying, and no deliverance ; it is with them as if it did *continually* Thunder and Lighten tempestuously.

119. For

119. For the kindled Spirits of God generate themselves *thus*.

I. First the hardnesse generateth a hard, raw, *rough*, cold and astringent quality.

II. Secondly, the sweetnesse is grown *faint*, like a glowing coal, when there is no more sap in the wood, that Gaspeth, and there is *no* refreshment for it.

III. Thirdly, the Bitternesse *teareth* like a Hot Plague, and is as Bitter as Gall.

IIII. Fourthly, the Fire *burneth* as a fierce wrathful Sulphur.

V. Fifthly, Love is an *Enmity* here.

VI. Sixthly, the sound is a meer Beating *Rumbling* or Cracking, like the noise of a fire, breaking forth out of a hollow place, as if it were great *Claps* of Thunder.

VII. Seventhly, the Circuit Region Court or *Residence* of the Body is a house of *mourning*.

120. Their food is *abomination*, and groweth from the fiercenesse of all qualities; Lamentation and woe; and that for Ever without End; there is no Time there. *Another King* sitteth on their Throne, which keepeth or holdeth a Judgment for Ever, they are onely his *Footstool*.

121. O, Beauty, *Pleasure* and Voluptuousnesse of this world! O *Riches* and proud Statelinesse! O Might and *Power*! Thy unrighteous Judgment and great *Pomp* with all thy pleasure and voluptuousnesse lyeth all together on a Heap, and is become a hellish Fire!

122. Now eat and drink, now trim and dresse thy self therewith, and domineer therein, thou fair Goddesse,

Goddeſſe, how art thou become a *whore*, and thy
ſhame and reproach continueth for ever.

The Eleventh Chapter.

VII.

Of the Seventh Qualifying or Fountain Spirit in the Divine Power.

I.

THe *Seventh* Spirit of God in the Divine
Power is the *Corpus* or Body which is gene-
rated out of the other *Six* ſpirits, wherein
All heavenly figures ſubſiſt, and wherein all
things Image and form themſelves, and wherein all
Beauty and Joy riſeth up.

2. This is the very ſpirit of Nature, yea *Nature
it ſelf*, wherein apprehenſibility or comprehenſibility conſiſteth, and wherein all Creatures are formed in Heaven and on Earth. Yea *heaven* it ſelf is
therein formed; and *Naturality* in the whole Deity,
conſiſteth in *this* Spirit.

3. If it were not for this Spirit, there would be
neither Angel nor man, and God would be an *unſearchable* Being, ſubſiſting *onely* in an unſearchable
Power.

Queſtion.

4. Now the Queſtion is : How is this form? Or
in what manner is this ſo?

Anſw.

Answer.

If thou art a Rational Mercurial spirit, which *presseth* through all the seven Spirits of God, and beholdeth proveth and examineth them, how they are, then thou wilt by the *explanation* of this seventh Spirit, conceive and understand the *Operation*, and the *Being* of the whole Deity, and apprehend it in thy Sense or Mind.

5. " But if thou *understandest* nothing by this Spirit, " then let this book alone, and (*Richte*) *Judge*, neither " of the cold nor of the warmth therein : for *thou* art " too hard bound and captivated in *Saturnus*, and " art not a Philosopher in this world.

6. Let thy (*Richten*) *Judging* alone, or else thou wilt receive thy *evil* wages for it ; therefore I will have thee faithfully warned of it. Tarry till thou commest into the other life, for then the heavenly Gate *will* be opened to thee, and then thou also wilt understand this.

Gregorius Rickter Primarius Zu Gorlitz. Gregory Rickter the Primate or Superintendent of the Clergy at Gerlitz.

Now observe the depth.

7. Here I must *lay hold* on the whole divine Body in the Midst or center at the Heart, and explain the whole Body, how Nature is or existeth, and there you will see *the highest ground*, how all the seven Spirits of God *continually* generate one another, and *how* the Deity hath neither Beginning nor End.

8. Therefore behold and see the Longing desired pleasure of thy Spirit, the eternal divine *Joyfulnesse*, and the heavenly delight and corporeal Joy, which in all eternity hath *no* End.

Now Observe.

9. When the flash riseth up in the Center, then the divine birth standeth in its full operation: in God it is continually and *Eternally* thus: but *not so* in us poor fleshly children.

10. In this Life, the triumphing divine birth lasteth in us Men, only *so long* as the flash lasteth, therefore our *knowledge is but in part*, whereas in God, the flash standeth unchangeably alwaies Eternally thus.

11. Behold, all the seven Spirits of *God* are generated alike together at once; none of them is the first, and none of them is the last ; but we must have an Eye to the Kernel, and consider how the divine Birth or *Geniture* riseth up, otherwise man understandeth it not.

12. For the creatures cannot comprehend *at once*, all the seven Spirits, one in another, but they look upon them ; But when one Spirit is touched or stirred, then that toucheth or stirreth all the other, and then the Birth or Geniture standeth in full Power.

13. Therefore it hath a beginning *in Man*, but none *in God*; and therefore I must also write in a *creaturely* manner, or else thou *canst not* understand it.

14. Behold all the seven Spirits without the flash, were a dark Valley, but when the *flash* riseth up between the Astringent and Bitter qualities, in the Heat, then it becometh *shining* in the sweet water, and in the flames of the Heat, it becometh Bitter and triumphing and Living, and in the astringent it becometh Corporeal, Dry and *Bright*.

15. And

15. And now thefe four Spirits move themfelves in the flafh, for all the four become living therein, and fo now the power of thefe four rifeth up in the flafh, as if the *Life* did rife up, and the *power* which is rifen up in the flafh, is the Love, which is *the fift Spirit.*

16. And that power moveth fo very pleafantly and amiably in the flafh, as if a dead Spirit did become living, and were fuddainly in a Moment fet into great clarity or *brighneſſe.*

17. Now in this moving, one power toucheth or ftirreth the other: and firſt the aftringent beateth or ftriketh, and the heat maketh in that beating or ftroak, a *clear* ringing found, and the bitter Power divideth the ringing, and the water maketh it mild and foft and fo mitigateth it; And this is *the fixth Spirit.*

18. And now the Tone in all the *five* fpirits rifeth up like a melodïous pleafant Muſick, and remaineth fo ftanding; for the aftringent quality exficcateth or drïeth it up.

19 So now, in the fame found that is *gone forth,* which now fubfifteth being dryed, and is the power of *all the fix* qualifying or fountain fpirits, and is as it were the *Seed* of the other fix fpirits, which they have there compaƈted or incorporated together, and made a Spirit thereof, which hath the quality of *all* the Spirits: And that is *the Seventh Spirit of God* in the divine power.

20. Now this Spirit fubfifteth in its colour like Azure or Heaven-*Blew*, for it is generated out of all the fix Spirits; and when the flafh which ftandeth in the midft or Center in the Heat, *fhineth* into the other Spirits; fo that they rife up in the flafh, and ge-

nerate the seventh Spirit ; then the *flash* riseth up also in the birth of the *six* Spirits together in the seventh.

21. But because the Seventh hath no *peculiar* quality in it, therefore cannot the flash in the seventh be brighter, but it receiveth from the seventh, the *corporeal* Being of all the seven Spirits, and the flash standeth in the midst or *Center* of these seven Spirits, and is generated from all the seven.

22. And the seven Spirits are the *Father* of the Light, and the Light is their Sonne, which they alwaies continually generate thus from Eternity to Eternity , and the light enlightneth and alwaies Eternally maketh the seven Spirits living, and joyfull, for they all receive their rising and *Life* in the power of Light.

23. Again, they all generate the light, and all are together alike the Father of the Light, and the light generateth no one Spirit, but maketh them *all* living and *Joyful*, that they alwaies continually stand in the Birth.

24. Behold I will shew it thee once more, that so by *any means* thou mayst apprehend it, that this high work *may not* passe away in vain without Profit to *thee*.

25. The astringent quality is the *first* Spirit, and that attracteth or draweth together and maketh all Dry : The sweet quality is the *second* Spirit, and that softneth or mitigateth it : Now the *third* Spirit is the bitter Spirit, which existeth from the fourth and first.

26. And so when the third Spirit in its rage *rubs* its self in the astringent, then it kindleth the *fire*, and then the *fierceneffe* in the fire riseth up in the astringent.

aftringent.   In that fiercenesse now the bitter Spirit becometh *self-subsisting*; and in the sweet it becometh meek or *Mild*, and in the hard it becometh *Corporeal*, and so now it subsisteth, and is also the *fourth* Spirit.

27. Now the flash in the power of these *four* goeth forth in the heat, and riseth up in the sweet spring water or fountain ; the bitter maketh it *triumphing*, the aftringent maketh it *shining*, dry, and corporeal, and the sweet maketh it meek or *Mild*; and so it receiveth its first shining or Lustre in the sweet, and here now the flash, or the light subsisteth in the midst or Center, *viz.* in the *Heart*.

28. Now when that Light, which standeth in the midst or Center, shineth *into* the four Spirits, then the power of the *four* Spirits riseth up in the light, and they become living, and *Love* the light; that is, they take it into them, and are impregnated with it, and that Spirit which is so taken in, is the Love of the Life; which is the fifth Spirit.

29. Now when they have taken the love into them, then they qualifie Act or *operate* for great Joy: for the one seeth the other in the Light, and so the one toucheth or stirreth the other.

30. And then the tone riseth up ; and the hard Spirit beateth striketh or *thumpeth*; but the sweet maketh that beating or striking *Mild*; and the Bitter *divideth* it , according to the condition or kind of every quality , the fourth causeth the *ringing*, the fift causeth *joyfulnesse*, and the compacted incorporated sounding is the *Tone* or Tune or the *Sixth* Spirit.

31. In this Tone riseth up the *power* of all the six Spirits, and becometh a palpable Body, to speak after

ter an Angelicall manner, and fubfifteth in the power of the other fix Spirits, and in the light; and this is the *Body* of Nature, wherein all heavenly Creatures Ideas Figures and Sprouts or Vegetations, are Imaged or fafhioned.

The Holy Gates.

32.

But the *Light*, which fubfifteth in the midft or Center in all the Seven Spirits, and wherein standeth the *Life* of all the feven Spirits; and whereby all feven become triumphing and Joyful, and wherein the heavenly *joyfulneffe* rifeth up;

33. That is *it*, which all the feven fpirits do generate, and that is the *Sonne* of all the feven fpirits, and the feven Spirits are its *Father*, which generate the Light; and the Light generateth in them, the *Life*; and the *Light* is the Heart of the feven fpirits.

34. *And this Light is the true Sonne of God, whom we Chriftians worfhip and honour, as the Second Perfon in the holy Trinity.*

35. *And all the feven Spirits of God together, are God the Father.*

36. For no one fpirit of them is *alone* or without the other; they all feven generate one another; for if one were *wanting*, the other could not be.

37. But

37. But the *Light* is another *Person,* for it is *continually* generated out of, or from the seven spirits, and the seven spirits rise up continually in the light; and the powers of these seven spirits go forth continually in the glance or *splendor* of the light in the seventh * Nature-spirit, and do form and Image all in the *seventh* Spirit; *And this out-going or Exit in the Light is the Holy Ghost.*

* or *spirit* of *Nature.*

38. The flash, or stock or Pith, or the Heart, which is generated in the powers, remaineth standing in the *midst* or Center, and that is the Sonne; and the Splendor or *Glance* in all the powers, goeth forth from the Father and the Sonne, in all the powers of the Father, and formeth and imageth in the seventh Nature-spirit, all, according to the power and operation of the seven Spirits, and according to their *Distinction* and impulse. *And this is the true Holy Ghost, whom we Christians honour and adore for the Third Person in the Deitie.*

39. Thus, O blind Jew, Turk and Heathen, thou seest that there are *Three Persons in the Deitie,* thou canst not deny it, for thou livest and art or hast thy being *in the Three Persons,* and thou hast thy life from them, and in the power of these three Persons, thou *art to rise* from the Dead at the Last Day, and live Eternally.

Note.

Note.

40. Now if thou haft lived well and *holily* in the Law of Nature, in this world; and haft * *not* extinguifhed the half Flafh, which is the Sonne of God, which *teacheth* thee the Law of Nature in thy feven qualifying or fountain fpirits; and haft not put it out through a fierce elevation, which runneth on contrary to the † Knowledge of Nature; * Then wilt thou with all Chriftians, live in eternal Joy.

* Note.

† or Con-fcience.

* Note.

Note.

P.

41. [" *The* Law of Nature *is the* Divine *Ordi-*
" *nance out of the Center of Nature, he that*
" *can live therein, needs no other Law, for*
" *he fulfilleth the will of God:*]

* or Nefcience Ignorance or not belie-ving.

42. For it lyeth not in thy * unbelief, to hinder it; thy unbelief doth *not take away* or make void the truth of God: but *Faith* bloweth up the Spirit of *Hope,* and *teftifieth,* that we are Gods Children. The Faith is generated in the flafh, and wreftleth fo long with God, till it *overcometh* and gets the victory.

43. Thou *Judgeft* us, and thereby thou judgeft thy felf, in that thou bloweft up the zealous or Jealous Spirit in Anger and Wrath, which extinguifheth thy Light. * But if thou art grown on a *fweet* Tree, and *fuppreffeth* the evil influence or *fuggeftions,* and liveft well and holily in the Law of Nature, which sheweth thee very well, what is *Right*: If thou art not indeed grown out from a *fierce* or wrathful Twig or Branch,

* Note.

Q.   [" *Here is meant or* underftood, *out of or from a very*

" *very wicked Seed, where out there often*
" *groweth a Thistle : though yet there were*
" *a remedy, if the will were but once broken:*
" *but it is a Rare and Pretious thing ; How-*
" *ever indeed on a Good Tree it is often so*
" *that some branches do also wither.*

Note.

45. Moreover thou art blind. For who shall separate thee *from the love of God,* in which thou art born or Generated, and *wherein* thou livest ; if thou perseverest and continuest therein, till the End? who shall separate thee from God, in whom thou hast li ved *here* ?

46. That which thou hast *sowen* in the Ground, that will spring up, be it Rye, Wheat, Barley, Tares or Thorns ; that which is not combustible or capable of the final or last Fire, that will not burn at all : but God will not corrupt or spoil *his good Seed himself;* but will husband, *Till,* and manure it, that it may bear *fruit* in the Eternal life.

47. Seeing then, *all* live and have their Being in God, why do the *weeds* Glory and boast against the *wheat* ? Dost thou think, that God is a Dissembler, and that he regardeth or respecteth *any mans person,* or *name* ?

48. What Man was the Father of us All ! was it not *Adam* ? And when his Sonne *Cain* lived *wickedly* before God ; why did not his Father *Adam* help him ? But here it may be said : He that *finneth, shall be punished,* Ezek. 18. 4, 20.

49. If **Cain** had not *quenched* or extinguished his light, *who* could have *separated* him *from the love of God?*

50. So thou also, thou boastest thou art a Christian, and knowest the light, why dost thou *not* walk therein? Dost thou think the *Name* will *make* thee *Holy?* Tarry friend, till thou comest thither into the other world, then thou wilt know it by experience. Behold! *many* a Jew, Turk, and Heathen will *sooner* enter into the Kingdom of Heaven, who had indeed *their Lamps well Trimmed and Furnished;* then thou who Boastest.

Question.

What Prerogative or Advantage then have the Christians?

Answer.

51. Very much; For they *know the way of life*, and know *how* they should rise from the Fall: but if any *will lye still,* then he must be thrown into the *Ditch,* and there must perish with all the *wicked* Heathens.

52. Therefore take heed what thou dost, and consider what thou art; thou *judgest* others, and art *blind* thy self.

53, But the Spirit saith thou hast no cause for it, *viz.* to Judge him who is *better* then thou: Have we not all *one* flesh, and our life subsisteth in God, be it in his Love, or in his Anger? for *what thou sowest, that thou shalt reap.*

Note,

Note.

54. God is not the Cauſe thereof that thou art loſt : for the law, to do right or righteouſneſs, is written in *Nature* and thou haſt *that very Book* in thy Heart.

55. Thou knoweſt very well, that thou *ſhouldeſt* deal well and friendly with thy Neighbour; alſo thou knoweſt well that thou ſhouldeſt *not vilifie* thy own life ; that is, thou ſhouldeſt not bemire and *defile* thy own body and ſoul and lay open their ſhame.

56. Surely *herein* conſiſteth the Pith and kernell, and the Love of God. God doth not regard any mans *Name* or *Birth*, but he that moveth or acteth in the Love of God, moveth in the *Light*, and the light is the Heart of God.   Now he that *ſitteth* in the Heart of God, who can ſpew him out from thence ? none, for he is begotten or Generated in God.

57. O thou blind *half dead* world, ceaſe from thy Judging, O thou blind Jew, Turk and Heathen deſiſt from thy *calumniating*, and ſubmit thy ſelf in obedience to God, and walk in the Light, then thou wilt ſee, *how* thou ſhouldeſt riſe from thy Fall, and how thou ſhouldeſt Arme thy ſelf in this world againſt the helliſh *fierceneſſe* and wrath, and how thou mayſt overcome, and live *with God*, Eternally.

58. Moſt certainly, *there is but One God*, but when the vail is put away from thy Eyes, ſo that thou ſeeſt and knoweſt *him*, then thou wilt alſo ſee and know *all* thy brethren whether they be *Chriſtians*, *Jews*, *Turks*, or *Heathens*.

59. Or doſt thou think, that God is the God of you *Chriſtians* only ? Do not the *Heathens* alſo live in

God

God *whosoever doth* right or *righteousnesse, God* loveth and *accepteth him,* Act. 10. 35.

60. Or, what didst thou know, that art a Christian, *how God would* Redeem and deliver thee from Evill? what friendship and *familiarity* haddest thou with H I M? or what covenant haddest thou made with H I M, *when* God caused his Sonne to become Man or be incarnate, to redeem *Mankind?* Is He only *thy* King? Is it not written, *He is the comfort of all the Heathen,* Haggai. 2.8.

61. Hearken, *By one man sin came into the world, and pressed through one upon all,* Rom. 5. 18. *and through one came the Redemption into the world, and pressed through one upon all,* what therefore lieth in *any mans* knowledge? No! indeed thou didst not know, how God would deale with thee, when *thou wert Dead* in Sins.

62. Now as *Sin* without distinction raigneth through one Man over all, so *Mercy* and Redemption raigneth through one over all.

63. But unto those Heathens, Jews and Turks, *blindnesse did befall,* yet for all that, they stand in an anxious Birth, and *seek* for a rest, they *desire* Grace, though they seek not for it at the right mark or in the right Place or Limit: but *God* is *every where,* and looketh upon the ground of the *Heart.*

64. But if in their anxious Birth the Light be generated *in them;* what art thou, that judgest them?

65. Behold! thou blind Man, I will demonstrate this to thee, thus; Go into a Medow, there thou seest *several* sorts of Herbs, and flowers, thou seest some that are Bitter, some Tart, Sweet, Sowre, White, Yellow, Red, Blew, Green, and many various sorts.

66. Do

66. Do they not all grow out of the *Earth* ? Do they not stand one by another ? Doth the one *Grutch* the beautious form of the other ?

67. But if one among them lifteth up it self too high in its growth, and so *withereth*, becaufe it hath not Sap enough; How can the *Earth* help it ? Doth it not afford its Sap to *that* as well as to the other.

68. But if *Thorns* grow among them, and the Mower cometh to reap his crop, he cutteth them down together, but he cafteth out the Thorns and they are to be *burnt* in the fire: but the various flowers and good Crop, he gathereth and caufeth it to be brought into his Barn.

69. Thus it is alfo with Men, there are *diverfities* of Gifts and accomplifhments Endowments or Aptitudes, one it may be is much *Lighter* or brighter in God then an other, but all the while they do not *wither in the Spirit,* they are not rejectible, but when the *Spirit* withereth, then that is good and ufefull for nothing, but for fewell, and is only as wood for the Fire.

70. But if the Turks be of an *aftringent* Quality, and the Heathens of a *Bitter,* what is that to thee ? Is the light becom *fhining* in the aftringent and bitter qualities, then it giveth Light alfo.

71. But thou art generated in the Heat, where the light rifeth up in the *fweet* fpring or fountain-water, have a care, left the Heat *burn* thee, it is time, thou fhouldft do well to *Quench* that.

Queftion.

72. Thou fayeft: Is it *right* then that the Hea-thens, Jewes and Turks, fhould perfevere in their *blindneffe* ?

                                               Anfw.

Anſwer.

73. No; but this I ſay; How can he ſee, that hath *no Eyes*? for what doth the poor Lay *or* vulgar man know, of the *Tumults* which the Prieſts have in their drunkenneſſe? He goeth on in his ſimplicity, and generateth anxiouſly, in his *Spiritual* Birth.

Queſtion.

74. But then thou ſayeſt: Hath *God* blinded the Turks, Jews and Heathens?

Anſwer.

No; but when God kindled the light for them, then they lived after the pleaſures *voluptuouſneſſe* and Luſts of their own Hearts, and would not be led or directed *by the Spirit*, and ſo the *outward* Light extinguiſhed.

75. But it is not therefore ſo *totally* extinguiſhed, that it *could not* be generated in Man; for man is out of or from God, and liveth in God, be it either in Love or in Wrath.

76. Now if man be in a Longing, ſhould he not be *impregnated* in his Longing: and ſo if he be impregnated once, then he can generate alſo. But becauſe the *outward* Light doth nor ſhine to him, *therefore* he doth not know his Sonne, whom he hath generated.

77. But when the Light *ſhall ariſe* on the Laſt Jugment Day, then he will *See* HIM.

78. *Behold, I tell thee a myſtery: the time is already, that the*

the Bridegroom crowneth his Bride!

79. Gueſſe Friend, where lyeth the *Crown* ? Toward the *North* ; For in the Center of the aſtringent quality the light will be clear and bright.

80. But from whence cometh the *Bridegroom* ? From the midſt or Center, where the Heat Generateth the light, and goeth toward the North into the aſtringent quality, there the Light groweth *Bright.*

81. What do theſe toward the *South* ? They are in the Heat fallen *aſleep*, but a ſtormy Tempeſt will awaken them, among theſe many will be terrified to *Death.*

82. Then what do thoſe in the *Weſt* ? their Bitter quality will rub it ſelf with the other, but when they taſte the ſweet water, then will their ſpirit be *mild* and meek.

83. But what do thoſe in the *Eaſt* ? thou art a lofty Proud *Bride*, from the beginning, the Crown was alwayes offered to thee from the beginning, but thou thoughtſt thy ſelf *too Fair* already ; thou liveſt as the reſt do.

Of the Divine and Heavenly Natures operation and property.

84. Now if thou wilt *know*, what kind or manner of Nature there is in *Heaven*, and what kind of Nature the Holy *Angels* have; alſo what kind of Nature

Adam

Adam had before his Fall, and what, properly, the holy heavenly and *Divine* Nature, is: then observe the circumstances exactly concerning this *seventh* qualifying or fountain-spirit of God, as followeth.

85. The seventh qualifying or fountain spirit of God is the qualifying or fountain-spirit of *Nature*: for the *other* six do generate the seventh; and the seventh, when it is generated, is then as it were the *Mother* of the six, which encompasseth the other six, and generateth them again: for the *corporeal* and *natural* Being consisteth in the seventh.

Observe here the Sense :

86. The *six* rise up in a full or compleat Birth according to the power and *condition* of each of them, and when they are risen up, then is their power mingled one in another, and the hardnesse *dryeth* it, and is as it were the whole Being.

87. This corporeal exsiccation or drying, I call in this book, the Divine S A L I T T E R, for it is * therein *the Seed of the whole Deity,* and † is as it were a Mother, which receiveth the Seed, and alwayes generateth fruit again, according to all the Qualities of the *Seed.*

* in the Seventh fountain spirit of Nature.
† the said seventh Spirit.

88. Now in this rising up of the six spirits, there riseth up also the *Mercurius,* Tone, or Sound, of all the six Spirits, and in the Seventh Nature-spirit it subsisteth.

Note.

96. As, &c. ————————

89. [" By the word * SALITTER, *in this book, is* " *understood,* How out of the Eternal " Center of Nature, *the* Second Prin- " ciple

" ciple groweth and springeth up out of
" the first, Just as the Light springeth up
" out of the fire, wherein two *Spirits* are
" understood, viz. I. First a Hot, II. Se-
" condly, an Aërial one, whereas in the
" aërial life, the true vegetation or grow-
" ing consisteth, and in the fire-life, is, the
" cause of the *Quality.*

" 90. So, when it is written, the Angels are created
" out of God, then it is understood or
" meant, *Out of* Gods Eternal Nature,
" wherein is understood or meant the seven
" forms, and yet the divine *holy* nature
" is not understood to be in the Fire, but in
" the Light.

" 91. And yet the Fire giveth or holdeth forth to us
" a Mystery of the *Eternal Nature*, and
" of the *Deity* also, wherein a *Man* is to un-
" derstand, two principles of a twofold
" source, viz. I. a Hot, Fierce, Astrin-
" gent, Bitter, Anxious, Consuming One
" in the fire-soarce. *And* out of the fire
" cometh the II. viz. the light, which
" dwelleth in the Fire, but is not appre-
" hended or laid hold on by the fire; also it
" hath another source then the fire hath,
" which is, Meeknesse, wherein there is a
" desire of Love, where then in the Love-
" desire another will, is understood, then
" that which the Fire hath.

" 92. For the fire will consume all, and causeth a
" high rising in the source, and the meek-
" nesse of the light, causeth Entity or Sub-

F f   stantiality,

" ſtantiality, *viz. In the eternal light it*
" *cauſeth the water-ſpirit of Eternal life ;*
" *And in the third principle of this world,*
" *it cauſeth water, together with the exi-*
" *ſtency or Original of the Ayr.*

" 93. *Thus the Reader is to underſtand this book as*
" *concerning Three Principles or Births,*
" *viz one is the original of the Eternall*
" *Nature, in the eternal will or deſire of*
" *God ; which deſire driveth it ſelf on in*
" *great anguiſh till it come to the* fourth
" *form, viz. to the Fire.*

" 94. *wherein the ſecond, which is the Light, exiſt-*
" *eth, and repleniſheth the Eternal Liber-*
" *ty beſides or beyond Nature, wherein we*
" *underſtand the holy* Ternarie *in the*
" *Light, without or beyond Nature, in the*
" *power of the Light, in the Liberty, as*
" *another or ſecond ſpring or ſource without*
" *Being ; and yet united with the fire's*
" *Nature, viz. as Fire and Light together*
" *in One.*

" 95. *And the third principle of this world is gene-*
" *rated and created out of the Firſt, that*
" *is, Magically : as is clearly demonſtra-*
" *ted in our* ✱ Second *and* † Third Book,
" *unto which this Book is onely an Intro-*
" *duction, and is the* firſt Book, *which was*
" *not ſufficiently apprehended by the Au-*
" *thour at the firſt time; though it appea-*
" *red clearly enough, yet all of it could not*
" *be conceived ; alſo it was as when a Tor-*
" *rent or ſtormy Showre of Rain paſſeth*
" *over*

" *over a place, from whence Vegetation and*
" *Springing exifteth: for, therein, is the*
" *Seed of the whole Deity :*]

------96.

As in the *mother*; and then the feventh generateth all manner of Fruits and Colours according to
the *Operation* of the Six.

97. But here thou muft know, that the *Deity* doth
not ftand ftill, but worketh and rifeth up without
intermiffion, as a pleafant wreftling, moving or
ftruggling;

98. Like *two* creatures, which in *great Love* play
together, Embracing ftruggling and wreftling one
with the other; now the one is above, by and by
the other, and when *one* hath overcome, it yeeldeth
or giveth over, and lets the *other* rife up again.

99. Thou mayft alfo underftand it thus in a fimilitude, as when *Seven Perfons* had begun a friendly
Sport and Play, where one gets the upper hand
above another, and a *third* comes to help *that one*
which is overcome; and fo there is a pleafant friendly fporting amongft them; whereas indeed they all
have one and the *fame* agreement or Love-will together, and yet ftrive and fight or vie one againft the
other in a way of *Love* in fporting and paft-
time.

100. And thus alfo is the *working* of the fix Spirits of God in the feventh; fuddenly *one* of them
hath a ftrong rifing up, fuddenly *another*; and thus
they wreftle in love one with another.

101. And when the Light rifeth up *along* in this
ftriving, then the Holy Ghoft moveth in the power
of the Light in the Play of the other fix fpirits, and

so in the seventh there *spring up* all manner of fruits of life, and *all manner* of Colours and vegetations or Ideas and forms.

102. Now as that quality is which is *strongest*, so the Body of the fruit is Imaged, and the Colours also, in this striving, or wrestling the *Deity* formeth it self into infinite and insearchable variety of kinds and manners of Images or Ideas.

103. For, the seven spirits are the *seven*-head-Sources or springs, and when *Mercurius* riseth np therein, that stirreth all, and the bitter quality moveth it, and *distinguisheth* it, and the astringent *dryeth* it up.

104. [" Nature *and the* Ternarie *are not one and*
" *the same, they are distinct, though the*
" Ternarie *dwelleth in* Nature *but un-*
" *apprehended, and yet is an eternall*
" Bind, *as is plainly expounded in our*
" Second *and* Third *Book.*

Now observe here, how the Imaging in Nature is in the seventh Spirit.

105. The sweet water is the *beginning* of Nature, and the astringent quality draweth or attracteth it together, that it becomes natural and *creatural*, to speak in an Angelical way.

106. Now being drawn together, it looketh like *Azure* or Skie-colour Blew, but when the light or flash riseth up therein, then it looketh like the pretious Jaspis, or *Jasper stone*, or as I may call it in my
language

language, a Glassie Sea, on which the Sun shineth, and that very clear and Bright.

107. But when the bitter quality riseth up therein, then it divideth and formeth it self, as if it were *alive* or lively, or as if the Life did rise up there, in a *greenish* flourishing manner and form, like a Green Flash of Lightening, to speak after the manner of men, even so that it dazleth a mans Eyes, and *blindeth* him.

108. But when the Heat riseth up therein, then the Green form inclineth to a half Red or *Ruddy* form, as when a Carbuncle stone shineth from the Green flash or B*eam* of Light.

109. But when the Light, which is the Sonne of God, shineth into this Sea of Nature; then it getteth its *yellowish* and Whitish Colour, which I cannot compare with any thing; but you must be content to stay or tarry with this aspect or vision, till you *come into* the other Life.

110. For this now is the true Heaven of Nature, which is out of or from God. wherein the *Holy Angels* dwell, and out of which they were created in the beginning.

111. Behold now, when the *Mercurius* or Tone in this Nature Heaven, riseth up, there the Divine and Angelical joyfulnesse riseth up, for therein rise up Forms, Imagings, Colours, and Angelicall *Fruits*, which blossome curiously, grow, spring, flourish, and stand in *Perfection*, as to all manner of Bearing or fruit Trees, Plants and springing growths, of a Gracious comely lovely amiable blessed prospect vision or sight to be looked upon, with a most delicious lovely pleasant Smell and Taste.

112. *But*

112. *But here I speak with an Angels Tongue, thou must not understand it Earthly, like to this world.*

113. It is with *Mercurius* in this manner or form, also; thou must *not* think, that there is any hard beating, striking, toning or sounding, or whistling and Piping, in the Deity, as when one taketh a Huge Trumpet, and Bloweth in it, and maketh it to Sound.

114. O *no*, Dear Man; thou half dead Angel, that is not so, but all is done and consisteth, in *power*: for the Divine Being standeth in power: but the holy Angels sing, ring and Trumpet forth, with clear and *shrill sounding* : for to that End God hath made them out of himself, that they should encrease and multiply the Heavenly Joy : [*and therefore were the Angels made out of God.*]

115. Also such an Image was *Adam*, as God created him, before his *Eve* was made out of him; but the corrupted *Salitter* did wrestle with the Wellspring of Life *in Adam*, till it overcame. And so *Adam* became faint, which made him fall into a *Sleep*. Here he was undone : And if the Bamhertzigkeit, or the *Mercy* of God had not come to help him, and made a *woman* out of him, he should have continued still asleep.

Of

Of this we will speak in its proper Place.

116. This, as is mentioned above, is that fair Bright and holy Heaven, which is thus in the *Totall Deitie*, which hath neither Beginning nor End, whither no Creature with its fenfe *can* reach.

117. Yet thou fhalt know this, that alwaies in a place fuddenly *one* quality fheweth its felf *more powerfully*, then the other, fuddenly the fecond prevaileth, fuddenly the third, then fuddenly the fourth, fuddenly again the fifth, fuddenly the fixth, then again fuddenly the feventh.

118. Thus, there is an *Eternal wreftling*, working, and friendly amiable rifing up of Love ; where then in this rifing up, the Deity continually *fheweth* it felf *more* and *more* wonderful, more incomprehenfible and more unfearchable.

119. So that the holy Angels cannot fufficiently *enough* rejoyce themfelves, nor fufficiently enough converfe walk and moft lovingly fport therein, nor fufficiently enough fing, that *Te Deum Laudamus*, We praife thee, O God, *in Halelujah's*, as to each quality of the Great God, according to his wonderfull Revelation, and Wifdome, and Beauty, and Fruit, and Form.

120. For the qualities rife up *Eternally*, and fo there is not with them or among them, either Beginning, Middle or End.

121. And although I have written here ; how all is come to be, and how all is framed *formed* and Imaged, and how the Deity rifeth up, yet for all that

thou

thou muſt not think, that it hath any Reſt ceaſing or extinction, and that afterward it riſeth up thus *again*.

122. O no: but I muſt write in *part* or by pieces, for the Readers better underſtanding, that he might thereby apprehend *ſomewhat*, and ſo attain the Sence and Meaning thereof.

123. *Neither* muſt thou think, that I have climbed up aloft into Heaven, and beheld it with my *carnall* or fleſhly Eyes. O, no; hear me, thou *half-dead* Angel, I am as thou art, and have no greater light in my *outward* Being, then thou haſt.

124. Moreover, I am a *ſinful* and mortall man, as well as thou, and I muſt every day and hour grapple ſtruggle and fight with the Devill who afflicteth me in my corrupted loſt Nature, in the fierce or wrathful quality, which *is* in my fleſh, as in all Men, continually.

125. Suddenly I get the better of him, ſuddenly he is too hard for me; yet for all that he hath *not* overcome or conquered me, though he often getteth the *advantage* over me : *for our life is as a perpetuall warfare with the Devill.*

126. [" *This Strife and Battle is about that moſt* " *High Noble Victorious Garland, till the* " *corrupted periſhed Adamical Man is* " *killed and* dead, *in which the Devill* " *hath an* acceſſe *to Man.*

127. " *Of which the Sophiſter will know nothing : for* " *he is not generated of God, but is* born " *of Fleſh and Blood : and though in-* " deed

" deed the Birth *ſtandeth* open for and
" towards him, yet he will not enter ; for
" the Devil withholds him : God blindeth
" None.]

128. If he buffetteth me, then I muſt *retire* and give back, but the Divine power helpeth me *again*, then he alſo getteth a Blow, and often loſeth the day, in the fight.

129. But when he is overcome, then the heavenly Gate openeth *in my ſpirit*, and then the ſpirit ſeeth the Divine and heavenly Being, not externally without the Body, but in the fountain or well-ſpring of the *Heart* there riſeth up the flaſh in the *ſenſibility* or Thoughts of the Brain, and therein the ſpirit doth contemplate or meditate.

130. For *Man* is made out of all the powers of God, out of all the ſeven Spirits of God, as the *Angels* are alſo. But now ſeeing Man is *corrupted*, therefore, the Divine Birth doth not *alwayes* ſpring qualifie or operate in him, no, nor in all men neither : And though indeed it ſpringeth in him, yet the *high light* doth not preſently ſhine in all men ; and though indeed it doth ſhine, yet it is incomprehenſible to the corrupted Nature.

131. For, the Holy Ghoſt will not be caught held or *retained* in the *ſinful* fleſh ; but riſeth up like a flaſh of lightning ; even as fire flaſhes and ſparckles out of a Stone, when a man ſtrikes fire upon it.

132. But when the flaſh is caught in the fountain of the Heart, then the Holy Ghoſt riſeth up in the ſeven qualifying or fountain ſpirits, into the Brain

like

like the Day-break, Dawning of the Day, or Morning Redneſſe : and therein *ſticketh* the mark Aime or ſcope, and knowledge.

133. For in *that light,* the one ſeeth the other, feeleth the other, ſmelleth the other, taſteth the other, and heareth the other, and is as if the whole Deity did riſe up therein.

134. And *herein* the ſpirit ſeeth into the depth of the Deity; for in God, near and afar off, is all one; And that ſame God, of whom I write in this Book, is as well in his *Ternarie* in the Body of a Holy ſoul ; As in Heaven.

135. From this God I take my knowledge, and from no other thing, neither will I know *any other thing,* then that ſame God, and the ſame it is which maketh that aſſurance in my ſpirit, that I *ſteadfaſtly* believe, and truſt in him.

136. And though an Angel from heaven ſhould tell this to me, yet for all that I *could not* believe it ; much leſſe lay hold on it, for I ſhould alwayes doubt, whether it were certainly ſo or no : But the *Sun* it ſelf ariſeth in my ſpirit, and therefore I am moſt *ſure* of it, and I my ſelf do ſee the proceeding and Birth of the holy Angels and of *all things,* both in heaven and in this world.

137. For the Holy Soul is *one ſpirit with God,* though indeed it is a Creature, yet it is *like* to the Angels : Alſo the Soul of Man ſeeth much deeper then the Angels ; for the Angels ſee onely to the heavenly Pomp, but the Soul ſeeth *both* the Heavenly and the Helliſh, for it liveth *between* both.

138. Therefore it muſt undergo many hard Bangs and pinches, and muſt every day and hour wreſtle

and

and ftruggle with the devill, that is, with the * *hel-*
lifh qualities, and fo it liveth in great danger in this
world : and therefore this life is very well called,
the *Valley of mifery,* full of anguifh, a *perpetual* hurliburly pulling and haling, worrying warring fighting, ftruggling and ftriving.

* or devillifh
conditions
inclinations
and paffions
in us.

139. But the cold and *half-*dead Body doth not
alwayes underftand this fight of the Soul : The Body
doth not know how it is with it, but is heavy and
anxious, it goeth from one room or *bufineffe* to another, and from one Place to another ; it feeketh for
eafe and reft.

140. And when it cometh thither, where it *would
be,* yet it findeth no fuch thing : then doubtings and
unbelief fall in between and come upon it; fometimes it feems to it as if God had *quite* caft it off:
but it doth *not* underftand the fight of the Spirit, how
the fame is fometimes down, and fometimes gets
aloft.

141. And what vehement and furious warre and
fight there is betwixt the *hellifh* and *heavenly* Quality, which fire the Devils *Blow up,* and the Holy Angels *Quench* it; I leave to every Holy Soul to confider of.

142. Thou muft know, that I write not here as a
Story or Hiftory, as if it were *related* to me from
another, but I muft continually ftand in that Combat or Battle, and I find it to be full of heavy ftri-
vings, wherein I am often *ftruck down* to the ground,
as well as all other Men.

143. But for the fake of the violent fight, and
for the fake of the *earneftneffe,* which we have together, this Revelation hath been given me, and the

vehement

vehement driving or impulse, to bring it so to paſſe as to ſet all this down in *Paper*.

144. But what the Totall ſequel is, which may follow upon, and after this, I do not *fully* know : onely ſometimes, future Myſteries in the depth, are *ſhewed* to me.

145. For when the flaſh riſeth up in the Center, one ſeeth through and through, but cannot well apprehend or lay hold on it; for it happeneth to ſuch a one as when there is a Tempeſt of *Lightening*, where the flaſh of fire openeth it ſelf, and ſuddenly vaniſheth.

146. So it goes alſo in the Soul, when it preſſeth or breaks quite through in its fight or *Combat*, then it beholdeth the *Deity*, as a flaſh of Lightening; but the ſource quality or fountain of Sins, covereth it ſuddenly again; For the *Old* Adam belongeth * to the Earth, and doth not, with *this* fleſh, belong * to the Deity.

147. I do *not* write this for my own Praiſe, but to that end, that the Reader may know, wherein my Knowledge ſtandeth, that he might not ſeek that from me, which I have not, or think me to be *what I am not*.

148. But what I am, *that*, all men are, who wreſtle in JESUS CHRIST our King, for the *Crown* of the Eternal Joy; and live in the *Hope* of Perfection; the *beginning* whereof is at the Day of the Reſurrection, which is now *ſhortly* near at Hand: which, in the circle of the riſing or Horizon of the Eaſt in the flaſh, is very *well* to be ſeen, in which Nature ſheweth it ſelf as if it would be Day-Break.

149. There-

149. Therefore take heed, that you be not found asleep in your *Sinnes*: surely the prudent and the wise will take notice hereof, but the wicked will *continue* in their Sins.

150. They say, What ayles the Fool, when will he have done with his Dreaming ? This is, Because they are asleep in *fleshly* Lusts, Well, well; you shall see what kind of Dream this will Bee :

151. I would fain take ease and rest in my *meeknesse*, if I were not put upon this work; but that God who hath *made the* world, is *too* strong for me, I am the work of his Hands, he may set me and place me, *where* he will.

152. And though I must be a *by-word* and Spectacle of scorn to the World and Devils, yet my hope is in God, concerning the Life to come, in Him I will *venture* to hazard my self, and not resist, or *strive* against the Spirit. *Amen.*

I.

The

The Twelfth Chapter.

† rise original Geniture or Springing forth.

Of the Nativity and † proceeding forth or descent of the Holy Angels, as also of their Government, Order, and Heavenly joyous Life.

1.

T.

VErbum Domini, *The word of the Lord,* " *comprised the Qualifying or fountain-* " *spirits by the* Fiat ; *that is, the saying,* " *Let there be, Angels ; into a will, and* " *that is the Creation of the Angels:*]

Question.

2. Now the Question is ; What is properly an Angel ?

Answer.

Behold, when God $\begin{cases} \mathfrak{Schuff} \\ created \end{cases}$ the Angels ; then he created them out of the *seventh* qualifying or fountain spirit, which is Nature ; or the *Holy Heaven.*

3. The

3. The word { **Schuff** / Created } thou must understand

thus, as when a man sayes, * drawn together, or † driven together, as the Earth is *driven* or Compacted together: In like manner, when the whole God did move himself, then the astringent quality drew or drove together the *Salitter* of Nature, and *dryed* it, and so the Angels came to be : now *such* as the Quality was, in every place, *such* also was the Angel.

*attracted.

† Compacted.

Observe the depth.

4. There are seven Spirits of God, all these *seven* have moved themselves, and the *Light* therein hath moved it self also, and the *Spirit*, which goeth forth out of the seven Spirits of God, hath moved it self also.

5. Now the Creator intended, according to his *Ternarie*, to create three * Hoasts, not one from another, but one *by* another, as in a circle or sphear.

* *Armies Bands* or *Companies.*

6. Now Observe: *as* the † Spirits were therein in their moving boyling or rising up, *so* also were the Creatures; In the midst or Center of each Hoast was the *Heart* of each Hoast incorporated or compacted together, out of which an Angelical or Great or Chief-Prince, proceeded, or came to be.

† seven Spirits of God.

7. And as the *Sonne* of God is generated in the midst or center of the seven Spirits of God, and is the life and heart of the seven Spirits of God; so there was *one* Angelical King created in the midst or center of his circumference sphear extent or * Region out of Nature, also out of Natures Heaven, out

* or *Province.*

out of the *power* of all the seven qualifying or fountain spirits; and that now was the heart in one Hoast, and had in him the quality might power and strength of his *whole* Hoast, and was the fairest amongst them or of them all.

8. Just as the Sonne of God is the heart and *Lif* and strength of all the seven Spirits of God, so is also that *one* King of Angels in his Hoast.

9. And as there are seven principal qualities in the *divine* power out of which the heart of God is generated; so there are also some mighty *Princely* Angels created in each Hoast, according to each Head or chief quality; The number of which I do not *exactly* know, and they are with or near the King, *Leaders* of the other Angels.

10. Here thou must know, that the Angels are *not* all of one quality, neither are they equal or alike one to another in Power and Might: Indeed, *every* Angel hath the power of all the seven qualifying or fountain-spirits, but in every one there is somewhat of one Quality more predominant and strong then another, and according to that quality is he glorified also.

11. For such as the *Salitter* was, in every place, at the time of Creation, such also was the Angel that came forth, and according to *that* quality, which is strongest in an Angel, he is also named and glorified.

12. As the *Flowers* in the Meadowes do every one receive its colour from its quality, and is named also according to its quality, so are the Holy Angels also: some are strongest in the *astringent* quality, and those are of a * Brownish Light, and are nearest of Quality to the Cold.

* Dusky or Grey, or dim white like twilight.

13. And

13. And ſo when the Light of the Sonne of God ſhineth on them, then are they like a browniſh or *purple* flaſh of Lightening very Bright and clear in their quality:

14. Some are of the quality of the *water*, and thoſe are light, like the holy Heaven; and when the light ſhineth on them, then they look like to a *Cryſtalline* Sea.

15. Some are ſtrongeſt in the *Bitter* quality, and they are, like a * green Pretious ſtone, which ſparkleth like a flaſh of Lightening; and when the light ſhineth on them, then they ſhine and appear as a *Greeniſh Red*, as if a Carbuncle did ſhine forth from it, or as if the Life had its Original there.   *or Emeraud.*

16. Some are of the Quality of *Heat*, and they are the Lighteſt and brighteſt of all, *Yellowiſh* and Reddiſh; and when the Light ſhineth on them, they look like the flaſh or Lightening of the Sonne of God.

17. Some are ſtrongeſt in the quality of *Love*, and thoſe are a Glance of the heavenly Joyfulneſſe, very light, and *Bright*, and when the light ſhineth on them, they look like * *Light-Blew*, of a pleaſant Gloſſe Glance or Luſtre.   * *Azure* or *Watchet.*

18. Some are ſtrongeſt in the quality of the *Tone*, or Sound, and thoſe are Light or bright alſo; and when the Light ſhineth on them, they look like the *riſing* of the flaſh of Lightning, as if ſome thing would lift it ſelf aloft there.

19. Some are of the Quality of the *totall* or whole Nature, as a General mixture, and when the light ſhineth on them, they look like the holy *Heaven*, which is formed out of all the Spirits of God.

20. But the King is the heart of all the qualities,

and hath his circumference * *Court* Quarters or Residence in the midst or Center, like a fountain : And as the *Sun* standeth in the midst among the Planets, and is a King of the Stars, and the heart of *Nature* in this world : so great also is a *Cherubin* or King of Angels.

21. And as the other six planets with the Sun are Leaders of Hoasts, and give up or submit their will to the Sun, that it may raign and *work* in them : so all the Angels give up or submit their will to the *King*, and the *Princely* Angels are in *Councel* with the King.

22. But thou must know here, that they all have a *Love-will* one to another, none of them grutcheth the other his Form and *Beauty* : For as it goeth among the spirits of God, so it goeth among these.

23. They all have *joyntly* and equally the Divine Joy, and they equally enjoy the heavenly Food, therein there is no difference.

24. Only in the Colours and *strength* of power there is a difference, but *no* difference at all in the perfection : for every one hath in them the power of all the spirits of God ; therefore when the light of the Sonne of God shineth on them, then each Angels quality sheweth it self by the *Colour*.

25. I have reckoned up onely some few of the forms and colours of them, but there are a *great many* more that might be written down, which I will omit for brevity sake.

26. For as the Deity presenteth it self *infinitely* in its rising up, so there are insearchable many *varieties* of colours and forms among the Angels : I can shew thee no *right* similitude of it in this world but

in

in the *blossoming* field of flowers in *May*, which yet is but a *dead* and Earthly Type.

Of the *Angelical Joy.*

Question.

27. Now it may be asked : *what* then is it, which the Angels do in heaven; or *why*, or to what End and purpose hath God created them ?

Answer.

28. Ye greedy covetous griping persons may observe this , you who in this world *seek* after Pride, State, dignity, Honour, Fame, Glory, Power, Money and Goods, and *squeeze* out the sweat and blood of the poor oppressed and distressed, and spend their Labours upon your Gallantry bravery and statelinesse, and *think* your selves Better then plain and simple Lay-vulgar people, and suppose it is *that* God hath created you for.

Question.

Why hath God created Angel-Princes, and hath not made them all *Equall* , or alike.

Answer.

29. Behold *God is the God of Order :* and as it is, goeth, and boyleth, in his Government in himself, that is, in his Birth or Geniture, and in his rising up, so also is the *order* of the Angels.

30. Now as there are in him, *chiefly* seven qualities, whereby the *whole* Divine Being is driven on,

and

and sheweth it self infinitely in these seven qualities, and yet these seven qualities are the Chief or *Prime* in the infinitenesse, whereby the divine Birth or Geniture stands eternally in its Order unchangeably.

31. And as in the *Midst* or Center of the seven Spirits of God, the heart of Life is generated whence the divine Joy riseth up, *thus* also is the order of Angels.

32. The Angel-Princes were created according to the spirits of God, and the Cherubin according to the heart of God : And as the divine *Being* worketh, so also do the Angels.

33. That quality which riseth up in Gods Being, and chiefly sheweth it self in its *working*, as in the rising up of the Tone or Tune, or of the divine working, wrestling and fighting ; that Angelical Prince, which is most strongly *addicted* to that Quality, begins in his Rank or File and Round, with his Legions ; with singing, ringing forth, dancing, rejoycing and Jubilating.

34. This is *heavenly Musick*, for here every one singeth according to the voice of his quality, and the Prince leadeth the Qnire or *Chorus* ; as a Chantour or singing-Master with his Scholars, and the *King* rejoyceth and Jubilateth with his Angels, to the honour of the great God, and to the encreasing and multiplying of the heavenly Joyes : and that, is in the Heart of God, as a Holy *Sport* or Scene ; and to that end also are they created for the Joy and Honour of God.

35. Now when the heavenly Musick of the Angel riseth up, then, in the heavenly Pomp in the Divine *Salitter* ; there rise up all manner of Vegetations

Spring-

Springings or Sprouts, alſo all manner of figures ſhapes or *Ideas*, and all manner of colours; for the Deity preſenteth ſheweth or diſcovereth it ſelf, in *endleſſe* and unſearchable varieties of kinds, colours, Ideas, forms, and Joyes.

36. Now, that qualifying or fountain-Spirit in the *Deity* which doth ſhew it ſelf then in a ſingular manner with its riſing up, and *Love-wreſtling*; as having become the Prince or Chief of them; that *very* Angel-Prince belonging to it, beginneth inſtantly his heavenly Muſick with his own Legions, according to his Quality, with ſinging, ringing forth, Piping melody, and in all the manners of heavenly *Skill* and Art, which riſeth up in the Spirits of God.

37. But when the Center in the Midſt riſeth up, that is, when the Birth or Geniture of the Sonne of God, ſheweth it ſelf in a ſingular manner, as a *Triumph*; then there riſe up the Muſicks melodies or Joyes, of all the *three* Kingly Governments or Royal Regiments of the whole Creation of all the Angels.

38. What manner of Joy this *muſt* be, let every Soul conſider: I, in my corrupted nature, cannot apprehend it, much leſſe can I write it.

39. By this ſong I invite or Cite the Reader into the other Life; there himſelf will be alſo of that Quire or *Chorus*, and then firſt will he give credit to this ſpirit; what he doth not underſtand here, that he will have there *apparently* in his view.

40. Thou muſt know, that this is not forged out of a Stone; but when the flaſh riſeth up in the Center, *then* the Spirit ſeeth and knoweth it.

41. Therefore look to it, and be not too ſcornfull

in

in this Place, elfe thou wilt be found a fcorner and mocker before God, and then well mayft thou *fare,* as King *Lucifer* did.

Now it may be asked.

Queftion.

What do the Angels then when they fing Not?

Anfwer.

42. Behold! What the Deity doth, that they do alfo : When the Spirits of God *lovingly* generate one in another, and rife up one in another, as in a loving faluting, Embracing, kiffing, and feeding one another : in which Tafte and Smell, the *life* rifeth up, and the eternal refrefhing ; of which thou mayft read before at Large.

43. Then the holy Angels alfo walk and *Converfe* one with another friendlily, gracioufly amiably and bleffedly in the heavenly Circumference or Region, and do behold the wonderful and pleafant form or *profpeft* of heaven, and eat of the gracious amiable bleffed and delicate fruits of *Life.*

Now

Now thou wilt Ask:

Question.

What do they Talk of, one with another?

Answer.

44. Behold! thou Pompous ſtately *lofty* and Proud Man; the world is even *too narrow* for thee here, and thou thinkeſt there is *none* like thee, or Equal to thee: bethink thy ſelf in this, whether thou haſt *in thee* the manner quality or condition of an Angel or of a Devill.

To whom now ſhall I liken the Angels?

45. I will liken them to *little* children, which walk in the fields in *May,* among the *flowers,* and pluck them, and make curious Garlands, and Poſeys, carrying them in their hands *rejoycing,* and alwayes talk together of the ſeveral forms or ſhapes of *curious* flowers, *leading* one another by the hand, when they go to gather flowers.

46. And when they come home, they *ſhew* them to their Parents, and they alſo rejoyce in their children, and are merry and *cheerly* with them.

47. So do the Holy Angels likewiſe, they **take** one another by the *Hand,* and walk together in the
curious

curious *May* of heaven, and parly or talk of the pleafant and fair Spring or *fruits* in the heavenly Pomp, and feed on the *delicate* bleffed fruits of God, and make ufe of the beautiful heavenly Flowers for their play or fport in their *Scenes,* and make curious Garlands, and rejoyce in the delicious pleafant May, of God.

48. Here is nothing but a Cordial or Hearty loving, a meek and gentle love, a friendly courteous difcourfe, a gracious amiable and *bleffed* Society, where the one alwaies delighteth to fee the other, and to honour one another.

49. They know of *no* malice, *cunning* fubtlety or deceit, but the divine fruits and pleafant lovelineffe are *common* among them, one may make ufe of thefe things, *as well* as the other, there is no diffavour or hatred, no Envy, no contrary or *oppofite* will, but their hearts are knit together in Love.

50. In this, the *Deity* hath its higheft Delight, as Parents have in their children, that its dear and beloved children in heaven, behave themfelves fo well, and fo friendlily : for the Deity in it felf playeth *or fporteth* alfo thus, *one* qualifying or fountain-fpirit in the other.

51. And therefore the Angels can do no other, then their Father doth, as alfo our Angelical King JESUS CHRIST teftified, when he was with us on earth, as it is written in the Gofpel, where he faith; *Verily the Sonne can do nothing of himfelf; but what He feeth his Father do, that the Sonne doth alfo,* John 5. 19. Alfo *if you do not convert, and become like children, you cannot come into the Kingdom of heaven,* Matth. 18. 3.

52. Whereby he meaneth, that *our hearts* fhould be knit together in Love, as the Holy Angels of God are, and that we fhould deal friendly courteoufly and kindly one with another, and love one another, and *prevent* one another in kindneffe and *refpects*, as the Angels of God do.

53. *Not* that we fhould *Deceive* and belye one another, and tear the Bread out of others Mouthes for very greedineffe and great Covetoufneffe, neither fhould one *outbrave* another, in Statelineffe, Fafhions, and *deportment*, and fo defpife another who cannot ufe his flie crafty fubtile Devillifh Policy and *Tricks*.

54. O, no : the Angels in heaven do *not* fo, but they love one another, and rejoyce in the Beauty and lovelineffe of others, and none efteemeth or accounteth himfelf excellenter then the other, but *every* one hath his Joy in the other, and rejoyceth in the *others* fair Beauty comely form and Lovelineffe, whence then their love one towards another rifeth up, fo that they lead one another by the Hand, and friendlily Kiffe one another.

Obferve the Depth.

55. As, when the flafh of life rifeth up in the Center of the *Divine power*, wherein all the fpirits of God attain their Life, and highly rejoyce ; there, is a loving and *Holy* Embracing, Kiffing, Tafting, Touching or Feeling, Hearing, Seeing and Smelling. So alfo there is among the Angels ; when the one feeth, heareth, feeleth or toucheth the other, then there rifeth up *in his heart* the flafh of Life, and one fpirit embraceth the other ; as it is in the Deity.

I i

Obferve here, the Ground, and higheft Myftery of Gods Angels.

56. If thou wilt now know, from *whence* their Love, Humility and friendlineffe cometh, which rifeth up in their heart, then Obferve that which followeth :

57. Every Angel is Conftituted , as the *whole* Deity is, and is as a *little* God.   For when God conftituted the Angels, he conftituted or framed them *out of Himfelf*.

58. Now God is the fame in one place, as he is in another, God is *every where* the Father and Sonne and Holy Ghoft.

59. In thefe three Names and *Powers*, ftandeth Heaven and this world , and all whatfoever thy heart can think upon : and though thou fhouldft draw a little Circle, which thou canft hardly look into or which thou canft hardly difcern, even leffe then the *fmalleft Point* thou canft imagine: yet even *in that* is the *whole* Divine power, and the Sonne of God is generated *therein*, and the Holy Ghoft *therein* goeth forth from the Father and the Sonne ; if not in Love, then in wrath, as it is written, *with the holy thou art Holy, and with the perverfe thou art perverfe*, Pfal. 18. 26.

60. They which *ftir up* the wrath of God upon themfelves, which wrath ftandeth alfo in *all* the fpirits of God, in that place, where it is awakened, ftirred up, or *provoked* : On the other fide , where the

the love of God is awakened or ftirred up, there it ftandeth alfo in the *full* Birth or Geniture of the *whole* Deity of or in the place or thing wherein it is awakened.

61. And herein there is *no* difference, the Angels are created one as well as another, *all* out of the Divine *Salitter* of the heavenly Nature : onely this is the difference betwixt them ; that when God conftituted them, each Qcality in the great Motion ftood in the *higheft* Geniture or rifing up.

62. Hence it is come to paffe, that the Angels are of *various* and Manifold Qualities, and have feveral colours and Beauties, and yet all out of or from God.

63. Yet *every* Angel hath *all* the qualities of God in him, but one of them is ftrongeft in him, according to which he is Named, and glorified in that Quality.

64. Now, as the qualities in God *alwaies* generate, raife up, and heartily Love, the one the other, and the one alwayes getteth its *life* from the other ; And as the flafh in the fweet water rifeth up in the heat, from whence the Life and the Joy have their Original : fo it is alfo in an Angel, his *internal* Birth or Geniture is no otherwife then that which is diftinct from him or without him, in God.

65. And, as the Sonne of God, without or diftinct from the Angels, is generated in the middle or Centrall fountain *Spring*, in the heat, in the fweet water, out of or from *all* the feven fpirits of God, and re-enlighteneth back again all the feven Spirits of God ; *whence* they have their Life and Joy.

66. So alfo in like manner, the Sonne of God in an Angel, is generated in the Angels middle or cen-

trall

trall fountain Spring of the *heart* in the heat in the
fweet water ; and re-enlightneth back again all the
feven qualifying fpirits of *that* Angel.

67. And as the Holy Ghoft goeth forth from
the Father and the Sonne, and formeth, Imageth
figureth or frameth and loveth *All* : even fo the Holy Ghoft goeth forth in the Angel, *into* his fellow Brethren, and Loveth them, and rejoyceth with
them.

68. For there is no difference between the Spirits
of God and the Angels, but *only this* ; that the Angels are *Creatures,* and their *Corporeal* Being hath a
beginning ; but their *power,* out of which they are
created, is God himfelf, and is from Eternity, and
abideth in Eternity.

69. Therefore their agility is as nimble and fwift
as the *Thoughts* of a Man, where ever they would be
there alfo they are Inftantly ; moreover they can be
Great or Small, as they pleafe.

70. *And this is the true Being
of God in Heaven, yea Heaven it
felf ;* If thy Eyes were opened, thou fhouldft fee
it plainly and clearly on Earth in *that* place, where
thou art at prefent.

71. For feeing God can let the fpirit of Man fee
it, which is yet ftaying in the Body, and can reveal
or manifeft himfelf to him *in the flefh,* furely he can
well do it alfo when he is, out of the flefh, if he pleafeth.

72. O thou finful Houfe of *this* world, how art
thou encompaffed with *Hell* and *Death,* awake, the
hour of thy Regeneration is at hand, the Day-break-
eth

eth, the Day-spring Dawning or Morning-Redneſſe sheweth it self.

73. O thou Dumb and Dead world, *why* doſt thou require or demand *Signes* and Wonders? Is thy whole body chilled and benummed? wilt thou not awake from sleep?

74. Behold a *great sign* is given Thee, but thou sleepeſt and seeſt it not: Therefore the Lord will give Thee a sign in his zeal or Jealouſie which thou haſt awaked and *provoked* with thy *Sins.*

Of the whole Heavenly delight-fulneſſe of all the Three Kingdomes of Angels.

75. Here the Spirit sheweth, that where every Angel is conſtituted ſtated or ſettled, there *that Place* in the heavenly Nature, wherein, and out of which he is become a creature, is his *own* ſeat; which he poſſeſſeth by Right of Nature, as long as he abideth *in Gods Love.*

76. For it is the Place, which he hath had from *Eternity,* before he was become a Creature, and that *Salitter* ſtood in the ſame place, out of which he exiſted, and *therefore* that ſeat remaineth to him, and is his, by right of Nature, as long as he moveth in Gods Love.

77. But thou muſt not think, as if God were tyed to it, and cannot or may not *expell* him from thence, if he ſhould move or ſtirre otherwiſe, then God had conſtituted ſettled or *ſtated* him at firſt.

78. For

78. For as long as he abideth in obedience, and in love; the Place is *his*, by right of Nature; but when he elevateth himſelf and kindleth that place in the wrathful fire; then he ſets his Fathers Houſe on fire, and becomes a contrary will or *oppoſite* to the Place, out of which he is made, and maketh TWO out of that, which was ONE, before his Elevation.

79. Now when he doth ſo, then he *keeps* his corporeal Right of Nature to himſelf, and that Place alſo keepeth *its* own to it ſelf : but ſeeing the *Creature*, which hath a beginning, will oppoſe or ſet it ſelf againſt the Firſt Being, which was before the Creature was, which had no beginning, and will needs ſpoil the Place, which is *none* of its making, wherein it was created a creature in the Love, and will *turn* that love into a wrath-fire, then it is equal and juſt, that the Love ſhould ſpew up the wrathfire forth together with the Creature.

† Lawes Cuſtomes Statutes Ordinances and Polities.

80. From hence alſo the †RIGHTS in this world exiſt or have their original. For when a ſonne reſiſteth his Father, and ſtriketh his Father, then he loſeth his Fatherly or Paternal *inheritance*, and his Father may thruſt him out of his Houſe : but ſo long as he continueth in obedience to his Father, the Father hath no right authority or Lawfull Power to Diſ-inherit him.

* *Jus.*

81. This worldly * *Right* taketh its original from Heaven; as alſo many other worldly Rights, which are written in the Books of *Moſes*, take their beginning and original from the *Divine Nature* in Heaven, which I ſhall demonſtrate plainly in its due place from the true ground in the Deity.

Now ;

Now ; one might Object and say ;

Objection.

Then an **Angel** is fully bound and tyed to that place, in which he is created, and must not stir, nor can stir from thence.

Answer.

82. No : as little as the *Spirits of God* are or will be tyed in their rifing up; that they fhould not move one among another, fo little are the *Angels* alfo tyed to their place at all.

83. For as the fpirits of God rife up continually one in another, and have a Sport or Game of Love in their Birth or Geniture, and yet every fpirit keepeth his natural *feat*, or place, in the Birth or Geniture of God, wherein it *never cometh to paffe*, that the Heat is changed into the Cold, or the Cold into the Heat, but each keepeth its natural place or *Pofture*, and the one rifeth up in the other, from whence the life hath its Original.

84. So the Holy Angels move walk or *converfe* in all the three Kingdoms, one among another, whereby they conceive, or receive their *conceptions*, one from the other; *that is*, from the others Beauty comely form, friendlineffe courtefie and vertue, every one receiveth his higheft joy, and yet *each* keepeth his naturall feat or Place, in *which* he is become a creature, for his *own* propriety.

85. Like one in this world, that when he hath a dear and near kinfman, which *returns* home from
forraign

forraign Parts of the world, whom he had a very *hearty* defire, and earneft longing to *fee* ; there is joy and friendly faluting and bidding welcome, alfo a friendly loving difcourfe or conference between them, and fo he treateth this loving and wellcome *Gueft* in the beft manner that he can : yet this is but cold water, in *refpect* of the Heavenly.

86. And *thus* the Holy Angels do one towards another ; when the Army or Company of one Kingdome cometh to the other, or when the Army or Company of one princely Quality cometh to an Army or Company of another princely Quality, there is nothing but meer loving Entertainment faluting and *embracing* reception ; a very gracious amiable and bleffed difcourfe and friendly refpect, a very gracious amiable *bleſſed* and loving walking and playing together ; a moft *chaft* and humble exercife ; a friendly kiffing and leading one another up and down, here beginneth the lovely Quire and fet *Dancing*,

87. Like little Children, when they go in *May* to gather *flowers*, where many often meet together, there they talk and *confer* friendly, and pluck or gather many fundry forts of flowers.

88. Now when this is done, they carry thofe flowers in their Hands, and *begin* a fportfull Dance, and fing from the joy of their Heart rejoycing. Thus alfo do the Angels in Heaven, when the *Forraign* Armies or Companies meet together,

89. For the corrupted Nature in this world, *labours* in its utmoft power and diligence, that it might bring forth heavenly forms, and many times little children might be their Parents School-mafters and *Teachers*, if Parents could but underftand, or would

but

but take *notice* of them; But now adayes the Corruption is Lamentable both with Young, and Old, and the Proverb is verified,

**Wie die Alten Sungen,
So Lerneten die Jungen.**

*As the Old ones Sing,
So th' Young Learn to Ring.*

90. By this high *humility* of the Angels, the Spirit admonisheth the children of this world, that they should view and *examine* themselves, whether they bear such a love one to another? whether there be such humility among them? what kind of Angels do they think they are? and whether are they like to *these* or no? Being they have in them in possession, the *third* Angelical Kingdome.

91. Behold the Spirit will here a little present before thy Eyes, what *manner* of love, humility, and courteous friendlinesse there is in thee, thou fair Angelical *Bride*; behold I pray thee thy Dresse, Ornament, and Attire, what excellent delight and pleasure may thy *Bridegroom* take in thee, thou beloved Angel, that dancest daily with the Devil,

I.

92. First, If one be now adayes a *little* prefer'd or advanced, and getteth but a little while into an Office, then, others are no more so good as he, or fit for his company that are in *no* preferment, he counteth the vulgar or Lay-Man his Footstool, he instantly endeavoureth by cunning and craft to get the vulgar or Lay-mans *Goods* under his disposing, if he

K k   cannot

cannot compasse it by Tricks, and *designs*, then he doth it by force, to satisfie his high-mindednesse.

93. If a simple man cometh before him, that *cannot place* his words handsomely, then he taketh him up short, as if he were a *Dogg*: and if he hath any businesse before him, then he regards only *those* that are of *worldly Esteem*, and lets them carry the cause, *Right or Wrong*: Take heed friend; what manner of princely Angel indeed thou art: Thou wilt find it well enough in the following Chapter, concerning the fall of the Devil; that will be *thy* Looking-Glasse to see thy self in.

II.

94. Secondly, If one now adayes hath learnt more in *worldly Sciences*, or studied more then the vulgar or Lay-man, in an instant, no vulgar or Lay-man is to be compared to him, because he cannot *Expresse* himself, or speak according to Art, he hath *no skill* in the others proud Gauge and Garb.

95. In brief, the *Simple* plain man must be his *Fool*, whereas he himself is indeed a Proud Angel, and is in *Love* but a *dead* Man. This sort of *Party* will have its *Looking-Glasse* in the following Chapter.

III.

96. Thirdly, If one be *Richer* now adayes, then the other, then the *Poorer* Man is counted the Fool: and if he can wear but better and more fashionable *Clothes* or Apparel then his Neighbour, then the poorer man is *no more* worthy or good enough to be in his Company.

97. And so the Old Song is now adayes in full force and Practice: which is this;

**Der Reich den Armen Zwinget,
Und Ihm sein sweisse abdringet,
Daß nur sein Grosse klinget.**

*The Rich man doth Constrain the Poor,
And Squeezeth out his Sweat so sore,
Tha.'s own great Wealth abroad may roar.*

These Angels also are invited as Guests to the next Chapter for their Looking-Glasse to see themselves in.

IIII.

98. Fourthly, There is for the generality such a *devillish* pride and statelinesse, and such over-topping one another, such despising, belying, entrapping circumventing over-reaching cheating deceiving betraying, extorting Usury, coveting, envying and hating one another: that the world *burneth* now as in the hellish fire: Woe, woe for Ever!

99. O World *where* is thy Humility? *where* is thy Angelical Love? *where* is thy courteous friend-linesse? At that very instant when the Mouth saith, God save thee; then if the *Heart* were seen it might be said; Beware, look to thy self: for it bids the Devil take thee.

100. O thou Excellent Angelical Kingdom, how comely dress'd and Adorned wert thou once? how hath the Devill turn'd thee into a *murtherous* Denne? Dost thou suppose thou standest now in the flower of thy Beauty and Glory? No! thou standest in

the

the *midſt* of Hell : if thine Eyes were but opened, thou wouldſt ſee it.

101. Or doſt thou think, that the Spirit is *drunken,* and doth not ſee thee ? O, it ſeeth thee very well : thy ſhame ſtandeth quite naked before God, thou art an unchaſt wanton laſcivious woman, and goeſt a whoring day and night, and yet thou *ſayſt,* I am a chaſt Virgin.

102. O, how fair a Looking-Glaſſe art thou, in the preſence of the Holy Angels : do but ſmell to thy ſweet Love and Humility, doth it not ſmell or favour juſt like *Hell* ? All theſe parties are invited as Gueſts, to the following Chapters.

Of the Kingly Primacy, or of the power and Authority of the Three Angelical Kings.

103. As the Deity in its Being is Threefold, in that the Exit out of the ſeven Spirits of God ſheweth and generateth it ſelf as *Threefold,* viz. Father Sonne and Holy Ghoſt, *One* God ; wherein the whole Divine Power conſiſteth, and all whatſoever is therein ; and they are the *Three Perſons* in the Deity, and yet are not a divided Being, but in one another as *one.*

104. So alſo when God moved himſelf and Created the *Angels,* there came to be *Three* ſpeciall Angels out of the beſt Kernel of Nature, out of the Being of the *Ternary* in the *Nature* of God, and in ſuch power authority and Might as the Ternary in the
the

the seven Spirits of God, and is again the Life and Heart of all the seven Spirits.

105. And so also, the *Three* Angelical Kings, *each* of them in the manner kind and Nature of his Hoast or Army, is risen up, and is a Natural Lord of his Place or Region, over the Regiment or *Dominion* of his Angels; but the Ternary of the Deity retaineth that *Place*, which is unalterable or unchangeable to it self: and the King retaineth the Dominion of the Angels.

106. Now as the Ternary of the Deity is one only Being or Substance in all *Parts* in the whole Father, and is united together, as the Members in Mans *Body*, and all places are as *one* Place, though one place may have a different condition frame and * *Constitution*, distinct from the other, as also the members of men have; yet it is the Body of God.

* *Office* or *Function*.

107. So also are the Three Angelical Kingdomes *united* one in another, and not each *severed* asunder: No Angelical King ought to say: This is my Kingdome: or that there ought *no other* King to come thereinto; though indeed it is his first *beginning* original natural inheritance; and remaineth also to be his: yet *all* other Kings and Angels are his true Naturall Brothers, generated out of or from one Father, and do inherit their Fathers Kingdom.

108. And as the qualifying or fountain Spirits of God, have *each* of them the Natural seat or possession of its Birth or *Geniture*, and retaineth its Naturall *Place* to it self, and yet is, together with the other spirits, the one only Spirit; so that if the other were not, *that* would not be neither, and thus also they rise up One in the other.

109. So it is also with the Chief or *Principall* of the Holy Angels in his Constitution; and is in no

other

other *manner* then as it is in God ; and therefore they live all friendlily peaceably and blessedly one *with another*, in their Fathers Kingdom, as loving dear brethren ; there are no Bounds or Bars how far any should go, and how far not.

Queſtion.

Upon what do the Angels walk? or upon what do they ſtay or ſet their Feet ?

Anſwer.

110. I will here ſhew thee the right Ground, and it is *no* otherwiſe in Heaven, then as thou here findeſt in the letter, for the Spirit looketh into this Deep, very unremoveably or *ſteadfaſtly*, alſo it is very apprehenſible.

111. The *whole* Nature of the Heaven, ſtandeth in the power of the ſeven qualifying or fountain-ſpirits, and in the ſeventh conſiſteth *Nature* or the apprehenſibility of all the Qualities : this now is very lightſome and ſolid as a Cloud, but very *tranſparent*, and ſhining, like a Cryſtalline Sea, ſo that a man can ſee through and through it all : Yet the whole depth upward and downward is wholly *thus*.

112. Now the Angels alſo, have ſuch Bodies, but more dry and cloſe compacted or incorporated together, and their body alſo is the kernel, of or out of Nature, even the beſt or faireſt ſplendor and *brightneſſe* of or out of Nature.

113. Now

113. Now upon the seventh spirit of God their Foot doth stay, which is solid like a Cloud, and clear and bright as a Crystalline Sea, wherein they walk upward and downward, which way soever they please. For their Agility or Nimblenesse is as swift as the *Divine power* it self is, yet one Angel is more swift then another, and that answerably according to their Quality.

114. In that seventh spirit of Nature, rise up also the Heavenly fruits and colours, and whatsoever is apprehensible or comprehensible, and is like to such a * *Forme*, or manner, as if the Angels did dwell *betwixt* Heaven and Earth in the Deep, where they ascend and descend, and where ever they are, there their foot resteth, *as if* it stood upon the Earth.

* *Text Forma.*

115. Antiquity hath represented the Angels in Picture, like Men with Wings, but they have *no need* of any Wings, yet they have Hands and Feet, as Men have, but after a Heavenly manner and kind.

116. At the Day of the Resurrection from the Dead, there will be no difference between the Angels and Men, they will be of one and the *same kind of forme*; which I shall shew plainly in its due place, and our *King* JESUS CHRIST clearly testifieth the same, where he saith, *In the Resurrection they are like the Angels of God,* Matth. 22. 30.

Of

Of the Great Glory Brightneſſe and Beauty of the Three Angelical Kings.

117. This is the very *Billet* or Staffe, which is flung at the *Dog*, to make him run away, becauſe of this Song, Lord *Lucifer* could pull and tear off the Hair of his Head and Beard for grief ſorrow and Pain.

Obſerve here the depth.

Concerning the King or Great Prince
MICHAEL.

118. MICHAEL ſignifieth the Great *ſtrength* or power of God ; and beareth the name operatively actually and in *Deed* : For he is incorporated or conſolidated together, out of the ſeven qualifying or *fountain* ſpirits, as out of a Kernel or ſeed of them, and ſtandeth here now, as in the ſtead of God the Father.

119. The meaning is *not*, that He is God the Father, who conſiſteth in the ſeven ſpirits of the *whole* Deep, and is not creaturely ; but, the meaning is, that in Nature among the Creatures there is alſo ſuch a kind of Creature, as is *like* God the Father,

as

as he is in the seven qualifying or fountain spirits, which is to raign among the *Creatures.*

119. For when God made himself creaturely, then he made himself creaturely according to his *Ternarie*; And as in God, the *Ternarie* is the greatest and chiefest, and yet his wonderful proportion, form and variety *cannot* be measured, in that he sheweth himself in his operation so *variously* and manifoldly. So also he hath created Three principal Angel-Princes, according to the *highest* Primacy of his *Ternarie.*

120. After that, he created the Princely-Angels, according to the seven qualifying or fountain spirits, answerable to their Quality, *viz.* GABRIEL, an Angel or Prince of the Tone, sound, or of swift or speedy Messages; as also R A P H A E L, and others beside in the Kingdom of MICHAEL.

121. Thou must not understand this, as if these Royal Angels were to Rule in the *Deity,* that is, in the seven qualifying or fountain-spirits of *God,* which are without or distinct from the creatures; no, but each over his Creatures, or the creatures of his *own* Dominion.

122. For as the *Ternarie* of God raigneth over the infinite or *Endlesse,* Being and over the figures and several *various* forms or Ideas in the Deity, and changeth varieth and Imageth or frameth the same.

123. So also are the three Angelical Kings, Lords over *their* Angels even to the heart and deepest Ground, though they *cannot* corporeally or Bodily vary or change themselves, as God himself *can,* who hath created them; yet they rule them (*viz.* the Angels) Corporeally, and are bound or united to them; as body and soul are bound one to another.

124. For

124. For the King is their *Head,* and they are the *Members* of the King; and the * Qualifying or fountain Princely Angels are the Kings *Counsellours* or † *Officers* in his Affaires, like the five Senses in Man, or as the Hands and Feet, or the Mouth, Nostrils, Eyes and Ears, whereby the King *executeth* or accomplisheth his Affairs.

* or facultating potentiating.

† instruments in Employment.

125. Now as all Angels are bound to the King, so is the King also bound to *God* his Creator, as Body and Soul : the Body, signifieth God; and the Soul the Angelical King, which is in the Body of God, and is become a *Creature* in the Body of God, and abideth eternally in the Body of God, as the soul doth in its Nest, and therefore also hath God so highly glorified him, as his own *propriety,* or as the Soul is glorified in the Body.

126. Thus the King or Great Prince *Michael* Looks like God the Father in his glorification, clarity, or brightnesse, and is a King and prince of God upon the *Mount* of God, and hath his Office in the Deep, wherein he is created.

127. That circumference or space, Region or Province, wherein he and his Angels are created, is *his* Kingdom, and he is a *loving* Sonne of God the Father in Nature, a *Creaturely* Sonne, in whom the Father delighteth.

128. Thou must *not* compare him with the Heart or Light of God, which is in the whole Father, which hath neither Beginning nor End, as well as God the Father himself.

129. For this Prince *is* a Creature, and *hath* a Beginning, but he is *in* God the Father, and is bound and united with him *in his Love,* as his dearly beloved Sonne, whom he hath created out of himself.

130. There-

130. Therefore he hath set upon him the *Crown* of Honour, of Might Power and Authority, so that there is in heaven no higher nor Excellenter, nor mightier then He is, *except* God himself in his *Ternarie.* And this is one King; rightly described, with a true ground, in the knowledge of the Spirit.

Of the second King LUCIFER, so now called, because of his Fall.

131. King LVCIFER, shut thy Eyes here a little, and stop thy Ears a little, that thou mayst neither hear nor see, or else thou wilt be horribly *ashamed*, that another sitteth upon thy Seat, and so thy shame shall be fully discovered yet before the End of the world, which thou hast kept so closely *concealed* in secret and suppressed, ever since the begining of the world, wheresoever thou couldst: I will now describe thy Kingly Primacie, not for thee, but for the *benefit* of Man.

132. This High and Mighty, Glorious and Beauteous King, *lost* his right name in his Fall : for he is now called LVCIFER, that is, One carried forth or expell'd out of the Light of God.

127. His name was *not so* at the beginning : for he was a creaturely Prince or King of the Heart of God in the bright Light, even the Brightest among the *three* Kings of Angels.

Of * his Creation.

134. As *Michael* is Created according to the quality manner and property of God the Father ; So was *Lucifer* Created according to the quality, condition, and Beauty of God the Sonne, and was bound to and united with him in Love, as a dear Sonne or Heart, and his heart also ſtood in the *Center* of Light, as if he had been God himſelf ; and his Beauty or Brightneſſe tranſcended all.

135. For his circumference conception or chiefeſt mother, was, the Sonne of God, and there he ſtood as a King or Prince of God.

136. His Court, Province, place, Region or Quarters, wherein he dwelt with his whole Army or Company, and wherein he is become a *Creature*, and which was his Kingdome ; is the created Heaven and this world, *wherein* we dwell with our King JESUS CHRIST.

137. For our King ſitteth in Divine *Omnipotence*, where King *Lucifer did* ſit, and on the Kingly throne of *expulſed* Lucifer, and the Kingdome of King Lucifer is now become HIS ; O Prince *Lucifer*, how doſt thou reliſh that ?

138. Now as God the Father is bound and united in great love with his Sonne ; ſo was King Lucifer alſo bound with King *Michael* in great love, as One heart or One God, for the fountain or wellſpring of the Sonne of God *hath* reach'd even into the heart of Lucifer.

139. Onely that the Light, which he had in his Body, he had it for his *own* propriety, which while

it

it shone with or agreeable to the Light of the Sonne of God, which was Externally, without or distinct from him, they both qualified incorporated and united together as one thing, though they were two, yet they were bound or united together, as Body and Soul.

140. And as the light of God raigneth in all the *powers* of the Father, so he also did raign in all *his* Angels, as a mighty King of God, and did wear on his Head the fairest Crown of Heaven.

141. Here at present I will leave him a little *scope*, because I shall have so much to do concerning him, in the *second* Chapter. Let him prance a little yet, here, in the *Crown*, it shall suddenly be plucked away from him.

Of the third Angelical King called URIEL.

142. This gracious amiable Blessed Prince and King, hath his *Name* from the Light, or from the flash, or going forth of the Light, which signifieth rightly, *God the Holy Ghost.*

143. For as the Holy Ghost goeth forth from the Light, and formeth figureth and *Imageth* all, and raigneth in all; such also is the power and gracious amiable blessednesse of a Cherubin; who is the King and heart of all his Angels; that is, when his Angels do but *behold* him, they are all then affected and *touch'd* with the will of their King.

144. For, As the will of the heart affecteth and stirs all the members of the Body, so that the whole
Body

Body doth as the *Heart* hath *Decreed* or concluded: Or as the Holy Ghost riseth up in the Center of the Heart, and enlightneth all the Members in the *whole* Body : so the Cherubin with his whole Glance or Lustre and will, *affecteth* all his Angels, so that they all are together, as one Body, and the *King* is the heart therein.

145. Now this glorious and Beautiful Prince is Imaged and framed according to the kind and *quality* of the Holy Ghost, and is indeed a glorious and fair Prince of God, and is united with the other Princes in Love, as *one* heart.

146. These are now the *Three* Princes of God in the Heaven. And when the *Flash* of *life*, that is, the Sonne of God, riseth up in the middle or central circle in the qualifying or fountain spirits of God, and sheweth it self triumphantly, then the Holy Ghost also riseth upward triumphantly : In this rising up, the Holy *Trinity* also riseth up in the heart of these three Kings, and each of them triumpheth also according to his kind and Quality.

147. In this rising up, the Armies or Companies of *all* the Angels of the *whole* Heaven become triumphant and joyfull, and that Melodious *TE DEUM LAUDAMUS* (WE PRAISE THEE O GOD) riseth up.

148. In this rising up of the heart, the *Mercurius* in the heart, is stirred up or awakened, as also in the whole *Salitter* of Heaven there riseth up in the Deity, the *miraculous* wonderful and fair Beautiful Imaging of heaven in several manifold various colours and manners, and each spirit presenteth it self in its own peculiar form.

149. I

149. I can compare it with Nothing save onely with the most * *Pretious* Stones or Jewels ; as

| a Jerubin. Cherubins. | a *Rubie's,* b *Emeraud's,* c *Topaze's,* d *Onix'es, Saphir's, Diamonds, Jasper's,* e *Jacinct's, Ametist's,* f *Beril's,* g *Sardis'es,* h *Carbuncles.* |
| c Delfin. Topazes. | |

and such † *Like.*

* Such as are mentioned, Exod. 28. 17. & Ch. 39. 10. Rev. 21. 19.
a or Sardius'es.
b or Chrysoprasus'es.
d or Sardonix'es.
e or Ligure's.

for Turkoise's. g or Achate's or Calcedonie's. h or Chrysolichus'es. † as Opal's, Granat's, Vermilion-stones, Gold-stones, &c.

150. In *such* manner and Colours, the * Heaven of Gods Nature sheweth or presenteth it self in the rising up of the spirits of God : and now when the Light of the Sonne of God *shineth* therein, then it is like a Bright clear *Sea* of the colours of the abovementioned Pretious Stones or Jewels.

* or *Gods Nature's Heaven.*

Of the wonderful proportion, alteration or variation, and rising up of the Qualities in the heavenly Nature.

151. Seeing then the Spirit giveth the *form* and manner of Heaven to be known ; I cannot chuse but write it thus down, and let his will be done, who will have it so.

152. And although the Devil will raise scorners and mockers to *vilipe* it, I do not much regard that: I am satisfied with this gracious amiable and blessed *Revelation* of God ; they may mock so long, till they find it by experience with Eternal Shame, then the fountain of woe Lamentation and sorrow will surely *Gnaw* them.

153. Also I have not gone up to Heaven, and *beheld*

held it with my fleshly Eyes, much leffe hath any told it me ; For though an Angel fhould come, *and tell it me*, yet I could not apprehend or *conceive* it without enlightening from God, much *leffe* believe it.

154. For I fhould alwayes ftand in Doubt, whether it were a good Angel, fent of God or no, feeing the Devil can transform or cloath himfelf in the form of an Angel of light, to feduce Men, **2** *Corinth.* 11. 14.

155. But becaufe it is *generated* in the Center or Circle of Life, as a bright fhining light, like unto the heavenly Birth, or rifing up of the Holy Ghoft, with a fiery driving or impulfe of the fpirit, therefore I cannot refift or withftand it, though the *world* alwaies make a mock of me for it.

156. The Spirit teftifieth, that there is yet a very little time remaining, and then the Flafh in the whole circle of this world, will rife up, to which end this fpirit is a fore-runner, *Meffenger,* and Proclaimer of the Day.

157. And then whatfoever man, is not found in the *Birth* of the Holy Ghoft at that time ; in him the Birth will never rife at all, but he abideth in the quality or fource of darkneffe, as a dead hard Flint ftone, in which the fource or quality of fierceneffe wrath and corruption rifeth up Eternally.

158. And there he will be a mocker eternally in the Birth of the hellifh *Abomination* : for whatfoever quality the Tree is of, fuch alfo is its fruit.

159. Thou liveft betwixt Heaven and Hell, into whichfoever thou *foweft*, in that thou fhalt *reap* alfo, and thar will be thy food in Eternity : If thou foweft fcorn and contempt, thou wilt alfo reap fcorn
and

and contempt, and that will be thy food.

160. Therefore, O child of Man! have a care, truſt not too much upon *worldly* wiſdome, it is blind, and is born blind, but when the flaſh of life is generated *therein*, then it is no more blind, but ſeeth.

161. For, *John* 3.7. Chriſt ſaith; *You muſt be born anew, or elſe you cannot enter into the Kingdome of heaven.*

162. Truly it muſt be generated in ſuch a manner, in the * Holy Ghoſt; which riſeth up in the ſweet ſpring or fountain-water of the heart, in the Flaſh.

* the printed Copie Holineſſe of God.

163. *And therefore hath Chriſt ordained or Inſtituted the Baptiſm or New Birth or Regeneration of the Holy Ghoſt, in the Water, becauſe the birth of the light riſeth up in the ſweet water in the * Heart.*

* printed Copie, Brain,

164. Which is a very great myſtery, and hath been alſo kept *ſecret* from all men ſince the beginning of the world, *till now* : which I will demonſtrate and deſcribe plainly in its due place.

Now Obſerve the Form and Poſture of Heaven.

165. When thou beholdeſt this world, thou haſt a *Type* of heaven;

M m   I. The

I. The *Stars* fignifie or denote the Angels : for as the ftars muft continue unaltered, till, to the End of this Time, fo the *Angels* alfo in the *Eternal Time* of heaven muft remain unaltered for ever.

166. II. The *Elements* fignifie or denote the wonderfull proportion variety *change* and alteration of the form and pofture of Heaven : For as the Deep between the Starres and Earth alwaies alter and change in their *form*, fuddenly it is fair bright and Light, fuddenly it is lowry and dark; now wind, then rain; now fnow, fuddenly the Deep is Blew or *Azure*, fuddenly greenifh, by and by whitifh, then fuddenly again Dusky.

167. Thus alfo is the change and alteration of *Heaven*, into many feveral colours and *forms*, but not in fuch a manner and kind as in this world, but all, *according* to the rifing up of the Spirits of God, and the Light of the Sonne of God fhineth therein Eternally : But the rifing up in the birth differs in the *Degrees* more at one time then at another.

And therefore the wonderful wifdome of God is incomprehenfible.

168. III. The *Earth* fignifieth or denoteth, the Heavenly Nature, or the feventh * fpirit of Nature, in which the Idea's, or *Images* forms and Colours rife up :

169. IIII. And the *Birds or Fowles Fifhes and Beafts* fignifie or denote the feveral forms or fhapes of figures in Heaven.

170. Thou art to know this, for the fpirit in the Flafh teftifieth the fame, that in Heaven there arife

all

all manner of figures or shapes like the Beasts Fowles Birds and Fishes of this world, but in a *heavenly* form or manner, clarity or brightnesse and kind, as also all manner of Trees, Plants and Flowers.

171. But as they rise, so they go away again, for they are not incorporated or compacted together, as the *Angels* are : for these figures are so formed in the Birth of the rising qualities in the spirit of Nature, or *Nature-spirit.*

172. If a figure be Imaged in a spirit, so that it it *subsisteth* ; and if another spirit wrestleth with this, aud gets the *better*, then it comes to be divided, and indeed changed or altered, all according to the *kind* of the qualities ;

And this is in God as a holy Sport Play or Scene.

173. *Therefore* also the Creatures, as Beasts, Fowls or Birds Fishes and Worms in this world ; are not created to an Eternal Being, but to a *transitory* one, as the figures in Heaven also *passe away.*

174. This I set down here onely for a manuduction or introduction : you will find it described more at large, concerning the *Creation* of this world.

The

The Thirteenth Chapter.

Of the terrible, dolefull and Lamentable miferable Fall of the Kingdome of Lucifer.

I.

I Would have all proud, covetous, envious, and wrathfull men *invited* to look into this Glaffe; and there they will fee the original of their pride, covetoufneffe, envy and wrath, alfo the *iffue* and final requital or wages thereof.

2. The *Learned* have produced many and various Monfters concerning the beginning of Sin, and Original of the Devil, and fcuffled one with another about it; every one of them, thought he had the Axe by the Handle, yet it continued hidden from them *all*, till this very time.

3. But fince it will henceforth be *fully* revealed, as in a clear Looking-Glaffe, therefore it may well be conceived, *that the Great Day of the Revelation of God is now near at hand,* wherein the fierceneffe and the kindled fire will be *feparated* from the Light.

4. Therefore let none make himfelf ftark blind,
for

for *The time of the Restitution, of whatsoever man hath lost, is now near at Hand : the Day Dawneth, or, the Morning-Redness breaketh forth ; It is high Time to awake from sleep.*

Question.

Now it may be Asked :

What is the source or fountain of the first Sin of Lucifers Kingdom?

Answer.

5. Here we must *again* take in Hand the highest depth of the Deity ; and see, Out of what, King Lucifer, became a Creature, or what was the first source or fountain of Evil or *Malice* in him ?

6. The Devil and his *crew* continually excuse themselves, and so do all wicked men, which are begotten in corruption, saying ; God doth them *wrong*, in thrusting them out or rejecting them.

7. Nay, this present world doth dare to say, that God hath *Decreed* or concluded it so in his *predestinate* purpose and counsel ; that some men should be *Saved*, and some should be *Damned*, and say, to

that

that end also God hath rejected Prince *Lucifer*, that he should be a spectacle of Gods *wrath*.

8. As if Hell or Malice and Evil, *had been* from Eternity, and that it was in Gods predestinate purpose, that Creatures should and *must* be therein; and so they pull and *hale* and bestir themselves to prove it by *Scripture*, though indeed they neither have the knowledge of the *true* God, nor the *understanding* of the Scriptures: though some erroneous things also are *brewed* from the Scriptures.

9. Christ saith, *the Devil was a murtherer and Lyar from the beginning, and did not stand in the Truth*, John 8. 44. But being these Justifiers and Disputers assist the Devil so stedfastly, and *pervert* Gods truth, and change it into Lies, in that, they *make* of God a thirsty and fierce wrathful Devil, and such a one, as hath created and still willeth Evil, and so all of them, together with the Devil, are *joyntly* murtherers and Lyars.

10. For, as the Devil is the *Founder* and Father of Hell and Damnation, and hath himself built and *prepared* for himself the Hellish *quality* to be his Royal Seat; so also such Writers and *Scriblers* are the *Master*-Builders of Lies and Damnation, who help to confirm and Establish the Devils Lies, and to make of the Merciful loving and friendly God, a murtherer and furious *Destroyer*, and so pervert and turn the truth of God into Lies.

11. For God saith in the Prophet:

As true as I live, I have no delight or pleasure, in the death of a Sinner,

ner, but that he turn and live,
Ezek. 33. 11. And in the *Psalms* it is thus; *thou art not a God, that haft plea-sure in wickednesse,* Psal. 5. 5.

12. Besides, God hath given Lawes to man, and hath *forbidden* the Evil, and *commanded* the Good. Now if God would have the Evil, and also the Good, then he should be at Odds with himself, and it would follow, that there would be destruction or destructivenesse in the *Deity*, one quality running counter against the other, and the one spoiling and corrupting the other.

13. Now how all this is come to passe, or how *wickednesse* hath taken its First Source, original and beginning, I will declare in the highest simplicity in the greatest depth.

14. To which End the spirit inviteth and citeth, summoneth or *warneth* all men that are seduced into Errours by the Devil, that they come and present themselves before the Looking-Glasse of this *School* wherein they shall see and inspect the murtherous Devil into his very heart.

15. Then he that will not take heed and *beware* of his Lies, whilest he may very well do it, there is no *Remedy* for him neither here nor hereafter: he that soweth and will *sowe,* with the Devil, must *Reap* with the Devil also,

16. *In the Center of the flash it is shewed, that the Harvest is white already: wherein every one will*

will Reap, what he hath Sown.

17. Here, my *Entrusted* Talent, which I have received, I will let out for rent profit and encrease as I am commanded to do, and he that will deal with me in *this* way of gain or usury, it shall be free for him, he may freely do it; *whether* he be a Christian, a Jew, a Turk, or a Heathen; they will be all alike advantagious to me; my Ware-house shall stand open for every one, let none fear Exacting tricks or deceit, for he that cometh to *deal with me* in my Wares, shall be justly rightly and fairly dealt with.

18. Every one should here, have a care, to deal so well that he bring in some Gain of *use-money* for his Master: for I am afraid, that every Merchant will not be *fitted* in my Warres for his turn ; for to some they will be very strange and *uncouth*, neither will every one understand my Language Phrase and Expression.

19. I would therefore have every one warned, that he deal circumspectly and *warily*, and not be conceited, that he is rich, and cannot grow poor; truly I have very admirable and *wonderfull* wares to Sell, every one will not have understanding and skill to know what to do with them.

20. Now if any one should in a dull humour fall upon them, and plunge himself into perdition, let him bear his own blame; he hath need of a light *in his Heart*, that his *Understanding* and Mind may be well governed.

21. Else let him forbear to come into my Ware-house, or he will but deceive his own expectation; for the Ware which I have to sell is very Pretious and

and Dear, and requireth a very fharp and acute *underftanding*: therefore have a care, and do not climb aloft, where you fee no Ladder is, elfe you will fall.

22. But to me is fhewen the Ladder of *Jacob*, upon which I am climb'd up, even into heaven, and have received my Ware, which I have to fell and vent: Therefore if any one will climb up after me, let him take heed that he be not drunken, but he muft be girt with the fword of the Spirit.

23. For he muft climb through a horrible deep, a *giddineffe* will frequently come into his head; and befides, he muft climb through the midft or center of the Kingdom of Hell, and there he will feel by experience what a *deal* of fcoffings and upbraidings he muft Endure.

24. In this combate, I had many hard tryals to my *hearts* grief: my Sun was often eclipfed or *extinguifhed*, but did rife again; and the oftner it was eclipfed or put out, the *brighter* and clearer was its rifing again.

25. I do not write this for my own *praife*, but only for an *Item* or hint, that if it go fo with you, you fhould not defpair about it, for there belongeth and is requifite a mighty endurance hard labour and ftoutneffe, for him that fighteth with the Devil, *betwixt* Heaven and Hell: for He is a potent Prince.

26. Therefore have a care, that thou put on the Coat of Mayl or *Habergeon of the Spirit, elfe do not venture to come *near* my Ware-houfe, that my wares be not ill handled by thee, and fo be prejudicial to thee.

* Corflet or Breft-plate.

27. Thou muft *renounce* the Devil and the world,

if thou wilt enter into this fight, elfe thou wilt not overcome: But if thou *overcomeft not*, then let my book alone, and meddle not with it, but *ftick* to thy Old matters, *elfe* thou wilt receive but evil wages for thy pains: *be not deceived, God will not be mocked,* Gal. 6. 7.

28. Truly it is a narrow and ftrait paffage, or *entrance*, through the Gates of Hell; for them that will preffe *in* to God: they muft endure many *pangs* crufhings and fqueezings from the Devil.

29. For the *humane* flefh is very young and tender, and the *Devil* is rough and hard, alfo dark, hot, bitter, aftringent and cold: and fo thefe *two* are very ill *match'd*.

30. Therefore I ferioufly exhort the Reader, and would have him faithfully warned, as it were with a *Preface* to this Great Myftery, that if he do *not* underftand it, and yet longeth and would fain have the meaning or underftanding thereof, that he would pray to God for his Holy Spirit, and that he would *enlighten* him with the fame.

31. For, without the illumination thereof you will *not underftand* this Myftery; for there is a ftrong Lock and Bar before it *in the fpirit of Man*, that muft be firft unlockt or opened, and that *No man* can do, for the Holy Ghoft is the *onely* Key to do it withall.

32. Therefore if thou wilt have an open Gate into the Deity, then thou muft move ftirre and walk *in* God's Love, this I have fet down here for thy Confideration.

Now

Now Obferve :

33. Every Angel is created in the *feventh* * Qualifying or fountain-fpirit, which is † NATURE, out of which his Body is compacted or incorporated together, and his Body is given him for a propriety, and the fame is *free* to it felf, as the whole Deity is free.

* or *faculty.*

† NATURA.

34. He hath no impulfe or driving without or diftinct from himfelf, his impulfe and mobility ftandeth *in his Body,** which is of fuch a kind and manner, as the *whole* God is ; and his light and knowledge, as alfo his life, is generated in that manner, as the whole Divine Being is generated.

* *viz. the Body.*

35. For the Body is the incorporated or compacted fpirit of Nature, and encompaffeth or inclofeth the other fix Spirits; thefe generate themfelves *in the Body,* juft as it is in the *Deity.*

36. Now *Lucifer* had the faireft Beautifulleft and powerfulleft Body, in Heaven, of or among *all* the Princes of God, and his Light, which he hath, and is continually generated in his Body, that hath incorporated *with* the heart or Sonne of God, as if they were *One* thing.

37. But when he faw that he was fo fair and beautiful, and found or felt his inward birth and great power or authority, then his fpirit, which he had generated in his Body, which is his ANIMAL (or animated) or *Life-*fpirit, ———

[*Note,* The *Author calls the foulifh Birth the* ANIMAL *Birth ; from* Anima, *which fignifieth the Soul; but being the Scripture otherwife underftandeth by the word* Animal, *the perifhed or corrupted Soul, or* Animalem hominem, *the Animal man or*

N n 2   *the*

the corrupted Natural Man, that is, the Adamical beaftial Man ; *and fo he being adverti-fed of it, he altered that Expreffion, and ufed it no more any further.*

——or Sonne or Heart ; exalted it felf, *intending* to triumph over the Divine Birth, and to lift up or extoll it felf *above* the Heart of God.

Here Obferve the Depth.

38. In the middle or central fountain or well-fpring, which is the Heart ; where the Birth rifeth up ; the aftringent or harfh quality rubs it felf with the Bitter and Hot, and there the *light* kindleth, which is the *Sonne,* of which it is alwayes impregnated in its Body, and that enlighteneth and maketh it *living.*

39. Now that light in *Lucifer* was fo fair bright and Beautiful, that he *excelled* the bright form of heaven, and in that light was perfect *Underftanding :* for all the feven qualifying or fountain fpirits generate that fame light.

40. But now, the feven qualifying or fountain-Spirits are the Father of the Light, and may *permit* or fuffer the Birth of the Light to be as much as they pleafe : and the light *cannot* exalt or raife it felf higher, then the qualifying or fountain-fpirits will permit, or give it leave.

41. But when the Light is generated, then it *enlightneth* all the feven qualifying or fountain fpirits, fo that all feven are Underftanding ; and do all feven give their will to the *Birth* of the Light.

42. But now, every one hath power and Might to *alter* its will in the Birth of the light, according as there

there is *need* : now if that be fo, then the fpirit cannot triumph thus, but muft lay down its *prancing* Pomp.

43. And therefore it is that all feven fpirits are in full power, every one of them hath the Reines in its hand, that it may hold in and *check* the *generated* fpirit, from triumphing any higher, then is *fit* for it.

44. But the feven fpirits, which are in an Angel, which generate the light and underftanding, they are bound and united with the *whole* God, that they fhould not qualifie any other way, either higher or *more* vehemently, then God himfelf; but that there fhould be one and the fame *manner* and way between *them both*.

45. Seeing they are but a part or *peece* of the whole, and not the whole it felf, for God hath therefore created them out of *himfelf*, that they fhould qualifie operate or Act in fuch a manner form and way as God himfelf doth.

46. But now the qualifying or fountain fpirits in *Lucifer* did not fo, but they feeing that they fate in the higheft Primacie or *Rank*, they moved themfelves fo hard, and ftrongly, that the fpirit, which they generated was very fiery, and climbed up in the fountain of the heart, like a Proud *Damfell* or Virgin.

47. If the qualifying or fountain fpirits had moved qualified or acted gently and lovely, as they *did* before they became creaturely, as they were *univerfally* in God before the Creation, then had they generated alfo a gentle lovely mild and meek Sonne in them, which would have been *like* to the Sonne of God ; and then the Light in *Lucifer* and the Light

of

of the Sonne of God had been *One* thing, one qualifying operating acting and affecting, one and the same lovely kissing, Embracing and struggling.

48. For the great Light, which is the Heart of God, would have *played* meekly mildly and lovingly with the *small* Light in *Lucifer*, as with a young sonne, for the *little* sonne in Lucifer should have been the dear *little* brother, of the Heart of God.

49. To this End God the Father hath created the Angels, that as he is manifold and *various* in his Qualities, and in his *alteration* or variegation is incomprehensible in his Sport or *Scene* of Love ; so, the *little* spirits also, or the little Lights of the Angels, which are as the Sonne of God, should play or sport very *gently* or lovely in the great light before the Heart of God ; that the Joy in the Heart of God might here be *encreased*, and that so there might be a holy Sport Scene or play in God.

50. The seven spirits of Nature in an Angel should play and rise up *gently* in God their Father, as they had done before their creaturely Being, and rejoyce in their New-born sonne, which they have generated out of *themselves*, which is the Light and Understanding of their Body.

51. And that light should rise very gently or mildly in the Heart of God, and *rejoyce* in the light of God, as a child with its Mother, and so there should be a Hearty loving, and friendly kissing, a very meek and pleasant Taste or relish.

52. In this the Tone should rise up, and sound, with *singing* and ringing forth ; in praising and jubilating: also all the qualities should rejoyce therein, and every spirit should *exercise* or practise its Divine work or labour, as God the Father *Himself* doth.

53. For

53. For the seven spirits had this in perfect knowledge, for they were united and *actuated* with God the Father, so that they *could all* see, feel, taste, smell and hear, what God their Father *did*, or wrought and made.

54. But when they elevated themselves in a sharp or strong kindling, then they did *against* Natures Right, otherwise then God their Father did, and this was a stirring quality of rising up, *against* or contrary to the whole Deity.

55. For they kindled the *Salitter* of the Body, and generated a high triumphing Sonne, which in the astringent quality, was hard, rugged or rough, dark and cold; in the sweet, was *burning* bitter and fiery: The Tone was a hard *fiery noise*; The Love was a lofty *Emnity* against God.

56. Here now stood the kindled Bride in the seventh Nature-spirit, like a *Proud Beast*; now she supposed she was beyond or above God, nothing was like her now: Love grew *cold*, the Heart of God could not touch it, for there was a *contrary* will or opposition betwixt them. The Heart of God moved very meekly and lovingly, and the heart of the Angel moved very darkly *hard* cold and fiery.

57. And the heart of God should now *unite* and qualifie with the Heart of the Angel, but that could *not* be; for there was now hard against soft, and soure against sweet, and dark against light, and fire against a pleasant gentle warmth, and a hard knocking or rumbling against a loving melodious song.

Question.

Queſtion.

Hearken Lucifer, *Where ly-*
eth the fault now, that thou art
become a Devill? Is God in fault,
as thou lyingly ſayſt?

Anſwer.

58. O no, *thou* thy ſelf art faulty, the qualifying
or fountain Spirits in thy Body, which thou thy ſelf
art, have generated thee *ſuch* a little ſonne : Thou
canſt not ſay, that God hath kindled the *Salitter*, out
of which he made thee, but thy qualifying or fountain ſpirits have done it, whereas thou wert clearly before, a Prince and King of God.

59. Therefore, when thou ſayſt, God Created
thee thus, or that he hath *without ſufficient* cauſe ſpewed thee up out of thy place : then art thou a Lyar
and Murtherer. For the *whole* heavenly Hoaſt or
Army beareth witneſſe againſt thee, that thou haſt
thy ſelf erected and prepared this fierce Quality for
thy ſelf.

60. If it be not ſo, then go before the face of
God, and *Juſtifie* thy ſelf. But thou ſeeſt it plain
enough without that ; and beſides, thou dareſt not
look on that matter : Wouldſt not thou *fain* have a
friendly kiſſe of the Sonne of God, that thou mightſt
once be eaſed or refreſhed ? if thou art in the Right,
then do but once look upon HIM : perhaps thou
mayſt be made ſound or whole again.

61. But

61. But ftay a little, *another* fitteth on thy Throne; He is kiffed, and he is an obedient fonne to his Father, and doth as the Father doth.

62. Stay yet a little while, and the *Hellifh* fire will kiffe thee; in the mean while, make much of this Latine till more groweth out of it; thou wilt *fuddenly* lofe thy Crown.

Now one might Ask:

What then in Lucifer, *is properly, that Emnity againft God; for which he was Thruft and driven out of his place?*

63. Here I will fhew you exactly the Pith Kernel and *Heart* of Lucifer, and then you will fee, what a Devil is, or *how* he is become a *Devil*. Therefore take heed, and do not Invite or Entertain him as a Gueft, for he is the Arch-fworn Enemy of God, and of all Angels and Men, and that in his Eternity.

64. Now if thou underftandeft and apprehendeft *this* aright, then thou wilt not make of God a Devil; as fome do, which fay: *God hath created the Evil,* and that his will is, that fome men fhould be Loft; which men, that fo fay, help to encreafe the Devils *Lies,* and bring upon themfelves the fevere Judgment, by their perverting Gods *truth,* and fo turning them into Lies.

Now Obferve.

65. The whole Deity hath in its innermoft or beginning Birth, in the Pith or kernel, a very tart terrible

O o   rible

rible *sharpneſſe*, in which, the aſtringent quality is a very horrible, tart, hard, dark and cold attracting or drawing together, like *winter*, when there is a fiery bitter cold froſt, when water is frozen into Ice, and beſides is very Intolerable.

66. Then think or ſuppoſe if in ſuch a hard Winter, when it is ſo cold, the *Sun* ſhould be taken away, what kind of hard Froſt, and how very rough *fierce* and hard darkneſſe would it be, wherein no life *could* ſubſiſt.

67. After ſuch a manner and kind is the aſtringent quality in the innermoſt kernel or Pith *in it ſelf*, and to it ſelf alone, without the other qualities *in God* ; for the auſtereneſſe or ſeverity maketh the attracting or drawing together, and fixation or Glutinouſneſſe of the body, and the hardneſſe dryeth it *Creature-* up, ſo that it ſubſiſteth * as a Creature.

ly.　68. And the bitter quality is a *tearing*, penetrating, and cutting bitter quality or ſource : *or it divideth* and driveth forth the hard and aſtringent Quality, and maketh the mobility.

69. And betwixt theſe two qualities is heat generated from its hard and fierce bitter rubbing, tearing and raging, which riſeth up in the Bitter and hard quality, as a *fierce* wrathful kindling , and preſſeth quite through, as a *hard* fiery *Noiſe*.

70. From whence exiſteth the hard Tone, and in that riſing up, or climbing, it is invironed and *fixed* in the aſtringent quality, ſo that it becometh a Body, which ſubſiſteth.

71. Now if there were *no* other quality in this Body, which could quench the *fierceneſſe* of theſe four * or were. qualities, then there * would be a perpetual Emnity therein. For the bitter * would be againſt the aſtringent,

astringent, in that it stormeth and teareth so vehemently therein, and *breaketh open* the astringent.

72. And then the astringent also would be against the bitter, in that it attracteth, draweth together and holds fast, the bitter, *captive,* that it could not have its own course.

73. And the Heat would be against both, in that with its fierce wrathful kindling and rising up, it maketh all hot, *burning*, and raging, and is fully or totally against the cold.

74. And so the Tone would be a great Emnity in all the other, in that it penetrateth forcibly through all like a *Tyrant.*

75. *And thus, this is the very deepest and innermost hidden Birth of God,* according to which, he calleth himself *an angry* zealous or *Jealous God,* as may be seen by the Ten Commandements on Mount *Sinai,* Exod. 20.5. Deut. 5.9.

76. And in this quality standeth *Hell* and Eternal Perdition, as also the eternal Emnity and murtherous Den, and such a creature the *Devil* is come to be.

77. But now, seeing he is a sworn Arch-enemy of God, and though indeed the Disputants and Helpers of the Devil will needs force it so, in *arguments*; that God willeth the good and also the evil, and that he hath created *some* men to Damnation; therefore and thereupon the Spirit of God *citeth* them upon pain of eternal Emnity, to come before this Looking-Glasse, wherein their *Heart* shall be laid open; and they shall see, *what God is, and who*

the

the Devil is, or *how* he is become a Devil.

78. If thy heart be not bolted and barred up in death, through thy *stubborn* wilfulnesse aed Blasphemy, and *drown'd* in horrible sins, purposing not to desist from them, or leave them, then *awake*, and behold; I take Heaven and Earth; also the Stars and Elements, and all the Creatures, and Man himself also in his whole substance, to witnesse, and so I will prove it also *plainly* and clearly in its due place, with all these forementioned things, especially, when we come to treat of the *Creation* of all the Creatures.

79. If these things will *not* give thee satisfaction; then pray to God, that He would *open* thy Heart, and then thou wilt know and *see* Heaven and Hell, as also the *whole* Deity with all its qualities; and then no doubt thou wilt forbear, and justifie the Devil no more : *I am not able to open thy heart for thee.*

Now observe the true * Birth or Geniture of God.

80. Behold, as I have mentioned above; the Birth or Geniture of God in its innermost Being, in *these* four qualities; is thus Sharp or Tart.

Thou must understand it exactly.

81. The astringent quality is thus sharp in its own proper quality in *it self*: but it is not alone, or without the other; neither is it generated of or in it self, as being wholly free, but the other six Spirits generate

generate it, and they also hold it by the Reins, and may let their Reins and *authority* go as far only, as they please.

82. For, the sweet spring or fountain water is suddenly a whip scourge or Lash upon the astringent quality, and mitigateth softneth or suppleth it, so that it groweth very thin, gentle mild and soft, as also very *Bright.*

80. But that it is thus sharp in it self, is to the end, that a *Body* may be Imaged or framed through its attracting or drawing together, otherwise the Deity *would not* subsist, much *lesse* a creature.

84. And in this sharpnesse, God is an All-comprehensible and all-fixing or all-fastning sharp God: for the Birth Geniture and sharpnesse of God is *thus* every where.

85. But if I shall describe the Deity in its Birth or *Geniture* in a small round circle, in the highest Depth, then it is *thus*

In a Similitude.

86. As suppose a WHEEL standing before thee, with seven *wheeles* one so made in the other, that it could go on *all* sides, forward, backward, and crosse wayes, without need of any turning back or stopping.

87. And in its going, that, alwayes one wheel in its turning about *generateth* the other, and yet none of them do vanish out of sight, but that all seven be visible, or in *sight.*

88. And the seven Wheeles alwaies generating the *Naves* in the midst or center according to their turning about, so that the Nave stand alwaies free

without

without alteration or removing ; whether the wheeles go forward or backward or croſſe waies, or upward or downward.

89. And the Nave alwaies generating the *Spoaks*, ſo that in their turning about, they ſtand right and direct from the *Nave* to the *Felleys* of the wheel : and yet none of the *ſpoaks* to be out of ſight, but ſtill turning about, thus one with another, going whitherſoever the *wind* drive it, and that without need of any turning back or *ſtopping*.

Now obſerve what I ſhall inform you in the application of this.

90. The *ſeven wheeles* are the ſeven Spirits of God, the one alwaies generating the other ; and are like, the turning about of a wheel, which hath ſeven wheels *one in another*, and the one alwaies wheeleth it ſelf otherwiſe then the other in its *ſtation*, and the ſeven wheeles are Felleyed, or *hooped* Round with Felleys, like a round *Globe.*

91. And yet that a man may ſee all the ſeven wheeles turning round about ſeverally apart, as alſo the whole *fitneſſe* or compaſſe of the frame, with all its Felleys and Spoaks and Naves.

92. And the *ſeven Naves* in the midſt or Center being as it were *one Nave*, which doth fit every where in the turning about, and the wheeles continually generating theſe Naves, and the Naves generating the Spoaks continually in all the ſeven wheeles, and yet none of the wheeles, as alſo none of the Naves, nor any of the Felleys or Spoaks *to be out of ſight*, and as if this wheel had *ſeven* wheeles, and yet were all but *one wheel*, and went alwayes
forward

forward, whitherſoever the wind drove it.

Now Behold, and Conſider.

93. The ſeven wheeles one in another, the one alwaies generating the other, and going on every ſide, and yet none out of ſight, or turning back: theſe are the *ſeven* qualifying or fountain *Spirits* of God the Father.

94. And they generate in the ſeven wheeles, in each wheel a Nave, and yet there are not ſeven Naves, but only *One,* which fitteth in all the ſeven wheeles: And this is the Heart or *innermoſt* Body of the wheeles, wherein the wheels run about, and that ſignifieth the *Sonne* of God.

95. For all the ſeven Spirits of God the Father generate continually in their circle, and that, is the ſonne of all the ſeven ſpirits, and all thoſe qualifie or *act* in his Light, and is in the midſt or Center of the Birth, and *holds together* all the ſeven ſpirits of God, and they in their Birth turn about therewith, thus.

96. That is, they clime either upward or downward, backward or forward or croſſe-wayes, and ſo the Heart of God is *alwayes* in the midſt or center, and fitteth alwaies every qualifying or fountain Spirit.

97. Thus there is *One* Heart of God, and *not* ſeven, which is alwaies generated from all the ſeven, and is the heart and *life* of all the ſeven.

98. Now the *Spoaks*, which are alwaies generated from the Naves and Wheeles, and which do fit all the wheeles in their turning, and are their Root, ſtay, and faſtning, in
which

which they ſtand, and out of which they are generated ; ſignifie God the *Holy Ghoſt*, which goeth forth from the Father and the Sonne, even as the Spoaks go out from the Nave and Wheel, and yet *abide* alſo *in* the wheel.

99. Now as the Spoaks are many, and go alwaies about with and in the wheel ; ſo the Holy Ghoſt is the *Workmaſter* in the wheel of God, and formeth, Imageth and frameth all, in the whole or total God.

100. Now this wheel hath ſeven wheels one in another, and one Nave, which is fitted in all the ſeven wheels : and all the ſeven wheels *turn on that one Nave*: Thus God is one God, with ſeven qualifying or fountain ſpirits, and yet is but one God, juſt as theſe ſeven wheeles are but *One* wheel.

Now Obſerve:

101. The wheel in its incorporated ſtructure and frame ſignifieth the *aſtringent* quality, which attracteth or draweth together the whole corporeal Being of the Deity, and holds it, and dryeth it, ſo that it *ſubſiſteth.*

102. And the *ſweet* ſpring or fountain-water is generated by the driving about or *riſing up* of the ſpirits, for when the light is generated in the Heat, then the aſtringent quality is amazed or terrified for great Joy, and this is a ſubmitting or lying down, or growing thin, and the *hard* corporeal being, ſinketh down like a meekneſſe or mildneſſe.

103. And ſo now the terrour or the *glance* of the Light riſeth up in the aſtringent quality very *gently* and ſhivering, and trembleth ; which now in the

water

water is bitter, and the Light dryeth it, and maketh it friendly and sweet.

104. Now therein standeth *life* and *joy*: for the terrour or flash riseth up in all the qualities, like the wheel afore mentioned, which turneth about, and then there all the seven spirits rise up one in another, and generate themselves, as in a *Circle*, and the light is shining in the midst or Center of the seven Spirits, and re-shineth back again in all the spirits, and all the spirits *triumph* therein, and rejoyce in the light.

105. And as the seven Wheeles turn about upon one Nave, as upon their Heart, which *holds* them, and they hold the Nave; so the seven spirits generate the Heart, and the *heart* holds the seven spirits, and so there arise *voyces,* and *divine* joyfulnesse, of * hearty loving and kissing.

106. For when the spirits with their light move, or boyl, turn about and rise one in another, then the life is *alwayes* generated: for one spirit alwaies affordeth to the other its taste or relish, that is, it is *affected* with the other.

107. Thus the one tasteth and feeleth the other, and the Tone presseth forth from all the seven spirits *towards* the Heart, and riseth up in the heart in the flash of the light, and then rise up the voices and *joyfulnesse* of the Sonne of God, and all the seven spirits triumph and rejoyce in the Heart of God, each according to its quality.

108. For in the Light in the *sweet* water, all astringency, and hardnesse, and bitternesse, and heat, are mitigated and made pleasant; and so there is, in the seven spirits nothing else but a *pleasant* striving strugling

* or *Glorious.*

ling

ling and wonderful generating like a divine holy Sport or Scene of God.

109. But their sharp or Tart Birth, of which I have written above, abideth *hidden* as a kernel, for it becometh mitigated by the light and sweet water.

110. Just as a sour bitter green Apple is *forced* by the Sun, that it becometh very pleasant or lovely to be eaten, and yet all its qualities are tasted: so the Deity keepeth its qualities also, but striveth or struggleth gently, like a pleasant lovely Sport or Scene.

111. But if the qualifying or fountain spirits should *extoll* or lift up themselves, and penetrate suddenly one into another, driving hard, rubbing and thronging, crowding or squeezing; then the sweet water would be *squeezed out*, and the fierce heat would be kindled, and then would rise up the *fire* of the seven spirits, as in *Lucifer.*

112. *This is now the true Birth or Geniture of the Deity, which hath been so from eternity in all Corners and Places whatsoever, and abideth so in all Eternity.*

113. But in the Kingdom of *Lucifer,* † the *Destroyer;* it is otherwise; as I have written above concerning the *fierceneſſe;* and in this world which is now half kindled also, it is likewise after another manner;

manner; and will be so till the day of the Restitution; of which I shall write when I treat concerning the *Creation* of this world.

114. Now in this glorious lovely and heavenly *Salitter* or divine Qualities, the Kingdom of *Lucifer* also was created without any greater motion, then the other.

115. For when *Lucifer* was created, he was altogether *perfect*, and was the fairest Prince in heaven, adorned and indued with the fairest *clarity* or Brightnesse of the Sonne of God.

116. But if *Lucifer* had been spoiled or destroyed in the moving of the Creation, as *he pretendeth*, then he had *never had* his Perfection, beauty and clarity; but would have been *presently* a fierce dark Devill, and not a Cherubin.

Of the glorious Birth and beauty of King Lucifer.

117. Behold thou murtherous and lying spirit! here I will describe thy *Royall Birth*, how thou wert in thy Creation, how God created *thee*, and how thou becamest so beautiful, and to what *end* God created thee.

118. If thou sayst any other thing then this, which Heaven and Earth, and all the Creatures testifie, then thou Lyest, nay the whole *Deity* testifieth against thee; that God created thee for his *praise* out of himself, to be a Prince and King of God, as he did Prince *Michael* and Prince *Uriel*.

Now

Now Observe:

119. When the Deity moved it self to Creation, and would form Image or frame Creatures in *its Body*, it kindled not the qualifying spirits, else they would have *burnt* Eternally, but it stirr'd them very gently or softly in the astringent quality.

120. That, drew or attracted the Divine *Salitter* together, and dryed it so that it became a *Body*, and so the whole divine power of all the seven qualifying or fountain-spirits of that place or Room, as far as that of the Angels *reached*, was captivated in the Body, and became the propriety of the Body, which neither can nor shall, be destroyed again, in *Eternity*, but shall remain the Bodies propriety or proper own, in Eternity.

121. Now the captivated or incorporated power of all the seven qualifying or fountain spirits had its *propriety* in the Body, and is risen in the Body, and hath generated it self in the same manner as the *Deity* generateth it self from all the seven qualifying or fountain spirits.

1:2. One quality hath alwaies generated the other alike, and none of them have vanished or gone out of sight, just as it is in the *whole* Deity : and then the whole Body, as it is also in the Ternarie, generated it self just as the Deity generateth it self without or distinct from the Body, in the *Ternarie*.

123. But this I must mention here ; *viz.* that *Lucifer*, the King, was incorporated together out of his whole Kingdome, as the Heart of the whole place or Room thereof, so *far* as his whole Angelical Hoast or Army reached when it was created, and

so far as that circumference or circle, Region or Quarter, reach'd, wherein He and his Angels became a creature, and which God before the time of Creation had enclosed or concluded as a Room or Space for a Kingdom, whose circuit or Extent comprehendeth *Heaven and this world*; as also the *Deep of the Earth*, and of the whole Circle Sphear or Circumference of this *whole world* of the Heavens and Stars.

124. And according to the qualities were his qualifying or fountain Princes created, which are his Kingly Counsellours, and so also were all his Angels created.

125. Yet you are to know, that *every* Angel hath *all* the seven spirits in him, but one of the seven is chief or principal.

Now behold!

126. When the King was thus incorporated or *compacted* together, as one comprehending his whole Kingdom, then instantly, the same hour, and in the same *Moment*: when he was incorporated or compacted together: the birth of the Holy *Trinity* of God, which he had for a propriety in his Body,

[ss *Understand in the Liberty*, not *essentially*, but
“ *as the fire shineth forth or gloweth through the*
“ *Iron that is flaming hot, and the Iron remai-*
“ *neth Iron still*; or *as the light replenisheth*
“ *or filleth the Darknesse, the dark source or*
“ *quality being changed into Light, and so be-*
“ *cometh joyful, and yet in the Center remain-*
“ *eth a darknesse, which is understood to be*
“ *Nature*;

" *Nature ; for a spirit is repleninish'd onely*
" *with the Majestie:]*

rose up and generated it self without, distinct from
the Creature, in God.

127. For in the driving together of the Body presently likewise rose up the Birth also in great triumph, as in a New-born King, *in God* ; and all the
seven qualifying or fountain spirits shewed themselves very joyful and *triumphing*.

128. And instantly in the same *Moment* the light
was generated and rose up out of the seven spirits in
the Center of the heart, as a new-born sonne of the
King, which also instantly in a Moment, clarified
or brightened the *Body* of all the seven qualifying or
fountain spirits from the Center of the Heart; and
externally from without, the light of the Sonne of
God clarified or brightened it.

129. For the Birth of the new Sonne in the Heart
of *Lucifer* also penetrated through the whole Body,
and was glorified from the Sonne of God, which was
without distinct from the body, and was friendlily
welcommed with the *greatest* Beauty of Heaven, according to the Beauty of God the Sonne, and it was
to him as a loving Heart of propriety, with which
the whole Deity qualified or *operated*.

130. And then instantly also the spirit of the new
born sonne in the Heart, went forth from the light of
Lucifer through his *Mouth*, and united qualified or co-
operated with the holy Spirit of God, and was with
highest Joy received and embraced, as a dear *little*
Brother.

131. Now here standeth the Beautious Bride:
what shall I write of her now ? was she not a *Prince*
of God ; as also the most beautiful; moreover in
Gods

Of the horrible, proud, and henceforth doleful Lamentable

Beginning of Sin.

The higheft Depth.

Obferve here.

132.

When King *Lucifer* was thus fairly glorioufly Beautioufly highly and holily framed or built, he fhould *furely* have now begun to praife, honour and magnifie his *Creatour*; and fhould do that, which God his Creator doth.

133. *Viz.* God his Creator qualifieth or operateth very *meekly*, lovingly and Joyfully, and one qualifying or fountain-fpirit of God alwaies loveth the other, and bringeth its *affection* into the other, and alwaies helpeth the other to Image form and frame all in the *heavenly Pomp.*

134. Whereby, in the heavenly pomp alwaies fuch fair beautious forms, Ideas, *figures*, and vegetations, fpring up, as alfo *various* colours and fruits ; and this the qualifying or fountain fpirits of God do, *in God*, as a holy Play Sport or Scene.

Now-behold!

135. Seeing then God had incorporated or compacted together out of himfelf, *Eternal Creatures*, they fhould not qualifie or operate in the heavenly pomp

in

in such a way and manner, as to be *like* God himself.

136. No, by no means; for they were not thus Imaged or framed to *that End*: For, the Creator had for this cause incorporated or *compacted* the Body of an Angel together, to be more dry, then he is in his Body; that he might be and *remain to be* God; so that the qualities should be harder and tougher, that the Tone or Sound might be loud clear and shrill.

137. So that, when the seven qualities in an Angel, in the Center of the heart, do *generate* the Light and the spirit or *understanding*; that then, that same spirit, which in the light of the heart, goeth forth at the mouth of the Angel, in the *Divine* power; should as a loud clear shrill sound in the power of all the qualities *in God*; sing and ring forth as a melodious *Musick*, and in the forming Imaging framing or qualifying of God, rise up as a pleasant hearty loving voyce; in *Gods forming*.

138. And when the Holy Ghost formeth the heavenly fruit, then should the Tone, which should rise up in the praising of God, from the Angels, be also together in the *forming* or Imaging of the fruit; and so on the other side again, the fruit should be the *food* of the Angels.

139. And therefore also we pray in *Our Father,* saying,

$$\left\{ \begin{array}{c} \text{GIB uns unser Taglich Brodt,} \\ \text{GIVE } us\ our\ daily\ Bread, \end{array} \right\} \text{Mat. 6.11}$$

so that the *Tone* or word $\left\{ \begin{array}{c} \text{GIB,} \\ \text{GIVE} \end{array} \right\}$ which, we thrust

forth from our *Center* of the Light, through the animated, animal or * Soulish spirit, out at the *Mouth*

forth

forth from us, into the divine power; should in the divine power, as a * fellow-forming or † fellow-generating, *help* to Image or frame

*co-forming.
† co-generating.

{ **Unfer Taglich Bzodt**

Our daily Bread,

which afterwards { **Der Vater gibet Uns** } for

{ *the Father giveth to Us* }

Food. *

140. And then when *our* Tone is thus incorporated in *Gods* Tone, so that the fruit is formed Imaged or framed, it must needs be *wholesome* or healthfull for us, and so we are in Gods Love, and have that food to make use of, as by the right of Nature, being our spirit in Gods Love did *help* to Image and form the same.

141. *Herein standeth the innermost and greatest depth of God,*

O, Man, consider thy self! I will more *largely* declare it, in its due place.

142. Now for such an end hath God created the Angels, and they do so too: for their *spirit*, which in the Center or heart goeth forth from their light in the power of all the seven qualifying or fountain-spirits, *that* goeth forth at their Mouth, as God the Holy Ghost goeth forth from the Father and Sonne, and helpeth to form Image or frame all, in God (that is to say, in the Divine Nature) through the *Mercurius* song and speaking and Sport or Scene of Joy.

143. For, as God worketh in Nature to the producing of *all* manner of forms, Ideas, Images vegetations springings, fruits and colours: so do the Angels

* printed Copie, (*in fide et dilectione Dei.*)

gels

gels also in very great simplicity or sincerity; and though they should *scarce* touch the least Twigg, or scarce rejoyce in the beautious flowers in the heavenly *May*, and discourse and confer never so little, weakly meanly or simply thereof; yet neverthelesse that very Tone or speech riseth up together in the Divine *Salitter*, and helpeth to co-Image and frame or form all.

144. Thou hast many *examples* thereof in this world, that if some Creature or Man look upon a thing, it perisheth because of the Poison or venome in the Creature: On the other side again, some men, as also Beasts and other Creatures can with their Tone or words change or *alter* the malignity or evilnesse of a thing, and bring it into a *right* form.

145. And that how in the Divine Power, which all the Creatures are subjected to; for all whatsoever it is that liveth and moveth, is in God, and *God himself is all*, and all whatsoever is form'd or framed, is formed *out of* HIM, be it either out of Love or out of Wrath.

The Head Spring or fountain Vein of

Sinne.

146. Now *Lucifer* being so Royally Imaged or framed, that his spirit in his forming and imaging rose up in him, and was received or embraced of God very excellently and lovingly, and was set or put into *Glorification*; then instantly he should have begun his Angelical *Obedience* and course, and should have moved (as *God himself* did) as a loving son in the house

house of his Father, and that he did not.

147. But when his light was generated in him in his heart, and that his qualifying spirits were instantly affected or *invironed* with the high light, they then became so highly rejoycing, that they elevated themselves in their Body against the Right of Nature, and presently began as it were a Higher *statelier*, more Pompous or Active qualifying or Operation, then God himself *exercised.*

148. But these spirits elevating themselves thus, and triumphing so eagerly and vehemently one in another, and rising up against the right of Nature, by that means they kindled the qualifying or fountain spirits too exceeding much; *viz.* the astringent Quality attracted or compacted the *Body* too hard together, so that the sweet water was *dryed* up.

149. And the powerful and great Bright Flash, which was risen up in the sweet water in the *Heat*, from whence the bitter Quality existeth in the sweet water, that rubb'd it self so horribly hard with the astringent quality, as if it would break in pieces for great *Joy.*

150. For the flash was so Bright, that it was as it were intolerable to the qualifying or fountain spirits, and therefore the bitter quality or source trembled and rubb'd it self so hard in the astringent, that the heat was kindled *contrary* to the Right of Nature, and the astringent also dryed up the sweet water by its hard attracting together.

151. But now the quality of Heat was *so severe*, furious and eager, that it bereaved the astringent quality or source of its power: for the heat existeth in the fountain or source of the *sweet* water.

152. But

152. But the sweet water being dryed up through the astringent attracting together, therefore could not the Heat any more rise to a flame or to any light, (for the light existeth in the unctuosity or *Oylinesse* of the water;) but *glowed* like a red hot Iron, or like Iron not quite glowing, but very *dimly* and darkly : or as if you should put a very hard *stone* into the fire, and should let it lye there in great heat, as long as you please, yet it would not be *glowing* light, because it hath too little water, or *Oylinesse* in it.

153. Thus now the Heat kindled the dryed water, and the light could *no more* elevate and kindle it self, for the water was dryed up, and was quite consumed by the fire or great Heat.

154. The meaning is not here, as if the spirit of the water were *swallowed* up or devoured, which dwelleth, in all the seven qualities, but its Quality or upper place or *predominancy* was changed into a dusky hot and sour Quality.

155. For here in this place the sour quality hath taken its *first original* and beginning, which now also is *inherited* in this world ; which is not in Heaven in God, after *such* a manner at all, nor in any Angel : for it is, and signifieth, the house of *affliction* trouble and misery, and is a forgetfulnesse of all Good.

156. Now when this was done, the qualifying or fountain spirits *rubb'd* themselves one upon another in that manner and way, as I have mentioned *above* concerning the *Figure* of the Sevenfold wheel, for they use thus to rise up one in another, and to taste one another, or to *affect* one another, from whence life and love existeth.

157. Now in all the spirits there was nothing else but a meer *Hot Fiery Cold* and *Hard* corruption,

and

and so one evil quality tasted the other, whereby the whole Body grew so very fierce and wrathfull; for the Heat was against the Cold, and the Cold against the *Heat.*

158. And so the sweet water being dryed up, the bitter quality (which existed and was generated by the *first flash*, when the light kindled it self;) rose up in the Body through all the spirits, as if it would *destroy* the Body, and so raved and raged like the rankest or worst Poison.

159. And from thence existed the *first* Poison, wherein we poor men now in this world have enough to *chew* upon ; and thereby the bitter *poisonous Death* is come into the flesh.

160. In this raging and tearing now, the life of *Lucifer* was generated, that is, his *dear* little sonne in the circle or center of his heart : and what manner of life and dear little sonne came to be, I offer to any *Rational* Soul to consider of.

161. For *such* as the Father was, *such* was the Sonne also, *viz.* a dark, astringent, Cold, hard, bitter, hot, sour, stinking, fountain or source, and the Love stood in the Bitter quality, in its *penetrating* taste and relish ; and became an emnity against all the qualifying or fountain spirits in the Body of the high-minded *arrogant* King.

162. Thus the Tone rose up through the penetrating of the bitter quality through the *heat* and *dryed* water, and through the astringent hard quality ; into the *heart*, into the little new dear sonne.

163. And here the spirit *went forth* ; and as He was generated in the *heart*, so he went forth now at the *Mouth*, but how welcome a Guest he was before

fore God, and in God, alſo before the Holy Angels of the other Kingdoms, I leave to *thee* to conſider of.

164. He ſhould now have united with the Sonne of God, as one Heart and one God : Alas for ever ! Who can write or expreſſe this ſufficiently.

The Fourteenth Chapter.

How Lucifer, *who was the Beautiouſeſt Angel in Heaven, is become the moſt horrible Devil.*

The Houſe of the murtherous Denne.

I.

HEre *King Lucifer* pull thy Hatt down into thy Eyes, leſt thou ſhouldſt ſee how man will take off thy Crown away from thee, thou canſt *no more* Rule in Heaven ; ſtand ſtill a little while, we muſt firſt *view* thee, and obſerve what a Beautious fair Bride thou art ; and whether the filth of thy whoredom may *not* be cleanſed and waſhed away from thee, that thou mayſt be fair again, we will a little deſcribe thy *chaſtity* and vertue.

2. *Come on* ye Philoſophers and ye Lawyers and Advocates,

Advocates, that justifie and defend King *Lucifer* ! Come near and bring him to the *Barre*, whilest he hath yet the *Crown upon him*, for here we will hold a *Court* of Judgment against Malefactours, for him ; If ye can *maintain* his cause to be right, then he shall be your King ; if not, then he shall be turn'd out and cast down into Hell ; and another shall get his Royall Crown, who will *Govern* Better then He.

Now Observe :

3. When *Lucifer* had thus horribly spoiled and destroyed himself, all his qualifying or fountain spirits were Emnity against God, for they all qualified or acted much *otherwise* then God, and so there came *to be* an eternal Emnity betwixt God and *Lucifer.*

But now it might be Asked :

Question.

How Long did Lucifer stand in the Light of God ?

The Depth.

Answer.

4. When the Royall Body of *Lucifer* was incorporated or compacted together, in that very *Hour* the Light kindled it self also in *Lucifer.*

5. For

5. For as ſoon as his qualifying or fountain ſpirits in the framing of the Body *began* to qualifie or operate, and to generate themſelves, according to the right of Nature, *then* roſe up the flaſh of life in the heart in the ſweet ſpring or fountain water, and ſo the Royall Body was *ready furniſhed or compleat,* and the ſpirit went forth in the heart from the light through the mouth *into* the Heart of God.

6. And ſo he was a moſt exceeding beautifull Prince and King, and very *dear* and acceptable to the Divine Being, and was received and *embraced* with great Joy.

7. In like manner alſo the ſpirit *went forth* from the heart into all qualifying or fountain veins of the Body, and kindled all the ſeven ſpirits, and ſo the Royall Body was glorified *in the twinkling of an Eye,* and there he ſtood as a King of God, in an unſearchable clarity, or Brightneſſe, tranſcendently *excelling* the whole heavenly Hoaſt or Army.

8. Now in this clear and light flaſh the ſeven ** or infected.* qualifying or fountain ſpirits were *inſtantly* * affected as a man kindleth a fire, for they were affrighted at the terrible clarity or brightneſſe of their ſpirit, and ſo inſtantly at the *firſt* flaſh *ſuddenly* became highly triumphing riſing aloft extream ſtately, and overjoyful, and ſo moved themſelves towards a *higher Birth.*

9. But if they had *continued* in their ſeats, and ** viz. the ſeven ſpirits of Nature which they were conſtituted of.* had qualified or operated, as * they had done from eternity, then that high Light had *not hurt* them.

10. For they were *not* new ſpirits made of any *new* thing, but they were the *Old* ſpirits, which had

no

no beginning; which had been in God from Eternity; and *knew very well* the Right of the Deity and of Nature, *how* they should move and stir.

11. Also when God figured or framed the Body together, he did *not* aforehand destroy the qualifying or fountain spirits, but figured or framed the Body of King *Lucifer* together out of the kernel of that which was the *best*, wherein was the best knowledge of all.

12. Else if the qualities had been dead aforehand, they had had need of a new Life, and it wonld have been in *doubt*, whether the Angels *could* have subsisted Eternally.

Conceive it aright.

13. God created Angels out of himself, therefore, that they might be harder and dryer incorporated or compacted together, then the Ideas, figures, shapes or forms, which through the qualifying or operating of the Spirits of God in Nature, rise up, and also through the moving of the spirits *vanish* or passe away again, that their light in their hardnesse should shine the clearer and *Brighter*, and that the Tone of the Body should sound the clearer and shriller, whereby the joyfulnes should increase the more, in God. *This was the cause, that God created Angels.*

14. But that it is said, the Angel generated *a new Light*, or *a new Spirit*, that, is thus to be understood,

15. When the qualifying or fountain Spirits

were incorporated or compacted together, then the light ſhone much brighter and clearer in the Body, and from or out of the body, *then it* did *before,* in the *Salitter :* for there then roſe up a much clearer and brighter flaſh in the body, then before, whileſt the *Salitter* was Thin and Dim.

16. And therefore the qualifying or fountain ſpirits alſo became ſtately and Proud, and ſuppoſed they had a *much fairer* little ſonne or Light then the Sonne of God was ; and therefore they would alſo the more earneſtly and eagerly qualifie or operate, and elevate themſelves, and ſo deſpiſed the qualifying or Acting which is in God their Father, and the Birth of the Sonne of God, as alſo the *Exit* or going forth of God the Holy Ghoſt ; and ſuppoſed, *they could do it,* becauſe they were ſo gloriouſly incorporated or compacted together, therefore they would now *exalt* themſelves gloriouſly and ſtately, and ſhew forth themſelves, as if they were the moſt fair and Beautious *Bride,* of Heaven.

17. *They knew very well,* that they were not the whole or Totall God, but were onely a *piece* or *part* thereof; they alſo knew very well, how *far* their Omnipotence reached or extended, and yet they would no more have their *Old* condition, but would be higher then the whole or *Total God,* and ſuppoſed, thereby they ſhould have their place Region Quarters or Court above the whole or Total Deity, above *all* Kingdoms *whatſoever.*

18. And therefore they elevated or extol'd themſelves, intending to kindle or *enflame* the whole God, and to Govern or rule the whole God by their power and might. All forms and *Ideas* ſhould riſe up in the

the qualifying and acting of their Spirit. He would be *Lord of the Deity*, and would not endure any Corrival.

19. *Now this is the Root of Covetousnesse, Envy, Pride and*   * * or *Anger*.
Wrath ; For in the *fierce* qualifying or acting and boyling, rose up the wrath, and burnt like fire of Heat and Cold, and was also *bitter as Gall.*

20. For the qualifying or fountain spirits had *no outward* impulse upon them gotten into them, but the impulse to Pride elevated it self *within* the Body, in the councel of the seven qualifying or fountain spirits, these *agreed* and united in a compact, that they would be God alone.

21. But because they could not begin it in their Old seat, and so bring it to effect, they therefore *dissembled* or playd the Hypocrite together, and flatter'd one with another, and so combined, intending to extoll themselves against the Birth of God, and would needs qualifie or work in the *highest depth*, and then nothing could be like them, being they were together the *most Mighty* Prince in God.

22. The Astringent quality was the *first* Murtherer flatterer and Hypocrite, for when it saw, that it generated so fair and bright a Light, then it compressed it self together *yet harder*, then God had created it to be, intending to be *much more* terrible, and to draw together all in its whole Region Circuit or circumference, and keep it *fast* as a *stern* severe Lord :

23. And so in a degree then it had Effected somewhat from whence Earth and Stones have their *Original* :

ginal : which I will write of, when I treat concerning the *Creation* of the World.

24. The Bitter Quality was the *ſecond* Murtherer, which when it roſe up in the Flaſh, did *tear* with breaking and great Power in the Aſtringent quality, as if it would break the *Body* in pieces.

25. And the aſtringent quality permitted it, or elſe it was very well able to have *ſtayd* and captivated the Bitter ſpirit, and to bathe or *ſteep* it in the ſweet water, till his high mind had been *allayed* and gone : But it would needs have *ſuch a little Brother*, becauſe it was ſo ſerviceable to its turn ; Elſe, being the bitter ſpirit *taketh* its original from it, as it were from its Father, it could well have *ſtopped* or hindred that.

26. The Heat is the *third* Murtherous ſpirit, which *killed* its Mother the *ſweet* water, but the aſtringent ſpirit is the cauſe thereof, for by its ſtern ſevere *attracting* together and hardening, it hath thus vehemently awakened and kindled the fire by the bitter Quality : for the fire is the *Sword* of the aſtringent and Bitter quality.

27. But being the fire riſeth up in the ſweet water, therefore it ſelf hath the *whip* or ſcourge in its own power, and might have *ſtayd* or kept back the aſtringent quality in the water, but it alſo became a *flatterer*, or hypocrite, and diſſembled with the *great* quality, *viz.* the aſtringent, and did *help* to deſtroy the ſweet water.

28. The Tone is the *fourth* Murtherer : for it taketh its *ringing* found in the fire in the ſweet water, and riſeth up very gently and lovely in the *whole* Body.

29. Yet it did not ſo here, but after it was riſen
up

up in the water, in the aftringent quality, it rofe up
fo *furioufly* like a Thunder-Clap, whereby it would
prove and fhew forth *its New Deity*: And fo the fire
rofe up, as when there is a *Tempeft* of Lightning, intending thereby to be *fo great*, as to be above all
things in God.

30. And this they practifed fo long, till they had
murthered their mother the fweet water: and therein
the whole *Body* became a dark valley, and there was
no more remedy or Council in God that could help
here: For, Love was turn'd into Emnity, and the

whole Body became a black dark $\begin{cases} \text{Teuffel.} \\ Devill. \end{cases}$

Teuffel.
quafi
Teu-fall.

31. Of the word (**Teuffel**): **Teu-** hath its origi-
ginal from hard beating Drumming, or Thumping;
and the word or fyllable, **-fell**, hath its originall

from the $\begin{cases} \text{falle,} \\ \text{fall,} \end{cases}$ and fo Lord Lucifer is called

$\begin{cases} \text{Teuffel,} \\ Devill, \end{cases}$ and is no more called a *Cherubin* or Se-

raphin.

Here

Here it may be Asked:

Queſtion.

Could not God have hindered and prevented the Pride of *Lucifer*, that he might have abſtained from his high-mindedneſſe?

Anſwer.

32. This is a high Queſtion, on which all thoſe lay hold that *juſtifie* and plead the Cauſe of the Devil; but they are all *Cited* to appear at the Court of Juſtice held for Tryal of Criminal *Malefaƈtours*: let them have a care *how* they plead for their Maſter, elſe the Sentence of Judgment will be *pronounced* againſt him, and he will loſe his *Crown.*

The wonderfull Revelation.

33. Behold King *Lucifer* was the Head in his whole Region Circuit or Circumference, alſo he was a *mighty* King, and was created out of the *kernell* or marrow of his whole Region and circumference, alſo he would fain have kindled that whole circumference by his Elevating, that ſo all might have burned and qualified, or operated *as he* did in his own body.

34. Though indeed the Deity without or diſtinƈt from his Body, would have meekly and gently qualified or *aƈted* towards him, and have *enlightned* and exhorted him to *Repentance*; yet now there was no

other

other will in *Lucifer*, but that he would *needs* rule over the Sonne of God, and kindle that whole Region or circumference, and in such a way *himself* would be the *whole* God, above and over all the Angelical Hoasts or Armies.

35. Now when the Heart of God with his *meekneße* and *Love* made haste toward *Lucifer*, he despised it, and thought *himself* far better then it, and then storm'd back again with fire and coldneße in *hard* Claps of Thunder *against* the Sonne of God, suppoſing he muſt be in ſubjection under him, and that He himſelf was *Lord*. For he *despiſed* the Light of the Sonne of God.

Queſtion.

Then thou Askeſt:

How? Had he ſuch Power?

Anſwer.

36. Yes, he had; for he was a *great part* of the Deity; and beſides, was from or out of the kernel thereof, for he made an *attempt* alſo upon that King and Great Prince *MichaEL*, to ſpoil and deſtroy him, who at laſt *fought* with him, and overcame him, in whom the power of God in *Lucifer*'s Kingdom fought vehemently alſo againſt *its* King, till at laſt he was thruſt down from his Kingly ſeat, as one that was *vanquiſhed*, *Apocal.* 12.

Objection

Objection.

Now thou wilt ſay :

God ſhould have enlightned his *Heart* that
he *might* have Repented.

Anſwer.

37. No! He would receive no other Light then
his own, for he *ſcorn'd* the Light of the Sonne of
God, which did ſhine without, diſtinct from his
Body, being he had ſuch a *glittering* light in himſelf,
and ſo elevated himſelf more and more, till his
water———

[" *This here, is* the water of eternal Life, *Gene-*
" *rated in the Light of the* Majeſtie, *but in*
" *the Center it is like the Sulphur or Brimſtone*
" *ſpirit, or to Aqua-*fortis, *or the water of ſe-*
" *paration*]

——— was quite dryed up and burnt, and his light
was quite put out, and then *all was done* with
him.

Concerning the Fall of all his Angels.

One might Ask.

Queſtion.

How comes it, that at this time all his
Angels did fall alſo?

Answer.

38. As *this* Lord commanded, so *his* Subjects obeyed: when he elevated himself, and would be God, his Angels seeing it, *follow'd* their Lord, doing as he did, all made a proffer to *assault* and storm the Deity.

39. For they were all in subjection under him, and he ruled *in all* his Angels, for He was created out of the Pith or kernel of that *Salitter*, out of which his Angels were *all* created, and he was the Heart and Lord of all his Angels.

40. *Therefore* they all did as he did, and all would sit in the Primacie of the Deity, and would rule powerfully in the whole Region Circuit or circumference, over and above the *whole* Divine power: They were all of one *will*, and would not suffer *the same* to be taken from them.

Now thou wilt Ask.

Question.

Did *not* the whole Total or Universal God *know* this, before the time of the Creation of Angels; that it would so come to passe?

Answer.

41. No: for if God had known it before the time of the Creation of Angels, it had then been an eternal *predestinate* purposed will in God to have it so, and it had been *no Emnity* against God, but God had

S ſ   indeed

indeed at the beginning created and made *him* a Devil.

42. But God did create and make him *a King of Light*, and when he became diſobedient and would be above the whole or *Total* God; then God did *ſpew him out* of his ſeat; and in the midſt or *Center* of *our Time* did create another King out of the ſame Deity, out of which Lord *Lucifer* was Created: [underſtand it aright; out of the *Saliter*, which was without *diſtinct* from the Body of King *Lucifer*:] and did ſet him on the Royal Throne of *Lucifer*, and did give him might authority and Power, as *Lucifer* had, before his Fall.

43. And the ſame King is called JESUS CHRIST, and is the Sonne of God and of Man.

44. And this I will demonſtrate clearly and at Large in its proper Place.

Note.

[" 45. *This is explained in the Second and Third*
" Book: *God knew this very well according*
" *to his* wrath, *but* not *according to his*
" Love, *according to which*, God *is cal-*
" *led* God: *into which no fierceneſſe nor*
" perturbation entereth, neither is there
" any ſearching in the Love concerning the
" Helliſh Creature.

" 46. *This foregoing Question is thus underſtood or*
" *Meant;*

" *meant ; as when I say ;* God knoweth
" not the Evil ; *Also* God willeth not
" the Evil, *according to the Tenure of the*
" *Scripture, then I understand, or mean,*
" *that in his Love (which alone is the one*
" *onely * * Good, and is alone called* God;)   * or Goodnesse.
" *there is* no *glimpse of Evil revealed or*
" *manifested ; otherwise if any evill were*
" *revealed or manifested therein, then the*
" *Love were not the Eternal* Meeknesse
" *and* Humility.

" 47. *But in the outspeaking of his word, wherein the*
" *Nature of the spiritual World existeth,*
" *wherein perceptibility or Sensibility is*
" *understood to consist, and wherein* God
" calleth himself an angry *zealous or*
" Jealous God, and a confuming fire :
" *Therein indeed* God hath known the
" Evil *from eternity, and that in case*
" *he should once move himself* † *therein,*   † in that according to
" *that the source or* Quality *thereof, would*   which he is
" *become creaturely also, but therein is he*   called a Confuming fire.
" not called God, *but a* confuming
" fire.

" 48. *I understand the abovesaid* Question *magi-*
" *cally, taking notice how* Gods Love *and*
" wrath *differ, and are distinguished, and*
" *how the Knowledge of Evil, viz. of the*
" Devil *and* Fall *is discerned to differ*
" *from his well-spring or source, from*
" *whence the* Fall *also took its* Origi-
" nal.

" 49. *And so also in* Gods Love *there is onely the*
" *fountain and knowledge of* Joyfulnesse,

" for

" *for every Science or Root cauſeth or pro-*
" *duceth its like.*

" 50. *For if I ſhould ſay, Gods Love had willed*
" *the Evil, or that there were* * *a falſe*
" *Science or Root in Gods Love and Meek-*
" *neſſe, then I ſhould ſpeak contrary to the*
" *Scripture : for what Gods love knoweth*
" *ſenſibly or feelingly in it ſelf, that it*
" *alſo willeth, and nothing elſe.*

" 51. *From hence, in the Creation,* Good *and* Evil
" *is exiſted : and I exhort the Reader to*
" *conceive our very deep ſenſe aright, and*
" *not miſtake or go aſtray here, but to read*
" *our* other *writings, where theſe things*
" *are ſufficiently explained:*]

Of the great Sin, and contrary or oppoſite will; and of the Eternal Emnitie, of King Lucifer, together with his whole Hoaſt or Army againſt God.

52. This is the right *Looking-Glaſſe* of Man ; before this Court of Juſtice for Malefactours the Spirit inviteth and citeth all men to ſtand, as before a Looking-Glaſſe ; wherein they may ſee themſelves, and what the *hidden Secret Sin* is.

53. This hath remained hidden ever ſince the
World

World began, and was never so fully and altogether revealed in any *Heart* of man: I also my self do wonder much more then the Reader can wonder, at this high Revelation or manifestation.

54. I do *not* write this for my own Glory; for my Glory standeth in my Hope of that which is to come: I am a poor sinner as well as other Men, and ought also to come before *this Glasse*;

55. But I marvel, that God should reveal himself thus fully to such a *silly* Man, and that he thus *impelleth* him also to set it down in writing: whereas there are many *learned* Writers, which could set it forth and expresse it better in a more *flourishing* style, and demonstrate it more exactly and fully then I, that am but a *scorn* and *Fool* to the world.

56. But I neither can nor will oppose him: for I often stood in great striving *against him*, that if it were not his impulse and will, that he would be pleased to take it *from me*; but I find, that with my striving against him I have but meerly gathered *stones* for this Building.

57. Now I am climb'd up and mounted so very high, that I dare not look back, for fear a giddinesse should take me, and I have now but a short *length* of Ladder to the Mark: when I go *upward*, I have no giddinesse at all; but when I look back, and would return, *then* am I giddy, and afraid to fall.

58. Therefore have I put my confidence in the strong God, and will *venture*, and see, what will come of it. I have no more but one Body, which neverthelesse is mortal and corruptible, I willingly venture *that*; if the light and knowledge of *my* God do but remain with me, then I have sufficiently enough for *this life and the life to come*.

59. Thus

59. Thus I will not be angry with my God, though for his *Names ſake* I ſhould endure ſhame ignominie and reproach, which ſpringeth buddeth and bloſſometh for me *every day,* ſo that I am almoſt enured to it : I will ſing with the Prophet *David,* Pſal. 73. 26. *Though my Body and Soul ſhould faint and fail ; yet thou, O God, art my truſt and confidence ; alſo my ſalvation, and the Comfort of my heart.*

60. *Sinne* hath *Seven* kinds forms ſpecies or ſorts ; among which there are *four* ſpeciall wellſprings or ſources : and the **Eighth** Kind or Sort is the *Houſe of Death.*

Now Obſerve.

61. The *Seven Forms* are the ſeven qualifying or fountain ſpirits of the Body ; *viz.* the *Aſtringent* Quality, the *water,* the *Bitter,* the *Heat,* the *Sound,* the *Love,* the *Nature* or beginning from the other Six : And when theſe are kindled, Each ſpirit generateth a *ſeveral* Emnity againſt God.

62. Out of theſe Seven are generated *other four* new ſonnes, and they together are the *new God,* which is wholly againſt the *old God,* as two profeſſed Armies of Enemies, which have ſworn Eternal Emnity one againſt the other.

The firſt Sonne is **Pride.**

The ſecond Sonne is **Covetouſneſſe.**

The third Sonne is **Envy.**

The

The fourth Sonne is *Wrath*.

63. Now let us view these in the Ground, from whence *all* hath its Original, and see how it is an Emnity against God : and therein you will see, what is the beginning and *Root of Sin*, and wherefore *in God* it *cannot* be suffered or endured.

64. Therefore come on ye *Philosophers* and *Lawyers*, you that will maintain and undertake to prove it, that God also created the *Evill*, and that he willeth the same; also that it is his *predestinate* purpose, that the *Devil fell*, and that many *Men* are *Damned*; else he could have altered all, and turned it some other way.

The Citation or Summons.

65. Here the Spirit of our Kingdom *citeth* you, together with your Prince *Lucifer*, whom you defend and Justifie ; the *third* time, before the final Court of Justice for Criminal Malefactours, give in your answer there;

66. For as to these *seven* Kinds or Forms, and *four* new Sonnes, the Right shall be prosecuted in the heavenly Fathers *House*.

67. If you can prove and maintain, that the *seven Spirits of Lucifer*, have of Right and Equity generated these *four* New Sonnes, so that they of *Right and Equity* should Govern Heaven and the whole Deity; then King *Lucifer* shall be Re-inthroned again and set upon his Seat, and his Kingdom shall be reduced to him again.   68. If

68. If *not*, then a *Hell* or Hole, Burrough or Dungeon ſhall be given to him for an Everlaſting Priſon, and *there* ſhall *He* together with his Sonnes be Priſoners for *Ever*: And you ſhould take heed left a Court of Juſtice be held and paſſe upon you alſo.

69. Now ſeeing then you will plead the Right of the *Devils* Cauſe ; wherewith ſhall he requite you? or what *Fee* ſhall he reward you with? He hath nothing in His power but the helliſh abomination ; . what will then be your recompenſe? Gueſſe Sir : even the beſt of all that he hath ; the Beſt fruits and Apples in his Orchard, and beſt perfumes and incenſe of his *Garden*.

Of the Firſt *Kind or* Form.

70. The *firſt* ſpirit is the *Aſtringent* or Harſh Quality, which in God is a gentle attracting or drawing together, a drying and cooling or refreſhing, and is made uſe of in and for the Imaging or framing of things, and though in its Depth it be ſomewhat Sharp or *Tart*, yet it tempereth it ſelf with the *ſweet water,* ſo that it is meek ſoft pleaſant and full of Joy.

71. And when the light of the ſweet water commeth *into it*, then it willingly, friendlily and freely *yeeldeth* up its birth thereunto, and maketh it dry, and ſhining *Bright*.

72. And when the Tone or *Tune* riſeth up in the Light, then it alſo giveth up its Tone Tune and ringing ſound very *gently* and brotherly thereunto.

73. Alſo it receiveth the *Love* from all the ſpirits.

74. *Alſo*

74. Also the *Heat* favoureth it, giving way friendly, that it may be cooled, and so it is a friendly will, in and with *all* the Qualities ; It readily helpeth also to Image or frame the spirit of *Nature*, and to form therein all manner of shapes, figures, fruits and Growths, or vegetations according to the *will* of all the six spirits.

75. It is a very *humble* Father to its children, and loveth them *heartily*, and playeth with them friendly : for it is the right *Father* of the *other six* spirits, which are generated in it, and it helps to generate them all.

76. Now when God constituted *Lucifer* with his Hoast or Army, he created them out of *this* friendly Deity, out of himself, out of the Place of Heaven and of this world, there was no other matter to make them of, this living *Salitter* was very gently and softly attracted or drawn together without any *killing* or flaying it, or without any *great* stirring or motion.

77. These Spirits thus incorporated or compacted together had the knowledge, the skill and the eternal infinite er beginninglesse *Law*, of God, and knew full well, I. How the Deity had generated them.

78, II. They knew also well, that the heart of God had the *Primacie* in the whole Deity : III. They knew well also, that they had no more for their proper own, to deal with and to *dispose of*, then their own compacted incorporated *Body*; for they saw very well, that the Deity generated it self without, severally distinctly, apart from their body, as it had done *from Eternity*.

79, IIII. They knew likewise very well, that the

T t   the

they were not the *whole* Room or Place; But were
therein to encreaſe the Joy and wonderful proportion variety and *Harmony* of that ſame place, and
were to *accord*, qualifie and act friendlily with that
Room or Place of the Deity, and friendlily affect the
Qualities, that are without diſtinct from their Bodies.

80. V. They had alſo *all power* to diſpoſe of all
the Ideas, figures and growths or vegetations, as they
would, all was a hearty Love-play Sport or *Scene* in
God, they had not at all moved God their *Creator*
to any contrary will, though they had *broken* all the
heavenly Ideas figures or vegetations and growths,
and had made of them all, *Horſes to Ride on*; God
had ſtill alwaies cauſe enough of *other*, to come up
inſtead of them; for it had all *been* but a play or
Scene in God.

81. For to that very *End* alſo they were created,
that they ſhould play and ſport with the Ideas,
figures and growths or vegetations, and *diſpoſe* of
them for their *own* uſe as they pleaſed.

82. For, the Ideas or figures have in a manner framed themſelves thus from eternity, and *have paſſed away* and altered *again* through the qualifying or
fountain ſpirits: *for this was the Eter-*
nall Play Sport or Scene of God,
before the Times of the Creation
of the Angels.

that is, have
come and
gone perpe-
tually.

83. Thou haſt a very good *Example* and Inſtance
of this, if thou wilt but ſee, and wilt not be ſtark
blind here : *viz.* In the Beaſts, Fowles, and all vegetations or growths in this world : *all theſe were* created

ted aforehand, e're Man was created, who is and signifieth the second Hoast or Army, which God created *instead* of expell'd *Lucifer*, out of the Place of *Lucifer*.

Question.

But now : What did the Astringent or harsh quality, do in *Lucifer* ?

Answer.

84. When God had thus *gently* incorporated it or compacted it together, then it found and felt it self to be mighty and powerful, and saw that it retained a *Body* as fair and excellent, as the figures were that were without distinct from it : *thereupon* it became high minded, and elevated it self in its Body, and would be more severe and eager, then the *Salitter* was, which was without distinct from its Body.

85. But being † it could not do any thing *alone*, it *flattered* and playd the hypocrite with the other Spirits, so that they followed it as their *Father*, and did all as they saw it do, each in its own Quality.

† the Astringent or harsh Spirit.

86. Now being thus agreed, they generated also *such* a spirit which did come forth at the Mouth, at the Eyes, at the Ears and at the Nostrils, and affected or *mixed* it self with the *Salitter* that was without distinct from the Body ;

87. For, the intent and purpose of the astringent or harsh quality, being it was so glorious, when the kernel was incorporated or compacted together out of the whole Kingdom, *viz.* its intent was, that it also through *its* spirit, which it did generate by or with the other spirits, would rule powerfully

with the fharpneffe Externally without its own Body, in the whole *Salitter* of God, and that all fhould ftand and be in or under its *own* Power and Authority.

88. It would Image frame and form all through its own fpirit, which it *generated*; as the whole Deity did, It would have the *Primacie* in the whole Deity : This was its purpofe.

89. But being it could not effect it in its true *Natural* feat, it thereupon elevated it felf, and kindled it felf.

90. And fo by this kindling it kindled its *fpirit* alfo, which now went forth at the Mouth, the Ears, the Eyes and the Noftrils as a very fierce *furious* fpirit, and ftrove againft the *Salitter* in its place, as a furious ftorming raging Lord, and kindled the *Salitter*, and attracted or drew all forcibly together.

Thou muft underftand it aright.

91. The aftringent or harfh Quality, in the fpirit that *went forth*, kindled the aftringent or harfh Quality which was in the Place of its *Region*, or in Nature, *viz.* in the feventh qualifying or fountain Spirit, and ruled powerfully in the aftringent quality in the *Salitter*, and that, the Aftringent Quality in the *Salitter* would not have, but ftrove with the fweet water againft this fpirit, but all would *not* help, the ftorm grew hotter and hotter, the longer the greater, till at length the aftringent or harfh Quality of the *Salitter* was kindled.

92. And fo when this was done, then the ftorm grew *fo hot*, that the aftringent quality drew the *Salitter* together, fo that *hard ftones* proceeded from it, whence the ftones in *this* world have their Original :

And the water in the *Salitter* was also attracted or drawn together, so that it became very thick, as it is now at present in this world.

93. But when the aftringent quality was kindled in *Lucifer*, then it became very Cold: for the *Coldneffe* is its own proper fpirit, and thereupon now it kindleth with its cold fire alfo, all, in the *Salitter*.

94. And hence the water of this world became fo cold dark and thick, and hence it is that all is become fo hard and palpable, which was *not* fo before the Times of the Angels.

95. And this now was a great contrary will in the *Divine Salitter*, a great Battel and ftrife, and an Eternall *Emnity*.

But now thou wilt fay :

Objection.

God fhould have withftood him, that it might not have come fo far.

Anfwer.

96. O, Dear Blind Man ! it was not a Man nor a Beaft that ftood here before God ; But it was *God* againft *God* ; one ftrong one againft another : Befides, How fhould God withftand him ? with the friendly *Love* ? that could not avail, for, *Lucifer* did but *fcorn* and difpife *that*, and would himfelf be God.

97. Should God withftand him then with Anger or Wrath, which indeed muft be done at *length* ; then God muft have kindled himfelf in his qualities in the *Salitter*, wherein King *Lucifer* dwelt, and

muft

must in the strong zeal or Jealousie strive and fight against him, which he did : and so this striving made this kingdom so dark *waste* and evil, that another Creation must *needs* afterwards follow upon it.

98. Ye Philosophers and *Jurists* or **Lawyers** of Prince *Lucifer*, here you must first defend the astringent or harsh quality in *Lucifer*, and *answer* whether it hath dealt righteously or *no*, and prove it in Nature. I do not *accept* of your extorted wrested bowed stretch'd and far-fetch'd Texts of Scripture, *brought in* by head and shoulders for a *proof*, but I will have living Testimonies.

99. And I will set before you also *living* Testimonies, *viz.* the created and comprehensible Heaven, the Stars, the Elements, the Creatures, the Earth, Stones, Men, and lastly your dark, cold, hot, hard, rough smoaky wicked Prince *Lucifer* himself : *all these* are come into this present condition, through his *elevation*.

100. Here bring in your *defence*, and answer for your spirit ; if not, it will be condemned. For this is Gods *Jus* Right or Law, which hath no begining, that the child, which is generated of the mother, should be *Humble* before the mother, and be obedient to her ; for it hath its life and Body from the *mother*, who hath generated it.

101. Also the *house* of the Mother, as long as the mother liveth, is not the childs proper own ; but the mother keeps the child with her in love, she nourisheth it, and putteth on it the best and bravest *Attire* which she hath, and giveth the same to it for its *own*, that her joy may be encreased by the child, and that she may have *Joy* in it.

102. But when the child *rebelleth* and resisteth against

againſt the mother, and takes away all from the mother, and *domineers* over her, and moreover ſtriketh at her, and forceth her to change into a *low* condition, contrary to Right and Equity : then it is but *Juſt*, that the child ſhould be expell'd out of the houſe, and left to ſit behind the *Hedge*, and quite loſe its childs portion and Inheritance.

103. And *thus* it was between God and his child *Lucifer*. The Father did put on him the faireſt Attire, *hoping* to have Joy in him : But when the child got the *Robe* and Ornament, he deſpiſed the Father, and would *domineer* over the Father, and would ruine his Fathers houſe ; and beſides, ſtruck at the Father, and would not be *adviſed* or taught to do otherwiſe.

Of the ſecond *Species form ſort or ſpirit, of* Sins *beginning, in* Lucifer.

104. The *Second* Spirit is the *water* : And as the aſtringent or harſh quality is the *Father* of the other ſix ſpirits, which attracteth or draweth them together, and ſo *holds* them : ſo the ſweet water is the *Mother*, in which all ſpirits are conceived, kept and generated, that ſoftneth and moiſtneth or ſoaketh them, wherein and whereby they get their life, and then the *light* of joyfulneſſe riſeth up therein.

105. Thus King *Lucifer* in the ſame manner did get the ſweet water for his corporeal Government, and indeed the very kernel and *Beſt* thereof. For God put on to his little ſonne the Beſt Ornament, Robe and Attire of all, hoping to have great Joy in him.

Queſtion.

Queftion.

Now what did this *aftringent* or harfh Quality with its *Mother* the fweet
Water?

Anfwer.

106. It flattered with the *Bitter* Quality, and
with the *Heat,* and perfwaded them that they fhould
elevate themfelves and be *kindled,* and fo together
they would deftroy their mother, and turn her into
a *four* form or property, whereby they would domineer with their fpirit very fharply, over the *whole*
Deity, all muft bow down and crouch to them, and
they would form frame figure and image all with
their *fharpneffe.*

107. According to this falfe or wicked conclufion,
and refult they *agreed* to do one and the fame thing,
and fo *dryed up* the fweet water in *Lucifer's* Body, the
heat kindled it, and the aftringent dryed it, and then
it became very four and *fharp.*

108. And when in this qualifying or acting they
had generated the *Spirit* of *Lucifer,* then the *life* of
the fpirit, which rifeth up in the water, as alfo the
light, became very four and fharp.

109. And now this four fpirit alfo *ftormed* with
all its powers againft the fweet water, which was
without diftinct from the Body, in Gods *Salitter,* and
thought, it *felf* muft needs be the Prime and chief,
and fhould in its *own* power, form frame and Image
every thing.

110. And this was the *Second Emnity* againft God,
from whence is exifted the *four* quality in this
world,

world, for it was not so from Eternity ; as you have an *Example* thereof in this ; *viz.* if you set any *sweet* thing in the *warmth*, and let it stand therein, it groweth *sour* of it self : as also Water, Beer or Wine in a vessell will do ; but none of the other qualities do alter, but only into a *stinck*, which is caused by the Quality of Water.

Now thou wilt Ask :

Question.

Why did God suffer Lucifers *Evil spirit* which proceeded out of the Body of Lucifer, to come *into Him*? could he *not* hinder it?

Answer.

111. Thou must know, that betwixt God and Lucifer there was no other difference, then there is between *parents* and *their Children* ; nay, there was yet a *nearer* relation between them : For as Parents generate a child out of their Body according to their Image, and keep it in their house, as a natural *Heir* of their Bodies, and cherish it : this near also is the *Body* of Lucifer to the Deity.

112. For God had generated him out of his body, and therefore also made him the Heir of his Goods, and gave him the whole Region or Extent of the place in which he created him, for a Possession.

The highest Depth.

113. But here thou must know, what it was, that *Lucifer* did fight against God *with*, and so *moved God to Anger*. For, he could *not* do it with his Body: for his Body reached no further, then the place, where he then stood; he could Effect *little* with that, but it was *something else*.

Be attentive here.

114. The spirit, which is generated from or out of all the seven qualifying Spirits in the *Centre* of the Heart; the same doth (while it is yet in the Body, when it is generated) qualifie mix or *act* in and with God, as one substance or thing, neither is there any difference.

115. And when that *same Spirit*, which is generated in the Body, seeth any thing through the Eyes, or heareth through the Ears, or smelleth through the Nostrils, then it is already in *that thing*, and worketh laboureth or acteth therein as in its own propriety.

116. And if the same be pleasing to it, it eateth thereof, and is *affected with the thing*, and wrestleth therewith, and maketh a mixture or *Temper* together: let the thing be as far off as it will, even so far as the *Original ng* of its Kingdom, in God, reacheth; so far can the Spirit give to or rule in a *Moment*, and is withheld or hindred by Nothing.

117. For it is, and comprehendeth the *Power*, as God the Holy Ghost doth; and in this there is no difference at all betwixt God the Holy Ghost, and the

the Spirit of the Body, *save onely* this, that the Holy Spirit of God, is the *whole fulnesse,* and the spirit of the Body is but a *Piece,* or *Part,* which presseth through the whole Fulnesse, and where ever it cometh, there it is mixed or *affected* with the place, and presently ruleth *with* God in the same place.

118. For it is of God and in God, and cannot be withheld or hindred, save onely by the *seven* Nature-spirits of the Body, which generate the animated or Soulish spirit; they have the *Reins* in their Hand, and generate it as they please.

[" *Gods Spirit hath all the qualities fountains or*
  " *sources, but distinguisheth it self in three*
  " *Principles, where three sources or qualities*
  " *arise, the first in the* fire *according to the*
  " *first principle, and the second in the* light
  " *in the second principle, and the third in the*
  " *spirit of this world in the* Aeriall *and*
  " *Astrall source:*]

119. When the astringent or harsh quality; as the *Father,* formeth the Word or *Sonne,* or Spirit, then it stands captive in the Center of the Heart, and is examined or *tryed* by the other spirits, whether it be good or no. Now if it please the fire, then the fire letteth the *flash* (in which the Bitter spirit standeth) go through the *sweet* water, wherein it conceiveth the *Love,* and goeth therewith into the astringent Quality.

120. Now when the flash returns with the Love into the astringent quality again, together with the *new* generated spirit or *will* ; then the astringent quality *rejoyceth* in the New young Sonne, and elevateth it self.   Vv 2   121. Then

121. Then the *Tone* layes hold thereon, and goeth forth therewith at the Mouth, Eyes, Ears, and Noſtrills, and executeth that which is decreed in the councel of the ſeven ſpirits : for as the *Decree* of the Councel is, ſo alſo is the ſpirit ; and the *Councel* can alter the ſame, as it will.

122. Therefore the original Luſt ſticketh in the circle of the Heart, in the *Councel* of the ſeven ſpirits; and as they generate the ſpirit, ſo alſo it is.

123. And ſo in this manner Lord **Lucifer** brought the *Deity* into Anger and Wrath :

Y.

> [" *that is, Kindled the* Eternal Nature *according*
> " *to the firſt* Principle :]

Being he, together with all his Angels, as a *malicious Devil,* fought or ſtrove againſt the Deity, intending to bring and ſubdue the *whole* Circumference Circuit or Region under his *innate* Spirits, that they ſhould form frame figure and Image all, and the whole Circumference Region or Extent ſhould *bow, yield,* and ſuffer it ſelf to be ruled and formed by the kindled *ſharpneſſe* of the innate ſpirits.

† or as this condition is in Angels, ſo there is ſuch a condition in Man alſo.

124. And † as this hath a Being or ſubſtance *form* or condition in Angels, ſo it hath alſo a being ſubſtance *form* or condition in Man. Therefore bethink and conſider your ſelves, *you,* that are proud, covetous, theeviſh, Extorting Uſurers, calumniating, Blaſphemous, Envious, and Whoriſh or Laſcivious, what manner of little ſonne or *Spirit* you ſend into God.

Z.

> [" *The ſoul was originally comprehended in the Eter-*
> " *nal Nature with the word* Fiat, *which is Gods*
> " *Nature according to the firſt* Principle *and*
> " *eternal Original of Nature ; and if it kindleth*
> " *it*

" it self in the Originall, *then it kindleth Gods*
" wrath *in the eternal Nature:*]

Objection.

Thou wilt say :

We do not send this *into God*, but only into our
Neighbour, or into his work which we ●
like and have a † Mind to.

† or med=
dle with in
our Minds.

Answer.

125. Now shew thou me any *Place*, to which
thou sendest thy Covetous or Lustful spirit, be it to
Man, Beasts, Garments, Fields, Money, or any *thing*
whatsoever, where God is *not :* from him is all, and
he is in all, * Himself is *All*, and he upholdeth and
supporteth all.

* *Note.*

Objection.

Then thou wilt say :

But he is with his *wrath* in many things which
are so hard and Evill, that they are not
suitable to or capable of the Deity.

Answer.

126. Yes, dear Man, all this is true ; The wrath
of God is certainly *every where* all over, In Silver,
Gold, Stones, Fields, Garments, Beasts and Men,
and all whatsoever is comprehensible and palpable;
otherwise they would not be so hard and harsh to
be felt as they are.

127. But

127. But thou muſt know, that the *kernel* of Love alſo, ſticketh in all in the hidden Center, unleſſe it be too too altogether Evill, and *ſo* Evill a thing Man hath *no* liking to at all, neither.

     * " *God poſſeſſeth* all, *onely, as to* Nature
       " *He is not the* eſſence, *He poſſeſſeth* himſelf.

Or doſt thou think thou doſt well, if thou batheſt or ſoakeſt thy ſelf in Gods wrath? take heed, that it doth *not kindle* thy Body and Soul, and ſo thou wilt *burn* therein eternally, as befell *Lucifer*.

128. But when God ſhall bring forth the hidden things, at the End of this time, then you will diſcern, in what Gods love or wrath hath *been*. Therefore have a care, and take heed, and *turn* thy Eyes from Evil, or elſe thou undoeſt thy ſelf, and ſo bringeſt thy ſelf into *Perdition*.

129. I take Heaven and Earth to witneſſe, that I have performed here, as God hath revealed it to me, that it is his Will.

130. Thus hath King *Lucifer*, in his body turned the ſweet water into a ſowr ſharpneſſe, intending therewith, in his haughty-mindedneſſe, to *rule* in the *whole* Deity.

131. And he hath brought it ſo far to paſſe, that, in this world, with that ſharpneſſe he reacheth *into* the *heart* of all living Creatures, as alſo into vegetables, leaves and graſſe, and into all other things, as a King and Prince of this world.

132. And if the Divine Love were *not yet* in the whole

whole nature of this world, and if we poor Men and Creatures had not in and about us *the Champion in the Fight*, we should *all* perish in a Moment in the hellish horrible Abominations,

133. Therefore we sing very rightly thus;

Mitten wir im Leben seynd, Mit dem Toot umbfangen;
Wo sollen wir dan fliehen hin, dass wir Gnad erlangen?
    Zu dir Herr Christ alleine.
Da ist nun Der Held im streit, Zu dem wir fliehen mussen,
    Welcher ist unser Konig,
        JESUS CHRISTUS.

In the midst of this our Life, Death doth us round embrace,
whither shall we flie away, that we may obtain Grace ?
    To thee Lord Christ alone.

This is the Champion in the Fight,
To Him 'tis we must flie,
Who is, Our King,
JESUS CHRIST.

134. He hath the Fathers Love in him, and fighteth in *Divine Power* and Might against the kindled hellish Abomination. To Him we must flie: and he it is that preserveth and *retaineth* the Love of God in all things in this world; else all would be lost and perish.

Nur hoff, wart, und bett.
Es ist noch ein kleine Zeit.
Wie des Teufels Reich daniet leit.

    Now Hope, pray, and wait
    But a small Time, and then strait
    Th' Devil's Kingdom will be quite down laid.

                                    135. Ye

135. Ye Philofophers and Jurifts or Lawyers, that make God to be as a Devill, in faying, That He willeth Evill: bring in your Plea, and anfwer once more here, and try whether you can *maintain* your Caufe to be juft; if not, then the fowr *fharp* Tart *fpirit* in Lucifer fhall be alfo condemned, as a Deftroyer; and the enemy of God, and of all his *heavenly* Hoafts and Armies.

The Fifteenth Chapter.

Of the Third *Species kind or form and manner of* Sinnes *beginning in* Lucifer.

1.

THe third Spirit in God is the *Bitter* Spirit, which exifteth in the flafh of Life; for the flafh of Life rifeth up in the fweet water through the rubbing or *fretting* of the aftringent and hot quality: but the body of the flafh abideth in the fweet water, fubfifting very meekly as a *Light* or heart, and the flafh is very trembling, and by the terrour, and fire, and water, and aftringent fpirit, it becometh bitter through the *original* of the water, in which it rifeth up.

2. And that flafh or raging terrour, or bitter fpirit is caught or laid hold on by the aftringent quality, and in the clear bright light in the aftringent fpirit, is *Glorified*, and exceeding highly Joyfull: which now is the mobility or the root of life, which in the aftringent quality Imageth frameth and formeth the Word, or maketh it *diftinct or* feverall; fo that in

the

the body, a Thought or Will doth exist.

3. Now this highly triumphing and Joyous spirit is very fitly and excellently, in the Divine *Salitter*, used to the Imaging or framing; because it chiefly moveth in the tone or Tune, and in the Love, and is *nearest* to the heart of God in the Birth, and bound or united therewith in joy, which indeed is it self also the spring and source of Joy, or the *rising up* in the heart of God.

4. And there is no difference here but onely such as is between the Body and Soul in Man : and so the *Body* signifieth or Resembleth the seven qualifying spirits of the Father ; and the *Soul* signifieth or Resembleth the onely begotten Sonne of God the Father.

[" *The spirit of the Soul signifieth* or represenseth
    " *the Heart of God ; and the* Soul, *the Eye of*
    " *God in the first principle : as is declared in*
    " *our Third Book, concerning the Threefold Life*
    " *of Man :*]

5. Now as the Body generateth the soul, so the seven Spirits of God generate the Sonne : and as the Soul is a peculiar *distinct* thing when it is generated, and yet is *united* with the Body, and cannot subsist without the Body ; so also is the *Sonne* of God, when he is generated, a peculiar severall distinct *thing* also, and yet cannot subsist without the *Father*.

Now Observe :

6. Just in such a Kind and manner was also the bitter quality in Lucifer, and had no cause to elevate it self, neither had it any *driving* to it from any thing, but followed the proud loftinesse of the astringent

quality, as its Father, and supposed also, it would reign in *its* kind and manner over the whole Deity, and so kindled it self in its elevation.

7. Now when it had *half* generated the animated or soulish spirit in the Body, that spirit became in this kind and manner a fierce, stinging, raging, kindled, and tearing spirit, bitter as *Gall*, and is rightly the Quality of Hell fire, a very fierce and Enimicitious hostile Being.

8. Now when this spirit in the animated or soulish spirit out of or from the heart of *Lucifer* and his Legions, roved [*or speculated*] into the Deity; [" *that is, brought its will thereinto, as into the* Genitrix :] then it was no other but a tearing, breaking, murthering and poisonous *burning* : concerning which Christ said ; *The Devil is a Liar and murtherer from the beginning* ; *and hath not continued in the truth*, Joh. 8. 44.

9. But *Lucifer* intended, by that means, to be above God, none could domineer and rule so terribly as himself, all must stoop to him ; he would with his spirit in the whole Deity, Rule as a powerfull King over all; being he was the fairest and *beautifullest*, he would needs *also* be the most *Potent*.

10. But he saw and knew very well the meek and *humble* Being, in God his Father : moreover he knew also very well, that it stood in such meeknesse from eternity, and that he also should generate in such meeknesse, as a loving and *obedient* Sonne.

11. But now being he was so beautiously and gloriously Imaged or formed as a King in Nature, his beautious form and feature tickled him, and so he thought with himself, *I am now God* ; and

formed

formed or framed out of God; who can vanquish me? or who can alter or change me? I *my self* will be Lord; and with my sharpnesse rule in all things, and my *Body* shall be the Image, which shall be worshipped; I will prepare and erect for my self a *new* Kingdom: for the whole circumference Extent or Region is mine, *I am God alone*, and none else.

12. And in his pride he struck and smote himself with darknesse and blindnesse, and made himself a *Devill*, and that he must be and abide so *Eternally*.

[" *He knew in God, onely the* Majestie, *and not the*
  " Word *in the Center, which hath the Fanne*
  " *or Casting shovell:* He blinded himself with
  " *the astringent* darknesse; *for he would needs*
  " *inflame himself, and rule in the fire over the*
  " *light, and over the* Meeknesse:]

13. Now when these Evil Devillish Spirits [understand the Center of the Genitrix:] moved or boyled in Gods *Salitter*, and Imagined Speculated or roved thereinto, then there was nothing but stinging, burning, murthering Robbing, and a meer Opposite or contrary will.

14. For the Heart of God delighted in Love and *meeknesse*; and *Lucifer* would needs turn the same by force into a Raging Tyranny: And so there was nothing but Enmity and a contrary or Opposite will; for by force he kindled the *Salitter* of God, which had *rested* from Eternity and stood in its Meeknesse.

15. Concerning this kindling in this circumference or Extent, it is, that God calls himself an angry Zealous or Jealous God, against those that hate him, Exod. 20. 5. Deut. 5. 9. that is, against those, who

kindle

kindle his wrath and *fierceneſſe yet more,* with their *diabolical* ſpirits, with ſwearing, curſing, blaſpheming, and all manner of furious fierceneſſe and wrath, which *ſticketh* in the Heart, with pride, covetouſneſſe, envy, and Anger; all that, whatſoever is in thee, thou caſteſt into God; ["*that is, into the Genitrix of Nature, and therefore that muſt be proved and tryed through the fire, and the Soul's ſpirit alſo, and the wickedneſſe or malice muſt abide and remain in the Fire:*]

d.

Now thou Askeſt:

How can that be?

Anſwer.

16. When thou openeſt thy Eyes, and feeſt the † Being of God; then thou *prickeſt,* as it were with Thorns, into the Being of God, and moveſt or ſtirreſt up the Wrath and Anger of God.

† Which is every where in this world in every Creature.

17. And when a Tone or Noiſe ſoundeth in thy *Ears,* ſo that thou receiveſt or catcheſt it up from the Being of God; then thou infecteſt it, as if thou didſt dart Thunder-Claps into it.

18. Conſider what thou doſt with thy *Noſtrills,* and with thy *Mouth,* whence thy dear newborn little ſonne ruſheth forth with thy ſpeech, as a little ſonne of all the ſeven ſpirits, and obſerve whether it doth not *ſtorm* and aſſault in Gods *Salitter,* as *Lucifer* did? O! there is no difference at all in this.

19. But again on the other ſide, God ſaith; *I am a merciful God to thoſe that love me; Thoſe I will do good to, and bleſſe them, to a thouſand Generations,* Exod. 20. 6. Deut. 5. 10.

Here

Here Observe :

20. And such are those, who contrary to the kindled wrath-fire, do with their *Love*, meeknesse, and industrious earnest yernings and *kindlings* of love, with their prayers *Quench* the wrath-fire, and presse on against the kindled fiercenesse.

21. And here indeed is many a hard Blow or Crushing : for the kindled wrath-fire of God falls many times so heavy upon them, that they know not *where* to bestow themselves; heavy Mountains lye upon them, the *Love-Crosse* presseth sore, and is heavy.

22. But this is their Comfort and *strong Helmet* against the fiercenesse, and the kindled fire; according as the Kingly Prophet *David* saith, *To the* Honest or *the upright the light riseth up in the darknesse,* Psal. 112.4.

23. And in this strife and fight against the wrath of God, and the kindled fiercenesse of the *Devils,* and of all *wicked* Men; the Light riseth up in the heart of the Honest and upright; and the friendly Love of God *embraceth* him, that he may not despair in his Crosse; but strive further still against the wrath and fiercenesse.

24. If there were not at all times some honest upright Men on Earth, who *quench* the wrath of God with their opposing ; the Hellish fire had kindled it self long ago; and then it would have well been seen *where* Hell is, which men do *not* now believe.

25. But thus saith the Spirit ; assoon as the fiercenesse

neſſe overcometh the oppoſition of love in this world, then the *fire* kindleth it ſelf, and then there is *no* more *time* in this world.

26. But, that the fierceneſſe doth terribly burn now at preſent, it needs no proof here, for it is known as clear as the Day, by *wifull experience.*

Behold there riſeth up yet, a little fire, in the oppoſition againſt the wrath, out of a ſingular eſpeciall Love-reſtraint of God: when this groweth weak alſo, then is the End of this Time.

27. But whether *Lucifer* hath done rightly, in that he hath awakened and ſtirr'd up the fierceneſſe in the *Salitter* of God, whence this world is become Stinging, Venomous, Thorny, Rocky, Envious and Evill falſe or wicked; let the *Atturneys*, Proctors, Advocates, and defenders of *Lucifer*, anſwer plead and juſtifie it if they can; if *not*, then this third *Bitter* ſtinging venomous ſpirit ſhall be *condemned* alſo.

Of the Fourth *Kind Species form or manner of Sin's beginning in* Lucifer.

28. The Fourth Spirit of God is *Heat*, which is generated between the bitter and aſtringent quality, and is conceived or bred in the ſweet water, and is *ſhining* and giving light, and is the true fountain of life.

29. For

29. For in the sweet water, it is very meek, from whence Love existeth, and is onely a loving *warmth* and no fire.

30. And though indeed it be in the hidden kernel of the fires quality or Originall; yet that fire is not kindled or burning, for it is generated in the *sweet* water.

31. Now where the water is, there is not burning fire, but a pleasing warmth and gentle qualifying or *vivifying*; but if the water should be dryed up, then there would be burning fire *there.*

32. Thus Lord *Lucifer* thought also, if he did but kindle his fire, then he might domineer forcibly in the Divine power: but he thought it would have burnt *Eternally*, and also have given Light; his purpose was not to put out the Light, but he would have it burn continually in the fire: he thought he would dry up the water, and then the light would move stirre or *shine* in the burning fire.

33. But he *knew not*, that if he kindled the dryed water, that the kernel, that is, the unctuosity oyl or heart of the water would be *consumed*, and that the light would turn into darknesse, and the water turn into a sowr *stinck.*

34. For the oyl or unctuosity in the water is generated through meeknesse or well-doing, and that is the unctuosity oyl unction marrow or fatnesse, wherein the Light becomes *shining*. But if the unctuousnesse be burnt up, then the water is turn'd into a sowr stinck, and moreover becometh very dark.

35. And thus it befell the Pride of *Lucifer*, he triumph'd a little while with his kindled Light; but when his light was *spent* and burnt up, then he became a Black Devill.   36. But

36. But he suppofed he would Eternally reign thus in his burning light in the whole Divine power, as a very terrible God, and fo with his fire-fpirit he *wreftled* with the *Salitter* of God, intending to kindle the whole circumference or Extent of his Kingdome.

37. And indeed he hath done fomewhat, in that he hath fet the *Divine* power into a burning, which appeareth even in the Sun and Stars; alfo the fire in the *Salitter* in the Elements, is often kindled, fo that it feemeth as if the *Deep* were of a burning fire; of which, I fhall fpeak in another place.

[" *He ftept back out of the* meekneffe *into the anxi-*
" *ous* fire-will; *and fell into* darkneffe. *The*
" *Reader is advertifed, that he muft not under-*
" *ftand in any place, as if the Devill had kindled*
" *or fired the Light of* God, *no, but the forms of*
" Nature *only, out of which, the* light *fhineth.*
" *For he hath not comprehended the Light, as lit-*
" *tle as the fire doth, which cannot lay hold on the*
" *Light: But he entred into the fire, and is ex-*
" *pelled into the Darkneffe; and hath neither*
" fire *nor* light *befides without or diftinct from*
" *his* creature.] *or own* Creaturelineffe.

38. Now in this quality, King *Lucifer* hath prepared for himfelf the right Hellifh Bath or Lake. He *dares not* fay, that God hath framed or erected the Hellifh quality for him; but he himfelf hath done it: Moreover he hath *offended* the Deity, and turn'd the powers of God into a hellifh Bath or Lake, for his own *Eternal habitation*.

39. For when he and all his Angels had kindled

in their Bodies the qualifying or fountain spirit of the fire, then the unctuousnesse marrow or fatnesse *burnt* in the sweet water, and the flash or terrour, which riseth up fiercely in the birth of the light, became raging and tearing, burning and stinging, and a being or substance of a meer *opposite or con-*trary will.

40. And here, in this quality, the *Life* was turn'd into *a Sting of Death;* for through Heat the bitter quality grew so fierce, stinging, raging and burning, as if the whole body were meer fiery Stings; these did tear and rage in the astringent quality, as if one did thrust *fiery* Pins, Needles or red-hot Bodkins through the Body.

41. On the other side, the *cold fire* of the astringent quality was in a mad furious rage against the heat, and against the bitter venom or Poison, like a great Uproar or hurliburly; and now furthermore, in the Body of *Lucifer*, there was nothing else but a murthering, rubbing, fretting, burning and stinging, a most horrible hellish fire.

42. This *fire-spirit*, and right Devils-spirit, elevated it self now also in the Center of the heart, and would *rule* through the animated or soulish spirit————

  [" *Hereby is understood the* spirit of the will, *out of*
    " *the* Center, *which is generated out of the* Ge-
    " nitrix, *viz. out of the seven qualifying or foun-*
    " tain *spirits ;* which is the Image of God.]
———— in the *whole* Divine power, and kindle the whole *Salitter* of God as a new and potent God : and so the formings and Heavenly Imagings, should rise up in a horrible fiery Qvality, and suffer themselves

to be Imaged and framed according to this *fierce-nesse.*

43. Now when I write of the animated or *fou-lish spirit,* then thou must exactly know, *what it is,* or *how it is,* else thou

† or Nati-vity.

wilt read this Birth or † Geniture in vain, and it will happen to thee, as it did to the wise Heathens, who climbed up to the very face or countenance of God, but could not *see* it.

* or Soulish spirit.

44. The * *Spirit of the Soul* is very much subtiler and more incomprehensible then the Body, or the seven qualifying or fountain spirits, which hold retain and form the Body; for it goeth forth from the seven spirits; As God the Holy Ghost, goeth forth from the Father and the Sonne.

45. The seven qualifying or fountain Spirits have their compacted or incorporated Body, out of Nature, that is, out of the seventh Nature-spirit in the *Divine* power; which in this Book, I call *the Salitter of God,* or the *comprehensibility,* wherein the heavenly figures or shapes arise.

46. And that is *a spirit,* as all the rest of the seven Spirits are, onely the other six are an incomprehensible Being therein: for the Divine power generateth it self in the comprehensibility of the seventh Nature-spirit, as it were hidden or concealed, and incomprehensible to the Creatures.

47. But the animated or *foulish* spirit generateth it self in the heart out of or from the seven qualifying or fountain spirits, in that manner as the Sonne of

of God is generated; and keepeth its feat in the heart, and goeth forth from that *Seat* in the Divine power, as the Holy Ghoft from the Father and the Sonne; for it is of fuch a fubtilneffe as the Holy Spirit of God hath, and uniteth qualifieth or operateth with God the Holy Ghoft.

48. And when the animated or foulifh Spirit goeth forth out of the Body, then it is *one* thing with the hidden Deity, and is together the midft or center in the Imaging or framing of a thing in Nature, as God the Holy Ghoft himfelf is.

49. An example whereof you have in this: as when a *Carpenter* will build a curious houfe or Artificial piece of Architecture, or any other *Artift* goeth about the making of fome artificiall work, the *Hands* which fignifie *Nature*, cannot be the firft that begin the work; but the feven Spirits are the firft Workmafters about it, and the animated or foulifh fpirit fheweth the form figure or fhape of it to the feven fpirits.

50. And then the feven fpirits Image or frame it, and make it comprehenfible, and then the hands *firft* begin to fall to work, to make the Structure according to the Image or frame contrived: For a work muft be firft brought to the fenfe, before you can make it.

51. For the Soul comprehendeth the *higheft* fenfe, it beholdeth what God its Father acteth or maketh, alfo it Co-operateth in the heavenly Imaging or framing: And therefore it maketh a defcription draught platform, or modell, for the Nature-fpirits, fhewing how a thing fhould be Imaged or framed.

52. And according to this delineation or prefigu-

ration of the Soul, all things in this world are made; for the corrupted soul worketh or endeavoureth continually, to bring forth or frame heavenly forms, but cannot bring that to Effect, for the *materials* for its work are onely the earthly corrupted *Salitter*, even a *half-dead* Nature, wherein it cannot Image or frame heavenly Ideas shapes or figures.

53. By this you may understand, what great *power* the spirits of the expelled Angels have had in the heavenly Nature; And what manner of substance this perdition or *Corruption* is of; How they have corrupted and spoiled Nature in heaven in their place with their horrible kindling; from whence the horrible fiercenesse which is predominant in *this* world is exifted.

54. For the kindled Nature burneth still continually untill the laft Judgment Day, and this kindled fire fource or quality is an Eternall *Emnity* against God.

55. But yet whether this kindled fire-fpirit hath *Right* therein; and whether God himfelf hath kindled it, from whence the wrath-fire is exifted; let the Electionifts or Predeftinarians, or thofe that difpute fo about Election, juftifie it, and prove it in *Nature*, if they can; if not, then this fire-fpirit is to be condemned alfo.

Of the Fifth *kind Species form or manner of* Sin's *beginning, in* Lucifer *and his Angels.*

56. The fifth qualifying or fountain fpirit in the Divine power, is the Gracious amiable and bleffed *Love*, which is the very Glance or afpect of *meeknesse* and humility, which is alfo generated in the flafh of life.   57. For

57. For the flash as a Crack penetrateth suddenly, whereby Joy exifteth, and then the ftock of the kindled light in the fweet water, abideth ftanding, and *preffeth* gently after the flafh through the fire, even into the aftringent quality, and mitigateth the fire, and mollifyeth foftneth or fuppleth the aftringent quality, which is alfo a Birth or geniture of the water.

58. But when the fire tafteth the *mild* fweet and pliant Tafte, then is it mitigated and formeth it felf into a meek warmth, very lovingly, and there rifeth up a very *friendly* life in the fire, and penetrateth the aftringent Quality with this pleafing lovely gentle warmth, and allayeth or ftilleth the *cold fire*, and mollifieth or fuppleth the hardneffe, attenuateth the thick, and maketh the dark to be Light.

59. But when the Bitter flafh together with the aftringent and fire-fpirit, tafteth this meekneffe, there is nothing elfe then but a meer longing, defiring and replenifhing, a very gentle pleafant tafting, wreftling, kiffing, and love-Birth : For the *fevere* births of all the qualifying or fountain fpirits in this penetrating, become very gentle, pleafant, humble and friendly, and the very *Deity* rightly fubfifteth therein.

60. For in the firft four qualifying or fountain fpirits ftandeth the Divine Birth or Geniture, therefore they muft be very Earneft and ftrong alfo, though they have among them too, their *meek mother* the fweet water, and in the fifth ftandeth the gracious amiable and bleffed Love, and in the fixth the Joy, and in the feventh the framing Imaging or *comprehenfibility*.

61. Now *Lucifer* ! come on, with thy Love : how haft

haft *thou* behaved thy felf, is *thy* Love alfo fuch a Well-fpring or fountain as this? We will now view that alfo, and examine what manner of *loving Angel* thou art turned into.

Obferve.

62. If *Lucifer* had not elevated and kindled himfelf, then his fountain of Love would be no other then that in God, for there was no other *Salitter* in him, then there is in God.

63. But when he elevated himfelf, *intending* to rule the whole Deity with his animated or foulifh fpirit, then the ftock and heart of light, which is the kernel marrow or pith of *love* in the fweet water, became a fierce and *corroding* crouding fire fource or quality, from whence, in the whole body exifted a very trembling, burning, government and Birth or Geniture.

64. Now when the animated or foulifh fpirit was *generated* in this fevere and aftringent fire's-Birth, then it preffed very furioufly forth from the Body into Nature, or the *Salitter* of God, and *deftroyed* the gracious amiable and bleffed love in the *Salitter*: for it preffed very fiercely furioufly and firily, as a raging Tyrant, through all, and fuppofed, that it felf *alone* was God; it *felf* alone would govern with its fharpneffe.

65. From *hence* now is exifted the great contrary oppofite will and Eternall Emnity between God and *Lucifer*; for the power of God moveth very *foftly* meekly pleafantly and friendly, fo that its Birth cannot be conceived of or *apprehended*, and the fpirits of *Lucifer* move and tear very *harfhly*,

aftrin-

aftringently firily fwiftly and furioufly.

66. An example whereof you have in the kindled *Salitter* of the Stars, which becaufe of this kindled fierceneffe, muft *Roul* with the vanity, even to the laft Judgment Day : And *then* the *fierceneſs* will be feparated from them, and be given to King *Lucifer*, for an Eternal houfe.

67. But that this is a great oppofite contrary will in God, needs no proof : but a Man may think, in cafe fuch a fierce fire fource or quality fhould rife in his Body, what an *untowardneſſe* and contrary will he fhould have in him, and how often the whole Body would be in a rage and fury.

68. Which indeed befalls thofe, who lodge the Devil within them, but fo long as he is but a Gueft, he lyeth *ſtill* like a Tame Whelp : but when he becometh the *Hoſt* himfelf and Mafter of the houfe, then he ftormeth and maketh *havock* in the Houfe, as he did to the Body of God.

69. And therefore it is, that, the wrath-fire of God, is yet in the Body of God which is in this world, till the End, and many a creature is fwallowed up and *devoured* in the wrath-fire, of which much is to be written, but is referred to its proper place.

70. But now whether God himfelf hath created and kindled this Emnity and fierce fire-fource in *Lucifer*, they are to plead for and juftifie, which difpute for Predeftination, Forefeeing, and the Election of Grace, and they are to prove it in Nature, if they can ; if not, then this *corrupted* fire-fource, which ftands in the place or ftead of Love, fhall be condemned alfo.

Of the Sixth *Species Kind form or manner of* Sin's *beginning in* Lucifer, *and in his Angels.*

71. The Sixth qualifying or fountain spirit in the Divine power is the *Mercurius* or *Tone* or Tune, wherein the distinction and heavenly Joy riseth up.

72. This spirit taketh its original in the fire-flash, that is, in the bitter quality, and riseth up in the flash through the *sweet* water, wherein it mitigateth it self, so that it becometh clear and bright, and is reserved and kept in the astringent quality, and there it *toucheth* or stirreth all the spirits : and from this touching or stirring riseth up the Tone ; its rising source or quality standeth in the flash, and its Body or Root standeth in the sweet water in the *Love*.

73. Now this Tone or Tune is the *Divine Joyful-neße*, the triumphing, wherein the Divine and meek Love-play sport or scene in God riseth up, as also the formings Imagings and all manner of *Ideas* shapes and Figures.

74. But here thou must know, that this quality penetrateth very gently and pleasantly with its touching or stirring, through all the Spirits, in such a way and manner, as when a *pleasant* and meek fire of Joy riseth up in the heart of a man, in which fire of Joy, the animated or soulish Spirit triumpheth as if it were in *Heaven*.

75. Now this spirit doth *not* belong to or concern the Imaging or framing of the body, but to the distinction *diversifying* and mobility, especially to the Joy, and to the distinction or difference in the Imaging or shaping.

76 And

76. And when the animated or foulifh Spirit in the Center of the heart, in the midft or Center of the feven qualifying or fountain fpirits is generated, fo that the *will* of the feven Spirits is incorporated or compacted together, then the Tone bringeth it forth from the Body, and is its *Chariot*, on which the fpirit rideth, and executeth that, which is Decreed in the *Council* of the feven fpirits.

77. For the Tone goeth through the animated or Soulifh fpirit into the nature of God, and into the *Salitter* of the feventh qualifying or fountain fpirit in the *Divine* power, which is its receptive or beginning Mother, and uniteth qualifieth or co-operateth with the fame in the forming or framing, and alfo in the diftinguifhing or diverfifying of the Imaging or *fhape.*

78. Therefore when King *Lucifer* changed or *tranfmuted* his high-minded prancing Nagg or Palfrey in the Tone, into a firy † refting, in all the feven fpirits; that was a terrible contrary or *oppofite* will in the *Salitter* of God.

† *or* Reftive-neffe.

79. For when his animated or foulifh fpirit was generated in his body, then he *ftung forth* from his Body into the *Salitter* of God, as a fiery Serpent, out of a hole.

80. But when the Mouth *opened to fpeak,* that is, when the feven fpirits had incorporated or compacted the word together, in their will, and fent it through the Tone into the *Salitter* of God, then it was no otherwife, then if there went a fiery Thunder-bolt into Gods Nature; or as a fierce Serpent, which tyrannizeth raveth and rageth, as if it would *tear* and rend Nature all to pieces.

81. Hence that taketh its original; that the De-

vill

vill is called *the old Serpent,* Apocal. 12.
9. and alfo, that there are Adders and *Serpents* in
this corrupted world ; moreover, all manner of vermine, or venomous Broods of Worms, Toads, Flies,
Lice and Fleas, and all fuch like things whatfoever;
and from hence alfo *Tempeftuous* weather of Lightning, Thundring, Flafhing and Hail-ftones take their
Originall in this world.

Obferve :

82. When the Tone rifeth up in the Divine Nature, then it rifeth up gently from all the feven qualifying or fountain fpirits *joyntly* together, and generateth the word, or Ideas figures and fhapes very
gently :

83. That is, when one qualifying or fountain
fpirit attracteth a will to the Birth or Geniture, then
it preffeth very *gently* through the other qualifying
or fountain fpirits even into the *Center* of the Heart,
and there that will is formed and approved by all
the fpirits.

84. And then the other fix fpirits fpeak it forth
in the Tone, out from *Gods* animated or foulifh fpirit, forth, underftand out from the heart of God, out
from the Sonne of God, which abideth ftanding in
the center as a compacted *incorporated* Word.

85. And the flafh out of that fame Word, or the
ftirring of the Word, which is the Tone, goeth forth
very finely and gently from the Word, and executeth
effecteth or performeth the will of the Word.

86. And that fame *forthgoing* from the Word is
the Holy Ghoft, which formeth frameth and Imageth

geth all whatſoever was Decreed in the center of the heart, in the *Councel* of the ſeven ſpirits of God the Father.

87. In ſuch a gentle way and manner ſhould King *Lucifer* alſo have generated qualified or operated, and according to the *Right* of the Deity, with his animated or ſouliſh ſpirit in the *Salitter*, or in the Nature of God, have *helped* to Image or frame things as a *dear* ſonne in Nature.

88. Juſt as a ſonne in the Houſe helps his Father to drive or *manage* his work, according to his Fathers way and profeſſion Kind and Art : and ſo ſhould *Lucifer* alſo with his Angels, in the *great Houſe* of God the Father, according to the manner and way of God, have *helped* with his animated or ſouliſh ſpirit, to Image all the forms Ideas and vegetations in the *Salitter* of God.

89. For the whole *Salitter* ſhould be a Houſe of pleaſure and *delight* for Angelicall Bodies, and all ſhould riſe up according to the delight of their ſpirit, and Image themſelves ſo, that they ſhould never at all have *any* diſpleaſure in any figure ſhape or creature, but their animated or ſouliſh ſpirit ſhould be Co-operative in every Imaging ;

[" *The* Imaging *out of the heavenly* Eſſences, *is*
" performed Magically, *all according to the*
" *will and ability or potentiality of Nature*
" *and the Creatures :*]

and then the *Salitter* ſhould have been the Creatures proper own,

90. If they had but continued in their meek Birth or Geniture according to the *Divine Right*, their all had Been their own, and their will would have been alwaies *fulfill'd* eternally ; and nothing had Been

among them and in them but meerly the Joy of Love, to speak after an Earthly manner, as it were an *Eternal Laughing* and a perpetuall rejoycing in an eternal hearty delight. For God and the creatures had been one heart and one will.

[" *The Image out of or proceeding from the Soul's fire,*
" *and the Love, and the Divine Center, are*
" *in one Being:*]

91. But when *Lucifer* exalted himself, and kindled his qualifying or fountain spirits, then the animated or soulish spirit went forth in the *Tone* out of or from all the Bodies of *Lucifers* Angels, into the *Salitter* of God, as a fiery Serpent, or *Dragon*, and Imaged or framed all manner of fiery and poisonous forms and Images, like to wild cruel and Evill Beasts.

92. And from hence these wild fierce and Evill Beasts have their *original* in this world. For the Hoast or Army of *Lucifer* had kindled the *Salitter* of the Stars and of the Earth, and *half* kill'd spoyl'd and destroy'd it.

93. But when God, after the fall of *Lucifer*, made the Creation of this world, then all was created out of the same *Salitter*, wherein *Lucifer* had his Seat: And so afterwards the creatures also in this world must needs be created out of that same *Salitter*, which now form themselves according to the condition or kind of the kindled Qualities Evill and Good.

94. And that Beast, which had most of the fire, or the Bitter or the astringent quality, in the *Mercurius*, that became also a bitter, hot, and fierce Beast, all according as the quality was predominant or chief in the Beast.

95. This I set down here only for a manuduction: you

you will find it demonstrated more at large, concerning the *Creation* of this world.

96. Now whether this fiery Tone or *Dragon-spirit* in *Lucifer* and in his Angels be right, and whether God hath thus created him, let the Atturneys or Advocates of *Lucifer,* which make God to be as a Devill, justifie it here by their Answer, and prove it in *Nature* if they can, whether God be such a God, as willeth the Evill, and as hath created the Evill.

97: *If not,*then shall this spirit also be condemned to the Eternall Prison: and they should give over their lying and blaspheming of God; or else they are *worse* then the wild Heathen or Pagans, which know nothing of God ; *who* notwithstanding, live in God, and shall *sooner* possesse the Kingdom of heaven, then many of these blasphemers of God shall, which I shall demonstrate also in its proper Place.

The Sixteenth Chapter.

Of the Seventh *Species kind form or manner of* Sin's beginning *in Lucifer,* and his *Angels.*

HEre thou shouldst open thy Eyes *wide,* for thou wilt see the hidden secret things, which have been kept hidden from all men since the world began. For thou wilt see the murtherous Denne of the *Devill,* and the horrible sin, Emnity, and Perdition.

2. The Devill hath taught man *Sorcery* or *witch-*

craft, thereby to strengthen and fortifie his Kingdom.
But if he had revealed to man the right true funda-
mentall Ground, which did lurk behind or *under* it,
many would have altogether let it alone, and not
have medled with it at all.

3. *Come on ye Jugglers and
Sorcerers or Witches*, you that go a
wooing and a whooring after the Devill: Come to
my School; I will shew you, how with your *Ne-*
cromancie or Art you are carried into Hell.

4. You *tickle* your selves with this, that the Devill is in subjection to you, and ye suppose that ye
are gods: Here I will describe the Originall and
Ground of *Necromancie*, for I am become also a † sear-
cher into Nature, but not after your way and manner, but to *discover your shame* by a Divine Revelation, for an advertisement to this last world, and
for a sentence of Condemnation upon *their* skill and
knowledge: for the Judgment followeth upon knowledge.

† Nature
Kundiger.
Naturalist
Physicus, or
Natural Phi-
losopher.

5. Being the Bow of *fiercenesse* is already Bent,
let every one look to himself, lest he be found in the
limit of the Mark. *For the time is at*
hand, to awake from sleep.

6. Now the seventh form or the seventh spirit in
the divine power, is **Nature**, or the issue or
exit from the other six. For the astringent qualy
attracteth the *Salitter* together, or the Fabrick or
product of all the six spirits, even as a Magnet or
Loadstone attracteth to it self the *Salitter* of the
Iron: and when it is attracted together, then it is a
compre-

comprehensibility; in which the six spirits of God qualifie act or operate, in an *incomprehensible* way or manner.

7. This Seventh spirit hath a colour and condition or kind, of its own, as all the other spirits have: for it is the *Body* of all the spirits, wherein they generate themselves as in a Body: Also out of this spirit, all *figures* shapes and forms, are Imaged or fashioned: moreover the Angels also are created out of it, and *all* † *Naturality standeth therein*.

† Naturelinesse, or the universall Nature.

8. And *this Spirit* is alwayes generated from the six, and subsisteth alwaies *continually*, and is never missing or wanting, nor doth ever passe away, and it again continually generateth the six; for the other six are in this seventh, as in a Mother inclosed or encompassed; and they receive their nourishment power and strength *alwayes*, in their mothers Body or Womb.

9. For the Seventh spirit is the *Body*, and the other six are the *Life*, and in the middle center is the heart of *Light*, which the seven spirits continually generate as a Light of Life; and that Light is their Sonne, and the boyling *mobility* or Penetration through all the spirits, expandeth it self aloft in the Heart, in the exit or rising up of the Light.

10. And this is that spirit of all the seven, which goeth forth out of the heart of God, which formeth frameth and Imageth all in the seventh, and wherein the qualifying or fountain spirits, with their *Love-wrestling* present and shew themselves infinitely.

11. For the Deity is like a wheel, which with its

its *Felleys* and *Spoaks*, and with all the *Naves*, turneth about, and is felleyed together as seven wheeles, so that it can go any way forward, backward, downward, upward, and crosse-wayes, without turning back.

12. Whereas yet alwayes the form of all the seven *wheeles* and the One onely *Nave* in the Center of all the wheeles, is fully in sight, and so it is not understood, how the wheel is made; but the wheel alwaies appears admirable *wonderfull* and marvellous with its rising up, and yet abideth also in its own Place.

13. In such a manner the Deity is continually generated, and neverpasseth away, ceaseth, or vanisheth out of sight; and in this manner also is the *Life* in Angels and Men, continually generated.

14. But according to the moving of the seven spirits of God, the figures and Creatures of the *transitorinesse* are *formed*, and not thus generated: though indeed the Birth or geniture of all the seven spirits sheweth it self *therein*, yet their quality standeth onely in the seventh Nature-spirit, which the other six spirits do form figure frame *alter* and *change* according to their *wrestling* and rising up.

15. And therefore also the figures and *transitory* forms and creatures are changed, according to the condition of the *seventh* Nature-spirit, in which they rise up.

16. But the Angels are not onely Imaged or framed out of the seventh Nature-spirit, as the transitory creatures are, but when the Deity moved it self to the creating of Angels, then in *every* circle, wherein each Angel was incorporated or compacted together; there the Deity with its *whole substance* and
being

being, was *incorporated* or compacted together———

["*Understand*; the two *Eternal Principles, viz.*
"the Fire *and the* Light, *and yet not the qua-*
"*lity or source of the Fire, But the Essence*
"*of it* :]

———and became a Body, and yet the Deity continued in its *seat*, as before.

Understand this well :

17. The Angels Body or the *comprehensibility*, is
from or out of the *Seventh* spirit, and the Birth or
Geniture in that Body, is, the *Six* qualifying or fountain-spirits ; and the spirit or the heart, which the
six spirits generate in the center of the Body, in which
the Light riseth up, and the animated or soulish spirit out of the Light, which also qualifieth uniteth
or operateth with the *Deity*, without, distinct from
the Body : that signifieth the Heart of God, out of
which the Holy Ghost goeth forth.

18. And it also was from or out of the heart of
God co-united or mixed in the Body of the Angel in
their first compacting or *incorporating* together ;
therefore the Angels Government in the *Mind* generateth *it* self, as the Deity doth.

19. And as in the Seventh Nature-spirit of God,
which existeth out of the other six, there doth *not*
stand the whole perfect knowledge of the other six
spirits; for it *cannot* search or dive into their deep
Birth or Geniture, in that they are its *Father*, and
generate it out of themselves.

20. No more doth the whole full and *perfect*
knowledge of God stand in the *Angelical* Body, but
in the *Spirit*, which is generated in the Heart, which

goeth

goeth forth from the Light, which qualifieth or operateth also with the heart and spirit of God, wherein the whole full and *perfect knowledge* of God standeth: but the Body cannot apprehend that animated or soulish spirit; as also the seventh Nature-spirit comprehendeth not the *deepest birth* or Geniture of God.

21. For when the seventh Nature-spirit is generated, then it is dryed by the astringent Quality, and is as it were staid and kept by its Father, and cannot *go back* again into the Deep, that is, into the Center of the Heart, where the Sonne is generated, and from whence the Holy Ghost goeth forth, but must hold still as a *Generated* Body, and must give way to the qualifying or fountain Veins, that is, to the *spirits*, to qualifie work and labour therein as they Please.

22. For it is the proper house and habitation of the six spirits, which they continually build according to their pleasure, or as a Garden of delight, into which, the Master of it, *soweth* all manner of Seeds according to his pleasure, and then enjoyeth the fruit thereof.

23. Thus the other six spirits continually erect this garden of delight and pleasure, and *sowe* their fruits thereinto, and feed upon it to strengthen their Might and joy: and this is the Garden, in which the Angels dwell, and walk up and down in, and *wherein* the heavenly fruit groweth.

24. But the wonderfull proportion or variety of Harmony which appeareth in the growths or vegetations and figures or forms in this Garden, ariseth from the *qualification* or operation, and from the loving wrestling or strugling of the other spirits.

25. For

25. For that which is predominant or chief in the ſtriving, Imageth or formeth the growth and vegetation according to its kind, and the other alwayes *help* to promote it ; one while one is at it, by and by the other, then the third, and ſo on.

26. And *therefore* alſo there ariſe ſo many ſeveral growths vegetations and figures, as are altogether inſearchable and incomprehenſible to the *Bodily Reaſon* of the Angels; but to the animated or *ſouliſh Reaſon* of the Angels, they are wholly fully and perfectly comprehenſible.

27. And this is alſo wholly hidden as to my Body, but *not* as to my animated or ſouliſh ſpirit, for ſo long as it qualifieth or worketh with and in God, it comprehendeth the ſame, but when it falls into *Sin*, then the Door is ſhut againſt it, and the Devill bolteth it up faſt, and it muſt be ſet open again with great labour and induſtrie of the *ſpirit.*

28. I know very well, that the wrath of the Devil will mock and ſcoff in the hearts of wicked men, at *this Revelation.* For he is mightily aſhamed becauſe of this revelation, he hath alſo given my ſoul many a Pang and Cruſh for it: but I leave it to Gods direction, that will have it ſo ; I cannot reſiſt him, though my earthly Body ſhould go to wrack for it, yet my God will *glorifie me* in my knowledge.

29. The Glorification of *this* my knowledge, I deſire, and no other ; for I know, that when this my ſpirit in my new body, which I ſhall get at the Day of my *Reſurrection,* out of this my now *corrupted* Body ; ſhall ariſe, that it will appear like the Deity, as alſo like the holy Angels.

30. For the triumpning Joyous Light, in my ſpirit ſheweth me it ſufficiently, in which I have alſo

searched, into the depth of the Deity, and described it rightly according to my gifts, and the impulse of the spirit, though in great *feeblenesse* and weaknesse, in that my *original* and *actual-sins* have often bolted the Door against me, and the Devil hath danced before it, as a whorish woman, and rejoyced at my Captivity and anguish ; yet that will bring *very little* profit to his Kingdom.

31. Therefore I must now look for no other then his fierce wrath, *but my stay trust and Refuge is the Champion in the Fight*, who hath often delivered me from his Bands, in whom I will *fight* against him, till my departure out of this Life.

Of the terrible, lamentable and miserable perdition of Lucifer *in the* Seventh Nature-*Spirit.*

The Sad mourning House of Death.

32. If all Trees were Writers or Clerks, and all Branches were Pens, and all Hills were Books, and all Waters were Ink, yet they could not *sufficiently describe* the lamentable misery, which *Lucifer*, together with his Angels, hath brought into his place or *whole space* of that World wherein he was Created.

33. For he hath made the House of *Light* to be a House of *Darknesse*, and the House of *Joy* to be a House

House of Mourning Lamentation and Sadnesse; that which was the house of pleasure delight vivifying and *refreshing*; he hath made to be a House of thirst and *hunger*; the House of *Love* to be a House of eternal *Emnity*, and the house of *meeknesse* to be a House of knocking rumbling *thundring* and lightning; the house of *Peace* to be a House of lamenting and eternal *Howling*; the House of *laughing* to be a House of eternal trembling and *Horrour*.

34. The Birth or Geniture of light, munificence and *well-doing* to be an eternall hellish Pain and *Torment* : the *food of pleasing relish* to be an eternal Abomination and Stinck, a *Loathing* of all fruits; and the house of *Lebanon* and Cedars, to be a Stony and *Rocky* House of Fire; the *sweet* sent or relish to be a *stinck* and a house of ruine and desolation, an End of all Good; the *Divine Love* to be a black, cold, hot, eating *corroding*, and yet not consuming *Devill*, who is an *Emnity* against God and his Angels; and so he hath all the heavenly Hoasts or Armies against him.

Now Observe :

35. The *Learned* have had many Disputations Questions Conceits and Opinions concerning the fierce malignity and evil that is in all the Creatures, even in the very Sun and Stars in this world; moreover, there are some so very poisonous and venomous Beasts, Worms and Vegetables in this world, that thereupon Rational men have justly *wondred*; and some have concluded peremptorily, *That God must needs have also willed the Evill,* being He hath Created

fo much that is Evil: And fome have laid the blame and fault thereof upon the Fall of *Adam*, and fome have imputed it to the work and doings of the Devill.

36. But being all the Creatures and vegetables were created *before* the Time of man, therefore the fault ought *not* to be laid upon man: for man gat not the *beaſtial Body* in his creation, but it firſt came to be fo in his Fall.

37. Neither hath man brought the malignity poiſon and venom into the Beaſts, Birds, Worms, and Stones, for he *had not* their Body, otherwiſe if he had brought malignity and fierceneſſe or wrath into all Creatures, then he could *never* have looked for mercy at Gods Hands; no more then the Devill.

38. Poor Man did not fall out of a reſolved purpoſed will, but through the poiſonous venomous *infection* of the Devil, elſe there had been no Remedy for him.

39. Now this true information thou wilt find deſcribed here following, not from a zeal, to vilifie any body thereby, but *in Love*, and as a humble information and inſtruction from the Abyſſe of my ſpirit, and for an aſſured comfort to the poor ſick old *Adam*, which now lyeth at the point of his *Laſt departure* from hence out of this world.

40. For *in Chriſt* we are all one Body, therefore alſo this ſpirit would heartily fain have it fo, that its fellow Members might be *refreſh'd* with a draught of the precious Wine of God *before* their departure from hence, whereby they might encounter and ſtand in the great fight with the Devil, and obtain the *Victory*, that the victory of the Devill in this modern Drunken world might be diſappointed and

deſtroyed,

deftroyed, and the great Name of the LORD might be Sanctified.

Now behold!

41. VVhen King *Lucifer* together with his Angels fo glorioufly beautifully and divinely created, as a Cherubin and King in God, then he fuffered his bright beautious form to *befool* him, in that he faw how noble, glorious and fair a Spirit *rofe up* in him.

42. Then *his* feven qualifying or fountain fpirits thought they would elevate and kindle themfelves, and fo they alfo would be as fair, glorious and mighty, as the animated or *foulifh fpirit*, and thereby would domineer, by their own Power and Authority in the *whole* Court Circumference Dominion or extent as a New God.

43. They faw very well, that the animated or *foulifh fpirit*, qualified mixed or operated with the Heart of God, and thereupon they were refolved, they would elevate and *kindle* themfelves, hoping to be as bright illuftrious, deep, and Almighty as the *deepeft* Ground in the Center of the Heart of God.

44. For they thought to elevate the natural Body, which was compacted together or incorporated out of the Nature-fpirit of God, up into the *hidden Birth* or Geniture of God, that their feven qualifying or fountain fpirits might thus be as high, and as all compact as felf, as the animated or foulifh fpirit.

45. And the animated or foulifh fpirit fhould triumph over the Center of the Heart of God, and the Heart of God fhould be fubjected under it; and fo the feven Spirits of God fhould Image, frame and

form

form all, by *their* animated or foulifh fpirit.

46. And this High mind, and felf-will, was directly and *wholly* againft the Birth or Geniture of God : for the Body of the Angels fhould abide and remain in its feat, and *be* Nature, and as an humble mother, hold ftill and be quiet, and fhould not have the Omnifcience and own felf rational comprehenfibility of the Heart, or of the deepeft Birth or Geniture of the *holy Trinity*; but the feven fpirits fhould generate themfelves in their Natural Body, as is done in God.

47. And their comprehenfibility fhould not be in the *hidden kernel*, or in the innermoft Birth or Geniture of God, but the animated or foulifh fpirit, which they generate in the Center of their Heart; fhould *qualifie* mix or operate with the innermoft Birth or Geniture of God, and *help* to form all figures fhapes and Images, according to the pleafure delight and will of the feven fpirits, whereby in the Divine pomp, all might be but *One* Heart, and *one* will.

48. For the Birth or Geniture of God alfo is thus; the feventh Nature-fpirit doth not *reach back* into its Father, which generateth it, but holdeth ftill and is quiet as a Body, and letteth the Fathers Will, which is, the other fix fpirits, to form and image in it, how *they* pleafe.

49. Neither doth any one fpirit particularly and feverally reach with its corporeal Being, after the Heart of God, but includeth clofeth or *joyneth* its will with the other, in the Center, to the Birth or Geniture of the Heart, fo that the Heart and the feven Spirits of God are *One* will.

50. For this is the Law of the *comprehenfibility* that

that it do not elevate it self up into the *incomprehensibility*: for the power, which in the Center or midst, is compacted together or incorporated out of all the seven spirits; is incomprehensible and unsearchable, but *not* invisible, for it is not the power of one spirit alone, but of all seven.

51. Therefore one spirit in its own Body, besides and distinct from its † instanding or innate instant Birth or Geniture, *cannot* reach into the whole Heart of God, and examine try and search all, for it comprehends, besides and distinct from its instanding Birth or Geniture, onely its *own* Birth or Geniture in the heart of God; but *all* the seven spirits *joyntly* together comprehend the whole heart of God.

† Instehen-
den Ge-
buhrt.

[" *And so also in Man, but understand it as to the*
" *Image of God, viz. in the Soul's spirit, not*
" *in the fiery Essence of the soul, but in the Es-*
" *sence of the* Light, *wherein the* Image *of* God
" *standeth :*]

k.

52. But in the instanding or innate Birth or Geniture of the spirits, where the one still generateth the other, there *every* spirit generateth all the seven spirits, but yet only in the rising flash of the life.

53. But the Heart, when it is generated, is singular, or distinct; *viz. a peculiar Person* ; and yet not separated from the Spirits; but the spirits cannot transmute or change themselves in their first Birth or Geniture one into another.

54. Also the second cannot change it self into the third, which is the *exit* of the spirit; but every Birth or Geniture abideth in its seat, and yet all the Births or Genitures together, are but the *One* Only *God.*

55. But

55. But being the Body of *Lucifer* was created out of Nature and the most *outward* Birth or Geniture, therefore it was unjustly done, that he should elevate himself into the *innermost* and deepest, which he could not do * in the Divine Right, but must so elevate and kindle himself onely, that thereby the qualifying or fountain-spirits might be set or put into the sharpest penetrating and *Infecting.*

56. I verily suppose indeed, that thou fair Necromancer, hast changed thy self to purpose; and mayest well teach men also *thy Black Art*, that they perhaps might also become such potent Gods, as *thou* art.

57. Ye blind and proud Necromancers, Jugglers and Sorcerers, your Art consisteth in your changing the *Elements* of your Body by your conjurations and Instruments of the Qualities or qualifying Properties, which you make use of to that purpose, and ye think ye have *Right* so to do; but is it not against the Birth or Geniture of God? If you think so, make that appear.

58. How can you well suppose, that you can change your selves into *another form?* Indeed you suffer the Devill thus to play the Ape with you, and *cheat* you: and all this while you are but *blind* in your own skill, though you have learned your Art never so well, yet you do not know the Scope it driveth at; for the Pith and Heart therein, is the changing or altering of the qualifying or fountain-spirits, as *Lucifer* did, when he would needs be God.

Now thou Askest :

How can that be ?

Answer.

59. Behold, when the corporeall qualifying or fountain spirits set their will into Sorcery or Witchcraft, then the animated or soulish spirit, which they generate, and which, in the *Astral Elementary* Quality ruleth in the hidden and deepest Center; is clearly already a Sorcerer or Witch, and hath changed transformed or metamorphosed it self into Sorcery or *Witchcraft.*

60. But the Bestial Body cannot follow so suddenly and nimbly, but must be charmed to it, by *Characters* and *Conjurations,* and some instruments for that purpose, whereby the animated or soulish spirit maketh the bestial Body invisible, and changeth it into such a form, as the will of the qualifying or fountain spirits *was,* at the beginning of its purpose to a *Metamorphosis,* or Transmutation.

61. The Bestial flesh cannot well *change* it self, or put it self into another Birth or Geniture, but is brought into a slender and inferiour Base form, as of a Beast, of Wood, or such like thing, which hath its Body qualifying or boyling in the *Elements,* as in their fountain.

62. But the Astral spirits can well cloath themselves in another form or shape, but that continueth *onely so long,* as the Birth or Geniture of Nature above their Pole or Zenith permitteth them.

63. For when it changeth it self with its *wheeling* and penetrating, so that another qualifying or foun-

tain spirit becomes chief or predominant, then their
Art lyeth down upon the ground; and *their Deity* in
the first qualifying or fountain spirit, in which they
had begun their Art, hath an *End*.

64. Now if it be to last *any longer*, then it must be
made again *afresh* according to the qualifying or
fountain spirit then ruling at that Present, or the
Devill with his animated or soulish spirit must be in
the astrall spirits of the Body, which instantly and
suddenly changeth it, or else *his Art* is here at an
End also.

65. For Nature will *not* suffer it self to be Juggled
with, at all times and houres, as the spirits would
have it, but all must be done, according to that
spirit, which then at that present time is Lord and
chief or *predominant*.

66. It is *not* that Spirit of God which is Lord and
chief in Nature, which *causeth* or maketh the Jug-
ling, but it is made, in the *fiercenesse* of the *Salitter*,
which Lord *Lucifer* hath kindled with his elevation,
which is *his* eternal Kingdom.

67. But when the power or might of that spirit
is allayed, then the kindled fire can be *no more* useful
to the Juggler.

68. For the wrath-fire in Nature, is not, during
this Time of the world, the Devils *own* house of his
power; for the love standeth *hidden* in the Center of
the wrath-fire, and *Lucifer*, together with his Angels, lyeth imprisoned in the *outward* wrath-fire even
untill the Judgment of God: then, he will have the
wrath-fire separated from the Love, for an eternall
Bath or Lake, and doubtlesse he will wash his Jug-
lers Head and Face withall.

69. This I set thee down here for a **Warning**, that thou mayst know, what manner of *Ground* Sorcery or Witchcraft hath, not in such a way as if I would write any heathenish sorcery or witchcraft, neither have I studied any; but the animated or soulish spirit beholdeth their Juggling, which in the *Body* I do not understand.

70. But being it runneth counter clean contrary to the Love and Meeknesse of the Birth or Geniture of God, and is a contrary or *opposite* will in the Love of God, so that he is loath without pressing necessity driveth him to it to hurt Man; therefore will the spirit have the *wrath-Bath* or Lake of Nature, set apart to be an Eternal Parching or drying place, for Jugglers, perverters or changers of Gods Ordinance or Order. And therein they may practise and shew forth *their* new Deity.

Of the Kindling of the wrath-Fire.

71. Now when King *Lucifer*, together with all his Angels, kindled himself, then the wrath-fire rose up *instantly* in the Body, and the gracious amiable and blessed *Light* was extinguisht in the animated or soulish spirit, and became a fierce furious Devillish Spirit, all according to the *kindling* and will of the qualifying or fountain spirits.

72. Now this animated or soulish spirit was bound or united with the Deity, in Nature, and could qualifie mix or operate in and with the same, as if it were one and the same thing: and that now stung forth out of the Bodies of the Devills into the Nature of God, like a Theef and a *Murtherer*, that

desired

desired to Rob murther and spoil all, and bring all under its power, and so kindled all the Seven spirits in Nature, and then there was nothing else but an Astringent, Bitter, fiery and cracking *burning* tearing and raging.

73. Thou must *not think*, that the Devill hath thus powerfully and mightily overcome the Deity: No ; but he hath kindled the wrath of God, which indeed had otherwise *rested Eternally* in secret, and so he hath made the *Salitter* of God to be a Murtherous *Denne* ; for if fire be cast into a heap of straw and kindled, it will *burn.*

74. Moreover, the wrath-fire of God doth *not reach* in Nature into the innermost kernel of the Heart, which is the Sonne of God; much lesse into the Secret glory or Holinesse of the Spirit; but into the Birth or Geniture of the six qualifying or fountain spirits, in the *place* where the seventh is generated.

75. For in that place or in this Birth or Geniture is Lord *Lucifer become* a *Creature,* and his dominion did reach no further or deeper then so : but if he had continued in the *Love,* then his animated or soulish spirit had reach'd even to the *Center* of the Heart of God, for Love presseth or penetrateth *through* the whole Deity.

76. But when his Love was extinguisht, then the animated or soulish spirit could *no more* reach into the heart of God, and so his attempt was in vain, but he raved and raged in nature, that is, in the seventh qualifying or fountain spirit of God.

77. But being the power of all the seven spirits stood *in this One* ; therefore also all the seven were kindled in the wrath, but yet only in the *outward* and

compre-

comprehensible qualification or constitution.

78. For the Devill could not touch the heart, neither could he touch the *innermost* Birth or Geniture of the qualifying or fountain spirits; for his *Glory* of the seven spirits was already mortified in the first flash of kindling, and was presently held captive and imprisoned in the first *exit* of the animated or soulish Spirit.

79. In *this Hour* King *Lucifer* prepared for himself, the Hell and eternal Perdition, which now standeth in the *outermost* qualifying or fountain spirit of the Nature of God, or in the outermost Birth or Geniture of this world.

80. But when *Nature* kindled it self thus horribly, then the house of joy came to be a house of trouble affliction and misery : for the astringent quality became kindled in *its own* House, which is a very hard cold and dark Being, like a cold hard frosty Winter, which only attracted the *Salitter* together, and dryed it up, so that it became rugged cold and sharp like Stones, wherein the heat was captivated imprisoned and also attracted together, and so formed or framed into a hard cold, dark Being.

81. When this was done, the Light in Nature was extinguish'd in the outermost Birth or Geniture also, and all became very dark perished and *spoiled* ; the water became very cold and thick, and staid here and there in the *Clefts* : this is the original of the Elementary Water on Earth.

82. For before the Times of the world the water was very Thin or rarified like Ayr, and then the life was generated therein also, which *water* is now so *mortal* corrupted perished and spoiled, and so rolleth and runneth to and fro.

83. The

83. The Gracious amiable and bleſſed Love, which roſe up in the flaſh of the life, became a fierce and bitter venom or Poiſon, a very murtherous Denne, *a Sting of Death* : the Tone or Tune became like the hard knocking or Loud *Rumbling* of ſtones, and a houſe of Lamentation.

84. Briefly, all was a meer dark and miſerable Being in the whole Circumference Extent or Dominion, in the outermoſt birth or Geniture of the Kingdom of *Lucifer*.

85. But thou muſt not think, that Nature was thus *corrupted* and kindled even to the innermoſt ground, but only the outermoſt Birth or Geniture; but the innermoſt, in which the ſeven qualifying or fountain ſpirits generate themſelves; retain'd its own Right to it ſelf, being the *kindled* Devill could *not* reach into it.

86. But now the inner Birth or Geniture hath the Fanne or Caſting-ſhovel in its Hand, and will one Day *purge* its floor, and give the Chaffe or huſks to the Kingdom of *Lucifer* for Eternal food.

87. For if the Devil *could* have reach'd into the innermoſt Birth or Geniture, then inſtantly the whole Circumference Court or Extent of his Kingdome would have been the kindled *burning Hell*.

88. But now he muſt lye *captivated* and Impriſoned in the outermoſt Birth or Geniture even till the laſt Judgment Day, which is at hand, and very near *to be Expected*.

89. But *Lucifer* hath kindled *his qualifying or fountain ſpirits* even in the innermoſt Birth or Geniture, and now *his* qualifying or fountain ſpirits generate an animated or ſouliſh *Devills* ſpirit, which is an eternal Enemy of God.

90. For

90. For when God was angry in *his* outermost Birth or Geniture in Nature, then it was not his purposed *determinate* will, to be kindled; neither hath he effected that kindling : but he hath drawn the *Salitter* together, and thereby hath prepared an eternal *Lodging* for the Devil.

91. For he cannot be expell'd *quite out* away beyond God, into another Kingdom of Angels; but a place must be *reserved* to him for a Habitation.

92. Neither would God *presently* give him the kindled *Salitter* for an eternal Habitation, for the *internal* Birth or Geniture of the spirits stood yet *hidden* therein.

93. For God intended to do somewhat *else* with it, and so King *Lucifer* should be kept a *Prisoner*, till another Angelical Hoast or Army, out of the same *Salitter*, should come in *his* stead; which are *Men.*

94. Now come on ye Atturneys Lawyers and Advocates of *Lucifer*, maintain the Cause of your King now, and shew whether he hath done Right, in kindling of the *wrath-fire* in Nature: if not, then he must *burn* therein eternally, and your *Lies* against the Truth must burn with him.

95. These are the Seven kinds species forms or manners of Sin's beginning and eternal *Emnity* against God.

Now followeth briefly concerning the Four *new little* Sonnes *of* Lucifer, *which he hath generated in himself in his corporeal Regiment : for which he was expell'd from his Place, and is become* the Horriblest Devill.

Of the First Sonne

Pride.

Now it may be asked :

What *moved* Lucifer to this ? *that he* would *needs be above God ?*

Answer.

96. Here thou must know, that *without* distinct from himself he had no impulse at all to his Pride, but his Beauty and brightnesse *deceived* him; when he saw that he was the fairest and beautifullest Prince in Heaven, then he *despised* the friendly qualifying mixing Operating and generating of the Deity, and thought with himself that he would *rule* with his Princely power in the whole Deity, all must stoop and bow to *him.*

97. But when he found, that he could not effect it, then he kindled himself, intending to do it *some other* way, and so then, the Sonne of Light became a Sonne of Darknesse; for he *himself* consumed the power of his sweet water, and made it to be a sowr stinck.

Of the Second Sonne,

Covetousnesse.

98. The second Will was *Covetousnesse*, which grew out of Pride, for *Lucifer* thought with himself, that he would *reign* over all Kingdoms, as a Sole God; all should bow to him, he would form and frame *all* with his own power; and besides also his *beauty* so deceived him, that he thought he would have all in his sole possession alone.

99. This Modern World should do well to speculate on this Pride and Covetousnesse, and to consider, *How* it is an Emnity against God, and that thereby they go *headlong* to the Devill, and there must have their Jawes and Throat open eternally to rob and devour, and yet find nothing but *hellish* Abomination.

Of the Third Sonne

* *Envy.*

* or *Spite.*

100. This Sonne is the very † *Gout* of this world; † *Podagra.* for it taketh its original in the flash of Pride and Covetousnesse, and standeth on the Root of Life as pricking and bitter Gall.

101. This spirit also came at first from Pride, for Pride thought and said to it self, Surely thou art *beautifull* and mighty *potent*: and Covetousnesse thought, and said to it self, All must be *Thine*; and Envy thought and said to it self, Thou must *kill* all with thy stinging, which is not obedient unto thee;

and

and thus it Stung at the other Gates of Angels, but all was in vain, for its power and might reach'd *no further*, then in the Extent of the *place*, out of which it was created.

Of the Fourth *Sonne*

* *Wrath.*

102. This *Sonne* is the very *burning* Hellish Fire, and taketh its original also from Pride. For when *Lucifer* with his hatefull and Odious Envy could *not* fill his Pride and Covetousnesse, then he kindled the *wrath-fire* in himself, and roared therewith, into Gods Nature, as a fierce Lion, and from whence then arose the wrath of God and *all Evil.*

103. Of which much were to be written, but you will find it more apprehensibly, at the place concerning the Creation : For there are to be found *living* Testimonies Enough, so that none need doubt, whether the things be so or no.

104. Thus King *Lucifer* is the beginning of *Sin*, and *the Sting of Death*, and the kindling of Gods wrath, and the beginning of all Evill, a corruption perdition and destruction of this world, and whatever evill is done, there, *he is the first Author* and *Causer* thereof.

105. Also he is a murtherer and Father of Lies, and a founder of Hell, a spoyler and corrupter and destroyer of all that is *Good*, and an eternal Enemy of God, and of all good Angels and Men ; against whom, I, and all men that think to be saved, must daily and hourly *struggle* and fight, as against the worst and Archest Enemy.

The

The final *Condemnation.*

106. But being God hath *accurfed* him as an eternal Enemy, and *condemn'd* him unto eternal Imprifonment, where he now feeth his hour-Glaffe more and *more* plainly before his Eyes: And being his hellifh Kingdom is *revealed to me* by the Spirit of God; fo I curfe him alfo together with and amongft all holy Souls of Men, and renounce and *defie* him as an eternal *Enemy*, who hath often fpoyled and Torn up my Vineyard.

107. Moreover I defie alfo all his † Lawyers and † Helpers, and will with the Divine Grace from hence forth *fully* reveal his Kingdom; and demonftratively prove, that *God is a God of Love and Meekneffe, who willeth not the Evill,* Pfal. 5. 5. and *who hath no pleafure in the perdition of any, but willeth that all men fhould be* helped or *faved,* Ezek. 18. 23. & 3. 3. 11. And then I will fhew and prove alfo, that *all Evill* cometh from the Devil, 1 *Tim.* 2. 4, and taketh its original from him.

Of the final *Fight and* Expulfion *of* King *Lucifer, together with* all his Angels.

108. Now when this horrible Lucifer as a *Tyrant*, and raging fpoiler of all that is Good, fhewed himfelf thus terribly, as if he would kindle and deftroy *all*, and bring all under his Jurifdiction; then all the heavenly Hoafts and Armies were againft him, and he alfo againft *them all*, there now the fight began: for all ftood moft terribly, one *party againft another.* 109. And

109. And the great Prince MICHAEL with his Legions fought against him, and the Devill with his Legions had *not* the *victory*; but was driven from his place, as one vanquished, *Apoc.* 12.

Now it may be Asked :

What manner of fight was this ? how could could they fight one with another *without* weapons ?

Answer.

110. The Spirit alone understandeth this *Hidden* secret ; which must fight Daily and Hourly with the *Devill*, the outward flesh *cannot* comprehend it; also the Astral spirits in Man cannot understand it, neither is it comprehended by man at all, unlesse the animated or soulish spirit unite qualifie and operate with the *innermost* Birth or Geniture in Nature, in the Center, where the Light of God is set opposite against the Devills Kingdom, that is, in the Third Birth or Geniture in the *Nature* of this world.

111. When it uniteth qualifieth or operateth with God in *this seat*, then the animated or soulish spirit carrieth it into the *Astrall* ; for the Astrall must in this Place fight hourly with the Devill.

112. For the Devill *hath* power in the outermost Birth or Geniture of Man, for his seat is there, the murtherous Denne of Perdition, and the House of misery and *woe* : wherein the Devill *whetteth* the Sting of Death, and through his animated or *soulish* spirit, he reacheth in into the Heart of Man in his outermost Birth or Geniture.

113. But

113. But when the Astrall Spirits are *enlightned* from the animated or soulish spirit, which in the Light uniteth with God, then they grow *fervent* and very Longing and desirous of the light: on the other side, the animated or soulish spirit of the Devil which ruleth in the outermost Birth or Geniture of Man, is very terrible and angry, and of a very contrary or *opposite* will.

114. And then there riseth up the striving or *fighting fire* in Man, just as it rose up in Heaven with *Michael* and *Lucifer*, and so the poor Soul comes to be miserably crushed *stretched*, tormented, and put upon the Wrack.

115. But if it get the victory *with its piercing penetration*; then it bringeth its light and knowledge into the outermost Birth or *Geniture* of *Man*: for it presseth back with force through the seven Spirits of Nature which I *call* here the Astrall Spirits, and as an assessor governeth also in the *councill* of Reason.

116. And then man first knoweth what the Devill is; how much an Enemy he is to him, and how *great* his power is; also how he must fight with him, very *secretly* every day hour and Moment.

117. Which thing *Reason*, or the outward Birth, or *Geniture* of Man, without the experience of this fight or battle *cannot* comprehend: for the Third or outermost Birth or Geniture in Man, which is the *carnal* or fleshly Birth; and which man, through the first Fall in his Lusts, hath raised and prepared for himself; is the Devils Castle or *Fort* of Prey or Robbery and dwelling House, wherein the Devill, as in a *Bullwark*, fighteth with the Soul; and giveth it many a bland thump upon its Breast, which goes to the very Heart.   118. Now

118. Now this Birth of the *Flesh*, is *not* the Mansion House of the soul ; but in its strife it goeth in with its Light into the *Divine* power, and fighteth against the Murther of the Devil.

119. On the other side, the Devil with his Poison shooteth and *darteth* at the seven qualifying or fountain spirits, which generate the soul, intending to destroy and to *kindle* them, that thereby he may get the whole Body for his own propriety.

120. Now if the soul would fain bring its light and knowledge into the *Humane* Mind, then it must fight and strive hard and stoutly, and yet hath a very *narrow* passage to enter in at, it will be often knockt down by the Devill, but it must stand to it here, like a *Champion* in the battel. And if it now gets the *Victory*, then it hath conquered the Devill ; but if the Devil prevails and gets the better, then the soul is *captivated*.

121. But being the fleshly Birth or Geniture is not the soul's *own* proper House, and that it cannot possesse it as an *Inheritance*, as the Devil doth, therefore the Fight and Battel lasteth so long, as the House of Flesh lasteth.

122. But if the House of Flesh be once destroyed, and that the Soul is not *yet* conquered or vanquished in its House, but is free and unimprisoned ; then the fight is *ended*, and the Devil must be gone from this spirit *Eternally*.

123. Therefore this is a very difficult *Article* to be understood ; nay it cannot be understood at all unlesse it be by experience in *this* fight : though I should write *many* Books thereof, yet thou wouldst understand *nothing* of it, unlesse thy spirit stand in *such* a Birth or Geniture, and that the knowledge be

generated in thy self; otherwise thou canst neither comprehend *nor believe* it.

124. But if thou comprehendest this, then also thou understandest the strife or the Fight, which the *Angels* held with the Devils : for *the Angels have not Flesh nor Bones,* no more have the Devills.

125. For their Bodily or *Corporeal* Birth standeth onely in the seven qualifying or fountain spirits, but the animated or *soulish* Birth in the Angels, uniteth mixeth or operateth with God; but it is *not* so in the Devils.

126. Therfore thou must here know, that the Angels with their animated or *soulish* Birth , in which they qualifie and unite with God, have striven and fought in *Gods power* and Spirit against the kindled Devills, and turn'd them out from the Light of God, and driven them together into a *Hole,* that is, into a narrow Court Quarter or Compasse, like a Prison, which is the place or space in upon and above the Earth up to the Moon, who is a Goddesse of the Earthly Birth or Geniture.

127. So far reacheth their Extent now, till the Last Day, and then they will get a House in that Place, where the *Earth* now is and standeth,——

[" *That is, in the outermost Birth in the Darknesse,*
" *wherein they reach not the second Principle*
" *and source or fountain of the* Light :]

—— and this will be called *the burning Hell.*

128. Lord *Lucifer,* wait for it , and in the mean while take this for an assured Prophesie concerning

it :

it : for thou wilt get the kindled *Salitter* in the outer-most Birth or Geniture, which thou thy self haft so prepared and fitted, to be thy *Eternall House* to dwell in.

129. But not in such a form as it now standeth, but all will be *separated* in the kindled wrath-fire, and the dark, hot, cold, rugged, hard, bitter, stinking relicks dregs or drosse, will be *left thee* for an eternal Inne and Lodging.

130. And thou wilt be such an Eternal Almighty God therein, as a *Prisoner* in a deep Prison or Dungeon ; where thou wilt neither attain nor see the Eternall light of God : But the kindled bitter wrath of God will be thy *Grate* Bolts and bounds, out of which thou canst never Get.

The Seventeenth Chapter.

Of the lamentable and miserable *State and Condition of the* Corrupt perished Nature, *and Original of the four Elements,* instead of the Holy Government of God.

I.

ALthough God be an Eternal Almighty Regent or Governour, whom none can resist, yet *Nature,* in its kindling, hath now gotten a very monstrous strange government, such as was *not,* before the times of the wrath.

2. For the six qualifying or fountain spirits did generate the seventh Nature-spirit before the Times of the wrath, in the Place of this world ; very meekly.

ly and *pleasantly*, as is now done in heaven, and not so much as the least spark of Wrath or Anger did rise up therein.

3. Moreover, all was very Bright and light therein, neither was there need of any *other* Light; but the fountain or well-spring of the Heart of God enlightned *all*, and was a light in all, which did shine every where all over incessantly without any obstacle: For Nature was very rarified and thin or Transparent, and all stood meerly in power, and was in a very pleasant *lovely* Temper.

4. But as soon as the fight began, *in Nature*, with the proud Devil; then in the seventh Nature-spirit, in the Court Region or Extent of *Lucifer*, which is the place of this world, all gat *another* form and operation.

5. For Nature gat a Twofold source, and the outermost Birth or Geniture in Nature, was kindled in the wrath-fire, which † fire, now, is called the † *Nature-Fire, Gods Anger, Hell.* 𝖜𝖗𝖆𝖙𝖍 𝖔𝖋 𝕲𝖔𝖉, or the *burning Hell.*

Note.

6. Here is required, most Inward Sense or Perception to understand this; for the place, where the Light is generated in the heart, only comprehendeth it, the *outward* Man doth not comprehend it at all.

7. But behold! when *Lucifer* with his Hoast or Army stirred or *awakened* the wrath-fire in the Nature of God, so that God was moved to anger in Nature in the place of *Lucifer;* then the outermost Birth or Geniture in Nature gat *another* quality, which was very Fierce, Astringent, Cold, Hot, Bitter, and Sowr.

8. The

8. The moving or Boyling spirit, which *before* qualified or operated very meekly in Nature, that became in its outermost Birth or Geniture very elevating and *terrible*, which now in the outermost Birth is called the *Wind,* or the Element of *Ayr,* in regard of its elevation or expansion.

9. For when the seven spirits kindled themselves in their outermost Birth or Geniture, then they generated such a *violent* moving spirit; and so the sweet water, which before the times of the wrath was very rarified and thin and incomprehensible, grew very thick and elevated and swelled, and the astringent quality grew very sharp and Cold-firie, or fierce-cold, for it got a strong attracting together, like *Salt.*

10. For the Salt-water or * Salt, which still to this Day is found in the Earth, hath its original and descent from the *first kindling* of the Astringent Quality: and so the Stones also have their beginning and descent from thence, as also the Earth.

11. For the astringent quality now, attracted the *Salitter* very strongly together, and dryed it, whence the *bitter* Earth is proceeded, but the Stones are from the *Salitter,* which at that Time stood in the power of the Tone or Tune.

12. For, as Nature with the working, wrestling, and rising up of its Birth or Geniture, stood in the time of the kindling, Just *such* a *Matter* attracted it self together.

Now it may be Asked:

How then is a comprehensible or palpable Sonne come to be out of an incomprehensible Mother?

Answer.

13. Thou haſt a *Similitude* of this, in that the Earth and Stones are proceeded out of the incomprehensibility.

14. For behold the Deep between Heaven and Earth is alſo incomprehenſible, and yet the Elementary Qualities at *ſometimes* generate living comprehenſible fleſh, therein, as Graſhoppers, Flyes and Worms or creeping things.

15. Which is cauſed by the *ſtrong* attracting together of the qualities, in which attracted *Salitter* the life is ſuddenly generated; For when the heat kindleth the aſtringent Quality, then the life riſeth up, for the Bitter quality ſtirreth it ſelf, which is the original of life.

16. So in like manner the *Earth* and *Stones* have their deſcent; for when the *Salitter* kindled it ſelf in Nature, then all became very rugged thick and dark, like a thick dark Miſt or Cloud, which the aſtringent quality dryed up hard with its coldneſſe.

17. But, being the Light in the outermoſt Birth was extinguiſhed, the Heat alſo was captivated in the Comprehenſibility or palpability, and could *no more* generate its Life: from thence *Death* did come into Nature, ſo that Nature or the corrupt Earth could no more help it, and thereupon *another* crea-tion,

tion of Light muſt needs follow, or elſe the Earth would have been an *Eternal* undiſſolvable Death, but now the Earth generateth or bringeth forth fruit in the power and kindling of the *created* Light.

Now one might ask :

What is the condition then of this *Two-fold* Birth or Geniture ? Is God then extinguiſht in the kindling of the wrath-fire, in the place of this world, ſo that nothing is there elſe but a *meer* wrath-fire ? or is the *One* onely God become a Two-fold God ?

Anſwer.

18. Thou canſt not better comprehend apprehend or underſtand this then in and by thy *own Body*, which through the firſt fall of *Adam* with all its Birth or Geniture, fitneſſe faculties and will, is become juſt ſuch a Houſe.

19. Firſt, thou haſt the *Beaſtial* Fleſh, which is come to be ſo through the Luſtfull longing Bit of the Apple : for it is the Houſe of *Corruption* ; For, when *Adam* was made out of the corrupted *Salitter* of the Earth, that is, out of the Seed or *Maſſe or Lump, which the Creator extracted out of the corrupted Earth ; he was not then at firſt, ſuch fleſh ; elſe his Body had been created *Mortall*, but he had *an Angelicall powerfull Body,* in which, he ſhould ſubſiſt Eternaily, and ſhould eat Angelical fruit, which did grow for him in Paradiſe before his fall ; *before* the LORD curſed the Earth.

20. But

20. But being the Seed, or Masse or Lump, out of which *Adam* was made, was somewhat infected with the corrupt disease or malady of the Devill, *Adam therefore* long'd after his Mother, that is, to eat of the fruit of the corrupted Earth, which then in its outward comprehensibility was become so Evil, and in the wrath-fire was become so hard palpable and comprehensible.

21. But being *Adams spirit* long'd after that fruit, which was, of the Quality of the corrupted Earth, *therefore* also Nature formed or framed such a Tree for him, as was *like* the corrupted Earth.

22. For *Adam* was the Heart in Nature, and therefore his animated or soulish spirit did *help* to Image fashion or frame *this Tree*, of which he would fain eat.

23. But when the Devill saw, that the *Lust* was in *Adam*, then he stung lustily and briskly at the *Salitter in Adam*, and infected the *Salitter*, out of which *Adam* was made, *yet* more and more.

24. And now then *it was time*, that the Creator should frame a *wife* for him, which afterward set the *Same on work*, and did eat of the evill or corrupt fruit: Else if *Adam* had eaten of the Tree, *before the woman* had been made out of him, then it would have been far *worse* then it is.

25. But being this requireth a high and deep Description, as also requireth much Room, therefore seek for it concerning the *Fall* of *Adam*, where you will find it largely described.

So, now I return to the forementioned Similitude.

26. Now when *Adam* did eat of the fruit, which was Good and Evill, then he suddenly gat *such a Body* also: The fruit was corrupt or perished and palpable.

able, as to this day all fruits now on Earth are, and so such a fleshly and palpable or comprehensible Body *Adam* and *Eve* gat instantly.

27. But now the flesh is *not* the whole Man: for this flesh cannot comprehend or apprehend the Deity, else the flesh were not Mortal and corruptible, or fading and transitory; for Christ saith, *John* 6. 63. † *It is the Spirit that quickneth, the flesh profiteth nothing.*

† or *The Spirit is the Life.*

28. For *this flesh* cannot inherit the Kingdom of heaven neither, but is only a *Seed* which is sowen into the Earth, out of which will grow an impalpable or incomprehensible Body, such as the *first* was, before the Fall. But the Spirit is eternal life, which uniteth qualifieth or mixeth with God, and comprehendeth the *internal* Deity in Nature.

29. Now as Man in his *outward* Being is *corrupted*, and as to his fleshly Birth or Geniture, is in the wrath of God, and is moreover also an *Enemy* of God, and yet is but one Man, and not Two: and on the other side, in his spiritual Birth or Geniture he is a Child and *Heir of God*, which ruleth and liveth with God, and qualifieth mixeth or uniteth with the innermost Birth or Geniture of God: Thus also is the Place of this world come to be.

30. The outward comprehensibility or * Palpability in the whole Nature of this world, and of all things which are therein, standeth all in the *wrath-fire* of God: for it is become thus through the kindling of Nature; and Lord *Lucifer* with his Angels, hath his dwelling now in the same outward Birth or Geniture which standeth in the wrath-fire.

* or *feelableness.*

31. But now the Deity is *not separated* from the outward Birth or Geniture, so, as if they were *Two* things

things in this world; if so, Man could have *no Hope*, and then this world did not stand in the Power and Love of God.

32. But the Deity *is* in the outward Birth, hidden, and hath the Fanne or Casting shovel in its hand, and will one Day cast the chaffe and the kindled *Salitter* upon a Heap, and will draw away from it its inward Birth or Geniture, and give them to Lord *Lucifer* and his *Crew* of followers for an Eternal House.

33. In the *mean while* Lord *Lucifer* must lye *captive* and Imprisoned in the outermost Birth in the Nature of this world, in the *kindled* wrath-fire : and therein he hath great Power, and can reach into the *Heart* of all Creatures with his animated or soulish spirit in the outermost Birth or Geniture, which standeth in the wrath-fire.

34. *Therefore* the Soul of man must fight and strive continually with the Devill, for *he still presents before it the Swine-Apples of Paradise,* ——

[" *That is, the fierce source of Malignity, wherewith* " *the Soul is infected :*]

—— and invites it also to Bite thereof, that he thereby may also bring it into his Prison :

35. And if that will not succeed to his purpose, then he strikes many a hard blow at the stomack ready to choak it, and that man must continually *lye under the Crosse,* affliction, and misery, in this world.

36. For he hideth the Noble Grain of Mustard-

seed,

feed, fo that, *Man doth not know himſelf* : And then the world ſuppoſeth, that he is thus plagued and ſmitten of God, whereby the Devils Kingdom remaineth alwaies *hidden* and undiſcovered.

37. But ſtay a little : thou haſt given me alſo many a Blow, I have experimentall knowledge of thee , and here I will open thy Door to thee a little, that *another alſo* may ſee what thou art.

The Eighteenth Chapter.

Of the Creation *of Heaven and Earth ; and of the* firſt Day.

1.

MOſes writeth in his firſt Book *as if* he had been *Preſent,* and had beheld all with his Eyes ; but without doubt he received it in writing from his Forefathers : it may be, *He might have* well diſcerned ſomewhat *more* herein in the Spirit then his Forefathers.

2. But becauſe at that time, when God created Heaven and Earth, there was *yet no Man* which ſaw it, therefore it may be concluded, that *Adam* before his Fall, while he was yet in the deep knowledge of God, did know it in the Spirit only.

3. But yet when he fell, and was ſet into the *outward* Birth or Geniture he knew it no more; but had onely a *Remembrance* of it, as of a dark and ſecret *Action* or *Hiſtory,* and ſo left it to his Poſterity.

4. For it is manifeſt, that the firſt World before the Deluge or Flood, knew *as little* of the qualities

and

and Birth or Geniture of God, as this last world wherein we now live: for the external fleshly Birth or Geniture could *never* apprehend or *understand* the Deity, otherwise somewhat more would have been written of it.

5. But being through the *Divine Grace* in this High Article, this Great Mystery hath been somewhat revealed to *me*, in *my spirit* according to the inward Man, which qualifieth mixeth and uniteth with the Deity, therefore I *cannot* forbear to describe it according to my *Gifts*: And I would have the Reader faithfully admonished, not to be offended at the *Simplicity* of the Author.

6. For I do it not out of a desire of *Boasting* and vain-glory, but in a humble information to the Reader, that thereby the works of God might be *somewhat* better known, and the Devils Kingdom revealed and laid open, being this present Modern world moveth and liveth in all malice wickednesse and *Devillish* vicious Blasphemies, that it might once see, in what kind of power impulse or driving it liveth, and in what kind of *Inne* it taketh up its Lodging.

7. And try, whether I may happily with the *entrusted* Talent get gain of Usury, and not return it to my God and Creator again singly and empty, without improvement, like the *lazie* servant, who had stood idle in the vineyard of the Lord, and would require his wages without having laboured at all.

8. But if the Devil should raise Mockers and despisers, who would say; It doth not become me to climb so *high* into the Deity, and to dive so *deeply* thereinto:

9. To

9. To all of them, I give this for an Anſwer : That I am not climbed up into the Deity, neither is it Poſſible for ſuch a mean man, as I am, to do it; but the Deity is climbed up into me, and from *its Love* are theſe things revealed to me, which otherwiſe I in my half-dead fleſhly Birth or Geniture muſt needs have let alone altogether.

10. But being I have ſuch an impulſe upon me, I let *him* act and move in me, who knoweth and un-derſtandeth what it is, and whoſe pleaſure it is that I ſhould do it; I poor man of Earth, Duſt and Aſhes, could *not* do it. But the ſpirit inviteth and Citeth all ſuch mockers and deſpiſers before the *innermoſt* Birth or Geniture of God in this world , to deſiſt from their wickedneſſe and malice : If not, then they ſhall be ſpewed out as *Helliſh chaffe* into the *outermoſt* Birth or Geniture in the wrath of God.

Now Obſerve :

11. ＊When God was now moved to Anger in the *Third* Birth or Geniture in the Court Quarters or Region of *Lucifer,* which was all the ſpace and room or Extent of this world, then the light was *extin-guiſh'd* in the third Birth or Geniture, and all be-came a Darkneſſe, and the *Salitter* in the third Birth or Geniture was rough, wild, hard, bitter, ſowr, and in ſome parts ſtinking, *Muddy* and Brittle, all according to the Birth or Geniture of the qualifying or fountain ſpirits, then at that time working.

12. For in that place wherein the *aſtringent* qua-lity was predominant, there the *Salitter* was attract-ed together and dryed, ſo that hard dry *Stones came to be ；* but in thoſe places, where the aſtringent ſpi-rit,

rit, and the bitter were equally alike predominant, there ſharp ſmall Gravel and *Sand* came to be, for the raging bitter ſpirit brake the *Salitter* all to pieces.

13. But in thoſe places, where the *Tone* together with the aſtringent ſpirit, were predominant in the water, there Copper, Iron, and ſuch like rocky Oar of Minerals came to be, but where the *water* was predominant, together with all the ſpirits joyntly and equally; there the wild Earth came to be, and the water was here and there like a cloud or vapour held *captive* in the Clefts and veins or ſpaces of the Rocks: for the aſtringent ſpirit, as the Father of corrupted Nature, held it captive with its ſharp *attracting* together.

14. But the *Bitter* ſpirit is the chiefeſt cauſe of the black Earth, for through its fierce bitterneſſe the *Salitter* became kill'd in its outermoſt Birth or Geniture, from whence exiſted the wild or *Barren* Earth.

15. But the *Heat* in the aſtringent ſpirit chiefly helped to make the Hardneſſe; but where that came to be, there it generated the nobleſt and *pretiouſeſt Salitter* in the Earth, as Gold, Silver, and Pretious Stones.

16. For when the *ſhining Light* by reaſon of the hard, dry and rough matter became extinguiſh'd, then it was together dryed up and incorporated in the Heat, which is the Father of the Light.

Yet you muſt underſtand it, thus:

17. *Viz.* where the Hot ſpirit in the *ſweet water* was predominant in Love; there the aſtringent ſpirit attracted the matter together, and ſo thereby the

nobleſt

nobleſt Oar of minerals and Pretious Stones were generated.

18. But concerning Pretious Stones, as Carbuncles, Rubies, Diamonds, Smaragds or Emerauds, Onixes and the like, which are of the *beſt* Sort, they have their Original where the *flaſh* of the light roſe up in the Love. For that Flaſh becometh generated in the meckneſſe, and is the Heart in the Center of the qualifying or fountain ſpirits; therefore thoſe Stones alſo are Meek, full of vertue, delightſome pleaſant and lovely.

Now it might be Asked:

Why, Man in this world is ſo in love above all other things, with Gold, Silver, and Pretious Stones, and uſeth them for a † Defence or Protection, and the maintenance of his Body?

† Eccleſ.7.12. with Money and Treaſures, men defend themſelves, as with a ſhield.

Anſwer.

19. Herein lyeth the *Pith* or kernel; for Gold, Silver and Pretious Stones, and all bright Oars of Minerals, have their Original from the *Light,* which did ſhine before the Times of wrath in the outermoſt Birth or Geniture of Nature; that is, in the *ſeventh-*Nature-ſpirit: And ſo now ſeeing every Man, is, as the whole Houſe of this world is, therefore all his qualifying or fountain ſpirits love the *kernel* or the beſt thing that is in the corrupted Nature, and that they uſe for the defence protection and † maintenance of themſelves.

† or Livelihood.

20. But the innermoſt kernel, which is the Deity, that they can no where comprehend, for the *wrath* of

the

the fire lyeth before it, as a ſtrong * wall, + or *Bull*
and this wall muſt be broken down *wark.*
with a very ſtrong ſtorm or aſsault,
if the Aſtrall ſpirits will ſee into
it. But the Door ſtandeth Open to the Animated
or Souliſh ſpirit, for it is withheld by Nothing, but
is as God himſelf is in his innermoſt Birth or Geniture.

Now then it might be asked :

How ſhall I then underſtand my ſelf in or according to the Threefold Birth or
Geniture in Nature ?

The Depth !

21. Behold, the *Firſt* innermoſt aud deepeſt Birth
or Geniture ſtandeth in the Center, and is the *Heart*
of the Deity, which is generated by the qualifying
or fountain ſpirits of God ; and this Birth or Geniture is the *Light*, which though it be generated out
of the qualifying or fountain ſpirits ; yet no qualifying or fountain ſpirit of it ſelf alone can comprehend it, but every qualifying or fountain ſpirit comprehendeth only its own inſtanding innate place or
ſeat in the light, but *all* the ſeven ſpirits joyntly together comprehend the whole Light, for they are
the Father of the Light.

22. Thus alſo the qualifying or fountain ſpirits of
Man do not *wholly* comprehend the innermoſt Birth
or Geniture of the Deity, which ſtandeth in the
light, but every qualifying or fountain ſpirit reacheth

eth with *its* animated or *soulish* Birth or Geniture into the Heart of God, and uniteth qualifieth or mixeth in that Place *therewith.*

23. And that is the hidden Birth or Geniture in Nature, which no Man by his own Reason, wit, or *capacity* can comprehend ; but the *Soul* of that Man, which standeth in the Light of God onely comprehends it, and *no* other.

The Second Birth or Geniture in Nature, are the seven Spirits of Nature.

24. This Birth or Geniture is more *intelligible* and comprehensible, but yet also only to *the chil-dren of this Mysterie;* the Plow-man doth not understand it, though he seeth, smelleth, tasteth, heareth, feeleth it, yet he looks on *it,* but knoweth not *how* the Being thereof is.
[" *By this is meant or understood the corrupt* Reason *in*
" *its own wit ingenuity or capacity, without the*
" *Spirit of God:* The Doctor *as well as the*
" Plow-man *is here meant, the one is as blind*
" *concerning the* Deity, *as the other, and some-*
" *times the* Peasant *or* Plowman *exceeds the*
" *Doctor in knowledge, if he cleave close to God:*]
25. Now these are the Spirits, wherein all things stand both in Heaven and in this world, and from these the *third* and outermost spirit is generated, wherein corruptibility standeth.
26. But * this Spirit, or this Birth hath *seven* kinds or species, *viz.* the Astringent, the Sweet, the Bitter, the Hot ; these four generate the *comprehensibility* in the third Birth or Geniture.
27. The fifth Spirit is the Love, which existeth
from

from the Light of the life, which generateth *ſenſi-bliity* and *Reaſon.*

28. The ſixth Spirit is the Tone, which genera-teth the *ſound* and Joy, and is the ſpring or ſource riſing up through all the ſpirits.

29. In this ſixth Spirit now ſtandeth the ſpirit of life, and the will, or Reaſon and *Thoughts* of all the Creatures ; and all Arts, Inventions, Formings and Imagings of all that which ſtandeth in the *Spirit* in the *incomprehenſibility.*

30. The ſeventh Spirit is Nature, in which ſtand-eth the corporeal Being of all ſix ſpirits, for the ſix ſpirits generate the ſeventh. In this ſpirit, ſtandeth the corporeal being of Angels, Devils and Men, and is the *Mother* of all the ſix ſpirits, in which they ge-nerate themſelves, and in which they alſo generate the light, which is the Heart of God.

Of the Third *Birth or Geniture.*

31. Now the third Birth or Geniture is the com-prehenſibility or palpability of Nature, which was rarified and Tranſparent lovely pleaſant and Bright, *before* the time of Gods wrath, ſo that the qualify-ing or fountain ſpirits could ſee *through* and *through* all.

32. There was neither Stone nor Earth therein, neither had it need of any ſuch created or contracted Light, as now, but the light generated it ſelf *every where* in the Center, and all ſtood in the Light.

33. But when King *Lucifer* was created, then he excited or awakened the wrath of God in this *third* Birth or Geniture ; for the Bodies of the Angels came to be *Creatures* in this Third Birth.

34. Now

34. Now then feeing the Devils kindled their own Bodies, intending thereby to domineer over the whole Deity, *therefore* the Creator alfo in his wrath kindled this *third* fpirit, or this third Birth or Geniture in Nature, and imprifoned the Devill therein, and made an eternal Lodging therein for him, that he might not be *higher* then the *whole* God.

[" *Underftand, in the outward fources or Qualities:*
  " *for, the outermoft of all, is alfo the Innermoft of*
  " *all :*]

35. But feeing the Devils kindled themfelves out of Pride *wantonneffe* and wilfulneffe, *therefore* they were quite thruft out from the Birth or Geniture of the Light, and they can neither lay hold of, or comprehend it, *Eternally.*

36. For the Light of their Heart, which qualified mixed or united with the heart of God, they have extinguifht *that* themfelves, and inftead *thereof* have generated a fierce, hot, aftringent, bitter, and hard ftinging Devillifh Spirit.

37. But now thou muft *not think*, that thereupon the whole Nature or Place of this world is become a meer bitter wrath of God. No; here lyeth the Point: the *wrath* doth not comprehend the innermoft Birth or Geniture in Nature, for the *Love* of God is yet hidden in the Center, in the whole place of this world, and fo the Houfe, which Lord *Lucifer* is to be in, is *not fully* feparated, but there is ftill in all things of this world, both Love and wrath *one in another*, and they alwaies wreftle and ftrive one with another.

38. But the Devils cannot lay hold on the wreftling

ling of the Light, but only on the wrestling of the Wrath, wherein they are *Executioners* or Hangmen, to execute the Justice or Law, which was pronounced in Gods wrath, against *all* wicked Men.

39. Neither *ought* any man to say, that he is generated in the wrath-fire of the totall corruption or perdition, *out of Gods predestinate purpose.* No: the corrupted Earth doth not stand, *neither,* in the totall wrath-fire of God, but only in its *outward* comprehensibility or palpability wherein it is so hard, dry and bitter.

40. Whereby every one may perceive, that this Poison and *fiercenesse* doth not belong to the Love of God, in which there is nothing but *Meeknesse.*

41. Yet I do not say this, as if every Man were *Holy* as he cometh from his mothers womb, but as the Tree is, so is its Fruit. Yet the Fault is not Gods, if a *Mother* beareth or bringeth forth a child of the Devil; but the Parents wickednesse.

42. But if a wild twigg be planted in a Sweet Soyl, and be *ingrafted* with some other of a better and sweeter Kind, then there groweth a Mild Tree, though the twig were *wild.* For here all is possible; as soon is the good changed into Evill, as the Evill into Good.

43. For every Man is *free,* and is as *a God* to himself; he may *change* and alter himself in this life either into wrath or into light: such Cloaths or Garments as a man puts on, such is his ornament or lustre: and what manner of Body soever man *soweth* into the Earth, such a Body also groweth up from it, though in another form clarity and Brightnesse: yet all according to the quality of the *Seed.*

44. For if the Earth were *quite* forsaken of God,

    then

then it could never bring forth *any* Good Fruit, but meer bad and Evil Fruit. But being the Earth standeth yet in Gods Love, therefore his wrath will not burn therein Eternally, but the Love *which hath overcome* will spew out the wrath-fire.

45. And then will the burning Hell begin, when the Love and the wrath shall be *separated.* In this world the Love and the wrath is one in another in *all* creatures, and that which overcometh in the wrestling, inheriteth the House of or by Right, whether it be the Kingdom of Hell or of Heaven.

46. I do not speak so, as if the Beasts in their Birth or Geniture, were to inherit the Kingdom of Heaven; *No;* for they are like the corrupted Earth, Evil and good; but if they be sown again into their mother the Earth, then they are Earth.

47. But the *Salitter* in a good Beast shall not therefore be left to the Devil for a propriety, but will in the separated part, in the Nature of God, Eternally blossom——

P. 〔" *That is,* their Figure *will stand as a Shadow upon*
　　" the holy *Ground,* in the wonders, *viz. in the*
　　" eternal Magia :〕

——and bring forth other *heavenly* figures. But the †*from or be-* Salitter of the Beast † of Gods wrath will in the *longing to.* wrath of God bear eternal *Hellish* Fruits.

48. For if the Earth be once kindled, then in the wrath, burneth the Fire; and in the love, the Light: and then *all* will be separated, for the one cannot comprehend the other *any more.*

49. But in this Time every thing hath a *Twofold* source and quality ; whatsoever thou buildest and sowest here in the *spirit,* be it with words, works or Thoughts, *that* will be thy Eternal House.

50. Thus

50. Thus thou seest and *understandest*, out of what the Earth and Stones are come to be: but if that kindled *Salitter* should have continued to be thus in the whole Deep of this world, then the whole place thereof would have been a *dark valley*, for the Light was imprisoned together also with and in the *Third* Birth or Geniture.

51. Not that the Light of the Heart of God in its *innermost Birth*, is imprisoned; No, but that Lustre and the shining thereof in the *third* Birth or Geniture was together incorporated or compacted in the *outermost* comprehensibility, and therefore it is that Men are in Love with all those things, which stand in *that Salitter*.

52. But being the whole Deep in the third Birth or Geniture was very dark in regard of the *corrupted Salitter* of the Earth and Stones, *therefore* the Deity could not endure it to be so, but created and compacted the Earth and Stones together as in *one Lump*, or as on a Heap.

Concerning which, Moses *writeth thus:*

Im   Anfang   schuff GOTT,
At   the Beginning,   Created,   GOD,

Himmel und Erden. Genesis 1.1.
Heaven and Earth.

53. These words must be considered exactly, † what they are. For the word (**Im**) conceiveth it self in the *Heart*, and goeth forth to the *Lips*, but there is captivated and goeth back again sounding, till it come to the place from whence it went forth.

54. And

† or, how these *German* words are framed in the Articulation by the Instruments of Speech: that what they signifie according to the Language of Nature, may be understood.

† Voyce of God.

54. And this fignifieth now, that the † Sound went forth from the Heart of *God,* and encompaffed the whole place or Extent of this world, but when * it was found to be *Evil,* then the Sound return-ed again into its own place.

* the place of this world.

55. The word or fyllable (**An-**) thrufteth it felf out from the Heart and *preffeth forth* at the Mouth, and hath a long following † preffure ; but when it is fpoken forth, then it *clofeth* it felf up in the midft or Center of its Seat with the * upper Gums, and is *half* without, and *half* within.

† or murmu-ring Sound,

* or Palate.

56. And this fignifieth, that the Heart of God had a Loathing againft the *corruption,* and fo thruft away the corrupted Being from himfelf, but *laid hold* on it again in the midft or Center at the Heart.

57. And as the Tongue breaketh off or divideth the word or fyllable, and keeps it half without, and half within : fo the Heart of God would *not wholly* rejeƈt the kindled *Salitter,* but the malignity malice and malady of the Devill, and the other part fhould be re-edified or built again *after* this Time.

58. The word or fyllable (**-fang**)goeth *fwiftly* from the heart out at the mouth, and is *ftaid* alfo by the hinder part of the Tongue, and the Gums; and when it is let loofe, it maketh *another* fwift preffure from the Heart, out at the Mouth.

59. And this fignifieth the fuddain *Rejeƈtion* at the riddance and thrufting out of the Devils, together with the corrupted *Salitter* : for the ftrong and fwift fpirit thrufteth the breath *ftrongly* away from it, and *retaineth* the true Tone of the word, or the expreffion, with it at the hindermoft Gumme, and that is, the true fpirit of the word or fyllable.

60. And this fignifieth, that the corrupted *fierce-*
neffe

*neſſe.*is thruſt out eternally from the light of God, but the inward ſpirit, which is *loaden* therewith againſt its will, ſhall be ſet again in its firſt Houſe.

61. The laſt following preſſure (-**ang**) ſignifieth, that the innermoſt ſpirits in the corruption are not *altogether* pure, and therefore they need a ſweeping away, *purging,* or conſuming of the wrath, in the fire, which *will* be done at the End of this Time.

62. The word (**Schuß**) conceiveth it ſelf *above* and *under* the Tongue, and ſhutteth the Teeth in the upper and lower gummes, and ſo preſſeth it ſelf *cloſe* together, and being held together, and ſpoken forth again, then it openeth the Mouth again ſwiftly, like *a Flaſh.*

63. And this ſignifieth the aſtringent ſpirit's *ſtrong* driving together of the corrupted *Salitter* as a Lump on a Heap.

64. For the Teeth *retain* the word, letting the ſpirit go forth *leiſurely* between the Teeth : And this ſignifieth, that the aſtringent quality holdeth the Earth and Stones *firmly* and faſt together ; and yet for all that, *letteth* the ſpirits of the Earth ſpring up, grow and bear Bloſſoms out of the aſtringent ſpirit : which ſignifieth the *Regeneration or Reſtitution of the ſpirits of the Earth.*

65. But that the Mouth is ſwiftly opened again *after* the word is Ended, it ſignifieth concerning the Deep above the Earth ; that God the Lord will nevertheleſſe dwell there, and *reſerve* his Regiment for himſelf, and hold the Devil as a Priſoner in the wrath-fire.

66. The

66. The word (**GOTT**) conceiveth it self in the *midst* or Center upon the Tongue, and is thrust thither out of the Heart, and leaveth the Mouth *open*, and stayeth sitting on its Royall Seat, and soundeth without and within: but when it is spoken forth, then it maketh *another* pressure between the upper Teeth and the Tongue.

67. And this signifieth; that when God created Heaven and Earth, and all the Creatures, he *nevertheless* remained in his Divine, Eternal, Almighty Seat, and *never* went away from it at all, and that HEE alone is ALL. The Last pressure, signifieth the sharpnesse of his spirit, whereby in a Moment he *effecteth* all in his whole Body.

68. The word (**Himmel**) conceiveth it self in the Heart, and is thrust forth to the Lips, there it is *shut* up, and the syllable (-**mel**) setteth the Lips open again, and is held on the middle of the Tongue, and so the Spirit goeth forth on *both Sides* of the Tongue out of the Mouth.

69. And this signifieth, that the *innermost* birth is become shut up from the outermost, by the horrible Sins, and is incomprehensible to the outward corrupted Birth or Geniture.

70. But being it is a word with a *Twofold* syllable, and that the second syllable -**mel** openeth the mouth again, it signifieth, that the *Gates* of the Deity are become opened again.

71. But that by the word or syllable -**mel** it is conceived again upon the Tongue, and held fast with the upper Gumms, and that in the mean while the spirit *slippeth* forth on both sides of the Tongue.

72. This signifieth, that God would again give to this corrupted Kingdome or Place in
God,

God, a *King* or *Great* Prince, who should open again the innermost Birth or Geniture of the clear and Bright *Deity*, and thereby the Holy Ghost should go forth on both sides, that is, out of the innermost Depth of the Father and of the Sonne; and should go forth *again* into this world, and should new regenerate this world again, through the *New King.*

73. The word, **und**, conceiveth it self in the Heart, and is staid and compacted or *incorporated* by the Tongue on the upper Gummes; but when it is *let loose*, it maketh another pressure from the Heart, out at the Mouth.

74. Now this signifieth the difference or *distinction* between the Holy and the Earthly Birth or Geniture. This syllable cometh indeed from the Heart, but is staid by the Tongue on the upper Gummes, so that one cannot *yet* perceive what kind of word it is: And this signifieth, that the earthly and corrupt Birth or Geniture, cannot lay hold on, or apprehend the innnermost Birth or Geniture, but is foolish and silly †.

75. The last pressure from the Heart, signifieth, that * it will indeed qualifie mix or *unite with* the innermost Birth or Geniture in its sensibility perception or Thoughts, but *cannot* apprehend it in its Reason; therefore this syllable or word alone by it self is Dumb, and hath no signification or understanding in it alone, but is used onely for distinction sake, with some *other* word.

76. The word **Crden**, is thrust forth from the Heart, and is conceived on the *hinder* part upon the Tongue at the hinder Gummes, and *trembleth*: the

† *a foolish or silly Virgin.*
* *the Earthly Birth.*

Tongue

Tongue is used about the first syllable **Er** yet not

† or staggers. steadily, but it † recoiles inward at the neather gummes, and *croucheth* as it were before an enemy trembling.

77. The other syllable -**den**, is conceived by the Tongue and the *upper* Gumms, and leaveth the Mouth open, and the spirit of formation goeth forth at the *Nostrills*, and will not go forth together in this word out at the *Mouth* ; and though it carrieth forth somewhat indeed along with it, yet the true Tone or Noise of the true spirit goeth onely forth through or at the Nostrils, or Organ of Smelling.

This is a great Mysterie :

78. The word or syllable **Er** signifieth the *kindled* astringent and bitter quality, the earnest *severe* wrath of God, which trembleth at the hinder part of the Gummes, before which the Tongue is as it were afraid, and croucheth at the neather gums, and flieth as it were from an Enemy.

79. The word or syllable, **den**, conceiveth it self on the Tongue again, and the spirit attracteth the power and vertue out of the word, and therewith goeth forth *another way* at the Nostrills, and so goeth therewith up into or *towards* the Brain before the Royal Seat. And this signifieth, that the outermost *Salitter* of the Earth is *eternally* rejected from Gods Light and *Holinesse.*

80. But, that the Spirit layeth hold on the *power* and vertue of the word, and goeth another way through the Nostrills into the Brain before the Throne of the Senses or *Thoughts* ; it signifieth, that God will *extract* the Heart of the Earth from the wrath of wickednesse, and *use* it to his eternal Royal Praise.   *Observe.*

Observe.

81. He will extract from the Earth the *Kernel*, and the Best or the Good Spirit, and will *Regenerate* it anew, to his honour and Glory.

82. *Here, O Man, consider thy self well,* and mind, What manner of seed thou sowest into the Earth, the very same will spring up, and bear Blossoms and fruit *for ever,* either in the Love or in the Wrath.

83. But when the good shall be separated from the Evil, then thou wilt live in *that part,* which thou hast laboured for, here, be it either in Heaven or in Hell-fire.

84. *In † what soever thou endeavourest, Labourest and actest here, into that thy Soul goeth, when thou Dyest.*

† Whether Heavenly or Hellish, Good or Evil matter or thing.

85. Or dost thou think, that my spirit hath suck'd this which I have set down here out of the corrupted Earth, or out of an Old Felt Hatt, or Old Shoe?

86. Truly no; for the spirit at this Time of my description and setting it down did *unite* and qualifie or mix with the deepest Birth or Geniture of God; in *that,* I have received my knowledge, and from thence it is sucked, not in great Earthly Joy, but in the anxious Birth or Geniture, *perplexity* and Trouble.

87. For what I did hereupon undergo suffer and endure from the Devill and the Hellish quality,

which

which as well doth rule in my *outward* Man, as in all Men whatsoever: this thou canst not apprehend, unlesse thou also *Dancest* in this Round.

88. Had not our Philosophers and Doctors alwaies plaid upon the Fiddle of Pride, but on the *Musicall Instrument* of the Prophets and Apostles, there would have been far another knowledge and *Philosophy* in the world.

89. Concerning which in regard of my imbecillity, want of Literature or Learning and study, as also the flownesse and dullnesse of my *Tongue,* I am very *insufficient,* but not so slender in the knowledge: Only I cannot deliver it in profound Language and the *Ornament* of Eloquence, but I rest contented with my gift I have received, and am a

Philosopher among the Simple.

Concerning the Creation of the Light in this world.

90. Here shut the Eyes of thy *Flesh,* a little, for here they will profit thee nothing, being they are *blind* and dead; and open the Eyes of thy spirit, and then I will rightly *shew thee,* the Creation of God.

Observe:

91. When God had driven the corrupted *Sulitter* of Earth and Stones, which had generated it self in the outermost Birth, by the *kindling,* together on a Heap as in a Lump, then, for that cause, the third Birth or Geniture in Nature in the *Deep,* above the Earth, was not pure and Bright, because the wrath of God did *yet turn* therein.

92. And

92. And though the innermost Birth or Geniture was light and Bright, yet the outermost, which stood in the wrath-fire, could not *comprehend it*, but was altogether dark.

93. For *Moses* writeth, in *Genesis* 1.

Und es war Finster auff der Tieffe:

And it was Dark on the Deep:

The word (**auff**) *on*, signifieth the *outermost* Birth or Geniture, and the word (**in**) signifieth the *innermost* Birth or Geniture.

94. But if the innermost Birth had been dark, then the wrath of God had *rested* in this world Eternally, and it would never have been Light : but the wrath hath *not* thus touched or reached the Heart of God.

95. Therefore He is a sweet, friendly, Bounteous, Good, Meek, Pure and *Mercifull* God, according to his Heart in the *innermost* Birth or Geniture in the place of this world, and still continueth to be so : and his meek Love presseth forth from his Heart into the *outermost* Birth or Geniture of the wrath, and quencheth the same, and therefore, **Sprach Er**, he said, **Es werde Licht.**

Let there be Light.

Here observe the sense in the Highest Depth !

96. The word (**Sprach**) or *said*, is spoken after the manner of Men : Ye Philosophers, open your Eyes, I will in my simplicity teach you, the [**Sprach Gottes**] the Speech Speaking or Language of God, as, when he saith a thing ; and indeed, it *must be* so.

97. The word, **Sprach**, conceiveth it self *between* the

the Teeth, for they bite or *joyn close* together, and the spirit hisseth forth through the Teeth, and the Tongue boweth or *bendeth* in the middle, and setteth its forepoint, as if it did listen after the hissing, and were *afraid*.

98. But when the spirit conceiveth the word, that *shuts* the Mouth, and conceiveth it at the hinder gums upon the Tongue in the hole or *hollownesse*, in the bitter and astringent Quality.

99. And there the Tongue is *terrified*, trembleth and croucheth to the neather Gums, and then the spirit *cometh* forth from the Heart, and closeth the word, which conceiveth it self at the hinder Gums in the astringent and bitter quality, in the wrath; and goeth forth mightily and strongly through the fiercenesse, as a King and Prince, and also *openeth* the mouth, and ruleth with a strong spirit from the heart through the *whole* Mouth within, and also without the Mouth, and maketh a mighty and *long syllable*, as a spirit which hath broken the wrath.

100. Against which the wrath with its *snarling* in the astringent and bitter Quality at the hinder gums in the hollow on the Tongue *struggleth*; and keeps its right to it self, and keepeth its seat in its Place, and lets the *meek* spirit come forth from the heart, through it, and thundreth with its snarling after it, and so *helps* to form or frame the word, yet with its *thundring* cannot get away from it seat, but abideth in its hollow Hole, as a Captive Prisoner, and looketh *terribly*.

This

This is a great Mysterie,

101. Here observe the sense and meaning, if thou apprehendest it, then thou *understandest* the Deity aright, if not, then thou art yet blind in the Spirit.

102. *Judge not,* else here thou runnest counter against a strong Gate, and wilt be imprison'd : if the wrath-fire catcheth thee, then thou wilt remain *eternally* therein.

103. Thou Child of Man : Behold now, how great a *Gate* of Heaven, of Hell, and of the Earth, as also of the whole Deity, the spirit openeth to thee.

104. Thou shouldest *not* think, that God at that time did speak in that way as Men do, and that it was but a *weak* impotent word, like *Mans* word.

105. Indeed Mans word conceiveth it self just in such a *form,* manner, proportion, quality, and correspondency ; onely the *half dead* Man doth not understand it : And this understanding is very noble dear and precious, for it is generated onely in the knowledge of the *Holy Ghost.*

106. But Gods Word, which He spake then in power, hath encompassed Heaven and Earth, and the heaven of heavens ; yes, and the *whole* Deity also.

107. But it frameth ann conceiveth it self first between the Teeth closed or *clapp'd* together, and *hisseth,* which signifieth, that the Holy Ghost at the beginning of the Creation went through the firmly closed *wall* of the Third and outermost Birth or Geniture, which standeth in the *wrath-fire* in this world.   108. For

108. For it is written, *And it was dark on the Deep, and the Spirit of God moved on the water.* The *Deep* signifieth the *innermost* Birth or Geniture; and the *darkneſſe* signifieth the *outermost* corrupt Birth or Geniture, in which the wrath burned. The *water* signifieth the allaying or *Mitigation* of the spirit.

109. But that the spirit doth *hiſſe* through the Teeth, it signifieth, that the spirit *is gone forth* from the heart of God through the wrath: but, that the Teeth remain *closed* together, whileſt the spirit hiſ-ſeth, and do not open themſelves, it signifieth, that the wrath *hath not* comprehended or reached the Holy Ghoſt.

110. But that the Tongue doth *crouch* towards the neather gums, and is ſharp at the point, and will not be uſed about the hiſſing; it signifieth, that the *outward Birth* or Geniture, together with all the Creatures which are therein, † *cannot* comprehend or reach to apprehend the *Holy Spirit,* which goeth forth out of the innermoſt Birth or Geniture out from the Heart of God, neither can they hinder him by their power.

† The Natural man cannot perceive the things of God. query the Text.

111. For he goeth and penetrateth through *all* ſhut or cloſed Doors, Cloſets and Births, and needs no Opening of them; as the Teeth cannot ſtay or hinder the spirit or *breath* from going or *paſſing* through them.

112. But that the Lips ſtand open, when it is come hiſſing through the Teeth, it signifieth, that * he with his going forth out of the Heart of God, in the Creation of this world, hath *opened* again the *Gates* of heaven, and is gone through the Gates of Gods wrath, and hath left the *wrath* of God ſtrongly ſhut

* the Holy Ghoſt.

shut and bolted up, and hath left the Devil his eternal kindled wrath-house close locked up, out of which he cannot come Eternally.

113. It further signifieth, that the Holy Ghost in like manner hath an *open Gate* in the wrath-house of this world, where he may drive and perform his work, *incomprehensibly* as to the Gates of Hell, and where he gathereth or congregateth a *holy Seed* to his eternal Praise, against or without the will of the strong fast shut hellish Gates, and altogether incomprehensibly as to *them*.

114. But as the spirit effecteth his going forth, and his conceived or intended will, through the Teeth, and yet the *Teeth* do not stir ; *nor can* comprehend the will of the spirit : so the Holy Ghost also, without the apprehension or comprehension, either, of the *Devill* or of the *wrath* of God, buildeth or erecteth continually a holy Seed and Temple in the house of *this* world.

115. But that the whole word **Sprach** [said] formeth or conceiveth it self at the *hinder* gummes on the Tongue in the *hollow* hole in the Center of the astringent and bitter quality, and *snarleth* ; it signifieth, that God hath conceived or framed the place of this world at the heart in the midst or Center of it, and hath built to himself again a house to his praise, against all the grumbling murmuring and *snarling* of the Devill ; in *which* he ruleth with his Holy Ghost.

116. And as the spirit goeth forth from the heart through the grumbling murmuring and snarling of the bitter and astringent quality very *strongly* and powerfully, and with its going forth ruleth in the astringent and bitter quality, incomprehensibly as

to the aftringent and bitter quality, as a potent King: fo alfo the Spirit of God ruleth in the *outermoft* Birth or Geniture of this world (in the wrath-houfe) *mightily,* and generateth to himfelf a Temple therein incomprehenfibly as to the wrath-houfe.

117. But that the aftringent and bitter fpirit doth fo *grumble* and murmur, when the fpirit from the Heart goeth through its Houfe, and ruleth powerfully: it fignifieth, that the wrath of God, together with the Devils, are in the houfe of this world, fet in oppofition to the Love, fo that *both* thefe, all the time of this world, muft fight and *ftrive* one againft the other, as two Armies in the Field; *from whence alfo wars and fightings among Men, and among Beafts, and All Creatures have their Original.*

118. But, that the aftringent and bitter quality conceive themfelves *together* with the word, and unite and agree one with another, and yet the fpirit of *the* Heart onely fpeaketh forth the word at the Mouth: it fignifieth, that *all* Creatures, which were onely produced and put forth by the word, *viz.* the Beafts, Fowls, Fifhes, Worms, Trees, Leaves, Herbs and Graffe, were formed from the *whole* Body, being Good and Evill.

119. And that, in all thefe, there *would ftand* both the angry and corrupt quality, and alfo the love of God; and yet all would be *driven on* by the fpirit of Love, though thofe two would difturb, rub, plague, fqueeze and *vex* one another.

Note

120. Whereby then, in many a Creature the wrath-fire would be so very *hard kindled*, that the Body together with the spirit, will afford and produce an Eternal wrath-*Shitter* in Hell.

121. For, the spirit, which is generated in the Heart, must in its Body walk through the midst or Center of the *Hellish* Gates, and may very *easily* be kindled, they are as wood and fire, which will burn, if thou pourest no water in among them.

122. *O man, thou wert not created together with and as the Beasts, by the word, from Good and Evil; and if thou hadst not eaten of good and Evil, then the Wrath-fire would not have been in thee, but by that means thou hast also gotten a bestial Body: It is done, The Love of God take pity, and have Mercy in that behalf.*

123. But, that a co-conceiving and compacting of the word together in the Astringent quality at the hinder gums upon the Tongue, the Mouth openeth it self wide, and the compacted and united spirit goeth forth together at the Mouth, which Spirit is

generated

generated *both* out of the Heart, and also out of the astringent and bitter quality: it signifieth, that the creatures would live in great anguish and *adversity*, and would not be able to generate through one Body, but through *Two*.

124. For the Astringent and bitter quality receives the power from the spirit out of the Heart, and infecteth or affecteth it self therewith: And therefore is Nature now become *too weak* in the spirit of the heart, and is not able to elevate its own innermost Birth of the Heart, and *for that cause* Nature hath brought forth a Male and a Female.

125. Thus it denoteth also the Evil and Good will, in the whole or *universall* Nature, and in all the Creatures; that there would be a continuall wrestling fighting and destroying, from whence this world is *rightly called* a valley of Misery, full of Crosses, Persecutions, Toyles and Labours. For when the spirit of Creation entred into the midst and *interposed* its power, it was fain to make and form the Creation in the *midst* or center of the Kingdom of Hell.

126. And now seeing the outermost Birth or Geniture in Nature, is *Two-fold*, that is, both Evill and Good, *therefore* it is that there is a *perpetual* tormenting, squeezing, lamenting and howling; and the Creatures in this life are subject to torments, and afflictions, so that *this Evill World is justly call'd a murtherous Denne of the Devill.*

127. But, that the astringent and bitter spirit *sitteth still* in its seat at the hinder gums on the Tongue, and

and *thrusteth* forth the word at the Mouth, and yet cannot get away from thence ; it signifieth, that the Devil and the wrath of God *would* indeed be domineering in all the Creatures, yet should not have *full power* in them, but must *stay* in Prison, and there would belch forth or blow into all the creatures, and plague them, but should *not* overcome them, unlesse the Creatures themselves are minded to tarry there, in that place : or love to live in the qualities, and be of the conditions of the Devill, and wrath of God.

128. Just as the *Meek* spirit of the Heart goeth through the astringent and bitter quality, and overcometh it ; and though it be indeed infected with the astringent and bitter spirit, yet it *teareth* and breaketh thorough, as a Conquerour : but if it should *wilfully* sit still in the hollow hole in the astringent and bitter spirit, and suffer it self to be taken captive, and *would not* fight, then the fault were its own.

129. And thus it is also with those Creatures, which will continually *sowe* and *reap*, in the Hellish fire, especially **that man,** who liveth in a *continual desire* of Pride, Covetousnesse, Envy and Wrath, and will at *no time* fight and strive against them with the spirit and fire of *Love* ; such a one himself *pulleth* the wrath of God, and the burning hellish fire, upon his Body and Soul.

130. But, that the Tongue doth crouch so much towards the neather gums when the word goeth forth, it signifieth and denoteth the animated or *soulish* spirit of the Creatures, especially of *Man.*

131. The word, which conceiveth it self at the upper Gums, and which qualifieth or uniteth with

the

the aſtringent and bitter ſpirit, ſignifieth the *ſeven ſpirits of Nature*, or the Aſtrall Birth or Geniture, in which the Devill ruleth, and the Holy Ghoſt *oppoſeth* him therein, and overcometh the Devill.

132. But the Tongue ſignifieth the *Soul*, which is generated from the ſeven ſpirits of Nature, and is their *Sonne*: and ſo now when the ſeven ſpirits will, *then* the Tongue muſt ſtirre, and muſt perform their *demands*.

133. If the Aſtrall ſpirits *would not* prove falſe, and would not wooe the Devill to commit adultery with him, then they would *hide* the animated or *ſouliſh* ſpirit, and hold it faſt in their *Bands* as a Treaſure, when *they fight* with the Devill: Juſt as they hide and cover the Tongue; when they wreſtle with the aſtringent and bitter quality; as their beſt Jewel.

134. Thus you have a ſhort and *real* Introduction concerning the word, which God hath ſpoken; rightly deſcribed in the knowledge of the *Spirit* faithfully imparted according to my Gifts, and the *Talent*, I am entruſted with.

Now it may be Asked:

What then is it that God *Spake*, when He ſaid;

Let there be light, and there was Light?

The Depth.

135. The *Light* went forth from the innermoſt Birth or Geniture, and kindled itſelf in the outermoſt.

Note

Note.

It *gave again* to the outermost, a *natural* peculiar Light of its own.

136. Thou must *not think*, that the Light of the Sun and of Nature is the Heart of God, which shineth in secret. No; thou oughtest not to *worship the* Light of Nature, it is not the Heart of God, but it is a *Kindled Light* in Nature; whose Power and Heart standeth in the unctuosity or *fatnesse* of the sweet water, and of all the other spirits in the *third* Birth or Geniture; and is *not* called God.

137. And though it be generated *in* God and *from* God, yet it is but the *instrument* of his handy-work, which cannot apprehend and *reach back* again to the clear Deity in the deepest Birth or Geniture, as the flesh cannot apprehend or reach the Soul.

138. But it must *not* so be understood, as if the Deity were *separated* from Nature; no, but they are as Body and Soul: *Nature* is the Body, and the *Heart of God* is the Soul.

Now a Man might Ask:

What kind of Light then was it, which was kindled; was it the Sun and Stars?

Answer.

139. No: the Sun and Stars were *first* created but on the Fourth Day, out of *that* very Light: there was a Light arisen in the seven spirits of Nature, which had no peculiar distinct *seat* or place, but did shine every where all over, but was not

bright

bright like the Sun, but like an azure Blew and Light, according to the kind and manner of the qualifying or fountain spirits; till afterwards the right Creation and kindling of the *fire* in the water in the astringent spirit, followed, *viz.* the Sun.

The Nineteenth Chapter.

Concerning the Created Heaven, *and the form of the* Earth *and of the* Water, *as also concerning* Light *and* Darknesse.

Concerning *Heaven.*

I.

THe true *Heaven,* which is our own proper humane Heaven, into which the Soul goeth when it parteth from the Body, and into which *Christ our King* is entred; and from whence it was that he came from his Father, and was born, and became *Man* in the Body or Womb of *the Virgin Mary*; hath hitherto been *close hidden* from the children of men, and they have had many Opinions about it.

2. Also the learned have scuffled about it with many strange scurrilous writings, falling one upon another in calumnious and disgraceful *terms*, whereby the holy Name of God hath been reproached, his Members wounded, his Temple destroyed, and the holy Heaven *profaned* with their calumniating and malitious Enmity.

3. *Men*

3. *Men have alwaies* been of the Opinion, that Heaven is many hundred, nay many thousand Miles distant from the face of the Earth, and that God dwelleth onely in that Heaven.

4. Some † *Naturalists* or Artists have undertaken to measure that height and distance, and have produced many *strange* and monstrous devices. Indeed, *before* this my knowledge and *Revelation* of God, I held *that* onely, to be the true Heaven, which, in a round Circumference and sphear, very azure of a Light Blew colour, Extends it self *above* the Stars, supposing that God had therein his *peculiar Being*, and did *rule* onely in the *power* of his holy Spirit in this world.

† *Physiol. Studiers of Natural Philosophy called Physicks. or the Mathematicians.*

5. But when this had given me many a hard blow and *repulse*, doubtlesse from * the Spirit, which had a great Longing yerning towards me, at last I fell into a very *deep Melancholy* and heavy sadnesse, when I beheld and contemplated the great Deep of this world, also the Sun and Stars, the Clouds, Rain, and Snow, and considered in my spirit the *whole* Creation of this world.

* *the holy Spirit.*

6. Wherein then I found to be in all things, *Evil and Good*, Love and Anger; in the inanimate creatures, *viz.* in Wood, Stones, Earth, and the Elements, as also in Men and Beasts.

7. Moreover, I considered the little spark of light, *Man*, what he should be Esteemed for, with God in *comparison* of this great work and fabrick of Heaven and Earth?

8. But finding that in all things there was Evill and Good, as well in the *Elements* as in the Creatures, and that it went as *well* in this world with the wicked, as with the vertuous honest and Godly, also

that the *Barbarous* People had the beſt Countries in their poſſeſſion, and that they had *more Proſperity* in their wayes, then the vertuous honeſt and Godly had.

9. I was *thereupon* very Melancholy *perplexed* and exceedingly troubled, no Scripture could *Comfort* or ſatisfie me, though I was very well acquainted with it, and *verſed* therein; at which time the Devil would by no means ſtand Idle, but was *often* beating into me, many Heatheniſh Thoughts, which I will here be ſilent in.

10. But when in this *afflifion* and trouble I elevated my ſpirit, which, then I underſtood very little or nothing at all what it was, I *earneſtly* raiſed it up into God, as with a great ſtorm or onſet, wrapping up my whole Heart and Mind, as alſo all my *Thoughts* and whole will and reſolution, *inceſſantly* to wreſtle with the Love and Mercy of God, and not to give over, unleſſe he bleſſed me, that is, unleſſe he *enlightened me with his holy Spirit*, whereby I might *underſtand* his will, and be rid of my ſadneſſe.

And then the ſpirit did break thorough.

11. But when, in my reſolved zeal, I gave ſo hard an aſſault ſtorm and onſet upon God, and upon all the Gates of Hell, as if I had had more reſerves of vertue and power ready, with a *reſolution* to hazard my life upon it, which aſſuredly were not in my ability, *without* the aſſiſtance of the Spirit of God; *ſuddenly* after ſome violent Storms made, my ſpirit *did break thorough* the Gates of Hell, even into the innermoſt Birth or Geniture of the Deity, and there I was *embraced* with Love, as a Bride-groom

groom embraceth his dearly beloved Bride.

12. But the greatnesse of the triumphing that was in the spirit, I *cannot expresse* either in speaking or writing: neither can it be compared with any thing, but with *that*, wherein the life is generated in the midst of Death, and it is *like* the Resurrection from the Dead.

13. In this light my spirit suddenly saw through all, and *in and by* all the Creatures even in Herbs and Grasse it knew God, Who he is, and How he is, and What his will is: and suddenly in that light my will was set on by a Mighty *impulse*, to describe *the Beeing of God.*

14. But because I could not presently apprehend the *deepest* Births of God in their *Beeing*, and comprehend them in my *Reason*, there passed almost *Twelve* years, before the exact understanding thereof was given me.

15. And it was with me as with a young Tree, which is planted in the Ground, and at first is young and *tender*, and flourishing to the Eye, especially if it comes on lustily in its growing: But doth not bear fruit *presently*; and though it blossometh, they fall off; also many a cold wind, frost and snow, puffe upon it, *before* it comes to any growth, and bearing of Fruit.

16. So also it went with this spirit; the first fire was but a *Seed*, and not a constant lasting Light: *since that time* many a cold wind blew upon it; but the Will never extinguished.

17. This Tree was also often tempted to try whether it would bear Fruit, and shew it self with Blossoms; but the *Blossoms* were struck off till this very

time, wherein it standeth in its *first* Fruit in the growth or vegetation.

17. *From this Light now it is, that I have my knowledge,* as also my *will impulse and driving,*

and therefore I will set down this knowledge in writing according to my Gift, and let God work his will; and though I should *Irritate* or enrage the whole world, the Devill, and all the Gates of Hell, I will look on and wait what the LORD intendeth with it.

18. For I am too too *weak* to know his Purpose; and though the spirit affordeth in the *Light* to be known some things, which are *to come,* yet, according to the outward man I am too weak to comprehend the same.

19. But the animated or *soulish* spirit, which qualifieth or uniteth with God, that comprehends it well, but the *bestial Body* attains onely a Glimpse thereof, Just as if it lightned: for this is the posture of the innermost Birth or Geniture of the soul; when it teareth through the *outermost* Birth or Geniture in the elevation of the Holy Ghost, and so breaketh through the Gates of Hell; but the outermost Birth presently *shuts* again: for the *wrath* of God bolteth up the firmament, and holds it captive in its Power.

20. And then the knowledge of the outward Man is *gone,* and he walketh up and down in an *afflicted* and anxious Birth or Geniture, as a woman with child, who is in her travel, and would *alwaies fain* bring forth her child, but *cannot,* and is full of Throes.

21. Thus

21. Thus it goeth also with the bestial Body, when it hath *once tasted* of the sweetnesse of God, then it continually hungreth and thirsteth after it: But the *Devil* in the power of Gods wrath opposeth exceedingly, and so a Man in such a course must *continually* stand in an anxious Birth or Geniture, and so there is nothing but fighting and warring in his Births or Genitures.

22. I write not this for mine own glory, but for a *comfort* to the Reader, so that if perhaps he be minded to walk with me upon my *Narrow* Bridge, he should not suddenly be discouraged dismayed and distrustfull, when the Gates of Hell and Gods wrath meet him, and *present* themselves before him.

23. When we shall come together *over* this narrow Bridge of the fleshly Birth or Geniture, to be in yonder green Medow, to which the wrath of God doth *not* reach or come, then we shall be fully *requited* for all our damages and Hurts we have sustained: though indeed at present the world doth account us for *fooles*, and we must suffer the Devill in the power of Gods wrath, to Domineer, Rush and roar over us: It should not trouble us, for it will be more excellent *Reputation* to us in the other life, then if in this Life we had worn a Royal Crown: and there is so very *short a time* to get thither, that it is not worth the being called a *Time*.

Now Observe :

24. If thou fixest thy Thoughts concerning Heaven, and wouldst *fain conceive* in the Mind What it is, and Where it is, and How it is ; thou *needest* not

to.

to ſwing or caſt thy Thoughts many thouſand Miles off, for, that Place or that Heaven is *not thy* Heaven.

25. And though indeed that is united with thy Heaven, as *one* Body, and ſo together is *But the One* Body of God, yet thou art not in that very place, which is become a *Creature* aloft many hundred thouſand Miles off, but thou art in the *Heaven* of this world, which containeth alſo in it juſt ſuch a Deep, as is not of any Humane Number, [or is Circumſcriptive].

26. For, the *true Heaven* is every where, even in that very Place where thou ſtandeſt and goeſt, and ſo when thy ſpirit apprehendeth the innermoſt Birth or Geniture of God, and preſſeth in *through* the aſtral and fleſhly geniture, then it is *clearly* in Heaven.

27. But that there is aſſuredly a *pure* glorious Heaven in all *the* three Births or Genitures aloft above the Deep of this world, in which Gods Being together with that of the holy Angels riſeth or *ſpringeth up*, very purely, brightly beautiouſly and joyfully, is *undeniable,* and he is *not* born of God that denyeth it.

But thou muſt know,

28. That the place of this world with its innermoſt Birth or Geniture uniteth or qualifieth with the Heaven aloft *above us,* and ſo there is one Heart, one Being, one Will, *one God, All in All.*

29. But that the place of this world, is not called Heaven, and that there is a firmament or faſt incloſure between the *upper* Heaven above us; it hath this underſtanding or meaning, as followeth.

30. The

30. The upper Heaven compriseth the two Kingdoms, that of *Michael* and that of *Uriel*, and of all the holy Angels, which are *not fallen* with *Lucifer*, and that Heaven *continueth* as it was from Eternity, before the Angels were created.

31. The Other Heaven is this world, in which *Lucifer* was a King, who kindled the outermost Birth or Geniture in Nature, and that now is the *wrath* of God, and cannot be called God or Heaven, but *Perdition*.

32. Therefore the upper Heaven includeth it self up so far in its outermost Birth or Geniture, and reacheth so far as the *wrath* of God reacheth, and so far as the Government or Dominion of *Lucifer* hath reached, for the corrupted or perished Birth or Geniture cannot comprehend the *Pure*.

33. That is, the outermost Birth or Geniture of this world cannot comprehend the outermost Birth or Geniture of Heaven *aloft* above this world, for they are one to the other as the Life and the Death, or as a *Man* and *a Stone* are one to the other.

34. And therefore there is a strong firmament or inclosure between the *outermost* Birth or Geniture of the upper Heaven, and that of this world : for the firmament between them is *Death*, which ruleth and reigneth every where in the outermost birth in *this* world, and this world is so bolted up therewith, that the *outermost* Birth of the *upper* Heaven cannot come into the outermost Birth of this world, there is a great Cliff or Gulph between them. And therefore in our outermost Birth or Geniture we cannot *see* the Angels, neither can the Angels dwell with us in the *outermost* Birth of this world, but in the *innermost* they dwell with us.

36. And

36. And so when we fight with the Devill, they keep off his Blowes in the innermost Birth, and are the Defence and Protection of the *holy* Soul.

37. Therefore we can neither see nor comprehend the holy Angels: for the outermost Birth of *their Body* is incomprehensible to the outermost Birth or Geniture of this world.

38. The second Birth of this world standeth in the life, for it is the *Astral* Birth, out of which is generated the *third* and holy Birth or Geniture, and therein Love and wrath *strive* one with the other.

39. For the second Birth standeth in the seven qualifying or fountain spirits of this world, and is in all places, and in all the Creatures, as also in Man: But the Holy Ghost also ruleth and reigneth in the *second* birth, and helpeth to generate the *third* holy Birth or Geniture.

40. But this third Birth or Geniture is the clear and *holy Heaven*, which qualifieth or uniteth with the Heart of God without distinct and above all Heavens, as one Heart; also they are the one Heart, which holdeth and *beareth up* or sustaineth the place of this world, and holdeth the Devil Captive in the outermost birth in the Anger fire, as *an Almighty incomprehensible* God.

41. *And out of this Heart,* JESVS CHRIST *the Sonne of God, in the Womb or Body of the Virgin* Mary, *went into all the three Births or Genitures, and assumed*

aſſumed them really, that He might through and with his innermoſt Birth or Geniture, take the Devill Death and Hell Captive in the outermoſt Birth, and overcome the wrath of God as a King and Victorious Prince; and in the power of his Geniture or Birth in the fleſh, preſſe thorough all Men.

42. And ſo by this entring of the innermoſt Birth of the Heart of the Heaven of this world, into the *Aſtrall* and outermoſt, is JESUS CHRIST, the Sonne of God and of *Mary*, become the *Lord* and *King* of this our Heaven and Earth, who ruleth and *reigneth* in all the three Births or Genitures over Sin, the Devil, Death, and Hell, and ſo *we with him*, preſſe through the ſinful corrupted and outermoſt dead Birth or Geniture of the fleſh, *through Death* and *the wrath of God* into our Heaven.

43. **In this Heaven** now ſitteth **Our King** JESUS CHRIST, at the right hand of God, and encompaſſeth or ſurroundeth all the three Births, as *an almighty Sonne of the Father,* who is preſent in and throughout all the three Births in this world in all Corners and Places, and comprehendeth, holdeth, and beareth up or ſuſtaineth all,

all, as a new Born Sonne of the Father, in the power and upon the Seat or *Throne* of the *once* Great mighty Potent, and *now expell'd*, accursed, and Damned, King *Lucifer* the Devill.

44. Therefore thou child of man, be not discouraged, be not so timorous and pusillanimous: for if thou sowest in thy zeal and earnest sincerity *the seed of thy Teares*, thou dost not sow it in Earth, but in *Heaven*; for in thy astral Birth, thou sowest, and in thy animated or soulish Birth, thou reapest, and in the Kingdom of heaven thou, possessest and enjoyest it.

45. While thou livest in this strugling or *striving* Birth or Geniture, thou must Buckle and suffer the Devil to ride upon thee: but so hard as he striketh thee, so hard thou must strike him again, if thou wilt defend thy self. For when thou fightest against him, thou *stirrest* up his wrath-fire, and destroyest his Nest, and this is then, as a great *combustion*, and as a great strong Battel maintained against him.

46. And though thy Body perhaps is put hard to it and suffers pain in misery, yet it is much worse with him when he is vanquished, for then he roareth like a Lion, which is *robbed* of her young whelps, for the fiercenesse and wrath of God *tormenteth* him: but if thou lettest him Lodge *within* thee, then he groweth fat and *wanton*, and will *vanquish thee*, in Time.

47. Thus thou hast a real description of *Heaven*: And though perhaps *thou* canst not in thy Reason conceive it: Yet *I can* very well Conceive it, therefore consider Rationally and seriously upon it: What God is.

48. Thou seest in this world Nothing but the

Deep

Deep, and therein the Stars, and the Birth or Geniture of the Elements: now wilt thou say, God is *not* there? 'pray then what was there in that place *before* the time of the world? Wilt thou say, there was Nothing: then thou speakest *without* Reason, for thou must *needs* say, that God was there, or else nothing would there have come to be.

49. Now if God were *there* then, who hath thrust him *out* from thence, or vanquished him, that he should be there *no* more? But if God be there, then he is indeed in his *Heaven,* and moreover, in his *Trinity.*

50. But the Devil hath kindled the Bath or Lake of wrath, whence the Earth and Stones, also the Elements, are become so fluctuating, as also cold bitter and hot, and so hath † *destroyed* the outermost † *killed or* Birth or Geniture.   *murthered.*

51. Whereupon now this Treatise and my whole purpose is to describe, how it is come to be living and *revived* again, and how it regenerateth it self again. And from * thence also in the Creatures the * *the wrath beastial Flesh* is come to be, but *Sin* in the Flesh is   *Bath.* the *wrath* of God.

Another *Question,* which is chiefly treated of in this *Book,* is this, *viz.*

Where then shall the Wrath of God become?

Answer.

52. Here the spirit answereth, that at the *End* of the Time of *this* corrupted Birth or Geniture, *after* the Resurrection from the Dead, this place or space, where the Earth now is, will be given to the *Devill*

for

for a propriety or Possession and *House of wrath*, yet *not* through and in all the three Births or Genitures, but onely in the *outermost*, in which he *now* standeth: But the innermost will hold him Captive in its might and strength, and use him for a *footstool*, or as the Dust under its foot, which innermost Birth he will never be able either to comprehend or to *touch*.

53. For it hath *not* this understanding or meaning, that the wrath-fire should be *extinguished*, and be no more; for then the Devils also must become *Holy* Angels again, and live in the holy Heaven: but that *not* being so; a Hole Burrough or Dungeon in this world must remain, to be *their* Habitation.

54. If Mans Eyes were but *opened*, he should see God every where in his Heaven; for Heaven standeth in the innermost Birth or Geniture every where.

55. Moreover *when Stephen saw the Heaven opened, and the Lord JESUS at the right hand of God*, there his spirit did not first swing it self up aloft into the upper Heaven, but it penetrated or pressed into the *innermost* Birth or Geniture, wherein Heaven is every where.

56. Neither must thou think, that the *Deity* is such a kind of Being as is *onely* in the upper Heaven, and that the Soul when it departeth from the Body, goeth up *aloft* into the upper Heaven many hundred thousand Miles off,

57. It *needeth* not do that, but it is set or put into the innermost Birth, and there it is with God, and *in* God, and with all the holy Angels, and can suddenly be above, and suddenly beneath, it is not *hindred* by any thing.

58. For in the innermost Birth, the upper and neather

neather Deity is *one Body*, and is an open Gate: the Holy Angels converse and walk up and down in the innermost Birth of this world *by* and *with* our King JESUS CHRIST, as well as in the uppermost world aloft in their Quarters Courts or Region.

59. And where then would or should the Soul of Man *rather* be, then with its King and Redeemer JESUS CHRIST. For, near and afar off in God is *one* thing, *one comprehensibility*, Father Sonne and Holy Ghost, every where, all over.

60. The Gate of the Deity in the upper heaven is *no other*, also no brighter, then it is in this world; and where can there be greater Joy then in that place, where every hour and *Moment* beautiful loving dear new born children and Angels *come* to Christ, which are press'd or penetrated through Death into Life?

61. Doubtlesse they will make *large Relations* of many Fights; and where can there be greater *Joy*, then where, in the midst or Center of Death, life is Generated continually?

62. Doth not every soul bring along with it a *new Triumph?* and so there is nothing else, but an exceeding friendly welcoming and *Salutation* there.

63. Consider then the Soules of children come to their Parents, who in the Body did Generate them, whether Heaven *can choose* but be there? or dost thou think my writing is too Earthly?

64. If thou wert come to this Window, thou wouldst not then say, that it is earthly; And though I must indeed use the *earthly* Tongue, yet there is a true heavenly *understanding* couched under its, which in my outermost Birth I am not able to expresse either in writing or in Speaking.

65. I know very well, that the word concerning the

the three Births, cannot be comprehended or apprehended *in every Mans Heart,* especially where the
† *or fleshly* Heart is too much *steeped* soaked or drowned in † the
matters. flesh, and bolted and Barred up with the outermost
Birth.

66. But I cannot render it otherwise then as it is,
for it is just so: and though I should write *meer* Spirit, as indeed and truth it is no other, yet the heart
understandeth *onely* Flesh.

Concerning the Constitution and form of the
Earth.

67. Many Authors have written, that Heaven
and Earth were created out of NOTHING: but I
do wonder, that among *so many* excellent Men there
hath *not one* been found, that could yet describe the
true Ground; seeing the same God which now is,
hath been from Eternity.

68. Now where nothing is, there nothing can
come to be: All things must have *a Root,* else can
nothing grow: If the *seven Spirits of Nature* had not
been from eternity, then there would no Angel, no
Heaven, also no Earth, have come to be.

69. But the Earth is come from the corrupt *Salitter* of the outermost Birth or Geniture, which thou
canst not deny, when thou lookest on Earth and
Stones, for then thou must needs say, that *Death* is
therein: And on the other side also thou must needs
say, that there is a *Life* therein, otherwise neither
Gold nor Silver, nor any Plant, Herb, Grasse or Vegetable could grow therein.

Now one might Ask

Are there also all the three Births or Genitures therein.

Answer.

70. Yes: the Life presseth thorough Death: the *outermost* Birth is the Death: the *second* is the Life, which standeth in the wrath-fire and in the Love; And the *Third* is the Holy Life.

An

Instruction, or Information.

71. The outward Earth is a bitter stinck, and is dead, and that every man understandeth to be so. But the *Salitter* is destroyed or killed through Death: for thou canst not deny, but that *Gods wrath* is in the Earth, otherwise it would not be so astringent, bitter, fowr, venomous and poisonous, neither would it engender such poisonous venomous Evill worms and creeping things. But if thou shouldst say, that *God* hath created them *thus, out of his Purpose,* that is as much, as if thou shouldst say, that God himself is Evil, Malice, Malignity or Wickednesse?

Pray tell me; Why was the Devil expell'd or Thrust out?

72. Surely thou wilt say, because of *his Pride,* In that he would needs be above God.

But Guesse Sir, with *what* he would do so: *what* Power had he to do it?

Here tell me, if thou knowest any thing of it; if thou

thou knoweſt Nothing, be *ſilent* and attentive.

37. Before the Times of the Creation He ſate in the *Salitter* of the Earth, when it was yet Thin or Tranſparent, and ſtood in a heavenly holy Birth or Geniture, and was in the *whole* Kingdom of this world, therein it was neither Earth nor Stones, but a heavenly *Seed,* which was generated out of the ſeven qualifying or fountain ſpirits of Nature ; for therein ſprung up heavenly fruits forms and Ideas, which were a pleaſant *delightfull food* of Angels.

74. But when the *wrath* did *burn* therein, then it was killed and deſtroyed in Death : Yet not ſo to be underſtood, as if it were therefore altogether *quite* dead : For *how* can any thing in God dye *totally,* that hath had its Life from eternity ?

75. But I. the *outermoſt* Birth or Geniture was burnt up, frozen, drown'd, ſtupiſied, chilled, and ſtark benummed.

76. But II. the *Second Birth* or Geniture generateth the Life again in the outermoſt.

77. And III. the *Third* ✱ is generated between the firſt and the ſecond, that is, between Heaven and Hell in the *midſt* or Center of the wrath-fire, and the ſpirit preſſeth thorough in the wrath-fire, and generateth the *Holy* Life, which ſtandeth in the power of the Love.

78. And in this ſame Birth or Geniture ſhall *thoſe* Dead ariſe who have ſown a *holy* Seed, and *thoſe* who have ſown in the *wrath,* will ariſe in the Wrath-fire: for the Earth will *revive* and be living again : ſeeing the Deity in *Chriſt* hath regenerated *it* anew again through his *Fleſh,* and exalted *it* to the right hand of God : but the wrath-fire *abideth* in its own Birth or Geniture.

79. But

79. But if thou fayft, that there is *no* Life in the Earth, thou fpeakeft as one that is *blind*; for thou mayft fee plainly, that Herbs and Graffe grow out of it:

80. But if thou fayft, it hath but *one* kind of Birth or Geniture: thou fpeakeft again alfo like one that is *blind*: for the Herbs and Wood, which grow out of it, are *not* Earth, neither is the *fruit* which groweth upon a Tree, wood; fo alfo the power and *vertue* of the Fruit is *not* God, neither; but † God is in the Center, in the innermoft Birth in all the three natural Births or Genitures, *hiddenly*, and is not known, but onely † *in the Spirit of Man*; alfo the outermoft Birth in the fruit doth not comprehend conceive or contain *him*, but *he* containeth the outermoft Birth of the fruit, and formeth it.

† *Note how God is in all things, yet no Creature is He.*

Another Queſtion is,

Why then is the Earth fo Mountainy, Hilly, Rocky, Stony, and uneven?

Anſwer.

81. The Hills came to be fo in the driving together or *Compaction*: for the *corrupted Salitter* was more abounding in one place, then in another; accordingly as the wheel of God was, as to its innate inftanding or inftant qualifying or fountain fpirits.

82. For in *thofe* Places, where the fweet water in the ftanding wheel of God was chief or *predominant*, there much Earthly comprehenfible or *palpable* water came to be.

83. But where the aftringent Quality in the bitterneffe

terneſſe in *Mercurius* was chief or predominant, there much *Earth* and *Stones* came to be.

84. But where the Heat in the Light was chief or predominant, there much *Silver*, and *Gold*, as alſo ſome fair *clear Stones*, in the flaſh of the *Light* came to be; but eſpecially where the Love in the Light was chief or predominant, there the moſt *pretious Stones* or Jewels, as alſo the beſt pureſt and *fineſt Gold* came to be.

85. But when the Lump of the Earth was preſs'd and compacted together, then thereby the water came to be *ſqueezed* and preſſed forth : but where it was *incloſed* and preſs'd in with the aſtringent quality by hard Rocks, there it is yet in the Earth ſtill, and hath ſince that time worn and made ſome great Holes or *Veins* for its paſſage.

86. In thoſe places, where there are great Lakes and *Seas*, there the *water* was chief or predominant over that place in that Zenith or *Elevation* of the Pole; and there not being much *Salitter* in that place, there came to be as it were a Dale or Valley, wherein the water remained ſtanding.

87. For the thin water ſeeketh for the valley, and is an *humility* of the life, which did not elevate it ſelf, as the aſtringent, bitter and fire's Quality hath done in thoſe Creatures the *Devils*:

88. Therefore it alwaies ſeeketh the *Loweſt* Places of the Earth ; which rightly ſignifieth or reſembleth the ſpirit of *meekneſſe*, in which the life is Generated : as you may read concerning the Creation of Man, as alſo before, concerning the Species or condition of Water, Meekneſſe, and ſuch Qualities:

Of Day, and Night.

89. The *whole* Deity with all its Powers and operations, together with its innate or Instant *Being*, as also its rising up, penetration, changing and alteration; that is to say, the whole Machine fabrick and work, or the whole generating or production, is *all* understood in the *spirit* of † the Word.

90. For in what proportion or *Harmony* soever, or innate or instant generating or production of Qualities soever, the spirit comprehendeth conceiveth & formeth the Word, and goeth forth therewith ; Just *such* an innate or instant Birth, penetrating, rising, wrestling and overcoming, it hath also in *Nature*.

91. For when Man fell into Sin, he was *removed* out of the innermost Birth or Geniture, and set or put into the other *two*, which presently embraced him, and mixed qualified or united *with* him and *in* him, as in their own propriety, and so Man instantly received the spirit, and all generatings or productions of the *Astral* Birth, and also of the outermost Birth or Geniture.

92. Therefore now it Expresseth or speaketh forth *all words*, according to the innate instant generating or production of Nature : for the spirit of Man, which standeth in the Astrall birth, and qualifieth or uniteth with the totall universall Nature, and is as it were the whole Nature it self; that formeth the word, according to the innate instant Birth or Geniture.

93. When it seeth any thing, then it giveth a *Name* to it according to its Qualification or conditi-

† *Of every word or syllable in every Language or dialect of Language.*

on : and if it be to do so, then it must also form or *frame* or put it self into such a form, and generate it self also with its Tone Sound or Articulation, just so as the *thing* which it will give a Name to, doth generate or *Compose* it self.

And herein lyeth the kernell of the whole understanding of the Deitie.

94. I do *not* write this, and bring it to light, that others after me should presently fall a writing, and publish the conceits of his own spirit herein, and cry it up for *Sanctity* or a Holy Thing.

95. Hearken *friend*, there belongeth more then so to this : thy animated or *soulish* spirit, must first qualifie operate or *unite* with the innermost Birth or Geniture in God, and stand in the *Light*, that it may *rightly* know and understand the Astrall Birth or Geniture, and that it may have a free and *open Gate* into all the Births or Genitures, else thou wilt *not* be able to write a Holy and true Philosophie, but as it were full of † Lice and Fleas, and so thou wilt be found a Mocker against God.

† or many evil Beasts and Creeping vermine.

96. I conceive already, the Devill will get *many* a one to ride upon *his* proud prancing Nagg : and many will make themselves *ready* for the Journey before they be well *Girt* * : I will not bear the blame !

* with the Girdle of Truth.

97. For what I here *reveal* or manifest : I must do it ; for the time of Breaking through is at *Hand* : He that will *now sleep*, the stormy Tempest of the fiercenesse, will rouze him.

98. But now that every one might have a care of
his

his affairs and *doings*; I would have them faithfully warned according to the impulſe driving and will of the ſpirit.

Obſerve :

99. The Writer *Moſes* ſaith, *Gen.* 1. *God ſeparated the Light from the Darkneſſe, and called the Light Day, and the Darkneſſe, Night, ſo out of Evening and Morning, the firſt Day came to be.*

100. But being theſe words, *Evening,* and *Morning,* are contrary to the Current of Philoſophie and Reaſon, therefore it may be conceived, *that Moſes* was not the ſole Original Author thereof, but that it was derived down to him from his Foreſathers, who reckoned *all* the *ſix* Dayes of the Creation in one *continued courſe,* and preſerved and kept the memory of the Creation, from *Adam,* in an *obſcure* word, and *ſo left* it to poſterity.

101. For Evening and Morning were *not* before the Time of the *Sun* and *Stars,* which moſt certainly and really were firſt created but on the *Fourth Day,* which I ſhall demonſtrate from an aſſured certain ground, concerning the Creation of the Sun and Stars.

102. But there was *Day* and *Night,* which I will here declare according to my knowledge : Thou muſt here once more open the Eyes of thy ſpirit wide, if thou intendeſt to underſtand it ; if *not,* then thou wilt remain *blind.*

103. *And though* this great work in Man hath remained *hidden* till this very day, yet God be praiſed, it will now *once be Day,* for the Day-ſpring or Morning-Redneſſe *breaketh forth.* The Breaker-through or Opener of the innermoſt Birth ſheweth

and.

and prefenteth it felf with its *Red, Green,* and *white,* Flagg, in the outermoft Birth upon the *Rainbow.*

Obferve:

Now thou Objecteft:

How then could there be Day and Night, and not alfo Morning and Evening?

Anfwer.

104. *Morning,* and *Evening,* is and reacheth only up from the Earth to the Moon, and taketh its *Original* from the Light of the Sun, and this maketh Evening, and Morning, as alfo the *outward Day* and the *outward* dark *Night,* as every one knoweth.

105. But there was not a *twofold* Creation of Evening and Morning at that time; but when Evening and Morning did once begin, they kept their *conftant* courfe all along from that time to this.

Of the { **Day.** } { **Tage.** }

106. The word (**Tage**) conceiveth it felf at the Heart, and goeth forth at the mouth through the *way* or Paffage of the aftringent and bitter quality, and doth *not* awaken or rouze up the aftringent and bitter quality, but goeth *directly* through their place, which is at the hinder Gums upon the Tongue, *forth,* very foftly or *gently,* and incomprehenfibly as to the aftringent and bitter Quality.

107. But when it cometh forth upon the Tongue, then the Tongue and the upper Gums *clofe* the mouth,

mouth, but when the spirit thrusteth at the Teeth, and will go forth, then the Tongue *openeth the mouth* at the Teeth, and will go forth before the word, and doth as it were *leap* for Joy *forth* at the mouth.

108. But when the word breaketh thorough, then the Mouth *within* openeth wide, and the word conceiveth it self *once more* with its sound behind the astringent and bitter qualities, and rouzeth them up, as if they were *lazy* sleepers in the Darknesse, and goeth forth *suddenly* out at the Mouth.

109. And then the astringent quality *drayeth* after it as a drowzie Man, which is awakened from sleep: but the bitter spirit which goeth forth from the fire-flash, lyeth *still*, and heareth or regardeth *not*, *neither* doth move.

These are very great things, and not so slight matters, as the Country-Man supposeth.

110. Now, that the spirit first conceiveth it self at the heart, and breaketh through all *watches* and Guards till it come upon the Tongue, unperceived, or unobserved: it signifieth, that the Light Brake forth out of the Heart of God, through the *corrupted*, outermost, fierce, *dead*, bitter and astringent Birth or Geniture in the *Nature* of this world, incomprehensibly both as to Death and the Devill, together with the wrath of God, as it is written in the Gospel of St. *John*, 1. Chap. verse 5. *The Light shone in the Darknesse, and the Dark-*

Darkneſſe comprehended it not.

111. But that the Tongue and the upper Gums *cloſe* the Mouth, when the ſpirit cometh upon the Tongue: it ſignifieth, that the ſeven qualifying or fountain Spirits of Nature in *this* world, at the time of the Creation were *not mortified* and Dead through the wrath of God, but were *lively active and vigorous.* For the Tongue ſignifieth or denoteth the life of Nature, in which ſtandeth the animated *Souliſh* and Holy Birth or Geniture: for it is a † Type of the Soul.

† Prefiguration or Reſemblance.

112. But that the Spirit ſuddenly *affecteth* the Tongue, when it cometh upon it, whereupon it leapeth for Joy, and will go *before* the Spirit forth at the Mouth; it ſignifieth, that the ſeven qualifying or fountain ſpirits of Nature, which are called the *Aſtrall* Birth: when the Light of God, which is called the *Day,* roſe up in them, they ſuddenly gat the *Divine* Life and Will, and ſo highly rejoyced, as the Tongue in the Mouth here doth.

113. But that the *fore* Gums widen *inward,* and give room for the ſpirit to do as it pleaſeth: it ſignifieth, that the *whole* Aſtral Birth yielded it ſelf very friendly and Courteouſly to the *will* of the Light, and did not awaken the fierceneſſe in it.

114. But that the ſpirit, when it goeth forth at the Mouth, conceiveth it ſelf yet *once more* behind the aſtringent quality upon the Tongue at the hindermoſt gums, and awakeneth or rouzeth up the aſtringent quality, being as it were *aſleep,* and then goeth ſuddenly forth at the Mouth;

115. It ſignifieth, I. that the *aſtringent* ſpirit indeed muſt hold preſerve and Image or frame all in

the

the whole Nature, but it is *after* the spirit of the *Light* hath *first* formed it, and that then first the Light awakeneth the *astringent* spirit, and giveth all into the Hands *thereof* to hold or preserve it.

116. And that must be, because of the outermost comprehensibility or *Palpability*, which must be held and sustained by the *astringent* fiercenesse, else nothing would subsist in its *Body*, neither could the compressed Compacted Earth and Stones subsist; but would be again a broken Thick muddy and *dark Salitter*, such as at first *moved* in the whole Deep.

117. It signifieth also, 2°. that this *Salitter*, at last, when the spirit hath done with its *Creation*, and *work*, in this world; shall be rouzed up and *revived* at the Last Judgment Day.

118. But, that the spirit conceiveth it self *behind* the astringent quality, and not *in* the astringent quality, and so awakeneth or rouzeth it up : it signifieth, that the astringent Nature will *not comprehend* the Light of God in its *own* proper Way, but shall *rejoyce* in the Light of the *Grace*, and be awakened or raised up thereby, and *perform* the *will* of the Light, as the beastial Body of Man effecteth and performeth the will of the spirit, and yet these are *not two* severed Things.

119. But why the bitter spirit *lyeth still*, and neither heareth nor comprehendeth or apprehendeth the work of the spirit, it signifieth, that the bitter wrath-fire, which existeth in the flash of fire, at the time of the Birth or Geniture of the *Light*, and *still also*, is not awakened by the Light, also doth not comprehend it, but lyeth *Captive* imprisoned in the outermost Birth or Geniture, and must give leave

to

to the spirit of Light, to do its work in Nature, how it *pleaseth*, and yet can neither see, hear nor comprehend the *work* of the Light.

120. Therefore *no Man* ought to think, that the Devill is *able* to tear the works of the Light, out of his Heart, for he can neither see nor comprehend them : And though he rageth and raveth in the outermost Birth in the *Flesh* as in his Castle of Robbery or Fort of Prey; be not discouraged or dismay'd : onely take heed *thou thy self* bring not the works of wrath into the *Light* of thy Heart, and then thy soul will be *safe enough* from the *deaf* and *dumb Devill*, who is *blind* in the Light.

121. Thou shouldst not suppose, that which I write here, to be as a *doubtful* Opinion, questionable whether it be so or no : For, the Gate of Heaven and Hell standeth open to the spirit, and in the light presseth through them *both*, and beholdeth them, also proveth or Examineth them : for the Astrall Birth or Geniture liveth *between* them both; and must endure to be squeezed.

122. And though the Devil *cannot* take the Light from me, yet he *hideth* or *eclipseth* it often with the outward and fleshly Birth or Geniture, so that the Astrall Birth or Geniture is in *anxiety*, and in a straight, as if it were captivated or imprisoned.

123. And these onely are his *Blowes* and *Strokes*, whereby the Mustard Seed is overwhelmed, covered, and obscured : Concerning which also the Holy Apostle *Paul* saith, *that a great Thorn was* given him *in his Flesh, and he besought the Lord earnestly to take it from him, whereupon the Lord answered, Let my Grace be sufficient for thee, 2. Cor. 12. v. 7, 8, 9.*

124. For

124. For he was also *come to this* place, and would fain have had the Light without obstruction or hinderance as *his own in the Astrall Birth* or Geniture. But *it could not be*: for the *wrath* resteth in the *fleshly* Birth, and must bear or endure the corruption or putrefaction in the flesh: but if the fiercenesse should be *quite* taken away from the Astrall Birth or Geniture, then in that, he would be like God, and know all things, as God himself doth.

125. Which now at † present *that Soul* onely †*in this Life,* knoweth, which qualifieth operateth or *uniteth* with the *Light* of God, but cannot *perfectly* bring it back again into the *Astral* Birth or Geniture; for it is another Person.

126. Just as an Apple on a Tree *cannot* bring its Smell and Taste back again into the Tree or into the Earth, though it be indeed the sonne of the Tree; so it is also in *Nature.*

127. The *Holy Man* Moses was so high and deep in this Light, that the *Light* glorified *Clarified* or Brightned the Astrall Birth also, whereby the outermost Birth of the *Flesh* in his *Face* was clarified brightned or Glorified; and he also desired to see the Light of God *perfectly* in the Astrall Birth or Geniture.

128. But it could *not* be; for the Barre or Bolt of the *wrath* lyeth before it: for even the whole or universal Nature of the Astral Birth in this world *cannot* comprehend the Light of God, and therefore the Heart of God is *hidden* and concealed, which however, *dwelleth* in all places, and comprehendeth All.

129. Thus thou seest, that the *Day* was created before the time of the Sun and Stars: for when God

said,

faid, *Gen.* 1. v. 3. ***Let there be Light***
there the Light brake thorough the Darkneſſe, bu
the Darkneſſe did not comprehend it, but remained ſit
ing in its Seat.

130. Thou ſeeſt alſo, how the Wrath of God i
the *outermoſt Birth* of Nature lyeth hid, and reſteth
and *cannot* be awakened, unleſſe men *themſelve*
rouze or awaken it, who with their fleſhly-Birth o
Geniture qualifie operate, or unite with the wrath i
the *outermoſt* Birth of Nature.

131. Therefore if any one ſhould be *Damned* int
Hell, he ought *not* to ſay; that God hath done it, o
that he *willeth* it to be ſo; but *Man* awakeneth o
ſtirreth up the wrath-fire in *himſelf*, which if i
groweth *burning*, afterward qualifieth mixeth o
uniteth with Gods wrath, and the helliſh fire, a
one thing.

132. For when thy Light is extinguiſht, the
thou ſtandeſt in the Darkneſſe, and in the Darkneſ
the *wrath* of God is *hidden*, and ſo if thou awakene[
it, then it *burneth* in thee.

133. There is fire even in a Stone, but if you d
not ſtrike upon it, the fire remaineth *hidden*, but i
you ſtrike it, then the fire *Springs forth*; and then i
any combuſtible matter be near it, that will take fir
and burn, and ſo it cometh to be a Huge fire: an
thus it is alſo with *Man*, when he kindleth the reſ[
ing wrath-fire, which is otherwiſe at *Reſt*.

Of the { *Night.*
          Nacht.

134. The word (Nacht) conceiveth it self first
at the Heart, and the spirit *grunteth* with or in the
astringent Quality, yet not wholly comprehensible
to the astringent Quality; afterward it conceiveth
it self upon the tongue: But *all the while* it grunteth
at the Heart, the Tongue *shuts* the Mouth, till the
spirit cometh, and conceiveth it self upon the tongue,
but then it openeth the Mouth suddenly, and lets the
spirit *go forth.*

135. And now, that the word conceiveth it self
first at the Heart, and *grunteth* with or in the astringent Quality, it signifieth, that the Holy Ghost conceived it self *in the Darknesse* upon the Heart of God
in the Astrall Birth or Geniture of the seven qualifying or fountain spirits: But that it *grunteth* within
or at the astringent Quality, it signifieth, that the
Darknesse was a contrary or *opposite* will against the
Holy Ghost, at or against which, the spirit was *dif-*
pleased.

136. But that it goeth likewise through the *dark*
way or Passage, it signifieth, that the spirit goeth
forth also through the Darknesse, which is *yet* in a
quiet Rest, and generateth it to be Light, if it hold
still, and doth *not* kindle the fire.

Note.

137. Here is cause for the Judging world to see,
and consider; who *condemn Man in*
his

his Mothers Body or Womb,
whereas they do not know, whether the wrath-fire
of the *Parents* be *fully* kindled in the fruit, or not:
and feeing that the Spirit of God moveth alfo in the
Darkneſſe which ſtandeth yet in Quiet Reſt, and
can eaſily generate the Darkneſſe to be Light: And
moreover the *Hour* of Mans Birth or *Nativity* is very *helpful* and profitable for it: but in many it is very *hurtfull* and obſtructive, but not *compulſive.*

138. But that the Mouth ſhutteth, when the ſpirit conceiveth it ſelf upon the Heart, and that the
aſtringent quality grunteth againſt and *with* or *in* it,
it ſignifieth, that the whole Court Extent or Place
of this world was *very dark* in the Aſtrall, and alſo
in the outermoſt Birth or Geniture, and by the *ſtrong*
going forth of the ſpirit, became Light.

139. But that the bitter ſpirit is not *awakened,*
whileſt the ſpirit goeth through its Place, it ſignifieth, that the *dark Night* in the outermoſt Birth or
Geniture of this world hath *never* comprehended
the Light, alſo *never ſhall* comprehend it in all Eternity.

140. Hence it is, that the Creatures ſee onely
the *Aſtrall Light* with their Eyes, elſe if the darkneſſe were not yet in the outermoſt Birth or Geniture, then the Aſtrall ſpirit could ſee *through* Wood
and Stones, as alſo *through* the *whole Earth,* and could
not be hindred by any thing; Juſt as it is in Heaven.

141. But, now the Darkneſſe is ſeparated from
the Light, and *abideth* in the outermoſt Birth or Geniture, wherein the wrath of God reſteth till the
Laſt Judgment Day, but then the wrath will be
kindled

kindled, and the darknesse will be the House or Habitation of Eternal *Perdition*, wherein Lord *Lucifer* together with all wicked Men, which have sowen into Darknesse into the soyl of the wrath, shall have their eternal Dwelling and *Residence*.

142. But the Astrall Birth, in which the natural Light now standeth, and wherein the *holy* Birth is Generated, shall be *also* kindled at the End of this Time, and the wrath and the *holy* Birth shall be *separated* asunder, for the wrath shall not comprehend the holy Birth or Geniture.

143. But the wrath in the Astrall Birth shall be given to the House of Darknesse for a Life, and *the Wrath shall be called the Hellish fire:* And *the House of darknesse,* which is the outermost Birth, *shall be called Death:* And *King Lucifer* shall be the *God therein,* and his Angels and all Damned Men shall be his Ministers Officers and Servants.

144. In this Devouring *Gulf* or Throat will rise up all manner of *Hellish Fruits* and *Forms,* all according to the hellish quality and kind; as in Heaven there spring up *Heavenly fruits* and *forms* according to the heavenly quality and kind.

145. Thus you may understand, what the Creation of Heaven and Earth, signifieth and is, also what God made on the *first Day*. Though indeed the first Three Dayes were not *distinguisht* or severed asunder by Evening and Morning, but a Time is to be reckoned and accounted as of Twenty four Hours

Hours, as there is on high above the *Moon*, such a Time and Day.

146. Secondly, it is also therefore counted for a Humane Day, because doubtlesse the *Earth* instantly *began* its Revolution, and did turn Round about, once in such a period of Time, while God was separating, and so till he had separated, the Light from the **the Earth.* darknesse, and thus * it performed and finished its course the first Time.

The Twentieth Chapter.

Of the Second Day.

1.

IT is written thus, concerning the second Day: *And God said; Let there be a Firmament in the midst of the waters, and let it be a distinction or division between the waters: so there God made the Firmament, and divided the waters under the firmament, from the waters above the firmament: and it was so done. And God called the firmament, Heaven; and so out of the Evening and the Morning the second day came to be,* Gen. 1. v. 6,7,8.

2. This description sheweth once more, that the Dear Man *Moses* was not the Original Authour thereof; for it is written very Obscurely, and not fully expressed, though indeed it hath a very *excellent* understanding and meaning.

3. And without Doubt the *Holy Ghost* would not have it revealed, lest the Devill should know all the Mysteries in the Creation. For the Devil, doth

not

not know the Creation of the *Light*, viz. how Heaven is made out of the midst or Center of the water.

4. For he can neither see nor comprehend or apprehend the Light and holy generation or production, which standeth in the water of the Heaven, but the Generation or production only which standeth in the Astringent, Bitter, Sowr, and Hot Quality, from whence existed the *outermost* Birth or Geniture, which is his Royall Fort or Castle.

5. The meaning is *not*, that he hath *no* power in the Elementary water, to possesse it ; for the outermost corrupted Birth or Geniture in the Elementary water *belongeth also* to the wrath of God, and *Death* is also therein, as well as in the Earth.

6. But the spirit in *Moses* meaneth here, quite another *sort* of water, which the Devill can neither understand, nor comprehend : But if it should have been *declared* so long a time ago, then the Devill would have *learned* it from Man, and had without doubt strowed his hellish chaff *also* into it.

7. *Therefore* the Holy Ghost hath kept it hidden *almost* till the last Hour before the *Evening*, wherein his *Thousand yeares are accomplished, and then he must be let loose again for a little season,* as is to be read in the Revelat. ch. 20. v. 3.

[" *After that* Summer, *cometh the Last* Winter :
" *but the* Sun *will shine warm yet, before that*
" *Time* :]

8. But being he is *now loose* from the chains of Darknesse, God causeth Lights to be set up every where in this world, whereby Men might learn to
know

know him and *his feats* and wiles, and beware of him.

9. Whether he be *loose* or *no*, I offer it to every one to Confider; view but the world in the clear Light, and thou wilt find, that at prefent the *four new Sonnes*, which the Devill generated, when he was thruft out of Heaven; *do govern* the world, *viz.* 1. Pride, 2. Covetoufneffe, 3. Envy, 4. Wrath; Thefe rule the world at prefent, and are the *Devills* Heart, his animated or *foulifh* fpirit.

10. Therefore view the world very well, and then thou wilt find, that it *fully* qualifieth uniteth and Co-worketh with thefe *four new Sonnes* of the Devil. Therefore men have caufe to look circumfpectly to themfelves. For *this is the Time*, of which, all the Prophets have prophefied: and Chrift in the Gofpel, faying: *Thinkeſt thou, that the Sonne of Man will find any faith, when he ſhall come again to Judge the world,* Luke 18. v. 8.

11. The world fuppofeth, that it flourifheth now, and ftandeth in its *Flower*, becaufe the clear Light hath moved over it; But the fpirit fheweth to me, that it ftandeth in the *midſt* or Center of *Hell.*

12. For it forfaketh the Love, and hangeth on Covetoufneffe, Extortion and Bribery; there is *no Mercy at all* therein: Every one cryeth out, if I had but *Mone*! Thofe that are in Authority and power fuck the very Marrow from the Bones of Men of low Degree and Rank, and feed upon the fweat of their

Br *m* os

Browes. Briefly, there is nothing else but Lying, Cozening, robbing and murthering, and so may very justly be called the Devils *Nest* and dwelling House.

13. The *Holy Light* is now adayes accounted a meer History and bare knowledge, and that the spirit *will not work* therein ; and yet they *suppose*, that is Faith, which they professe with their *Mouthes*.

14. O thou blind and foolish world ! full of Devils. It is *not* Faith, to know, that Christ dyed for thee, and hath shed his Blood for thee, that thou mightest be *saved* : This *in thee* is but a meer History and knowledge, The Devil also knoweth as much, but it profiteth him *Nothing* : so thou also, thou foolish world, goest *no further*, but contentest thy self with the *bare* knowledge, and therefore this thy knowledge will *Judge* thee.

15. But if thou wouldst know, what the *true Faith is*, then observe : *Thy heart must not qualifie or co-operate with the four Sonnes of the Devill, in Pride, Covetousnesse, Envy, Wrath, Extortion, Oppression, Lying, Deceiving, Murther, and tearing the Bread out of thy neighbours Throat, studying day and night to do mischief, in bringing subtile Devices and designs to*

Nnn 2   *Effect,*

Effect, that thou mayſt give ſa-
tisfaction to the Proud Covetous
Envious and wrathful Devils, to
Court them, and exerciſe thy ſelf
in worldly pleaſures and voluptu-
ouſneſſe.

16. For thus ſaith the ſpirit in its zeal or in the Jealouſie of Gods wrath in this world: while thy *ſpirit* and *will* qualifieth or co-operateth with and in the four Abominations of the Devill, thou art not one ſpirit with God: and ſaith the ſpirit, though thou preſenteſt me every Hour with thy Lips, and *Prayeſt*, and *boweſt thy knees be-fore me*, yet I will accept none of thy Labour: Is not thy breath however continually before me? whar ſhall thy Incenſe be to me in my fierce wrath? doſt thou think, I will receive the Devil into my ſelf? *or exalt Hell into Heaven?*

17. Convert! Convert! and *ſtrive againſt the malice and wickedneſs of the Devill,* and incline thine heart towards the LORD thy GOD, and *walk in his will,* Heart will incline to me, ſaith the ſpirit, then will I alſo incline to thee: or doſt thou think, that I am falſe and wicked as thou art?

18. *Therefore* I ſay now, if thy heart doth not qualifie

lifie mix or Co-operate with *God* in thy knowledge: out of a true Purpose of *Love*, then thou art a Dissembler, Lyar, and Murtherer in the sight of God: for God doth not *hear* any mans **Prayer**, unlesse his Heart be fully directed and bent, in *Obedience* to God.

19. Wouldst thou fight against the Wrath of God ? then thou must put on the Helmet of *Obedience* and of *Love*, otherwise thou wilt not break thorough ; and if thou dost not break thorough, then thou fightest in *vain*, and remainest to be a Servant or Minister of the Devil in one way as well as in the other.

20. What will thy *knowledge* do thee Good, if thou wilt not strive and *fight* therein ? It is Just as if one knew of a great Treasure, and would not go for it, but though he knoweth he might have it, would rather *starve* for hunger in the *bare* knowing of it.

21. Thus saith the spirit, *many Heathens*, who have not thy knowledge, and yet strive or fight against the wrath, *will enter into the Kingdome of Heaven before thee.*

22. For who shall Judge them, if their Heart do qualifie unite or operate with God ? For, though they do *not* know him, and yet work and labour in his spirit, in Righteousnesse and in the *purity* of their Heart, in *true Love* one to another; *they testifie assuredly, that the Law of God is in their Heart ?* Rom. 2. 15.

23. But

23. But being thou knoweſt it, and doſt it *not,* and the other know it not, but yet *do it,* they with their Doing judge thy knowledge; and thou art found to be a hypocrite, diſſembler, and an unprofitable Servant, who wert put into the Vineyard of the Lord, and *wilt not work* therein.

24. What doſt thou ſuppoſe, the Maſter of the Houſe will ſay to thee, when he ſhall require and demand his *Talent,* which he entruſted thee with, *thou having buried it in the Earth?* will he not ſay, *thou Perverſe wicked ſervant, why didſt thou not put my Talent out upon uſe, and then I could have demanded the Principall and the Intereſt* or profit?

25. Note: And ſo the *ſufferings of Chriſt* will be quite taken from thee, and will be given to the Heathens, who had but *One Talent,* and yet made *Five* good, for it, to the Maſter of the Houſe; and thou muſt *howl with the Dogs.*

Now Obſerve:

26. Now if we will rightly conſider, How God ſeparated the *water under* the Firmament, from the water *above* the Firmament, then great Things are to be found herein.

27. For the water, which *reſteth on the Earth,* is as a corrupt periſhed and mortal or Dead Being or Thing as the Earth is, and belongeth alſo to the *outermoſt* Birth, which with its comprehenſibility, or as to its palpability ſtandeth in *Death,* even as the Earth and *Stones* do.

28. The meaning is *not,* that it is quite reprobated rejected or thruſt out from God: for the *Heart* therein belongeth yet to the Aſtrall Birth or Geniture, out

of

of which the *holy* Birth becometh Generated.

29. But Death standeth in the outermost Birth, and *therefore* is the palpable water *separated* from the impalpable.

Now thou wilt Ask :

How is that ?

Answer.

30. Behold the water, in the Deep *above* the Earth, which qualifieth mixeth or uniteth with the *Elementary* Ayr and Fire, that, is the water of the *Astrall* Birth or Geniture, wherein standeth the *Astral life*, and wherein *especially* the Holy Ghost moveth, and through which the *Third* and innermost Birth doth generate *incomprehensibly* as to the wrath of God therein : and that water to our Eyes seemeth like the Ayr.

31. But, that Water, Ayr, and Fire, are *one in another*, in the Deep above the Earth ; every intelligible Man may see and understand.

32. For thou seest that often the whole Deep is very *clear* and pure, and in *a quarter of an Hour* is covered with watery Clouds, that is, when the Stars from *above*, and the water upon the Earth from *beneath* kindle themselves, and so water is suddenly. there also generated ; which would *not be*, if the wrath did not also stand in the Astral Birth or Geniture.

33. But being *all* is corrupted, therefore must the upper water in the wrath of God, come to help the Astringent, Bitter, and Hot quality of the Earth, and allay mitigate and *quench* its fire, so that the life may
always

alwayes be generated, and that the holy Birth between Death and the wrath of God, may be generated also.

34. But, that also the Element of *Fire* is, and doth rule, in the Deep of the Air and Water; thou seeft in Tempefts of Lightning : alfo thou perceiveft, how the Light of the *Sun* kindleth the Element of Fire on the Earth with its *reflection*, although many times aloft in the upper Region towards the *Moon* it is very cold.

35. But now, God feparated the palpable water from the impalpable, and placed the palpable on the Earth, and the impalpable remained ftill in the Deep in its own Seat as it had been from Eternity.

36. But being the wrath alfo is in *that* water in the Deep above the Earth, therefore conftantly through the kindling of the Stars and of the water in the *wrath*, fuch palpable water generateth it felf, which with its outermoft Birth ftandeth in Death.

37. Which, being it qualifieth or *uniteth* with its innermoft Birth of the Aftrall Birth or Geniture, it cometh to help the *Salitter* of the *corrupted* Earth, and quencheth its wrath, whereby in the Aftrall Birth or Geniture all ftandeth in the Life, and fo the Earth generateth the *Life* through the *Death*.

The Gate of the Myftery.

38. But, that there is a *Firmament*, between the Waters; which Firmament is called *Heaven*; it hath this *underftanding* or meaning.

39. The whole Deep, from the *Moon* to the *Earth*, ftandeth all with its working in the wrathfull and com-

comprehensible or palpable Birth or Geniture: for the *Moon* is the Goddesse of the palpable Birth, and so the House of the Devills of Death and of Hell is in the circuit orb or Extent between the Moon and the Earth.

40. Where *therefore* the fierce *wrath* of God in the outermost Birth or Geniture in the Deep becometh daily kindled and blown up by the *Devills* and *all wicked* Men, through the Great Sins of Man, which still qualifie mix unite or co-operate with the *Astral* Birth or Geniture in the Deep.

41. Now Therefore God hath made the Firmament, which is call'd Heaven, *between* the outermost and innermost Birth, and that is a *Partition* or division between the outermost and innermost Birth or Geniture.

42. For, the outermost Birth of the water cannot comprehend the innermost Birth of the water, which is called Heaven, and which is made out of the midst or Center of the water.

["*Heaven is the Firmament, viz. the fire-Sea, or*
"*Sea-of-Fire out of the seven spirits of Nature,*
"*out of which, the Stars as a Quintessence were*
"*concreted incorporated or created by the word*
"*FIAT: And it hath, or containeth both fire*
"*and water, and hangeth in it self inwardly on*
"*the first Principle, and shall bring its wonders,*
"*with or as to the figure of them, into the Eter-*
"*nal; but its Birth or Geniture fadeth or passeth*
"*away:*]

43. Now the innermost Birth of Heaven *reflects strongly* upon the Earth, and holdeth the outermost water upon the Earth, together with the Earth also, strongly *captive.*

q.

43. And

44. And if that were not, then with the *Revolution* of the Globe of the Earth the water would be divided or diſſolved again; alſo then would the Earth Crumble, break, and moulder away in the Deep, [and all would be a *Chaos* again.]

45. But now therefore that Firmament between the outermoſt palpable water and the Inward; holdeth the *Earth* and the *palpable* water Captive.

But now thou mayſt Ask :

What? is the fire then a *Firmament* of that Heaven, which I can neither ſee nor apprehend?

Anſwer.

46. Yes; It is the Firmament *between* the clear Deity and the corrupt Nature, which thou muſt break through, when thou intendeſt to come to God; and it is that very Firmament, which doth not *quite* ſtand in the wrath, neither is it altogether or perfectly pure : concerning which it is written, *the very Heavens are not pure in the fight of God,* as in *Job* 15. 15. and at the laſt Judgment Day the wrath will be purged from them. For it is written, *Heaven and Earth ſhall paſſe away, but my word ſhall not paſſe away, ſaith Chriſt, Matth.* 24.35. *Mark* 13.31.

47. Now that *impurity* in that Heaven is the *wrath,* but the *purity* is the *word* of God, which he once ſpake, ſaying; *Let the water under*

under the Firmament be separated from the water above the firmament, Gen. I.

And that Word standeth, and is *comprised*, in the firmament of the water ; and holdeth the outward water together with the Earth, captive or *fixed.*

The Gate of the Deitie.

Observe here the hidden Mystery of God.

48. When thou beholdest the Deep above the Earth, thou oughtest *not* to say, that it is *not* the Gate of God, where God in his *holinesse* dwelleth : No, no, think not so : For the *whole* holy *Trinity* God the Father Sonne and Holy Ghost, dwelleth in the Center under the Firmament of Heaven, but that very Firmament cannot comprehend him.

49. Indeed all is as it were *one* Body, the outermost and inhermost Birth, together with the Firmament of heaven, as also the Astrall Birth *therein,* in and with which the wrath of God also qualifieth mixeth and uniteth ; but yet they are one to another as the Government frame or constitution in *Man.*

50. * The *Flesh* signifieth, 1°. The outward Birth or Geniture, which is the House of Death.   2°. The second Birth or Geniture in Man is the *Astrall*, in which the *Life* standeth, and wherein Love and wrath wrestle one with another :   And *thus far* Man himself knoweth himself : for the Astrall Birth genereateth the Life in the outermost, that is, in the *dead* Flesh : 3°. The Third Birth, is generated between the Astrall and outermost, and that is called the animated or *soulish* Birth or Geniture, or the

* *Note.* Three sorts of Births or Genitures in Man.

O o o 2   Soul:

Soul: and is as Large as the *whole* Man.

51. And that Birth or Geniture, the outward Man *neither knoweth nor comprehendeth*, neither doth the Aftrall comprehend it, but every qualify-ing or fountain spirit comprehendeth only its *innate* or inftant *Root*, which fignifieth, or refembleth the Heaven.

52. And that animated or foulifh Man muft preffe through the Firmament of Heaven to God, and *live* with God, elfe the whole man *cannot* come into Heaven to God.

53. For every Man, that defireth to be faved, muft with his innate inftant Births, or Genitures, be, as the *whole* Deity with all the three Births in this world, is.

54. Man cannot be abfolutely or *wholly pure with-out wrath and fin*, for the Births of the Depth in this world are not fully pure before the Heart of God, *Job* 15. v. 15. but alwayes Love and wrath *wreftle* one with another, whence God is called *an angry zealous God*, Exod. 20. 5. Deut. 5. 9.

55. Now as man is, in the Government or Order of his *Nativity* Birth or Geniture: Juft *fo* alfo is the whole Body of God in or of this world; but in the *water* ftandeth the *meek* Life.

56. As, I. Firft in the outward Body of God, in or of this world, there is the congealed, aftringent bitter and Hot *Death*, in which the palpable water is alfo congealed and Dead.

57. And therein now is the *Darkneffe*, wherein King *Lucifer* with his Angels, as alfo all *flefhly* or carnal wicked Men lye captive even with or in their *living* Bodies, as alfo the *Separated* fpirits of *damned* Men.

58. This

58. This birth can neither fee, hear, feel, fmell nor comprehend the *Heart* of God: but is * a Foolifh Virgin; which King *Lucifer* in his Pride hath caufed to be fo. * or *Folly*

59. And II. The fecond Birth is the Aftrall, which thou muft underftand to be the *Life* of the feven qualifying or fountain fpirits, wherein *now* the Love and the wrath is againft one another, and therein ftandeth the *upper* water, which is a fpirit of the life, and therein, or *between* is the Firmament of Heaven, which is made out of the midft or Center of the water.

60. Now this Birth or Geniture preffeth through the outward congealed Birth *quite through* Death, and the Aftral Life in the death, that is, in the congealed Earth, Water, and Flefh, of the Beafts and of Men, alfo of the Fowls, Fifhes, and Worms, or Creeping things.

61. And the Devil can reach *half* into this Birth, fo far as the wrath comprehendeth or reacheth, and no deeper, and thus far goeth his dwelling, and no Deeper; therefore the devill *cannot know,* how the other Part in this Birth hath a Root. And fo far Man is come in his knowledge from the Beginning of the world to this time, fince his Fall. But the other *Root,* called the Heaven, the fpirit hath kept that hidden and concealed from Man, till this Time, Left the Devill fhould have learned it from Man, and fhould have ftrowed Poifon into it, for Man, before his *Eyes.*

62. This *other Part* of the Aftrall Birth, which ftandeth in the Love in the fweet water, is the Firmament of Heaven, which holdeth the kindled wrath together with all the Devils, *captive.* For
they

they cannot enter thereinto, and in that Heaven dwelleth the *Holy Spirit,* which goeth forth from the Heart of God; and striveth or fighteth against the fierceneſſe, and generateth to himſelf a Temple in the *midſt* in the fierceneſſe of the wrath of God.

63. And in this Heaven dwelleth the Man, that *† or, alive in the Body here upon Earth.* feareth God, even with and in † the living Body : for that Heaven is as well in Man, as in the Deep above the Earth ; And as the Deep above the Earth is, ſo is Man alſo both in love and wrath, *till* after the departure of the ſoul : but then when the ſoul departeth from the Body, then it *abideth* either only in the Heaven of Love, or only in the Heaven of Wrath.

64. That Part which it here hath comprehended in its *departure,* that is now its Eternal permanent inceſſant dwelling Houſe, and from thence it can *never* get : for there is a great * *Cliff between them and the other :* as Chriſt ſpeaks of *the Rich man,* Luk. 16.26.

65. And in this Heaven the Holy Angels dwell amongſt us : and the Devils in the other Part : And in this Heaven, Man liveth *between* Heaven and Hell, and muſt endure and ſuffer from the fierceneſſe, many hard *Blowes,* Temptations, Perſecutions, and many times Torments and Squeezings.

66. * The *wrath* is called the *Croſſe,* and the *Love-Heaven* is called *Patience,* and the *ſpirit* that riſeth up *therein* is called *Hope* and *Faith,* which qualifieth mixeth or *uniteth* with God, and *wreſtleth* with the wrath *till it overcometh and getteth the victory,* 1 John 5.4.

* †
1. Croſſe.
2. Patience.
3. Hope.
4. Faith.

67. And herein lyeth the *whole* Chriſtian doctrine:
He

He that teacheth otherwise, doth *not* know, what he teacheth, for his doctrine hath no foot ground or foundation, and his heart alwaies tottereth wavereth, and doubteth and knoweth not what it should do.

68. For his *spirit* alwaies seeketh for *Rest*, but findeth it not, for it is impatient, and alwaies seeketh after *Novelties*, or some New thing; and when it findeth somewhat, it *tickleth* it self therewith, as if it had found some *new Treasure*, and yet no stedfastnesse stability or certainty in him, but he seeketh continually for Abstinence or for a Diversion.

69. *O ye Theologists, the Spirit here Openeth a Door & Gate for you* : If you will not now see, and feed your Sheep and Lambs on a green meadow, but on a dry seare Heath, you must be *accomptable* for it before the severe earnest and wrathfull Judgment of God; therefore look to it.

70. I take Heaven to witnesse, that I perform here what I must do : for the spirit *driveth me* to it, so that I am wholly captivated therewith, and cannot be freed from it, whatever may befall me hereafter, or ensue upon it.

The Holy Gate.

71. III. The Third Birth or Geniture in the Body of God in or of this world, is under the firmament of Heaven, hidden or concealed; and the Firmament of heaven qualifieth mixeth or uniteth therewith,

with, but yet not fully *Bodily*, but *creaturely*, as the Angels, and the Soules of Men do.

72. And this Third Birth or Geniture is the *Almighty* and *Holy* Heart of God, wherein our King *Jesus Christ* with his natural Body *sitteth at the right hand of God*, as a King and Lord of the whole Body or place of this world, who encompasseth holdeth and preserveth *all*, with his Heart.

73. And this Firmament of Heaven is his Throne or footstool, and the qualifying or fountain spirits of his natural Body *rule* in the whole Body of this world, and all is tyed bound or united with them, whatsoever standeth in the Astral Birth in the Part of *Love* : The other part of this world is tyed bound and united with the *Devill*.

74. Thou must *not think*, as *Johannes Calvus* or *Calvinus*, thought, which was, that the Body of Christ is *not an Almighty Being*, and that it comprehendeth or reacheth *no further* then a little Circumscribed Place wherein it is.

75. No; thou child of Man, thou errest, and dost not *rightly* understand the *Divine* Power ; Doth not every man in his Astrall qualifying or fountain Spirits *comprehend* the whole place or Body of this world, and the place *comprehendeth* Man ? it is all but *one Body*, onely there are distinct Members.

76. Why then should not the qualifying or fountain spirits in the naturall Body of Christ qualifie mix or unite with the qualifying or fountain spirits of *Nature*? Is not his Body also out of the qualifying or fountain spirits of Nature, and his heart animated or become soulish from or out of the *third Birth* or Geniture, which is the Heart of God, which comprehendeth all Angels and the Heaven of Heavens, even the *whole Father*.

77. Ye Calvinists, desist from your Opinion, and do not *Torment your selves* with the comprehensible or palpable Being; for *God is a Spirit;* John 4. 24. and in the comprehensibility or palpability standeth *Death.*

78. The Body of Christ is no more in the hard comprehensibility or palpability, but in the Divine comprehensibility or Palpability of Nature, like the Angels.

79. For our Bodies also at the Resurrection will have no more such hard Flesh and Bones, but be like the Angels; and though indeed all *forms* and *powers* shall be therein, and all *faculties* and *Members* even to the Privy Parts, and these shall be in another manner of form, and so also the Entralls and Guts, and yet we shall *not* have the *hard* comprehensibility or Palpability.

80. For Christ saith to *Mary Magdalen* in *Joseph's* Garden at the Sepulcher, after his resurrection: *Touch me not, for I am not yet ascended to my God and to your God,* Joh. 20. v. 17. As if he would say, I have *not* now the *Bestial Body* any more, although I shew my self to thee in my form or shape which *I had,* otherwise, thou, in thy bestial couldst *not see me.*

81. And so during the Fourty Dayes after his Resurrection he did *not* alwaies walk *visibly* among the Disciples, but *invisibly;* according to his heavenly and angelical Property; but when he would speak or *talk* with his Disciples, then he shewed or presented himself in a comprehensible or *palpable*

manner

manner and form, that thereby he might speak natural words with them, for the *corruption* cannot comprehend or apprehend the Divine [words or things].

82. Also it sufficiently appeareth, that his Body was of an angelical kind, in that he went to his Disciples *through the Doors being shut,* John 20.19.

83. Thus, thou must know now, that his Body qualifieth mixeth or uniteth with all the seven spirits in Nature in the Astrall Birth in the part of *Love*, and holdeth Sin, Death, and the Devill captive in its *wrath-Part*.

84. And thus thou now understandest, what God made on the *Second Day*, when he separated the water under the Firmament, from the water above the Firmament. Thou seest also, How thou art in this world *every where* in Heaven and also in Hell, and dwellest between Heaven and Hell in great Danger.

85. Thou seest also, *how* Heaven is *in* a Holy man, and that *every where*, wheresoever thou standest, goest or lyest, if thy spirit do but qualifie or co-operate with God, then as to *that Part*, thou art in Heaven, and thy *Soul* is in God. Therefore also saith Christ; *My Sheep are in my Hands, no man can pull them away from me,* John 10.

86. In like manner thou seest also, How thou art alwaies in Hell among all the Devils, as to the *wrath*, if thy Eyes were but open, thou wouldst see *wonderfull* things, but thou standest between Heaven and Hell, and canst see neither of them, and walkest upon a very *Narrow Bridge*.

87. Some

87. Some Men have many Times, according to or in the Sidereal or Astral spirit, entred in thither: being ravished in an *Extasie*, as men call it; and have presently known the Gates of Heaven and of Hell, and have told shewed and declared how that many men dwell in Hell *with* or *in* their living Bodies, or with their Bodies alive : And such indeed have been scorned derided or laugh'd at, but with great ignorance and indiscretion; for it is Just so as *they declare*: which I will describe also more at large in its due place, and shew in what manner and condition it is with them.

88. But that the water hath a *Twofold* Birth, I will here prove it also with or by *the Language of Nature*. For that is the *Root* or *Mother* of *all* the Languages, which are in this world; and therein standeth the whole *perfect* knowledge of *all* things.

89. For when *Adam* Spake at the first, he gave Names to all the Creatures, according to their qualities and innate Instant Operations, vertues or faculties. And it is the very Language of the totall universal Nature, but is not known to every One. For it is a hidden secret Mystery, which is imparted to me by the Grace of God from the Spirit, which hath a Delight and Longing towards me.

Now Obſerve:

90. The word 𝔚𝔞𝔰𝔰𝔢𝔯 [*water*] is thruſt forth from the Heart, and *cloſeth* the Teeth together, and paſſeth *over* the aſtringent and Bitter qualities and toucheth them not, but goeth forth *through* the Teeth, and the Tongue contracteth and rouzeth up it ſelf together with the ſpirit, and *helpeth* to hiſſe, and ſo qualifieth mixeth or *uniteth* with the Spirit, and the ſpirit preſſeth very forcibly through the Teeth. But when the ſpirit is *almoſt* quite gone forth, then the Aſtringent and Bitter ſpirit contracteth and rouzeth up it ſelf, and afterwards firſt qualifieth with the word, but yet it ſitteth ſtill in its ſeat, and afterwards *jarreth* mightily and ſtrongly in the ſyllable -**ſer.**

91. But now, that the Spirit conceiveth it ſelf at the Heart, and cometh forth, and cloſeth the Teeth together, and *hiſſeth* with the Tongue through the Teeth; it ſignifieth, that the *Heart of God* hath moved it ſelf, and made a *cloſure* round about it, which is the *Firmament* of *Heaven:* Alſo, as the Teeth do ſhut and *cloſe* together; and then the Spirit goeth through the Teeth : ſo alſo the ſpirit goeth forth from the heart into the *Aſtrall* Birth or Geniture.

92. And as the Tongue *frameth* it ſelf for the hiſſing, and qualifieth mixeth or uniteth with the ſpirit, and moveth therewith : ſo the ſoul of Man *coImageth* or frameth itſelf with the Holy Spirit, and qualifieth operateth or uniteth therewith, and preſſeth joyntly together in the power thereof, *through Heaven,* and ruleth together alſo therewith in the *word* of God.

93. But

93. But that the Aftringent and Bitter qualities awaken *behind* afterwards, and co-image afterwards to the framing of the word: it fignifieth, that indeed all is as it were *one* Body, but the Heaven and the Holy Spirit together with the Heart of God, hath its *proper* * Seat to it felf, and the Devill together with the wrath of God, can neither comprehend the Holy Spirit, nor the Heaven; but the Devill together with the wrath, *hangeth in* the outward Birth in the *word*, and the wrath helpeth to Image all in the outermoft Birth in this world, whatfoever ftandeth in the comprehenfibility or palpability: Juft as the aftringent and bitter qualities *rouze* themfelves behind *afterwards* to the framing of the word, and qualifie operate or unite therewith.

* *One Copy hath*, Lite.

94. But that the fpirit *firft* goeth over the aftringent and bitter qualities unperceived; it fignifieth, that the *Gate of God* is every where in this world *all over*, wherein the Holy Ghoft ruleth, and that the Heaven ftandeth open every where, even in the midft or center of the Earth: And that the Devill *no where* can either fee comprehend or apprehend the Heaven, but is a *grumbling* and fnarling Hell-Hound, which afterwards firft cometh out from behind, when the Holy Ghoft *hath* built or raifed to himfelf a Church and Temple; and deftroyeth it in the wrath, and *hangeth behind* at the word as an Enemy, who will not endure, that a Temple of God fhould be raifed or built in his Land or Country, whereby his Kingdom might be *leffened* or diminifhed.

The

The One and Twentieth Chapter.

Of the *Third Day.*

I.

ALthough *the Spirit* in the Writings of *Moses* hath kept the *Deepeſt* Myſteries ſecret hidden and concealed in the *Letter*, yet all is ſo very regularly deſcribed, that there is *no Defect* at all in the Order thereof.

2. For when God through the Word had created Heaven and Earth, and had *ſeparated* the Light from the Darkneſs, and had given a place to each of them, then preſently *each began* its Birth or Geniture, and qualifying or working.

3. On the *Firſt Day*, God drave together [or compacted] the Corrupt *Salitter* which came to be ſo in the kindling of his wrath: I ſay, God then drave it together or Created it through the *ſtrong* ſpirit; for the word Schuff [*created*] ſignifieth here, a Driving together, [or Compaction].

4. In this driving together or *compaction* of the corrupted wrath-*Salitter*, was King *Lucifer* alſo, as an Impotent Prince together with his Angels, *driven* into the Hole of the wrath-*Salitter* into that place, where the outward *half* dead comprehenſibility is generated, which is the place or Space between the Nature-Goddeſſe the *Moon*, and the Dead *Earth*.

5. Now when this was done, the Deep became clear,

clear, and with the hidden or concealed Heaven, the Light was *separated* from the Darkneſſe, and the Globe of the Earth in the great *wheel* of Nature was rolled or turned *once about* ; and accordingly there paſs'd the Time of *one Revolution, or of One Day, which containeth Twenty Four Hours.

**the Diurnal motion of the Earth 24 Hours.*

6. In the Duration of the *Second Day*, began the ſharp ſeparaticn; and the *incomprehenſible Cliff* between the Wrath and the Love of Light was made, and ſo King *Lucifer* firmly ſtrongly or faſt *bolted up* into the Houſe of Darkneſſe, and was *reſerved* to the final Judgment.

7. And ſo alſo the water of Life was *ſeparated* from the water of Death, yet in that manner as that they *hang* one to another in this Time of the world, *as Body and Soul*, and yet neither of them comprehend the other ; but the *Heaven* which was made out of the midſt or center of the water, is the *Cliffe* between them, ſo that the comprehenſible or palpable water is a Death, and the incomprehenſible or impalpable is the Life.

8. Thus now the incomprehenſible ſpirit, which *is God*, ruleth every where in this world, and repleniſheth or *filleth all*, and the comprehenſible hangeth or dependeth on him, and dwelleth in the Darkneſs, and can neither ſee, hear, ſmell, nor feel the incomprehenſible one, but ſeeth the works thereof, and is a *Deſtroyer* of them.

9. And now when God had bound up the Devill in the Darkneſſe through the *cloſure* of the Heaven, which Heaven is every where in all places ; then HEE began again his wonderful Birth or Geniture in the *ſeventh* Nature-ſpirit, and all generated again as it *had done* from Eternity.

10. For

10. For *Moses* writeth thus : *And God said, Let the Earth send forth Grasse and Herbs that yield a Seed, and the fruit Tree yielding or bearing fruit after its kind, and which hath its own seed in it self upon the Earth, and it was so done. And the Earth sent forth grasse, and the herb that yieldeth seed each after its kind, and the tree yielding fruit, and which hath its seed in it self, every one according to its kind, and God saw that it was good. And so out of Evening and Morning the Third Day came to be,* Gen. I. v. 11, 12, 13.

11. This indeed is very rightly and properly *described,* but the true ground sticketh *hidden* or concealed in the Word, and hath *never* been understood by Man. For Man since the Fall could never comprehend or *apprehend* the inward Birth or Geniture to perceive, How the heavenly Birth or Geniture is : but his *Reason* lay captivated in the outward comprehensibility or *palpability,* and could not penetrate and presse through Heaven, and see the inward Birth or Geniture of God, which also is in the corrupted Earth and *every where* in all Places.

12. Thou must *not* here think, that God hath made some *New* thing, which *never* was before. For if that were so, then there had been *another* God, which is not possible to be. For without, or *besides,* this one onely God, nothing is at all, for the Gates of Hell are *not any where* without beyond or *absent* from this one onely God; onely there is a *Partition* or distinction between the love in the light, and the kindled wrath in the Darknesse, so that the one cannot comprehend the other, and yet hang one to another as *one* Body.

13. The *Salitter,* out of which the Earth is come to be, *was* from Eternity, and stood in the seventh quali-

qualifying or fountain spirit, which is the *Nature-spirit*, and the other six have generated the seventh continually, and are incompassed or surrounded *therewith*, or lie captivated or inclosed therein as in their Mother, and are the power and life of the seventh, just as the *Astrall* Birth is, in the Flesh.

14. But when King *Lucifer* had stirred the wrath in this Birth or Geniture, and had with his *loftinesse* brought the Poison and Death into it, then in the wrathful Birth, in the fiercenesse, or *Sting* of Death, such Earth and Stones were Generated.

15. And upon this now ensued the *Spewing out* thereof: for the Deity could not endure such a Birth or Geniture in the Love and Light of God, but the corrupted *Salitter* must be *driven together* in a Lump, and Lord *Lucifer* also with it, so then presently the innate Light in the corrupted *Salitter*, went out or extinguished, and the *closure* of the Heaven between the Wrath and the Love was made, that so such *Salitter* might be generated *no more*, and that Heaven might hold the Wrath in the outermost Birth or Geniture in Nature captive in the Darknesse, and be an *Eternal* Partition or separation between them.

16. But this being accomplished in the Two Dayes, then on the *Third Day* the Light rose up in the Darknesse, and the Darknesse together with the Prince thereof, could not comprehend it:

17. For there, out of the Earth sprung up Grasse and Herbs, and Trees, and there now also it standeth written thus : *Each according to its kind,* Gen. 1. *v.* 12. In these words lyeth the *Kernel* of the eternal Birth or Geniture hidden

of

or concealed, and cannot be comprehended or apprehended by or with Flesh and Blood, but the Holy Ghoſt through the animated or ſouliſh Birth, muſt kindle the *Aſtrall* man, otherwiſe he is blind *herein*, and underſtandeth nothing but concerning Earth and Stones, alſo Graſſe, Herbs, and woodden Trees.

18. But now is it written here; *God* $\begin{cases} \text{ſprach,} \\ \text{ſaid,} \end{cases}$ *Let the Earth bring forth Graſſe, and Herbs, and fruit-full Trees.*

Obſerve here :

19. The word **Sprach**, [*Said*] is an *Eternal* word, and *was* before the times of the wrath ; from eternity *in* this *Salitter,* when it ſtood *yet* in the heavenly form and life, and now alſo it is *not quite* dead in its Center, but only in the comprehenſibility or *palpability.*

20. But now when the Light roſe up again in the outward comprehenſibility, or in Death, then the Eternal Word ſtood in its *full* Birth, and generated the *life* through and out of Death, and the corrupted *Salitter* brought forth fruit again.

21. But being the eternal *word* muſt qualifie mix or unite with the corruption in the Wrath, thereupon the *Bodies* of the fruits were Evill and Good. For the outward Birth or Geniture of the fruits muſt be out of or from the *Earth* which is in Death ; And the ſpirit or life muſt be out of the *Aſtral* Birth, which ſtandeth in Love and Wrath.

22. For thus ſtood the Birth or Geniture of Nature in the Time of the *Kindling,* and was thus together incorporated in the Earth, and muſt alſo in ſuch

a

a Birth spring up again :   For it is written ; *that the dead Earth should let the Grasse and Herbs, and Trees spring up, each according to its kind,* Gen. 1. 12. that is, according to the kind and quality, as it *had been* from eternity, and as it had been in the heavenly quality, kind and form.   For that is called *its own* kind, which is received in the mothers Body or Womb, and is its *own* by right of Nature, as its own peculiar Life.

23. Thus also the Earth brought forth *no* strange Life, but even that which *had been* in it from eternity ; And as before the time of the wrath it had brought forth heavenly fruit, which had a *holy* pure heavenly Body, and were the food of Angels : so now it brought forth fruits, according to its comprehensible palpable hard, Evil, wrathful, poisonous, venomous, *half-*dead kind : for as the Mother was, so were her children.

24. *Not* that the fruits of the Earth are thereupon *wholly* in the wrath of God : for the incorporated or compacted Word, which is immortal and *incorruptible*, which was from eternity in the *Salitter* of the Earth, sprung up again in the Body of death, and brought forth fruit out of the *dead* Body of the Earth : but the Earth comprehended *not* the Word, but the Word comprehended the Earth.

25. And now as the whole Earth was, together with the Word ; so was the fruit also, but the word remained in the Center of the *Heaven,* which is also in this place, hiddenly ; and this Birth or Geniture *caused* the seven qualifying or fountain spirits, out of or from the outermost, corrupt and dead Birth or Geniture *to form* the Body ; and it self, viz. the

Word or Heart of God remained in its heavenly feat fitting on the Throne of *Majeftie*, and filled the Aftrall and alfo the mortal Birth or Geniture, but to them was the holy life *altogether* incomprehenfible.

26. Thou muft not think, that thereupon the outermoft dead Birth or Geniture of the Earth hath gotten *fuch* a Life through the rifen word that fprung up, fo that it is *no more* a Death : No; that can never be, for that which is *once* dead in God, that, is really dead, and in its *own power* can never be living again, but the Word, which qualifieth mixeth or uniteth with the Aftrall Birth in the Part of the Love, that generateth the *Life* through the aftrall Birth or Geniture; through the Death.

27. For thou feeft plainly, How all the Fruits of the Earth, whatfoever it bringeth forth, muft *putrifie* and Rot; alfo they are a Death.

28. But, that the Fruits get *another* Body, then the Earth is; which is much fuller of vertue, fairer, or more beautifull; alfo of a better tafte relifh and fmell: it is, *becaufe* the Aftrall Birth or Geniture receiveth power or vertue from the Word, and formeth or frameth *another* Body, which ftandeth half in the Death, and half in the Life, and ftandeth *hidden* between the Wrath of God, and the Love.

29. But, that the Fruits upon the Body, are much pleafanter lovelier fweeter and milder, and with a Good Tafte and relifh: that, is even the *Third Birth* out of the Earth; according to which the Earth fhall be *purged* and cleanfed at the End of this time, and fhall be fet or put again into its *firft* Place, but the Wrath will abide in Death.

The

The richly joyfull Gate of Man.

30. Behold, thus faith the Spirit in the Word, which is the very Heart of the Earth, and which rifeth or fpringeth up in his Heaven, in the half flafh of the Life, wherewith my fpirit in its knowledge qualifieth mixeth or *uniteth*, and through which I write thefe words.

31. *Man is made out of the Seed of the Earth, out of an incorporated or compacted Maffe or Lump;*

   [" *Underftand out of the Matrix of the Earth, where-*
     " *in the Eye is twofold; the one in God, and the*
     " *other in this world; out of Three Princi-*
     " *ples :*]   r.

and not out of the wrath, but out of the Birth or Geniture of the Earth: and ftood in the Aftrall Birth or Geniture in *the part* of the Love, but wrath hung to him, which he fhould have put forth from himfelf as the the fruit putteth forth from it, the *bitterneffe* of the Tree.

32. And that *he did not*, but reached back from the Love into the wrath, and *lufted* after his dead or mortal Mother to eat of her, and to fuck her breaft, and to ftand *upon* her ftock.

                        33. Now

33. Now according to his wreſtling, ſo alſo it befell him, and ſo he brought himſelf with his outermoſt Birth or Geniture into the Death or *mortality* of his mother, and with his *life* he brought himſelf out from the Love into the Part of the *wrathful* Aſtral Birth or Geniture.

34. And there he ſtandeth now between Heaven and Hell in the *Face* of the Devill in his Kingdome, againſt whom the Devil *warreth* fighteth and ſtriveth continually, that he might either baniſh him out of his Country into the Earth, or make him a child of wrath in Hell.

And what is Now his Hope ?

Anſwer.

35. Behold! thou blind-Heathen: behold! thou Render Perverter Obſcurer and wreſter of the *Scriptures*, open thy eyes wide, and be not aſhamed at this ſimple plainneſſe; for God lyeth hid in the Center, and is yet much more *Simple* and plain, but thou ſeeſt him not.

36. Behold! thy ſpirit or thy ſoul, is generated from or out of thy Aſtral Birth or Geniture, and is the *Third* Birth *in thee*; Juſt as an Apple upon a Tree is the *Third* Birth or Geniture of the *Earth*, and hath not its vegetation in from or within the Earth, but from above the Earth: and if it were *a Spirit*, as thy ſoul is, it would not ſuffer the Earth any more to tye or *bind* it to corruption.

37. But thou muſt know, that the Apple on its ſtock or Branch, however with its innermoſt Birth or Geniture, qualifieth mixeth or uniteth with *the word of God*, through whoſe power it is grown out of the Earth. 38. But

38. But being the wrath is in its * Bodily or *Cor-* poreal Mother, therefore it *cannot* set or put it out from the Comprehensible or palpable Birth, but must remain with its Body in the palpablenesse or comprehensibility in Death.

* or *Mother of its Body.*

39. But in its power, in which its *life* standeth, wherewith it qualifieth mixeth or uniteth with the Word of God, it will in its mother in the power of the Word at the last Judgment Day be set or put again into its *heavenly* Place; and be *separated* from the wrathfull and dead or mortall palpablenesse, and spring up in the Heaven of this world, in a heavenly form, and be a *Fruit* for Men in the other Life.

[" *Here understand;* The power of the Principle, out
 " of which the Apple *and* All *groweth, shall in*
 " the Renovation *of the world spring up again in*
 " Paradise, *with the wonders :*]

s.

40. But being thou art made out of the *Seed* of the Earth,

[" *Red Earth,* is Fire and water, *conceived with or*
 " by the word Fiat, *out of the* Matrix *of the*
 " Earth; *but when* Man Imagined *or set*
 " his desire into the Earth, *he became Earth-*
 " ly.

t.

and hast set or put thy Body *back* again into thy Mother, therefore thy Body also is become a *palpable* dead or Mortal Body, such as thy Mother is.

41. And thy Body hath the same *Hope* which thy Mother the Earth hath, *viz.* that at the last Judgement Day, in the power of the word, it shall be set or put again into its *first* Place.

42. But being thy Astral Birth standeth here on Earth in the wrath, and qualifieth mixeth or uniteth

teth

teth with the Love in the Word, Juſt as the Fruit on the Tree doth : for the power of the fruit qualifieth or uniteth with the word; *Therefore thy Hope ſtandeth in God.*

For the Aſtrall Birth or Geniture ſtandeth in Love and Wrath; and, *that,* in this time it *cannot* prevent, in regard of the outermoſt Birth or Geniture in the *Fleſh,* which ſtandeth in Death.

43. For the dead or Mortal Fleſh hath encompaſſed the Aſtrall Birth, and Mans Fleſh is a dead *Carkaſſe,* whileſt it is yet in the Mothers body or womb, and is encompaſſed with Hell and Gods wrath.

44. But now the Aſtrall Birth generateth the animated ſouliſh Birth, *viz.* the *Third,* which ſtandeth in the word, where the incorporated or compacted word lyeth hidden in its Heaven.

[" *The* Sulphur *to be* [*production of the*] *Soul, is the*
" *firſt Principle in the eternall will-ſpirit, and*
" *cometh to Life in the third Principle, and ſo*
" *liveth between love and wrath, and hangeth*
" *to both :*]

v.

45. But now being, thou haſt thy *Reaſon,* and art not like the Apple on the Tree, but art Created an Angel and the ſimilitude or Image of God, *inſtead* of the Expulſed Devils, and *knoweſt* how thou canſt with thy Aſtrall Birth, in the part of Love, qualifie or unite with the Word of God ; *therefore thou canſt* in the Center in the Word, ſet or *put* thy animated or *ſouliſh* Birth into Heaven, and *thou canſt* with thy

* or, Body alive.

ſoul, even with thy * living Body in this Dead or Mortal palpability *rule* with God, in Heaven.

46. For the Word is in thy heart, *Deut.* 30. 14 *Rom.* 10. 8. and qualifieth or uniteth with the Sou

as if it were *one Beeing*; and if thy Soul standeth in the Love, then it also is one Beeing: And, thou mayst say, that according to thy soul thou sittest in Heaven, and livest and *reignest* with God.

[" *Understand*; *according to the spirit of the soul,*
" *with the Image out of the animated or soulish*
" *fire*:]

X.

47. For, the soul, which *apprehendeth* the Word, hath an open Gate in Heaven, and can be prevented by nothing, *neither* doth the Devill see the soul, because it is *not* in his Country or Dominions.

48. But being thy Astrall Birth standeth with the one part in the wrath, and that the Flesh through the wrath standeth in Death, *thereupon* the Devil, in the part of the wrath, seeth *continually* even *into* thy Heart, and if thou lets him have any Room or place there, then he teareth *that part* of the Astrall Birth, which standeth in the Love, *out* from the word.

49. And then thy Heart is a dark Valley; And if thou dost not Labour and work *quickly* again to the Birth of the Light, *then* he kindleth the wrathfire therein, and then shall thy soul be spewed out from the Word, and then it qualifieth or uniteth with the wrath of God, and so *afterward* thou art a Devil, and not an Angel, and canst not with thy animated or *soulish* Birth, reach the Gates of Heaven.

50. But if thou fightest and strivest with the Devill, and keepest the Gate of *Love* in thy Astrall Birth, and so departest from hence as to the Body, then thy Soul remaineth in the Word *quite hidden* from the Devil, and reigneth with God, even unto the Day of the Restitution of that which was Lost.

Rrr

51. But

51. But if thou ftandeft with thy Aftrall Birth in the *wrath* when thou departeft from hence as to the Body, and thy Soul not comprehended in the word; *then* thou canft never reach the Gates of Heaven, but into what thou haft fown thy feed, that is, thy *Soul*, in *that* very *Part* fhall thy Body alfo arife.

The Gate of the Power.

* or *find one another.*

52. But that, Soul and Body, fhall * come together again, at the Day of the Refurrection, thou mayft *perceive* fo much, here by the Earth. For the Creator faid; *Let the Earth bring forth Graffe and Herbs, and Trees bearing Fruit, each according to its Kind.* And then *each* fprung up according to its kind; and grew, and as before the time of the wrath it *had* a Heavenly Body, fo it got now an Earthly one, *anfwerable* to its Mother.

53. But it is to be confidered, how all was comprifed in the word at the great tumult and *uproar* of the Devill, *fo that* all fprung up in its *own Being* according to its *Power* vertue and kind, as if it had *never been* deftroyed or altered at all.

54. Now if it were thus at *that* Time, when there was fuch murthering and robbing, fure it will be much more *fo* at the Laft Judgment Day, when the Earth fhall be *feparated* in the kindled wrath-fire, and fhall be living again or revived, then *furely* it will be comprehended in the Word of Love, as it hath in the fame Word here generated its Fruit, of Graffe, Herbs and Trees, as alfo all manner of mineral Oars of Silver and of Gold.

55. But being the *Aftrall* Birth of the Earth ftandeth

eth in the Love, and the outward in Death, therefore will each remain in its feat, and fo Life and Death will *fever* themfelves.

56. And where now would the Soul of Man *rather* be at the day of Regeneration, then with its † *Fa-ther* ; that is, † *in the Body*, which hath Generated it ?

57. But being the Soul, all the *while* the Body had been in Death, remained *hidden* in the Word, and being the fame Word alfo holdeth the Earth in the Aftral birth in the *Love*, therefore it qualifieth mixeth or uniteth through the Word, *all* the time of its hiddenneffe and fecrefie, alfo with its *Mother* the Body, according or as to the *Aftral* Birth or Geniture in the Earth, and fo *Body* and Soul in the Word, were never feparated one from another, but live *joyntly* and equally together in *God*.

58. And though indeed the *Beftial* Body muft putrifie and Rot, yet its power and vertue *liveth*, and in the mean while there grow out of its power, in its Mother, fair beautiful Rofes *Bloffoms* and Flowers : and though it were *quite* burnt up and Confumed in the Fire, yet its power and *vertue* ftandeth in the four Elements in the *word*, and the Soul qualifieth mixeth or uniteth therewith : for the Soul is in *Heaven*, and the fame Heaven is *every where*, even in the midft or center of the Earth.

59. *O Dear Man view thy felf for a vvhile, in this Looking-Glaffe* ; thou wilt find it more largely to be read of concerning the Creation of Man : this I fet down *here* for this very caufe, that thou mighteft *the better* underftand the *power* of Creation, and that thou mighteft

the better conceive, and *fit* thy Self for, this Spirit, and so learn to understand *its Language.*

The open Gate of the Earth.

Now it might be Asked :

From or Out of what matter or power and *vertue* then did the Grasse, Herbs, and Trees spring forth ? what manner of substance or condition or Constitution hath this kind of Creature ?

Answer.

60. The simple saith, *God made All things out of Nothing* : but He knoweth not, That God ; neither doth he know, what He is : for when he beholdeth the *Earth,* together with the *Deep* above the Earth, he thinketh, verily, all this is *not* God, or else he thinketh, God is *not there.* He alwaies Imagineth with himself, that God dwelleth onely *above* the Azure Heaven of the Stars, and ruleth as it were, with some Spirit which *goeth forth* from him into this world ; and that *his Body* is not present here upon the Earth, nor in the Earth.

61. And just such Opinions and Tenents I have read also in the Books and Writings of Doctors (*der* † *Doctoren*): and there are also very many *Opinions* Disputations and Controversies arisen about this very thing among the *Learned.*

† Doct. The-sen, Learn-ed in Folly ; of verball Trifles.

62. But seeing God openeth *to me* the Gate of his Being in his great Love, and remembreth the *Cove-nant,* which he hath with Man, therefore I will faithfully

fully and earneftly according to my Gifts, *unfhut* and set wide Open *All the Gates of God*, fo far as God will give me leave.

63. It is *not* fo to be underftood, as that I am *fufficient* enough in thefe things, but only fo far as I am able to comprehend.

64. For, the Being of God, is like a Wheel, wherein many wheeles are made *one in another*, upward, downward, croffe-ways, and yet continually turn all of them together.

65. Which indeed when a man beholdeth the *wheel*, he highly marvaileth at it, and cannot *at once* in its turning learn to conceive and *apprehend* it : but the more he beholdeth the wheel, the more he learneth its Form or frame; and the more he learneth, the greater Longing he hath to the Wheel ; for he continually feeth fomewhat, that is more and more wonderfull, fo that a man can neither behold it or learn it *Enough*.

66. Thus, I alfo, what I do not *enough* defcribe in one place concerning this Great Myftery, that you will find in another place : and what I cannot defcribe in this book in regard of the Largeneffe of the Myftery, and my Incapacity, that you will find in the *other* following.

67. For *this Book* is the firft fprouting, or vegetation of this Twigg, which fpringeth or groweth Green in its Mother, and is *as a Child*, which is learning to go, and is not able to run a Pace at the *Firft*.

68. For though the Spirit feeth the Wheel, and would fain comprehend its form or frame in *every* Place, yet it cannot do it exactly enough, becaufe of the turning of the wheel : But when it cometh about
                                                    again,

again, so that the spirit can see the first apprehended or conceived form again, then *continually* it learneth more and more, and alwaies delighteth and loveth the wheel, and longeth after it *still* more and more.

Now Observe:

69. The Earth hath just such qualities and qualifying or fountain spirits, as the Deep above the Earth, or as *Heaven* hath, and all of them together belong to one only Body : and the whole or *universal* God is that one onely *Body* : but that thou dost not wholly and fully see and know him, *Sins are the cause,* with and by which, thou in this great Divine Body, Lyest *shut up* in the dead or mortal *Flesh,* and the power or vertue of the *Deitie* is *hidden* from thee, even as the *marrow* in the Bones is hidden from the *Flesh.*

70. But if thou in the spirit breakest through the Death of the Flesh, then thou seest the hidden God. For as the Marrow in the Bones penetrateth presseth or breaketh thorough, and giveth vertue power and strength to the *Flesh,* and yet the Flesh cannot comprehend or apprehend the Marrow, but onely the power and *vertue* thereof : no more canst thou see the hidden Deity in thy Flesh, but thou receivest its *power,* and understandest *therein* that God dwelleth in thee.

71. For the dead or *mortal* Flesh belongeth not * to the Birth of *life,* as that it can receive or conceive the life of the Light as a *propriety,* but the life of the Light in God riseth up in the dead or mortal

* or, *into.*

tal Flesh, and generateth to it self, from or out of the dead or mortal Flesh *another* heavenly and Living Body, which knoweth and *understandeth* the Light.

72. For this Body is but a *Shell*, from which the new Body groweth.

> [" *The new Body groweth out of the heavenly sub-*
> " *stantiality in the word, out of the Flesh and*
> " *Blood of Christ, out of the* Mystery *of the*
> " *Old Body :*]

y.

As it is, with a *Grain* of wheat in the Earth. The Husk or shell *shall not rise* and be living again, no more then it doth in the wheat, but will remain *for ever* in Death and in Hell.

73. Therefore, Man carrieth about with him here upon Earth, *in* his Body the Devil's Eternall Dwelling house. O thou fair excellent Goddesse! mayst thou not well Prance and Trick thy self *therein*, and in the mean while *invite* the Devill into the new Birth for a Guest, will it not profit thee very much ; take heed, thou dost not Generate a New Devill, who will remain in his *own* House.

74. Behold the Mystery of the Earth, As that Generateth or bringeth forth, so must thou Generate or bring forth. The Earth *is not* that Body, which groweth or sprouteth forth, But is the *Mother* of that Body, As also thy Flesh is not the spirit, but the *Flesh* is the Mother of the Spirit.

75. But now in Both of them, *viz.* in the Earth and in thy Flesh, there is the *Light* of the clear Deity hidden, and it breaketh thorough, and generateth to it self a Body according to the kind of *each* Body, for Man according to his Body ; and for the Earth, according to its Body ; for as the Mother is, so also is the *child.*   76. Mans

76. Mans Child, is the *Soul*, which is generated out of the Aſtral Birth from or out of the Fleſh; and the Earths child is the *Graſſe*, the Herbs, the Trees, Silver, Gold, and all mineral Oars.

Now thou Askeſt :

How then ſhall I do, that I may underſtand ſomewhat concerning the *Birth* or Geniture of the *Earth* ?

Anſwer.

77. Behold! the *Birth* of the Earth ſtandeth in its *Birth* or Geniture, as the *whole Deitie* doth, and there is no difference at all, but onely as to the *corruption* in the wrath, wherein comprehenſibility or palpability ſtandeth : that *only* is the difference or diſtinction, and is *the Death* between God and the Earth.

78. Thou muſt know, that all the ſeven ſpirits of God are *in* the Earth, and Generate, as they do in Heaven : For, the Earth is in God, and God never Dyed, but the outermoſt *Birth* or Geniture is *dead*, in which the wrath reſteth, and is reſerved, for King *Lucifer*; to be a Houſe of Death and of Darkneſſe, and to be an eternal Priſon or Dungeon.

Of the ſeven Spirits of God, and of their operation in the Earth.

79. The *Firſt* is the aſtringent Spirit, and that contracteth or draweth together in the Aſtral *Birth* of the ſeven qualifying or fountain ſpirits, a *Maſſe* or Lump in the Earth, through the kindling of the
ſuperiour

superiour *Birth* or *Geniture above* the *Earth*, and dryeth that up with its sharp *coldnesse*, just as it contracteth or draweth the water together, and maketh *Ice* thereof; so it also contracteth or draweth together the *water* in the Earth, and maketh thereof a dry Masse or Lump.

80. Then next, the *Bitter* spirit, which existeth in the fire-flash, is also in the *Matter* or Masse, and that cannot endure to be captivated or imprisoned in the dryed *exsiccated* Matter, but rubs it self against the astringent spirit in the dryed Masse or Lump, so long till it *kindleth* the fire; and so when that is done, then the Bitter spirit is terrified, and getteth its life.

Conceive this here aright.

81. In the Earth, thou canst not perceive, find, or search out any thing, *besides* the Herbs Plant or Vegetables and Metals, *more* then Astringency, Bitternesse, and water: *But* the water now therein is *sweet*, opposite to the other two Qualities: Also it is thin or Transparent, and the other two are Hard, Rough and Sowr, and alwaies the one is *against* the other. Thereupon there is a perpetual struggling fighting and wrestling, but in the struggling of these *three*, the *Life* doth not yet stand: but they are a dark valley, and they are three things which can never endure one another, but there is an eternal struggling amongst them.

83. And from hence *mobility* taketh its Originall, also Gods wrath which resteth in the hidden secresie, taketh its original from hence: and so also the *Original* of the Devil, of Death and of Hell, it

S s s   ariseth

arifeth from hence ; as you may read thereof, concerning the Fall of the Devill.

The Depth in the Center of the Birth or Geniture.

84. Now when thefe *three*, viz. the Aftringency, Bitterneffe and Sweetneffe rub themfelves one againft another, then the aftringent quality groweth predominant, for it is the ftrongeft, and *forcibly* attracteth or draweth the fweetneffe together, for the Sweetneffe is *meek* and extenfive in refpect of its *Suppleneffe*, and muft yield to be captivated or imprifoned.

85. And fo when that is done, then the Bitterneffe is alfo together captivated or imprifoned in the *Body* of the fweet water, and becometh alfo together dryed up, and then the Aftringent fweet and bitter are one in another, and ftruggle fo ftrongly in the *dryed* Maffe or Lump, till the Maffe be quite dry : For the Aftringent quality alwaies contracteth it together, and dryeth it more and more.

86. But when the fweet water can defend it felf *no* longer, then (*anguifh*) rifeth up in it, juft as in Man, when he is *Dying*, when the fpirit is departing from the Body, and fo the Body yieldeth it felf captive as a Prifoner to Death : juft fo the *water* alfo yieldeth it felf captive as a Prifoner.

87. And in this (anxious rifing up) an anguifhing Heat is generated, whereby a * *Sweat* preffeth forth, as it doth in a dying Man ; and that fweat qualifieth mixeth or uniteth with the aftringent and bitter qualities, for it is their fonne, which *they* have

* Humour or moifture.

genera

generated out of the sweet water, which they had *kill'd* and brought to Death.

88. Now when that is done, then the Astringent and Bitter qualities *rejoyce* in their sonne, understand in the Sweat, and each of them giveth to it their power vertue and Life, and stuffe it, like a greedy Gurmandizing Hogg, so that it *soon* comes to grow *full* and swelled : For the astringent quality, as also the bitter, alwaies draw the sap out of the Earth, and stuffe it into *their* young sonne.

89. But the Body, which was *first* contracted or drawn together out of the sweet water, remaineth dead or Mortal, and the † *Sweat* of the body, which qualifieth mixeth or uniteth with the astringent and bitter qualities, hath the *house* therein, where it spreadeth it self forth, groweth Grosse * full and Lusty or *wanton.*

† or *Juice* of the Body.

* *Fat, Luscious, Lascivious.*

90. But now the Two Qualities, *viz.* the Astringent and Bitter cannot leave their contention and opposition or contrary will, but wrestle *continually* one with another : The astringent is strong, and the bitter is *swift.*

91. And so now when the astringent grapleth with the bitter, then the bitter *leaps* aside, and taketh the sonne's sap along with it ; And then the astringent every where presseth hard after it, and would *fain* captivate it, then the Bitter rusheth out from the Body, and extendeth it self so far as it can.

92. But then when the Body begins to be *too straight* or narrow for it, that it can extend or stretch it no more, and that the contention be too great, then the bitter must yield it self captive. Yet for all that, the astringent *cannot kill* the bitter, but only holds it captive, and so the strife in them is so

great,

great, that the bitter *breaks out* of the body in
* ftrings like *Thrids*, and taketh fome of the Sonnes
fap or Body along with it.

*And this now is the vegetation or
growing and incorporating or im-
bodying of a Root in the Earth.*

Now thou Askeft :

How can God be, in that Birth or Geniture ?

Anfwer.

93. Behold! that is the Birth or Geniture of *Nature* : and fo now, if in thefe three qualities, *viz.* the
aftringent, bitter and fweet, the wrath-fire were not
kindled, then thou wouldft *plainly* fee, where God
is.

94. But now the wrath-fire is in all Three : for
the aftringent is *too very* cold, and contracteth or
draweth the Body *too hard* together, and the fweet is
too very thick and dark, which the aftringent foon
catcheth, and holds it captive, and dryeth it *too
much* : and then the bitter is *too ftinging*, murtherous
and raging ; and fo they cannot be reconciled to
agree.

95. Elfe if the Aftringent were not fo much *kindled* in the cold fire, and the water not fo thick, alfo
the bitter not fo *fwelling* rifing and Murtherous, then
they *Might* kindle * the *fire*, from whence the *Light*
would Exift, and from the light the *Love*, and fo out
of the fire flafh, the *Tone* would Exift : and then
thou fhouldft fee plainly, whether there would not
be

Left margin notes:
* *Fibræ.*

* or, that
Fire.

be a heavenly Body there; wherein the light of God would and doth *shine*.

96. But being the aftringent is too cold, and *dryeth* the water too much, thereupon it captivateth the *Hot* fire in its coldneffe, and killeth or deftroyeth the Body of the *sweet* water, and fo the bitter captivateth it, and dryeth it up.

97. And fo in this *exficcation* or drying up, the unctuoufneffe or *fatneffe* in the fweet water is killed or deftroyed, in which the fire kindleth it felf, and fo out of that unctuofity or fatneffe an aftringent and *bitter* fpirit comes to be. For when the unctuoufneffe or fat in the fweet water *dyeth*, then is it turn'd into an *anguifhing fweat*, in which the aftringent and bitter do qualifie mix or unite.

98. The meaning is not, that the water dyeth *quite*; no, that cannot be, but the aftringent fpirit taketh the fweetneffe or the unctuofity and *fatneffe* of the water captive in its *cold* fire, and qualifieth mixeth or uniteth therewith, and maketh ufe thereof for its Spirit : Its own fpirit being wholly *benummed*, and in Death, therefore it maketh ufe of the water for its Life, and draweth out its unctuofity or *fatneffe* to it felf, and bereaveth it of its power.

99. And then the water becometh an *anguifhing fweat*, which ftandeth between Death and Life, and fo the fire of the Heat *cannot* kindle it felf : For the unctuofity or *fatneffe* is captivated in the cold fire, and fo the *whole* Body remaineth a dark Valley, which ftandeth in an anguifhing Birth or Geniture, and cannot comprehend or reach the life. For the *life* which ftandeth in the Light, cannot elevate it felf in the hard, bitter, and aftringent Body : for it *is captivated* in the cold fire, but *not* quite dead.

100. And

100. And thou muſt ſee, that *all this* is really ſo: for Example, take a Root which is of a *Hot* quality, put it in *warm* water; or take it into *thy* Mouth, and make it warm and ſupple or moiſt; and then thou wilt ſoon *perceive* its life, and *active* or operative quality: But ſo long as it is without or *abſent* from the Heat, it is captivated in Death, and is *cold* as any other Root or piece of *wood* is.

101. And then thou ſeeſt, that the Body upon the Root is *dead* alſo: for when the vertue is gone out of the Root, then the Body is but a dead *Carcaſſe,* and can operate or Effect Nothing at all: and that is, *becauſe* the aſtringent and bitter ſpirit hath *killed* or deſtroyed the Body of the water, and attracted the *fatneſſe* or unctuoſity thereof to it ſelf; and thus they have drawn † or ſucked up the Spirit thereof, into the *dead Body.*

† Bred or hatched up their ſpirit in the dead Body.

102. Otherwiſe, if the ſweet water *could* keep its unctuoſity or *fatneſſe* in its own *power,* and that the aſtringent and the bitter ſpirit did rub themſelves one with another very *gently* in the ſweet water, then they would kindle the unctuoſity or fatneſſe in the ſweet water, and then the *Light* would inſtantly generate it ſelf in the water, and would enlighten the aſtringent and the bitter quality.

103. Whereupon they would get their true Life, and would be ſatisfied by the *Light,* and rejoyce highly therein, and from that *living Joy,* Love would ariſe up, and then the *Tone* would riſe in the fire-flaſh, through the *riſing up* of the Bitter quality in the aſtringent. And if that were done, there it would be a *Heavenly* Fruit, juſt as it ſpringeth up in Heaven.

104. But thou art to know, that the *Earth* hath all

all the qualifying or fountain spirits : for through the Devils kindling, the spirits of Life were incorporated or compacted together also in *Death*, and as it were captivated, but *not* quite murthered.

105. The *first three*, viz. the Astringent, Sweet, and bitter, belong to the Imaging or framing of the Body, and therein standeth the mobility and the *Body* or Corporeity : and these now have the comprehensibility or palpability, and are the Birth of the *outermost* Nature.

106. The *other three*, viz. the Heat, Love, and Tone stand in the incomprehensibility, and are generated out of the first Three ; and this now, is the inward Birth, wherewith the *Deity* qualifieth mixeth or uniteth.

107. And now, if the first three were *not* congealed or benumm'd in Death, so that they *could* kindle the Heat, then thou wouldst soon see a bright shining heavenly Body, and thou wouldst see plainly, *where* God is.

108. But being the first Three qualities of the Earth are congealed or benummed in death, therefore they *remain* also a Death, and cannot elevate their life into the *Light*, but remain a dark valley, in which, there *standeth* Gods Wrath, Death, and Hell, as also the Eternal Prison, and Source or Torment of the Devils.

109. *Not that* these three qualities of the outermost Birth, in which the wrath-fire standeth, are *rejected* and reprobated even to the innermost ; no, but onely the outward palpable Body, and therein the *outward* hellish source quality or Torment.

110. Here thou seest once more, how the Kingdom of God and the Kingdom of Hell hang one to
another,

another, as *one* Body, and yet the one cannot comprehend the other. For the *second Birth,* viz. the Heat, Light, Love and the Sound or Tone, is hidden in the outermost, and maketh the outward *moveable,* so that the outward gathereth it self together, and generateth a Body.

111. And though the Body standeth in the outward palpablenesse, yet is it formed according to the kind and *manner* of the inward Birth, for in the Inward Birth or Geniture standeth the *word,* and the Word is the Sound or Tone, which riseth up in the Light in the fire-flash through the bitter and the astringent quality.

112. But being the *Sound* of Gods Word must rise up through the astringent bitter Death, and generate a Body in the half-dead water, thereupon that Body is Good and also Evill, dead and living; for it must instantly attract the sapp of *Fiercenesse,* and the Body of Death, and stand in such a body and power, as the Earth its Mother doth.

113. But that the Life lyeth *hid* under and in the Death of the Earth, as also in the children of the Earth; I will here demonstrate *it* to you.

114. Behold! Man becometh weak faint and sick, and if *no remedy* be used, then he soon falls into Death. The sicknesse *caused* either by some bitter and astringent Herb, which groweth out of the Earth, or else *caused* by an evil mortiferous deadly water, or by severall mixtures of earthly Herbs, or by some evil stincking and rank flesh or Meat, and surfet from thence to *Loathing.*

115. Now if a Learned Physitian inquireth from the sick Person from what his Disease is *proceeded,* and taketh that which is the *cause* of the Disease, whether

whether it be Flesh, Water, or Herbs, and *diſtills* or *burneth* it to powder, according as the *Matter* is, and ſo burneth away the outward Poiſon thereof, which ſtandeth in *Death*; then, *in that* diſtill'd Water or burnt Powder the Aſtral Birth remaineth in its *Seat*, where life and death wreſtle o e with another, and are *both* capable of being raiſed up; for the *Dead Body* is gone.

116. And ſo now, if thou mingleſt with this water or powder, ſome good *Treacle* or the like, which holdeth *Captive* the riſing up and the power of the wrath in the Aſtrall Birth, and giveſt it to the ſick *party* or Patient in a little warm drink, be it Beer or Wine; then operateth the *innermoſt* and hidden Birth of the thing, which hath cauſed the *Diſeaſe* in man through its outermoſt dead Birth.

117. For when it is put into warm Liquor, then the *life* in the *thing* becometh riſing, and would fain raiſe it ſelf, and be kindled in the Light. ut it cannot becauſe of the *wrath*, which is oppoſite to it in the Aſtral Birth or Geniture.

118. But it can do thus much, *viz.* * it can *take away* the Diſeaſe from a Man: for the Aſtral Life *riſeth* up through Death, and taketh away the *power* from the Sting of Death: and ſo when that hath gotten the *victory*, then the Party becometh ſound again.

* or, it doth take away the diſeaſe.

119. Thus thou ſeeſt, how the power or *vertue* of the Word and eternal life in the Earth and in its *children* lyeth hidden in the center in Death, and ſpringeth up through Death, incomprehenſibly as to the Death, and continually travelleth in anguiſh to the Birth of *life*, and yet cannot flouriſh or budd till the Death be *ſevered* from it.

120. But it hath its Life in its Seat, and that *cannot*

Ttt   *not*

not be taken from it, but Death hangeth to it in the outermoſt Birth or Geniture, as alſo the wrath in Death : for the *wrath* is the life of Death and of the Devill : and in the wrath ſtandeth alſo the corporeal Being or the *Bodies* of the Devils, but the dead Birth or Geniture is their *Eternall* Dwelling Houſe.

The Depth in the Circle of the Birth or Geniture.

Now one might Ask :

What manner of ſubſtance hath it, or what is the condition thereof, that the Aſtral Birth of the *Earth* did begin its qualifying operating and generating one Day *ſooner* then the Aſtral in the *Deep* above the Earth : ſeeing the *fire* in the Deep *above* the Earth is much ſharper and eaſier to be kindled, then the fire *in* the Earth: and ſeeing alſo that the Earth muſt be kindled by the fire in the Deep *above* the Earth, elſe it can Bear no fruit?

Anſwer.

121. Behold ! thou underſtanding Spirit ; the Spirit ſpeaketh to *thee*, and *not* to the dead ſpirit of the fleſh : Open the Door of thy Aſtral birth wide, and elevate that one Part of the aſtral Birth in the *light*, and let the other in the *wrath* ſtand ſtill, and take heed alſo that thy animated or ſouliſh ſpirit do *wholly* unite with the Light.

122. And ſo when thou ſtandeſt in ſuch a *form*, then thou art as Heaven and Earth is, or as the whole Deitie

Deitie is with its Births or Genitures *in this world.*

123. But now if thou art *not thus*, then thou art blind herein, though thou wert the wittieſt and wiſeſt Doctor, that *ever* could be found in the world.

124. But if thou art *Thus*, then raiſe up thy ſpirit, and look through thy Art of Aſtrology, thy deep ſenſe, and meaſuring of Circles, and ſee if thou art *able* to apprehend it ? *It muſt be born IN THEE,* Elſe thou getteſt *neither* Grace nor Art

125. If the Eyes of thy Spirit ſhall ſtand open, then thou muſt generate *thus*, elſe thy Comprehenſibility is a Fooliſh Virgin, and it befalls thee as if a *Limner* ſhould offer to *pourtray* the Deity on a Table, and tell thee, It is made right, the Deity is juſt ſo.

126. Then the *Believer* and the Limner are *both* alike, both of them ſee nothing but only wood and Colours, and the one blind leadeth the other : *ſurely* thou art not to fight here with Beaſts; but with Gods.

Now Obſerve:

127. When the *whole* Deitie in this world moved it ſelf to the *Creation,* then not onely the *one* part did Move, and the other reſt; but all ſtood joyntly in the *Mobility,* Even the whole Deep, ſo far, as Lord *Lucifer* was King, and ſo far as the place of his Kingdom *reach'd,* and ſo far as the *Salitter* in the wrath-fire was *kindled.*

128. The motion of the three Births laſted the length of *ſix Dayes and Nights,* wherein all the *ſeven* Spirits of God ſtood in a *full* moving Birth or Geniture, as alſo the *Heart* of the ſpirits ; and the *Salit-*

ter of the Earth *turn'd about* in that while, *six times* in the great wheel; which wheel is the seven qualifying or fountain spirits of God; and at each turning about, or Diurnal Revolution, there was generated a several special fabrick or *work*, according to the *innate* Instant qualifying or fountain spirits.

129. For the *First* qualifying or fountain *spirit* is the Astringent, cold, sharp and hard Birth or Geniture, and that *belongeth* to the *first Day* in the Astrall Birth or Geniture, the Astrologers call it the *Saturnine*, which was performed on the First Day. For therein the hard dry sharp Earth and Stones came to be: and were incorporated or compacted together, moreover then was also generated the *strong* Firmament of Heaven; and the Heart of the seven spirits of God stood hidden in the hard sharpnesse.

130. Astrologers appropriate or attribute the *Second Day* to *Sol* or the Sun, but it belongeth to *Jupiter*, to speak of it Astrologically: for on the *second* Day the Light brake forth out of the *Heart* of the seven qualifying or fountain spirits through the hard quality of the Heaven, and caused a mitigation or allaying in the hard water of the Heaven, and the light became *shining* in that meeknesse and allay.

131. And then the meeknesse and the Hard water *separated* themselves asunder, and the hardnesse remained in its hard place, as a hard Death, and the meeknesse or softnesse penetrated through the Hardnesse in the power of the Light.

132. And this now is the *water of Life*, which is generated in the Light of God out of the hard Death. And thus the light of God in the *sweet water*

of

of Heaven brake through the aftringent and hard dark Death, and *thus* the Heaven is made out of the midft or Center of the water.

133. The hard Firmament is the aftringent qua-lity, and the *gentle* Mild or meek firmament is the water, in which the Light of Life rifeth up, which is *the Clarity or Bright Light of the Sonne of God.* And in this manner or form alfo the *knouledge,* and the light of life rifeth up in Man, and the whole light of God in this world ftandeth in *fuch* a Form, Birth, and rifing up.

134. The *Third Day* is very rightly attributed to *Mars,* becaufe it is a bitter, and a *furious* raging and ftirring fpirit. In the *third* Revolution of the Earth the bitter quality rubb'd it felf with the aftringent.

Underftand this thing rightly.

135. When the Light in the fweet water did *penetrate* through the aftringent fpirit, then the fire-*flafh* terrour or crack of the Light, when it kindled it felf in the water, rofe up in the aftringent and hard dead quality, and made all *ftirring,* from thence exifted the ~~Love, or felf, warmheartedneffe, or~~ ~~Defire,~~ *Nobility*

136. Now I fpeak here not *onely* of the Heaven above the Earth, but this ftirring and Birth or Ge-niture was alfo *in* the Earth and *every where.*

137. But being the heavenly fruits before the time of the wrath, fprung up *onely* in this ftirring of the feven qualifying or fountain fpirits, and vaniſh'd or *pafſed away* again by their ftirring, and fo changed

or

or *altered* themſelves ; *therefore* on the third Day of the Birth or Geniture of the Creation, they ſprung up alſo through the ſtirring of the fire-flaſh in the aſtringent quality of the Earth.

138. And though indeed the *whole Deity* is in the Center of the Earth *hidden*, yet the Earth could not for all that bring forth heavenly fruit, for the aſtringent quality had *ſhut* and barred the hard Bolt of Death upon it, and ſo the Heart of the Deity *remained* hidden in its meek and Light Heaven.

139. For the outermoſt Birth is *Nature,* and that ought not to reach *back* into the Heart of God, neither can it, but is the Body, in which the qualifying or fountain ſpirits generate themſelves, and ſhew forth and manifeſt their Birth or Geniture *by their fruits.*

The Two and Twentieth Chapter.

Of the Birth or Geniture of the Starres, and Creation of the

Fourth Day.

I.

Here now is begun the deſcribing of the Aſtrall Birth, and it ought well to be obſerved, what the *firſt title* of this Book meaneth, which is thus Expreſſed.

The

The Day-spring or Dawning in the East,

or

Morning-Redneſſe in the Riſing.

For here will a *very ſimple* Man be able to ſee and comprehend or apprehend the Being of God.

2. The Reader ſhould not make himſelf blind through his *unbelief* and dull apprehenſion : for here I bring in the whole or Totall Nature with all her children, for a *witneſſe* and demonſtration. And if thou art rationall, then look round about thee, and view thy ſelf, alſo conſider thy ſelf aright, and then thou wilt *ſoon find* from or out of what ſpirit I write.

3. For my part, I will obediently perform the command of the ſpirit, onely have thou a care, and ſuffer not thy ſelf to be *ſhut up* by or in an open Door: for here the Gates of knowledge ſtand open to thee.

4. And though the ſpirit will indeed go againſt the Current of ſome Aſtrologers, that is no great matter to me, for I am bound to *obey God rather then Men :* they are blind in or concerning the ſpirit, and if they will not ſee, then they may remain blind ſtill.

Now Obſerve :

5. Now when upon the *Third Day* the fire-flaſh roſe up out of the Light, which was ſhining in the ſweet water ; which flaſh is the bitter quality, which generateth it ſelf out of the kindled *terrour* or crack of fire in the water. 6. Then

6. Then the whole Nature of this world, became springing boyling and moving *in* the Earth, as well as above the Earth, and every where, and began to generate it self again in all things.

7. Out of the Earth *sprung up* Grasse, Herbs and Trees, and in the Earth silver, gold, and all manner of Oar came to be ; and in the Deep above the Earth sprung up the *wonderfull forming* of power and virtue.

8. But that thou mayest understand, what manner of *Subftance* and condition all thele things and Births or Genitures have, I will deferibe all orderly one after another, that thou mayst rightly understand the *Ground* of this Myftery.

And I will treat,

1. Of the *Earth.*
2. Of the *Deep* above the Earth.
3. Of the incorporating or compacting of the Bodies of the *Stars.*
4. Of the feven chief qualities of the *Planets,* and of their Heart, which is the *Sun.*
5. Of the *Four Elements.*
6. Of the outward comprehenfible or palpable Birth or Geniture, which exifteth out of this *whole Regiment* ; or Dominion.
7. Of the *wonderful proportion* and fitneffe or dexterity of the whole wheel of Nature.

9. Before this Looking-Glaffe I will now *invite* all Lovers of the Holy and highly to be Efteemed Arts, of *Philofophy, Aftrology, and Theology,* wherein I will Lay open the Root and *Ground* of them.

10. And though I have not ftudied nor learned
their

their Arts, neither do I know how to go about to meaſure Circles and *uſe* their Mathematicall Inſtruments and Compaſſes; I take no great care about that: However, they will have *ſo much* to learn from hence, that many will not comprehend the ground thereof *all* the dayes of their Lives.

11. For I uſe not their Tables Formula's or Schemes rules and wayes, for I have *not learned* from them, but I have another Teacher, or School-maſter, which is the whole or Totall NATURE.

12. From that *Whole Nature,* together with its innate inſtant Birth or Geniture, have I ſtudied and learned my *Philoſophie, Aſtrologie* and *Theologie,* and not from Men, or by Men.

13. But being Men *are Gods,* and have the knowledge of God the onely Father, from whom they are proceeded or deſcended, and in whom they Live, therefore I *deſpiſe not* the Canons Rules and Formula's of *their* Philoſophie, Aſtrologie and Theologie. For I find, that for the moſt part they ſtand upon a *right Ground,* and I will diligently *endeavour,* to go according to their rules and Formula's.

14. For I muſt needs ſay, that their Formula or Scheme is *my* maſter, and I have my beginning and *firſt* knowledge from their Formula or Poſitions: neither is it my purpoſe, to go about to amend or cry down theirs; for I cannot do it, neither have I *learned* them, but leave them ſtanding in their own Place and Worth.

15. But I will *not* build upon their Grounds, but as a laborious carefull ſervant, I will *digg* away the

Earth

Earth from the Root, that thereby men may fee the whole Tree with its Root, Stock, Branches, Twiggs and Fruits : And may fee that alfo my writing is *no new* thing, But that *their* Philofophie and *my* Philofophie are *one* Body, one Tree, bearing one and the *fame* fort of fruit.

16. Neither have I any *command*, to bring in complaints againft them, to condemn them, for any thing, but for their wickednefle and Abominations, as Pride, Covetoufnefie, Envy and Wrath, *againft* which the fpirit of Nature complaineth very exceedingly, and *not I* : for what can I do, that am *poor Duft and Afhes*, alfo very weak, fimple and altogether unable?

17. Onely the Spirit fheweth thus much, that *to them* is delivered and entrufted the *weighty* Talent, and the Key; and they are *drowned* in the pleafures of the flefh, and have *buried* their weighty Talent in the Earth, and have *loft* the key in their proud Drunkennefle.

18. The fpirit hath a long time waited on them and *importuned* them, that they would once open the Door, for the *clear Day* is at Hand, yet they walk up and down in their Drunkennefle, feeking for the Key, when they have it about them, though they *know it not*; and fo they go up and down in their proud and covetous Drunkennefle, alwaies feeking about like the Country man for his horfe, who all the while he went a feeking for him, was riding upon the *Back* of *that very* Horfe he looked for.

19. Thereupon *faith the Spirit of Nature, being they will not awake from*

from Sleep, and open the Door, I vvill therefore do it my self.

20. What could I simple vulgar *Lay-Man* teach or write of their high Art, if it were not given to me by the *Spirit* of Nature, in whom I live and † am? I am in the Condition or state of a vulgar or Lay-Man, and have no *Salarie* Wages or Pay for this writing: and should I then oppose the Spirit, that He should not *begin* to open, where and in whom he pleaseth? *I am not the Door,* but an ordinary woodden Bolt upon it: and now if the Spirit should pluck me out from thence, and fling me into the Fire, could I hinder it?

† subsist, or have my being.

21. But if I would be an *unprofitable* Bolt, which stubbornly would resist to be pull'd out, and should bolt up and *hinder* the Spirit in the opening, *would* not the Spirit be angry with me, tear me off, and cast me away, and provide a more profitable and a *fitter* Bolt? Then I should lye on the ground and be trampled under-foot, when as formerly I made so fair a shew upon the Door: what should this woodden Barre then serve for, but to be cast into the Fire and *burnt*?

22. Behold! I tell thee a Mystery, so soon as the Door is set *wide* open to its Angle, all uselesse fast-nailed sticking Bolts or Barres will be *cast away*, for the Door will *never* be shut any more at all, but standeth open, and then the *Four winds* will go in and out at it.

23. But the *Sorcerer* sitteth in the way, and will make many *so* Blind, that they will not see the Door: and then they return Home, and *say*; there is no Door at all, but that it is a meer Fiction, and so they go *thither* no more. Vvv 2 24. Thus

24. Thus men suffer themselves easily to be turn'd away, and so live in their *Drunkenneße.*

25. And now when this is done, then the Spirit is angry, which hath opened the Gates, because none will go OUT and IN at its Doors any more, and then it flings the Door-Posts into the Abyße, and then there is *no more Time* at all : those that are *within,* remain within; and those that are *without,* remain without.   AMEN.

Now it may be Asked :

What are the Stars ?

Answer.

26. *Moses* writeth concerning them thus : *And God said ; Let there be Lights in the Firmament of Heaven, to divide or distinguish the Day from the Night : and let them give figns and feasons, Dayes and Years : and let them be Lights in the firmament of Heaven to shine or give light upon the Earth, and it was so done. And God made two great Lights : the greater Light to rule the Day, and the lesser Light to rule the Night ; as also the Stars. And God set them in the Firmament of the Heaven, to shine or give Light upon the Earth : and to rule Day, and Night, also to divide or distinguish the Light from the Darkneße, and God saw that it was good, so out of the Evening and the Morning the fourth day came to be,* Gen. 1. *v.* 14, 15, 16, 17, 18, 19.

27. This description sheweth sufficiently, that the Dear man *Moses* was not the original Author thereof : for the first writer thereof did *not* know either the true God, or the Stars, what they were. And it is very *likely,* that the Creation, before the Flood, was

not

not described in writing, but was kept as a Dark word in their memories, and so delivered from one generation to another, till *after* the Flood, and till people began to lead Epicurean Lives, in all *voluptuousnesse.*

28. And then the *Holy Patriarchs,* when they saw *that, they described* the Creation, that it should not be quite forgotten, and that the *swinish* Epicurean world might have a Looking-Glasse in the Creation, wherein they *might see,* that there is a God, and that this Beeing of the world did not *so* stand from Eternity; whereby they might have a Glasse to look into, and so *fear the Hidden God.*

29. And it was the *Chiefest* Instruction and *Doctrine* of the Patriarchs before and after the Floud, that they *led* Men to the Creation: as *the whole book of* Job *also doth drive at* That.

30. After these Patriarchs came the *wise Heathens,* who went somewhat *deeper* into the knowledge of *Nature:* and I must needs say, according to the Ground of the Truth, that they in their Philosophie and Knowledge did come even before the face or Countenance of God, and yet could *neither* see nor know Him.

31. Man was so altogether *Dead* in Death, and so bolted up in the outermost Birth or Geniture in the dead Palpability: or else they could have Thought, that in this Palpability, there must *needs be a Divine power* hidden in the Center, which had *so* created this Palpability, and moreover preserveth upholdeth and ruleth the same.

32. Indeed they honoured prayed to or *worshipped* the Sun and Stars for Gods, but knew not how they were created or came to be; or out of what

they

hey came to be : for they Might well have thought, that they proceeded from somewhat, and that, *That,* which created them, must needs be Older and higher or Greater then *all the Stars.*

33. Besides, they had the Stones and the Earth for an Example, to shew, that they *must proceed* from somewhat, as also Men and all the Creatures upon the Earth. For all *give testimony,* that there must needs be in these things a mightier and greater *Power* at hand which had so created all these things, in that manner, as they are.

34. But indeed why should I write much of the *blindnesse* of the Heathens, are not *our* Doctors in their Crowned Ornaments of Hoods and Corner'd-Caps, *as blind as they ?* They know indeed that there is a God, who hath created all this, but they know not, *where* that God is, or *how* he is.

35. When they would write of God, then they seek for him *without,* and *absent* from this world, onely above in a kind of Heaven, *as if* he were some Image, that may be likened to *somewhat* : Indeed they *grant,* that, That God ruleth all in this world, with a Spirit ; but his corporeal propriety or *habitation* they will needs have in a certain Heaven aloft *many Thousand* Miles off.

36. *Come on ye Doctors ! if ye are in the Right, then give answer to the Spirit : I will ask you a few Questions ;* 1°. What do you think stood in the *Place* of this world, before the Time of the world? Or 2°. *Out of what* do you think the Earth and Stars came

came to be? Or, 3°. *what* do you think there is in the *Deep* of the Earth? Or, 4°. From *whence* did the Deep exist? Or, 5°. *How* do you think *Man* is the Image of God, wherein God dwelleth? Or 6°. What do you suppose *Gods wrath* to be? Or, 7°. What is *that* in man which displeaseth God so much, that he tormenteth and afflicteth man so, being he hath *created* him? And 8°. that he *imputeth Sinne* to Man, and condemneth him to eternal Punishment? 9°. Why hath he created *that*, wherein or wherewith Man committeth sin? Surely *that thing* must be far *worse*: 10o. Wherefore and *out of what*, is that come to be? Or 11°. What is the cause, or the beginning, or the Birth and Geniture of *Gods fierce wrath*, out of or from which, Hell and the Devil, are come to be? Or, 12°. *How comes it*, that all the creatures in this world do bite, scratch, strike, beat and worry one another, and yet sin is imputed *onely to Man*? Or, 13°. *Out of what* are Poisonous and venomous Beasts and worms, and all manner of Vermine come to be? Or 14o. *Out of what* are the holy Angels come to be? And 15o *what* is the *Soul* of Man? And lastly, 16°. *what is* the *Great GOD Himself?*

37. Give your direct and *fundamental* answer to this, and demonstrate what you say, and leave off your Verbal Contentions.

Now if you can demonstrate out of *all* your books and writings, 1°. that *you know* the true and onely God; and 2°. *How he is* in Love and Wrath: Also, 3°. *What* that God is? and 4°. if you can demonstrate, that God is *not in* the Stars, Elements, Earth, Men, Beasts, Worms, Leaves, Herbs and Grasse, also in Heaven and Earth; also that *all* this is not God
Himself,

Himfelf, and that *my* fpirit is *falfe* and *wicked* ; then *I* will be the firft, that will *burn* my book in the Fire ; and recall and recant *all* whatfoever I have written, and will accurfe it, and in all obedience *willingly* fubmit my felf to be inftructed by *you.*

38. I do not fay, that I cannot erre at all. For there are fome things, which are *not fufficiently* declared, and are defcribed as if it were from a *Glimpfe* of the great God, when the wheel of Nature whirl'd about *too fwiftly,* fo that Man with his half dead and dull capacity or apprehenfion cannot fufficiently comprehend it ; but what thou *findeft not fufficiently* declared in one place, thou wilt find it done in another; if not in this, yet in the other Books.

Now thou wilt fay :

It doth not become me, to ask *fuch* Queftions : for the *Deitie* is a Myftery, which no man can fearch into ?

Anfwer.

39. Hearken; If it doth not become *me* to ask, then it doth not become *thee* to *Judge mee.* Doft thou boaft in the knowledge of the Light, and art a *Leader* of the blind, and yet art *blind* thy thy felf ? How wilt thou fhew the way to the blind ? muft ye *not both* fall, in your blindneffe ?

But

But you will say:

We are not Blind : for we well see the way
of Light, though *none* can see
it rightly.

40. Ye teach others the way, and you are *almaies*
seeking after it your selves ; And so you *grope in the
dark,*and discern it not ! Or do you *suppose,* that it is
Sin, for any Man to *ask* after the way ?

41. *O ye blind Men! leave off
your contentions, and shed not innocent blood; also do not lay waste
Countries and Cities, to fulfill the
Devils will; but put on the Helmet of Peace, Girt your selves
with Love one to another, and
practise Meeknesse: Leave off
Pride and Covetousnesse, Grutch
not the different forms of one another, also suffer not the Wrath-
fire to kindle in you, but live in
Meeknesse, Chastity, Friendlinesse and Purity, and then you
are and live ALL in God.*

X x x   42. For

42. For thou needest *not* to Ask : *Where is God?* Hearken thou Blind Man : thou livest in God, and *God is in thee,* and if thou livest holily, then See the 14.Chap. 127 verse. *therein* thou thy self art God : For wherefoever thou lookest, there is God.

43. When thou beholdest the *Deep* betwixt the Stars and the Earth, *Canst* thou say, that is *not* God, or, there God is *not* ? O, thou miserable corrupted man ! Be instructed ; for in the Deep above the Earth, where thou seest and knowest *nothing,* and sayst, there is *nothing,* yet even *there* is the Light-Holy God in his Trinitie, and is generating *there,* as well as in the high Heaven aloft above this world.

44. Or dost thou think, that he *departed* and went away from his seat wherein he did sit from eternity, in or at the time of the Creation of this world ? O no ; that *cannot* be, for though He *would* himself do so, *He* cannot do it, for he himself is All : And as little as a member of the Body can be rent off from it self, so little can God also *be divided* rent or *separated* from Being *Every where.*

45. But that there are so many Formings figurings or framings in him, is caused by his Eternall Birth or Geniture, which first is Threefold, and out of or from that Trinitie, or Ternarie, it generateth it self *infinitely* or immensely unconceiveably.

46. Of *these* Births or Genitures I will here write, and shew to the children of the last world, *what God is,* *not* out of any Boasting or Pride, thereby to disgrace or reproach any body ! No ; the Spirit will instruct thee meekly and *friendly,* as a Father doth his children ; for the work is not from

my

† *my* fleshly Reason, but *the Holy Ghosts dear Revelation,* or *breaking through* in the Flesh.

47. In my *own* faculties or powers I am *as blind a Man,* as ever was, & am able to do nothing, but in the Spirit of God, *my* * *innate spirit* *seeth through* ALL, but not alwaies with long Stay or Continuance, onely when the Spirit of *Gods Love* breaketh thorough my spirit, then is the animated or *soulish* Birth or Geniture and the Deity one Being, one Comprehensibility, and one Light. —

* or, the Spirit that is generated, or rather regenerated in in me.

48. Am I *alone* onely so? No, *but All Men are so,* be they Christians, Jews, Turks or Heathens; in *whomsoever* Love and Meekneffe is, in *them* is also the Light of God.

If thou sayst, No, this is not so:

Confider.

49. Do not the Turks, Jews, and Heathens *live* in the fame Body, or Corporeity, wherein thou livest, and make ufe of that power and *vertue* of the fame Body, which thou ufeft, moreover they have even the fame Body, which thou haft; and the *fame God,* which is thy God, is *their God* alfo.

But thou wilt fay:

They know him not; alfo they **honour him not.**

Anfwer.

Answer.

50. Yes Dear Man, now boaſt thy ſelf that thou haſt hit it well! *Thou knoweſt* God indeed above others. Behold thou blind Man, where ever Love riſeth up in Meekneſſe, there the *Heart of God* riſeth up. For the Heart of God is generated in the meek water of the kindled Light, be it in Man, or any where elſe without Man, it is *every where* generated in the Center, between the outermoſt and innermoſt Birth or Geniture.

51. And whatſoever thou doſt but look upon, *there* is God, but the *comprehenſibility* ſtandeth in this world, in the wrath, which the Devil hath kindled; and in the hidden kernel in the midſt or center of the wrath the light or Heart of God is generated, *incomprehenſibly* as to the wrath, and ſo *each* of them remaineth in its Seat.

52. Yet for all that, I do *no way* approve or excuſe the *Unbelief* of the Jews, Turks and Heathens, and their ſtiff-necked ſtubbornneſſe, and their fierce wrath, furious malice and *hatred* againſt the Chriſtians. No; theſe things are *meer* Snares of the Devil, whereby he *allureth* Men to Pride, Covetouſneſſe, Envy and Hatred, that *he* may kindle in them the helliſh fire: neither can I ſay, that theſe four ſons of the Devil are *not* domineering in Chriſtendome, nay *indeed* in every Man.

Now thou ſayſt:

What then is the *difference* between Chriſtians, Jews, Turks and Heathens?

Anſwer

Answer.

53. *Here the Spirit openeth both Doors and Gates; if thou wilt not see, then be blind.*

54. The *first* I. difference is, which God hath alwaies held and maintained; that all *those*, who *know*, what God is, and how they should serve him, that they should be *able* by their knowledge to *presse through* the wrath into Gods Love, and *overcome* the Devil: but if they do it not, then they are *no better*, then those, that know it *not*.

55. But if he, that knoweth *not* the way, *presseth through* the wrath into the Love, then is he *like* him, who press'd thorough *by* his knowledge; but those that persevere in the wrath, and *wholly* kindle it in themselves, they are *all alike* one and other, be they Christians, Jews, Turks or Heathens.

Or *what* dost thou suppose it is, wherewith Man can serve God?

56. If thou wilt *Dissemble* with Him, and adorn or magnifie thy Birth, then I suppose thee to be a very fine Angel indeed: But He that hath *Love* in his heart, and leadeth a *mercifull* meek and lowly-minded life, and *fighteth* against malice and hatred, and *presseth through* the wrath of God into the Light, he liveth with God, and is *One Spirit* with God.

57. For God needeth no other Service, but that his creature, which is in *His* Body, do not slide back from *Him*, **but be Holy, as He is.**

58. There-

58. Therefore alfo God gave the Law to the Jews, that they fhould diligently ftudy and endeavour after *meek* Holineffe and Love, that thereby all the world might have them for their *Looking-Glaffe*: But when they grew proud, and boafted in their Birth, *inftead* of entring into Love, and turn'd the law of Love into the fharpneffe of wrath, then God *removed* their Candleftick and *went* to the Heathens.

59. *Secondly* II. There is this Difference betwixt the Chriftians, Jews, Turks and Heathens, that the *Chriftians know* the Tree of Life, which is CHRISTUS, CHRIST, who is the Prince of our Heaven and of this world, and ruleth in all Births or Genitures as a *King* in God his Father, and Men are *his* Members.

60. And now Chriftians know, how they may, *by the power* of this Tree, preffe out from *their* Death through *his* Death to him into his life, and raign and live with him, wherein they alfo with their *preffing through* with their *new birth,* out from *this Dead Body,* may be and are with him in Heaven.

61. And though the dead Body is in the *midft* or Center of Hell among all the Devils, yet for all that, the *new Man* reigneth with God in Heaven, and the Tree of life is *to them* a ftrong Gate, through which they *do* enter into Life: But of this thou fhalt find more largely in its proper Place. ▶

Now Obferve:

62. *Mofes* writeth, that God faid; *Let there be Lights in the Firmament of Heaven, which fhould therein give a Light to the Earth, and divide or diftinguifh Day*

Day and Night, alſo make Years and Times or Seaſons.

63. This deſcription ſheweth, that the firſt writer did *not* know, what the Stars are? But He took hold on the Deitie *at the Heart*, and look'd upon or had reſpect to the Heart, to conſider *what* the Heart and kernel of this Creation is, and the Spirit kept the Aſtral and outermoſt Dead Birth or Geniture *hidden from him*, and did onely drive him in *Faith* to the Heart of the Deitie.

64. Which is alſo the Principal Point, moſt neceſſary for Man : For when he layeth hold on *true Faith*, then he preſſeth through the Wrath of God, through Death into life, and reigneth with God.

65. *But being* Men *now at the* End *of this time , do liſten and long very much after the* Root *of the* Tree, *through which* Nature *ſheweth, that the time of the diſcovery of the* Tree *is at hand : therefore the Spirit will ſhew it to them : and the whole* Deitie *will reveal it ſelf; which is the* Day-ſpring dawning, *or* Morning-Redneſſe, *and the breaking forth of the great* Day *of God, in* which,

which, whatsoever is generated from Death, to the Regeneration of Life, shall be Restored and Rise again.

66. Behold, when God said, Let there be light, *then* the light in the *powers* of Nature, or the seven spirits of God rose up, and the Firmament of Heaven, which standeth in the *word*, in the Heart of the water, between the astrall and outermost Birth or Geniture was *closed* or shut up by or with the Word and Heart of the water, and the Astral birth is the Place of the *parting-mark* or Limit which standeth half in Heaven, and half in the Wrath.

67. For from or out of that half Part of the *wrath*, the Dead Birth generateth it self continually, and out of the other half Part, which reacheth with its innermost Degree even into the innermost Heart and *light* of God, generateth it self now continually through Death, and yet the Astrall Birth or Geniture is *not two*, but *One* Body.

68. But when in these *two Dayes* the Creation of Heaven and of Earth was compleated, and that the Heaven was made in the heart of the water, for a difference or *distinction* between the Light of God, and the Wrath of God, then on the *Third Day*, through the terrour or crack of the fire-Flash, which rose up in the heart of the water, and pressed through Death, incomprehensibly as to Death, there *sprung up* all manner of Ideas Forms and Figures, as was done *before* the time of the kindled wrath.

69. But being the water, which is *the Spirit* of the Astral Life, stood in the midst or Center of wrath,

and

and alſo in Death, thereupon alſo every Body formed it ſelf, as the Birth or Geniture to Life and mobility was.

Of the Earth.

70. But now, the Earth was the *Salitter*, which
was caſt up out of the innermoſt Birth, and ſtood in
Death : but when the fire-flaſh, through the Word,
roſe up in the water, then it was a terrour or *crack*,
from which exiſted the *mobility* in death, and that
Mobility in all the ſeven ſpirits, is now the *Aſtrall*
Birth or Geniture.

The Depth.
Underſtand this aright.

71. Now when on the the *Third Day* the fire-flaſh
in the water of death had kindled it ſelf, then the
Life preſſed forth *quite through* the dead body of the
water and of the Earth.

72. But yet the Dead water and Earth, comprehend *no more* then the flaſh or terrour or crack of the
Fire, where-through their mobility exiſteth : But
the Light which riſeth up very ſoftly Gently or
meekly in the fire-flaſh, that, *neither* the Earth, nor
the dead water, *can* comprehend.

73. But it retaineth its *Seat* in the kernel, which
is the unctuoſity or *fatneſſe*, or the water of life or
the Heaven ; for it is the Body of Life, which the
Death *cannot* comprehend, and yet it riſeth up in the
Death.

74. Neither can the wrath take hold of it or apprehend it, but the Wrath remaineth in the terrour

or

or crack of the Fire-Flaſh, and m aketh the *Mobility* in the dead body of the earth and the water.

75. But the Light preſſeth in very gently after, and formeth the Birth, which through the terrour or crack of the fire-flaſh hath gotten its *compacted* Body.

Of the Growths or Vegetables of the Earth.

76. When now the *wrathfull* fire-flaſh awakened and rouzed up the ſpirits of Nature, which ſtand in Death in the Earth, by its fierce terrour or crack ; then the ſpirits began, according to their peculiar *Divine* Right to generate themſelves, as they *had done* from eternity, and form figure or frame a Body together according to the innate inſtant qualities of *that* Place.

77. Now that kind of *Salitter* which in the time of the kindling of the wrath, *dyed* in Death, and as it did qualifie or operate at that time, in the innate ***or*, In-ſtanding.** * inſtant Life of the ſeven ſpirits of God, ſo alſo it *did* riſe again in the Time of the Regeneration in the Fire-Flaſh, and is not become any *New* thing, but onely another form of the Body, which ſtandeth in the comprehenſibility or *palpability* in Death.

78. But now *the Salitter* of the Earth and of the water is *no more* able to change or alter it ſelf in its dead Being, and ſhew forth it ſelf infinitely, as it did in the heavenly place or Seat ; but when the qualifying or fountain ſpirits form the Body, then it riſeth up in the power and vertue of the *Light.*

79. And the *Life* of the Light breaketh through the

the Death, and generateth to it another Body out of Death, which is not *conformable* to, or of the condition of the water, and the dead Earth, also doth not get *their* taste and smell, but the power of the Light presseth thorough, and tempereth or mixeth it self with the power of the Earth, and taketh from Death, its *Sting*, and from the wrath its poisonous venomous power; and presseth forth up together in the midst or center of the Body in the growth or vegetation, as a *Heart* thereof.

80. *And herein sticketh now the kernel of the Deitie in the Center in its Heaven, which standeth hidden in the water of Life: if thou canst now apprehend or lay hold on it.*

Of the Metalls in the Earth.

81. The *Metals* have the same substance, condition and Birth or Geniture, as the *vegetables* upon the Earth have. For the Metalls or Mineral Oares at the time of the kindling of the wrath in the innate instant Wheel of the seventh nature-Spirit, stood in the Fabrick *work* or operation of the Love, wherein the meek beneficence or well-doing generateth it self *behind* the Fire-Flash; wherein the Holy Heaven standeth, which in this Birth or Geniture, when the *Love* is predominant, presents or

sheweth

sheweth forth it self in such a gracious amiable and blessed Clarity or Brightnesse, and in such beauteous colours, like Gold, Silver, and Pretious Stones.

82. But Silver and Gold in the dead Palpability or Tangibility are but as a Dark stone in comparison of the Root of the heavenly Generating : but I set it down here only, that thou mayst know, from *whence* it hath its Original.

83. But being it hath been, the *excellenteft* rifing up and generating, in the holy heavenly Nature, therefore also it is loved by man above all other in this world. For Nature hath indeed *written* in Mans Heart, *that it is* better, then other Stones and Earth, but Nature could *not* reveal or manifeft to him, the ground thereof from whence it is come or proceeded, *whereby* now thou mayst Obferve the Day-fpring or Morning-Rednesse.

84. There are many feveral forts of minerall Oars, according as the *Salitter* in Natures Heaven was *predominant* at its rifing up, in the Light of Love: For every qualifying or *radical* fpirit in the heavenly Nature containeth the property or kind of *all* the qualifying or fountain fpirits, for it is ever infected or affected with the other, from whence the Life and the unfearchable Birth or Geniture of the Deitie, exifteth: But yet is predominant as to *one* Power, and that is its own Body, from whence it hath the Name.

85. But now every qualifying or fountain fpirit hath the property of the whole or Totall Nature, and its Fabrick or *work* at the time of the kindling of the wrath was together alfo incorporated in Death, and out of every Spirits fabrick or work,

Earth,

Earth, Stones, mineral Oars, and *water* came to be.

86. Therefore also in the Earth there are *found* according to the quality of Each Spirit, minerall Oars, Stones, water, and Earth; and therefore it is that the Earth is of so many *various* qualities, all as Each qualifying or fountain Spirit with its innate Instant Birth or Geniture, was, at the *time* of the kindling.

87. Nature hath likewise Manifested or *revealed* so much to man, that he knoweth, how he may melt away the strange or Heterogene matter from every qualifying or fountain Spirits strange infected innate Birth or Geniture: whereby that qualifying or fountain spirit might remain chief in its own Primacy.

88. You have an *Example* of this in Gold and in Silver, which you cannot make to be pure or fine Gold or Silver, unlesse *it be melted seven times in the fire*, Psal.12.7. But when that is done, then it remaineth in the middle or *Central Seat* in the Heart of Nature, which is the water, sitting in its own quality and *Colour*.

I.

89. First, the *astringent* quality, which holdeth the *Salitter* captive in the hard Death, must be melted away, which is the grosse stony *Drosse*.

I I.

90. Then Secondly, the astringent Death of the water is to be separated, from which proceeds a poisonous venomous water of separation or *Aquafortis*, which standeth in the rising up of the *fire-flash*, which is the evil Malignant, even the very worst source of all in Death, even the Astringent and Bitter *Death* it self;

for

for this is the Place, where the Life, which exifteth
*or *dyed* in the fweet water, * dyed in Death; And that fe-
the Death. parateth it felf now in the *fecond* Melting.

III.

91. Thirdly, the *Bitter* Quality, which exifteth
in the kindling of the water fire-flaſh is melted
away, for that is a Rager Raver Tyrant and deſtroyer; alfo no Silver nor Gold *can* fubfift, if that be not
killed or mortified, for it maketh all dry and Brittle,
and prefenteth or fheweth forth it felf in feverall
Colours; for it rideth through all fpirits, *affuming*
the Colours of all fpirits.

IIII.

92. Fourthly, the *fire* fpirit alfo, which ftandeth
in the horrible anguifh, and pangs of life, muft be
alfo melted away, for it is a continued Father of the
wrath, and out of or from that is generated the *Hel-*
lifh woe.

93. Now when the wrath of thefe four fpirits is
kill'd, then the minerall Oary *Salitter* ftandeth in
the water like a tough Matter, and looketh like that
fpirit, which is predominant in the minerall Ore:
† or *Tin-* and the light, which ftandeth in the *Fire,*† coloureth
ſtureth. it according to its own Qualitie, be it Silver or
Gold.

94. And now this matter in the fourth melting
Subſiſtent looks like Silver or Gold, but it is not yet * *fixt,* nor
is it tough or malleable and pure enough, its body
indeed is *Subſiſtent,* but not the Spirit.

V.

95. Now when it is melted a Fifth Time, then
the

the *Love*-spirit riseth up in the water through the *Light*, and maketh the dead Body living again, so that the matter, which remained in the first four Meltings, getteth power or *strength* again, which was the proper own of that qualifying or fountain-spirit, which was predominant in this Minerall Oar.

VI.

96. Now when it is melted the sixt Time, then it groweth somewhat *harder*, and then the *Life* moveth, which is risen up in the Love, and stirreth it self: and from this stirring existeth the *Tone* in the Hardnesse, and the mineral Oar gets a clear *sound*, for the Hard and dead beating or noise of the bitter fiery matter is gone away.

97. In this sixth Melting I hold, to be the *greatest* Danger for † Chymists about the * *preparing* of their Silver and Gold.   For there belongeth and is required a very subtile fire for it, and it may soon be burnt and made dead or Deaf; and it becometh very dim or blind, if the fire be *too* cold.   †*den Alchymisten.* * *or making.*

98. For it must be a middle or mild fire, to keep the spirit in the Heart from rising, it must be gently *Simpring*, then it getteth a very sweet and meek ringing sound, and continually rejoyceth, *as if* it should now be kindled again in the Light of God.

99. But if the fire be *too Hot* in the Fifth and Sixth Melting, then the new life, which hath generated it self in the Love in the rising up of the Lights power out of the water, is kindled again in the *fiercenesse* in the wrath-Fire, and the Mineral Oar becomes a burnt scum and *Drosse*, and the Chymist hath *dirt* instead of Gold.

VII.

VII.

100. Now when it is melted the Seventh time, then there belongeth and is required yet a *more* subtile fire, for therein the life riseth up, and *rejoyceth* in the Love, and will shew forth it self in infinity, as it had done in Heaven *before* the Time of the wrath.

101. And in this motion it groweth *unctuous* or fat and luscious or luxuriant, it increaseth and spreadeth it self, and the highest depth generateth it self very joyfully out of or from the *Heart* of the Spirit, just as if it would begin an *angelical Triumph,* and present or shew forth it self infinitely in *divine* power and form according to the Right of the Deitie: and thereby the Body getteth its greatest strength and power, and the Body coloureth or tinctureth it self with the *highest degree,* and getteth its true beauty excellency and vertue.

102. And now when it is *almost* made, then it hath its true vertue and colour, and there is onely *one* thing wanting, that the spirit cannot elevate it self with its *Body* into the Light, but must remain to be a dead stone ; and though indeed it be of *greater* vertue, then other Stones, yet the *Body* remaineth in Death.

103. *And this now is the earthly God of Blind men ;* which they Love and Honour, and *leave* the living God, who standeth hidden in the Center, sitting in his Seat. For the dead Flesh comprehendeth onely a *Dead God,* and longeth also onely after such a dead God.

But

But it is such a GOD, as hath Thrown many men headlong into Hell!

104. Do not take me for a Chymist, for I write onely in the *knowledge* of the spirit, and not from Experience. Though indeed I could here shew *something* else, *viz.* in *how many* Dayes, and in *what Hours* these things must be prepared: for Gold cannot be made in one Day, but a whole Moneth is requisite for it.

105. But it is not my purpose, to make *any* try-all of it, because I know not how to *manage* the Fire, neither do I know the colours or tinctures of the qualifying or fountain-spirits in their outermost Birth or Geniture, which are *Two* Great Defects; but I know them according to (another) or the Regenerate Man, which standeth *not* in the palpability.

106. At the Description of the *SUN* you will find more and deeper things concerning it: my intention is onely, to describe the whole or *Total Deitie*, as far as I am capable, in my weaknesse to apprehend, *viz.* How, *that* is in Love and Wrath, and how it doth generate it self now at present in *this* world.

You shall find more concerning Jewels and pretious stones at the description of the seven Planets.

Z z z

The

The Three and Twentieth Chapter.

Of the Deep above the Earth.

1.

WHen Man beholdeth the *Deep* above the Earth, he seeth nothing, but *Stars* and *Clouds* of water, and then he thinketh, Sure there must be another place, where the Deitie presenteth or sheweth forth it self, together with the *heavenly* and *Angelical* Government : He will needs have the Deep together with its regiment or Dominion *severed* from the Deitie : for there he seeth nothing, but *Stars*, and the regiment or Dominion *between*, is Fire, Air and Water.

2. Then presently he thinketh, God hath made this thus out of or from his *predestinate purpose, out of Nothing* ; How then *can* God be in this Being ? or, *Can* that be God Himself ? He continually Imagineth, that this is onely a *House*, wherein God ruleth and dwelleth by his *Spirit* : God cannot be such a God, whose being consisteth in the power of *this* government, or Dominion.

3. Many will dare to say, what *manner of God* would that Be, whose Body, Being, and Power or vertue standethror consisteth in Fire, Air, Water and Earth ?

4. Behold ! thou *unapprehensive* Man, I will
shew.

shew thee the true *ground* of the Deitie: *If* this whole or universal Beeing, be not God, *then* thou art not Gods Image: If he be any other, or strange God, then thou haft *no Part* in him: For thou art created out of this God, and liveft *in* this very God, and this very God continually giveth thee power, or vertue and Blessing, also meat and drink *out of Himself,* also all thy knowledge standeth in this God, and when thou *dyeft,* then thou art *Buried* in this God.

5. Now, if there be any *other* or strange God without and besides this God, who then shall make *thee* living again out of this God, in whom thou shalt be departed and turned to *duft* ? How shall that strange God, out of whom thou art *not* created, and in whom thou didft *never* Live, bring thy Body and spirit *together again?*

6. Now if thou art * of any *other* Matter, than God himself, *how* canft thou then be his Child ? or *how* can the *Man* and *King* Chrift be *Gods* Bodily or corporeal Sonne, whom he hath generated or begotten out of his *Heart* ?

* or, of any other Materialls.

7. Now, if his Deitie be *another* Beeing substance or thing, than his Body ; then there muft be a twofold Deitie in him, his Body *would* be of or from the God of this world, and his Heart would be of or from the *unknown God.*

8. *O, thou Child of Man!* open *the Eyes of thy Spirit, for I will shew thee here, the right and reall proper Gate of the Deitie, as in-*

Z z z 2 *deed*

deed that very One onely God will have it.

9. Behold! *that* is the true One only God, out of whom thou art created, and *in whom thou Liveſt* : and when thou beholdeſt the Deep and the Stars, and the Earth, then thou beholdeſt thy God, and in that ſame thou Liveſt, and alſo art or *haſt thy Beeing* therein, and that ſame God governeth or ruleth thee alſo, and out of or from that ſame God alſo thou haſt *thy Senſes,* and thou art a Creature out of or from Him and in him ; elſe thou hadſt been *Nothing,* or wouldſt never have been.

10. Now perhaps thou wilt ſay ; I write Heatheniſhly.

Hearken and behold! Obſerve the diſtinct underſtanding, *How* all this is ſo : for I write *not* Heatheniſhly or Babarouſly, but Philoſophically ; neither am I a Heathen, but I have the *Deep* and *true* knowledge of the One onely great God, who is ALL.

11. When thou beholdeſt the Deep, the Stars, the Elements and the Earth, then thou *comprehendeſt not* with thy Eyes, the bright and clear Deitie, though indeed it is *there* and *in them* ; but thou ſeeſt and comprehendeſt with thy Eyes, Firſt, Death, and then, the Wrath of God, and the Helliſh fire.

12. But if thou raiſeſt thy *Thoughts,* and conſidereſt *where* God is, then thou apprehendeſt the Aſtral Birth or Geniture, where Love and Wrath move one againſt another ; but when thou draweſt up the *Faith* in God, who ruleth in *holineſſe* in this Government or Dominion, then thou breakeſt thorough
Heaven.

Heaven, and apprehendeſt or layeſt hold on God at his *holy* Heart.

13. Now when this is done, then thou art as the whole or *totall* God is, who *himſelf* is Heaven, Earth, Stars, and the Elements, and haſt alſo ſuch a regiment or Dominion in thee, and art alſo ſuch a Perſon, as the *whole God,* in the place of this world, is.

Now thou ſayſt :

How ſhall I *underſtand* this : for the Kingdom of God and the Kingdom of Hell and of the Devill are *diſtinct* one from another, and *cannot* be one Body ? Alſo the Earth and Stones are *not* God ? nor the Heaven, Stars and Elements : *much leſſe* can a Man be God : for if ſo, he could not be *rejected* by God.

Here I will tell thee the ground of all by *degrees,* one thing after another : therefore keep the Queſtion in Mind.

Of the Aſtral Birth or Geniture, and of the Birth or Geniture of God.

14. *Before* the Times of the created Heavens, the Stars and the Elements, and before the creation of *Angels,* there was *no* ſuch wrath of God, no Death, no Devil, no Earth nor Stones, neither were there any Stars, but the Deitie generated it ſelf very *meekly* and lovingly, and formed framed and figured it ſelf in Ideas ſhapes and Images, which were incorporated

:porated according to the qualifying or fountain spirits in their generating, *wreſtling* and riſing up, and *paſſed away again* alſo through their wreſtling; and figured or framed themſelves into another form or condition, all according to the primacy or *predominancy* of each qualifying or fountain ſpirit, as you may read before.

15. *But obſerve here rightly,* the earneſt and *ſevere* Birth or Geniture, out of which the wrath of God, Hell and Death are come to be; which indeed have *been* from Eternity in God, but † *not accenſible nor elevable.*

† not kindled or Domineering.

16. For the whole or Totall *God* ſtandeth in *ſeven* Species or Kinds; or in a ſevenfold Form or Generating: and if theſe Births or Genitures were not, then there would be neither God nor Life, nor Angel, nor any Creature.

17. And *theſe* Births or Genitures have *no Beginning*, but have ſo generated themſelves from Eternity; and as to this Depth, *God Himſelf knoweth not what He is: For He knoweth no Beginning of himſelf, alſo he knoweth not any thing that is like Himſelf, as alſo he knoweth no End of himſelf.*

18. *Theſe ſeven* Generatings *in all* are *none of them* the firſt, the ſecond, or the Third, or Laſt, but they

are

are all Seven every one of them, both the firſt ſecond third, fourth and laſt: yet I muſt ſet them down one after another according to a *creaturely* way and manner, otherwiſe thou couldſt not underſtand it: For the *Deity* is as a Wheel with ſeven wheels made one in another, wherein a man ſeeth *neither* Beginning nor End.

Now Obſerve:

I.

19. *Firſt*, there is the *Aſtringent* quality, which is *alwaies* generated from the other ſix Spirits, which in *it ſelf* is hard, cold, ſharp like Salt, and yet *farre* ſharper. For a Creature cannot ſufficiently apprehend its ſharpneſſe, ſeeing it is not *ſingly* and alone *in* a creature; but according to the manner and kind of the kindled Helliſh quality, I know *How* it is: This aſtringent ſharp quality attracteth or draweth together, and in the Divine Love holdeth or *retaineth* the forms and Images, and *dryeth* them ſo, that they ſubſiſt or are *fixed*.

II.

20. The *Second* Generating is the *Sweet water*, which is generated *alſo* out of all the ſix ſpirits: for it is the Meekneſſe, which is generated out of the other ſix, and preſſeth it ſelf forth *in* the aſtringent Birth or Geniture, and *alwaies* kindleth the aſtringent again, and then quencheth and *mitigateth* it, that it be not too much aſtringent, as it might be in its own ſharpneſſe, if it were *not* for the water.

III.

III.

21. The *third* Generating is the *Bitterneffe,* which exifteth out of the fire *in* the water : for it rubbeth and vexeth it felf in the aftringent and fharp coldneffe, and maketh the coldneffe moveable, from whence *mobility* exifteth.

IIII.

22. The *Fourth* Generating is the fire, which exifteth from the mobility or rubbing in the aftringent fpirit, and that is now fharp *burning,* and the bitter is ftinging and raging. But when the fire-fpirit rubbeth it felf thus ragingly in the aftringent coldneffe, then there is an anxious *horrible* quaking Trembling and fharp oppofite contentious generating.

Obferve here the Depth.

23. *I fpeak here as to the kind and manner of the Devil, as if the Light of God had not yet kindled it felf in thefe four kinds : and as if the Deitie had a beginning, I can no other or nearer way offer it to your Judgment that you may underftand it.*

24. In this Fourth rubbing is a very hard and moft horrible fharp and *fierce* coldneffe, like a refined melted and very cold falt-water, which yet is

not

not water, but such a hard kind of power and vertue as is like Stones.

25. There is also *therein* a raging raving stinging and burning, and that water is continually as a Dying Man, when Body and Soul are parting asunder, a most *horrible anxiety*, a woful painful Birth or Geniture.

26. *O man! here consider thy self, here thou seest, from whence the Devil, and his fierce Wrathful Malice hath its original, as also Gods Wrath, and the Hellish fire, also Death and Hell, and eternal Damnation.*

Ye Philosophers observe that!

27. Now when *these four* Generatings rub themselves one upon another, then *heat* gets the Primacy and predominancy, and kindleth it self in the sweet water, and then instantly the Light riseth up.

Understand this rightly :

28. When the Light kindleth it self, then the fire-terrour or *crack* cometh forth *first*, as when you strike upon a Stone, the fire-crack is first, and then the light first conceiveth it self from the fire-crack.

29. Now the *fire-crack* in the water goeth through the astringent quality, and maketh it moveable, but the light generateth it self in the *water*, and becomes

A a a a   *shining*

shining Light, and is an impalpable meek and moſt richly loving Being, which neither I nor any other Creature can ſufficiently write or ſpeak of, but I *ſtammer* only like a Child, which would fain learn to Speak.

30. That ſame Light is generated in the midſt or *Center* out of theſe four *Species* out of the unctuoſity or fatneſſe of the ſweet water, and repleniſheth the whole Body of this Generating. But it is ſuch a meek, pleaſing, *well-doing*, well-ſmelling and well-taſting Reliſh, that I know *no ſimilitude* to liken it to, But where Life is generated in the midſt or Center of Death; or as if a Man did ſit in a huge ſcorching hot flaming fire, and were ſuddenly ſnatched out from thence, and ſet in ſuch a very exceeding eaſie place of refreſhment, where inſtantly all the ſmarting ſcalding pains which he felt afore by the *burning* of the Fire ſhould ſuddenly paſſe away, and he be put into ſuch a pleaſing temper and *ſoundneſſe*: Juſt ſo the Generating of the 4. Kinds or Species are ſet or put into ſuch a *ſoft* and meek well-doing, and refreſhment, *aſſoon* as the Light riſeth up in them.

Thou muſt underſtand me here aright.

31. I write and mean it in a creaturely kind and manner, as if a Man had been the Devils Priſoner, and were *ſuddenly* removed out of the Devils *fire* into the *Light* of God.

32. For the Light hath had no beginning in the generating of God, but hath ſhined or given Light *ſo* from eternity in the Generating, and God *himſelf* knoweth no beginning therein.

33. *Only*

33. *Only the Spirit here setteth Open for thee the Gates of Hell,* that thou mayst see, what is the condition of the Devils and of Hell, and what the condition of Man is, when the divine Light *extinguisheth* in him, so that he sitteth in the wrath of God, and then he *liveth* in such a Generating in such an anguish, Smarting Pains, woe and misery.

34. Neither can I declare it unto thee in any other manner: for I must write so, *as if the Generating or Geniture of God had or took a beginning, when things came to be thus ; but I write here very, really true, and Pretious dear words, which the Spirit alone understandeth.*

Now Observe :

The Gates of God.

35. The *Light,* which generateth it self from the Fire, and becometh shining in the water, and replenisheth or filleth the whole Geniture, and enlighteneth it, and mitigateth it ; *that, is the true Heart of God, or Sonne of God.* For he is *continually* generated out of the Father, and is another *Person* then the qualities and Geniture of the Father. Aaaa 2 36.For

36. For the Generating or Geniture of the Father *cannot* catch or comprehend the Light, and use it to its Generating, but the Light *standeth* by it self; and is not comprehended by any Geniture, and it replenisheth and enlightneth the whole Geniture, *viz. the onely begotten Sonne of the Father,* John 1.14. *And this Light I call in the humane Birth or Geniture, the animated or Soulish Birth,*

    [" *Understand, the Image, which Budded forth out*
    " *of the Essences of the Soul, according to the*
    " *similitude of God :*]

or the Birth or Geniture, which qualifieth mixeth or uniteth with this animated or soulish Birth or Geniture of God; and *herein* is Man's soul *one heart* with God, but *that is* when it standeth in this **Light.**

V.

37. The *fifth* Generating in God, is, when this *Light* thus very gently mildly and amiably presseth through the first four Births or Generatings, and then it bringeth along with it, the Heart and most pleasant *lovely* power and vertue of the sweet water, and so when the sharp Births or Genitures taste of it, then are they very meek and *richly full* of Love, and is as if continually the life did rise up in and from Death.

38. *There* each spirit tasteth of the other, and
                    getteth

getteth meer *new* strength and power, for the astringent quality groweth now very pliable and yielding, because it is mitigated by the power of the Light that springeth out of the sweet water, for it *warmeth* the coldnesse, and the sweet water maketh the *sharp* taste very pleasant lovely and mild.

39. And so in the sharp and fiery Births or Generatings there is nothing but a meer *longing of Love*, a tasting, friendly affecting, gratious amiable and blessed Generating; there is nothing but meer Love, and all wrath and Bitternesse in the Center is *Bolted up* as in a strong Hold. This generating is a very meek beneficiall well-doing, and the bitter spirit now is the *Living* Mobility.

VI.

40. Now the *Sixth* Generating in God, is; *when* the *Spirits* in their Birth or Geniture thus *taste*, one of another, for then they become very full of *Joy*: For the fire-flash or the sharpnesse out of or from the Birth or Geniture riseth up aloft, and moveth as the Ayr in this world doth.

41. For when one power or vertue *toucheth* the other, then they taste one another, and become very full of Joy; for the Light becometh generated out of all the powers, and presseth again through all the powers; whereby and wherein the *rising Joy* generateth it self, from whence the *Tone* or * *Tune* exists.

* melody or
Musick.

42. For from the touching and moving the living Spirit generateth it self, and that same Spirit presseth through all Births or Generatings, very *unconceiveably* and incomprehensibly to the Birth or Geniture, and is a very richly Joyfull pleasant lovely

sharp-

sharpnesse, like melodious sweet Musick.

43. And now when the Birth generateth, then it *conceiveth* or apprehendeth the Light, and speaketh or inspireth it again into the Birth or Geniture through the moving Spirit.

And this moving Spirit is the Third Person in the Birth or Geniture of God, and is call'd God the Holy Ghost.

VII.

44. The *seventh* Generating is, and keepeth its Birth or Geniture, and *Forming* in the Holy Ghost, and so when that goeth through the sharp Births or Genitures, then it goeth forth with the Tone, and so formeth and *Imageth* all manner of Figures, all according to the wrestling of the sharp Births or Genitures one with another.

45. For they wrestle in the Birth or Geniture *continually* one with another like a loving Play or Scene, and according as the Birth or Geniture is with the *colours* and taste in the rising up, so are the *figures* also Imaged.

46. *And this Birth or Geniture now is called,* GOD *the Father Sonne and Holy Ghost:* and neither of them is the First, and neither of them is the Last : though *I make* a distinction, and set the one after the other, yet neither of them is the first or the last, but they have all been from Eternity thus seated in the same *Equality* of Beeing. 47.I

47. I must write by *this* way of *distinction*, that the Reader may understand it: for I cannot write meer heavenly words, but must write humane words. Indeed all is rightly truly and faithfully described;

But the Beeing of God consisteth only in Power, and the Spirit only comprehendeth it, and not the dead or mortal Flesh.

48. *And thus thou mayst understand, what manner of Being the Deitie is, and how the three Persons of the Deitie are: thou must not liken the Deitie to any Image; for the Deity is the Birth or Geniture of all things.* And if there were not in the First four Species or kinds the sharp Birth or Generating, then there would be no mobility, neither could the Light kindle it self, and generate the Life.

49. But now this sharp Birth or Geniture is the *original* of mobility and of Life, as also of the Light, from whence existeth the *Living and Rational spirit*, which distinguisheth formeth and Imageth all in this Generating.

50. For the astringent cold Birth or Geniture is the *beginning* of all things, which, is astringent, severe, contracting and retentive, and formeth and

con-

contracteth the Birth together, and maketh the Birth thick or solid, so that out of it *Nature* commeth to *Bee* : and hence Nature and comprehensibility, hath its original in the whole Body of God.

51. Now *this Nature* is as a *dead* unintellectual Being, and standeth or consisteth not in the power of the Birth or Geniture, but is a Body, wherein the power generateth.

52. But it is the Body of God, and hath all power as the whole Geniture hath, and the generating spirits take their strength and power out of or from the *Body* of Nature, and continually generate again, and the astringent spirit continually compacteth or draweth it together, and dryeth it ; and thus the Body subsisteth, and the generating spirits also.

53. Now the other Birth or Geniture is *the Water,* which taketh its original in the Body of *Nature.*

Observe :

54. Now when the Light shineth *thorough* the astringent contracted Body, and mitigateth it, then the mild beneficient *well-doing* generateth it self in the Body, and then the hard power groweth very mild, and melteth as Ice in the Heat of the *Sun,* and is *extenuated* or rarified as water is in the Ayr ; and yet the stock of Nature as to the heavenly comprehensibility *remaineth* standing.

55. For the astringent and fire-spirit holdeth it fast, and the meek water, which melteth from the Body of Nature in the kindling of the Light, that goeth through the *severe* and earnest, cold and fiery

Birth

Birth or Geniture, and is very sweet pleasant and lovely.

56. Whereby now the earnest and *austere* Birth or Geniture is refreshed ; and when it tasteth thereof, it groweth capable to be raised up, and *rejoyceth*, and also is a joyful rising up, wherein the life of Meeknesse generateth it self.

57. For *this is the water of Life,* wherein the Love, in God, as also in Angels and Men, generateth it self : For it is all of one sort of Power Vertue and Birth or Geniture.

58. And now when the Births or Genitures of the powers taste the water of Life, then they quake or Tremble for very Love and Joy, and that trembling or moving, which riseth up in the midst or center of the Birth or Geniture, is *Bitter.* For it riseth up swiftly out of the Birth, when the water of life cometh into the Birth or Geniture; like a Joyful leaping or springing up of the Birth.

59. But being it riseth up so swiftly, that the Birth elevateth it self so suddenly *before* it be fully affected with the water of life, thereupon that terrour or crack keepeth its bitternesse which it hath out of or from the *austere* Birth : for the beginning or incaptive Birth or Geniture is very austere, cold, fiery and astringent.

60. Therefore also is the terrour or Crack now so *swelling* and trembling; for it moveth the whole Birth, and rubbeth it self therein, till it kindleth the fire in the hard fiercenesse, from whence the Light taketh its original : And then the trembling crack becometh enlightned with the *Meeknesse* of the Light, and goeth in the Birth or Geniture up and

down, and croſſe-wayes both upwards and down-wards like a wheel made with *ſeven* wheels one in another.

61. In this preſſing through and turning about exiſteth the *Tone*, according to the Quality of each ſpirit, and alwaies one power affecteth the other, for the powers are as *loving Brethren* in one Body, and the meekneſſe riſeth up, and the ſpirit generateth and ſheweth it ſelf infinitely.

62. For that power, which in the *turning about* ſheweth it ſelf the ſtrongeſt in the generating, according to that power, manner and colour the *Holy Ghoſt* alſo imageth ſhapeth or frameth the figures in the Body of *Nature*.

63. *Thus thou ſeeſt*, that *none* of the powers is the firſt, alſo none the ſecond, third, fourth or Laſt: but the laſt generateth the Firſt as well, as the firſt the Laſt, and the middlemoſt taketh its original from the Laſt as alſo from the Firſt, as well as from the Second, Third, or any of the reſt.

64. Thou ſeeſt alſo, that Nature cannot be *diſtinguiſh'd* from the powers of God, but is all one Body.

65. The Deitie, that is, the holy power of the Heart of God is generated *in Nature*, and ſo alſo the Holy Ghoſt exiſteth or goeth forth out of the Heart of the Light *continually*, through all the powers of the Father, and figureth all, and Imageth or frameth All.

66. This Birth or Geniture is now in *Three* diſtinct *Parts*, every one being ſeveral and *Total*, and yet *neither* of them is divided aſunder from the other.

The

The Gate of the Holy Trinity.

67. The whole Birth or Geniture which is the Heaven of all Heavens, as also this world, which is *in* the Body of the whole, as also the *place* of the Earth and of all creatures, and whatever thou canſt think on, *all that together is God the Father,* who hath neither beginning nor end, and wherefoever and whatfoever thou thinkeſt upon even in the ſmalleſt circle, that can be imagined, is the *whole* Birth or Geniture of God, perfectly inceſſantly and irreſiſtably.

68. But if in a Creature or in any Place the light be *extinguiſht,* then is the auſtere Birth or Geniture *there,* which lyeth hid in the Light in the innermoſt kernel ; *And this now is One Part.*

69. The ſecond part or the ſecond Perſon is the Light, which is continually generated from or out of all powers, and enlightneth again all the powers of the *Father,* and hath the fountain of all powers. But is therein diſtinguiſh'd from the Father as a *ſingular Perſon,* in that it cannot comprehend the Birth or Geniture of the Father, and yet is the Fathers *Sonne,* which is alwaies generated from or out of the Father : An Inſtance whereof you have in all the kindled *Fires,* in this world, do but conſider of it.

70. And

70. And the *Father* loveth this his onely begotten or innate *Sonne* therefore so heartily, *because* he is the Light and the meek beneficent well-doing in *his Body*, through whose power the Fathers *Joy* and Delight riseth up.

71. *Now these are two Persons,* and neither of them can apprehend retain or comprehend the other, and the One is *as great* as the other; and if either of them were not, the other could not be neither.

72. *Observe here ye Jews, Turks and Heathens, for it concerneth you; to you here are opened the Gates of God,* harden not your selves, for now is the acceptible time.

73. You are *not* forgotten of God at all, but if you convert, then the Light and Heart of God will rise up *in you,* as the bright Sun at Noon-day.

74. *This I write in the power and perfect knowledge of the great God, and I understand his will herein very well.* For I live and * *am* in him, and spring up with this work and Labour out of his root and stock, and it must be so : Onely take thou heed ; if thou blindest thy self, then there is *no* Remedy more; neither canst thou say, thou knewest *not* of it, therefore arise, for the Day breaketh !

* or have my Beeing in him,

75. *The third diversity, or the third*

third Person in the Being of God is the moving Spirit, which existeth from the rising up in the terrour or Crack, where *life* is generated, which now moveth in all powers, and is the Spirit of Life; and the *powers* can no more comprehend him or apprehend him, but he kindleth the powers, and by his moving maketh figures and *Images,* and formeth them according to that kind and manner, as the wrestling Birth standeth in *every* place.

76. And if thou art not *wilfully* blind, thou mayst know, that the *Ayr* is that very spirit, but in the Place of this world Nature is *kindled* therein very swellingly in the wrath-fire, which Lord *Lucifer* effected, and the Holy Ghost, who is the Spirit of Meckneste, lyeth *hidden* therein in his Heaven.

77. Thou needest not to ask, where that Heaven is. It is in *thy* Heart, do but open it, the *Key* is here shewed to thee.

78. *Thus there is one God and three distinct Persons one in another,* and neither of them can comprehend or withhold or fathom the Original of the other, but the *Father* generateth the Sonne, and the *Sonne* is the Fathers Heart, and his Love and his Light, and is an original of Joy, and the *beginning* of all Life.

79. And the *Holy Ghost* is the Spirit of Life, and a former, framer and Creator of all things, and a *performer* of the will in God, that hath formed and created out of or from the Body and in the Body of

the

the Father, all Angels and Creatures, and holdeth and formeth all *still* daily, and is the sharpnesse and the Living Spirit of God : *And as the Father speaketh or Expresseth the Word out of or from his powers, so the Spirit formeth or frameth them.*

Of the great simplicity of God.

80. Come on Brave Sir, upon thy Brown Nagg ! who *ridest* from Heaven into Hell, and from Hell into Death, and therein the sting of death lyeth : *view thy self* here thou worldly wise Man, that art full of *base* wit Cunning and subtile Policy.

81. Take notice ye worldly wise *Lawyers*, if you will not, come before this Looking-Glasse, even before the *bright* and clear face of God, and view your selves *therein*, then the Spirit presenteth to you the Birth or Geniture in the innermost astringent circle ; where wit cunning and prudence is generated, where the *sharpnesse* of the anxious Birth or Geniture of God is, for *there* your prudence cunning and deep reaching wit is *generated.*

82. Now if you will be Gods, and not Devils, then make use of the *Holy* and *meek Law* of God, if not, then you shall for ever Eternally generate in the a *stere* and severe Birth or Geniture of God.

This saith the Spirit, as the Word of God, and not of my dead or mortal Flesh.

83. Thou

83. Thou muſt know, that I do not ſuck it out from the dead or mortal *Reaſon*, but my ſpirit qualifieth mixeth or uniteth with God, and proveth or ſearcheth the *Deitie* how it is in all its Births or Genitures in its taſte and ſmell: and I find, that the Deitie is a very ſimple, *pure*, meek, loving and Quiet Beeing; and that the birth of the *Ternarie* of God generateth it ſelf very meekly, friendly, lovingly and unanimouſly, and the *ſharpneſſe* of the innermoſt Birth, *can never* elevate cr ſwell it ſelf into the meekneſſe of the Ternarie, but remaineth *hidden* in the Deep.

84. And the ſharpneſs in the hidden ſecreſie is called God's WRATH, and the *Being* of meekneſſe in the Ternarie or *Trinity*, is called GOD. Here nothing goeth out of or forth from the ſharpneſſe, which *periſheth*, or which doth kindle the wrath, but the ſpirits Play very *gently* one with another, like little children, when they rejoyce one with another, where every one hath his work, and ſo they *play* one with another, and lovingly kiſſe and court one another.

85. Such a work alſo the Holy Angels *exerciſe* themſelves in, and in the *Ternarie* of God there is a very meek, pleaſant, and ſweet beeing, where the Spirit alwaies elevateth it ſelf in the * Tone, and the one power toucheth the other, as if there were pleaſant Melodious Hymnes or Songs and *conforts* of muſicall Inſtruments plaid upon. * *Tune melody or Muſick.*

86. And as the riſing up of the ſpirits, in every place is, ſo the Tone alſo formeth it ſelf, but very *meekly*, and incomprehenſibly to the *Bodies* of the Angels, but very comprehenſibly to the animated or ſouliſh *Birth* or Geniture of Angels: and as the Deitie preſenteth it ſelf in each place, ſo the Angels alſo

also present themselves: For the Angels were created out of *this Being*, and have among them their Princes of the qualifying or fountain spirits of God, as they are in the Birth or Geniture of God.

87. Therefore as the Beeing of God presents or sheweth forth it self in the Birth or Geniture, so do the *Angels* also, and that power, which at any time hath the *primacie* in the Birth or Geniture of God, and rejoyceth out of the Heart of God in the *Holy Ghost*, that Power's Prince of the Angels beginneth also his Hymn, and Jubilateth with his Hoaft or *Army*, now one, then suddenly another, for the Birth or Geniture of God is like a *wheel*.

88. But when the *Heart* of God sheweth forth it self with its Clarity or Brightnesse, then there riseth up the whole Hoaft or Army of *all* the *three* Kingdoms of the Angels, and in this rising up of the Heart of God the *Man* JESVS CHRIST *is King and Chief*, he leadeth the Royal *Chorus* or Quire with all the holy Souls of Men till the Last Judgment Day: And then the Holy Men are *perfect* Angels, and the wicked *perfect* Devils, and that in its eternity.

89. *Here view thy self, thou witty suttle world, and consider, from whence thy prudence suttlety and vvit proceedeth.*

Now thou wilt say to me :

90. Doft not thou feek after deeper futtlety than we ? thou wilt needs clime into the moft hidden fecrets of God, which is not fit for any Man to go about. We feek only after humane Prudence and futtlety, but thou wouldft be equall with God, and knovv all; How God is, in every thing both in Heaven and in Hell, in Devils, Angels and Men. Therefore fure it is not unlawful to feek for a cunning fharp wit and after crafty Defigns, which bring Honour Povver or Authority and Riches.

A Reply.

91. If thou climeft up *this Ladder*, on which I climb up into the Deep of God, as I have done, then thou haft climbed well: I am not come to this meaning, or to this work and *knowledge* through my *own* Reafon, or through my *own* will and purpofe, neither

Cccc   have

have I fought this knowledge, nor fo much as knew any thing concerning it, I fought only for the *Heart* of God ; *therein* to hide my felf from the tempeftuous ftorms of the *Devil.*

92. But when I gat in thither, then this great *weighty* and hard Labour was laid upon me, which is, to Manifeft and *reveal* to the world, and to make known *The great Day of the LORD* ; and being they feek and Long fo eagerly after the *Root* of the Tree ; to reveal to them, what the whole Tree is, thereby to intimate, that it is *the Dawning or Morning Redneffe of the Day,* which God hath long ago *Decreed* in his Councel. AMEN.

93. Thus thou feeft, *what God is,* and *How his Love and Wrath* hath been from *eternity,* alfo how his Birth or Geniture is : and now thou canft *not* fay, that thou art *not* in God, or doft *not* live in God, or that God is any *ftrange* Thing, which thou canft not come at, but muft confeffe, that where thou art, *there* is the Gate of God.

94. Now if thou art *holy,* then as to thy *Soul* thou art with God in Heaven ; but if thou art *wicked,* then as to thy *Soul* thou art in Hell-fire.

Now Obferve further :

95. When God created the Angels, all of them were created wholly out of this Birth or Geniture of God, their Body was *compacted* or incorporated out of Nature, therein their *Spirit* and *Light* generated themfelves, as the Deitie generated it felf.
And

And as the qualifying or fountain ſpirits of God alwaies took their power and ſtrength out of or from the *Body* of Nature, ſo the Angels alſo, they took their power and ſtrength alwaies out of or from the Nature of God.

96. And as the Holy Ghoſt in Nature formeth and Imageth or frameth *all*, ſo the ſpirit of the Angels alſo qualified or united with the Holy Ghoſt, and did *help* to form frame and Image *all*, that all might be One Heart and will, and a meer delight and Joy: For the Angels are the Children of the Great God, which He hath generated in his Body of *Nature* for the multiplying of the divine Joy.

97. But here thou muſt know, that the *Bodies* of Angels cannot apprehend the Birth or Geniture of God, neither doth their Body *underſtand* it, their *ſpirit* onely underſtandeth it, but the Body holdeth ſtill, as the *Nature* in God doth, and lets the ſpirit co-work and Labour with God, and Play lovingly.

98. For the Angels Play before and in God, as little children play before their *Parents*, whereby the Divine Joy is increaſed.

99. But when the mighty potent Prince and King *Lucifer* was created, he would *not* do ſo, but elevated and ſwelled himſelf, and would be God alone, and kindled the wrath-fire in himſelf, and ſo did all *his* Angels alſo.

100. But when that was done, he roared with his kindled fire-ſpirit, abroad into the *Nature* of God, and then the whole Body in the Nature of God, as far as his Kingdom and Dominion *reach'd*, was kindled: But being his light was *inſtantly* extinguiſh'd, he could no more qualifie or unite with his Spirit in the *two* Births or Genitures, *viz.* of the Sonne

of

of God, and of the Holy Spirit of God, but remained standing in the *sharp* Birth or Geniture of God.

101. For the light of God and the Spirit of God, *cannot* comprehend the sharp Birth or Geniture, and *therefore* they are *two distinct Persons* : And so Lord *Lucifer* could no more touch, see, feel or taste the Heart of God and the Holy Spirit of God, with his *austere,* cold, and hard fire-Birth, but was *Spewed* out with his fire-spirit, into the outermost Nature, wherein he *had kindled* the wrath-fire.

102. And *that* Nature is indeed the Body of God, wherein the Deitie generateth it self, but the Devils cannot apprehend the *meek Birth* of God, which riseth up in the Light : For their Body is *dead* to the Light, and liveth in the outermost and austere Birth or Geniture of God, wherein the Light *never* kindleth it self again any more.

103. For their unctuousnesse or fatnesse in the sweet water is *burnt* up, and that water is turn'd into a sowr *stinck*, wherein the Light of God can no more kindle it self, and the Light of God can no more enter into it.

104. For the qualifying or fountain spirits of the *Devils* are shut up in the hard wrath, their Bodies are a hard *Death,* and their spirits are a fierce *Sting* of the wrath of God, and their qualifying or fountain spirits generate themselves continually in the innermost sharpnesse, according to the sharp * Law of the Deitie.

* right or Order.

105. For otherwise they cannot generate themselves, neither can they dye or passe away, vanish and be no more, but they *stand* in the most anguishing Birth or Geniture, and there is nothing in them but meer *fiercenesse,* wrath and malice; the kindled

fire-

fire-fource rifeth from eternity to eternity, and they can never touch nor fee nor apprehend the *Sweet* and *Light* Birth or Geneniture of God any more.

Of the kindled Nature.

106. But God hath *therefore* kindled Nature fo much and fo hard, and did fo kindle the burning in his wrath therein, that he might *thereby* build a dwelling houfe for the Devils, and keep them *Prifoners* therein, in that they were the children of wrath, in whom he muft rule with his fierce *Zeal* or Jealoufie, and they alfo in the wrath of God.

The Four and Twentieth Chapter.

Of the Incorporating or Compaction of the Stars.

Printed Copy. Of the Dead Nature, and of the Fourth Day.

1.

NOw when the *whole Body* of Nature in the Extent Space or Circumference of this world, was benumm'd or *deadned* as in the hard Death, and yet that the Life was *hid* therein, thereupon God moved the whole Body of the Nature of this world on the *Fourth Day*, and generated the Stars from or out of Nature out of the rifen Light. For the wheel of Gods Birth or Geniture *moved* it felf *again*, as it *had done* from eternity.

2. Indeed

2. Indeed it had moved on the *First Day*, and began the Birth or Geniture in the Body of the *corrupt* Nature: for on the *first* Day, the life *separated* it selfe from the Death, and on the *second* Day a firmament was Created *between*, and on the *third* Day the Life *brake forth* through Death. For there the light brake*forth* through the Darknesse, and made the dead body of Nature to spring flourish and to be stirring and agile.

3. For on the *third Day* the Body of Nature did travell *so* hard in anxietie, till the *Love fire* had kindled it selfe in the Death, and till the Light of life was broken forth through the *congealed* Body of Death; and sprung up out of Death; but on the third Day it stood onely in the *Fire crack*, from whence mobility exifted.

4. On the *fourth Day* the Light rose up, and made its seat in the house of death, and yet *Death* could not, nor cannot comprehend it: As *little* as the austere Birth of God, which standeth in the innermost kernel, from whence life exifteth, can apprehend the meeknesse, and the light of the meeknesse together with the Spirit in the meeknesse; *so little* also can the dead Darknesse of this world comprehend the Light of Nature; *no more* can the Devills neither.

5. But the light shineth through Death, and hath made its *Royall* seat in the midst or center in the *or, Divine* House of Death, and of Gods wraths, and generateth *Body.* to it selfe a *new* * *Body* of God, out of the house of wrath which subsisteth eternally in the Love of God in comprehensibly to the *old* kindled Body in the *outmost* Birth or Geniture.

Now

Now thou wilt Ask.

How shall I understand this?

Answer.

6. I *cannot* at all write it in thy Heart, for it is not for every Mans capacity, understanding and apprehension, especially where the Spirit standeth in the *House of wrath*, and doth *not* qualifie operate or unite with the Light of God. But I will shew it to thee in an Earthly *similitude*, that thou mightst if possible get a little into the *deep* Sence.

7. Behold and consider a *Tree*, on the outside it hath a hard grosse *Rind* or *Bark* which is Dead benumm'd, and without Vegetation, yet it is not *quite* Dead, but in a faintnesse or imbecillity, and there is a great difference between it and the Body, which groweth next under the Rind or Bark. But the Body hath its Living Power, and breaketh forth through the *withered* Rind, and generateth many faire *young* Bodys or *Twigs*, all which stand in the *old Body.*

8. But the *Rind* is as it were dead, and cannot comprehend the *Life* of the Tree, but only hangs to it, and is a *Cover* to the Tree in which worms doe Harbour, which in the End destroy the Tree.

9. And *thus* also is the whole House of this world: the *outward* Darknesse is the House of *Gods* Wrath, wherein the Devils dwell, and it is rightly the House of Death, for the Holy Light of *God* hath *dyed* therein.

   [" *Understand, it stepp'd into its principle, and is the* b b.
      " *outward substantiality in God, as it were dead*
      " *in our Esteem, whereas it liveth in God, but*
      " *in another Source or Quality*]   10. But

10. But the Body of this great House, which lyeth hid under the *Shell* or Rind of darkneſſe, incomprehenſibly to darkneſſe, *that* is the houſe of Life, wherein Love and Wrath *wreſtle* one with another.

11. Now the Love alwaies breaketh *through* the Houſe of Death, and generateth *holy* heavenly Twigs in the great Tree; which Twiggs ſtand in the Light: For they ſpring up through the ſhell or *skin* of Darkneſſe, as the Twiggs do through the ſhell or Bark of the Tree, and are *One Life* with God.

12. And the wrath ſpringeth up alſo in the Houſe of darkneſſe, and holdeth many a Noble Twigg *captive* in Death through its infection in the houſe of *fierceneſſe.*

13. And this now is the *Summe*, or the Contents, of the Aſtral Birth or Geniture, of which I here intend to write.

And now it may be Asked:

What are the Stars? or out of what are they come to be?

14. They are the *power* of the ſeven Spirits of God: for when the wrath of *God*, was kindled by the Devil, in this world, then the *whole Houſe* of this world in Nature or the outermoſt Birth or *Geniture* was as it were benumm'd or *chilled* in Death, from whence the *Earth* and *Stones* are come to be. But when this hard droſſe or *Scum* was driven together into a Lump or Heap, then the *Deep* was clear'd, but was very dark, for the light therein was dead in the *wrath.*

15. But now the Body of God, as to this world, could not *remain* in Death, but God moved himſelf with

with his feven qualifying or fountain fpirits to the *Birth* or Geniture.

But thou muft underftand this high thing rightly:

16. The *Light* of God, which is the *Sonne* of God, as alfo the Holy Ghoft, *died not*, but the Light, which is gone forth from or out of the heart of God *from eternity*, and hath enlightned Nature, which is generated out of the feven fpirits, that is *departed* or gone away from the hard *corrupted* Nature; from whence it is that the Nature of this world with its comprehenfibility or palpability hath *remained* in Death, and cannot apprehend the Light of God, but is a dark Houfe of Devils.

17. Upon this On the *fourth* Day of the Creation God *regenerated* anew the whole Houfe of this world with the qualities thereof, and hath *placed* or fet the qualifying or fountain fpirits in the Houfe of Darkneffe, that he might generate to himfelf again out of that, a *new Body*, to his praife honour and Glory.

18. For his purpofe was to create *another* Angelical Hoaft or Army, out of this Houfe; which was thus to be done: He would create an Angel, which was *Adam*, who fhould generate out of himfelf Creatures *like* himfelf, which fhould poffeffe the Houfe of the New Birth, and in the middle of Time, *their King* fhould be generated or born out of a Humane Body, and poffeffe the new-born Kingdom as a King of thefe Creatures, inftead of the *corrupted* and expell'd Lucifer.

19. And at the *fulneffe* or accomplifhment of this Time, God would adorn and Trim this Houfe with its qualities, as a Royal Government, and let thofe

D d d d   very

very qualifying or fountain spirits *possesse* the whole House, that they might in that House of darknesse and of Death, bring forth Creatures and Images again, as they *had done* from eternity, till the accomplishment or fulfilling of the whole Hoast or Army of the new created Angels, which were Men : And *Then*, God would bolt and barr up the Devil in the House of darknesse in an eternal Hole, and then kindle the whole House in its own Light again, *all but* the very Hole Hell or Dungeon of the Devils.

Now it may be Asked :
Why did not God bolt him up instantly, and then he had *not* done so much mischief ?

Answer.

20. Behold ! this was Gods *purpose*, and that must stand, *which is*, he would re-edifie out of the corrupted Nature of the Earth, or build again to himself an Angelical Hoast or Army : Understand, *viz.* a true Body, which should *Subsist* eternally in God.

21. It was not Gods intention at all to let the Devil *have* the whole Earth for an eternal dwelling house, but onely the Death and *fiercenesse* of the Earth, which the Devil had brought into it.

22. For *what* sin hath the *Salitter* committed against God, that it should stand totally in *Eternal* shame ? None ; It was onely a Body, which must hold still, when the Devil elevated or swelled himself therein.

23. Now if He should have instantly *left* it to the Devil for an Eternal dwelling House, then out of *that* place a New Body could *not* have been built. Now what Sin had that space place or *Room* committed

mitted againſt God, that it ſhould ſtand in eternal Shame? None: and therefore that were *unequall* to be ſo.

24. Now the purpoſe of God was, to make a curious excellent Angelical Hoaſt or Army out of the *Earth*, and all manner of Ideas forms or Images. For, in and upon that all ſhould Spring, and generate themſelves *anew*, as we ſee in mineral Oares, Stones, Trees, Herbs and Graſſe, and all manner of Beaſts; after a *heavenly* Image or Form.

25. And though thoſe Imagings were *tranſitory*, being they were not pure before God, yet God would at the End of this time, *extraſt* and draw forth the Heart and the kernel, out of the new Birth or Geniture, and *ſeparate* it from Death and Wrath, and the new Birth ſhould Eternally ſpring up in God, without, *diſtinſt* from this place, and bear Heavenly fruits *again*.

26. But the death of the Earth and the wrath therein ſhould be Lord *Lucifers* eternal Houſe, after the accompliſhing of the new Birth or Geniture: in the mean while Lord *Lucifer* ſhould lie *captive* in the Darkneſſe in the Deep above the Earth; and there he is now, and may *very ſhortly* expeſt his Portion.

27. And that this New Birth or Geniture might be accompliſhed, whether the Devil will or *no*, the Creator hath therefore in the Body of this world generated himſelf, as it were *creaturely* in his qualifying or fountain ſpirits, and all the Stars are nothing elſe but Gods *powers*, and the whole Body of this world conſiſteth in the ſeven qualifying or fountain ſpirits.

28. But that there are ſo many Stars of ſo manifold different effeſts and operations, it is from the *Infi-*

niteneſſe,

* *Infection*
or *Affect-*
ings.

niteneße, which is in the * efficiency of the feaven
fpirits of God, in one another, which generate themfelves infinitely.

29. But that the *Birth* or the *Bodys* of the Starrs
doe not change or alter in their *feat*, but do as they
did from eternitie, it fignifyeth that there fhall be a
conftant continued Birth or Geniture, whereby the
benumm'd Body of the Earth fhould continually and
conftantly, in one *uniform* operation, which yet ftandeth in the infiniteneße, be kindled againe, and generate it felfe a new, and fo alfo fhould the Houfe of
darkneße of the Deep above the Earth ; whereby
the new Body might continually and conftantly be
generated out of Death, till time fhould be accom-
plifhed, and the whole new borne Body.

Now thou wilt object and fay.

Then fure the Starrs are God, and they muft
be honoured and worfhipp'd as God ?

30.The wife Heathen alfo came to this who indeed
in their fharp or acute underftandings far *excelled*
our Philofophers, but the *right* Door of knowledge
hath remained yet *hidden* to them.

13. Behold ! the Starrs are plainly incorporated
or *compacted* out of or from God, but thou muft underftand the difference between them:for, they are
not the Heart, and the meek pure Deitie, which man
is to honour and worfhip as God, But they are the
innermoft and fharpeft *Birth* or Geniture, wherein
all things ftand in wreftling and *fighting*,wherein the
Heart of God alwaies generateth it felf, & the Holy
Ghoft *continually* rifeth up from the rifing of the Life

32. But the fharp *Birth* or Geniture of the Starrs
cannot

cannot apprehend the Heart of God again , nor the Holy Ghoſt ; but the Light of God , which riſeth up in the *anxiety,*together with the moving of the Holy Ghoſt remaineth *free* to it ſelf as the Heart, and ruleth in the mid'ſt or center of the *Cloſure* of the hidden Heaven, which is from ʼr out of the Water of Life.

33. For from the Heaven the Starrs have their *firſt kindling,* and are onely as a *inſtrument* , which God uſeth to the *Birth* or *Geniture.*

It is Juſt ſuch a *Birth,* as is in *Man;*the *Body* is even the *Father* of the ſoule, and when the *Body* ſtandeth in the anguiſhing *Birth* or *Geniture* of *God,* as the Starrs doe, and not in the fierce helliſh *Birth* , then the ſoul of Man qualifieth mixeth or *uniteth* with the pure *Deitie,* as a *Member* in or of his *Body.*

35. Thus alſo is the Heart or Light of *God* alwaies generated in the *Body* of this world , and that generated Heart is *one Heart* with the eternal beginningleſſe infinite Heart of *God* , which is in and above all Heavens.

36. It is *not only* generated in and from the Starrs, but in the *whole Body* of this world , but the Starrs alwaies kindle the *Body* of this World , that the *Birth* or *Geniture* may ſubſiſt *every* where:

But here thou muſt well obſerve this.

37. The light or the Heart of *God* taketh *not* its original barely from the wild rough Starrs , where indeed *Love* and wrath are one in another, but out of or from the *Seat* where the meek water of Life is continually generated.

38. For that water, at or in the kindling of the
wrath.

wrath was not apprehended by *Death*, but subsisteth from eternity to eternity, and reacheth to all the Ends and Parts of or in this world, and is *the water of Life*, which breaketh through Death, out of which the new Body of God in this world is *built*.

39. But it is *in* the Stars as well as in all Ends corners and places, but not in any place, comprehensible or *palpable*, but filleth or replenisheth all alike at once : It is also in the Body of Man, and he that thirsteth after this water, and *drinketh* thereof, *in him the light of life kindleth it self*, which is the heart of God, and there presently springeth forth, the Holy Ghost.

Now thou Askest :

How then do the Stars subsist in Love and Wrath ?

Answer.

40. Behold ! the Stars are risen or proceeded out † the first inward stirring of Life in the Child. of the *Kindled House* of Gods wrath, as the † mobility or stirring of a *Child* in the Mothers Body or Womb in Three * Months : But now they have * as Gen. 38, 24. attained their kindling from the eternal benummed water of Life, for that water in Nature was *never* dead.

41. But when God moved himself in the Body of this world, then on the *third Day* the anxiety, in the birth of this world rubbed it self, from whence the fire-flash existed, and the light of the Stars kindled it self in the water of Life.

42. For

42. For till the *third* Day from the time of the kindling of Gods wrath in this world, Nature in the anxiety was a *dark* valley, and ftood in Death, but on the third Day the life brake through Death, and the *New Birth* began.

43. For fo long, and not an hour longer, *the new born King and Grand Prince of this world*, JESUS CHRIST, *refted in Death*, and hath born or generated the *firft three* Dayes of the Creation of Nature, and that very Time; in Death to Light again, that this time might again be *one* Time with the *Eternal* Time, and that no Day of Death might be *between*: and that the Eternal Love, and the new born or Regenerated Love out of the new Body of Nature might be *one* Eternal *Love*, and that there might be *no* difference between the eternal Love, and the new-born or regenerated Love, but that the new-born Love might reach into the Being or Subftance, which was from Eternity, and *it felf* alfo be in Eternity.

44. Thus the new-born Love, which rofe out of the water of Life in the light *in* the Stars, and *in* the whole Body of this world, is wholly bound and united with the eternal beginningleffe infinite Love, fo that they are *one* Heart and *one* Spirit, which fupporteth and preferveth all.

45. In this kindling of the Light in the Stars and Elements, the Birth of Nature did not thereupon *wholly tranfmute* or change it felf into the holy Meekneffe, as it was before the Time of the wrath, *fo that* the Birth of Nature is now altogether holy and *pure*; No, but it ftandeth in its fharpeft, auftereft, and

and moſt anxious Birth, wherein the wrath of God *unceſſantly* ſpringeth up like helliſh-Fire.

46. For if Nature had *fully* chang'd it ſelf with its ſharp Birth into Love, according to the heavenly Right Law or Manner, then were the Devils again in the *Seat* of God.

47. And this thou mayſt very well perceive and underſtand in *Extream* Heat and Cold, as alſo by the Poiſon, Bitterneſſe and Sowrneſſe in this world ; all which ſtand in the Birth or Geniture of the *Stars*, wherein the Devil lyeth *Captive.*

48. The Stars are onely the kindling of the great Houſe : for the whole houſe is benumm'd in Death, as the Earth is, for the outermoſt Birth or Geniture is *dead* and benumm'd, as the Rind Shell or Bark of a Tree : but the Aſtral birth is the *Body* in which the Life riſeth up.

49. But it is in its Body very ſharp, yet the new Birth, which riſeth up in the water of Life , and preſſeth through Death, *mitigateth* it. But it cannot *alter* the *kernel* of the ſharp Birth, but is generated out of it, and *keeps* its holy new life to it ſelf, and preſſeth through the angry Death, and the angry Death comprehendeth it *not.*

50. Now this love and wrath is indeed one Body, but the water of Life is the heaven of *Partition* between them, ſo that the Love doth not receive or comprehend the Wrath, nor the wrath the Love, but the Love *riſeth up* in the water of Life, and receiveth into it ſelf from the Earth and auſtere Birth, the *power*, which is in the Light, which is generated out of the Wrath ; ſo that, the New Body is born out of the Old.

51. For the *old Body*, which ſtandeth in the *auſtere Birth*

Birth, belongeth to the Devil for a House, and the *new* belongeth to the Kingdom of Chrift.

Now it may be Asked:

Are not all the Three Perfons of the Deitie in the Birth or Geniture of Meeknefle, in this World?

Anfwer.

52. *Yes,* they are all three in this world in the *full* Birth or Geniture of Love, meeknefle, Holinefle and purity, and they are alwaies generated in fuch a fubitance and B.eing, as *was done* from Eternity.

53. Behold! God the Fat! er Spake to the People of Ifrael on Mount Sinai, w en he gave the Law to them, faying, *I am an angry zealous or Jealous God to thofe, that hate me,* Exod.20.5. Deut.5.9.

54. Now thou canit not make of tiis *One* onely Father, who is both Angry and alfo full of Love, *two* Perfois, but he is one onely *Father,* which continually generateth his heartily beloved *Sonne,* and from both thefe the *Holy Ghoft* goeth forth continually.

Obferve the depth in the Center.

55. The *Father* is the One onely being, who himfelf is ALL; who continually generateth his heartily beloved *Sonne* from eternity, and *in both* of them the *Holy Ghoft* is continually ftanding in the Flafh, wherein the Life is Generated.

56. But now from the aufteïe and *earneft* Birth or

Eeee Geniture

Geniture of the qualifying or fountain spirits of the Father, wherein the Zeale or Jealoufy and the wrath ftandeth, the *Body* of Nature alwaies cometh to be, wherein the *Light* of the Sonne, viz: of the Fathers Heart ftandeth, incomprehenfibly as to Nature.

57. For the light is in the Midft or Center of the *Birth* or Geniture, and is the place of *Life*, wherein the meek Life of God is generated from or out of *all* the powers of the Father, and in the fame place the *Holy Ghoft* goeth forth from the Father and the Sonne.

58. Now thofe powers of the Father, which ftand in the *kindling* of the Light, are *the holy Father, and the meek Father, and the pure Birth or Geniture of God*, and the Spirit, which rifeth therein, is the holy Ghoft; but the fharp Birth or Geniture is the Body, wherein this *Holy Life* is continually generated.

59. But when the Light of *God* fhineth through this fharp Birth or Geniture, then it becometh very meek, and is as it were like a Man that is afleep, in whom the Life *ftill moveth*, and the Body is in a fweet quiet reft.

60. And in this Body of nature now was the *kindling* made, for out of this Body the Angels alfo were created; and if *they had not* elevated and kindled themfelves in their Highmindedneffe; then their Body might have ftood eternally in a *ftillneffe* and in an incomprehenfible meekneffe, as it is in the *other* Principalities of Angels that are without, diftinct

ftinct from this world, and their ſpirit had generated it ſelf eternally in *their* Body of meekneſſe, as the holy *Trinitie* doth in the Body or Corporeity of God, and their inborn or *innate* ſpirit had been oneHeart, one Will, and one Love with or in the Holy Trinity : for to *that end* alſo they were created in the Body of God, to be a *joy* to the Deitie.

61. But Lord *Lucifer*, would *himſelfe* be the Mighty God, and kindled his Body, and excited or ſtirred up therein the *ſharp* Birth of God , and oppoſed the Light or bright Heart of God, intending to rule therein with his ſharpneſſe, which was a thing impoſſible to be done.

62. But being he elevated and kindled himſelf *againſt* the Right of the Deitie, thereupon the ſharp Birth in the Body of the Father *roſe up* againſt him : and took him as an angry Sonne Priſoner or *Captive*, in the ſharpeſt Birth, and therein now is his eternall *Dominion*.

63. But now when the Father kindled himſelf in the Body of the ſharpneſſe , he did *not* for all that *kindle* the holy ſource, wherein his moſt lovingHeart generateth it ſelf, and ſo thereupon his Heart ſhould ſit in the ſource of wrath. No ! that is impoſſible that it ſhould be , for the ſharp Birth *cannot* apprehend the holy and pure Birth , but the holy and pure preſſeth *quite* through the ſharp, and generateth to it ſelf a new Body , which ſtandeth again in meekneſſe.

64. And that new Body is *the water of Life* which is generated when the light preſſeth through the wrath, and the holy Ghoſt is the Former or framer therein : but *Heaven* is the Partition be-

tween love and wrath , and is the feat, wherein the wrath is tranfmuted or changed into Love.

65. Now when thou beholdeft the Sun and Stars, thou muft *not* think, that they are the *Holy* and pure God, and thou muft *not offer* to pray to them or aske any thing of them , for they are not the Holy God , but are the kindled *auftere* Birth or Geniture of *his* Body, wherein Love and Wrath *wreftle* one with another.

66. But the holy God is *hidden* in the *Center* of all thefe things in his Heaven, and thou canft neither fee nor comprehend him , but the *foul* comprehendeth him, and the Aftral Birth but half , for the Heaven is the Partition between Love and Wrath : That Heaven is every where, even in thy felfe.

67. And now when thou worfhippeft or prayeft to the *Holy God* in his Heaven then thou worfhippeft or prayeft to *him,* in *that* heaven, which is *in* thee, and that fame God with his light ; and therein the holy Ghoft *breaketh* through in *thy* Heart , and generateth thy *Soul* to be * a New Body of God , which ruleth

* or New Divine Body and raigneth with God in *his* Heaven.

68. For the earthly Body, which thou beareft , is one Body with the whole kindled *Body* of this world and thy body qualifyeth mixeth or uniteth with the whole body of this world; and there is no difference between the Stars and the Deep, as alfo the Earth and thy Body ; it is all one Body : This is the only difference ; thy Body is a *Sonne* of the whole ; and is in it felf as the whole Being it felfe, is.

69. And now as the new Body of this world generateth it felfe in *its* Heaven, fo the new man alfo generateth himfelfe in *his* Heaven, for it is all but *one* Heaven, wherein God dwelleth, and therein thy

thy new man dwelleth, and they *cannot* be divided afunder.

70. But if thou art wicked, then thy Birth or Geniture is *not capable* of Heaven, but of the wrath, and remaineth in the other part of the Aftral Birth or Geniture, wherein the earneft and *auftere* fire-fource rifeth up, and bolts it up into *Death*, fo long, till thou breakeft through Heaven, and *liveft* with God.

71. For inftead of thy Heaven thou haft the wrath-Devil fitting there; but if thou breakeft thorough, then *he* muft get him gone, and the Holy Ghoft ruleth and reigneth in *that* Seat, and in the other Part *viz.* the fiercenefle, the Devil *tempteth thee*, for it is his Neft, and the Holy Ghoft *oppofeth* him, and the new man lyeth in his own Heaven *hidden* under the protection of the Holy Ghof, and the Devil knoweth not the New man, for he is not in *his* Houfe, but in Heaven, in the Firmament of God.

72. *This I write as a Word, which is Generated in its Heaven, where the Holy Deity alwaies generateth it felf, and where the moving fpirit rifeth up in the Flafh of Life, even there this Word and this knowledge is generated, and rifen up in the Love-fire through the Zealous fpirit of God.*

73, 1.

73. I know very well, what the Devil intendeth; for, *that Part* of the earnest and austere Birth or Geniture, wherein Love and wrath are set opposite one to another, *seeth* into *his* very Heart. For when he cometh with his fierce and hellish Temptation, like a *fawning* Dogg, then he setteth upon us with his wrath in that part, wherein the austere Birth or Geniture standeth, and *therein* the Heaven is set in opposition to him, and there the fair *Bride* is known.

74. For he stingeth through the *Old* Man, with an intent, to spoyl or destroy the *New* ; but when the new riseth against him, then the Hell-Hound retireth, and then the new Man *seeleth* very well, what device the Hell-hound hath darted or spit into the astral Birth, and then is it time to Purge and scour it out.

75. But I find, that the *cunning'st* Devill is set against me, he will raise scorners and mockers, who will say, that I intend by mine *own conceit* to grope, dig deep and search out the *Deitie*. Yes, Mr. Scorner, thou art indeed an *obedient* son to the Devil, thou hast great cause to mock Gods children, *as if I* were able in mine *own* power to fathom the depth of the Deitie ; No ! but the Deitie searcheth the Ground *in me* : Or, dost thou think, that I am strong enough to stand against it ?

76. Indeed thou *proud* Man, God is a very meek, simple and quiet still Beeing, and groapeth not in the Bottom of Hell and Death, but *in his* Heaven, where there is nothing, but an Unanimous meeknesse ; therefore it is not *meet* for me to do *so*.

77. But behold ! it is *not* I that have made way for this, but thy desire and highly raised lofty Lust, hath moved the *Deitie*, to *reveal* to thee the desire of

thy

thy Heart in the higheſt *ſimplicity* in the *greateſt depth,* that it may be a witneſſe againſt thee, and denunciation of the earneſt ſevere Day of God;

78. *This I ſpeak to thee as a word of the earneſt Severity of God, which is generated or born in the Flaſh of Life.*

The Five and Twentieth Chapter.

Of the whole Body of the Stars Birth or Geniture, that is, the whole Aſtrologie, or the whole Body of this World.

I.

THe learned and highly experienced *Maſters* of Aſtrology or the Starry Art, are come ſo high and deep in their underſtanding, that they know the *courſe* and *Effects* of the Stars, what their conjunction, * influence and breaking through of their powers, and vertues denoteth and produceth; and How *thereby* wind, rain, ſnow and

* *infection*

* Good Hap, Bad Hap: Good Luck and Miſchance or Miſchiefe.

and heat is cauſed, alſo Good and Evill, * Proſperity and Adverſity, Life and Death, and all the drivings and *agitations,* in this world.

2. And indeed it hath a *true* foundation which I know in the ſpirit, to be ſo, but their knowledge ſtandeth onely in the Houſe of Death in the outward comprehenſibility or palpability, and in the beholding with the Eyes of the *Body*; but the root of *this Tree* hath hitherto remained hidden *to them.*

3. Neither is it my purpoſe, to write of the *Branches* of the Tree, and to invert or diſprove their knowledge, neither do I build upon *their* Ground, but I leave their knowledge to *ſit* in its own ſeat, being I have not ſtudyed it : but I write in the ſpirit of *my knowledge* concerning the root ſtock Branches and Fruits of the Tree ; as an induſtrious and laborious Servant to *his* Maſter ; in diſcovering the *whole* Tree of this world.

4. *Not* with an intent to ſet any new thing on foote, for I have *no* command to do ſo, but my knowledge ſtandeth in this Birth or Geniture of the *Stars,* in the Midſt or Center, where the *Life* is generated, and breaketh through Death, and where the *moving ſpirit* exiſteth and breaketh thorough, and in the impulſe and moving *thereof,* I alſo write.

5. Alſo I know very well, that the Children of the fleſh will *ſcorne* and mock at me, and ſay, I ſhould *look* to my own *Calling,* and not trouble my Head about theſe things, but rather be diligent to bring in *food* for me and my familie : and let thoſe meddle with *Philoſophy* that have ſtudyed it, and are *called* and appointed to it.

6. With ſuch an attempt the Devill hath given me ſo many aſſaults, and hath ſo *wearyed* me, that I have

have *often* resolved to let it alone, but my former purpose was too hard for me. For when I took care for the *Belly*, and to get my *Living*, and resolved to *give over* this businesse in hand, then the Gate of Heaven in my knowledge, was *bolted* up.

7. And then my soul was so *afflicted* in anxiety, as if it were captivated by the Devill, whereby *reason* gat so many checks and assaults, as if the Body were presently to fall to the ground, and the spirit would *not* give over, till it brake thorough againe through the Dead or *Mortall* Reason, and so hath broke open to peeces, the *Door of darknesse*, and hath gotten its seat againe, in the stead thereof.

8. Whereby I understand, that the *spirit* must be *tryed* through the *Crosse* & *Affliction*, and I have not failed of bodily Temptation, but was faine alwayes to stand *ready* for an encounter, so much hath the Devill set himselfe against *this*.

9. But when I perceived, that my Eternal *Salvation* was concerned therein, and that through my negligence the Gates of the Light would be shut against mee, which yet was the very *Firmament* and *Fort* of my Heaven, wherein my soul did *hide* it self from the storms of the Devill, which I took in, and *gained* with great toyle and many hard assaults, and stormings through the *Love* of God, by the breaking through of my *Redeemer and King* JESVS CHRIST, and therefore I leave my care to God, and will take my fleshly Reason *Captive*.

10. And I have chosen the Gate of knowledge of the Light, and will follow after the impulse and knowledge of the spirit, though my *bestial Body*

should

fhould be brought to beggery or quite fall to the ground, I regard none of thefe things: but will fay with the royal prophet David (P*fa.* 73.26.)

though my Body and Soul fhould faint and faile, yet thou O God art my Salvation, my comfort, and the refuge of my Heart.

11. In *thy* Name I will venture it, and will not ftrive againft *thy* Spirit : though the flefh be troubled, and muft endure miferie, yet *faith* in the knowledge of the Light, muft move and foare *above* Reafon.

12. And I know alfo very well that it is not fit for the difciple to fight againft *his Mafter*, and I know that the high experienced Mafters of Aftrologie do *far exceed* me in *their* way. But I labour in *my* calling, and they in *theirs*, left I fhould be found a Lazy Idle Servant to my Lord, at his coming, when he fhall demand the *Talent* he hath entrufted me with all ; but that I may prefent it to him with ufury, or profit and gaine.

13. Therefore I will not *bury his Talent in the Earth* but lend it *out upon ufury or intereft, left he fhould fay to me at that time, of his requiring it of me, Thou wicked floathfull Servant, why haft thou hid my Talent in the Darkneffe, and did'ft not put it out upon ufe, and fo now I might have received it with ufury, gain and profit? and fo then he will take it quite away from me, and give it to another, who hath gained many Talents with his one.* Therefore I will fow, let him water it, I leave the care to him.

Now observe.

14. The whole Houſe of this World, which ſtandeth in a viſible and comprehenſible or *Palpable* being, is the *old Houſe of God*, or the Old Body, which ſtood before the time of wrath in a *Heavenly* claritie and *brightneſſe :* But when the Devill ſtirred up the wrath therein, then it became a Houſe of darkneſſe and of *Death.*

25. Therefore then alſo the holy Birth or Geniture of God, as a ſpecial Body of it ſelfe; *ſeparated* it ſelf from the wrath , and made the Firmament of Heaven, between the Love and the Wrath , ſo that the Birth or Geniture of the Stars ſtandeth in the *middle :* underſtand it thus ; *viz :* with its outward comprehenſibility and *viſibility* it ſtandeth in the wrath of Death, and with the New Birth , riſing np therein , which ſtandeth in the middle or central ſeate, where the *cloſure* of Heaven is , it ſtandeth in the meekneſſe of the Life.

16. For Meekneſſe moveth againſt the wrath, and the wrath againſt the Meekneſſe , and ſo *both* are *diſtinct* Kingdoms in the *one* onely Body of this World.

17. But being the Love and Meekneſſe of God would not leave the Body or place of this kindled wrath world, ſticking in eternal wrath and ignominie, *therefore* he generated the whole old Body of this world *againe* into a rectified reformed Body, wherein life did rule in a *divine* manner and way, *though* in the kindled wrath, yet it muſt ſubſiſt according to the *Right of the Deitie, that out of it, a New Body might be generated, which ſhould ſubſiſt in holineſſe and purity, *in Eternity.* * Law and Order.*

18. For which cause there is appointed in God, a *Day of separation*, on which, Life and Wrath shall be separated *asunder*.

19. Now when thou beholdest the Stars, and the Deep, together with the Earth, then thou seest with thy bodily Eyes, nothing else but the *old* Body in the wrathfull Death, thou canst not see Heaven with *thy Bodily* Eyes; for the Blew or Azure Sphere which thou seest aloff, is *not the Heaven*, but is only the old Body, which may be justly called *the corrupted Nature.*

20. But that there *seemeth* to be a Blew or Azure Sphere *above* the Stars, whereby the place of this world is closed and shut out from the *holy* Heaven, as Men have thought *hitherto*: yet it is *not so*, but it is *the superiour water of Nature*, which is much brighter then the water below the *Moon*: And now when the *Sun* shineth through the Deepe, then it is as it were of a Light-Blew or Azure colour.

21. But how deepe or how large the place of this world is, *no Man* knoweth, though some *Natural* Phylosophers Mathematicians Astronomers or Astrologers *have* undertaken to measure the Deepe with their Measures of Circles; their measuring is but conjecturall or a measuring of somwhat that is *comprehensible* or Palpable: as if a Man would grasp the wind in his Fist.

22. But the true Heaven is every *where* all over, to this very time, and till the last Judgment Day, and the Wrath House of Hell and of Death is also in this world *every where*, even to the last Judgment day.

But

23. But the dwelling of the Devills is *now* from the Moon to the Earth , and in the deep Caves and Holes thereof : efpecially in Wildernefles and Defart Places, and where the Earth is full of Stones and Bitterneffe.

24. But their Kingly Regiment or Government is in theDeep in the fourCoafts orQuarters of theEquinoctial Line or Circle, of which I will write in *another* place.

25. But here I will fhew thee , 1°. How the *Body* of this World came to be , and 2°. How *it is* at prefent, and then 3° how the Regiment or *Government therein,* is.

26. The whole Body of this world is as a Mans Body, for it is furrounded in its utmoft Circle with the Stars and arifen powers of *Nature*, and in that Body the *feaven* fpirits of Nature, Governe, and the Heart of Nature ftandeth in the Midft or Center.

27. But the *Stars* in generall are and fignifie the wonderfull proportion or changing *variety* of God : For when God Created the Stars , he created them out of the rifing up of the *infinity* , out of the Old-Body of God, *then* further kindled.

28. For, as the feaven fpirits of God, had *before* the time of the wrath, generated themfelves infinitely by their rifing up and *Effectings*, whence rofe up fo many feveral varieties of figures and Heavenly Ideas or vegetations: So alfo theHolyGod formed his old body of *this corrupted Nature*, into as many and *various* powers as ever ftood in the Birth or Geniture in the Holyneffe.

Under-

Understand this high thing rightly.

29. Every Star hath a several peculiar propertie, which thou maist perceive by the curious *Ornament* of the budding blossoming Earth ; And the Creator hath *therefore* rebuilt and revived againe the old kindled Body into so many & *various* powers, that *through* this Old Life in the wrath, such a new life might generate it self therein, through the *closure* of Heaven, that, that *New Life* might have all the powers & operations, that ever the old had before the times of wrath, that it might qualifie mixe or unite with the *pure* Deitie distinct from this world, and that *it* might be *One* holy God, together with the Deitie without, distinct from this World.

30. Also the *New Birth* blossom'd in the time of the Creation, when Man *had not* spoiled or corrupted it, but by him Nature was still *more* corrupted and so God cursed the Ground. But being Man tookhold of the *fruit* of the *old* Body, thereupon the *fruit* of the *new* Body was hidden in its Heaven, and Man must now behold it *with* the new Body, and cannot partake of it with the natural Body.

31. Of which I have a great longing to eate, but I *cannot reach* to it, for Heaven is the closure or *Firmament* between the old and new Body. And therefore I must let it alone till I come into the *other Life*, and must give my bestial Body, *Mother Eve's Wrath-Apples to Eate.*

Concerning

The kindling of the Heart or Life, of this World.

32. When God had brought the Body of this world, in *two Dayes* into a right forme; and had made the Heaven for a *Partition* betweene the Love & the Wrath, then on the *Third* Day *the Love* pressed through the Heaven and through the wrath, and then instantly the old Body in Death stirr'd and *moved it selfe* to the Birth or Geniture.

33. Eor the *Love* is *hot*, and that kindled the fire-source or quality, and that rubb'd it selfe in the astringent and cold quality of benumm'd Death, till the astringent qualitie was *heated* on the *third* Day, whereby the mobilitie or the astringent Earth, became moveable.

34. For all stood in the fire-crak till the *fourth* Day, and then the Light of the * *Sun* kindled it self *SOL* for the whole Body stood in anguish or *Paine* in the Birth, as a woman in Travell.

35. The Astringent qualitie was the encompasser or *inclofer* of the life, in it now; the Heat was anxious, which was kindled through the Love of God, and did *thrust forth* the astringent qualitie as a dead Body, but the Heat retcined its seat in the mid'st or center of the Body, and so prest through.

36, But when the Light of the *Sun* kindled it self, then the *nex* Circle or Orb above the *Sun*, stood in the fire-crak, for the Sun or the Light was shining in.

in the Water, and the bitterneffe afcended alfo in the
fire-crack out of the water : But the light made very
great *hafte* after it, and laid hold on the fire crak, and
there it remained ftanding as a *Captive*, and became
corporeal.

* MARS   37. In this Revolution the Planet * *Mars*
came to be, whofe power ftandeth in the *Bitter* fire-
crak, for it is a Tyrant, Rager, Raver and Stor-
mer, like a *fire-crak*, moreover it is *Hot*, and a poifonous venomous enemie of Nature, through whofe
rifing up and Birth or Geniture in the Earth all manner of Poifonous Venomous evill Wormes and *Vermine* are come to be.

38. But being the Heat in the middle point or center
of the Body was *fo Mighty* Great, thereupon it extended it felf fo very largely, and opened the Chamber of Death fo wide before its kindling of the Light,
that it, the SUN, is the Greateft Star.

39. But affoon as the Light kindled it felf in the
heat, fo inftantly was that Hot place *caught* in the
Light, and then the Body of the *Sun* could grow *no*
bigger : For the light mitigated the Heat, and fo
the Body of the *Sun* remained there *ftanding* in the
mid'ft or center as a *Heart*, for the Light is the
Heart of Nature; *not* the Heat.

But here thou muft obferve exactly.

40. As far as the middle point or center hath
kindled it felf, *Juft* fo bigg is the *Sun*; for the *Sun* is
nothing elfe but a kindled *point* in the Body of Nature.

41. Thou muft not thinke, that there is any o-
ther

other power or vertue in it or belonging to it, then there is in the whole Deep of the *Body* every where, all over.

42. For fhould the Love of God, through its Heaven kindle the whole body of this world *through the Heate*, it would be every where all over as Light as it is now in the Sun.

43. And now if the *great Heat* were taken away from the *Sun*, then it would be *One* Light with God: but feeing that cannot bee in this time, therefore it remaineth a *King* and Regent in the *old* corrupted and kindled Body of Nature: and the clear Deitie remaineth hidden in the meek Heaven.

44. But the light of the meekneffe of the Sun qualifieth mixeth or *uniteth* with the pure Deitie, but the *Heat* cannot comprehend the light, and therefore alfo the place of the Sun remaineth in the Body of *Gods wrath*, and thou muft *not* worfhip, pray to or honour the *Sun* as God, for its p'ace or *Body cannot* apprehend the water of Life, becaufe of its *Fierceneffe*.

The Higheft ground of the SUN and of ALL the PLANETS.

45. And here I fhall have *adverfaries* enough who will be ready to cenfure mee, for they will not have regard, to confider *the Spirit*, but will mind their *old Rules*, and fay: Aftrologers underftand it better, who have written of *fuch matters*: and they will look On *this Great open Gate*, as a Cow looks on a new Barn Doare.

46. Deare

46. Deare Reader, I underſtand the *Aſtrologers* meanings and ſayings full well, and I have *peruſed* their writings alſo, and taken notice, how they deſcribe the courſe of the *Sun* and *Stars*, neither do I deſpiſe it, but hold that for the *moſt part* to be good and *right*.

47. But that I write otherwiſe then they in *ſome* things, I do it not out of ſelf will or conceipt and *ſuppoſition*, doubting, whteher it be ſo or *no*: I dare not make any *doubt herein*, *neither* can any man inſtruct mee herein.

48. I have *not* my knowledge by *Study*, indeed I have read the order and *Poſition* of the *Seaven Planets* in the Books of Aſtrologers: and find them to be *very* right, but the Root, how they came to be, & from what they are proceeded, I cannot learne it from *any* Man; for they know it *not*, neither was I preſent, when God created them.

49. But being the Deores of the Deep, and the Gates of wrath, and the *Chambers* of Death alſo are ſet open *in my* ſpirit through the Love of God; the ſpirit, *therefore*, muſt needs look thorough them.

50. And accordingly I find, that the Birth or Geniture of Nature ſtandeth to this Day, and generateth it ſelfe juſt ſo as it firſt took its beginning, and *whatſoever riſeth up* in this world, whether Men, Beaſts, Trees, Herbs, Graſſe Minerall Oars, or what it will, all riſeth up in ſuch a *qualitie* manner & forme, alſo every Life be it good or bad, taketh its original thus.

51. For this is the *Right* or Law of the Deitie, that every Life in the body of God, ſhould generate it ſelfe in *one* manner or uniforme way, though it be done through many *various* Jmagings, yet the *Lif*

hath

hath one uniform way, and Original, in all.

52. I fee not this knowledge with my *flefhly* Eyes, but with thofe Eyes, wherein life generateth it felf *in me*, in that feat the Gates of Heaven and Hell ftand open to me, and the *new Man* Speculateth into the midft or center of the Aftral Birth or Geniture, and to him the inner and outermoft Gate ftandeth *Open*.

53. While he yet fticketh in the *Old* Man of Wrath and Death, and fitteth alfo in his Heaven; he feeth through *both*, in fuch a manner alfo he feeth the Stars and Elements: For *in God* there is no place of hinderance: *for the Eye of the* LORD *beholdeth all.*

54. Now if my fpirit did not fee thorough *his* fpirit, then I were but a blind Stock, but being I fee the *Gates* of God in *my* fpirit, and have the impulfe to do it, I will therefore write *directly* according as I have *feen* it; and will not regard any *Mans Authority.*

55. Thou muft not conceive it fo, as if *my* Old man were a *living Saint* or Angel. *No*, friend, He fitteth with all Men in the houfe of Wrath and of Death, and is a *conftant* Enemy to God, and fticketh in his Sins Wickednefle and Malice, as all Men do, and is full of faults defects and *Infirmities.*

56. But thou muft know this, that he fticketh in a continual *anxious* Birth or Geniture, and would fain be rid of the wrath and wickednefle, and *yet cannot*: For he is as the whole houfe of this world, wherein alwayes love and wrath wreftle one with another, and the new Body alwaies generateth it felf in the midft or center of the *anguifh.* For fo it muft

be, if thou wilt be born anew, otherwise no man can reach the Regeneration.

57. Man is *alwaies* seeking *here* for soft Dayes of Ease for the Flesh, and after Riches beauty and Bravery, and knoweth *not*, that he sitteth therewith in the *chamber* of Death, where the Sting of wrath darteth into Him.

58. *Behold! I tell this to thee, as a word of Life, which I receive in the knowledge of the Spirit in the midst or center in the Birth or Geniture of the new Body of this World, over which the Man JESUS CHRIST is Ruler and King, together with his Eternall Father.*

59. Also I receive it from *before* the Seat of his Throne, where all Holy Soules of men stand before him, and rejoyce before him: *That the Defire of the flesh in soft pleasingnesse, to be Rich, to be Handsom, Beautiful & Fair, or to be Mighty or Potent, is a very Bath or Lake of hellish Wrath,* into which thou crowdest and runnest, as if thou wert drawn in with Cartropes: for there is very great danger therein.

60. But

60. But if thou wouldst know, how it is, behold I will tell thee in a Parable or similitude : When thou art pressed according to the *desire* of thy Heart, into Riches and Power, then is it with thee, as if thou *stoodst* in a deep water, where the water alwaies standeth up to thy very mouth, and thou feelest *no ground* under thy Feet, but thou swimmest with thy Hands, and struggling waverest thy self ; suddenly thou art deep in water, suddenly above water again, yet alway in a great Terrour and danger, Expecting to sinck down to the bottom ; the water coming often *into thy Mouth*, alwaies expecting Death by being Drowned.

61. Just in this manner thou sittest and no other, when thou art in the *pleasures* of the flesh, if thou *wilt not Fight*, thou canst not look for any Victory, but thou wilt be *murthered* in thy soft Bed of Down : For man hath a continual Hoast or *Army* before him; which fighteth with him continually; if he will not *defend* himself, then he is taken captive and slain.

62. But how can he defend himself, that *swimmeth* in a Deep water, he hath enough to do, to keep himself *up* struggling and wavering in the water, and yet neverthelesse he is there also assaulted and *stormed* by the Devils.

63. *O Danger upon Danger,* as our King Christ also saith; *It is very hard for a Rich man to enter into the Kingdom of Heaven ; a Camel will easier go through the Eye of*

a

a Needle, then a Rich man enter into the Kingdom of Heaven
Math. 19. 24. Mark. 10. 25.

64. But if any will bee new born again, he muſt
not yeeld himſelf to be a ſervant *to* Cove touſneſſe,
Pride, State and ſelf-power, to take *delight* in the
will or deſires of his Fleſh, but he muſt ſtruggle and
fight againſt *himſelf*, againſt the Devill, and againſt
all the *Luſts* of the Fleſh, and he muſt think and conſider that he is but a *Servant* and Pilgrim on Earth,
which muſt wander through many miſerable Seas of
danger into another world; and *there* he will be a
LORD, and his dominion will conſiſt in power and
perfect delight beauty and brightneſſe, *this I
tell as the word of the Spirit.*

Now obſerve.

Sol.

65. The * SUN hath its own Royall place to it
ſelf, and *doth not goe away* from that place, where it
came to be at the firſt; as *ſome ſuppoſe,* that it runeth
round about the Globe of the Earth in a Day & a
Night; and *ſome* of the Aſtrologers alſo *write ſo,* and
ſome have undertaken to meaſure, how far its Orb
and Circumference of its *ſuppoſed* Motion, is.

66. This opinion or ſuppoſition is *not right,* but
the *Earth roueth* it ſelfe about, and *runneth* with the
other Planets, as in a wheele, *round* about the *Sun.*
The Earth doth *not* remaine *ſtaying* in one Place, but
runneth round in a yeare, *once* about the *Sun* as the
* other Planets next the Sun, but † Saturne and Jupiter,

* Venus
Mercury
† Saturne
Jupiter
Mars

piter, as alſo Mars by reaſon of their great Orb circumference, and great height *cannot do it*, becauſe
they ſtand ſo high above and far diſtant from the
* SUN.   * *Sol.*

How it may be asked,

what is the SUN, and what are the other
PLANETS ? or how are they
come to be ?

67. Behold ! the *other Planets* are peculiar Bodys
of their own which have a corporeal proprietie of
themſelves, and are *not bound* to any ſetled or fixed
place, but only to their *Circle* Orb or Sphere wherein they runne their courſe. But the SUN is not ſuch
a Body, but is only a place or Locality kindled by
the *Light* of God.

Underſtand it aright.

68. The place, where the SUN is, is ſuch a
place, as you may chooſe or ſuppoſe *any where* above
the Earth ; and if God ſhould kindle the Light by
the Heat, then the *whole* world would be ſuch a meer
SUN; for that ſame power, wherein the *Sun* ſtandeth,
is every where, all over; and *before* the time of wrath,
it was every where all over in the place of *this world*,
as Light as the *Sun* is now, but not *ſo* intollerable.

69. For that heat was not ſo *great* as in the *Sun*,
and therefore the light alſo was very *meek*, and thus
in reſpect of the horrible fierceneſſe of the *Sun*, the
Sun is differenced or diſtinguiſht from the Meekneſſe of God. So that Man ſhould *not dare* to ſay,
that the *Sun* is an open Gate of the light of God : but

is

is as the Light in a *Mans Eye,*whereas alfo the place
of the Eye belongeth to the Body , but the Light is
different or *diftinct* from the Body.

70. And though indeed it exifteth by the *Heate*
in the water of the Body , yet it is a peculiar diftinct
thing , which the body *cannot* comprehend;and fuch
a diftinct difference there is *alfo* between God the
Father and the Sonne.

71. Thus on the *Fourth Day* in the anxious Birth
or Geniture of this world in the middle point or
Center of this World , the SUN is Sprung up and
ftandeth ftill in its Eternal *Corporeal* place, for it *cannot* rife up in *one* place , and fet in *another.*

72. For it is the onely and *Sole* natural Light of
this world , and befides it there is *no more* any true
Light in the Houfe of Death, and though it feemeth
as if the other Stars did *fhine* Bright and give *Light*
alfo, yet it is *not fo,* but they take all their luftre and
fhining Light from the *Sun*; as hereafter prefently
followeth.

The true Birth or Geniture and defcent of
the Sun and of the other Planets
Is juft thus as followeth.

73. Now when the Heaven was made for a *diftinction* or partition between the Light of God and
the *kindled corruption* of the Body of this world : then
was the Body of this world a *dark* valley , and had
no light that could have fhone forth in the *cutward*
Body befides the Heaven , there ftood all powers as
it were captivated in Death, and were in great *anguifh* , till they had heatt themfelves in the mid'ft

or

or center of the Body.

74. But when this was *done*, so that the anxious Birth or Geniture stood so severely in the *Heat*, then the Love in the Light of God brake through the Heaven of the *Partition*, and kindled the Heat.

75. And there rose up the shining light in the Heat, in the water, or in the fat or oylinesse of the water, and the Heart of the water kindled it selfe, and this was done in the *twinckling* of an Eye.

76. For assoon as the Light had rightly laid hold on the Body, the Body was captivated in the *Light*; and the Heat was captivated, and was changed into a *competent* Meeknesse, and could stand or extend *no* further in such Anguish.

77. But being the Heat was so terrified by the Light, thereupon its horrible fire-source was *allayed* and so could kindle it selfe no further, and so also the breaking through of the Love in the Light of God through the Heaven at this time, with its breaking thorough, extended or stretched it selfe *no* further out of or from Gods predestinated purpose: therefore also the *SUN* came to be no bigger.

Of the Planet *Mars*.

78. But when the *Sun* was kindled, then the horrible fire-crack went forth *upward* from the Place of the *Sun*, distant from the Place of the Sun, as a horrible Tempestuous *Flash*, and in its corporeall: Being took along with it the fiercenesse of the fire, *whereby* the water became very bitter, and the water is the kernel or stock of the *Crack*.

Hhhh 79. Now

79. Now the Aſtrologers write, that the Planet *Mars* ſtandeth aloft about 15750, Miles off from the *Sun*: which I contradict *not*, becauſe I meddle *not* with the meaſuring of Circles: And ſo farr that fire-crack went on a *ſuddain* from its own Place, till the light alſo laid hold on it, and then *it* alſo was captivated by the Light, and ſtaid, and took poſſeſſi- on of that Place.

80. But that the Light could lay *no ſooner* hold of it; was cauſed by the earneſt fierceneſſe and ſud- den flaſh, for it was not taken hold of by the *Light before* the Light had wholly or throughly affected or poſſeſſed it.

81. And there it is now as a Tyrant Rager and Stirrer of the whole Body of *this* world: for that is its very Office, that with its *Revolution* in the wheele of Nature it moveth and ſtirreth all, from whence every life taketh its Original.

Of the Planet *Jupiter*

82. Now when the bitter firecrack was captivat- ed by the *Light*, then the light in its own power preſſed yet *higher* in the Deepe, till it reach'd into the *hard* and cold ſeate of Nature. And there the power of the firſt going *forth* or riſing up from the *Sun* could not get Higher, but fitting ſtayed there corporeally, and took poſſeſſion of that *Place* for a Habitation.

But thou muſt underſtand this thing aright:

83. It was the power of the Light, which *ſtayed* in this place, which is a very Meek, friendly, gracious, amiable bleſſed, and ſweet Being.   The Aſtrologers write, that *this* Planet is diſtant aloft above Mars, about 7875 Miles : But it is the *Mitigator* of the deſtroying furious Raging Raving *Mars,* and an original of the Meekneſſe in every Life , an original alſo of the water, from which the life generateth it ſelf, as I ſhall mention hereafter.

84. Thus farr the power of the Life *reached* forth from the *Sun,* and *not* higher, but the luſtre or *ſhineing* thereof which hath its power alſo ; reacheth even to the *Stars,* and through the whole Body of this world.

But thou muſt underſtand this exaƈtly , from whence theſe two Planets are come to be.

85. When the power of the Heart of God preſſed forth out of the eternal *inexhauſtible* fountain of the water of life through the Heaven of the Partition , and kindled the water in the place of the Sun ; then the flaſh , underſtand the fire-flaſh did ſhoot forth or went forth out of the water, which was very terrible and bitter, out of which , Mars came to be.

86. After this Flaſh the power of the Light *ſhot* nimbly after it, like a meek elevated life, and overtook the fire crack , and mitigated it , ſo that it became ſomwhat *weaker*, and could breake no farther through the deepe, but ſtayed trembling.

87. But

87. But the power that was gone forth in the Light had *more* ſtrength then the fire-crack, and ſo it roſe up higher then the fire-crack, *Mars*, till it came very deep into Natures auſtereneſſe, and there it became *feeble* alſo, and *ſtayd* there.

88. From or out of this power the Planet *Jupiter* came to be, and not out of or from that *place*, where he is, but it alwaies kindleth that very place with its power, but it is as one of the *Houſehold* Servants in that place, who muſt alwaies walk about in the place of its office and ſervice. But the *Sun* hath a houſe of its Own, but *no other* Planet hath any Houſe of its Own.

89. *If we will rightly ſearch into the Original of the Stars Birth and Geniture or their beginning, then we muſt exactly know the Birth or Geniture of the Life, viz : How the Life generateth it ſelfe in a Body ; for theſe all are one kind of Birth or Geniture.*

90. He that doth not know nor underſtand *this*, he doth not at all know the Birth of the Stars, for, *all* concrete together, is *one* Body. Every Creature, when life is once generated in it, then afterwards its *Life* ſtandeth or ſubſiſteth in its Body, *as* theBirthorGeniture ofthe natural Body of this world doth, for every Life muſt be generated according to the right Law or

Ordinance

Ordinance of the *Deitie*, as the Deitie generateth it self continually.

91. If this be rightly confidered , which indeed , cannot be done, without a *fpecial illumination* of the holy God ; then firft of all a Man findeth the aftringent, cold and auftere *Birth* or Geniture which is the caufe of the *Corporeal* Nature, or of the imaging fafhioning or *framing* of a thing.

92. Now if it were not for this fevere and cold fharp contracting, compacting power, there would be *no natural* or corporeall being, neither could the Birth or Geniture of *God* fubfift , and all would be infearchable.

93. But in this hard,fevere and cold power ftandeth the corporeall being , or the *Body* , wherein the fpirit of life is generated, and out of that *fame* fpirit the light and *underftanding* is generated whereby then the fenfes andTryal or Probation of all powers, doth exift.

94. For when the *Light* is generated, it is generated, in the midft or *Center* of the Body, as a Heart or fpirit out of all powers, and there it ftandeth and remaineth in the place where it had its beginning , and goeth forth *thorough* all the powers.

97. For as it is generated out of all powers, and hath the *fountain* of all powers , fo with its fhining luftre alfo it bringeth the Fountain of all powers *into* each power, from *whence* then exifteth the taft and fmell, alfo feeing, feeling, and hearing; as alfo Reafon and underftanding.

96. Now as the originall and beginning of the life, in a Creature,is;fo is the *firft Regeneration* of the Nature of the *new* Life in the *corrupted* Body of this world: And he that *denyeth* it , he hath *not* the true under-

underſtanding,nor any knowledge of Nature, and ſo his knowledge is not generated in God, but he is a *Mocker* of God.

I

97. For, firſt behold ! thou *canſt not* deny it , that the *Life* in a creature exiſteth in the *Heate* of the Heart , and in that Life alſo ſtandeth the Light of the animated or *ſouliſh* Birth or Geniture.

98. Now the Heart ſignifyeth the *Sun* , which is the beginning of Life in this outward Body of this world:and now thou canſt not ſay,that the animated or ſouliſh Birth goeth away or *departeth* from the *Heart* , whil'ſt the Body ſtandeth in the mobilitie or *Life*.

99. No more doth the *Sun* go away or depart from *its ſeat* , but retaines and keeps its own place , as a Heart,to it ſelfe, and ſhineth forth as a Light or as a ſpirit of the *whole* Body.

100. For its Birth alſo, hath a beginning out of all powers; and therefore with its Light and Heate it is againe *one ſpirit* and Heart in the *whole* Body of this world.

II

101. And ſecondly thou canſt not deny neither,but that the *Gall* in a Creature, is *not* exiſted from the Heart,and yet is the *mobilitie* or ſtirring of the Heart, by a *Vein* that goeth from the Gall to the Heart,from whence the *Heate* exiſteth. But it hath its firſt original from the *flaſh* of Life, and ſo when the life generateth it ſelfe in the Heart, and the Light riſeth up in the water , then the *fire-crack* goeth before, which riſeth up out of the anxietie of the water in the Heate.

102.For when heat,is ſo *anxious* in the cold in the
aſtringent

aftringent qualitie that the Light kindleth it felfe through the *hidden Heaven* of the hart in the corporeity, then the anxious Death in the wrath ofGod is terifyed, and *departeth* as a crack or flafh from the Light, and climeth upward very terribly trembling and timorously, & the Light of the Heart *hafteth* after it and affecteth or poffeffeth it, and then it remaineth *fitting* ftill.

103. And this, is & fignifyeth the Planet *Mars*, for thus it is become a Being, & its *own quality* is nothing elfe but a Poifonous *Venomous* bitter fire-crack which is rifen up from the Place of the *Sun*.

104. But now it is alwaies a kindler of the *Sun*, juft as the Gall of the Heart, whence the *Heate*, both in the *Sun* and in the Heart, exifteth; and whence the Life taketh its Original in *all things*.

III.

105. Thirdly, thou canft not deny, but that the *Braine* in the Head in a Creature is the *power* of the Heart, for from the Heart all powers rife up into the Brayne, from whence, in the Brayne, the *fenfes* of the Heart exift : The *Brayn* in the *Head* taketh its original from the power of the Heart.

Obferve :

106. After the fire-crack of the Gall, or *Mars*, was departed from the Light of Life, then the power preffed out of the Heart of Life *after it*, even into the Head into the *auftere quality*, and when the power can rife up no higher, then it is ftayed or captivated by the auftere Birth, and is dryed up by the cold.

107. Now

107. Now here it stayeth, and qualifieth, mixeth or uniteth with the spirit of life in the Heart, and is a *Royal seate* of the spirit of the Heart, for thus far the spirit of the Heart's power presseth forth, and there is it *approved.*

108. For the Brayne sitteth in the severe Birth or Geniture, and in its *own Body* it is the meek power of the Heart, and signifieth the *new Birth* which is new regenerated in the midst or center of the austerenesse of Death and wrath, in *its* Heaven, and presseth forth through Death into Life.

109. For there the spirit or the *Thoughts* become a whole creaturely Person againe through the affecting or proving of all powers, which in Man I call the animated or *Soulish* Birth.

110. For when the new spirit in the Braine is well settled, then it goeth to its *Mother* againe, into the Heart, and then it standeth as a perfect spirit or will, or as a new born Person, which, in Man, is called the *Soul.*

111. Now behold! as the Braine in Man is a Being and *product,* so is the Planet *Jupiter* also, a being and product: for it hath his original from the rising up of Life, from the power, which is risen up out of the *water* of Life out of the *Place* of the *Sun,* through the Light.

112. And that power is risen up so high, that it is *caught* or captivated againe in or by the austere, hard and cold power, and there it remaineth *at a stand,* and by the first *Revolution,* or going forth is become corporeal, and became exsiccated or dried by the austere and cold power.

113. And is rightly the Braine in the *corporeall* Government of this World, from whence the senses
and

and Reafon are generated, alfo all Meekneffe and *wifdom* in Naturall things, but the right and *holy* fpirit in Man, is generated in the *hidden* Heaven in the *water of Life.*

114. The outward *Jupiter* is onely the Meekneffe and underftanding in the outward comprehenfibilitie or *palpable* things : but the *holy* fountain or wellfpring is incomprehenfible and unfearchable or unfathomable to *outward* Reafon. For the Aftral Birth or Geniture ftandeth with the *Roote* in the holy Heaven, and with the *Corporeity* in the wrath.

The Six and Twentieth Chapter.

Of the Planet, Saturnus.

I.

SAturn; that cold fharp auftere and aftringent Regent, takes its beginning and Original, *not* from the *Sun* ; for it hath, in its Power, the chamber of Death, and is a dryer up of all powers, from whence *Corporeity* exifteth.

2. For as the *Sun* is the Heart of the Life, and an original of all fpirits in the Body of this world : fo *Saturn* is a beginner of all corporeity and comprehenfibilitie or palpability, and in the power of *thefe* two Planets ftandeth the whole Body of this world : and there cannot be *any Creature* or imaging, nor any mobilitie, without the power of *thefe two,* in the natural Body of this world.

3. But *Saturnes* original is the earneſt *aſtringent* and auſtere anxietie of the whole *Body* of this world : for as in the time of the kindling of the wrath the Light in the outermoſt Birth or Geniture of this world, was *extinct*; which Birth or Geniture is the *Nature* or comprehenſibilitie or the riſing up of the Birth of all qualifying or fountain ſpirits; ſo alſo the *aſtringent qualitie* ſtood in its ſharpneſſe and ſevereſt Birth or Geniture, and attracted or contracted moſt *ſtrongly* and eagerly, the whole work or effect of the qualifying or fountain ſpirits.

Naturlig-keit.
Naturalneſſa

4. From whence the nthe *Earth* and *Stones* came to be, and were very rightly the Houſe of Death, or the encloſing or ſhutting up of the Life, wherein King *Lucifer* was captivated.

5. But when, on the firſt day, the Light *ſomwhat* brake forth again, through the word or Heart of God in the Root of the Nature or Body of this world, as a *chooſing* or appropriating of the *Day* or beginning of the mobilitie of Life, then the ſevere and aſtringent Birth or Geniture obtained againe a *glimpſe*, or riſing up of the life in the Birth or Geniture.

6. And from that time it ſtood as it were in an *anxious* Death, till *after* the third Day, when the Love of God preſſ'd through the Heaven of the Partition, and kindled the *Light* of the *Sun*.

7. But being the Heart or *power* of the Sun could *not open* the anxious Birth or qualitie of fierceneſſe and wrath, and *temper* the ſame, eſpecially aloft in that height above *Jupiter*, thereupon that whole circumferen. e or ſphere, ſtood in a *Horrible* anxietie juſt as a woman in travel, and yet could not awaken or raiſe the Heat, becauſe of the horrible coldneſſe and aſtringency.

8. But

8. But being the *mobilitie* neverthelesse was risen up through the power of the *hidden* Heaven, therefore nature could *not rest*, but was in anguish to the Birth, and generated out of or from the Spirit of sharpnesse, an astringent, cold and austere Sun or Starre which is *Saturne.*

9. For the Spirit of Heat, could not kindle it selfe, from whence the *Light* existeth, and out of or from the Light through the water, the *Love* and meeknesse exist, but it was a Birth or Geniture of an austere cold and severe *fiercenesse*, which is a dryer, spoyler, and enemie, of meeknesse, which in the Creatures generateth the *Hard Bones.*

10. But *Saturne* was *not* bound to its place, as the *Sun is*, for it is not a Corporeal place or space in the *roome* of the Deepe, but *Saturne* is a sonne which is born or generated out of the Chamber of Death, out of the kindled, hard, and cold anxietie, and is only one of the House-hold or family in that *space* or roome, in which it hath its Course and *Revolution*: For it hath its corporeall proprietie to it selfe, as a *Child*, when it is born or generated from the Mother.

[" Saturne *indeed was Created together with the*
" *wheele*, *when the FIAT Created the wheele*;
" *but it doth not goe forth or proceed from Sol.*]

11. But, *why* it did rise up thus from God out of the *austere* Birth, and what its *Office is*, I will mention hereafter, concerning the driving about or revolutions of the Planets.

12. But its height or distance cannot be *exactly* known : But I am fully perswaded that it is in the midst, in the deepe between *Jupiter* and the general Sphere of the fixed Stars or constellations, for it is

the Heart of the *Corporeity* in Nature.

13. For as the *Sun* is the Heart of Life, and a cause of the *spirits* of Nature; so *Saturne* is the Heart and the cause of all *Bodies* & Imagings formings and framings in the Earth, and upon the Earth, as also in the whole Body of this world.

14. And as in Man the *Skull* is a containent or incloser of the Brayne, wherein the *Thoughts* are generated: So the *Saturnine* power is an environer, dryer and containent of all Corporeity and comprehensibilitie or *Palpability*.

15. And as the Planet *Jupiter*, which is an unshutter, and Generator of meeknesse, and is *betweene* the fierce *Mars* and the austere *Saturne*, and generateth the Meeknesse and wisdom in the Creatures; so the Life and the Senses of all Creatures, are genenerated *between* these two *qualities*, especially the *new Body* of this world, as also the *new Man*, of which thou wilt finde more concerning the description of Man.

Of the Planet *Venus.*

16. *Venus* that gracious amiable and blessed Planet, or the kindler of *Love* in Nature, hath its original and descent or proceeding from the Springing up of the *Sun* also, but its condition, qualitie, being, and proceeding or descent, is *thus.*

Here observe this rightly and exactly.

17. When the *Love of God* kindled the place of the *Sun*, or the SUN, then there sprung up first out

of

of the anxietie, out of the Place of the *Sun*, out of the feaven qualifying or fountain fpirits of Nature; the terrible *fierce*, bitter, fire-crak, whofe Birth and principal or firft original is the *kindled bitter wrath* of God, in the aftringent qualitie, through the water.

18. And that, fprung up *firft*, in the kindling of the *Sun* out of the Chamber of Death, and was an awakener or roufer of Death, and a beginner of life, and climed up aloft very fiercely, and trembling, till the Light of the *Sun* layd hold on it, and affected or poffeffed it, and there it was caught or captivated by the meekneffe of the Light, and *ftayed*, from which the **Planet** Mars *came to be*,

19. After that fire-crack, the power of the light; which at the beginning had generated it felfe out of the unctuofitie or *fatneffe* of the water behind the fire crack; inftantly *fhot forth* after it like a mighty potencie or power, and took the fierce Fire-crack captive, and highly elevated it felfe aloft *beyond* it, as a Prince and fubduer of the fierceneffe, from whence now exifted the fenfibilitie of Nature, or the **Planet** Jupiter.

The Gate of Love.

20. But when the *two* fpirits, of the mobilitie, and of the Life, were rifen up out of the Place of the *Sun* through the kindling of the water; then the meekneffe, as a *feed* of the water, preffed downward in the Chamber of Death, with the power of Light, with a very gentle and freindly *affection* or influence from whence exifted the Love of Life, or the **Planet** Venus. But

But thou muſt here underſtand this high thing.

21. The Birth or the riſing or ſpringing up of the ſeaven Planets, and of all the Stars ; is *no otherwiſe*, then *as* the Life, and wonderfull proportion, variety and harmonie of the *Deitie*, hath generated it ſelfe from *Eternitie.*

22. For when King *Lucifer* had cauſed this place of the world to be appointed as a Houſe of wrath for him, & ſuppoſed thus fiercely & powerfully to Rule there in then preſently the Light inNaturewent out, wherin he ſuppoſed to be the Lord; & the whole Nature was *benumm'd* and congealed as a Body of Death, wherein was no mobilitie, and he muſt remaine there in *darkneſſe* as an Eternall Captive Priſoner.

23. But now the Holy God would *not let* this place of his Body, underſtand, *the ſpace or roome of this World*, ſtand in eternal *darkneſſe* and ignominie, and *leave* it to the Devills for their proper own, but generated a *new* Regiment or dominion ofLight,and of all the ſeaven qualifying or fountain ſpirits of the *Deitie*; which the Devill could *neither* apprehend *nor* lay hold on or touch; neither was it uſefull or profitable to him at all.

24. For he can no more ſee in the Light of the *Sun*,but in the darkneſſe,for he is not become aCreature in this Light, and therefore it is *not* profitable or uſefull to him.

25. But being there muſt be a new Government or dominion, it muſt needs be *ſuch* a one as the Devil could lay *no* hold on or touch, or that he could make no as his corporeall *proper owne.* *Now*

Now that is thus conſtituted.

26. The Love, or *word*, or Heart, that is, the innate or *onely begotten Sonne* of the Father, who is the Light, and meekneſſe, and the Love, and Joy of the Deitie: *As He himſelfe ſay'd, when he aſſumed the humanitie,* I am the Light of the World. John 8. 12.; He took the place of this world by the Heart, and ſate in the mid'ſt or center of this ſpace or roome, in *that* place, where the mighty Prince and King *Lucifer* did ſit before his fall, and there he was *new Borne* to be, a Creature.

27. And ſo out of this kindled place of the *Sun*, there exiſted and were chiefly generated, *ſix* ſorts of qualities, all according to the right Law or Order of the *divine* Birth or Geniture.

28.   1°, Firſt there aroſe the *fire-crack*, or the mobility in the Heate, & that is the beginning of Life in the Chamber of Death.

   2°, After this ſecondly, the Light in the unctuoſitie or *fattneſs* of the water became ſhining in the Heat, and that is now the *Sun*.

   3°, And thirdly when now the Light of the *Sun* had affected or poſſeſſed the whole *Body* of the *Sun*, then the power of Life, which roſe up out of the firſt affecting or poſſeſſing, *aſcended* as when wood is kindled, or when fire is ſtruck out of a Stone.

29. Then firſt is diſcerned the *Glance* or ſplendor, and out of the ſplendor, the fire-crack, and after the
fire

fire-crack the *power* of the kindled Body; and the Light with the power of the Body, elevateth it self inſtantly above the crack, and ruleth or reigneth *much higher* deeper and more powerfully then the fire-crack.

30. Alſo the power of the kindled Body in the outgone power without and beyond the fire, qualifi- eth mixeth or *uniteth* gently, pleaſantly and very ſenſibly: and herein rightly is underſtood the

Divine Being.

31. In the ſame manner alſo is the *exiſtency* of the *Sun*, and of the two Planets, *Mars* and *Jupiter*.

32. But being the *place* of the *Sun*, that is, the SUN it ſelfe, contained *all qualities* according to the Right of the Deitie, as alſo all *other* places had; thereupon inſtantly in the firſt kindling, *all* the qua- lities went upward and downward, and generated themſelves according to the eternall beginningleſſe infinite Law, and *Right*.

33. For the power of the Light, which did mitigate the aſtringent and bitter qualitie in the place of the *Sun*: and made it thinne like water or the Love of Life, that went downwards according to the Nature of Humilitie.

34. Out of *this* the Planet *Venus* exiſted: for in the Houſe of Death it is an *opener* of meekneſſe, or a kindler of the water, and a ſoft penetrater into the hardneſſe, a kindler of the Love, in * which the up- per Regiment or *Dominion*, as the bitter Heat, is de- ſirous or longing after *Mars*, and the heartie ſenſi- bilitie, is deſirous or longing after *Jupiter*.

35. From whence the affections or *inſinuations* exiſt: for the power of *Venus*, maketh fierce *Mars* or the

* *Venus*

the fire-crack mild, and mitigateth it, and maketh
Jupiter humble, elfe the power of *Jupiter* would
break through the hard Chamber, *Saturne*; and in
Men and Beafts, through the Scul or Brain-pan, and fo
the fenfibilitie would tranfmute it felf into highmindedneffe above the Birth-Right, or right Law or
order of the Geniture, of the Deitie, in the manner
and way of the *proud* Devill.

Of the planet *Mercurius.*

36. If we would exactly and *fundamentally* know
how the Birth or *beginning* is, of the Planets and
Stars, and of the Being of all Beings, in the deepe of
this world, we muft accurately confider the inftant
or *innate* Birth or beginning of *Life*, in Man.

37. For *that* taketh fuch a beginning and rifing,
and ftandeth alfo in fuch an Order, as the Birth or
Geniture of *the Being of all Beings* in the Body of this
World, doth.

38. For the inftant or innate wheele of the Stars
and Planets is *no* otherwife, then as the Birth of the
feaventh fpirit of Nature, before the time of the
world rofe up, wherein were formed images and figures, formes, fhapes, or Ideas, as alfo *heavenly fruits*,
according to the eternal right Law or Order of the
Deitie.

39. And in that, Man is created according to the
qualifying or fountain fpirits of God, and alfo out of
the *divine* Being, *therefore* mans Life hath fuch a beginning and rifing up as that of the Planets and Stars
was.

40. For the beginning, inftant or innate *State* and *Being* of the Planets and Stars is no other, then the beginning and impulfe or government and Dominion *in Man.*

41. And now as the humane Life rifeth up, fo hath alfo the Birth of the feaven Planets and Stars rifen or fprung up, and *therein* there is no difference at all.

The Center or Circle of the Birth of Life.

The great depth.

Di Me
dicos:

42. The fpirit citeth * the Phyfitians to come before this Looking-glaffe, efpecially Anatomifts and diffectors of Men who by their *Anatomy* would learne the Birth and rifing or fpringing up of *Mans Life*, and have murthered many *innocent* men, againft the Right and Law of God and of Nature, *hoping* thereby to find out the wonderfull proportion Harmony and forme of Nature, that they might thereby be *ufefull* to reftoring the Health of others.

43. But being they are found in Nature to be *Murtherers*, and Malefactors, againft the Law and Right of God and Nature, therefore the fpirit, which qualifyeth, mixeth or uniteth with God, doth *not* juftifie them in their murtherous way.

44. They might have had a *nearer* and *furer* way to learne the wonderfull Birth or Geniture of Nature, if their *lofty* Highmindedneffe and Devilifh Murtherous Luft would have given them leave, which

which hath perverted their true *divine* senses or understandings.

45. Their intent was onely to *fight* with Men and
not with Gods, therefore it is just they should receive
such a reward of their errour.

46. Come on ye crowned Ornaments of Caps
and Hoods, *&c!* Let us see whether a simple Lay-
man, may be able to search into the Birth or Geniture of Mans Life, in the knowledge of God ? if it
be *amisse*, then reject it; if it be right, let it *stand.*

47. I here set down this *description* of the Birth or
Geniture of Mans Life, to the end that the original
of the Stars and Planets may be the better conceived: at the description of the Creation of Man, thou
wilt find all more fundamentally and *deeply*, what the
beginning of Man, is.

Now observe.

48. The *Seede* of Man is generated in such a manner, as the wonderfull proportion harmony or form
of Nature in its wrestling and rising up, is generated from Eternitie.

49. For the *humane* Flesh, is, and resembleth, Nature in the Body of God, which is generated from
the other six qualifying or fountain spirits, wherein
the qualifying or fountain spirits, generate themselves againe, and shew forth themselves *infinitely*,
wherein forms and images rise up, and wherein the
Heart of God, or the holy cleare Deitie in the middle or central *seate* generateth it selfe *above* Nature
in that center, wherein the Light of Life, riseth up.

50. But now in Mans *Body* in the government or
dominion of the Birth or Geniture, there are *three*

feverall things, each of them being *diftinct* and yet are not divided *afunder* one from another, but all three together are one only Man, after the kind and manner of the *Ternarie* or Trinity in the divine Beeing.

51. The *Flefh* is not the Life, but is a dead inanimate being, which when the Government or Dominion of the fpirit *ceafeth* to qualifie or operate therein, foone becometh a dead *Careaffe*, and putrifieth and turnes to Duft or Afhes.

52. But now no *fpirit* can fubfift in its perfection without the Body, for affoon as it departeth from the Body, it loofeth its Government or *Dominion*. For the Body is the Mother of the Spirit in which the fpirit is generated, and in which it *receiveth* its ftrength and power, it is and remaineth a fpirit, when it is feperated and departed from the Body, but it loofeth its *Rule* Dominion or Government.

53. Thefe three Dominions or Regiments are the whole Man together with Flefh and Spirit, and they have feverally for their beginning and Dominion or Government, a *feavenfold* forme after the kind and manner of the feaven fpirits of God or of the feaven Planets.

54. Now as the Dominion or Government of Gods Eternall beginningleffe infinite Birth or Geniture is, fo alfo is the beginning and rifing or fpringing up of the feaven Planets and the Stars, and juft fo alfo is the rifing or fpringing up of *Mans Life.*

Now obferve.

55. When thou mindeft thinkeft and confidereft what there is in this world, and what there is without befides or diftinct from this world, or what

the.

the being of all Beeings, is; then thou speculateft, contemplateft, meditateft, in the whole Body of God, which is the Beeing of all Beings, and that is a beginningleffe *infinite* Being.

56. But in its own feate there is no mobilitie, rationability or comprehenfibilitie, but it is a *dark* Deepe which hath neither beginning nor End. Therein is neither thick nor thinne, opake nor tranfparent, but is a dark Chamber of Death, where nothing is *perceived*, neither cold nor warmeth, but it is the *End* of all things.

57. And this now is the Body of the Deepe, or the very reall Chamber of Death.

58. But now in this dark valley there are the *feaven* fpirits of God, which have neither Beginning nor End, and the one is neither the firft, fecond, third or laft.

59. In thefe *feaven* Dominions or Regiments, the Regiment divideth it felfe into *three* diftinct Beings, where the one is not without the other, nor can they be divided the one from the other: But thofe feaven fpirits doe each of them generate one another, from Eternitie to Eternitie.

60. The *firft* Dominion or Regiment ftandeth or confifteth, in the Body of all things, that is, in the whole Deepe, or Being of all Beings, which hath in all corners and places thereof in it felfe the *feaven* fpirits in poffeffion or in propriety indivifibly, or irrefiftibly for its proper own.

61. Now if thefe feaven fpirits in any one place *wreftle not* triumphingly, then in that place there is no mobilitie, but a deep *darkneffe*; and although the fpirits are perfect in that place, yet that place is a dark Houfe, as you may perceive and underftand by a dark Cave or Roome clofe fhut up,

in

in which the kindled spirits of the Planets and Stars *cannot* kindle the Elements.

62. But now the *Roote* of the seaven spirits is every where all over, but when there is no wrestling, then it standeth still and quiet, and *no* mobilitie is *perceived*.

63. And such a House is the whole Deepe without, within, and above all Heavens; which house is call'd the *Eternitie:* and such a House also is the *House of Flesh* in Man and in all Creatures.

64. And this Being, together, comprehendeth the Eternitie, which is *not called* God, but the UN-Almighty Body of Nature, wherein indeed the Deity is immortall or not Dead, but standing hidden in the kernel of the seaven spirits, and yet not comprehended or understood.

65. And such a House also, the *whole space* or extent of this world came to be; when the Deitie in the seven spirits had *hidden* it selfe from the horrible Devills.

66. And had so *continued*, if the seaven Planets and Stars had not risen or sprung up from Gods spirits, which opened a-gaine and kindled the Chambers of Death in the dark House of this world in all places every where, from whence existeth the regiment or *Dominion* of the Elements.

67. Moreover thou art to know also, that the regiment or Dominion of the seaven spirits of God in the House of this world, is not thereupon exsiccated or dried up in *Death*, that all must needs receive its Life and beginning from the Planets and Stars.

68. *No!*

68. *No!* for the cleare Deitie ftandeth every where hidden in the Circle in the *Heart* of the whole Deepe, and the feaven fpirits ftand in the body of the Deepe in anxietie and great longing, and are ftill kindled by the Planets and Stars, from whence exifteth the *mobilitie* and the Birth or Geniture in the whole Deepe.

69. But being the Heart of the Deitie *hideth* it felfe in the Body of this world in the outermoft Birth or Genitnre which is the corporeity, *thereupon* the corporeity is a dark Houfe, and all ftandeth in great anguifh and needeth a *Light*, to fhine in the Chamber of the darkneffe, which is the *Sun*, and that fo long till the Heart of God will *move* it felfe againe in the feaven fpirits of God in the Houfe of this world, and *kindle* the feaven fpirits.

70. And then the *Sun* and Stars will returne againe to their firft place and will *paffe away* in fuch a forme or manner, for the Heart and Light of God fhall give Light and fhine againe in the *Corporeity*, that is, in the Body of this world, and replenifh or fill all.

71. And then the anxietie *ceafeth*; for when the anxietie in the Dominion of the Geniture or Birth regiment, tafteth of the *fweetneffe* of the Light of God; fo that the Heart of God *triumpheth* together in the Birth Regiment, then all is richly full of Joy, and the whole Body *triumpheth.*

72. Which at prefent in this time, in the Houfe of this world *cannot* bee, becaufe of the fierce *Captive* Devill, which keepeth Houfe in the outermoft Birth or Geniture in the Body of this world, till the *Judgment* of God.

73. Now.

73. Now here thou may'st un-
derstand, Hovv the Heart of God
hath the Fann or Castingshovel in
its hand, and vvill one Day
cleanse his floor, vvhich I here-
with earnestly declare to you as
in the knowledge, in the Light
of Life, where the Heart in
the Light of Life, breaketh
thorough, and Proclaimeth the
Bright cleare Day.

Of Man and the Stars.

74. Now as the *Deepe,* or the House of this world
is a dark House, where the whole Corporeity generateth it selfe, and so is very thick, dark, anxiou ,and
halfe dead, and taketh its moving from the *Planets*
and *Stars* which kindle the Body in the outermost
Birth or Geniture, from whence existeth the mobilitie of the *Elements,* as also the figured and *Creature-*
ly being ; so also the Humane house of Flesh is a
dark valley, wherein is indeed the *anxietie* to the Birth
of Life, and it alwayes highly endeavoreth, intending to elevate it selfe into the Light, from whence
the *Life* might kindle it self.

75. But

75. But being the Heart of God did hide it selfe in the center or kernel, *therefore* it cannot be, & *thereupon* the anxietiegenerateth no more but *ONE Seed.* The House, of the flesh generateth a *Seed* of its liknesse to the propagating of a Man againe, and the House of the spirit in the instant or innate state of the seaven spirits generateth *in the Seed* another *spirit* after its likenesse, to the propagating of the *spirit of Man* againe.

76. And the House of the *hidden* Heart generateth also such a spirit as standeth *hidden*, in the Body, to the spirit of the House of Flesh as also to the spirit of the Astral Birth or Geniture : just as the *Heart of God* in the seaven spirits of God standeth hidden in the spirits in the Deepe of this world, and doth *not kindle* them, till after *this* enumeration or account of *Time* is out.

77. This *third* spirit is the soule in Man, and qualifieth, mixeth or *uniteth* with the Heart of God, as a Sonne or *little* God in the great *immense or unmeasureable* God.

78. Now these three distinct Dominions or Regiments are generated *in the seed*, which taketh its original in the flesh, as I have mentioned before within three leaves from this.

Now obſerve this hidden ſecret Myſterie.

*Yee * Naturaliſts, obſerve.*

* Phiſici
Natural
Philoſophers

The Gate of the Great myſterie.

79. Out of the *anguiſhing* Chamber in the Body of this world out of the ſeaven ſpirits of God, are riſen or ſprung forth the Stars, which *kindle* the Body of this world, and out of or from the Body the *fruit* or *ſeede* generateth it ſelfe, which is the Water, Fire, Aire, and Earth.

80. *The Earth is the fruit of the ſeaventh ſpirit of God, which is Nature or Corporiety*; wherein the other ſix ſpirits generate themſelves againe, and figure or frame the *Salitter* of the ſeaventh ſpirit into *infinite ſorts* of formes or ſhapes; ſo that the Earth alſo generateth its ſeed, which is the fruit of *vegetation*, as is apparent to the Eye.

81. Now *Mans* Houſe of Fleſh is alſo ſuch a houſe as the *dark* deepe of this world is, wherein the ſeaven ſpirits of God generate themſelves.

82. But being Mans Body is its proper own, and is a *Sonne of the whole* Body of God, *therefore* it generateth alſo a proper ſeede of its own according to the Government or Dominion of his corporeal qualifying or fountain ſpirits.

83. The Body taketh its *food*, from the ſeed of the ſeaven ſpirits of God, in the Body of the great Deepe, which is, Fire, Aire, Water and Earth.

84. Of

84. Of or from the Earth it taketh the Birth of the Earth or the Fruit, for it is much more Noble then the Earth : *It is an extracted Maſſe out of the Salitter out of the ſeaventh Nature ſpirit.*

85. For when the Body of Nature was *kindled* by the Devill, then the *word* or the Heart of God drew the *Maſſe* together, before the corrupted *Salitter* was preſſ'd together, which now is called the Earth becauſe of the hard fierceneſſe or corruption.

86. But when the Earth was *preſſed* together, then the *Maſſe* ſtood in the dark Deepe in the created Heaven *betweene* the anxious Birth or Geniture and the Body of the Heart of God, till the *ſixth Day*; and then the Heart of God breathed the Light of Life out of or from his Heart into the innermoſt or *third* Birth or Geniture of the *Maſſe*.

87. Now when this was done, then in the *Maſſe*, the ſeaven ſpirits of the qualities *began* to qualifie or operate, and in the *Maſſe*, the *ſeede* of the ſeaven qualifying or fountain ſpirits generated it ſelfe, as Fire, Aire, and Water, *as* in the Body of the Deepe.

88. *Thus* MAN *became a living Soul*, in that kind and manner, as the *Sun* is riſen or ſprung forth, and out of that the reſt of the ſeven *Planets.*

89. The *Light* in Man, which the Heart of God *had breathed in*, ſignifieth or reſembleth, the *Sun* which ſhineth in the whole Deepe; concerning which you will finde more cleerely, about the Creation of Man.

90. Now behold ! As in the Deepe of this world, through the *kindling* of the Stars a *feede* is generated out of the Body of the dark deepe, like the *Creaturely* Body : so also in like manner in *Mans* House of Flesh there is generated, a feede, according to the Eternal Birth-Right of the *feaven* qualifying or fountain spirits.

91. And in the *feeds* there are *three diftinct* things, whereof the one cannot fathom the other , and yet are in that *one* only feed, and qualifie,mixe or unite one with another, as one being, and is also *one being*, and yet also *three diftinct things*, according to the kinde and manner of the *Ternarie* or Trinity in the Deitie.

92. *Firft* there is the whole *Body* of Man, which is a dark House , and hath no mobilitie besides or *without* diftinct from the qualifying or operation of the feaven spirits,but is a dark valley,as the Body of the Deepe of this world is.

93. Now in the dark Body of Man there is such a Regiment or Dominion also as to the *feaven* spirits as is in the Body of the Deepe ; And when the fea-ven spirits qualifie or operate according to the *Birth-Right* of the Deitie , then out of the *wreftling* of the feaven spirits a *feede* generateth it felfe according to *their* likeneffe.

94. Now that feede hath firft a *Mother* , which is the dark *Chamber* of the House of Flesh.   Second-ly it hath a Mother, which is the *wheele* of the feaven spirits, according to the kind and manner of the fea-ven Planets.   Thirdly it hath a Mother which is ge-nerated in the Circle of the feaven spirits in the cen-ter , and is the *Heart* of the feaven spirits.

95. And

95. And this now is the *Mother of the soule*, which shineth thorough the seaven spirits, and maketh them living, and in their steed the seed qualifyeth mixeth or *uniteth* with the Heart of God: But it is *that seed* only, in which the Light is kindled; but in that, in which the wrath fire burneth there this third Mother remaineth *Captive* in the dark Chamber.

96. And though indeede it is the *third* Mother, yet it remaineth to be but a foolish Virgin, if the Light be *not* kindled in it; just as the Deepe of this world is * a foolish Virgin before the Heart of God in which the wheele of the seaven spirits standeth in such anxietie, in so much *corruption* and *redemption* in heate and cold as is apparent to the Eye.

97. But when the *third* Mother is kindled in the *Light* then it standeth in the created Heaven of the *holy* Life, & shineth through the *second* Mother, the seaven spirit, vherby the seven spirits get a friendly courtous will, which is the *Love* of the Life, as you may read in the Eighth Chapter of this Book, *Concerning the Love-Birth or Geniture of God.*

98. But the *third* Mother, they cannot constantly or *permanently* shine thorough, for it standeth in the house of darknesse, but they often cast a *Glimpse* upon it, even as if it lightened, whereby the third Mother *many times* becometh very longing, and rejoyceth highly, but is soone bolted up againe by the *fiercenesse of Gods wrath.*

99. The Devill also danceth at this Gate, for it is the Prison, wherein the *new* Man lyeth hidd, and wherein the Devill lyeth Captive.   100. But

100. But I meane, in the Houſe of the Deepe of this World; though indeed the Houſe of *Fleſh* and the Deepe, altogether qualifie mixe or unite one with another, as one Body, and is one Body, only they have diſtinct parts or Members.

The Deepe in the Center.

101. Now behold! When the *ſeede* is generated, it ſtandeth in the center or mid'ſt of the Body in the *Heart*: for there the *Mother* catcheth the Ternarie or Trinity.

102. *Firſt* the aſtringent ſpirit catcheth hold, and that draweth together a Maſſe or *Lump* out of the *ſweet* water, that is, out of or from the unctuoſitie or fatneſſe of the *Blood* of the Heart, or from the Sap or *Oyle* of the Heart.

103. Now that Oyle hath clearly the *roote* of the Ternarie or Trinity in it, viz: the *whole Man*, for it is juſt as when kindled Tinder is caſt into Straw.

Now it may be asked,

How commeth this to paſſe?

104. Here now is the true ground of *Man*; obſerve it exactly, for it is the Looking Glaſſe of the great Myſterie, the deepe ſecret of the *Humanitie*, about which all the learned ſince the beginning

ginning of the World have dan-
ced, and have fought after this
Doare, but have not found it.

105. *But I muft once mention*
that it is the dawning *or* Morning
Redneſs of the Day, *as the Doare*
keeper will have me doe.

Now Obferve.

106. Juſt as the firſt *Maſſe* was, out of which
Adam became a living Man : ſo alſo in like manner
is every *Maſſe* or *ſeede* of the Ternarie or Trinity in
every Man.

Obferve:

107. When the *Salitter* or Fabrick of the ſix qualifying or fountain ſpirits, which is the ſeaventh
Nature ſpirit in the *ſpace* or roome of this World,
was kindled, then the *word* or Heart of God ſtood e-
very where in the center or mid'ſt of the Circle of the
ſeaven ſpirits, as a *Heart*, which repleniſhed all at
once, *viz :* the whole ſpace or roome of this World.

108. But being the Deepe, that is, the *whole ſpace*
of this World, was the Body of the Father, underſtand the Father of (the Heart of God) underſtand
the Fathers *Body* ; and the Heart in the whole
Body did ſhine forth, viz : The Fathers *Luſtre* or
Brightneſſe then the corrupted *ſalitter* was
affected or poſſeſſed every where with the Light
                                              and

& the Heart of God could *not flye* out from it, but did *hide* its Luſtre and ſhining Light *in* the Body of the whole Deep, *from* the horrid kindled Spirits of Devils.

109. And when this was done, then the qualifying or fountain ſpirits became very fierce and *vehemently* ſtrugling, and the aſtringent ſpirit, as the ſtrongeſt, in the ſeaventh nature-ſpirit, drew very terribly together, the fabrick and effects of the other *five,* from whence the bitter Earth and Stones came to be, but were *not yet* driven together, but moved in the whole Deepe.

110. In this houre the *Maſſe* was drawn together; for when the Heart of God did hide it ſelfe in the *Salitter,* then it caſt a *glance* againe on the whole ſpace or Body, and thought how it might be *Remedied* againe, whereby another Angelical Kingdom might be in the Deepe of this world.

111. *But the Glance was the Love-ſpirit in the Heart of God, vvhich in that place of the Glance, affected or poſſeſſed the Oyle of the water, where before the Light was riſen up.*

112. *Here conſider* Saint Peters *glance that was caſt upon him in the houſe of* Caiphas, *it is the very ſame.*

113. As the Man casts a *Glance* on the woman, and the woman on the Man, and so the spirit of the Man, understand the *Roote* of the Love, which in the rising up of Life out of the *water*, riseth up through the *Fire*, as also the womans spirit doth; and so one spirit *catcheth* the other in that Oyle of the Heart, whereby presently a *Masse*, *Seede*, or driving will, or desire, to the *propagating* of a Man againe, ariseth in the *Masse*.

114. Just in such a way and manner, the *first Masse* also came to be, for the Love-Spirit in the Heart of God cast a Glance in the *Body* of the kindled wrathfull Father on the *water of Life*, whereby, and out of which, the *Love* in the fire-Flash arose or sprung up *before* the time of the wrath.

115. In this casting of the Glance, the one spirit caught the other, the unctuous *Oyle* or Water in the wrath, *conceived* from the Love-Spirit in the Heart of God, and qualified mixed or united with the same, and the astringent spirit drew the *Masse together*: and there was clearly a Birth, or a will, or desire, to the *producing* of a whole creature, just as the *Seede* in Man is.

116. But now, the Firmament of Heaven that is *betweene* the Heart of God, and the kindled hard Chamber of Death, was closed or shut up; else the *Life* in the *Masse* had suddenly kindled it selfe.

117. For the firmament was *within* in the *Masse* as well as *without* distinct from the *Masse*, which is the parting mark, or limit of *separation* between the Heart of God and the fierce Devills.

118. *Therefore* the *word* or Heart of God *must* blow up the moving-spirit in the *Masse*, which was first done but on the *sixt Day*; for very assured causes.

Mmmm   119. For

119. For if Heaven had not as a Firmament been *fhut up* in the *Maffe*, between the Heart of God and the corporeal qualifying or fountaine fpirits of the *Maffe*, then the *Maffe* might have *kindled* the *Soul*, from or by its *own* power, as it was with the Holy Angels.

120. But it was to be *feared*, that it would come to paffe, as it did with that faire little Son *Lucifer*, being the corporeal qualifying or fountain fpirits in the *Maffe*, were kindled in the *wrath-fire*.

121. Therefore Heaven *muft* be a Firmament, between the fparkle which had conceived from the Heart of God in the *firft* Glance, that though the Body *might happen* to perifh, yet the *holy Seed* might remaine, which is the *Soul*, which qualifyeth mixeth or uniteth with the Heart of God, out of which a *new Body*, might come to be; when the whole God fhould *kindle againe* the Deepe of this world in the Light of the Heart of God; and juft fo it is come to be with the *Body*: *The Love of God have mercy* and *take pitty on it.*

122. The deare man *Mofes* writeth *that God made Man out of a Clod of Earth*, as the Learned have rendred it. But *Mofes* was *not* prefent, when it was done.

123. But this I muft needs fay, that *Mofes* hath written very *right*, but the true underftanding or meaning, out of what the Earth proceeded, remained hidden to *Mofes* and them that have come after him in the *Letter*, and the fpirit hath kept it hidden to *this* very time.

124. It

124. It was also hidden from *Adam*, while he was yet *in Paradise*; but *now* it will *fully* be revealed: for the Heart of God hath set upon or assaulted the Chamber of Death, and will *shortly* breake quite thorough.

125. And therefore in these our present times, some *Beames* of the Day will more and more break thorough in the hearts of *some* men, and make known the Day.

126. *But when the Dawning or Morning Rednesse shall shine from the East to the West or from the rising to the setting, then assuredly, time will be no more; but the SUN of the Heart of God riseth or springeth forth, and* *RA. RA. R.P. will be pressed in the Wine Presse without the Cittie, and therewith to R.P.

* Behmes Epistle 23. vers. 12.

127. *These are hidden mystical words, and are understood onely in the Language of Nature.*

128. *Moses writeth very right,* that Man was created out of the Earth, but at *that* time, when the *Masse* was held by the word, then the *Masse* was

not Earth : But if it had *not* been held or kept by the word , then at that very houre it had become *Black* Earth , but the cold wrath-fire was in it already.

129. For at the very *houre*, when *Lucifer* elevated himselfe, the Father was moved to *wrath* in the qualifying or fountain spirits againft the *Legions* of Lucifer , and the Heart of God hid it felfe in the Firmament of Heaven , where the *Salitter*, effect, product or Fabrick, of the corporeity, was *burning* already, for without or diftinct from the Light, is the *dark* Chamber of Death.

130. But the *Mafse* was held or kept in the Firmament of Heaven, that it might *not* be congealed : for when the Heart of God *Glanced* on the *Mafse* with its hot Love, then the unctuofitie or oyle in the *Mafse*, which rofe up out of the water through the fire , out of which the Light rifeth up, and out of which the Love-Spirit rifeth up; caught hold of ## *the Heart of God* , and was *impregnated* with a *young Sonne*.

131. And that was the *Seed of Love*; for one Love embraced the other, the Love of the *Mafse* embraced and conceived from the Love out of the *Glance* of the Heart of God; and was thereby impregnated : and this is the Birth or Geniture of the *Soule* ; and as to *this Sonne*, Man is the Image of God.

132. But the qualifying or Fountain spirits in the *Mafse*, could not prefently be kindled thereby from the Soul; for the Soul ftood only in the feed in the *Mafse*, hidden with the Heart of God in its Heaven; till the Creator *blew* upon the *Mafse*, and then the qualifying or Fountain fpirits kindled the *Soule* alfo, and then both **Body** and **Soul** lived equally together.

133. In-

133. Indeede the Soul had its *Life*, *before*, the Body, but it stood in the Heart of God, hidden in the *Masse* in Heaven, and was a kind of holy Seed qualifying mixing or uniting with God, which is *Eternal*, incorruptible, and undeftroyable, for it was a *new* and pure Seed, for an Angel and Jmage of God.

134. But the Fabrick, effect, or product, of the whole *Masse*, was an extract, or attraction of the *word* of God, out of the Fabrick or effect of the qualifying or fountain Spirits, or of the *Salitter*, out of which the Earth came to be.

135. This extract was *not yet* become Earth, though it was the *Salitter* of the Earth, but was held or kept by the *word*.

136. For when the Love-Spirit out of the Heart of God Glanced on the *Salitter* of the *Masse*, then the *Salitter* did catch hold of it and conceive from it, and was *impregnated* in the Center of the Soul, and the *word* stood in the *Masse* in the *Sound*, but the *Light* abode in the Center of the *Masse*, in the Firmament of Heaven, standing hidden in the unctuous oile of the heart, and did *not* move it selfe forth out of the Firmament of Heaven, in the Birth of the qualifying or fountain Spirits.

137. Elfe if the *Light* had kindled it selfe in the Birth or Geniture of the Soul, then all the seaven qualifying or fountain Spirits, according to the eternall Birth-Right of the Deitie, had triumphed and qualifyed mixed or *united* in & with the Light, and had been a *Living* Angel; but being the wrath had cleerely already infected the Salitter, therefore that danger was to be *feared*, which befell *Lucifer*.

Now it may be Asked.

138. *Why were not many Masse's Created, at this time, out of which inftantly at once, there might have been a whole Angelical hoaft or Army, inftead of fallen Lucifer.*

139. *Why fhould there be fo long a time of ftay in the wrath.*

140. *And why fhould the whole Hoaft or Army be generated out of that one Maffe, in fo very long a Time?*

141. *Or did not the Creator at this time fee and know of the Fall of Man.*

Anſwer.

142. *This now is the very Doore of the bidden fecret myftery of the Deitie.* Concerning which the Reader is to conceive

conceive, that it is not in the power or capacity of any Man to difcerne or to know it, if the *Dawning* or *Morning-Redneffe*, did not break forth in the Center in the Soul.

143. For they are *divine* myfterics, which no Man can fearch into by his *own* Reafon, and I alfo efteeme my felfe moft unworthy of fuch a gift, and befides I fhall have many fcorners and mockers againft me; for the *corrupted* Nature is horribly *afhamed*, before the Light.

144. But for all that, I cannot forbeare : for when the divine Light breaketh forth in the Circle or Birth of Life, then the qualifying or fountain Spirits *rejoyce*, and in the Circle of the Life, reflect or look back into their Mother, into the *Eternity*, and they alfo look forwards into the Eternitie.

145. But it is not a conftant and *lafting* thing or being, clarifying or brightning, of the qualifying or fountain Spirits, much *leffe* of the *Beftial* Body, but it is the *Ray* of the breaking through of the *Light* of God with a firie impulfe, which rifeth up through the meek water of Life in the *Love*, and remaineth ftanding in *its* Heaven.

146. Therefore I can bring it no further, then from the *Heart* into the *Braine* before the Princely Throne of the Senfes, and there it is *fhut up* in the Firmament of Heaven, and goeth *not back* againe through the qualifying or fountain Spirits into the Mother of the Heart, that it might come on to the *Tongue*, for if that were done, I wouldtell it with my *mouth*, and make it known to the *World*.

147. But for that cause I will let it stand in *its Heaven*, and write according to my gifts, and with wonder and *admiration* expect what will become of it. For in the qualifying or fountain Spirits I cannot *sufficiently* comprehend or apprehend it, because they stand in the *anxious* Chamber.

148. As to the *Soul* I see it *very well*, but the Firmament of the Heaven is between, in which the Soul *hideth* it selfe, and there receiveth its *Rayes* from the Light of God; and in that respect it goeth *through* the Firmament of Heaven as a Tempest of *Lightning*, but very gently in a most amiable and pleasant delight and Joy.

149. So that I *cannot* in the comprehensibility in my *innate* instant or present qualifying or fountain Spirits, or in the Circle of Life, discerne or know it *otherwise*, for *the Day breaketh forth apace.*

150. For that cause I will *write* according to this knowledge, though the Devill should offer to assault and storm the world, which however he cannot doe: Yet his Houre-Glasse is showen to him and set before him.

† *That contend about Election and Predestination.*
151. Now come on you * Electionists and contenders about the Election of Grace, you that suppose *you only* are in the right, and esteeme a simple Faith to be but a *foolish* thing, you have danced long enough before this Doore, and have made your *boast* of the Scriptures, that they maintaine that God hath of Grace, *chosen some* Men in their Mothers Womb, to the Kingdome of Heaven, and reprobated or rejected *others.*

153. Here

152. Here make to your selves many *Masse's*, out of which there may proceed other manner of Men of other qualities, and *then* you may be in the right: But out of the *one* only *Masse* you can make no more then *one* only *Love* of God, which presseth forth, through the first Man, and so presseth through and upon *all*. If God should have permitted *Peter* or *Paul* to have written otherwise: however look you to the Ground, of the *Heart.*

152. If you lay hold on the Heart of God, then you have Ground *enough.*

154. If God give me Life for a little while longer, I will well shew you, *Saint Pauls* Election of Grace. ———

The Seven and Twentieth Chapter.

Note.

* See Behmes
third Epiftle.
to Abraham
von Somer-
feld, verſ. 30.
anno 1620,

" * I advertiſe the Reader who loveth God; that this
" booke the **Aurora or Morn-**
" **ing Redneſſe,** was not finiſh
" ed: for the Devil intended to put a ſtop to it
" and ſuppreſſe it, when he perceived that the
" Day would break forth therein. And
" the **Day** hath cleerly made haſte after the
" Morning Redneſſe, ſo that it is become ve-
" ry Light. There want yet about Thirtie
" ſheets to the end of it. But being the ſtorm hath
" broken them off, therefore it was not finiſhed;
" ~~and in the mean while it is come~~ to be Day,
" ſo that the Morning Redneſſe is paſſed a-
" way, ~~and ſince~~ that time, the worke hath
" gone on by Day. And it ſhall ſo ſtand, for
" **an eternal Remembrance,**
" being the defect herein, is ſupplyed in the
" ✝ other Books.

✝ Three
Principles.
Threefold
Life.
40 Queſtions,

Jacob Behme
1620.

The Dawning or Morning ... Infancie and Child-hood, and ... ... the Creation of all Beeings, but very myſtically, ... not ſufficiently cleere, but full of Magical Under-ſtanding, for there are ſome Myſteries therein, which are ... to come to paſſe.

Note.

This is the deepe hidden Magicall Book, which the Author at that time might not make clearer, but may now doe it, through the Grace of God, 1621.

Note

This book is written in a Magicall ſenſe or underſtand-ing, for the Author himſelfe only, who knew of no other Readers; he ſuppoſed, he made this work only for himſelf, but God hath diſpoſed it otherwiſe.

Note.

The Author expreſſed the firſt ſyllable MER, in the word MERCURIUS, with an A, as MAR, MARCU-RIUS, not without a ſpeciall Myſticall cauſe, with the firſt Vowell A; But becauſe the ſelfe conceited wiſe in Reaſon, diſlike it, accounting it but a Country vulgar expreſſion, Therefore the tranſcriber of the High Dutch Copie, from whence this was tranſlated, wrote it according to the com-mon received word, MERCURIUS.

* **The Corne groweth againſt the will of the Enemie; For that which is ſowne by God, no Man can prevent or hin-der the growing thereof.**

See the third Epiſtle to Abraham von ...

Lightning Source UK Ltd.
Milton Keynes UK
UKOW022240240413

209715UK00004B/101/P